Lecture Notes in Computer Science

Vol. 379: A. Kreczmar, G. Mirkowska (Eds.), Mathematical Foundations of Computer Science 1989. Proceedings, 1989. VIII, 605 pages. 1989.

Vol. 380: J. Csirik, J. Demetrovics, F. Gécseg (Eds.), Fundamentals of Computation Theory. Proceedings, 1989. XI, 493 pages. 1989.

Vol. 381: J. Dassow, J. Kelemen (Eds.), Machines, Languages, and Complexity. Proceedings, 1988. VI, 244 pages. 1989.

Vol. 382: F. Dehne, J.-R. Sack, N. Santoro (Eds.), Algorithms and Data Structures. WADS '89. Proceedings, 1989. IX, 592 pages. 1989.

Vol. 383: K. Furukawa, H. Tanaka, T. Fujisaki (Eds.), Logic Programming '88. Proceedings, 1988. VII, 251 pages. 1989 (Subseries LNAI).

Vol. 384: G. A. van Zee, J. G. G. van de Vorst (Eds.), Parallel Computing 1988. Proceedings, 1988. V, 135 pages. 1989.

Vol. 385: E. Börger, H. Kleine Büning, M. M. Richter (Eds.), CSL '88. Proceedings, 1988. VI, 399 pages. 1989.

Vol. 386: J.E. Pin (Ed.), Formal Properties of Finite Automata and Applications. Proceedings, 1988. VIII, 260 pages. 1989.

Vol. 387: C. Ghezzi, J. A. McDermid (Eds.), ESEC '89. 2nd European Software Engineering Conference. Proceedings, 1989. VI, 496 pages. 1989.

Vol. 388: G. Cohen, J. Wolfmann (Eds.), Coding Theory and Applications. Proceedings, 1988. IX, 329 pages. 1989.

Vol. 389: D. H. Pitt, D. E. Rydeheard, P. Dybjer, A. M. Pitts, A. Poigné (Eds.), Category Theory and Computer Science. Proceedings, 1989. VI, 365 pages. 1989.

Vol. 390: J.P. Martins, E.M. Morgado (Eds.), EPIA 89. Proceedings, 1989. XII, 400 pages. 1989 (Subseries LNAI).

Vol. 391: J.-D. Boissonnat, J.-P. Laumond (Eds.), Geometry and Robotics. Proceedings, 1988. VI, 413 pages. 1989.

Vol. 392: J.-C. Bermond, M. Raynal (Eds.), Distributed Algorithms. Proceedings, 1989. VI, 315 pages. 1989.

Vol. 393: H. Ehrig, H. Herrlich, H.-J. Kreowski, G. Preuß (Eds.), Categorical Methods in Computer Science. VI, 350 pages. 1989.

Vol. 394: M. Wirsing, J.A. Bergstra (Eds.), Algebraic Methods: Theory, Tools and Applications. VI, 558 pages. 1989.

Vol. 395: M. Schmidt-Schauß, Computational Aspects of an Order-Sorted Logic with Term Declarations. VIII, 171 pages. 1989 (Subseries LNAI).

Vol. 396: T. A. Berson, T. Beth (Eds.), Local Area Network Security. Proceedings, 1989. IX, 152 pages. 1989.

Vol. 397: K. P. Jantke (Ed.), Analogical and Inductive Inference. Proceedings, 1989. IX, 338 pages. 1989 (Subseries LNAI).

Vol. 398: B. Banieqbal, H. Barringer, A. Pnueli (Eds.), Temporal Logic in Specification. Proceedings, 1987. VI, 448 pages. 1989.

Vol. 399: V. Cantoni, R. Creutzburg, S. Levialdi, G. Wolf (Eds.), Recent Issues in Pattern Analysis and Recognition. VII, 400 pages. 1989.

Vol. 400: R. Klein, Concrete and Abstract Voronoi Diagrams. IV, 167 pages. 1989.

Vol. 401: H. Djidjev (Ed.), Optimal Algorithms. Proceedings, 1989. VI, 308 pages. 1989.

Vol. 402: T.P. Bagchi, V.K. Chaudhri, Interactive Relational Database Design. XI, 186 pages. 1989.

Vol. 403: S. Goldwasser (Ed.), Advances in Cryptology – CRYPTO '88. Proceedings, 1988. XI, 591 pages. 1990.

Vol. 404: J. Beer, Concepts, Design, and Performance Analysis of a Parallel Prolog Machine. VI, 128 pages. 1989.

Vol. 405: C. E. Veni Madhavan (Ed.), Foundations of Software Technology and Theoretical Computer Science. Proceedings, 1989. VIII, 339 pages. 1989.

Vol. 406: C. J. Barter, M. J. Brooks (Eds.), AI '88. Proceedings, 1988. VIII, 463 pages. 1990 (Subseries LNAI).

Vol. 407: J. Sifakis (Ed.), Automatic Verification Methods for Finite State Systems. Proceedings, 1989. VII, 382 pages. 1990.

Vol. 408: M. Leeser, G. Brown (Eds.), Hardware Specification, Verification and Synthesis: Mathematical Aspects. Proceedings, 1989. VI, 402 pages. 1990.

Vol. 409: A. Buchmann, O. Günther, T. R. Smith, Y.-F. Wang (Eds.), Design and Implementation of Large Spatial Databases. Proceedings, 1989. IX, 364 pages. 1990.

Vol. 410: F. Pichler, R. Moreno-Diaz (Eds.), Computer Aided Systems Theory – EUROCAST '89. Proceedings, 1989. VII, 427 pages. 1990.

Vol. 411: M. Nagl (Ed.), Graph-Theoretic Concepts in Computer Science. Proceedings, 1989. VII, 374 pages. 1990.

Vol. 412: L. B. Almeida, C. J. Wellekens (Eds.), Neural Networks. Proceedings, 1990. IX, 276 pages. 1990.

Vol. 413: R. Lenz, Group Theoretical Methods in Image Processing. VIII, 139 pages. 1990.

Vol. 414: A.Kreczmar, A. Salwicki, M. Warpechowski, LOGLAN '88 – Report on the Programming Language. X, 133 pages. 1990.

Vol. 415: C. Choffrut, T. Lengauer (Eds.), STACS 90. Proceedings, 1990. VI, 312 pages. 1990.

Vol. 416: F. Bancilhon, C. Thanos, D. Tsichritzis (Eds.), Advances in Database Technology – EDBT '90. Proceedings, 1990. IX, 452 pages. 1990.

Vol. 417: P. Martin-Löf, G. Mints (Eds.), COLOG-88. International Conference on Computer Logic. Proceedings, 1988. VI, 338 pages. 1990.

Vol. 418: K. H. Bläsius, U. Hedtstück, C.-R. Rollinger (Eds.), Sorts and Types in Artificial Intelligence. Proceedings, 1989. VIII, 307 pages. 1990. (Subseries LNAI).

Vol. 419: K. Weichselberger, S. Pöhlmann, A Methodology for Uncertainty in Knowledge-Based Systems. VIII, 136 pages. 1990 (Subseries LNAI).

Vol. 420: Z. Michalewicz (Ed.), Statistical and Scientific Database Management, V SSDBM. Proceedings, 1990. V, 256 pages. 1990.

Vol. 421: T. Onodera, S. Kawai, A Formal Model of Visualization in Computer Graphics Systems. X, 100 pages. 1990.

Vol. 422: B. Nebel, Reasoning and Revision in Hybrid Representation Systems. XII, 270 pages. 1990 (Subseries LNAI).

Vol. 423: L. E. Deimel (Ed.), Software Engineering Education. Proceedings, 1990. VI, 164 pages. 1990.

Vol. 424: G. Rozenberg (Ed.), Advances in Petri Nets 1989. VI, 524 pages. 1990.

Vol. 425: C.H. Bergman, R. D. Maddux, D. L. Pigozzi (Eds.), Algebraic Logic and Universal Algebra in Computer Science. Proceedings, 1988. XI, 292 pages. 1990.

Vol. 426: N. Houbak, SIL – a Simulation Language. VII, 192 pages. 1990.

Vol. 427: O. Faugeras (Ed.), Computer Vision – ECCV 90. Proceedings, 1990. XII, 619 pages. 1990.

Vol. 428: D. Bjørner, C. A. R. Hoare, H. Langmaack (Eds.), VDM '90. VDM and Z – Formal Methods in Software Development. Proceedings, 1990. XVII, 580 pages. 1990.

Vol. 429: A. Miola (Ed.), Design and Implementation of Symbolic Computation Systems. Proceedings, 1990. XII, 284 pages. 1990.

Vol. 430: J. W. de Bakker, W.-P. de Roever, G. Rozenberg (Eds.), Stepwise Refinement of Distributed Systems. Models, Formalisms, Correctness. Proceedings, 1989. X, 808 pages. 1990.

Vol. 431: A. Arnold (Ed.), CAAP '90. Proceedings, 1990. VI, 285 pages. 1990.

Vol. 432: N. Jones (Ed.), ESOP '90. Proceedings, 1990. IX, 436 pages. 1990.

Vol. 433: W. Schröder-Preikschat, W. Zimmer (Eds.), Progress in Distributed Operating Systems and Distributed Systems Management. Proceedings, 1989. V, 206 pages. 1990.

Vol. 434: J.-J. Quisquater, J. Vandewalle (Eds.), Advances in Cryptology – EUROCRYPT '89. Proceedings, 1989. X, 710 pages. 1990.

Vol. 435: G. Brassard (Ed.), Advances in Cryptology – CRYPTO '89. Proceedings, 1989. XIII, 634 pages. 1990.

Vol. 436: B. Steinholtz, A. Sølvberg, L. Bergman (Eds.), Advanced Information Systems Engineering. Proceedings, 1990. X, 392 pages. 1990.

Lecture Notes in Computer Science

Edited by G. Goos and J. Hartmanis

468

S.G. Akl F. Fiala
W.W. Koczkodaj (Eds.)

Advances in Computing
and Information – ICCI '90

International Conference on Computing and Information
Niagara Falls, Canada, May 23–26, 1990
Proceedings

Springer-Verlag

Berlin Heidelberg New York London
Paris Tokyo Hong Kong Barcelona

Volume Editors

Selim G. Akl
Department of Computing and Information Science
Queen's University
Kingston, Canada K7L 3N6

Frantisek Fiala
School of Computer Science
Carleton University
Ottawa, Canada K1S 5B6

Waldemar W. Koczkodaj
Department of Mathematics and Computer Science
Laurentian University
Sudbury, Canada P3E 2C6

ICCI '90 was organized in cooperation with IEEE Hamilton Section and sponsored
by the Natural Sciences and Engineering Research Council of Canada (NSERC),
Carleton University in Ottawa and Laurentian University in Sudbury

CR Subject Classification (1987): D.1–2, E.2–4, F.0–2, H, I.2

ISBN 3-540-53504-7 Springer-Verlag Berlin Heidelberg New York
ISBN 0-387-53504-7 Springer-Verlag New York Berlin Heidelberg

Printing and binding: Druckhaus Beltz, Hemsbach/Bergstr.
2145/3140-543210 – Printed on acid-free paper

Preface

This volume contains papers presented at the International Conference on Computing and Information, ICCI'90, held in Niagara Falls, Ontario, Canada, May 23-26, 1990. All papers have been reviewed by at least two independent referees nominated by the Program Committee members. A full list of referees is enclosed (p. 528).

ICCI'90 was an international forum for the presentation of new results in research, development, and applications in computing and information. The primary goal of the meeting was to promote an exchange of ideas and cooperation between practitioners and theorists in the interdisciplinary fields of computing, communication and information theory.

The conference was organized along four streams:

A - Information and Coding Theory, Statistics and Probability
B - Foundations of Computer Science, Theory of Algorithms and Programming
C - Concurrency, Parallelism, Communications, Networking, Computer Architecture and VLSI
D - Data and Software Engineering, Database, Expert Systems, Information Systems, Decision Making and AI Methodologies

The contribution of each stream to the success of the conference was noticeable. In fact, each stream was a kind of subconference and consisted of theoretical papers as well as presentations on performance issues and implementation techniques.

General Chair was F. Fiala, Carleton University, Canada.

Organizing Committee:

W.W. Koczkodaj, Laurentian University, Canada, Chair
M.W. Herman, Laurentian University, Canada
G. Steinke, University of Passau, Germany

Stream Chairs:

Stream A - David Chiu, University of Guelph, Canada
Stream B - Lane A. Hemachandra, University of Rochester, USA
Stream C - R.P. Hopkins, University of Newcastle upon Tyne, UK
Stream D - Jaretta H. and G. Daryl Nord, Oklahoma State University, USA

The ICCI'90 Program Committee:

S.G. Akl, Queen's University, Canada, Chair
M. Cosnard, Ecole Normale Superieure de Lyon, France
K. Culik, University of South Carolina, USA
M. El-Gabaly, Kuwait University, Kuwait
J. Grant, Towson State University, USA
M.A.W. Houtsma, University of Twente, The Netherlands

M.E.C. Hull, University of Ulster at Jordanstown, UK
P.L. Kannappan, University of Waterloo, Canada
R.L. Kashyap, Purdue University, USA
V. Kumar, University of Missouri-Kansas City, USA
M.A. Langston, University of Tennessee, USA
H. Meijer, Queen's University, Canada
W. Oettli, University of Mannheim, Germany
M.M. Orlowska, University of Queensland, Australia
R.A. Paige, Courant Inst. of Math. Sciences, USA
W. Smyth, McMaster University, Canada
Ch. Stary, Institute for Applied Informatics, Austria
I. Stojmenovic, University of Ottawa, Canada
Ph.C. Treleaven, University College London, UK
Ch.T. Zahn, Pace University, USA

Electronic Mail Contacts:

For Asia and Australia - D. J. Chen, National Chiao Tung University, Taiwan ROC,
For Canada - Lixin Tao, Concordia University, Canada,
For Europe - Kai Jakobs, Technical University of Aachen, Germany,
For USA and South America - Manuel Bermudez, University of Florida, USA.

We wish to express our sincere gratitude to K. Peacock, the Chairman of IEEE Hamilton Section, S. Swing, the Vice-Chairman of IEEE Hamilton Section, D. Goldsack, the Dean of Science, L. Reed, the Vice-President, Research, and M. Dewson, the Vice-President, Academic at Laurentian University. A special appreciation is forwarded to them as they have been a true source of support and encouragement in organizing the conference. We thank M.A. Langston, University of Tennessee, W. Smyth, McMaster University, and I. Stojmenovic, University of Ottawa, for their considerable contribution to the reviewing process. R.C. Kick, Tennessee Technological University and M. Bermudez, University of Florida, have provided their help in coordinating presentations during the event in Niagara Falls. We thank H. Jurgensen for his editorial remarks and we would like to express our gratitude and appreciation to volunteers: L. Bermudez, D. Fiala, and M. Koczkodaj for their assistance in registration and information services.

Many other people were involved in the organization of ICCI'90 and we wish to thank each and every one of them.

Selim G. Akl
Francisek Fiala
Waldemar W. Koczkodaj

Sudbury, June 1990

Table of Contents

1. Summaries of Invited Lectures 1

2. Theory of Computing, Algorithms and Programming 13

R.S. Maier - *The Asymptotic Evolution of Data Structures* 14

J.D.P. Rolim - *On the Formal Aspects of Approximation Algorithms* 24

E. Eberbach - *Selected Aspects of the Calculus of Self-Modifiable Algorithms Theory* . 34

J.G. Geske, D. Kakihara - *Almost-Everywhere Complexity, Bi-Immunity and Nondeterministic Space* 44

D. Sheinwald, R.C. Pasco - *Deriving Deterministic Prediction Rules from Reduction Schemes* 52

W. Pugh - *Probabilistic Analysis of Set Operations With Constant-time Set Equality Test* 62

C.S. Wallace - *Classification by Minimum-Message-Length Inference* 72

F. Henglein - *Fast Left-Linear Semi-Unification* 82

T. Jiang - *On the Complexity of (Off-line) 1-tape ATM's Running in Constant Reversals* 92

P. Dietz, R. Raman - *A Constant Update Time Finger Search Tree* 100

R.A. Baeza-Yates, G.H. Gonnet - *Average Case Analysis of Algorithms using Matrix Recurrences* 110

A.P. Heinz - *Finding Two-Tree-Factor Elements of Tableau-Defined Monoids in Time $O(n^3)$* 120

J.V. Tucker, J.I. Zucker - *Toward a General Theory of Computation and Specification over Abstract Data Types* 129

I.A. Stewart - *Using The Hamiltonian Path Operator To Capture NP* 134

J. Wang - *Some Remarks on Polynomial Time Isomorphisms* 144

A.K. Singh - *An Axiomatization of Wait-Freedom and Low-Atomicity* 154

R. Harrison, H. Glaser - *The Gamma Model as a Functional Programming Tool* . . . 164

A.A. Toptsis, C.T. Yu, P.C. Nelson - *Computing the Transitive Closure of Symmetric Matrices* 174

3. Data and Software Engineering 185

K.-C. Liu - *An Environment for Information System Prototyping: A System Simulation Approach* 186

V. Yodaiken - *A Logic-free Method for Modular Composition of Specifications* 196

K. Okamoto, M. Hashimoto - *On Real-Time Program Specification Description with a Data Model-Based Language* 206

W. Ogryczak, K. Studzinski, K. Zorychta - *DINAS: Computer-Assisted System for Multi-Criteria Transportation and Location Analysis* 216

S. Khanna - *Logic Programming for Software Testing* 225

S.M. Chung - *Block Concatenated Code Word Surrogate File for Partial Match Retrieval* 235

D.A. Swayne, J. Storey, D. C.-L. Lam, I. Wong, A.S. Fraser - *Applications Development Toolkits For Environmental Modelling and Monitoring* 245

M. Brown, B. Czejdo - *A Hypertext for Literate Programming* 250

G. Steinke, G. Hamann - *Ethics and Computers: Can Universities Set the Standards?* 260

W. Boswell, A.L. Tharp - *Alternatives to the B+-tree* 266

V.G. Winters - *Minimal Perfect Hashing For Large Sets of Data* 275

M.T. Özsu, K. Barker - *Architectural Classification and Transaction Execution Models of Multidatabase System* 285

H.J.A. van Kuijk, F.H.E. Pijpers, P.M.G. Apers - *Semantic Query Optimization in Distributed Databases* 295

V.Y. Lum, K. Meyer-Wegener - *An Architecture for a Multimedia Database Management System Supporting Content Search* 304

H.H. Zhou - *Adaptive Expert Systems and Analogical Problem Solving* 314

J. Place, V. Kumar, A. van de Liefvoort - *The Behavior of Database Concurrency Control Mechanisms under Bursty Arrivals* 324

4. Computer Architecture, Concurrency, Parallelism, Communication and Networking 335

P.W. Proszynski - *The Core Concurrency* 336

A. Colbrook, C. Smythe - *Concurrent Data Structures* 346

J. Julliand, G.-R. Perrin - *Asynchronous Functional Parallel Programs* 356

J.-M. Adamo, C. Bonello - *Symbolic Configuration for SuperNode Multiprocessors* . 366

W. Zhou, B. Molinari - *A Model of Execution Time Estimating for RPC-Oriented Programs* 376

M. Lu - *Parallel Computation of Longest-Common-Subsequence* 385

C. C.-Y. Chen, S. K. Das - *Parallel Breadth-First and Breadth-Depth Traversals of General Trees* 395

B. Yu - *Parallelism via Speculation in Pure Prolog* 405

K. Saleh, R. Probert - *Synthesis of Error-Recoverable Protocol Specifications from Service Specifications* 415

S.K. Kim - *A Parallel Algorithm for Path-Min Queries in Trees* 425

L. Chen - *Efficient Deterministic Parallel Algorithms for Integer Sorting* 433

C.D. Marlin, M. Oudshoorn, D. Freidel - *A Model of Communication in Ada using Shared Data Abstractions* 443

Z.-Q. Luo - *Communication Complexity of Computing a Collection of Rational Functions* 453

G.H. Masapati, H. Ural - *Electing a Leader in a Synchronous Recursively Scalable Network* 463

J.R. Just - *Analysis of a Self-Reconfigurating Process of Fault-Tolerant Distributed Computing Systems* 473

T.A. Marsland, L. Meng - *Control of Bottlenecks in a Network Database Machine* . . 483

B. Klaassen - *A Hierarchical Multirate Method for Circuit Simulation on Parallel Computers* 493

M.H. Nodine, D.P. Lopresti, J.S. Vitter - *I/O Overhead and Parallel VLSI Architectures for Lattice Computations* 497

D.D. Sherlekar - *Optimality of Gauge and Degree-sensitive VLSI layouts of Planar Graphs* 507

C. Chevli, H.Y. Youn - *An Efficient VLSI Network Bridge Architecture for Local Area Networks* 517

Index of Authors 527

List of Reviewers 528

1. Summaries of Invited Lectures

Keynote Address outline

Education for Computing Professionals
David Lorge Parnas
Queen's University, Kingston, Ontario

I. Computing Professionals are Information System Engineers

In this information age, computers should be viewed as links in a communication system. They serve to transform information from the form in which it was produced to the form in which it is needed. Those who produce such systems should be viewed as engineers, not scientists.

It is time to ask whether Computing Science undergraduate education is in the best interests of the students, their employers, and society.

II. The Historical Debate

In the early 60's, there was strong opposition to the establishment of Computing Science as a separate discipline; both mathematicians and Electrical Engineers predicted that graduates of Computing Science programs would understand neither mathematics nor engineering. Their predictions deserve reexamination.

III. Computing Scientists: Mathematicians, Engineers, or Scientists?

Today, I am appalled at the inability of many Computing Science graduates to use basic mathematics. Computing Science graduates have heard about a lot of mathematics, but they don't know how to use it.

Further, many of those who work in the more practical areas of Computing Science seem to lack appreciation for the routine systematic analysis that is essential to professional engineering.

In Computing Science theory and practice have diverged. While classical mathematical topics, such as graph theory, continue to have applications in computing, most of what is taught in Computing Science "theory" courses is not relevant in the practical areas.

IV. Computing Science Education

Graduates of Computing Science programs are weak on fundamentals because they spend too much time on programming, programming languages, compilers and operating systems. Most Computing Science graduates confuse existence-proofs with products, and toys with useful tools.

Many Computing Science graduates are almost completely ignorant of information theory. As a result, analysis of important practical issues, such as the design of data representations, is done on an intuitive level.

Reliability requirements force the introduction of redundancy in computer systems. Unfortunately, current Computing Science graduates are usually unfamiliar with all but the most naive approaches to redundancy.

Many Computing Science graduates end up programming parts of control systems, such as those that run nuclear plants or adjust flight surfaces on aircraft. Unfortunately, I do not know of a single Computing Science program that requires its students to take a course in control theory.

V. What went wrong?

Most Computing Science departments were formed by a multi-disciplinary team. The members of the team were mathematicians interested in computing, electrical engineers who had built or used computers, and physicists who had been computer users. The set of topics that was included was often the intersection of what the founders knew, not the union. Further, the educational programs were designed around the interests of the faculty rather than the needs of the students.

VI. An Engineering Program for Computing Professionals

I still believe that a special educational program for computing professionals is needed. When I look at the programs produced by Engineers and Scientists who did not have such an education, I see that they are not prepared to apply engineering discipline to software design.

In [1], I propose a curriculum designed to draw heavily on the offerings of other departments and to emphasise mature fundamentals. The proposal in [1] is intended to start a discussion, not to be the final word.

VII. Conclusions

The program I propose will not produce people who can immediately take over the responsibilities of an employee who has left or been promoted. That is not the role of a University. Universities need not be teaching the latest technology. Our graduates need the fundamentals that prepare them for a lifetime of learning to understand the latest technology.

VIII.Reference

[1] Parnas, D.L., "Education for Computing Professionals", IEEE Computer, vol. 23, no. 1, January 1990, pp. 17-22.

Invited Address outline

MERGING OF SCORES FOR DECISION MAKING IN PRACTICE AND THEORY

Janos Aczél
Centre for Information Theory and Quantitative Economics
University of Waterloo, Waterloo, Ontario, Canada N2L 3G1

Performances of technologies and people, qualifications etc. are measured by their *scores* in respect to benchmarks, relative to those of some base performance (qualification). *For the purpose of comparisons, in order to arrive at a decision* on purchasing, hiring, promoting, etc. we merge the scores into a single number. The determination of price indices or of the index of leading economic indicators is a similar problem.

In practice often (weighted) *arithmetic means* are taken, *which is mostly incorrect both in theory and in practice,* though, as we will see, *it does not make difference in practice if the scores differ little.*

The *theory adopts* the (more or less) *reasonable requirements of the practice as postulates.* It is, for instance, reasonable to expect that, if the merged relative score of A is greater than that of B, both relative to a base performance C, then the same should be the order of the merged relative scores of A and B relative to D (order-invariance).

Several such reasonable expectations (postulates) can be formulated. In most cases we can determine *all merging formulas (functions)* satisfying one or more of these postulates. *It seems to be safe to take the geometric mean* of the individual *relative sources.* Our mathematical tools are some *basic functional equations.*

Invited Address outline

Designing parallel algorithms for transputer networks

Michel Cosnard

Laboratorie d'Informatique du Parallelisme
Ecole Normale Superieure de Lyon, France

In this lecture we discuss some algorithm design methodologies for distributed memory computers and show how classical algorithmic tools (divide and conquer, master-slaves, and others) can be efficiently used to obtain parallel algorithms. We also study in detail performance issues related to memory repartitions of the data, load balancing, synchronisation, distributed termination detection, data partitioning, communications, etc.

We illustrate these considerations on number theory algorithms and:
- discuss various implementations of the sieve of Erathostenes and obtain a fully efficient algorithm,
- study in detail the parallel implementation of the quadratic factoring sieve for factoring large integers (used in RSA cryptographic codes) and show how superlinear speedups can be obtained.

The illustration these par experimental works results are performed on a network of 32 transputers.

Invited Address outline

Distributed Computers: Object-vs. Unix-Based and Beyond

R.P. Hopkins, Computing Laboratory, University of Newcastle upon Tyne, U.K.

In this paper we consider architectures for extensible multi-level networks of computers. Given that some of the component computers may support concurrent computation, and may themselves be multi-processor systems, it is desirable that there be a common parallel architecture at all levels such that the entire network can be seen as a single distributed multi-processor computer.

Firstly, we cover issues involved in distributed computers, discussing object-based and Unix-based approaches. We consider their underlying models of storage (and thus addressing), execution and machine organisation and the extent to which these models are consistently applicable at three levels of system structure: the "programming" level within individual modules; the "system" level of interactions between modules within a single computer or local network; and "intersystem" level of interactions between modules within different systems which can connect and disconnect autonomously and permanently. We argue that neither (essentially system level) approach scales down to the programming level; and that the object-based approach is less adequate than the Unix-based approach in scaling up to the intersystems level.

We then identify a general architecture, an extension and rationalisation of the Unix approach, which is motivated by the requirement for complete scalability. This architecture is based on applying recursivity to each of the three structures of storage, execution and machine organization; and thus obtaining locality of interaction, inward extensibility (replacing a single component with a sub-structure), and outward extensibility (coming previously independent components).

Next we discuss the three principal ways of organizing concurrent computation at the programming level, namely control-data-and demand-driven, and consider their application to network interaction between concurrent computations in different computers. We show how these different organizations, and their possible combination, are subsumed within the general recursive architecture by extending the set of instruction/data interaction modes beyond the usual two read/write modes. At the network level this gives rise to a set of four fundamental transaction types, comprising the conventional remote procedure call and remote data access, and a generalisation of each. Finally, we touch on an abstract operational semantics for the primitive operations of the architecture (such as address binding, write operations).

In summary, we develop a recursively structured architecture, with Unix as its starting point, which integrates multi-computer network organisation and multi-processor computer organisation into a single multi-level distributed computer organisation and supports, at the network and computer levels, both the conventional control-driven model of computation and the data-and demand-driven models, using a common, formally defined, set of architectural primitives.

Invited Address outline

THE STRATEGIC SIGNIFICANCE OF EXPERT SYSTEMS: OPPORTUNITIES AND RISKS

Russell C. Kick
Tennessee Technological University, Cookeville, TN, USA

The advent of expert systems as a cost-effective management tool is a double-edged sword. On the one side, an expert system when properly deployed, offers a significant opportunity for increasing long-run profit. A poorly conceived an d ineffective system, on the other side, exposes the firm to considerable risk, which, if realized, could threaten the very existence of the organization.

An expert system embodies the collective knowledge of a firm's best minds in areas such as marketing and production. This knowledge is then leveraged by making it available within the firm to less experienced personnel who may then transact business in the same manner as the expert from whom the knowledge was extracted. For example, a computer manufacturer has been using a set of expert systems to market computers on the basis of every salesperson being able to develop exact configurations tailored to individual customer needs and then coordinating sales with manufacturing so that computers are delivered on time. This strategic competitive advantage has increased sales by an estimated $40 million per year.

Because such expert systems are so integrated into the very core of a business, they expose the company to substantial risk. Should a strategically placed expert system not function properly, competition would gain the advantage and firm sales, growth, and profit would be jeopardized. Codifying the expertise of the company puts the company in a position where a competitor could steal valuable knowledge and the competitive advantage would be lost. Extraordinary security and control must be maintained if the expertise is to be properly protected and effective standards must be in place to make certain that expert systems are properly developed, operated, and updated if their great potential to increase revenues, control costs and quality, and bring about better asset management and productivity are to be realized. Computer professionals and management have the mutual responsibility for selecting strategic, highpay off applications for expert systems and for making certain they are properly developed in order to minimize risk.

Invited Address outline

Time-Space Optimal Parallel Algorithms

Michael A. Langston[*]

Department of Computer Science
University of Tennessee
Knoxville, TN 37996, USA

A parallel algorithm is "time-space optimal" if it achieves optimal speedup and if it uses only a constant amount of extra space whenever the number of processors is fixed. Although the quest for efficient parallel file rearrangement methods has been a long-standing topic of intense interest, the vast majority of the published algorithms fail to meet at least one of these criteria.

Only in very recent efforts have parallel techniques been devised that simultaneously optimize *both* time and space. For merging, as an example, it is now possible in principle to merge two sorted lists of total length n on an EREW PRAM with k processors in $O(n/k + log\ n)$ time and $O(k)$ extra space. This scheme is thus time-space optimal for values of $k \le n/(log\ n)$. It is also stable, modifies neither the key nor any other part of a record, and naturally leads to time-space optimal parallel sorting. Moreover, it is "efficient" in the usual sense (its speedup is within a polylogarithmic factor of the optimum) for *any* value of k, suggesting that it may have practical merit even for relatively small files.

As an attractive side effect of minimizing space, modeling parallel computing with a bounded number of processors reflects more faithfully any real parallel computing environment. Methods such as this may be particularly useful in external file processing, real-time systems and other environments in which space is a critical resource.

Perhaps the most useful new technique to arise from the search for asymptotic parallel time-space optimality is one based on the use of what has been dubbed a "displacement table". In general, such a table permits each processor to determine in parallel (without read conflicts) the number of its records that are to be displaced by records from subfiles handled by other processors.

Open questions pertaining to this general subject abound, including extending this approach to other file management problems, simplifying known methods, and employing this line of attack with other parallel processing models. In fact, it has already been successfully extended to multi-channel broadcast networks.

----

[*] - Dr. Langston is also affiliated with the Department of Computer Science, Washington State University, Pullman, WA 99164, USA. His research has been supported in part by the National Science Foundation under grants MIP-8603879 and MIP-8919312, and by the Office of Naval Research under contract N00014-88-K-0343.

Invited Address outline

EXECUTIVE SUPPORT SYSTEMS FOR STRATEGIC ADVANTAGE

Jeretta Horn Nord and G. Daryl Nord
Management Information Systems
Oklahoma State University
Stillwater, Oklahoma
BITNET: MGMTJHN@OSUCC and MGMTGDN@OSUCC

SUMMARY

An Executive Support System (ESS) is a Decision Support System (DSS) designed to meet the specific needs of executives. Executives are people at or near the top of an organizational hierarchy who exert a strong influence on the course taken by the organization. Only recently have executives realised that the computer is a cost effective tool which can assist and support business decisions. Still in its infancy, Decision Support Systems for executives will become a vital segment of management information systems.

Executive decisions, characterized as broad and highly unstructured, include strategic planning, tactical planning, and/or fire-fighting activities. Hypothetical questions such as the following are among those in which executives need technological support for strategic decision-making. What are the financial implications of opening three new stores? What is the best location for an additional company? What caused the drop in international sales? How long can we wait before building another plant? How much market share can be gained by implementing a new computer system?

Executive support systems can benefit decision making situations in which 1) expertise in scarce, vague, or dispersed; 2) humans suffer from cognitive overload; or 3) the decision maker fails to monitor all available information, or cannot simultaneously manipulate all available information to obtain optimal solutions in the desired time frame. In addition to decision support, good executive support systems should include tools for time management and team coordination, thereby providing standards, speedy decisions, and an image of professionalism.

Struggling to compete in an increasingly complex global environment, managers will increasingly rely on information technology to crystallize and communicate company strategy and transform their organizations to meet the competition. Research indicates that users of executive support systems feel a lot more confident about the decisions they have made, and, as a result of decision-support tools, have been able to reach decisions quicker. Thus, it is inevitable that executive support systems will become commonplace over the next decade to aid in strategic decision support for competitive advantage.

Invited Address outline

On the Semantic Enhancement of Information Systems Design

Maria E. Orlowska

Key Centre for Software Technology
Department of Computer Science, University of Queensland, 4072 Australia

For the last several years, recent trends towards the industrialization of expert systems and the semantic enhancement of information systems have led to a general agreement that there is some sort of relationship between the two fields.

The problem of designing a knowledge system (information system or expert system) is a complex one; it involves the analysis of an informal and often incomplete statement about an enterprise or organization and then formal application of the established theories.

A more fundamental view of the informal part of a design is concerned only with the deep semantic structure of the knowledge which is represented in the database or knowledge base and on the semantic specifications of the operations that can manipulate that knowledge. At this conceptual level, we can regards knowledge bases and databases as (state-varying) a collection of facts about some application areas and a collection of rules which determine the permitted collection of facts. This conceptual level of descriptions completely excludes any implementation or user presentation aspects, but includes linguistic aspects (which can be effectively used for design and validation).

In general, we focus on enhancements of existing information systems modelling methods by the development of a computer-based tool for the design of conceptual schemata for large systems, and finally the designing of high quality relational databases.

We describe a tool system (ESM) for detection of unwanted properties (such as implied fact types) of a conceptual schema and show how the system supports the design process. The system used a rigorous, information-content-preserving approach to schema transformation, but combines it with heuristic and user interaction. We show how normalization techniques, particularly the synthesis method originally developed to produce an initial relational schema from functional dependencies, apply in the redesign of NIAM (Nijssen Information Analysis Method) conceptual schemas. The redesign task is important in modifications of a schema towards minimization of knowledge representation for a particular application. We present our approach for identifying redundant relationships and to show how relationship inference can be supported by user interaction removing many unavoidable errors in the design process.

The system is implemented in the Key Centre for Software Technology at the University of Queensland. It is now undergoing testing for large database design projects. We conclude with further possibilities of improvements to the presented system.

Invited Address outline*

Theory of Rough Sets: A New Methodology for Knowledge Discovery

Zdzislaw Pawlak

Institute of Computer Science, Technical University of Warsaw, Warsaw, Poland

Intuitively, knowledge can be perceived as a body of information about some parts of reality, which constitute our domain of interest. This definition, however, fails to meet standards of precision and; at a closer look, it has multiple meanings, tending to mean one or several things, depending on the context and the area of interest.

We propose here a formal definition of the term "knowledge" and we show some of its basic properties. We realize that the proposed understanding of knowledge is not sufficiently general, nor is it in accordance with the widely assumed paradigm in the AI community nowadays - yet it seems to cover a variety of domains, particularly in AI-like machine learning, pattern recognition, decision support systems, expert systems and others.

We do not aim to form a new, general theory of knowledge, but we have in mind practical applications. We advocate a rough set concept (cf. [1]) as a theoretical framework for discussions about knowledge, particularly when imprecise knowledge is of primary concern. Our claim is that knowledge is deep-seated in the classificatory abilities of human beings and other species. For mathematical reasons we will often use equivalence relations instead of classifications since these two terms are mutually interchangeable and relations are easier to operate with.

Rough set theory constitutes the basis for new data analysis algorithms. It is a concept, not just a technique. For example, in mathematics we use integral and derivative concepts. Both concepts have a number of applications whose results depend upon the problem at hand. Why is the rough set theory approach so successful in data analysis? How does it differ from other methods like statistics? The answer is quite easy. Rough set theory has pioneered a new perspective on data. Internal relationships (rules governing the data) rather than its measures like totals, averages, regressions or similar characteristics are examined. The method has its roots in topology rather than in statistics. It "looks" at the inside data nature for unknown internal relationships instead of trying to get more and more data with higher and higher precision, which is the object of all statistical methods. The rough set theory facilitates investigation of data relationships, data reduction and significance, decision rules-generation , and many other data characteristics.

References

[1]   Kick, R.C., Koczkodaj, W.W., "Business Data Analysis by Rough Sets Theory", 1990, (manuscript of a paper to appear)

Invited Address (Special Session) outline

Is there Science and Technology (Funding) after the Cold War?

Barbara Simons
IBM Almaden Research Center, San Jose, USA

We are living in extraordinary times. The major upheavals in the political landscape of the world in recent months were not foreseen by any planner. Many of the institutions created to meet various countries' national needs in science and technology seem poorly adapted to the world we are entering.

A significant amount of the science and technology infrastructure in the United States has been supported directly or indirectly by the military build-up stemming from the Cold War. This phenomenon is not limited to industry; during the past few years, between 60% and 70% of federally funded academic computer science research has been supported by the Department of Defense. The remainder of the research is funded primarily by the Department of Energy, the National Aeronautic and Space Administration, both of which have non-trivial military components, and the National Science Foundation.

In the talk we shall:

- Present a brief history of funding of academic computer science in the United States.

- Discuss some of the issues and controversies related to the current system of funding in the United States.

- Consider possible options for a civilian-oriented science and technology base.

- Discuss how we might encourage national and international cooperation on science and technology issues, such as the environment, which are of general concern.

Audience participation will be encouraged. We hope that the talk will provide a forum in which we can compare funding strategies of different countries.

2. Theory of Computing, Algorithms and Programming

The Asymptotic Evolution of Data Structures*

Robert S. Maier

Department of Mathematics, University of Arizona,

Tucson, Arizona 85721, USA

rsm@math.arizona.edu (E-mail), +1 602 621 8322 (Fax)

Abstract

The evolution of certain pointer-based implementations of dictionaries, linear lists and priority queues is studied. Under the assumption of equiprobability of histories, *i.e.*, of paths through the internal state space of the implementation, the $n \to \infty$ asymptotics of the space and time costs of a sequence of n supported operations are computed.

For list implementations the mean integrated spatial cost is asymptotically proportional to $n^{3/2}$, and its standard deviation to $n^{3/2}$. For d-heap implementations of priority queues the mean integrated space cost grows only as $n^2/\sqrt{\log n}$, *i.e.* more slowly than the worst-case integrated cost. The standard deviation grows as $n^{3/2}$.

These asymptotics reflect the convergence as $n \to \infty$ of the normalized structure sizes to datatype-dependent deterministic functions of time, as earlier discovered by Louchard. This phenomenon is clarified with the aid of large deviation theory, and path integral techniques.

Keywords: dynamic data structures, expected costs, stochastic modelling, large deviations

1. Introduction

A number of authors [2,3,4,5,11,12,13] have derived asymptotic expressions for the average cost of long sequences of operations on such data structures as priority queues and dictionaries. Usually one assumes an *equiprobability of histories*: all possible sequences of alterations of the data structure are taken as equiprobable. This includes alterations consequent on the insertion of a datum, on the deletion of a datum, and on accessing the structure to query it or to alter a datum in some way without removing it.

This note treats the cases of list and d-heap implementations of priority queues, and the case of list implementations of linear lists and dictionaries. In the case of dictionaries, an arbitrary number of query types are allowed.

In this framework, results on list implementations have been obtained previously by the combinatoric techniques of Flajolet *et al.* [3,4,5] and the more probabilistic method of Louchard [12,13]. The present treatment extends theirs by covering heap implementations as well as lists. Much more importantly, it brings to bear the powerful and user-friendly formalism of path integration. This formalism originated in physics [14], and has close ties to the mathematical theory of large deviations [6,15]. It is only now being applied to the analysis of computing systems [8]. This is its first application to dynamic data structures.

It turns out that the *asymptotic determinism* recently discovered by Louchard [12] holds very generally: in the limit of long histories, the most likely evolutions of the data structure are those that cluster tightly around a deterministic path, which can be computed explicitly. Consequently the integrated space and time costs, when normalized, converge as $n \to \infty$ to deterministic values. In

*This work was supported in part by AFOSR grant 88-0189.

the case of list implementations [3,4,5,12] the limiting costs are quadratic in n, so that expected costs increase in the limit as fast as worst-case costs. For heaps the expected costs increase rather less rapidly: the integrated space cost as $n^2/\sqrt{\log n}$, and the integrated time as $n \log n$. In expectation the spatial cost differs markedly from its worst-case value, which is quadratic in n.

2. The Probabilistic Model

Suppose one wished to store records in and retrieve records from a pointer-based data structure, according to keys selected from some linearly ordered set. The simplest operations are insertion (I) and deletion (D). The data structure may also support queries and operations that modify the stored data without reshaping the structure; these operations will be referred to generically as "queries" and denoted $Q^1, \ldots, Q^l$. Datatypes that fit into this framework include

- Dictionaries ($DICT_l$). Support I, D and l distinct types of query.

- Linear lists (LL). Support I and D only, so that $LL = DICT_0$.

- Priority queues (PQ). Support I and D only. D is interpreted as a D_{min} or 'delete min' operation; it takes no arguments, and acts only on the key of minimum rank.

This note analyses lists (L), both unsorted (UL) and sorted (SL), and d-heaps (H_d), as implementations of these datatypes.

From the point of view of an external observer, the evolution of a a data structure is specified by an "operation word" w over the alphabet

$$\Sigma = \{I, D, Q^1 \ldots Q^l\}.$$

The only constraint on such words is that $\#(D) \leq \#(I)$ for any prefix of w, since y_j, the number of stored data (key/value pairs) after j operations, must not drop below zero. By assumption, that the data structure begins empty.

The set of allowed operation words of length n, $\Lambda_n \subseteq \Sigma_n$, is a natural set over which to randomize if one wishes to compute average performance. If one further restricts Λ_n by requiring that w satisfy $\#(D) = \#(I)$, so that the structure ends empty as well as begins empty, then the structure size as a function of time will be a discrete analogue of the Brownian excursion process.

But in defining a set of evolutions over which to average, one should really *annotate* the operation words by indicating the location of each alteration to the data structure. There is a a a one-to-one correspondence between *internal* histories and appropriately annotated words in Λ_n. For example,

$$I_0 Q_1^3 I_1 I_1 Q_2^1 D_2 Q_1^2 D_1 D_0 \tag{1}$$

is a possible history of length $n = 9$ for a list implemention of a dictionary. This word subsumes the operation word $I Q^3 I I Q^1 D Q^2 D D$ (representing two insertions followed by two deletions, interspersed with queries of various sorts), and the subscripts on each operation indicate the location of the accompanying alteration to the list. If a list has grown to size y, then there are $m(y, O)$ possible ways in which operation O can alter it, with $m(y, O)$ given by

$$m(y, O) = \begin{cases} y, & O = D, Q \\ y + 1, & O = I \\ 1, & O = D_{min}, \end{cases} \tag{2}$$

If the jth operation is O then r, the subscript on O, must satisfy

$$1 \leq r \leq m(y_j, O). \tag{3}$$

X	Y	$E\{S^{X,Y}/n^2\}$	$\sigma\{S^{X,Y}/n^2\}$
$DICT_0$	L	$2\pi^{-2}$	$(16\pi^{-4} - 3\pi^{-2}/2)^{1/2}n^{-1/2}$
$DICT_2$	L	$1/6$	$(1/6\sqrt{5})n^{-1/2}$
PQ	L	$1/6$	$(1/3\sqrt{5})n^{-1/2}$

Table 1: Asymptotics of the mean and standard deviation of the $S^{X,Y}/n^2$, following [4,5,12].

Similarly for the case of d-heaps one has

$$m(y, I) = \lceil \log_d(d-1)(y+1) \rceil$$
$$m(y, D_{min}) \sim \alpha \log_d(d-1)(y+1)$$

In the case of heaps $m(y, D_{min})$, the number of distinct alterations that can result from a single D_{min} operation, depends on the ordering of the stored keys as well as on y. Though the sift-down procedure invoked by the D_{min} operation could in principle terminate in any of $\lceil \log_d(d-1)(y+1) \rceil$ different ways, some may be incompatible with the present configuration of stored keys. It is difficult to average over the possible configurations, but one may assume $m(y, D_{min}) \sim \alpha \log_d y$, i.e., that on the average a sifted-down datum penetrates some fraction α of the distance to the bottom of the heap. The deterministic asymptotics of the heap size turn out to be independent of α.

The annotated strings ("schemata") of the form (1) make up the probability space over which we will compute expectations. The random variables of interest are the costs, including the integrated space cost

$$S = \sum_{j=1}^{n} y_j. \tag{4}$$

To distinguish among the different datatypes, one will write $S^{X,Y}$, in which the superscripts X and Y denote datatype ($DICT_l$, PQ) and implementation (SL, UL, H_d) respectively. Also of interest are the temporal costs

$$T^{X,Y} = \sum_{j=1}^{n} t^{X,Y}(O_j, y_{j-1}, r_j). \tag{5}$$

Here $t^{X,Y}(O, y, r)$ is the time needed to perform operation O on a structure of size y if it results in alteration r, and $\{O_j\}_{j=1}^{n}$ and $\{r_j\}_{j=1}^{n}$ are the operations and subscripts in the word w. A natural choice for t is

$$t^{X,Y}(O, y, r) = \begin{cases} r-1, & X = DICT_l, \ Y = SL, \\ & O \in \{I, D, Q_1, \cdots, Q_l\} \\ r-1, & X = PQ, \ Y = SL, \ O = I \\ 0, & X = PQ, \ Y = SL, \ O = D \\ 0, & X = PQ, \ Y = UL, \ O = I \\ y-1, & X = PQ, \ Y = UL, \ O = D \\ r-1, & X = PQ, \ Y = H_d, \ O = I \\ r-1, & X = PQ, \ Y = H_d, \ O = D. \end{cases} \tag{6}$$

since in all cases r is the number of pointers that must be dereferenced during the carrying out of operation O_r on the structure. This choice for t counts the number of comparisons that must be performed.

If one assumes that all schemata in Λ_n occur with equal probability, what is known about the distribution of the $S^{X,Y}$ and $T^{X,Y}$ for large n? The results of Flajolet et al. [4,5] and Louchard [12] for $Y = L$ are summarised in Table 1 and Table 2. Louchard, moreover, proved that these random variables are asymptotically Gaussian.

X	Y	$E\left\{T^{X,Y}/n^2\right\}$	$\sigma\left\{T^{X,Y}/n^2\right\}$
$DICT_0$	SL	π^{-2}	—
$DICT_2$	SL	$1/12$	$(1/6\sqrt{5})n^{-1/2}$
PQ	SL	$1/24$	$(1/6\sqrt{10})n^{-1/2}$
PQ	UL	$1/12$	$(1/6\sqrt{5})n^{-1/2}$

Table 2: Asymptotics of the mean and standard deviation of the $T^{X,Y}/n^2$, following [4,5,12].

In the following sections the elegant and user-friendly path integral formalism is used to rederive their results. It is also used to derive the asymptotics for d-heap implementations, and to extend the treatment of $DICT_l$ to arbitrary l.

The asymptotic determinism mentioned in Section 1 is manifested in Tables 1 and 2. For the list implementations that the tables cover, the integrated space and time costs are quadratic in n. Since that is also the worst-case behavior, it is reasonable to call $S^{X,Y}/n^2$ and $T^{X,Y}/n^2$ the 'normalized' costs. As $n \to \infty$ the variances of the normalized costs tend to zero, so they converge in probability to certain limiting values. This striking behavior will be rederived in the following sections. But in the case of heap implementations it will be shown that the integrated costs increase less rapidly in expectation than do the worst-case costs, and that a different normalizing factor must be used.

3. Asymptotics of the Random Process

Large deviation theory has proven itself a powerful tool in the analysis of random processes [6,15]. It will now be applied to the process y_j of Section 2, in terms of which the random variables $S^{X,Y}$ and $T^{X,Y}$ are defined.

Define the normalized data structure size, as a function of time, to be

$$x(t) := g(n)^{-1}y_{[nt]}, \quad t \in [0,1]. \tag{7}$$

The normalization factor $g(n)$ must be chosen to ensure well-behaved $n \to \infty$ limits. As noted at the end of the last section, $g(n)$ equals n if $X = L$. The appropriate $g(n)$ for heap implementations will be derived below.

To leading order in n, the normalized integrated space cost

$$S/ng(n) \sim \int_{t=0}^{1} x(t)\,dt \tag{8}$$

and the asymptotics of the random process $x(t)$ will determine those of $S/ng(n)$.

The probability measure on the space of $n \to \infty$ continuous limiting paths $\{x(t)\}_{0 \le t \le 1}$ can be obtained from the joint probability distribution of the $\{y_j\}_{j=0}^{n}$. Note first that the assumed equiprobability of operation words implies that an allowed size history y_j has relative probability

$$\prod_{j=1}^{n} m(y_{j-1}, O_j). \tag{9}$$

To leading order in n this is independent of the operations O_j, equalling

$$\begin{cases} \prod_{j=1}^{n}(y_j + 1), & X = DICT \\ \prod_{j=1}^{n}(y_j + 1)^{1/2}, & X = PQ, Y = L \\ \prod_{j=1}^{n}\lceil \log_d(d-1)(y_j+1)\rceil^{1/2} \times & \\ \quad \lceil \alpha \log_d(d-1)(y_j+1)\rceil^{1/2}, & X = PQ, Y = H_d \end{cases} \tag{10}$$

The priority queue case of (10) requires that the number of I and D (i.e., D_{min}) operations be equal. At this point one notes that the constant α does not affect absolute probabilities, and can be dropped.

To leading order in n, the weighting factors (10) are equal to

$$e^{\sum_{j=1}^{n} W^{X,Y}(y_j)} \tag{11}$$

in which the (X, Y)-dependent function $W^{X,Y}(y)$ is defined to be

$$W^{X,Y}(y) := \begin{cases} \log y, & X = DICT \\ (1/2)\log y, & X = PQ, Y = L \\ \log\log y, & X = PQ, Y = H_d. \end{cases}$$

This factor affects the relative probabilities of scaled paths $\{x(t)\}_{0 \le t \le 1}$ by weighting them by

$$e^{\int_0^1 V_n^{X,Y}(x(t))\, dt} \tag{12}$$

in which the (X, Y)- and n-dependent function $V_n^{X,Y}$ equals

$$V_n^{X,Y}(y) := \begin{cases} n\log x, & X = DICT \\ (n/2)\log x, & X = PQ, Y = L \\ n\log g(n)\log x, & X = PQ, Y = H_d. \end{cases} \tag{13}$$

This follows by substituting (7) into (11), and (in the case of heaps) keeping only the leading term.

However, to obtain a complete expression for the probability measure on the space of normalized paths, one must determine what it would have been in the absence of (9) or (12). That is to say, if y_j were an unbiased random walk built up from I, D and Q operations, what probability measure on the $\{x(t)\}_{0 \le t \le 1}$ would be obtained by taking the $n \to \infty$ limit? The answer depends on the increments $\Delta := y_j - y_{j-1}$, which are I.I.D. random variables of mean zero. They are distributed by

$$P\{\Delta = k\} = \begin{cases} 1/(l+2), & k = -1 \\ l/(l+2), & k = 0 \\ 1/(l+2), & k = 1 \end{cases}$$

if $X = DICT_l$, with the distribution for $X = PQ$ being the same as that for $X = DICT_0$.

According to large deviation theory, as developed by Ventcel and Freidlin [15,6] the limiting measure on paths $x(\cdot)$ is

$$e^{-(g(n)^2/n)\int_0^1 T^{X,Y}(\dot{x}(t))\, dt} \mathcal{D}x(\cdot) \tag{14}$$

in which, assuming $E\{\Delta\} = 0$,

$$T^{X,Y}(u) = \begin{cases} \sup_{\theta \in \mathbb{R}} \left[\theta u - \log E\{e^{\theta\Delta}\}\right], & g(n) \propto n \\ u^2/2\, E\{\Delta^2\}, & g(n) = o(n). \end{cases} \tag{15}$$

If $g(n) = \Theta(n)$, then $T^{X,Y}(u)$ is the Legendre transform of the generating function of the cumulants of Δ. In (14) $\mathcal{D}x(\cdot)$ is a 'flat' measure on the space of paths $x(\cdot)$.

The form of (14) allows one to determine the appropriate scaling to use as $n \to \infty$, i.e., to choose $g(n)$. Combining (14) with (12) one gets

$$e^{-\int_0^1 \left((g(n)^2/n)T^{X,Y}(\dot{x}(t)) - V_n^{X,Y}(x(t))\right)\, dt} \mathcal{D}x(\cdot). \tag{16}$$

To yield a well-defined limit as $n \to \infty$ the two terms in the exponent must have similar asymptotics. But by (13), $V_n^{X,Y}$ is proportional to n unless $X = PQ$ and $Y = H_d$, in which case it contains a factor $n\log g(n)$. One therefore chooses

$$g(n) = \begin{cases} n, & X = DICT \\ n, & X = PQ, Y = L \\ n/\sqrt{\log n}, & X = PQ, Y = H_d. \end{cases} \tag{17}$$

The leading-order term in the asymptotic measure (16) will accordingly be

$$e^{-h(n)\int_0^1 \left(T^{X,Y}(\dot{x}(t))-V^{X,Y}(x(t))\right)\,dt}\,\mathcal{D}x(\cdot) \tag{18}$$

in which the n-dependent factor in the exponent, now the same for both terms, is

$$h(n) = \begin{cases} n, & X = DICT \\ n, & X = PQ, Y = L \\ n/\log n, & X = PQ, Y = H_d. \end{cases} \tag{19}$$

$V^{X,Y}$ signifies $V_n^{X,Y}(t)$ with the n-dependence removed, namely

$$V^{X,Y} = \begin{cases} \log x, & X = DICT \\ (1/2)\log x, & X = PQ, Y = L \\ \log x, & X = PQ, Y = H_d \end{cases} \tag{20}$$

Define

$$L(x, \dot{x}) := T(\dot{x}) - V(x). \tag{21}$$

Then (18) may be written compactly as

$$e^{-h(n)\int_0^1 L^{X,Y}(x(t),\dot{x}(t))\,dt}\,\mathcal{D}x(\cdot). \tag{22}$$

To obtain an explicit expression for $L(x, \dot{x})$ one must first compute $T^{X,Y}(u)$. Equation (15) yields, after a bit of computation

$$T^{X,Y}(u) = \begin{cases} (\frac{l+2}{4})[(1+u)\log(1+u)+ \\ \qquad (1-u)\log(1-u)], & X = DICT_l \\ (1/2)[(1+u)\log(1+u)+ \\ \qquad (1-u)\log(1-u)], & X = PQ, Y = L \\ u^2/2, & X = PQ, Y = H_d. \end{cases} \tag{23}$$

(The logarithmic expressions are interpreted as equalling $+\infty$ if $u \notin (-1, 1)$.) By combining (23) and (20) one gets

$$L^{X,Y}(x, \dot{x}) = \begin{cases} (\frac{l+2}{4})[(1+\dot{x})\log(1+\dot{x})+ \\ \qquad (1-\dot{x})\log(1-\dot{x})] - \log x, & X = DICT_l \\ (1/2)[(1+\dot{x})\log(1+\dot{x})+ \\ \qquad (1-\dot{x})\log(1-\dot{x}) - \log x], & X = PQ, Y = L \\ \dot{x}^2/2 - \log x, & X = PQ, Y = H_d. \end{cases} \tag{24}$$

The interpretation of $L(x, \dot{x})$, and the exponential weight factor in (22), is discussed in the next section.

4. Limiting Paths and Expected Costs

As $n \to \infty$ the relative probabilities of the normalized data structure sizes are given by (18), which is of a somewhat unusual form. It implies that for finite n the most likely sizes, as functions of time, are those for which the integral

$$\int_{t=0}^1 L(x(t), \dot{x}(t))\,dt \tag{25}$$

is minimized, and that as $n \to \infty$ the model gives negligible weight to all others. This sort of "asymptotic determinism" was first discovered by Louchard [12] by other means, but in the

l	x_0	$t(z)$
2	1/4	$1 - \sqrt{1-z}$
6	3/16	$\frac{1}{4}\left[2 - (z+2)\sqrt{1-z}\right]$
10	5/64	$\frac{1}{96}\left[8 - (3z^2 + 4z + 8)\sqrt{1-z}\right]$

Table 3: The limiting normalized data structure size for $X = DICT_l$ and $Y = L$, with $l \equiv 2 \pmod 4$. Here z denotes $(x^*_{DICT_l,L}/x_0)^{4/(l+2)}$, and x_0 is the maximum size attained.

l	x_0	$t(z)$
0	π^{-1}	$\pi^{-1} \arcsin(z)$
4	$2/3\pi$	$\pi^{-1}\left[\arcsin(z) - z\sqrt{1-z^2}\right]$
8	$16/45\pi$	$\pi^{-1}\left[\arcsin(z) - (\frac{2}{3}z^3 + z)\sqrt{1-z^2}\right]$

Table 4: The limiting normalized data structure size for $X = DICT_l$ and $Y = L$, with $l \equiv 0 \pmod 4$. Here z denotes $(x^*_{DICT_l,L}/x_0)^{2/(l+2)}$, and x_0 is the maximum size attained.

framework of measures on path spaces it arises very naturally. It is reminiscent of the appearance of a deterministic path in the low-diffusion limit of exit time problems [6].

The problem of minimizing (in general, extremizing) such a functional of paths as (25) is familiar from the calculus of variations [1] and classical mechanics [7]. The extremizing path $x^*_{X,Y}(\cdot)$ will satisfy the Euler-Lagrange equation

$$\frac{d}{dt}\frac{\partial L}{\partial \dot{x}} - \frac{\partial L}{\partial x} = 0. \tag{26}$$

It turns out to be easier to solve this equation for $t(x^*)$ than for $x^*(t)$.

In the dictionary case $t(x^*)$ is particularly easy to compute if l is even. $t(x^*)$ is displayed in Tables 3 and 4: if $l = 2, 6, 10, \ldots$ then $t(x^*)$ is algebraic, but if $l = 0, 4, 8, \ldots$ then it involves a trigonometric function as well. If the number of query types is odd (for example, if $\Sigma = \{I, D, Q\}$ so that $l = 1$) then the integration is far more difficult; $t(x^*)$ must be expressed in terms of elliptic functions. That case is not explored further here. Even if l is even, it may be difficult to invert $t(x^*)$ to obtain $x^*(t)$ in terms of elementary functions. It can certainly be done if $l = 0, 2$ or 6. The expression for $x^*_{DICT_6,L}(t)$ is rather complicated, and is left as an exercise to the reader; it follows from the cubic formula. The expressions

$$x^*_{DICT_l,L}(t) = \begin{cases} \pi^{-1}\sin \pi t, & l = 0 \\ t - t^2, & l = 2 \end{cases}$$

for $x^*_{DICT_0,L}(t)$ and $x^*_{DICT_2,L}(t)$ agree with those found by Louchard [12].

Similarly if $X = PQ$ and $Y = H_d$ one can solve (26) to get

$$t(x^*) = \frac{1}{2}\operatorname{erfc}\left(\sqrt{\log(x_0/x)}\right), \tag{27}$$

erfc$(\cdot)$ denoting the complementary error function. Remarkably, this expression for $t(x^*_{PQ,H_d})$ does not contain d. The leading-order asymptotic behavior of the size of a d-heap, when subjected to a random sequence of n I and $D_{\min}$ operations, is independent of d. By (17) and (27), the maximum size attained by the heap is asymptotic to $n/\sqrt{2\log n}$.

For any choice of X and Y, from the asymptotic path $t(x^*)$ may be derived the asymptotics of $E\{S_{X,Y}\}$. By (8),

$$E\{S^{X,Y}\} \sim ng(n)\int_{t=0}^{1} x^*_{X,Y}(t)\,dt.$$

X	Y	$E\{S^{X,Y}\}$	$\|S^{X,Y}\|_\infty$
$DICT_l$	L	$4(l+2)^{-1}\Gamma(\frac{l+2}{2})^4\Gamma(\frac{l+2}{4})^{-4}\Gamma(l+2)^{-1}\,n^2$	$n^2/2$
PQ	L	$n^2/6$	$n^2/2$
PQ	H_d	$\pi^{1/2}n^2/2\sqrt{\log n}$	$n^2/2$

Table 5: The asymptotics of $E\{S^{X,Y}\}$ and $\|S^{X,Y}\|_\infty$, the expected and worst-case integrated space costs, as $n \to \infty$.

X	Y	$E\{T^{X,Y}\}$	$\|T^{X,Y}\|_\infty$
$DICT_l$	SL	$2(l+2)^{-1}\Gamma(\frac{l+2}{2})^4\Gamma(\frac{l+2}{4})^{-4}\Gamma(l+2)^{-1}\,n^2$	$n^2/2$
PQ	SL	$n^2/24$	$n^2/4$
PQ	UL	$n^2/12$	$n^2/4$
PQ	H_d	$O(n\log_d n)$	$n\log_d n$

Table 6: The asymptotics of $E\{T^{X,Y}\}$ and $\|T^{X,Y}\|_\infty$, the expected and worst-case integrated time costs, as $n \to \infty$.

That is to say, $E\{S^{X,Y}\}$ is $ng(n)$ times the area under the curve $x^*_{X,Y}(t)$. The resulting asymptotics are displayed in Table 5. The asymptotics of $E\{S^{PQ,L}\}$ are, as remarked, the same as those of $E\{S^{DICT_2,L}\}$. And to leading order $E\{S^{PQ,H_d}\}$ is independent of d. For the sake of completeness the asymptotic behavior of $\|S^{X,Y}\|_\infty$, the worst-case integated space cost, is also tabulated. For all choices of X and Y it is clearly $n^2/2$.

By direct computation one can confirm the results of Flajolet $et\ al.$ [4,5] and Louchard [12] on $E\{S^{X,L}\}$. If $l=0$ the asymptotic expression for $E\{S^{DICT_l,L}\}$ reduces to $2\pi^{-2}n^2$, and if $l=2$ it reduces to $n^2/6$. These were the results reproduced in Table 1.

From the differential equation (26) one can also deduce the leading-order asymptotics of the time cost $E\{T^{X,Y}\}$. In general it is harder to handle $T^{X,Y}$ than $S^{X,Y}$. By (4) the integrated space cost $S^{X,Y}$ is a random variable on the space of operation words, in fact on the space of paths y_j. But by (5) the integrated time is defined on a larger space, which includes the "annotations". These annotations specify the details of each operation (insertion, deletion or query of whatever type) on the data structure.

However, the asymptotics of $E\{T^{X,Y}\}$ follow easily from those of $E\{S^{X,Y}\}$. As noted in Section 2, the subscript r on an operation O_r, which indicates the location of the alteration performed on the structure, ranges uniformly between 1 and $m(y,O)$. To leading order in n its expected value is $m(y,O)/2$, so by (6) and (3)

$$E\{t^{X,Y}(O,y,\cdot)\} = \begin{cases} y/2, & X = DICT_l,\ Y = SL, \\ & \qquad O \in \{I,D,Q_1,\cdots,Q_l\} \\ y/2, & X = PQ,\ Y = SL,\ O = I \\ 0, & X = PQ,\ Y = SL,\ O = D \\ 0, & X = PQ,\ Y = UL,\ O = I \\ y, & X = PQ,\ Y = UL,\ O = D \\ \frac{1}{2}\log_d y, & X = PQ,\ Y = H_d,\ O = I \\ \frac{a}{2}\log_d y, & X = PQ,\ Y = H_d,\ O = D. \end{cases} \tag{28}$$

to that order.

But by comparing

$$E\{T^{X,Y}\} = E\left\{\sum_{j=1}^{n} t^{X,Y}\right\} = \sum_{j=1}^{n} E\{t^{X,Y}\},$$

the consequence of (6), with

$$E\left\{S^{X,Y}\right\} = E\left\{\sum_{j=1}^{n} y_j\right\} = \sum_{j=1}^{n} E\left\{y_j\right\}$$

one deduces

$$E\left\{T^{X,Y}\right\}/E\left\{S^{X,Y}\right\} \sim \begin{cases} 1/2, & X = DICT_i, Y = SL \\ 1/4, & X = PQ, Y = SL \\ 1/2, & X = PQ, Y = UL. \end{cases}$$

This formula allows one to fill in the first three lines in Table 6. The asymptotics of $E\left\{T^{PQ,H_4}\right\}$, however, require knowledge of α, the average "penetration depth" of the sift-down procedure.

5. Conclusions

The probabilistic analysis of dynamic data structures is largely an attempt to sense the 'typical' behavior of costs by averaging over as many different sequences of operations as possible. Common approaches include averaging over the $n!$ distinct ways of performing operations on n records [2], and choosing keys independently from a fixed real-valued distribution [10]. Both approaches are unexceptionable, and the latter seems at first sight related to the model treated here. Indeed Jonassen and Dahl [9] proved that in the case of priority queues the choice of an exponential distribution leads to an equiprobability of key ranks: if r_j is the relative rank of the key manipulated in the jth insert operation, then all allowed r_j are equally likely to occur.

But the averaging over equiprobable histories, defined in Section 2, is quite different. The costs are not averaged over exogenous sequences of operations. If one regards the relationship between the data structure and the schema that drives it as the relation between a server and a single client, then the averaging of this paper is really an averaging over all possible paths in the state space of the server.

This contrasts strongly with the model of Jonassen and Dahl, whose 'operation words' were Markov chains. This is because the model of equiprobable histories, though superficially similar, is inherently non-Markov: equiprobability of operation words is not the same as equiprobability of ranks of independently chosen keys. Under the assumption of equiprobability of operation words, allowed structure sizes $\{y_j\}_{j=0}^{n}$ will have relative probability $\prod_{j=1}^{n} m(y_{j-1}, O_j)$. And the dependence of y_j on the past, $i.e.$, on $\{y_k\}_{k=0}^{j-1}$, will not be exhausted by its dependence on y_{j-1}.

Of course non-Markov behavior is not unrealistic. After all, clients as well as servers have a notion of internal state, and it is not entirely reasonable to assume that the sequence of requests a client generates be a Markov chain. But it can have curious consequences. In particular, it can give rise to the phenomenon of asymptotic determinism. It is clear from this paper that asymptotic determinism will normally occur in a model of equiprobable histories. The normalized data structure size as a function of time, the random function $x_{X,Y}(\cdot)$, will tend to 'freeze' at $x_{X,Y}^*(\cdot)$. It is not difficult to check that at any normalized time t, the random variable $x_{X,Y}(t)$ will, for large n, be well approximated by a Gaussian random variable of variance $h(n)^{-1}$, with $h(n)$ the function defined in (19). As $n \to \infty$, this variance tends to zero.

In terms of the unnormalized data structure size $\{y_j\}_{j=0}^{n}$, this 'freezing' behavior can be explained as resulting from the interaction of two strong but competing effects: the weighting factor $\prod_{j=1}^{n} m(y_{j-1}, O_j)$, which greatly increases the likelihood that y_j will be large, and the disinclination of an unbiased random walk $\{y_j\}_{j=0}^{n}$ to deviate far from 0, in particular much farther than order $n^{1/2}$. These two effects suppress, respectively, paths with small y_j and large y_j. So normalized paths $x(t)$ that are either too large or too small become as $n \to \infty$ very unlikely. $x_{X,Y}^*(t)$ and the corresponding unnormalized y_j^* balance on the knife-edge where the two competing effects are most evenly matched.

Averaging over all internal histories of the data structure is the same as "fully exercising" it. So the extent to which the consequent unusual behavior — the freezing of $x(\cdot)$ near $x^*_{X,Y}(\cdot)$ and, except in the case of d-heap implementations of priority queues, the growth of expected costs at the same rate as worst-case costs — does not occur in real-world applications of data structures should serve as a measure of the extent to which those applications fail fully to explore the data structure state space.

References

[1] N. I. Akhiezer, *The Calculus of Variations*. Blaisdell, New York, 1962.

[2] B. Bollobás and I. Simon, "Repeated Random Insertions into a Priority Queue." *J. Algorithms* **6** (1985), 466–477.

[3] L. Chéno, P. Flajolet, J. Françon, C. Puech and J. Vuillemin, "Dynamic Data Structures: Finite Files, Limiting Profiles and Variance Analysis." In *Proceedings of the 18th Allerton Conference*, pp. 223–232. Monticello, Ill., 1980.

[4] P. Flajolet, J. Françon and J. Vuillemin, "Sequence of Operations Analysis for Dynamic Data Structures." *J. Algorithms* **1** (1980), 111–141.

[5] P. Flajolet, C. Puech and J. Vuillemin, "The Analysis of Simple List Structures." *Inform. Sci.* **38** (1986), 121–146.

[6] M. I. Freidlin and A. D. Wentzell, *Random Perturbations of Dynamical Systems*. Springer-Verlag, New York, 1984.

[7] H. Goldstein, *Classical Mechanics*. Addison-Wesley, Reading MA, 1950.

[8] N. J. Günther, "Path Integral Methods for Computer Performance Analysis." *Inf. Proc. Lett.* **32** (1989), 7–13.

[9] A. Jonassen and O.-J. Dahl, "Analysis of an Algorithm for Priority Queue Administration." *BIT* **15** (1975), 409–422.

[10] A. Jonassen and D. Knuth, "A Trivial Algorithm Whose Analysis Isn't." *J. Comput. System Sci.* **16** (1978), 301–322.

[11] R. Kemp, *Fundamentals of the Average Case Analysis of Particular Algorithms*. Wiley, New York, 1984.

[12] G. Louchard, "Random Walks, Gaussian Processes and List Structures." *Theor. Comp. Sci.* **53** (1987), 99–124.

[13] G. Louchard, B. Randrianarimanana and R. Schott, "Dynamic Algorithms in D. E. Knuth's Model: A Probabilistic Analysis," in *Automata, Languages and Programming: Proceedings of ICALP '89*, Springer-Verlag, 1989.

[14] L. S. Schulman, *Techniques and Applications of Path Integration*. Wiley, New York, 1981.

[15] S. R. S. Varadhan, *Large Deviations and Applications*. SIAM, Philadelphia, 1984.

On the formal aspects of approximation algorithms

José D. P. Rolim
Department of Mathematics and Computer Science
Odense University
Campusvej 55, Odense 5230 M
Denmark

Abstract

Formal aspects of approximated solutions to difficult problems are considered. We define an approximation machine and its language as a formal model of computation. We strengthen previous results by showing the interpretation of the complexity classes with density in terms of approximation languages. In particular, we analyze the worst-case, the best-case and the average-case complexity related to the formal languages of approximation machines. The relationship between density of a complexity class and the "goodness" of an approximation is also investigated.

1. Introduction

Several models of languages have been introduced in the literature and several models of complexity case analysis have been studied. Our inability to solve the dilemma $P = NP$ has stimulated the study of the structure of the complexity classes [1, 8] . For example, the notion of density of *hard* languages is closely related to the *size* of the *hard* part of a *hard* problem [4, 6, 9, 13] . On the other hand, we must cope *in practice* with NP-complete problems. This necessity has been of great incentive to the study of approximation algorithms for hard problems [2, 3, 7] . Usually, a *good* approximation algorithm is a solution that works nicely in the average case complexity, but does not work so well from the worst-case point of view [5] . In this paper, we are concerned with the formalization of an approximation solution in terms of formal languages and its machine characterization. We study the density of an approximation solution related to the complexity classes of the worst, best and average cases analysis.

We start, in section 2, by defining approximation languages and approximation machines. In section 3, we relate the complexity classes of the worst-case to the approximation languages with density 1. In section 4, we give an interpretation of complexity classes with density $d(n)$. We prove that the recursive languages of a complexity class bounded by $f(n)$ with density $d(n)$ are precisely those languages L which can be approximated by $f(n)$ bounded machines agreeing with L with *probability* at least $d(n)$. As a corollary of this result, we show that a language is recognized in best-case $f(n)$ if and only if there exists an approximation algorithm for L. In order to study the average case complexity, we introduce the notion of probability in the concept of approximation languages and machines. We show, in section 5, that a language L can be recognized with median bounded by $f(n)$ if and only if there exists an approximation algorithm bounded by $f(n)$ with density $\frac{1}{2}$ for L. We also show that if a language is recognized within mean $f(n)$, then there exists an approximation language for L bounded by $f(n)$ with density strictly greater than zero everywhere. We conclude, in section 6, by pointing out some open question on the formalization of approximation problems and commenting some relevant lines of research in the area.

2. Approximation Languages

We use the standard definition of a deterministic multitape Turing machine with a two-way read-only input tape and a finite number of read-write working tapes; for space bounds we consider only the number of tape cells used on the working tape. All the machines in this paper are *deterministic* and so the term *machine* without qualifications means *deterministic multitape Turing machine*. We use $T(M,w)$ $(S(M,w))$ for the number of time steps (working tape cells) used by machine M on input w or ∞ if M does not halt on input w. Function f is *time (space) full constructible* if there is a machine M such that $T(M,w) = f(|w|)$ $(S(M,w) = f(|w|))$ for every input w.

We turn to the question of formalizing the notion of approximation. Given a language L, which might require a lot of resource time or space to recognize, maybe we can be satisfied with another language L', which costs less time or space to recognize. Obviously, we are not satisfied with any language L'. We require that L' solves part of the problem that L is supposed to represent. By solve we mean determine the correct answer, i.e. whether a word w belongs to L or not, and provide a proof that it is correct [5] . This is different from the sense in which approximations are often defined for functions, in which case one often demands that the approximation function be always easy and give an answer *close to* the correct one [11] .

We say that languages L and L' agree on word w if w is in L if and only if w is in L'. Given an off-line deterministic Turing machine M', we select from the definition of M' a set of states I. We require that whenever M' halts for word w in some state $s \in I$ then $L' = L(M')$ and the language L agree in word w, that is, word w belongs to L if and only if it belongs to L'. We want the language L', which is an approximation for L, to agree a *lot* with L and to be recognized in a moderate amount of time or space. Moreover, we want to be able to *prove* that L agrees with L' *often*. One approach is to single out a set of states and demand that when the machine halts in that state set we *know* that it is correct and that it halts in those states *often*.

Definition 2.1 Let L and L' be languages over input alphabet Σ^*.

(1) We say that L' is in $APPROXIMATION - DTIME(L, f(n), d(n))$ if there is an off-line multitape deterministic Turing machine M' accepting L' with a special set I of states of M' satisfying the following.

(i) M' is of worst-case time complexity $f(n)$, i.e., for all w, M' halts on w within time $f(|w|)$.

(ii) If M' halts for input w in some state $s \in I$, then L and L' agree on w.

(iii)
$$d(n) \leq \frac{|\{w : M' \; halts \; on \; w \; in \; a \; state \; of \; I\}|}{|\Sigma|^n}$$

(2) We say that L' is in $APPROXIMATION - DSPACE(L, f(n), d(n))$ if there is an off-line multitape deterministic Turing machine M' accepting L' with a special set I of states of M' satisfying the following.

(i) M' is of worst-case space complexity $f(n)$, i.e., for all w, M' halts on w within time $f(|w|)$.

(ii) If M' halts for input w in some state $s \in I$, then L and L' agree on w.

(iii)

$$d(n) \leq \frac{|\{w : M' \text{ halts on } w \text{ in a state of } I\}|}{|\Sigma|^n}$$

Note that $d(n)$ is a lower bound for the number of "good" words. The set of these *good words* is sometimes called the *definite part* of L in the literature. [6] Machine M' is a formalization of an approximation machine and L' the corresponding language formalization. Furthermore, these definitions of $APPROXIMATION$ sets are strengthenings over previous notions of polynomial time approximation algorithms [10] .

3. Worst-case Complexity

We want to relate the sets $APPROXIMATION$ and the complexity classes of the worst-case complexity. We recall the concept of a worst-case complexity class. Consider a Turing machine M and let $T(M, w)$ denote the running time of M on input w and $S(M, w)$ the space spent by M on w. We can, for the worst-case complexity, define the functions:

$$T_{max}(n) = max\{T(M, w) : |w| = n\}$$

$$S_{max}(n) = max\{S(M, w) : |w| = n\}$$

The family of languages accepted by deterministic multitape off-line Turing machines for which $T_{max}(n) \leq f(n)$ is called $DTIME(f(n))$ The family of languages accepted by deterministic multitape off-line Turing machines for which $S_{max}(n) \leq f(n)$ is called $DSPACE(f(n))$

Notice that the pattern of the names of complexity classes is the same and meant to be mnemonic:

$$DBOUND(f(n))$$

for the class of languages accepted by deterministic multitape off-line Turing machines within $BOUND\ f$.

We would like to relate the new complexity classes, namely the $APPROXIMATION$ sets, to the traditional worst-case complexity classes $DBOUND(f(n))$. The next result implies that the worst-case complexity corresponds to the approximation complexity with density function 1.

Theorem 3.1

$$L \in DBOUND(f(n))$$

if and only if

$$APPROXIMATION - DBOUND(L, f(n), 1) \neq \emptyset$$

Proof: Consider L accepted by machine M within bound $f(n)$ everywhere. This machine when viewed as approximation machine, with the set of internal states exactly the same as the set I, is an approximation language with density 1 and vice-versa. $\diamond$

4. Best-case Complexity

The notion of density has been associated with complexity classes to give a measure of the sparseness of the class [9] . We recall some basic concepts related to sets and to their density. We say that a deterministic Turing machine M *respects the bound* $f(|w|)$ on input w if M on input w halts within $f(|w|)$ steps for time complexity or if M on w visits no more than $f(|w|)$ working tape cells for space complexity. Thus, for example, we would like to say that a Turing machine M is of time complexity $f(n)$ with density function $d(n)$ if for all n the number of words of length n that respect the bound $f(n)$ is at least $d(n)$. Intuitively, $d(n)$ is a lower bound on the number of "good" words. More formally, we define the complexity measure as follows.

Definition 4.1 Let M be a Turing machine with input alphabet Σ and let $d(n)$ be a function such that $0 \le d(n) \le 1$ for all n.

(1) We say that M is a Turing machine of time complexity $f(n)$ with density function $d(n)$ if for all n

$$d(n) \le \frac{|\{w : |w| = n \,\&\, T(M, w) \le f(n)\}|}{|\Sigma|^n}$$

(2) M is a Turing machine of space complexity $f(n)$ with density function $d(n)$ if for all n

$$d(n) \le \frac{|\{w : |w| = n \,\&\, S(M, w) \le f(n)\}|}{|\Sigma|^n}$$

Based on the above definition, we can join languages into families of languages as follows.

Definition 4.2 Let $d(n)$ and $f(n)$ be functions in N such that $0 \le d(n) \le 1$ for all n. Then:

(i) $DSPACE(f(n), d(n))$ is the class of languages recognized by deterministic Turing machines of space complexity $f(n)$ with density function $d(n)$.

(ii) $DTIME(f(n), d(n))$ is the class of languages recognized by deterministic Turing machines of time complexity $f(n)$ with density function $d(n)$.

Note the similarity between the definitions of a complexity class with density and of an approximation language. More formally, we can switch from one definition to another as a consequence of the next result.

Theorem 4.1 Let $f(n) \ge n$ be a monotonic increasing time constructible function and L be a recursive language. Then:

$$L \in DTIME(f(n), d(n))$$

if and only if

$$APPROXIMATION - DTIME(L, f(n), d(n)) \ne \emptyset$$

Proof: Suppose L recursive and let M be a deterministic always halting Turing machine accepting L. Let $L' = L(M')$ be in $APPROXIMATION - DTIME(L, f(n), d(n))$ with machine M' operating in time $f(n)$ and selected set of states I and consider a deterministic Turing machine M_1 which behaves on input w as follows.

(i) Simulate M' on w.

(ii) If M' does halt on a state of I, then accept w if and only if M' accepts w.

(iii) Otherwise, simulate M on w, accepting w if and only if M accepts w.

Consider any word w. If M' halts in a state of I, then M_1 accepts w if and only if M' accepts w. But, whenever M' halts in a state of I, machine M' accepts w if and only if w is in L. Furthermore, if M' does not halt in a state of I, then machine M_1 simulates machine M on input w; thus w is in $L(M_1)$ if and only if w is in $L(M) = L$. Therefore, for any word w, w is in $L(M_1)$ if and only if w is in L. Therefore, the language accepted by machine M_1 is L.

Conditions (i) to (ii) take at most $f(|w|)$ computation steps, since M' is of worst-case complexity $f(n)$. Then any word accepted in time $f(n)$ by M' takes no longer than $f(n)$ when processed by M_1. But there are at least $|\Sigma|^n d(n)$ of these words, since $L' \in APPROXIMATION - DTIME(L, f(n), d(n))$.

Therefore, by the definition of the complexity classes,

$$L = L(M_1) \in DTIME(f(n), d(n)).$$

Conversely, suppose $L \in DTIME(f(n), d(n))$. There is machine M accepting L within time bound $f(n)$ and density $d(n)$. Consider machine M' with $I = \{Y, N\}$ and set of accepting states $F = \{Y\}$ which behaves on input w of size n as follows.

(i) Set a $f(n)$ counter on a working tape of M'. and simulate machine M for $f(n)$ steps on input w.

(ii)If M halts and accepts w, then M' accepts w halting in state Y. If M halts and rejects w, then M' rejects w halting in state N.

(iii) If M does not halt within $f(n)$ steps, then M' rejects w, halting in a state not in I.

We have to prove that $L' = L(M')$ is in $APPROXIMATION - DTIME$ $(L, f(n), d(n))$ Machine M' halts within $f(n)$ steps. Further machines M' and M agree on all words accepted/rejected in step (ii) with M' halting in a state in I. These are precisely the inputs accepted or rejected by M within $f(n)$ steps. Since M operates in time $f(n)$ with density $d(n)$, then M and M' agree on at least $|\Sigma|^n d(n)$ of these words. Thus, $L' \in APPROXIMATION - DTIME(L, f(n), d(n))$.◊

Theorem 4.1 provides a strong relationship for time bounds between the complexity classes with density and the approximation languages. The analog of the theorem for space bounds are easy to establish. Thus, we have the following.

Theorem 4.2 Let $bound = \{time, space\}$, $f(n) \geq n$ be a monotonic increasing $bound$ constructible function and L be a recursive language. Then

$$L \in DBOUND(f(n), d(n))$$

if and only if

$$APPROXIMATION - DBOUND(L, f(n), d(n)) \neq \emptyset$$

Theorem 4.2 gives another interpretation for the classes $DBOUND(f(n), d(n))$ in terms of approximation languages; it says that the recursive languages of the complexity class $DBOUND$ are those languages L which can be approximated by $f(n)$ bounded machine agreeing with L on w with probability at least $d(|w|)$ if we consider all the words of length n have the same probability of occurring.

As a consequence of Theorem 4.2, we can easily relate the notion of best-case complexity to the approximation formalization. First, we recall the concept of a best-case computation. Consider a Turing machine M with running time $T(M, w)$ and space $S(M, w)$ on input w. We can, for the best-case complexity, define the functions:

$$T_{min}(n) = min\{T(M, w) : |w| = n\}$$

$$S_{min}(n) = min\{S(M, w) : |w| = n\}$$

The family of languages accepted by deterministic multitape off-line Turing machines for which $T_{min}(n) \leq f(n)$ is called $DTIME - BEST(f(n))$ The family of languages accepted by deterministic multitape off-line Turing machines for which $S_{min}(n) \leq f(n)$ is called $DSPACE - BEST(f(n))$.

Corollary 4.3 Let $bound = \{time, space\}$, $f(n) \geq n$ be a monotonic increasing $bound$ constructible function and L be a recursive language. Then:

$$L \in DBOUND - BEST(f(n))$$

if and only if there exists $d(n) > 0$ everywhere such that $APPROXIMATION - DBOUND$ $(L, f(n), d(n)) \neq \emptyset$.

Proof: We prove for time bounds, the proof for space bound is analogous and left to the reader. The proof is based on the proof of Theorem 4.1. Suppose that L is recognized in best-case $f(n)$ by some machine M. Then there exists at least one word for which M respects bound $f(n)$. An approximation machine based on M would simulate M by $f(|w|)$ steps on input w accepting w if and only if M does it. Otherwise, the approximation machine rejects w, for example. Since, there exists at least one 'good' word for every length n, the density $d(n)$ of the approximation machine is strictly greater than zero everywhere.

Conversely, if $L' = L(M')$ is an approximation for L with density $d(n) > 0$ then we can build an algorithm M for L based on L' as follows. M simulates M'. If M' halts on a state not in the special set I, then M must simulate another machine for L, which is possible since L is recursive by hypothesis. Otherwise, M and M' agree on w. Since, $d(n) > 0$ for M', then $|\{w : |w| = n \ \& \ T(M, w) \leq f(n)\}| > 0$. But then, there is at least one word for which M respects bound $f(n)$ for any length n. So, $L \in DTIME - BEST(f(n))$. $\diamond$.

5. Average-case Complexity

There are many ways in which an algorithm can work well *on average*. The standard approach assumes a probability distribution on the problems instances and require the algorithm to be bounded on certain kind of average (mean, median, etc.).

In this section, we study the average case analysis from an abstract point of view. We start enlarging our notion of approximation machines by considering a probability distribution on the inputs. Then, we specify the approximation classes defined to the median case and to the mean case complexity.

Let Σ denote a finite input alphabet, Σ^n denote words in Σ^* of length n and let X be a random variable taking values in Σ^*. We assume that we are given the conditional probability $P[X = w/n]$ of X taking value w in Σ^n given that X takes a value in Σ^n. Therefore, for any fixed value of n, we know how the words are distributed within this fixed length n. Thus, $P[X = w/n]$ can be seen as a generic probability distribution on n and $\sum_{w \in \Sigma^n} P[X = w/n] = 1$ for every n. If, for example, we assume an uniform distribution, i.e. $P[X = w/n] = |\Sigma|^{-n}$, we can move back to the standard complexity theory without probability. Otherwise, we suppose that this family of probability distribution is known. We suppose that this probability distribution is positive, i.e. every word w of length n has a non-zero probability of occurrence, $P[X = w/n] > 0$ for all w and n.

Definition 5.1 Let L be a language over Σ^*. We say that L' is in $APPROXIMATION - DTIME(L, f(n), d(n), P[X = w/n])$ if there is an off-line multitape deterministic Turing machine M' accepting L' with a special set I of states of M' satisfying the following.

(i) M' is of worst-case time complexity $f(n)$, i.e., for all w, M' halts on w within time $f(|w|)$.

(ii) If M' halts for input w in some state $s \in I$, then L and L' agree on w.

(iii)

$$d(n) \leq P[M' \text{ halts on } w \text{ in a state of } I/|w| = n] =$$

$$= \sum_{|w|=n:\ M' \text{ halts on } w \text{ in } s \in I} P[X = w/n].$$

Notice that conditions (ii) and (iii) of Definition 5.1 imply that L and L' agree on w with *at least* probability $d(|w|)$, since

$$d(n) \leq P[M' \text{ halts on } w \text{ in a state of } I/|w| = n] =$$

$$= \sum_{|w|=n:\ M' \text{ halts on } w \text{ in } s \in I} P[X = w/n]$$

$$\leq \sum_{|w|=n:\ L \text{ and } L' \text{ agree on } w} P[X = w/n]$$

We can define $APPROXIMATION - DSPACE(L, f(n), d(n), P[X = w/n]$ in a similar way.

5.1. The Median Case Complexity

Usually when we talk about expected complexity, we require that some kind of average (mean, median) over all words of length n be bounded by a function of n in all points. We start with the concept of median complexity.

We recall informally the concept of median. Suppose we have the values $v_1, v_2, ...v_k$ each one with given probability $P[X = v_i]$ for $1 \leq i \leq k$. The median of these values denoted by m is the least element v_i such that $P[X \leq v_i] \geq \frac{1}{2}$.

Let M be a deterministic Turing machine and let w be a word of length n. We define $T_{median}(n, P[X = w/n])$ as the median of the running time on words of length n by M with probability distribution $P[X = w/n]$. We define $S_{median}(n, P[X = w/n])$ as the median of the space spent on words of length n by M with probability distribution $P[X = w/n]$.

Definition 5.2.1 Let $T(M, w)$ and $S(M, w)$ be respectively the running time and the space spent on w by machine M. Let $P[X = w/n]$ be positive. We define:

(i) $T_{median}(n, P[X = w/n])$ is the least $T(M, y)$ such that $|y| = n$ and

$$\sum_{|w|=n:T(M,w)\leq T(M,y)} P[X = w/n] \geq \frac{1}{2}$$

(ii) $S_{median}(n, P[X = w/n])$ is the least $S(M, y)$ such that $|y| = n$ and

$$\sum_{|w|=n:S(M,w)\leq S(M,y)} P[X = w/n] \geq \frac{1}{2}$$

Once we have defined the median complexity measures as above, we can define the median complexity classes as follows.

Definition 5.2.2 We define:

(i) $MEDIAN - DTIME(f(n), P[X = w/n])$ is the family of languages L for which there is a deterministic Turing machine M accepting L with $T_{median}(n, P[X = w/n]) \leq f(n)$ for all n and probability distribution $P[X = w/n]$.

(ii) $MEDIAN - DSPACE(f(n), P[X = w/n])$ is the family of languages L for which there is a deterministic Turing machine M accepting L with $S_{median}(n, P[X = w/n]) \leq f(n)$ for all n and probability distribution $P[X = w/n]$.

The next theorems relate the median complexity classes to the approximation classes.

Theorem 5.2.1 Let L be a recursive language. Then

$$L \in MEDIAN - DTIME(f(n), P[X = w/n])$$

if and only if

$$APPROXIMATION - DTIME(f(n), \frac{1}{2}, P[X = w/n])$$

$$\neq \emptyset$$

Proof: Suppose that L is in $MEDIAN - DTIME(f(n), P[X = w/n])$. Thus, there is a deterministic Turing machine M accepting L for which $T_{median}(n, P[X = w/n]) \leq f(n)$, for some positive $P[X = w/n]$. Let $T(M, w)$ denote the running time on word w by machine M. Thus:

$$\sum_{|w|=n:T(w)\leq f(n)} P[X = w/n] \geq$$

$$\sum_{|w|=n:T(w)\leq T_{median}(n,P[X=w/n])} P[X = w/n],$$

since $T_{median}(n, P[X = w/n]) \leq f(n)$.

But $\sum_{|w|=n:T(w)\leq T_{median}(n,P[X=w/n])} P[X = w/n] \geq \frac{1}{2}$, since $T_{median}(n, P[X = w/n])$ is the median of the values $T(M, w)$ for words w of length n. Therefore, an approximation machine built as in the proof of Theorem 4.1 will approximate L and have $\sum_{|w|=n:T(M,w)\leq f(n)} P[X = w/n] \geq \frac{1}{2}$. But then $APPROXIMATION - DTIME(L, f(n), \frac{1}{2}, P[X = w/n])$ is non-empty.

Conversely, if the recursive language L has an approximation in $APPROXIMATION - DTIME(L, f(n), \frac{1}{2}, P[X = w/n])$, then there exists a deterministic Turing machine M built as in the proof of Theorem 4.1 accepting L for which: $\sum_{|w|=n:T(M,w)\leq f(n)} P[X = w/n] \geq \frac{1}{2}$. However, the median $T_{median}(n, P[X = w/n])$ is by definition the *least* element $e(n)$ for which $\sum_{|w|=n:T(M,w)\leq e(n)} P[X = w/n]$ is greater or equal $\frac{1}{2}$. Thus $f(n) \geq T_{median}(n, P[X = w/n])$ and so L is in $MEDIAN - DTIME(f(n), P[X = w/n])$. $\diamond$

By techniques similar to those in the proof above, we can relate the approximation complexity classes to others median complexity classes.

Theorem 5.2.2 Let L be a recursive language. Then:

$$L \in MEDIAN - DSPACE(f(n), P[X = w/n])$$

if and only if

$$APPROXIMATION - DSPACE(f(n), \frac{1}{2}, P[X = w/n])$$

$$\neq \emptyset$$

Notice that the theorems above give a useful interpretation of the median-complexity classes, since the results of traditional complexity theory hold for the approximation complexity classes as shown in [12]. Therefore, we can apply the results of the worst-case complexity theory to the median-case complexity classes.

5.2. The Mean Case Complexity

We turn to the complexity classes related to the concept of mean. Let M be a Turing machine with running time $T(M, w)$ and space spent $S(M, w)$ on word w of length n. Let $P[X = w/n]$ be a positive probability distribution. We define $T_{mean}(n, P[X = w/n])$ as the mean of the running time of M on words of length n and $S_{mean}(n, P[X = w/n])$ as the mean of the space spent by M on words of length n with probability distribution $P[X = w/n]$.

Definition 5.3.1 Let $T(M, w)$ and $S(M, w)$ be the running time and the space spent on w by machine M, respectively. Let $P[X = w/n]$ be positive. We define:

$$(i) T_{mean}(n, P[X = w/n]) = \sum_{|w|=n} T(M, w) P[X = w/n].$$

$$(ii) S_{mean}(n, P[X = w/n]) = \sum_{|w|=n} S(M, w) P[X = w/n].$$

The complexity classes for the mean case complexity can be defined as follows.

Definition 5.3.2

(i) $MEAN - DTIME(f(n), P[X = w/n])$ is the family of languages L for which there is a deterministic Turing machine accepting L with $T_{mean}(n, P[X = w/n]) \leq f(n)$.

(ii) $MEAN - DSPACE(f(n), P[X = w/n])$ is the family of languages L for which there is a deterministic Turing machine accepting L with $S_{mean}(n, P[X = w/n]) \leq f(n)$.

The next results show that any language in a complexity class of the type $MEAN - DBOUND(f(n))$ belongs to a corresponding approximation complexity class for some density function.

Theorem 5.3.1 If a language L is in $MEAN - DTIME(f(n))$, then there exists a positive density function $d(n)$ for which $APPROXIMATION - DTIME(L, f(n), d(n), P[X = w/n]) \neq \emptyset$

Proof: Let L be in $MEAN - DTIME(f(n), P[X = w/n])$. Then there exists a deterministic Turing machine M accepting L for which $T_{mean}(n, P[X = w/n]) = \sum_{|w|=n} T(M, w) P[X = w/n] \leq f(n)$.
Let

$$d(n) = \sum_{|w|=n : T(M,w) \leq f(n)} P[X = w/n] \geq$$

$$\sum_{|w|=n : T(M,w) \leq T_{mean}(n, P[X=w/n])} P[X = w/n],$$

since $f(n) \geq T_{mean}(n, P[X = w/n])$.

But there exists a word w of length n for which $T(M, w) \leq T_{mean}(n, P[X = w/n]) \leq f(n)$. So $d(n)$ as defined is strictly greater than zero everywhere, since $P[X = w/n]$ is positive. Thus, there exists a density function $d(n)$ positive everywhere for which $APPROXIMATION - DTIME(L, f(n), d(n), P[X = w/n]) \neq \emptyset$. $\diamond$

Theorem 5.3.2 If a language L is in $MEAN - DSPACE(f(n))$, then there exists a positive density function $d(n)$ for which $APPROXIMATION - DSPACE(L, f(n), d(n), P[X = w/n]) \neq \emptyset$

Notice that the propositions above have been shown in only one direction. Given that L is of mean-complexity $f(n)$ then there exists an approximation for L. The other way around, i.e. "does L' in $APPROXIMATION - DBOUND(L, f(n), d(n), P[X = w/n])$ imply that L is in $MEDIAN - DBOUND(f(n), P[X = w/n])$"? is an open problem. Certainly, it does hold if $d(n) = 1$ almost everywhere. Another issue here is whether there is any relationship between $MEAN - DBOUND(f(n), P[X = w/n])$ and $MEDIAN - DBOUND(f(n), P[X = w/n])$ or not.

References

[1] S. Ben-David, B. Chor, O. Goldreich, and M. Luby. Towards a theory of average case complexity. In *Proceedings 21th Annual ACM Symposium on Theory of Computing*, Seatle, Washington, 1989.

[2] A. Goldberg, P. Purdom, and C. Brown. Average time analysis of simplified davis-putnan procedures. *Information Processing Letters*, 15:72–75, 1982.

[3] A. V. Goldberg and A. Marchetti-Spaccamela. On finding the exact solution of a zero-one knapsack problem. In *Proceedings 16th Annual ACM Symposium on Theory of Computing*, New York, 1984.

[4] J. Hartmanis. On sparse sets in NP-P. *Information Processing Letters*, 16:55–60, 1983.

[5] D. S. Johnson. The NP-completeness column: An ongoing guide. *Journal of Algorithms*, (5):284–299, 1984.

[6] K. Ko and D. More. Completeness, approximation and density. *SIAM Journal of Computing*, 10:787–796, 1981.

[7] J. C. Lagarias and A. M. Odlyzko. Solving low-density subset sum problems. In *Proceedings 24th Annual Symposium on Foundations of Computer Science*, Los Angeles, 1983.

[8] L. A. Levin. Problems complete in average instance. In *Proceedings 16th Annual ACM Symposium on Theory of Computing*, 1984.

[9] N. A. Lynch. Approximations to the halting problem. *J. Comput. Syst. Science*, 9:143–150, 1974.

[10] C. H. Papadimitriou and M. Yannakakis. Optimization, approximation and complexity classes. In *Proceedings 20th Annual ACM Symposium on Theory of Computing*, pages 229–234, 1988.

[11] A. Paz and S. Moran. Non deterministic polynomial optimization problems and their approximation. *Theoretical Computer Science*, 15:251–277, 1981.

[12] J. Rolim. Towards a complexity theory for approximation languages. paper presented at the 3rd. Symposium on Complexity of Approximately Solved Problems at Columbia University, New York, April 1989.

[13] J. Rolim and S. Greibach. On the IO-complexity and approximation languages. *Information Processing Letters*, 28(1):27–31, 1988.

SELECTED ASPECTS OF THE CALCULUS OF SELF-MODIFIABLE ALGORITHMS THEORY

Eugeniusz Eberbach

Jodrey School of Computer Science, Acadia University

Wolfville, Nova Scotia, Canada B0P 1X0

E-Mail BITNET: eugene@AcadiaU.CA, FAX: +1 902 542 7224

Abstract

In this paper the introductory concepts and chosen applications of the Calculus of Self-modifiable Algorithms (CSA) are presented. The CSA model is a theory for describing parallel behavior. In contrast to the well-known Hoare's CSP and Milner's CCS parallel computing theories, the CSA model was designed as a theory within Artificial Intelligence. It considers self-modifiable algorithms which are mathematical models of processes with the possibility of applying modifications to their own behavior. The CSA model unifies artificial intelligence methods and parallelism, two fundamental aspects of new generation computers. The most important features of the CSA model are the self-modifiability of programs (changeability of code) and the optimization of control (minimizing cost of algorithm execution).

Keywords: self-modifiable algorithm, foundation of AI, computation models, fixed-point semantics, parallel programming languages and methodologies

1 INTRODUCTION

There are at least seven main classes of programming languages [24]: procedural, object-oriented, logic, functional (applicative and single-assignment) and knowledge-based (production rules and semantics networks) languages.

A **Calculus of Self-Modifiable Algorithms** (CSA for short) can be viewed as a theory representing an eight class.

The wide use of artificial intelligence methods and different forms of parallelism are a main feature of new generation computers. The current state of research is characterized by a lack of suitable and applicable theories allowing to describe both intelligent and parallel behavior, and by difficulties with understanding, as well as lack of precise definitions of such ambiguous and changeable notions as learning, reasoning, experience, knowledge, faults, and so on. It would seem that CSA solves most of these problems.

A notion of self-modifiable algorithm has been introduced in [2] as a mathematical model of a program (process) with the possibility of applying modifications to its behavior. Subsequently the definition was modified a few times (what seems to be in accordance with the idea and the essence of the self-modifiable algorithm itself - applied simply to creation of its definition) to give, finally, the current form [5,6].

From the formal point of view, the theory considers special cases of complete lattices and covers both nondeterminism and parallelism. It consists of two parts: fixed point semantics and optimization. Fixed point semantics describes a history of algorithm computation, and optimization is responsible for the improvement of the algorithm activity by minimizing its cost.

The *self-modifiable algorithms* seem to be appropriate tools for building expert systems (which are a characteristic feature of fifth generation computers) as well as for learning (which is a crucial problem of the sixth generation). They can describe parallel and fault-tolerant computing that are common features of both future generations. We believe that it will be possible to build both systems with a dominating role of hardware (for instance, in the form of neural computers) and with dominating software (e.g. self-learning expert systems) working on the basis of the described theory. The scope of applications of the theory of self-modifiable algorithms is very wide, including expert systems, machine learning, adaptive systems, pattern recognition, neurocomputing, fault-tolerant systems, distributed and parallel computing, new computer architectures and languages. In the U.K., CSA has been applied to a new generation computer project, and in the U.S. to a fault-tolerant project.

In section 2 we present a brief outline of the theory of self-modifiable algorithms. In section 3 we describe certain applications of the Calculus of Self-Modifiable Algorithms. In this paper more formalized aspects of the theory as the description of the fixed point semantics and the solutions of optimal problems will not be presented. For these reasons we do not introduce the notions of the self-modifiable algorithm net, extended regular expressions, and the cost system.

2 SELF-MODIFIABLE ALGORITHMS

Self-modifiable algorithms are a mathematical model of processes (programs) with possibilities of modifications to its behavior. They describe a single (recursive or iterative) modifiable program or systems of cooperating modifiable programs. An idea of a self-modifiable algorithm has been introduced in [2], and the current definition is based on [5,6].

Let , denote a binary relation of parallel composition, let ∘ be a sequential composition, and let • be a general composition (parallel or sequential one); and let their reflexive and transitive closures will be denoted by $^{\pm}$, * , and $^{⊞}$, respectively.

By a **recursive self-modifiable algorithm** we mean any system:

$$MA = (S, D, A, M, \sigma, \varepsilon, Step) \text{ , where}$$

S - is a nonempty set of **control states**

D - is a set of **data**

A - is a set of **actions** (proper actions)

M - is a set of **modifications** (modification actions), $(\forall x, y \in S, D, A, M \ / \ x \neq y) \ x \cap y = \emptyset$

$\sigma \in S$ - is the **initial control state** of MA

ε - is the **terminal control state** (goal) of MA (the empty symbol)

$Step \subseteq S \times T^{\pm} \times S^{⊞}$ - is the **one-step relation** (elementary transitions, productions) of MA. In other words, Step is the subset of triples of the form (s_1, a, s_2), where $s_1 \in S$, $a \in T^{\pm}$, $s_2 \in S^{⊞}$. The set $T = D \cup A \cup M \cup \{\varepsilon\}$ will be called the set of **transits**. $a = a_1 , ... , a_m$, where $a_1, ..., a_m \in T$, and parallel composition of transits $a_1 , ... , a_m$, which appear in one-step relation, will be called a **vectorial action,** and will be denoted by $(a_1 , ... , a_m)$. $s_2 = s_{21} • ... • s_{2p}$, $s_{21}, ..., s_{2p} \in S \cup \{\varepsilon\}$.
$s_{21} • ... • s_{2p}$ forms a recursive stack of control states. □

The interpretation of particular components of the self-modifiable algorithm is the following:

S - is a set of control states (snapshot images) describing in the form of Boolean expressions (conditions with operations "or" ∨, "and" ∧, "not" ¬) the current state of the algorithm computation. The conditions for instance concern the current set of data or the goal of the computation.

D - is a set of data for set A (mainly for the set A but sometimes also for the set M). Data can be simple, as for example integer or real numbers, characters, logical values or they may be structured as arrays, records, symbolic data (strings, trees), relations, etc. Data are *passive* but they can change between particular control states.

A - is a set of actions. Actions are *active* and they operate exclusively on data D and control states S; and at the same time, they can be data themselves for modifications M. The set of actions can be identified with instructions of "classic" imperative programming languages.

M - is a set of modifications. Modifications are the essence of the self-modifiable algorithm. They are *active* and operate upon actions, modifications, but they can operate additionally on data , control states and on complex structures (as e.g. one-step relation or the whole self-modifiable algorithm). The foregoing means that modifications are applicable to actions and that there exist modifications applicable both to actions and data (it is the most significant difference between modifications and proper actions. It can be said that actions are such "degenerated" modifications, which operate exclusively on data and control states.). Modifications are simply a generalization of actions. They cause generation of new instructions and change old instructions (actions and modifications) of the algorithm. Analogues of modifications can be found in knowledge representation languages (see e.g. Lenat's RLL metarules [11,16]).

σ - is the initial control state describing the input data and what the algorithm should do (its goal).

ε - is the terminal control state describing what has been done (the goal of the algorithm).

$Step$ - the interpretation of the one-step relation is the following: $(s_1, (a_1 , ... , a_n), s_2) \in Step$ means that transits $a_1, ..., a_n$ (vectorial action $(a_1 , ... , a_n)$) have been initiated in parallel in control state s_1 (some of them can be continuation actions - this means that they could be initiated before). Later transits $a_1, ..., a_n$ are executed in parallel, and after termination of some of them (sometimes of all), an algorithm achieves control state s_2. Transits not terminated in state s_2 will be continued (as continuation transits) in the next vectorial action started from control state s_2. $s_2 \in S^{\boxplus}$ - this means that $s_2 = s_{21} \bullet ... \bullet s_{2p}$, $s_{22}, ..., s_{2p} \in S \cup \{\varepsilon\}$, i.e. if $\bullet = \circ$, where $\circ$ denotes the operation of sequential composition, s_2 describes stack LIFO (from: Last In First Out) of control states with top s_{21} and bottom s_{2p} (more exactly, we have then a *sequential recursion*). In the next step, state s_{21} will be active, and $s_{22}, ..., s_{2p}$ wait in stack for erasing (by POP operations) their predecessors. Due to the stack behavior, we are capable of describing recursive procedures and therefore this class of the self-modifiable algorithms have been called *recursive* ones. If $\bullet = $, (where , is a parallel composition), we have a *parallel recursion*. This means that $s_{21} , ... , s_{2p}$ will initiate new sequences of transits in parallel.

A self-modifiable algorithm with the empty set of modifications ($M = \emptyset$) is simply a traditional algorithm (program) and will be called a **modified algorithm** (by other algorithms, if such ones exist).
A self-modifiable algorithm with the empty sets of data and actions ($A \cup D = \emptyset$) will be called a **modifying algorithm** (modifying other algorithms).

A self-modifiable algorithm with productions of the form $Step \subseteq S \times T^{\pm} \times (S \cup \{\varepsilon\})$ will be called an **iterative self-modifiable algorithm** (without recursion). It describes an iterative program (process) with the possibility of modifications but without recursion.

Self-modifiable algorithms can be hierarchically ordered according to the number of transit levels, which operate one upon another (see Figure 1). It is useful, in particular, for the definition of necessary and sufficient conditions for learning or adaptation. It also permits one to understand the nature of "intelligent" behavior of self-modifiable algorithm programs compared to traditional ones [5]. The modifications consist, in fact, of an infinite hierarchy of sets working one upon another, which have been combined in a single set for the practical reason.

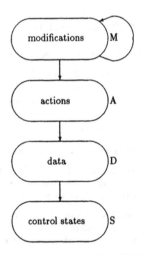

Figure 1: Hierarchy of cooperating self-modifiable algorithms elements

The structure of control states, data, actions and modifications, represented only by their names, is too poor to describe intelligent behavior (see e.g. [11,15,16]). Therefore each component of the self-modifiable algorithm has to have a more complex structure. Control states, transits and the whole algorithm take a similar uniform representation. This representation has analogies with Minsky frames [17], Lenat units [11,15], Pascal records [25], Pawlak information systems [18], and objects from object-oriented programming [10].

Control states have the frame-like (unit, object, information system, record) form, as shown in Table 1. Control states describe in the form of Boolean expressions the goal of the computation and the current set of data. The formal description has the form of disjunctions of conjunctions of atomic conditions in negated or simple form. This has been motivated by two facts:

- any predicate can be written using disjunction ($\vee$), conjunction ($\wedge$) and negation ($\neg$)

- such a form is more suitable to the production rules-like formal description of transits.

The sets FAppl, FSim, FPar and BAppl, BSim, BPar are useful for the construction forward and backward canonical sets of equations, respectively. Such sets of equations (more precisely, their solutions: the *least fixed points*), describe the strings of transits between two control states.

name	is-a	informal description	formal description	generalizations	specializations	analogies
	control state	in natural language	disjunction of conjunctions of atomic conditions in simple or negated form	control states containing a given state	control states contained in a given state	states which intersections with a given state are nonempty

cost	transit data	FAppl	BAppl	FSim	BSim	FPar	BPar
between a given state and terminal and initial states (real or expected)	e.g. in recursive calls of procedures	forward applicable transits	backward applicable transits	subsets of forward potentially simultaneously applicable transits	subsets of backward potentially simultaneously applicable transits	subsets of forward appl. to FSim vectorial actions	subsets of backward appl. to BSim vectorial actions

Table 1: Structure of control states

Transits i.e. data, actions and modifications, also have a frame-like structure, as shown in Table 2.

name	is-a	informal description	formal description			generalizations	specializations	analogies	
			pre	act	post			pre	post
	data	in natural	if pre(t)			types of:	types of	the same	
	or	language	then act(t)			○	○	pre or post	
	action		fi post(t)			, ∪	, ∪		
	or					∪	∪		
	modification					*	*		
						●	●		
						±	±		
						●	●		
						...	...		

domain	cost	history
transits on which it operates	"beyond-real" number	the average time of execution, how many times considered and executed, how many times decreased and increased the distance to the goal of MA

Table 2: Structure of transits

One of the important components of transits is the **cost** representing the weight of the transit. The costs, represented by real numbers (more precisely **beyond-real numbers** [2]), can have different interpretations, such as, for instance, weights in the neural-computing sense [14], values of transits, time of execution, real cost of execution, probability, beliefs, Lenat's level of interestingness [15,11], penalty, subjective impression, a linear composition of all of the above factors, and so on. The beyond-real numbers are similar to complex numbers, and were introduced in order to specify the cost of iteration (recursion) with an unknown number of repetition. The cost of iterated and non-iterated parts of the program are represented then by a beyond-real number, consisting of two ordered real numbers, respectively [2].

The formal description of transits has the form based on production rules [11,16,17] and Petri nets [19]:

if precondition **then** activity **fi** postcondition ,

where *precondition* and *postcondition* are conjunctions of negated or simple conditions, and *activity* describes what the transit actually does (i.e. the proper contents of a datum, action or modification). Such form of transits is decided by three facts:

- post is useful in generating explanations,

- we have a symmetric possibility both for forward and backward chaining (in building, for instance, forward or backward canonical sets of equations),

- only such form is complete, compared to Petri nets, where we have both pre- and postcondition places (note that production rules have only preconditions).

The following operations are performed on transits:

○ - operator of **sequentialization** (sequential composition),
interpretation: $a \circ b$ means that a is executed first, next b,

, - operator of **parallelization** (parallel composition, vectorial action),
interpretation: a , b means that both a and b are executed in parallel (in particular, simultaneously),

∪ - operator of **union** (excluding choice),
interpretation: $a \cup b$ means that if some condition is satisfied then a is executed else b is executed,

⊌ - operator of **modifiable union** (nondeterministic choice),
interpretation: $a \uplus b$ means that either a or b is executed and selection of one of them is arbitrary,

* - operator of **sequential iteration**,
interpretation: a^* means that a is executed sequentially a finite number of times until some condition is satisfied,

● - operator of **modifiable iteration**
interpretation: $a^\bullet$ means that a is executed sequentially an arbitrary and a finite number of times,

± - operator of **partation** (parallel iteration),
interpretation: $a^\pm$ means that a is executed in parallel a finite number of times until some condition is satisfied,

● - operator of **modifiable partation**,
interpretation: $a^\bullet$ means that a is executed in parallel an arbitrary and a finite number of times,

Additionally, we have the operations:

- of modifiable iteration of iteration, iteration of modifiable iteration, modifiable partation of partation, and partation of modifiable partation to close the class of extended regular expressions for iterative self-modifiable algorithms,

- and parallel and sequential recursion for recursive self-modifiable algorithms.

The foregoing operations have the following analogues in programming languages:

○ corresponds to ; from procedural languages

, has some analogies with parallel operator ‖ from the CSP theory [12] (PAR from OCCAM [13])

∪ corresponds to construction **if-then-else** from procedural languages

⊌ has some analogies with Dijkstra's guarded if-fi commands [1] and nondeterministic ALT from OCCAM [13] and corresponds to construction: if a then b or c (pure nondeterminism)

* corresponds to **sequential while** from procedural languages

● has no equivalents in deterministic programming languages, and corresponds to nondeterministic sequential while (it has some analogies with Dijkstra's guarded do-od commands)

± corresponds to **parallel while**

● has no equivalents in deterministic programming languages and corresponds to nondeterministic parallel while.

Specialization of transits means that there exist other transits from which we can build a given transit using the above operations. This is like the call and the body of procedure on different levels of abstraction, and a transit is replaced by the composition of others. For example, the specialization of type $\circ$ of a means that there exist such b and c that $a = b \circ c$. Generalization describes the opposite process.

A single self-modifiable algorithm can be extended to the systems of cooperating algorithms: *Sequential Modifiable Algorithm System, Quasi-Concurrent Algorithm System, or Parallel Modifiable Algorithm System* [5]. In particular, the last one - the Parallel Modifiable Algorithm System PMAS - seems to be most suitable to model tightly or loosely coupled multicomputer systems.

The input-output behavior of self-modifiable algorithms is described as the solutions (the least fixed points) of some sets of equations. These sets of equations can be built starting from the initial control state (forward equations) or from the terminal control state (backward equations). Their solutions contain redundant threads of transits, therefore they are optimized by removing operators connected with nondeterminism (for instance: by removing modifiable union, modifiable iteration and modifiable partation). Optimization uses the costs of transits and operations as the main criterion to find the best algorithm to realize a given goal. Examples of self-modifiable algorithms have been presented in [5,9].

3 CHOSEN APPLICATIONS

We will present chosen applications of the Calculus of Self-Modifiable Algorithms.

3.1 Programming Language

Programs of the Calculus of Self-Modifiable Algorithms language [5], which we refer to as the CSA-language, consist of written in any sequence declared transits and two control states: the initial and the terminal (goal) ones. The process described by the CSA-language program (realized by the CSA-language Inference Engine) is nothing else than a self-modifiable algorithm. The programs written in a CSA-language are in general self-modifiable (thus such language is a suitable tool for writing learning programs).

We differentiate 3 classes of transits: data, actions and modifications. Each transit has structured frame-like structure. One of important components of such a structure is just the cost representing the weight of the transit.

Control, i.e. a set of sequences of transits of the language is not defined a priori by a programmer. This function, based on the **optimization mechanism**, performs the Inference Engine of the language. Generally, the Inference Engine of the language can work by the generate-and-test method (using matching mechanism for construction of elementary actions) or by the use-of-abstraction method (by generalizations and specializations of transits). The process of problem-solving is separated into particular segments (it depends on the complexity of the problems, i.e. an easy problem - to the end of the program, a very complex problem - only one-step ahead). Every segment of the algorithm is constructed in 3 phases: select ($\approx$ generate), examine ($\approx$ test), and execute. The basic method of work is by specialization and generalization of transits (use-of-abstraction method). If the resulting relation is unknown, then a mechanism, similar to matching, is used (generate-and-test method).

The Inference Engine chooses appropriate transits and builds from them (completing lacking control states) forward or backward canonical set of equations (data or goal-driven control). Next, such a set of equations is solved in the sense of the least fixpoints. Its solution, the so-called resulting relation, contains all possibilities together. Therefore the resulting relation is optimized and the best (the cheapest) solution is executed.

The programming in the CSA-language has some similarities with:

functional programming - in an analogous way, as the functional program can be viewed as nested λ - expressions, the executable program of the CSA-language (its resulting relation) these are nested expressions with operators

$$\circ, \, , \, \cup, \, \cup, \, ^*, \, ^\bullet, \, \pm, \, \underline{\bullet} \, ,$$

logic programming - by its control strategy, but in comparison with Prolog a solution is found, not by backtracking but by use of parallelism, and the start can be made from the initial as well as from the terminal control states,

knowledge-based programming - by production rules-like form of transits,

parallel procedural programming - by flow of control tokens between control states. Procedures are also expressible in the CSA-language,

object-oriented programming - transits with their data can be viewed as objects. Classes of object-oriented languages consist of data and actions and modifications (methods) applicable to data. In the case of the CSA-language, we have the opposite situation: we define a priori actions and modifications, and then data (domains), on which they operate, are defined.

3.2 Parallel Architecture

We can differentiate at least 7 main classes of computer architectures, namely: control flow, data flow, reduction, actor, logic, rule-based and connectionist (e.g. neural) computers [24]. The **Cost-Driven Machines** [3,4,9], based on the self-modifiable algorithm model for computation, can be interpreted as an eighth-class of computer architectures.

The main principle of their work is the following: **minimum of costs of the part or entire realized program(s) causes the execution of instruction(s).**

Cost-Driven Machines are simply a computer architecture realization of the self-modifiable algorithm(s).

Cost-Driven machines can be built as parallel, sequential, multi- or single-tasking, multi- or single-processor. They can be realized mainly as the software systems (e.g. as Transputer-like hardware + expert system working in the self-modifiable algorithm style), or with dominated role of hardware (as e.g. neural-like computers, where hardware fulfills ideas of the self-modifiable algorithms).

The work of Cost-Driven machines consists of 3 phases. At the select phase, particular instructions (transits) are completed (by matching) and one equation, or a few equations, or a complete set of equations, is built (it corresponds to work one step ahead, a few steps ahead, to the end of program). Such set of equations contains in parallel all possibilities (a complete or incomplete tree of transits). At the examine phase, these equations are solved and the optimal solution is found. The optimal resulting relation as an executable program is performed in the last execute phase.

The class of languages most suitable to program Cost-Driven machines is represented by the CSA-language. The Cost-Driven machines have the ability to learn from its behavior.

Cost-Driven Machines have some similarities with:

neural networks - by the optimization control looking for a minimum of costs

control and data flow computers - by flow of control and data tokens between particular control states, releasing execution of particular transits (transits represent data as well as instructions - thus both control and data flow)

reduction computers - by the executable programs which have the form of nested expressions

knowledge based and logic computers - by the same main field of application, i.e. knowledge processing and the possibility to generate different algorithms (programs) using the same knowledge base.

3.3 Machine Learning

The main properties of the learning systems are:

- their changeability (transits, control states and one-step relation)

- the optimization-like manner of their work

- the system possesses a certain knowledge about its activity and can use this knowledge for improvement of its behavior

- changes, usually, are irreversible, i.e. the system cannot return to its previous state (before learning).

We can interpret learning as a goal-directed process of modifications giving as a result better (cheaper) data, actions or modifications. After the learning, the system possesses a self-knowledge about its adaptation.

Therefore we can say that a learning system is a special case of an adaptive system, and thus also of a self-modifiable algorithm, because an adaptive system is nothing else but a self-modifiable algorithm.

From the above, it follows that concepts of the adaptive and learning systems are very similar. Learning systems are a subclass of adaptive systems. Both cases, i.e. the adaptive and learning systems, are easily expressible with the self-modifiable algorithms formalism. The third condition implies that a self-modifiable algorithm-learning system should have a nonempty set of modifications. This is true in a general case of learning systems. Even Boltzman machines [24] have modifications. Data for these are Boltzman machine examples for recognition, actions have the reduced form of weights (weights represent relations between examples - thus they are actions of the self-modifiable algorithm-learning Boltzman machine), finally modifications - these are learning algorithms changing weights. The same can be said about perceptron algorithms [14,16].

Learning systems improve their data and rules and the same can be said about the self-modifiable algorithms. The self-modifiable algorithms can learn from examples, from instruction, by analogy, from observation, and by discovery. Learning can be connected with data, actions or modifications. The necessary condition for learning for a given set of transits is that MA should have both a nonempty set operating on this optimized (taught) one and a nonempty set operating on the optimizing set (i.e. the teaching set should consist of two components being at least one and two levels higher than the taught one).For example if learning is connected with the set of data (learning from examples) then actions and modifications M of the self-modifiable algorithm should be nonempty, etc. Its sufficient condition is the achievement of minimum of costs of the resulting relation for two sets of transits: the taught one and adapting the taught set - this last one differs them from the adaptive systems.

By means of the self-modifiable algorithms we can express both supervised learning (with the teacher - i.e. we have two self-modifiable algorithms: a modifying algorithm (teacher) and a modified one (student)) and self-learning (a single self-modifiable algorithm).

3.4 Expert System

Expert systems realize a goal-directed process of problem-solving (modifications). As the result we receive a nonempty resulting relation satisfying a given goal (i.e. we reduce cost of Resfin in comparison with the infinite cost of the empty resulting relation).

Therefore, an expert system can be viewed also as a self-modifiable algorithm(s).Such expert system-self-modifiable algorithm has all components of expert systems:

Knowledge Base - these are simply actions, data, modifications and segments (parts) of the self-modifiable algorithm,

Inference Engine - is a part of MA (usually permanent) responsible for control strategy of the self-modifiable algorithm. In addition it can contain parts responsible for explanation and knowledge acquisition,

Working Memory - is a place where Inference Engine performs all computation (building sets of equations, calculating fixpoints, costs, optimization).

An expert system-self-modifiable algorithm can work forward or backward (solving forward or backward canonical set of equations, or both together). Its Inference Engine can work by the generate-and-test method (using matching mechanism for construction one-step relation) or by use-of-abstraction method (by generalizations and specializations of transits). The process of problem-solving is separated into particular segments (depending on the complexity of the problems, i.e. an easy problem - to the end of the algorithm; a very complex problem - only one step ahead). Every segment of the algorithm is constructed in 3 phases: select ($\approx$generate), examine ($\approx$test) and execute.

Knowledge Acquisition is also the feature possessed by the Expert System-self-modifiable algorithm (because learning is expressible by the MA formalism). Extended, production rules-like forms of transits are useful for explanation purposes.

In comparison with "traditional" expert systems, we may gain the following new possibilities:

- instead of any solution satisfying a given goal, the *optimal* solution is found

- a recursive solution (if we use a recursive self-modifiable algorithm)

- solutions of many problems together in sequential, concurrent or parallel manner (if we use the systems of self-modifiable algorithms)

- an automatic knowledge acquisition (self-learning)

- the simplicity of explanations.

3.5 Pattern Recognition

Pattern recognition is a goal-directed process of classification. As the result we receive the cheapest (i.e. error-free) data classification.

From this it follows that pattern recognition systems are also a special case of self-modifiable algorithm(s). Pattern recognition is based on **inductive classification methods**. Classified objects are simply data of the self-modifiable algorithm and the process of their classification is described by actions and modifications of MA. Actions and modifications seek out the least generalization (maximally specific conjunctive generalization - see e.g. [16]) of particular subsets of data (classes of objects). In terms of the self-modifiable algorithm, this means that optimization is concerned with data only (because usually algorithm of classification is permanent). The cost of data can represent the penalty for improper classification.

Very often, algorithms of classification improve the percentage of proper classified samples after a learning process. This is known as **learning from examples**. We discriminate learning from positive and negative examples. Adding negative examples increases speed of learning.

Very often, algorithms of classification depend on changing weights of connections (representing relations) between particular objects. In case of the self-modifiable algorithm, the classified objects - these are data of MA, weights - actions of MA, algorithms of classification - modifications of MA.

Neural computers are the hardware (architecture) realization of the classification algorithms. These algorithms are capable of learning from examples, therefore the process of pattern recognition (seen as the self-modifiable algorithm) can be realized by neural-like hardware.

The other potential applications of CSA: fault-tolerant computing, adaptive systems, semantics of programming languages, and the integration of different styles of programming, have been described in [5,7,8,9].

4 CONCLUSIONS

The proposed approach should be understood as a tentative creation of a universal theory for parallel and intelligent systems applied in different domains of future generation computers. CSA is a such prototype and can be classified as a theory for problem-solving, integrating different styles of programming. It should be a candidate for the theory of AI. The scope of potential applications of the theory of self-modifiable algorithms is very wide. The Calculus of Self-modifiable Algorithms has been used to describe the formal semantics and laws of programming for procedural parallel PARLE [7,21] - the main language of the ESPRIT-1588 SPAN Project [20], and an object-oriented parallel IIR [8] - an Idealized Intermediate Representation language for the Kernel System of the SPAN Project. This confirms the likelihood that CSA is capable of integrating different styles of programming. The fault-tolerant application of CSA for the Boeing avionics project has been studied at Wichita State University [22,23].
In the future, investigations should go in two directions:

- to demonstrate theoretically that the proposed methods are tractable and effective for some classes of problems. This will probably lead to specialization and refinement of the theory from its too-general scope,

- to demonstrate empirically the same things, for instance, by implementing a simple CSA language.

ACKNOWLEDGEMENTS
    I would like to thank Philip C. Treleaven for inviting me to join his Architecture Group at University College London and for providing the occasion to apply self-modifiable algorithms to the ESPRIT Project-1588, otherwise known as "SPAN: Parallel Computer Systems for Integrated Symbolic and Numeric Processing". The work of the author was partially supported by an operating grant from the National Sciences and Engineering Research Council of Canada, No. OGP0046501, and a general NSERC grant.

References

[1] Dijkstra E. W. : Guarded commands, nondeterminacy and formal derivation of programs ; Comm. ACM , 18, 8 (1975), 453-457.

[2] Eberbach E. : Algorithms with Possibilities of Selflearning and Selfmodification ; Fundamenta Informaticae 6, 1 (1983), 1-44.

[3] Eberbach E., Just J. R. : On Fault-Tolerance Mechanisms in Distributed Computer Systems ; Microprocessing and Microprogramming 16, (1985), 239-244.

[4] Eberbach E. : A Cost-Driven Machine:Fault-Tolerance and Learning ; AMSE Review, 6, 2, (1987), 37-47.

[5] Eberbach E. : Self-Modifiable Algorithms and Their Applications ; Research Note RN/88/27, Department of Computer Science, University College London, (June 1988).

[6] Eberbach E. : Self-Modifiable Algorithms: Towards a Theory of Artificial Intelligence ; Proc. Intern. Conf. on Computing and Information ICCI'89, Toronto, Canada, vol.II, 1989, 261-266.

[7] Eberbach E. : Formal Semantics for PARLE - a Target Machine Language of the ESPRIT SPAN Project ; Tech.Rep. SPAN-WP1-26, University College London, (Jan 1989).

[8] Eberbach E. : Formal Semantics and Laws of Programming for IIR - an Idealised Intermediate Representation ; Tech.Rep. SPAN-WP1-28, University College London, (June 1989).

[9] Eberbach E., Just J.R., Koczkodaj W.W. : An Approach to Optimal Reconfiguration Strategies for Fault-Tolerant Multiprocessor Systems ; Advances in Modelling and Simulation, vol.20, no.1, (1990), 39-47.

[10] Goldberg A,Robson D. : SMALLTALK-80:The language and its implementation ; Addison-Wesley, 1983.

[11] Hayes-Roth F., Waterman D.A., Lenat D.B. : Building Expert Systems ; Addison-Wesley, 1983.

[12] Hoare C. A. R. : Communicating Sequential Processes ; Prentice-Hall, 1985.

[13] INMOS Ltd : The OCCAM programming manual ; Prentice Hall , 1984.

[14] Kohonen T. : An introduction to neural computing ; Neural Networks 1, 1 (1988), 3-16.

[15] Lenat D.B., Brown J.S. : Why AM and EURISKO appear to work ; Artificial Intelligence 23, (1984), 269-294.

[16] Michalski R.S., Carbonell J.G., Mitchell T.M. : Machine Learning.An Artificial Intelligence Approach ; Tioga, Palo Alto, 1983.

[17] Minsky M. : A framework for representing knowledge ; In:Winston,P.(ed) The psychology of computer vision, McGraw-Hill, New York, 1975.

[18] Pawlak Z. : Information systems-theoretical foundations ; Information Systems 6, 3 (1981), 205-218.

[19] Petri C.A. : Kommunikation mit Automaten ; Schriftung des Rheinisch-Westfalischen Institutes fur Instrumentelle Mathematik an der Universitat Bonn, Heft 2, Bonn, 1962.

[20] Refenes A. N., Clough J. R., McCabe S. C., and Treleaven P. C. : SPAN: Parallel Computer Systems for Integrated Symbolic and Numeric Processing ; Proc. ESPRIT'88 Conf. Putting the Technology to Use, North-Holland, vol.I, Brussels (1988), 877-890.

[21] Refenes A. N., Eberbach E., McCabe S. C., and Treleaven P. C. : "PARLE: A Parallel Target Language for Integrating Symbolic and Numeric Processing", Proc.Conf.on Parallel Architectures and Languages Europe PARLE 89, Lecture Notes in Computer Science 366, Springer-Verlag, Eindhoven, The Netherlands, (1989), vol.II, 181-198.

[22] Tomayko J.E. : Software Requirements Specification for the Cost-Driven Machine for Software Reallocation ; Boeing Military Airplanes and the Wichita State University, 1989.

[23] Tomayko J.E., Eberbach E. : Applying Formal Methods and Proofs to the Verification of Distributed Systems, unpublished manuscript, Wichita and London, 1989.

[24] Treleaven P. C., et al : Computer Architectures for Artificial Intelligence ; in: Future Generation Computers. Lect.Notes in Computer Science, Springer-Verlag, vol.272, 1986, 416-492.

[25] Wirth N. : The programming language PASCAL ; Acta Informatica 1, 1 (1971), 35-63.

Almost-Everywhere Complexity, Bi-Immunity and Nondeterministic Space

John G. Geske[†]
Department of Computer Science
Michigan State University
East Lansing, Michigan 48825

Diane Kakihara
Department of Computer Science
Michigan State University
East Lansing, Michigan 48825

Abstract

We show that the complexity-theoretic notion of almost-everywhere complex functions is identical to the recursion-theoretic notion of bi-immune sets in the nondeterministic space domain. Furthermore we derive a very strong separation theorem for nondeterministic space — witnessing this fact by almost-everywhere complex sets — that is equivalent to the traditional infinitely-often complex hierarchy result. The almost-everywhere complex sets constructed here are the first such sets constructed for nondeterministic complexity classes.

Keywords: Nondeterministic space complexity; immune sets; almost-everywhere complexity; hierarchy theorems.

1 Introduction

A recent thrust in complexity theory is in constructing sets with known *lower bounds*. More precisely, we are interested in sets with nontrivial lower bounds for all but finitely many strings. Such sets have proven to be particularly useful in studying the mathematical structure of complexity classes.[4][6]

Recall that if a language $L \notin \text{DTIME}(t)$ for some time function t, then for every deterministic Turing machine M that recognizes L there exist infinitely many inputs x for which the running time of M on x is slower than $t(|x|)$. This leaves open the possibility that there exists some other infinite set of inputs which M can recognize within time bound t. This notion of *infinitely-often complexity* is the basis for all deterministic and nondeterministic complexity classes. In many applications one wants to know that $L \notin \text{DTIME}(t)$ (or DSPACE, NTIME, or NSPACE) *almost-everywhere*, that is, for every deterministic Turing machine M that recognizes L, M runs for more than $t(|x|)$ steps for all but finitely many strings x. [3][10]

[†]This author was supported in part by the National Science Foundation under grant CCR 8811996.

Balcázar and Schöning [2] relate this notion of almost-everywhere complexity to the recursion-theoretic notion of bi-immune set. Given a complexity class C, an infinite set A is C-*immune* if no infinite subset of A is in C. An infinite, co-infinite set A is C-*bi-immune* if both A and $\overline{A}$ are C-immune. At least for deterministic complexity classes, almost-everywhere complexity and bi-immunity are equivalent notions. A comprehensive review of these results for deterministic time complexity classes is presented in Geske, Huynh and Seiferas [5]. Specifically, they prove much stronger hierarchy theorems for deterministic time than the traditional "infinitely-often" theorems — they show that these separations can be witnessed by bi-immune sets. The analogous result for deterministic space was proved by Meyer and McCreight [9].

The case for nondeterminism is not as clearly understood. Geske, Huynh and Seiferas point out the inherent difficulty of deriving similar results for nondeterministic complexity classes. Allender, Beigel, Hertrampf, and Homer [1] have investigated these issues for nondeterministic time. They presented a hierarchy theorem, not as tight as the existing hierarchy theorems for nondeterministic time, in which the witness to this separation is an immune set. They failed to achieve the strong separation results obtained by Geske, Huynh and Seiferas, but they showed that their result is the best possible for nondeterministic time using relativizable techniques.

In this paper we examine the problem of nondeterministic space. We show that there is a natural relationship between almost-everywhere complexity and bi-immunity in nondeterministic space complexity classes that mirror the results achievable in deterministic complexity classes, and are significantly stronger than the results obtainable for nondeterministic time. Moreover, there is an analogous strong hierarchy theorem for nondeterministic space that is equivalent to that achievable for deterministic space.

2 Main Results

Defining almost-everywhere complexity in terms of nondeterministic machines poses unique problems not encountered in the deterministic case. Resource bounds for nondeterministic machines depend only on the resources of *accepting* computation paths. Therefore, language acceptance for nondeterministic machines is an asymmetric proposition. Allender, Beigel, *et. al.* [1] point out that, due to this asymmetry, immunity appears to be the natural notion to consider when defining almost-everywhere complexity for nondeterministic time-complexity classes. They ignore *rejecting* paths in deriving the following definition for a.e. complexity for nondeterministic time.

Definition 1 *A set A is* NTIME(t)-*almost-everywhere complex if and only if for every nondeterministic machine recognizer M for the set A, the shortest accepting path for any string x in A is longer than* $t(|x|)$.

From this definition, the following result is immediate.

Theorem 1 *Let t be a time-constructible function. A set A is* NTIME(t)-*almost-everywhere complex if and only if A is* NTIME(t)-*immune.*

They then prove the following result:

Theorem 2 *Let T and t be monotone nondecreasing time-constructible functions such that, for some k, $T^{(k)}(n) = \omega(2^{t^{(k)}}(n))$, and such that, for all large n, $t(T(n)) \leq T(t(n))$. Then there is a set in* NTIME(T(n)) *which is immune to* NTIME(t(n)).

Allender, Beigel, *et. al.* admit that it is rather unsatisfying to allow the possibility of infinitiely many inputs that are *rejected* easily. Nevertheless, they show that the above result is the best possible using relativizable proof techniques.

The equivalence one would really like to establish is almost-everywhere complexity with bi-immunity. We show that for nondeterministic space, the above problems do not arise. Due to the very elegant work of Immerman [8] and Szelepcsényi [12] showing nondeterministic space is closed under complementation, it is possible to consider rejecting paths of nondeterministic space-bounded machines. This observation motivates the following:

Definition 2 *A set A is* NSPACE(s)-*almost-everywhere complex (*NSPACE(s) *a.e. complex) if for every nondeterministic Turing machine M that recognizes A, M uses more than $s(|x|)$ space (tape cells) on an input string x, and this is true for all but finitely many input strings.*

It follows that if a set A is NSPACE(s)-almost-everywhere complex, then for any s space-bounded nondeterministic machine M that recognizes A and all but finitely many input strings x, all accepting *or rejecting* computation paths require more than $s(|x|)$ space. This definition of a.e. complexity is analogous to the notion of a.e. complexity for deterministic time and space classes, and it is significantly stronger than the notion of a.e. complexity for nondeterministic time given in Definition 1. This is made precise in the following theorem.

Theorem 3 *Let s be a space-constructible function. A recursive set A is* NSPACE(s)-*bi-immune if and only if A is* NSPACE(s)-*almost-everywhere complex.*

This result precludes the troubling possibility of having infinite sets of strings that can be rejected easily. An immediate consequence of Theorem 3 is that all of the following theorems can be restated in terms of almost-everywhere complexity.

Before we present our final theorems we digress and introduce some standard notation. Let Σ denote the binary alphabet $\{0,1\}$ and Σ^* the strings over Σ. $|w|$ denotes the length of the string $w \in \Sigma^*$. We assume a total ordering on $\Sigma^* = \{w_i \mid i \geq 1\}$ such that shorter strings precede longer ones, and strings of the same length are ordered lexicographically. As a computational model we use the *multiple-tape off-line Turing transducer* — a multiple worktape Turing machine with a read-only input tape and a write-only output. A transducer T *accepts* a string x if there is a computation by T on input x that halts in a distinguished accepting state. $L(T)$ denotes the set of strings accepted by transducer T. T *computes* a value y on an input string x if there is an accepting computation of T on x for which y is the output. Let $\{T_i\}_{i \in \mathbb{N}}$ be an effective enumeration of nondeterministic Turing transducers so that for every recursive set A there exists some T_i such that $A = L(T_i)$; φ_i denotes the partial multi-valued function computed by transducer T_i.

A further characterization of bi-immune sets follows from the work of Balcázar and Schöning [2]. Recall that given a set Σ^*, a relation $R \subseteq \Sigma^* \times \Sigma^*$ is *finite-one* if for every $y \in \Sigma^*$, $R^{-1}(y)$ is finite.

Theorem 4 *Let s be a space-constructible function, $s(n) \geq \log n$. A recursive set A is* NSPACE(s)-*bi-immune if and only if for every nondeterministic $s(n)$ space-bounded transducer T, $\varphi_T(A) \cap \varphi_T(\overline{A}) = \emptyset$, φ_T is finite-one.*

Proof. Assume a set A is not NSPACE($s(n)$)-bi-immune. Then there exists an infinite subset A_1 of A (or $\overline{A}$) such that $A_1 \in$ NSPACE($s(n)$). Define $\varphi : \Sigma^* \to \Sigma^*$ by $\varphi(x) = y$ for all $x \in A_1$, where y is some fixed string in A_1, and $\varphi(x) = x$ for all $x \in \overline{A_1}$. Clearly $\varphi(A) \cap \varphi(\overline{A}) = \emptyset$, and φ is not finite-one. φ is computable nondeterministically in $s(n)$ space. Note that this last statement follows since NSPACE($s(n)$) is closed under complementation.

Conversely, assume there exists an φ computable nondeterministically in $s(n)$ space, $\varphi(A) \cap \varphi(\overline{A}) = \emptyset$ and φ is not finite-one. Then there exists a $y \in \Sigma^*$ such that $\varphi^{-1}(y) \subseteq A$ is infinite, $\varphi^{-1}(y) \in$ NSPACE($s(n)$) and so, A is not NSPACE($s(n)$)-complex. $\square$

The standard nondeterministic hierarchy theorems for time and space are proven with *translational* methods that make use of "padding" arguments. (See for instance Seiferas, Fischer, Meyer[11] and Ibarra[7].) Geske, Huynh, and Seiferas [5] have pointed out that such methods cannot be used to prove almost-everywhere complex results. While this proves to be disastrous for nondeterministic time, we note that the power of Immerman's counting technique allows us to *diagonalize* over nondeterministic space classes. Our final result is to show that, as with deterministic time complexity classes and deterministic space complexity classes, it is possible to separate nondeterministic space complexity classes with bi-immune sets,

Theorem 5 *If s_2 is a space-constructible function, s_1 and s_2 are at least $\log n$, and $s_1(n) = o(s_2(n))$, then there is a NSPACE(s_1)-bi-immune set in NSPACE(s_2).*

The construction of a NSPACE(s_1)-bi-immune set is based on a finite-injury priority argument. Such a construction is given in Figure 1. Given the function s_2, we construct a recursive bi-immune set A inductively on the enumerated strings of Σ^*. We consider the following infinite enumeration of *restraining conditions*:

$$R_i : \varphi_i \text{ is not finite} - \text{one} \Rightarrow \varphi_i(A) \cap \varphi_i(\overline{A}) \neq \emptyset.$$

A condition R_j is *satisfiable* if its antecendent is true. A satisfiable condition R_j is *satisfied* if $\varphi_j(A) \cap \varphi_j(\overline{A}) \neq \emptyset$.

At each stage we attempt to satisfy the least (smallest indexed) restraining condition that has not yet been satisfied. In the construction, S is a set of restraining conditions (transducer indices) to be considered. The proof of Theorem 5 then reduces to proving the following two intermediate results:

Lemma 1 $A \in$ NSPACE($s_2(n)$).

Proof. We show that there exists a nondeterministic Turing machine that executes the algorithm given in Figure 1 in space $s_2(n)$. On an input x of length n, the time to cancel machines from previous stages requires space $s_2(n)$. Each simulation is run within $s_2(n)$ space. (Note that for a machine to do this requires that $s_2(n)$ be space-constructible.) Therefore the simulations require at most $s_2(n)$ space, and the total space necessary to execute the algorithm is $O(s_2(n))$, and we arrive at our desired result.□

Lemma 2 *For every $s_1(n)$ computable φ_j that is not finite-one, R_j is satisfied.*

stage i
  begin
    Let $S := \{1, \ldots, i-1\}$;
    Within space $s_2(n)$ execute as many previous stages as
      possible, beginning with stage 1, removing elements
      out of S that have been satisfied during previous
      stages;
    for each $j \in S$ **do**
      Within space $s_2(n)$ simulate T_j to determine whether
        there is a string $w < w_i$ such that $T_j(w) = T_j(w_i)$;
    if yes then begin
               Let $\hat{j}$ be the least transducer index with
                 this property;
               Let $\hat{w}$ be the least string $\hat{w} < w_i$ with this
                 property;
               {* Note that $T_{\hat{j}}$ is diagonalized by the fol-
                 lowing statement *}
               if $\hat{w} \in A$ **then** add w_i to $\overline{A}$
                        else add w_i to A
      end
  end stage i

Figure 1: Inductive construction of an NSPACE($s_1(n)$) a.e. complex set

Proof. Let T_l be a $s_1(n)$ time-bounded transducer such that φ_l is not finite-one and $\varphi_l(A) \cap \varphi_l(\overline{A}) = \emptyset$. Because of the conditions placed on $s_2(n)$ we can assume without loss of generality that at some stage i in the construction, for all indicies $j < l$, either $j \notin S$, i.e., R_j has already been satisfied, or φ_j is finite-one. So, l is the smallest satisfiable index in S at stage i, and remains the smallest satisfiable index at all future stages until R_l is satisfied.

The space required to simulate T_l on an input of length n is $s_1(n)$. We are only allowed to simulate T_l for $s_2(n)$ steps. However, since φ_l is not finite-one, and by the conditions placed on $s_2(n)$, there exist strings w_j, w_k such that $|w_j| < |w_k|$, $\varphi_l(w_j) = \varphi_l(w_k)$, and w_k is a sufficiently large string such that $s_1(|w_j|) < s_2(|w_k|)$. Therefore there is enough space to complete the simulation and witness the fact that $\varphi_l(w_j) = \varphi_l(w_k)$. If $w_j \in A$ then $w_k \in \overline{A}$, otherwise $w_j \in \overline{A}$ and $w_k \in A$. In either case $\varphi_l(A) \cap \varphi_l(\overline{A}) \neq \emptyset$ and R_l is satisfied.$\square$

Our desired result follows from the observation that if Lemma 2 holds then the conditions of Theorem 4 are satisfied.

3 Conclusions

We have examined the relationship between bi-immunity and almost-everywhere complexity in nondeterministic space complexity classes, and we have found that this relationship is analogous to the deterministic case. We have been able to derive very strong separation theorems for nondeterministic space that are as strong as the traditional hierarchy theorems. The bi-immune sets constructed here are the first such sets constructed for a nondeterministic complexity class.

The strength of our result is due to our ability to diagonalize over nondeterministic space. It is important to note that it is the *technique* developed by Immerman that allows this result — not the fact that nondeterministic space is closed under complementation. Allender, Beigel, *et. al.* [1] have shown that their hierarchy theorem for nondeterministic time — an immunity result — is about the best that can be hoped for using relativizable proof techniques. The most natural relationship one would expect is between almost-everywhere complexity and bi-immunity; we have been unable to achieve this result, *even under the assumption that nondeterministic time is closed under complement.* Indeed, it appears that new techniques must be developed to achieve stronger nondeterministic time results.

References

[1] E. Allender, R. Beigel, U. Hertrampf, and S. Homer. A note on the almost-everywhere hierarchy for nondeterministic time. To appear in STACS 90, Lecture Notes in Computer Science.

[2] J.L. Balcázar and U. Schöning. Bi-immune sets for complexity classes. *Mathematical Systems Theory*, 18(1):1–10, 1985.

[3] L. Berman. On the structure of complete sets: almost everywhere complexity and infinitely often speedup. In *Proc. 17th IEEE Symposium on the Foundations of Computer Science*, volume 17, pages 76–80, 1976.

[4] J.G. Geske. *On the structure of intractable sets.* PhD thesis, Iowa State University, 1987.

[5] J.G. Geske, D. Huynh, and J. Seiferas. A technical note on bi-immunity and almost everywhere complexity. To appear in Information and Computation.

[6] J.G. Geske, D. Huynh, and A. Selman. A hierarchy theorem for almost everywhere complex sets with application to polynomial complexity degrees. In *STACS 87, Lecture Notes in Computer Science Vol. 247, pp. 125-135.* Springer-Verlag, Berlin, 1987.

[7] O.H. Ibarra. A note concerning nondeterministic tape complexities. *Journal of the ACM*, 19:608–612, 1972.

[8] N. Immerman. Nondeterministic space is closed under complement. In *Proc. Structure in Complexity Theory*, volume 3, pages 112–115, 1988.

[9] A.R. Meyer and E.M. McCreight. Computationally complex and pseudo-random zero-one valued functions. In Z. Kohavi and A. Paz, editors, *Theory of Machines and Computations, pp. 19-42*. Academic Press, New York, 1971.

[10] M.O. Rabin. Degree of difficulty of computing a function and a partial ordering of recursive sets. Technical Report 2, Hebrew University, Jerusalem, Israel, 1960.

[11] J.I. Seiferas, M.J. Fischer, and A.R. Meyer. Separating nondeterministic time complexity classes. *Journal of the ACM*, 25:146–167, 1978.

[12] R. Szelepcesényi. The method of forcing for nondeterministic automata. *Bull. European Association Theoretical Computer Science*, pages 96–100, 1987.

Deriving Deterministic Prediction Rules from Reduction Schemes

Dafna Sheinwald   Richard C. Pasco

IBM Almaden Research Center, Dept. K52/802

650 Harry Road, San Jose, CA 95120-6099

USA

Abstract

Deterministic Prediction in progressive coding of images is investigated. *Progressive coding* first creates a sequence of resolution layers by beginning with an original image and reducing its resolution several times by factors of two. Next, the resultant layers are losslessly encoded. The lowest-resolution layer is encoded first, then each higher resolution image is built incrementally upon the previous, until the original image is finally encoded. Coding efficiency may be improved if knowledge of the rules which produced the lower-resolution image of each pair is used to *deterministically predict* pixels of the higher, so they need not be encoded.

We address this problem: given reduction rules expressing each low-resolution pixel as a function of nearby high-resolution pixels and previously-generated low-resolution pixels, find a complete set of rules, each of which deterministically predicts the value of a high-resolution pixel when certain values are found in nearby low-resolution pixels and previously-coded high-resolution pixels. We show that this problem is NP-Hard by analogy to the well-known Satisfiability problem, then propose a recursive algorithm for solving it in optimal time as a depth-first tree search. The effectiveness of prediction is shown to vary depending on the sequence order in which the pixels are processed; we prove upper bounds on the effectiveness and demonstrate how to find the optimal order. Reduction rules taking their inputs from an area of pixels (template) larger than 2×2 are shown to exhibit an interdependence between their input pixels such that certain combinations are impossible; we show a sequence order of processing that addresses correctly this phenomenon. Finally, we demonstrate how multiple template positions lead to a recursion in prediction which further enhances predictability. This work serves as a basis for both working software implementation and for future research into unsolved problems which we identify.

Keywords: *deterministic prediction, progressive coding.*

1. Introduction

In *progressive coding* of images (two dimensional arrays of finite alphabet) one first creates a list of reduced versions of the processed image. The first image in the list is the original one, and each of the subsequent elements is a reduction by a factor of two in both dimensions of its immediate predecessor, and is composed of the same alphabet as the original image. Then, the lowest resolution version of the image (last in the list) is encoded using a lossless data compression code, then the second to lowest resolution version of the image is encoded, using a lossless code in conjunction with the fact that the decoder already knows the lowest resolution version of the image, and so on, towards higher and higher resolutions. The main advantage of a progressive coding scheme is that by traversing the list from last item to first, a low resolution version of the image is *quickly* displayed, and then can be gradually refined. This way, the pixels that compose a low resolution version of the image (or several layers of low resolutions) convey more information as to the flavor of the original image, to a human inspection, than the same number of pixels that compose one region of that original image do.

In this paper we deal with the commonly used reduction schemes that comprise a *template* T which specifies the relative positions of a few high-resolution and low-resolution pixels, and a function R over the alphabet of the image and its reduced versions. We define *cell* as the relative position of a pixel selected by the template to the pixel being computed. Template T is shifted in a predetermined order, (usually raster order), on the high resolution image and its low-resolution counterpart being produced, thereby assumes different contents in different positions. R defines a value for a low-resolution pixel in each of these positions, given the contents T assumes there.

Since the reduction is by two-to-one (2:1) in each dimension, the template is shifted horizontally in steps of two high-resolution pixels, and vertically in steps of two high-resolution lines. Thus, each specific high-resolution cell of T is positioned on every other line of the high-resolution image, and in each such line, on every other pixel. Also, the low-resolution cells of T must use only values of pixels already produced. We assume some predetermined boundary conditions, for example all zero beyond edges, for positions which cause some of the template's cells to be laid beyond the edges of the low-resolution and/or the high-resolution images.

The reduction process is recursive: a reduced version yielded by one reduction serves as the high-resolution input to the next. For simplicity we will deal with one pair of consecutive images in the above mentioned list: a high-resolution image denoted H and its low-resolution version L. Our results can be carried over to all pairs of the list.

Given the reduction scheme, deterministic prediction rules can be derived, by which values of pixels of H could be uniquely determined by the values of their previously-coded neighbors and some of L's pixels. Encoding of these high-resolution pixels can be avoided, thereby compression efficiency is enhanced. Deriving these rules is the major problem we deal with in this paper.

As an illustration, suppose that the images are binary, that T includes only four high-resolution cells in the shape of a 2×2 square, and that R is the OR function. Observing a zero in L, in position p, the decoder can tell, without reading anything from the code stream, that all four pixels of H that yielded p are zero. The quality demanded of the reduction scheme renders such a simple scheme unacceptable. Typically, T includes ten to twenty cells, and R is quite complicated, often expressed as a large look-up table. By the cells of T, one can recognize whether it is the case that some pixels of H or L may be covered by T in several positions;

i.e., these pixels may contribute to the value of more than one (low-resolution) pixel of L. This case contributes to the complication of deriving deterministic prediction rules, as will be shown in Section 3.

In this paper we present algorithms for deriving deterministic prediction rules for *any* given reduction scheme. Our results are for bi-level images (every pixel is either black or white, i.e., the alphabet is $\{0,1\}$), and are readily generalized to larger alphabets.

In Section 2 we derive deterministic rules using the pixels covered by the template's cells when positioned in one position. We prove that the algorithm we present for deriving these rules is optimally efficient. Also, we prove some properties of the number of rules, and discuss ways to maximize that number. In Section 3 we derive rules using unions of the sets of pixels covered by several adjacent positions of the template. Some concluding remarks are given in Section 4.

2. Deriving Rules in One Position of the Template

We impose some linear order on the template cells, and denote $T = (c_1, c_2, \dots , c_n)$. That is, in one position, T covers n pixels, some of them belong to L and some of them to H. The associated function of the reduction scheme is $R: \{0,1\}^n \to \{0,1\}$.

2.1 The problem is hard

Suppose we are given some Boolean reduction function (accepting n input bits), the values of its first $k - 1$ input bits (for some $k \le n$), and the value of its output bit. We would like to infer the value of the k-th input bit. To do this, we examine those combinations of possible values of it and the remaining $n - k$ input bits which produce the given value of the output bit (if there are any such combinations), to see if the desired bit is the same for all of them. If so, we can *deterministically predict* its value from the given values. More specifically, we state the DPR problem:

The Deterministic Prediction Rules Problem (DPR)

Given a Boolean reduction function R, $z = R(x_1, x_2, \dots , x_{k-1}, x_k, x_{k+1}, \dots , x_n)$, DPR asks whether there are an index k, $1 \le k \le n$, specific Boolean values $P, b_1, b_2, \dots , b_{k-1}$, for the variables $z, x_1, x_2, \dots , x_{k-1}$, and another Boolean value b, such that both conditions hold:

[D1]   There exists at least one combination of values $b_k, b_{k+1}, \dots , b_n$ for the remaining variables $x_k, x_{k+1}, \dots , x_n$ such that $P = R(b_1, b_2, \dots , b_n)$.

[D2]   In *every* such combination, the value b_k is the same, $b_k = b$.

In other words, the combination $P, b_1, b_2, \dots , b_{k-1}$ implies $b_k = b$, not in the empty sense only.

By a linear transformation from the Satisfiability problem (cf. [GJ]), we can prove the following theorem (see the full proof in [SP]):

Theorem 1

DPR is NP-Hard. ∎

2.2 An Exhaustive Search for Solutions for DPR

The reduction function $R(x_1, x_2, \ldots, x_n)$ may be drawn as a binary tree, with the branches ordered such that x_i establishes the i-th branch from the root, and with leaves labelled with the value returned by R. Figure 1 shows such a tree where $R(x_1, x_2, x_3)$ is the "majority-of-three" function.

The following recursive algorithm, *Deter*, receives a Boolean vector x of n components and an index k as input parameters. It is first invoked with an arbitrary vector of length n and with $k = 1$. *Deter* presumes knowledge of reduction function R, and traverses, depth-first, the tree associated with R, recording for each node the set of all possible labels on leaves reachable from that node. At each node where the set of outcomes of one branch differ from those of the other, a *DP rule* may be stated: If the function returns an outcome obtainable from one branch but not from the other, then it is obvious which branch was taken.

```
 1  function Deter(x: [1..n]; k: integer): set of 0..1;
 2  var set0, set1: set of 0..1;
 3  begin
 4      if k = n + 1 then return({R(x)})
 5      else begin
 6          x[k] := 0;
 7          set0 := Deter(x, k + 1);
 8          x[k] := 1;
 9          set1 := Deter(x, k + 1);
10          for all P ∈ set0 − set1
                print(P, x[1], x[2], ... , x[k − 1] ↦ "x[k] = 0");
11          for all P ∈ set1 − set0
                print(P, x[1], x[2], ... , x[k − 1] ↦ "x[k] = 1");
12          return(set0 ∪ set1);
13      end;
14  end;
```

Theorem 2

For a given Boolean function R of n variables, *Deter* makes *one* pass on all 2^n different assignment of values to the x_i. During this pass, it outputs *all* combinations of $P, b_1, b_2, \ldots, b_{k-1}$ and b that satisfy [D1] and [D2] (i.e., all deterministic prediction rules).

Proof: By lines 6-9, it is clear that *Deter* is invoked 2^n times, and that R is invoked *once* for each of the 2^n different values of the binary vector x of length n. Altogether, assuming printing of a prediction rule consumes a constant time (as can be done by outputting all rules as paths on a tree), a time complexity of $O(2^n)$ for *Deter*, which by Theorem 1 is optimal.

It is easy to verify by induction on k that, for an invocation of *Deter* with specific values of $k, x[1], x[2], \ldots, x[k-1]$, the following hold in line 10 for $b = 0,1$:

$$setb = \bigcup_{x[k+1], x[k+2], \ldots, x[n]} \{R(x[1], x[2], \ldots, x[k-1], b, x[k+1], \ldots, x[n])\}.$$

This easily implies the correctness of the algorithm. See [SP] for the full proof. ∎

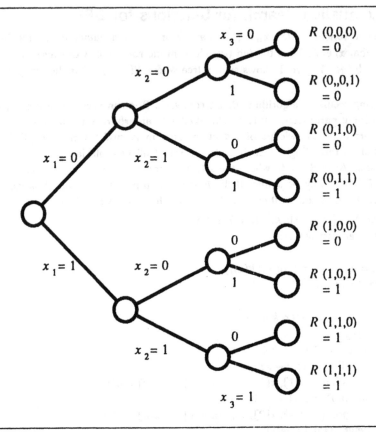

Figure 1. Binary tree representation of majority-of-three reduction function.

2.3 Optimal order of variables

The definitions of deterministic prediction rules depend on the index order of the arguments of R. The two-dimensional template T does not impose any specific linear order on its cells. In this subsection we discuss how the order of processing the pixels covered by the template affects the number of usable deterministic prediction rules. Note that this order must be identical to the coding order, because the decoder must know the values upon which to base its prediction of subsequent values.

Let o be an index-ordering, that is a permutation $\{1, 2, \ldots, n\} \rightarrow \{1, 2, \ldots, n\}$ mapping the sequence order of prediction to the indices of position in the template. The binary tree $Tr(R, o)$, corresponding to R and o, has $x_{o(i)}$ establishing the i-th branch, $i = 1, 2, \ldots, n$, and has $R(b_1, b_2, \ldots, b_n)$ labelling the leaf reached from the root by taking branches according to $b_{o(1)}, b_{o(2)}, \ldots, b_{o(n)}$. Given a vector $\vec{b} = b_1, b_2, \ldots, b_n$ and an index k, $1 \leq k \leq n$, we check at the node reached from the root according to $b_{o(1)}, b_{o(2)}, \ldots, b_{o(k-1)}$, whether all leaves labelled with $R(b_1, \ldots, b_n)$ require taking the next branch according to $b_{o(k)}$ (i.e. all leaves reachable from the alternate branch $\bar{b}_{o(k)}$ have the opposite label $\bar{R}(b_1, \ldots, b_n)$). If so, the next branch is deterministically predictable under sequence order o; we say that the effectiveness of $\vec{b}$ at its $o(k)$-th component is 1. Otherwise, the effectiveness is 0. Formally,

$$ef(R, o, \vec{b}, k) \; \underset{=}{\Delta} \; \begin{cases} 1 & \text{if, for all } \vec{b'} \text{ with } b'_{o(1)}, \cdots, b'_{o(k-1)} = b_{o(1)}, \cdots, b_{o(k-1)}, \\ & (R(b') = R(b)) \mapsto (b'_{o(k)} = b_{o(k)}) \\ 0 & \text{otherwise} \end{cases}$$

The overall effectiveness of the ordering is now defined as

$$ef(R, o) \; \underset{=}{\Delta} \; \sum_{k=1}^{n} \sum_{\vec{b} \,\in\, \{0,1\}^n} ef(R, o, \vec{b}, k) \; .$$

An obvious modification of *Deter* can serve to compute $ef(R, o)$ for given R and o in $O(2^n)$ steps, which is optimal because (1) DPR is NP-hard and (2) for any index-ordering o, $ef(R, o) = 0$ if and only if R is single-valued (either a tautology or a contradiction), that is, if and only if the answer to DPR is NO. In [SP] we present a dynamic programming algorithm that in $O(n\, 3^n)$ steps determines the most effective index-ordering. By the previous remark, the time complexity of this algorithm is polynomially equivalent to the best possible.

Some observations on the achievable effectiveness conclude this subsection For a node v of $Tr = Tr(R, o)$ let $v0$ and $v1$ denote the vertices reached from v by taking a branch dwon, let $Tr(v)$ denote the subtree rooted by v, let *zero*(v) denote the number of leaves l in $Tr(v)$ labelled "0", and let *one*(v) denote the number of leaves l labelled "1". A node $v \in Tr$ is said to be *balanced* if $|zero(v0) - zero(v1)| \leq 1$, and *unbalanced* otherwise. A function is *balanced* if its associated tree has all nodes balanced, and *unbalanced* otherwise. Let the cardinality $\lfloor R \rfloor$ of R denote the minimum of the number of b such that $R(b) = 0$ and the number of b such that $R(b) = 1$, and let I denote the natural ordering: $I(j) = j$, $j = 1, 2, \ldots, n$.

Theorem 3

Balanced functions maximize $ef(R, I)$ over all functions R with $\lfloor R \rfloor = m$.

Proof: By induction on the minimum distance from any leaf of $Tr(R)$ to any unbalanced node in the tree. See [SP] for the full proof. ∎

Theorem 4

$\max\{ef(R, o): o \text{ is arbitrary and } \lfloor R \rfloor = m\} = \max\{ef(R, I): \lfloor R \rfloor = m\} = p + m\,l$, where $0 < p \leq m$ and $0 < l$ are the unique integers satisfying $2^n = p\, 2^l + (m - p)\, 2^{l-1}$.

Proof: By induction on m. See [SP] for the full proof. ∎

Corollary: $\max\{ef(R, o): \text{ any } R \text{ and } o\} = \max\{ef(R, I): \text{ any } R\} = 2^n$ ∎

The upper bound of Theorem 4 is not tight. As an illustration, consider the function $R(b_1, b_2, b_3)$ with $R(0,0,0) = R(1,0,0) = R(1,0,1) = R(1,1,0) = 0$ and $R(b_1, b_2, b_3) = 1$ for the other four vectors (b_1, b_2, b_3). Under each of the six possible orders of its three variables, the overall effectiveness of the function is 6, whereas by Theorem 4 the effectiveness is upper bounded by 8.

3. Deriving General Rules

This section is relevant to templates that include more than four high-resolution cells.

3.1 Dependence between variables

As an example of a reduction scheme, consider the template comprising three low-resolution cells and 3×3 high-resolution cells of the form

$$
\begin{array}{cc}
\begin{array}{cc} l_1 & l_2 \\ l_3 & p \end{array} &
\begin{array}{ccc} h_1 & h_2 & h_3 \\ h_4 & h_5 & h_6 \\ h_7 & h_8 & h_9 \end{array}
\end{array}
\tag{1}
$$

A Boolean function $R: \{0,1\}^{12} \rightarrow \{0,1\}$ defines p as a function of $l_1, l_2, l_3, h_1, h_2, \ldots, h_9$.

Note that when the template includes more than four high-resolution cells, some pixels contribute to the values of more than one low-resolution pixel. Here h_1, for example, contributes to l_1, l_2, l_3, and p. Thus we observe an interdependence between the arguments of function R, the degree of which depends on the specific function R. If we knew the surroundings (pixels covered by the template T while computing l_1, l_2 and l_3) we might find that some of the combinations of values for $c_1, c_2, \ldots, c_n = l_1, l_2, l_3, h_1, h_2, \ldots, h_9$ could not possibly be assumed by T as its contents in the given surroundings.

Surrounding is not defined for *Deter*, and hence impossible combinations are not detected by it. This leads to two kinds of consequences: output of superfluous rules for conditions which never occur, and omission of potentially useful rules which could be obtained by utilizing knowledge of impossible conditions. As an example of the first kind, suppose that P is included in *set0* only for impossible c's and that P is not a member of *set1*. That is,

$$(\forall c[k], c[k+2], \ldots, c[n] : R(c) = P)(c[k] = 0 \text{ and } c \text{ is impossible}) \,.$$

In other words, the combination $P, c[1], c[2], \ldots, c[k-1]$ is impossible, and will never be met while coding H. Nevertheless, since $P \in set0$ and $P \notin set1$, line 10 of *Deter* will output a superfluous rule of the form $P, c[1], c[2], \ldots, c[k-1] \mapsto ``c[k] = 0"$. As an example of the second kind, suppose that P is included in *set0* for possible c's, and in *set1* only for impossible c's. That is,

$$(\forall c[k], c[k+2], \ldots, c[n] : R(c) = P)(c \text{ is possible} \mapsto (c[k] = 0)) \,.$$

Hence, if the combination $P, c[1], c[2], \ldots, c[k-1]$ is met while coding H, then it is part of a possible c, and therefore, it suffices to predict $c[k] = 0$. But line 10 of *Deter* outputs no rule of the form $P, c[1], c[2], \ldots c[k-1] \mapsto ``c[k] = 0"$, since $P \in set1$ by our assumption. Note again that the terms "possible" and "impossible" are surrounding-dependent.

Adjusting reducing order (the order in which the template is shifted on H and L) and coding order to each other can eliminate the problem of not outputting applicable rules for some pixels. See [SP].

3.2 Predicting over Multiple Template Positions

When coding and reducing orders are given, and we want to exploit the predicting potential of the reduction scheme on all cells of the template, we can solve the dependence problem as follows. First, we find the size and shape of the area that includes the influencing surroundings as well as the area covered by the template where we want to make the prediction. Then, we apply an exhaustive search over all possible values of pixels in that area, and derive and apply rules in a manner analogous to the use of *Deter*. The problem with this is threefold: (i) the size and shape of that area are indefinite and depend on the closeness of the pixel to be predicted to the margins of the image; (ii) the search for rules grows exponentially with the size of the area; and (iii) the exhaustive search for a match between the vicinity of the processed pixel and any of the prediction rules, which is done for every pixel during the coding process, consumes enormous time as the number of pixels comprising the rules grows. In this subsection we use a new approach for predicting. We do not derive prediction rules and then, while coding, try to apply them. Instead, we combine the coding process with gathering and processing pieces of information, and keep them handy for effective use when needed to determine predictability of pixels. That information processing is in the form of either predictions within one position of the template or operations on data associated with pairs of adjacent template positions. Thereby the complexity of deriving rules and implementing prediction is kept low.

We assume here that both reducing order and coding order are raster, the most commonly used order. For practical reasons, due to the very large size of images in an overwhelming number of applications, the lines of H, and their counterparts in L, are coded a few at a time. Processed lines are not dealt with again at a later point of the coding. Upon completion of the coding of some lines, the coding process continues to subsequent lines that are read in from a file or from an input buffer. Although there are pathological cases of reduction schemes where the knowledge of low-resolution pixels of bottom lines conveys information about the values of high-resolution pixels of far top lines, in most quality reduction schemes, the low-resolution pixels "represent" only the respective 2×2 high-resolution pixels and their immediate vicinity. In light of the above, we shall restrict our search for information applicable for prediction to only a few consecutive high-resolution lines (including the processed line) and their low-resolution counterparts.

For simplicity, we assume that $c_1, c_2, \dots, c_l$ are the low-resolution cells of the template, and $c_{l+1}, c_{l+2}, \dots, c_n$ are the high-resolution cells indexed in the coding order. Also, we assume that the high-resolution cells of the template form a rectangular shape. If this is not the case, we can add dummy cells to the template, without letting their contents affect the reduction result. Rectangularity will ease the analysis of overlapping of two adjacent positions of the reduction template.

We derive all rules of the form $P, c_1, c_2, \dots, c_l \mapsto \{A_1, A_2, \dots, A_j\}$, with $0 \le j$ and the set $\{A_i\}$ consisting of all the assignments of values to cells $c_{l+1}, c_{l+2}, \dots, c_n$ such that $P = R(c_1, c_2, \dots, c_n)$. The assignments A are vectors of length $n - l$ with $A[i]$ being the value assigned to c_{l+i}. These rules are derived without taking surroundings into account. A variation of *Deter*, can derive these rules during one pass on all 2^n possible values of $c_1, c_2, \dots, c_n$.

Let G denote the grid of templates formed by locating a template for each pixel of L, as positioned for determining that pixel during the reduction process. Here we consider the template to include the low-resolution cell to which the result of the reduction function is assigned. Thus, for example, the template of (1) consists of 13 cells, including p. While encoding or decoding H, the low-resolution cells of each $t \in G$ assume the values of the corresponding pixels of L, and the high-resolution cells that cover already-processed pixels of H assume their values. The templates overlap on H, since they include more than four high-resolution cells. When templates cells extend beyond edges of H or L, these cells assume some predetermined value m (the same value assumed during the reducing process).

Our algorithm maintains a processing buffer B which holds a few consecutive lines of G at a time, being the lines that cover the current coded line of H. During the coding of H a new line of templates is loaded to B upon starting the coding of every other line of H. At the same rate, although not necessarily simultaneously, template lines leave the buffer. $H(B)$ and $L(B)$ denote the portions of H and L, respectively, covered by the templates of B. For each $t \in B$ we maintain a set $S(t)$ of the possible assignment of values to the high-resolution cells of t. This set shrinks as information gathered in the course of processing rules out more and more assignments. Note that the last line of B covers the current coded line of H and all yet uncoded lines of $H(B)$. Some notations are in order: (1) Let t_1 and t_2 be two adjacent templates of B. We say that $A_1 \in S(t_1)$ *agrees* with $A_2 \in S(t_2)$ if assigning A_1 to t_1 and A_2 to t_2 does not raise a conflict on the pixels covered by both templates. We say that $A_1 \in S(t_1)$ agrees with some high-resolution pixels covered by t_1, if assigning A_1 to t_1 does not raise a conflict on these pixels. (2) For a pixel h of the coded line, we denote by $t(h)$ the leftmost template of the bottom line of B that covers h. (3) Let w denote the number of templates in one line of G (which is also the number of pixels in one line of L). We index the templates of the bottom line of B from left to right as $t_1, t_2, \ldots, t_w$.

Our Algorithm for Predicting and Coding:

Suppose that the buffer B is loaded with r consecutive template lines $Q_1, Q_2, \ldots, Q_r$ of G and we are about to process a pixel h of H. Suppose that $t(h)$ covers h with its i-th high-resolution cell c_{l+i}. If for some Boolean value b, $A[i] = b$ for all $A \in S(t(h))$, then h is predicted to have the value b. If a uniformity as to the value of h is not found, then h is coded and every $A \in S(t(h))$ which does not agree with the value of h is removed. Then, we consider the position of the next pixel for processing, h'. If h and h' share the same line of H, then in case that $t(h') = t(h)$ we start with the processing of h'; otherwise, $t(h')$ must be immediately to the right of $t(h)$ and we remove from $S(t(h'))$ every assignment that does not agree with at least one member of $S(t(h))$. If h and h' do not share the same line of H, then either (i) Q_r is the lowest line of G that covers the line of h', or (ii) Q_{r+1} (the line following Q_r in G) is the lowest line of G that covers h'. In the first case, we sequentially for $i = w-1, w-2, \ldots, 1$ remove from $S(t_i)$ every member which disagrees with all members of $S(t_{i+1})$. In the second case, the line Q_{r+1} of G is loaded into B and becomes its bottom line, and then the sets $S(t)$, $t \in Q_{r+1}$, are formed sequentially from right to left on Q_{r+1} as follows: First, $S(t)$ is initialized according to the rules we derived, with the assignments implied by the values at the low-resolution cells of t. Then, every member which disagrees with all members of the set associated with the template immediately above t is removed from $S(t)$. In case that t has cells extending beyond the margins of H, every member which disagrees with the predetermined value m is removed. Finally, every member which disagrees with all members of the set associated with the template immediately to the right of t (if t is not the rightmost template of Q_{r+1}) is removed. Whenever the processing of h completes the processing of its line, we check if the first line Q_1 of B does not cover the line of h'. If so, it is removed from B. At this point the algorithm proceeds to the processing of h'. ∎

Analyzing our algorithm, we first show by induction on the number of processed pixels of H that upon starting the processing of each pixel the sets $S(t)$, $t \in B$, are the maximal sets that satisfy: [S1] Every $A \in S(t)$, $t \in Q_r$, agrees with the already-processed high-resolution pixels covered by t inside the margins, and with the predetermined value m outside; [S2] Every $A \in S(t)$, $t \notin Q_r$, agrees with the already-processed high-resolution pixels, that are not covered by a template of Q_r, and with the predetermined value m covered by t; [S3] $S(t)$ is a subset of the set of assignments implied by the values of the low-resolution cells of t according to the rules we derived; [S4] For every $t_1, t_2 \in Q_r$, with t_2 immediately to the right of t_1, and t_2 is not right from $t(h)$, it holds that every $A_2 \in S(t_2)$ agrees with at least one $A_1 \in S(t_1)$; [S5] For every $t_1, t_2 \in Q_r$, with t_2 immediately to the right of t_1, and t_1 is not left from $t(h)$, it holds that every $A_1 \in S(t_1)$ agrees with at least one $A_2 \in S(t_2)$; and [S6] For every $t_1, t_2 \in B$, with t_2 immediately above t_1, it holds that every $A_1 \in S(t_1)$ agrees with at least one $A_2 \in S(t_2)$; By the maximality of the sets $S(t)$ we mean that no more assignments can be added to them without violating [S1] – [S6]. Note that every $S(t)$ includes a member that equals the actual contents of $H(B)$ covered by t. These amount (see [SP] for details) to the following theorem:

Theorem 5

If h is predicted by any prediction rule based on high-resolution pixels that precede h and on low-resolution pixels of the part of L from $L(B)$ up, then h is also predicted by our algorithm. ∎

It is possible that low-resolution pixels of lower parts of L can exclude more assignments from $S(t(h))$ toward the processing of h and thus enhance predictability. We can tune our algorithm to include in B also lower lines of G. In this case, the sets S include assignments for the high-resolution pixels covered by a few vertically adjacent templates of G: columns of templates that cover the still unprocessed part of $H(B)$. The trade off between the complexity of managing large sets of long assignment vectors and prediction potential is to be considered, and the proper number of template lines to be included in B is to be accordingly determined.

4. Conclusions

We have used deterministic prediction in a system for progressive coding of bi-level images. We found that the compression improved by 7 to 10% for prediction within single template positions. Predicting on multiple template positions was found to improve compression performance further, but less than 1%.

The algorithms presented in this paper are a guide to development of practical programs for exploiting the ultimate potential of deterministic prediction. A working implementation may or may not take advantage of every technique we have explored.

Future research along the lines of this paper include:

- Developing metrics for measuring the trade-offs between the benefits of deterministic prediction and its complexity of implementation.

- Deriving prediction rules for *relations* between high-resolution pixels, rather than values of single pixels. The assignment sets $S(t)$ introduced in Subsection 3.2 can serve as an example of relations. This form of prediction should be used in conjunction with a coding system that takes advantage of the restriction which the predicted relation imposes on the possible contents of sections of the image.

- Studying the interaction between deterministic prediction and adaptation carried out also on predicted pixels in adaptive coding systems.

References

[GJ]   Garey, M.R., and Johnson D.S. *Computers and Intractability: A Guide to the Theory of NP-Completeness*. San Francisco: W.H. Freeman & Company, 1979.

[KN]   Knuth, D.E., *The Art of Computer Programming*. Addison-Wesley, 1973.

[SP]   Dafna Sheinwald and Richard C. Pasco, *Deriving Deterministic Prediction Rules from Reduction Schemes*. Proceedings of International Conference on Computing and Information, ICCI'90. Canadian Scholars' Press Inc., May 1990.

Probabilistic analysis of set operations with constant-time set equality test

William Pugh

Institute for Advanced Computer Studies and Department of Computer Science
University of Maryland , College Park
pugh@cs.umd.edu, (301)-454-5694

Abstract: We analyze the implementation of set operations using binary tries. Our techniques are substantially simpler than previous techniques used for this problem, and allow us to analysis not only the expected performance but also the probability distribution of the performance. We show that by making use of constant-time equality tests, we can achieve better performance than any previously known method for performing set operations. In particular, for two sets A and B of n elements that differ in only k elements, we can perform any set operation such as $A \cap B$ in only $O(k \log n)$ expected time (without knowing in advance anything about the differences between A and B).

Keywords: Analysis of algorithms, Data structures, Probabilistic analysis

We describe results on the use of binary hash tries to represent sets. Binary hash tries use a binary trie [Knu73] data structure based on the hash keys of the elements (alternatively, assume our elements are uniformly distributed integers). We describe how this representation allows constant time equality tests for sets. We then shown how these equality tests can be incorporated into the algorithms for operations such as set union to produce better asymptotic time bound than any previously described algorithm for set operations. We derive these results using new probabilistic analysis techniques that are much simpler than previous techniques used for analyzing binary hash tries and provide not only the expected performance of the set operations but also the probability distribution of the performance of the algorithms.

Our results include allowing constant time equality tests for sets. We also show that the expected time required to compute $A \ op \ B$, where $op \in \{ \cup, \cap, -, \subseteq \}$, is bounded by

$$O(\ |S_2| \ (1 + \log(\ |S_3| \ / \ |S_2| \ )) \ )$$

where S_2 and S_3 are the middle and largest of the sets $A - B$, $B - A$, $A \cap B$. If the sets A and B differ in only k elements, the expected time required to calculate $A \ op \ B$ is therefore only

$$O(k \ (1 + \log(|A \cap B| / k)) \ ).$$

This is better than the performance of any previously known implementation of set algorithms.

1 Binary Hash Tries

Each node of a binary hash trie is labeled with a binary string (possibly the empty string). A subtree whose root is labeled L represents a set whose elements all have hash keys with L as a prefix. Thus, the root of a complete binary hash trie is labeled with the empty string, since it represents all elements. If all the elements represented by a node have the same hash key, that node is a primitive set: a leaf node containing a sorted list of all the elements represented by the node. If a node represents zero elements, it is an empty set leaf node. Otherwise, the node is an interior node. An interior node labeled L has two children labeled $L0$ and $L1$.

2 Constant time equality tests for data structures

We assume in our algorithms that we have a technique available for performing constant time equality tests for data structures. All known techniques for doing this prevent us from destructively updating data structures, but we don't have any need to do this anyway. One technique for doing constant time equality tests is hashed-consing [Got74] [All78] [SL78]. Although hashed-consing does produce poor worst-case time for creating new records, it rarely takes more than constant-time in practice. In our analysis, we assume constant-time equality tests and record creation. Hashed-consing is discussed in appendix A.

Note that our analysis techniques do not depend on the availability of constant-time equality tests. If the set algorithms are rewritten so that they do not use equality tests between tries, set operations take

$$O(|A|(1 + \log(|B|/|A|)))$$

expected time to compute A op B (assuming w.l.g. $|A| \le |B|$).

3 Unique representations & Constant time equality tests for sets

Constant expected time equality tests for data structures do not automatically give us constant expected time equality tests for sets. The representation scheme we use for sets must also provide unique representations: two data structures represent the same set if and only if the two data structures are equal. For example, using a sorted list of the elements of the set allows constant expected time equality tests for sets, but an unsorted list of the elements of the set does not (e.g., the lists [1,2] and [2,1] would both represent the set {1,2}). Using binary hash tries gives us a unique representation for sets.

4 Set algorithms

The algorithms for performing set operations are the obvious divide and conquer algorithms. To compute S op T, we first check for any of the cases that allow quick termination: $S = \emptyset, T = \emptyset$ or $S = T$. For set union, intersection, difference and for subset tests, we can return a result in constant–time in any of these situations. For example, if $S = \emptyset$ then $S \cup T = T$ and if $S = T$ then $S \cup T = S$.

If both S and T are interior nodes, the computation is done using the obvious divide and conquer technique. For union, intersection and difference, if $S =$

InteriorNode(S', S") and *T = InteriorNode(T', T")*, then our preliminary result is *InteriorNode(S' op T', S" op T")*. This result is preliminary because we must then check if it can be simplified. If one of the results is the empty set and the other is a leaf node (either empty or a primitive set) then we simply return the leaf node. The divide and conquer step for the subset test is similar : $S \subseteq T \equiv S' \subseteq T' \wedge S" \subseteq T"$.

If S and T are both primitive sets (i.e., a non–empty leaf nodes) with the same hash key, then *op* is performed on the primitive sets.

The remaining cases are fairly obvious to derive.

5 Analysis

In our analysis, we make the assumption that all elements have distinct hash keys. Since, unlike hash tables, the size of our data structures do not depend number of possible hash keys, we can use long hash keys. In practice, the small number of hash key collisions seen should have no significant impact. We also assume that all sets have sizes that are a power of 2. This allows us to use $\lg n$ instead of $\lceil \lg n \rceil$ in our calculations. Our results should provide good estimates for sets that do not have a size that is a power of 2, but an upper bound can be obtained by rounding up all set sizes to the next power of 2.

5.1 Random Variables and Probabilistic Upper Bounds

In this section, we briefly present a method for analyzing both the expected performance and the probability distribution of the running times of probabilistic algorithms. A *random variable* has a fixed but unpredictable value and a predictable probability distribution and average. If X is a random variable, Prob$\{ X = x \}$ denotes the probability that X equals x and Prob$\{ X \le x \}$ denotes the probability that X is at most x. For example, if X is the number obtained by throwing an unbiased die, Prob$\{ X \le 3 \} = 1/2$. We use $E(X)$ to denote the mean value of the random variable X and $V(X)$ to denote the variance of X. For conciseness, we sometimes refer to a property of the probability distribution of a random variable as a property of the random variable itself.

It is often preferable to find simple upper bounds on values whose exact value is difficult to calculate. To discuss upper bounds on random variables, we need to define a partial ordering on the probability distributions of random variables:

Definition 1 ($=_{prob}$ and $\le_{prob}$). Let X and Y be random variables. We define equality and partial orderings on the probability distribution of random variables as follows:

$$X =_{prob} Y \text{ iff } \forall\, x, \text{Prob}\{ X \le x \} = \text{Prob}\{ Y \le x \} \text{ and}$$
$$X \le_{prob} Y \text{ iff } \forall\, x, \text{Prob}\{ X \le x \} \ge \text{Prob}\{ Y \le x \}. \;\square$$

We use negative binomial distributions in our analysis.

Definition 2 (*negative binomial distributions* — *NB(s)*). Let s be a non-negative integer and p be a probability. The term *NB(s)* denotes a random variable with the *negative binomial distribution* equal to the distribution of the number of failures seen before the sth success in a series of random independent trials where the probability of a success in a trial is $1/2$. $E(NB(s)) = s$ and $V(NB(s)) = s/2 \;\square$

Negative binomial distributions can be summed in the obvious manner. For example:

$$NB(s_1 + s_2) =_{prob} NB(s_1) + NB(s_2)$$

5.2 Analysis techniques

In our analysis, we make use of a *hash-space tree*. A hash-space tree is complete binary tree with leaves at a depth equal to the length of the hash keys used (the root is at depth 0). The root of a hash-space tree is labeled ε. An interior node labeled L has two children, labeled $L0$ and $L1$. We define several terms regarding sets and hash-space trees.

Definition 3 (*select(L, S)*). Let S be a set and L be a label. Define $select(L, S) = \{ x \in S \mid L$ is a prefix of $hash(x) \}$.

Definition 4 (*depth/level*).The *depth* or *level* of a node n in a hash-space tree is the length of the label of n.

Definition 5 (*matching*). An element x *matches* a node n in a hash-space tree iff the label of n is a prefix of the hash key of x. $\square$

In our analysis, we will talk about dyeing selected nodes of a hash-space tree with certain dyes. After we have applied two or more dyes, we will talk about the colors of the nodes.

Definition 6 (*dyes* and *colors*). A node is *dyed* a tint if the node contains that tint dye. A node is *colored* a color if the final color of a node is that color. To make this distinction clearer, tints appear in *italics typeface* and colors appear in roman typeface. $\square$

5.3 The depth of leaf nodes

We first look at the depth of leaf nodes. This corresponds to the number of bit examinations for a successful search in a trie.

Lemma 1. For an element x and a set S that contains x, the depth of the leaf node for x in the trie representing S is equal to the number of purple nodes generated by dyeing *red* all the nodes in a hash-space tree that match an element in $S - \{x\}$ and dyeing *blue* all the nodes that match x.

Proof. Start with an uncolored hash-space tree. Dye *red* all the nodes that match an element in $S - \{x\}$. Dye *blue* all the nodes that match x (*red* + *blue* yields purple). A coloring for a sample set is shown in Figure 1 (white nodes are nodes that do not match any element in S). Let n be the highest blue node (i.e., the blue node with the shortest label), and let p be the parent of n. L_n be the label of n and L_p be the label of p. Since $|select(L_n, S)| = 1$ the node n labeled L_n in the binary tree representing S will be a primitive set leaf node (assuming the parent of n is an interior node). Since $|select(L_p, S)| > 1$, the node p labeled L_p in the binary tree representing S will be an interior node. Therefore, n is the leaf node corresponding to x. The depth of n is equal to the number of purple nodes.

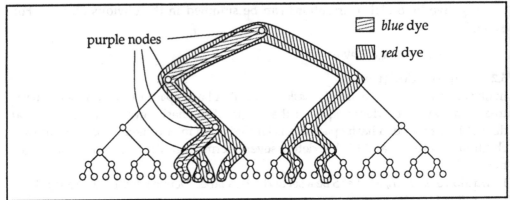

FIGURE 1 – Shows the result of dyeing blue the nodes in a hash-space tree that match x and dyeing red nodes that match elements in S – {x}.

Lemma 2. For an arbitrary set S and an element x, when dyeing *red* all the nodes in a hash-space tree that match an element in $S - \{x\}$ and dyeing *blue* all the nodes that match x, the number of purple nodes generated is bounded as shown below.

$$(\text{# of purple nodes}) \leq_{prob} \lg \; |S| + 1 + NB(1)$$

Proof. Let p_i = the probability that the level i node that matches x is colored purple. We know that the node at level i that matches x is either purple or blue, so p_i is the probability that the level i node that matches x contains *red* dye (i.e., is dyed *red*).

Consider level $\lg \; |S|$. There are $|S|$ nodes at this level, and it is possible that they will all be dyed *red*. There are no more than $1 + \lg \; |S|$ purple nodes at or above level $\lg \; |S|$. Consider level $i + \lg \; |S|$ ($i > 0$). There are $2^i |S|$ nodes at this level and only $|S|$ of them can be dyed *red*. The hash key of x is unrelated to the hash key of any element in $S - \{x\}$. Therefore, $p_{i + \lg N} \leq 1/2^i$. This gives a distribution for the number of purple nodes that is $\leq_{prob} \; \lg N + 1 + NB(1)$. $\square$

Theorem 1. For an element x and a set S containing x, the depth of the leaf node for x in the trie representing S is bounded as shown below.

$$(\text{depth of the leaf node for } x) \leq_{prob} \lg \; |S| + 1 + NB(1)$$

Proof. Follows directly for Lemma 1 and Lemma 2.

This result gives an upper bound on the expected level of leaf nodes of $\lg \; |S| + 2$. Using a more complicated analysis, Knuth [Knu73] derives a value of approximately $\lg \; |S| + 1.33275$.

5.4 Performance of set operations on disjoint sets
We now examine the cost of set operations for disjoint sets, as a warm-up for analyzing set operations on arbitrary sets.

Lemma 3. For two disjoint sets A and B and a set operation $op \in \{\cup, \cap, -, \subseteq\}$, the amount of computation required to compute $A \; op \; B$ is proportional to the number of purple nodes generated by dyeing *blue* all nodes in a hash-space tree matching elements in A and by dyeing *red* all the nodes matching elements in B (i.e., the amount of computation is proportional to the number of nodes in the hash-space tree that match elements from both sets).

Proof. In an uncolored hash-space tree, dye *blue* all the nodes that match elements in A. Dye *red* all the nodes that match elements in B. Purple nodes correspond to non-trivial computations. White nodes correspond to computing $\varnothing \; op \; \varnothing$. Blue nodes correspond to computing $S \; op \; \varnothing$. Red nodes correspond computing $\varnothing \; op \; S$. The computation associated with a trivial node might be performed only if the parent of that node is non-trivial. Since we assume all elements have distinct hash keys, all atomic set operations take constant time and the computation associated with each node takes constant time. The time required to compute $A \; op \; B$ is therefore proportional to the number of nodes colored purple, which are exactly those nodes that match elements from both sets.

We will need to introduce a new term in our next lemma, so we first define it.

Definition 7 (*Overlap*(A, B, k)). Let A and B be disjoint sets s.t. $|A| \leq |B|$ and let k be a non-negative integer such that $k \leq \lg |B|$. We define *Overlap*(A, B, k) to be the number of nodes deeper than level k that match elements in both A and B. $\square$

Lemma 4. For two *disjoint* sets A and B (assuming w.l.g. $|A| \leq |B|$) the number of purple nodes generated when all the nodes that match elements in A are dyed *blue* and all the nodes that match elements in B are dyed *red* is bounded as shown below.

$$(\text{\# of purple nodes}) \leq_{prob} 2\,|A| + Overlap(A, B, \lg |A|)$$

Proof. There are only $2|A|$ nodes at or above level $\lg |A|$. Follows from definition of *Overlap*.

Lemma 5. $Overlap(A, B, k) \leq_{prob} |A| \; (\lg|B| - k) + NB(|A|)$

Proof. For each element x in A do the following step: Start with a white hash-space tree and dye *red* all the nodes that match elements in B. Dye *blue* all the nodes that match x. By Lemma 1, the number of purple nodes generating by this dyeing operation is $\leq_{prob} (\lg |B| + 1 + NB(1))$. Since $k+1$ of these are at or above level k, the number of purple nodes deeper than level k generated by this dyeing operations is $\leq_{prob} (\lg |B| + NB(1) - k)$.

If we repeat this step for all the elements in A, the sum of the number of purple nodes generated in each step is an upper bound on the number of purple nodes generated when all the nodes that match elements in A are dyed *blue* and all the nodes that match elements in B are dyed *red*.

The hash keys of the elements of A are independent. The upper bound we have obtained is independent of the hash keys of the elements of B. Therefore the sum of $|A|$ independent $NB(1)$ distributions is $NB(|A|)$. $\square$

Lemma 6. For two *disjoint* sets A and B (assuming w.l.g. $|A| \le |B|$) the number of purple nodes that are generated when all the nodes that match elements in A are dyed *blue* and all the nodes that match elements in B are dyed *red* is bounded as shown below.

$$(\text{\# of purple nodes}) \le_{prob} |A|(2 + \lg|B| - \lg|A|) + NB(|A|)$$

Proof. Follows directly from Lemmas 4 and 5.

Theorem 2. For two disjoint sets A and B (assuming w.l.g. $|A| \le |B|$), the number of non-trivial computations required to compute A *op* B is $(|A|(2 + \lg|B| - \lg|A|) + NB(|A|))$ whose expected value is $O(|A|(1 + \log(|B|/|A|)))$.
Proof. Follows directly from Lemmas 3 and 6. $\square$

5.5 Performance of set operations on arbitrary sets

We have now developed the techniques and terminology to allow us to analyze the performance of set operations on arbitrary sets.

Lemma 8. For arbitrary sets A and B and a set operation $op \in \{\cup, \cap, -, \subseteq\}$, the amount of work required to compute A *op* B is proportional to the number of multi-dye nodes (nodes colored purple, green, orange or brown) that result when dyeing *blue* nodes that match elements in $A - B$, dyeing *red* nodes that match elements in $B - A$ and dyeing *yellow* nodes that match elements in $A \cap B$.

Proof. Starting with a white hash-space tree, dye the nodes as described above. Nodes whose final colors are red, blue, white or yellow are trivial nodes. A blue node corresponds to computing S *op* $\varnothing$. A red node corresponds to computing $\varnothing$ *op* S. A white node corresponds to computing $\varnothing$ *op* $\varnothing$. A yellow node corresponds to computing S *op* S. Therefore, the amount of computation is proportional to the number of non-trivial nodes, which are the multi-dye nodes.

Lemma 9. Let *yellowSet*, *blueSet* and *redSet* be the smallest, middle and largest of the sets $A - B$, $B - A$, and $A \cap B$. The number of multi-dye nodes is bounded as shown below.

$$
\begin{aligned}
(\text{\# of multi-dye nodes}) \le_{prob}\ & 2\,|\textit{blueSet}| \\
& + |\textit{yellowSet}|\,(\lg|\textit{blueSet} \cup \textit{redSet}| - \lg|\textit{blueSet}|) \\
& + |\textit{blueSet}|\,(\lg|\textit{redSet}| - \lg|\textit{blueSet}|) \\
& + NB(|\textit{blueSet}| + |\textit{yellowSet}|).
\end{aligned}
$$

Proof. For each set, dye the matching nodes in the tree the appropriate tint. The resulting tree looks like Figure 2. We want to count the number of multi-dye nodes.

number of multi-dye nodes
$\le$ number of multi-dye nodes at level $\lg|\textit{blueSet}|$ or higher

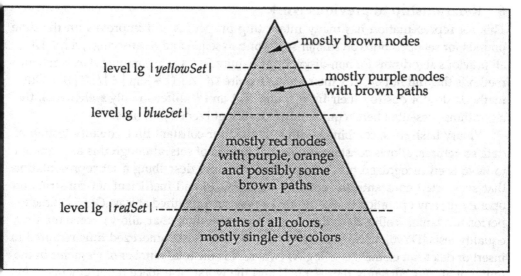

level lg |yellowSet| - - - - - - - - - mostly brown nodes

mostly purple nodes
with brown paths

level lg |blueSet| - - - - - - - - - - - - -

mostly red nodes
with purple, orange
and possibly some
brown paths

level lg |redSet| - - - - - - - - - - - - - - - - - -

paths of all colors,
mostly single dye colors

FIGURE 2 – Coloring that results when nodes are dyed as described.

+ number of nodes dyed *yellow* also dyed *red* or *blue* (i.e., green, orange and brown nodes)
  at a level deeper than lg |blueSet|
+ number of nodes dyed both *red* and *blue* (i.e., purple or brown nodes)
  at a level deeper than lg |blueSet|
$\leq$ number of nodes at level lg |blueSet| or higher
  + Overlap(yellowSet, blueSet ∪ redSet, lg |blueSet|)
  + Overlap(blueSet, redSet, lg |blueSet|)

Since the hash keys of the elements in *yellowSet* and of the elements in *blueSet* are independent, the negative binomial distributions that result from expanding *Overlap* can be summed.

number of multi-dye nodes
$\leq_{prob}$ 2 |blueSet|
  + |yellowSet| (lg |blueSet ∪ redSet| − lg |blueSet|) + NB(|yellowSet|)
  + |blueSet| (lg |redSet| − lg |blueSet|) + NB(|blueSet|)
$\leq_{prob}$ 2 |blueSet|
  + |yellowSet| (lg |blueSet ∪ redSet| − lg |blueSet|)
  + |blueSet| (lg |redSet| − lg |blueSet|)
  + NB(|blueSet| + |yellowSet|). □

Theorem 3. Let S_1, S_2, S_3 be the smallest, middle and largest of the sets $A - B$, $B - A$, $A \cap B$. The time required to perform $A\ op\ B$ is bounded by a value that is proportional to

$$2|S_2| + |S_2|\lg(|S_3|/|S_2|) + |S_1|\lg(|S_3 \cup S_2|/|S_2|) + NB(|S_2|+|S_1|)$$

which has an expected value that is $O(\ |S_2|\ (1 + \log(|S_3|/|S_2|))\ )$.

Proof. Result follows from Lemmas 8 and 9. □

6   Relationship to previous work

This set representation has many interesting properties and improves on the time bounds for set operations on similar sets. For two sets A and B satisfying $|A| \le |B|$, all previous algorithms for non-disjoint sets require $\Omega(|A|)$ to compute A *op* B and all methods that did not destroy their inputs require $\Omega(|A|\,(1 + \log(|A|/|B|)))$. Our methods do not destroy their inputs, and if A and B differ in only k elements, the algorithms presented here require only $O(k + k\log(|A \cap B|/k))$ time.

Binary hash tries, combined with a method for constant-time equality testing of data structures, allows constant-time equality tests of sets, although this appears not to have been recognized previously. The first paper describing a set representation that supported constant-time equality tests [SG76] had inefficient set construction operations; any operation that computed a new set S required at least $O(|S|)$ time to perform. Daniel Yellin describes a set representation that allows constant time equality tests [DY90]. In his representation, the worst-case amortized time required to insert or delete an element is $O(\log N)$ (where N is the total number of elements in the union of all sets currently represented) and the worst-case space requirements of his method are $O(k^2 N)$ (where k is the total number of sets). In comparison, with our method the expected cost to insert or delete an element is $O(\log n)$ and the expected space requirements of his method are $O(n)$. His method does have the advantage of providing good worst-case amortized time bounds, but his space costs are very high, and that fact the update costs are based on N, rather than on the number of elements in the set being manipulated, could be a severe disadvantage in many situations.

Pardo [Par78] also analyzed set operations on binary tries. However, his analysis was much more complicated and achieved poorer results. The bounds he obtains on the expected number of operations required to compute $A \cup B$ are

$$O(|A|\,(1 + \log(|B|/|A|)))$$

Our algorithms give better results primarily because our algorithms take advantage of the fact that (A *op* A) is a trivial computation. Pardo did not analyze the probability distribution of the time performance of the set algorithms on binary tries, and it is unclear if the techniques he used could be extended to analyze set operations taking advantage of constant–time equality tests.

References

[All78]   John Allen. *Anatomy of LISP*, McGraw Hill Book Company, NY, 1978.

[DY90]   Daniel Yellin, Representing Sets with Constant Time Equality Testing, ACM-SIAM Symposium on Discrete Algorithms, 64-73. January 1990.

[GK76]   Eiichi Goto and Yasumasa Kanada. Hashing Lemmas on Time Complexities with Applications to Formula Manipulation, *Proceedings of the 1976 ACM Symposium on Symbolic and Algebraic Computation*, pp 154-158.

[Par78]   Luis Isidoro Trabb Pardo. *Set Representation and Set Intersection*, Ph.D. thesis, Stanford University, 1978

[SG76]   M. Sassa and E. Goto. A hashing method for fast set operations. *Inf. Proc. Let.* 5(2):31–34, June 1976.

[SL78]   J.M. Spitzen and K.N. Levitt. An example of hierarchical design and proof, *Communications of the ACM*, 21(12):1064–1075, December 1978.

Appendix A – Hashed consing

Hashed consing is a technique that has been used in pure–LISP implementations (i.e., LISP without side effects) to store cons cells uniquely and provide constant-time equality tests [Got74] [All78] [SL78]. In LISP, cons cells are created only by function *cons*. When hashed consing is used, CONS is modified so that it never allocates a new cons cell that would be equal to an already existing cons cell – instead, a pointer to that already existing cons cell is returned. When hashed consing is used, EQ tests true equality (i.e., EQ and EQUAL are the same predicate). Thus, hashed consing allows constant expected time equality tests.

Hashed-consing is not limited to just cons cells. In a functional language other than LISP, we would use hashed-consing techniques whenever a new record is created. In other functional languages, hashed-records would be used (whenever a new record is created, ...).

Hashed consing cannot be used in a system in which destructive updates of cons cells occur; such updates would have unintended side effects. Hashed consing also complicates garbage collection. A cons cell *c* should be collected if the only pointers to *c* are from the hash table.

CLASSIFICATION BY MINIMUM-MESSAGE-LENGTH INFERENCE

C. S. Wallace
Computer Science, Monash University
Clayton, Vic. 3168 Australia

Keywords: Classification, Unsupervised learning, Minimum message length, Induction, Coding, Statistical inference.

ABSTRACT

Although classification is perhaps the oldest practical application of MML inference, the early algorithm was subject to weakly inconsistent estimation. The same problem is inherent in any MML inference which infers many discrete "nuisance" parameters. A solution has been found using a novel coding trick, which could be useful in many inductive inferences.

1. INTRODUCTION

Classification was the first practical problem to be addressed by the Minimum Message Length (MML) inference method (Wallace & Boulton 1968, Boulton & Wallace 1970, 1973). The resulting Snob programs have been used successfully in fields from the taxonomy of seals to the texture of clouds, the diagnosis of depression, and patterns of juvenile delinquency. In inductive or statistical problems where each new datum introduces a new unknown ("nuisance") parameter, classical Maximum Likelihood methods will commonly give inconsistent estimates of global parameters. When the nuisance parameters are real-valued, MML inference avoids inconsistency by automatically choosing to state estimates of the nuisance parameters to limited precision. However, when the nuisance parameters are discrete, simple application of MML inference has hitherto also been prone to inconsistency. The original Snob algorithm was subject to just this problem, because the inferred parameters describing the membership of inferred classes are discrete "nuisance" parameters. In this paper we develop a method for, in effect, the imprecise statement of discrete inferences, and its application to MML classification. The new method removes inconsistency in this application, and should be a useful tool in applying MML to other problem domains.

2. MINIMUM MESSAGE LENGTH (MML) INFERENCE

2.1 *General Principle*

We regard intrinsic classification as a limited form of inductive inference. The class structure derived from the known data is regarded as a kind of theory about the objects observed, which, like any inductively-derived theory, cannot be deduced from the data and cannot be proved to be correct. We draw on a general metatheory of inductive inference which is briefly outlined below.

Given some data or observations, we define an "explanation" of the data as a message having two parts. The first part states some theory or hypothesis about the objects of study. The second part states in full the data, using a language or code which would be optimal in the sense of least expected message length were the stated theory true. For definiteness, suppose that the data is given in the form of a binary string, and that the explanation is encoded as a binary string. We assume that the theory, possibly in conjunction with prior knowledge, implies a probability distribution over the set of possible data strings. By standard coding theory, the length of the second part is just minus the logarithm base 2 of the probability of finding the observed data if the theory were true., i.e., minus the log likelihood. The length of the first part, which states the theory, will depend on the language or code used to express the theory. We assume this code to be non-redundant. In particular, if a prior probability distribution can be specified over the (perhaps infinite) set of possible theories, we assume the part 1 code to be efficient in the above sense, in which case the length of the first part will be minus the logarithm of the prior probability of the theory. Note that the use of any non- redundant code for the expression of a theory is equivalent to the assumption of a prior probability distribution, namely the unique distribution for which that code would be efficient. An explanation is regarded as acceptable if its length is less than that of the data string. Of all acceptable explanations, if any, the shortest is preferred. If the data are totally random in the sense of Chaitin (1966) there will be no acceptable explanation, and no non-trivial theory about the data.

In a simple case where the set of possible theories is a discrete set of non-parameterized probabilistic hypotheses, each with a known prior probability, choosing the theory which yields the shortest explanation is exactly equivalent to the Bayes rule of choosing the hypothesis of highest posterior probability, given the data. More generally, even where a prior probability distribution over the set of possible theories may not be easy to determine, the use of any reasonable non-redundant code for the expression of the theory has the effect that complex theories, requiring a lengthy description, are penalized relative to simpler theories.

When some or all of the possible theories have unknown real-valued parameters whose values must be estimated from the data, the set of possible theories becomes or includes a continuum, and it is no longer possible to assign a non- zero prior probability to each theory. Equivalently, it is impossible in a part 1 of finite length to specify an arbitrary parameter value in a continuum of possible values. We have shown (Wallace and Freeman 1987) that the shortest explanation is then achieved when part 1 specifies an estimated parameter value (usually) close to the Maximum Likelihood estimate, and specifies it to a precision comparable to the expected error in the estimate. For instance, if the chosen theory involves a Normal distribution with unknown mean, and the data provide N independent random values drawn from this distribution, then part 1 of the explanation will optimally include a value for the mean close to the sample mean and stated to a precision of order $\sigma/\sqrt{N/12}$, where sigma is the (known or estimated) standard deviation of the Normal distribution. If part 1 states the estimated mean to higher precision, e.g. to more binary places, the length of part 1 is thereby increased. If a lower precision is used, part 1 is shortened, but part 2, which encodes the data using a code optimized for the estimated mean, will become longer because its coding will be optimized for a mean differing substantially from the sample mean. In general, the volume of the precision quantum to which an estimated parameter vector is rounded is proportional to the reciprocal of the square root determinant of the Fisher information matrix, that is, the matrix of expected second derivatives of the log likelihood function. Thus, if the log likelihood is expected to have a narrow peak, the estimate will be stated with high precision (small rounding quantum).

The MML approach to inductive inference is more fully described by Wallace and Freeman (1987), and Georgeff and Wallace (1984). Note that MML is a criterion for assessing and comparing inductively-derived theories and explanations based on these. It does not prescribe any general algorithm for inductive inference. In comparing two different acceptable explanations of the same data, the difference in explanation length is equal to the log posterior odds ratio in the simple case of a discrete set of non-parameterized possible theories. When the estimation of real-valued parameters is involved, a similar interpretation is plausible but not yet fully investigated. However, it seems reasonable to accept that a difference of more than about 10 binary digits shows strong preference for the theory giving the shorter explanation.

2.2 *The Classification Message*

We suppose the data to be a matrix comprising D "attribute values" for each of N "things". Some of the attribute values may be missing. Our aim is to partition the things into classes so that the things in a single class may be treated as equivalent at some level of discourse. Snob2 assumes that within a single class, the attributes of the things have a simple multivariate distribution. Continuous (real-valued) attributes are assumed to have a Normal distribution, discrete (e.g. binary) attributes are assumed to have a multinomial distribution, and it is assumed that different attributes are uncorrelated. The distribution parameters are all regarded as unknown, and may have different values in different classes.

To describe such a theory in part 1 of an explanation, several message fragments are concatenated which encode, in turn:
   (a) The number of classes
   (b) The relative abundance of each class
   (c) For each class, the distribution parameters of each attribute.
   (d) For each thing, the class to which it is estimated to belong.

The details of the encoding, and of the calculation of the length of part 1, may be found in Wallace and Boulton (1968). The coding assumes conventional "colourless" priors for the above parameters.

Part 2 comprises a section for each thing giving the attribute values for that thing using a code optimized for the attribute distribution stated in (c) for the class to which the thing is assigned in (d). In the shortest explanation of the above form for a given data set, each thing is assigned to that class most likely to contain such a thing, and the parameters estimated for each class are close to the Maximum Likelihood estimates based on the things assigned to that class.

Theories of this kind essentially amount to hypothesising that the observed things are drawn from a multivariate distribution which is a mixture of a number of different simple distributions. Equivalently, such a theory represents the inference of the existence and effect of an unobserved discrete variable, whose value for each thing has a (probabilistic) effect on the observed attributes of the thing. This kind of theory, while it has obvious limitations, seems reasonably appropriate where the "things" may be regarded as individuals sampled from a (potentially) large population. It is probably not appropriate where the "things" to be classified are themselves populations, and the set of "things" is exhaustive. Thus we would not suggest the use of this kind of theory where the set of "things" was the set of species forming a small genus.

3. PARTIAL ASSIGNMENT

In explanations generally (not just classifications) the length is minimized when the theory (part 1) specifies unknown parameters to a precision comparable to the expected estimation error. The consequences of departing from this rule are more than simply a lengthening of the explanation. It will often happen that if an excessive precision is used, minimization of the explanation length with respect to the estimated parameter values will lead to estimates which are biased or even inconsistent. For example, if we assume that part 1 states the parameters of a Normal distribution to very high precision, minimization of the message length with respect to the standard deviation will (assuming the usual 1/sigma "colourless" prior) yield the Maximum Likelihood estimate sqrt(v / N) where v is the sample variance and N the sample size. By contrast, if the "optimum" precision is used, one gets the unbiased estimate sqrt(v / (N-1)). Inconsistent estimates may arise by a similar phenomenon if the number of parameters to be estimated increases with the sample size. Unfortunately, the original classification explanation described above suffers from just this problem. There is an unknown parameter associated with each thing, viz. the class to which it belongs. An estimate of this is stated in (d) of part 1, and appears as a definite statement naming the thing's class. But, at least for some things, the class to which the thing belongs may not be determined beyond reasonable doubt, and so should in some sense be stated to limited "precision". The result was that minimization of the message length led to inconsistent estimates of class attribute distribution parameters.

The effect can be seen by considering a simple case where each thing has a single continuous attribute value, and the things in the data are drawn from a two-class population. The single attribute then has a density distribution which is the sum of two different Normal densities. Assume for simplicity that they have the same standard deviation and equal abundance. If the two means are well separated, so that the two Normal curves do not overlap appreciably, there is no problem, because almost all things will have attribute values allowing them to be assigned to one or other class with high confidence. However, suppose the means are separated by only twice the class standard deviation. Then a substantial fraction of the things drawn from one class will have attribute values nearer to the mean of the other class, and would be assigned to it. The effect of this assignment is that the mean of the values of all the things assigned to the class of higher mean is higher than the true mean of the class, and similarly the mean of the other class will be underestimated. The estimated means will be further apart than the true means, and the estimated standard deviation in each class will be lower than its true value. These errors will not decrease with increasing sample size, so the estimates are inconsistent. If the means are separated by less than about three times the true standard deviation of each component, the shortest explanation (indeed the highest likelihood) is achieved by a one- component model, no matter how large the sample.

A major improvement incorporated in Snob2 overcomes the above defects. It bases the message length on a way of encoding the explanation which in effect specifies class membership only as precisely as is warranted by the data. Suppose the explanation being considered hypothesises a model with two equally abundant classes. The explanation may be rearranged as:

    (a) A statement of the number of classes (2).
    (b) For each class in turn:
        (i) Its abundance (0.5)
        (ii) The distribution parameters of attributes in the class
    (c) For each thing in turn:
        (i) Its supposed class.
        (ii) Its attribute values, using a code optimized for this class.

We will be concerned with (c). In encoding the data for a thing, the original scheme chose to assign it always to that class giving the shorter total length for (c)(i) and (c)(ii). This choice amounts to choosing the class of higher likelihood. Suppose that for some thing both classes give almost equal lengths, differing by less than one bit. Then the thing could be assigned to either class without significantly affecting the length of the explanation, and the data really do not allow the class of the thing to be estimated with any definiteness. Rather than choosing the marginally superior class in such a case, we may choose the class on some other basis without serious consequences. We will in fact choose the class by examining the first binary digit of the (c) fragment for the next thing (assuming the thing in question is not the last in the data list). Assume that this rule is applied to all things where the two classes give lengths differing by less than one bit.

Now consider the decoding of an explanation encoded in this way. Having decoded a thing's attribute values, and knowing from parts (a) and (b) the distribution parameters of both classes, any receiver of the explanation can at this stage compute the length that the (c)(i) and (c)(ii) fragments for this thing would have had if we had assigned the thing to the other class. The receiver can note that the length would have differed by less than one bit, and hence detect that we have treated this thing as ambiguous. Assuming the receiver knows the rule for choosing the class of an ambiguous thing (as he is assumed to know the other coding conventions), he can tell from our choice of class what was the first digit of the (c) fragment for the next thing. Hence we need not include this digit in the explanation, thus shortening it by one bit.

The above device may be generalized. Suppose that in some explanation (not necessarily a classification) there is some segment of data, not the last to be included in part 2, which could be encoded in several different ways within the code optimal for the "theory" stated in part 1. Let the lengths of the several possible code segments be $L(1), L(2), \dots$ etc.

    Define $p(j) = 2 ** (-L(j))$ $j = 1,2,\dots$

These $p(j)$ values may be identified with the probabilities of getting the data by each of several mutually-exclusive routes all consistent with the "theory". In our case, they are the probabilities of there being such a thing in each of the classes.

Define P = Sum over all j of p(j);   q(j) = p(j) / P, j = 1,2,...

To choose the encoding for the data segment, first construct a code optimized for the discrete probability distribution { q(j), j = 1,2,... }. Note that this distribution is the Bayes posterior distribution over the mutually-exclusive routes. From the standard theory of optimum codes, the length m(j) of the code word in this code for route j will be m(j) = - log (q(j)), the code will have the prefix property, and every sufficiently long binary string will have some unique word of the code as prefix. Now examine the binary string encoding the remainder of the data, i.e., the data following the segment being considered. This string must begin with some word of the above code, say the word for route k. Then encode the data segment using route k, hence using a code segment of length L(k). By an obvious extension of the argument presented for the crude trick, the first m(k) bits of the binary string for the remainder of the data need not be included in the explanation, as they may be recovered by a receiver after decoding the present data segment.

Consider the net length of the string used to encode the data segment, i.e. the length of string used minus the length which need not be included for the remaining data. The net length is

$$
\begin{aligned}
L(k) - m(k) &= - \log p(k) + \log q(k) \\
&= - \log (p(k) / q(k)) \\
&= - \log P \\
&= - \log (\text{Sum over } j \text{ of } p(j))
\end{aligned}
$$

Merely choosing the shortest of the possible encodings for the data segment would give a length of
     - log (Max over all j of p(j)).

The coding device therefore has little effect when one possible coding is much shorter (more probable a posteriori) than the rest, but can shorten the explanation by as much as log (number of possibilities) if they are all equally long. A more detailed account of the general application of this coding technique is given by Wallace (1989). When used in the construction of a classification explanation, this coding device has the following effects:

(a) Each thing but the last may be encoded more briefly. We ignore the fact that the saving is not available for the last thing.
(b) Although the form of the explanation states a class for each thing and encodes it as a member of that class, the net length of the description is the same as would be achieved by a (much more complex) code which made no assignment of things to classes, but instead was optimized for the sum of the densities of the classes.
(c) The estimation of the number of classes and their parameters become consistent. Given sufficient data, two classes with different distributions will be distinguished by minimization of the message length, no matter how much they overlap.
(d) The device effectively makes a fuzzy choice of class assignment. The probability that the thing will be assigned to a particular class is given by the posterior distribution q() for that thing over the classes. The program treats each thing as

being partially assigned to all the classes. Notionally, a fraction q(j) of the thing is assigned to class j, and its attribute values contribute with weight q(j) to the estimates of the distribution parameters of class j. The net message length required for the description of the thing is computed directly from the sum of the distribution densities of the classes (- log P).

4. SIGNIFICANCE OF ATTRIBUTES

A further change from the coding model of the earlier programs is that Snob2 can decide whether or not a particular attribute is significant in the definition of a class. In part 1 of the message, in which the classes are described, the specification of the distribution parameters of an attribute in a class is now preceded by a single bit which declares whether or not the attribute is "significant" in the class. If so, specifications of its distribution parameters to appropriate precision follow as in the earlier programs. However, if the attribute is declared "insignificant", its distribution within the class is assumed to be the same as its distribution over the whole population, and no parameter specification is required. This device reduces the disruptive effects of attributes which turn out to have no bearing on the class structure.

5. COMPARISON WITH AUTOCLASS II

A program for numerical classification called Autoclass II has been developed by P. Cheeseman (1988) which bears interesting similarities to the present work. The class model of both programs is identical. Both model the given data by a density in attribute space which is the sum of simple multivariate densities, one per class. Like Snob2, Autoclass II assumes a prior distribution over the number of classes, a prior density of the abundances of the classes, and independent prior densities over the distribution parameters of the simple class densities. However, Autoclass II is not based on a message length criterion, but instead makes a more direct Bayesian inference of the number of classes J.

Let V be the vector of abundance and distribution parameters needed to specify a model with J classes. Let P(J) be the prior probability of having J classes, and let h(V) be the prior probability density of the parameters V. Let X denote the data, i.e. the set of attribute values for all things, and let P(X|V) be the probability of obtaining data X given the J-class model specified by V. The joint probability P(J,X) of J and X is then

P(J) * integral dV * h(V) * P(X|V)
and the posterior probability P(J|X) of J given the data is
P(J,X) / (Sum over j of P(j,X))

Autoclass II aims to estimate the number of classes J by maximizing P(J|X). Having estimated J by the above scheme, it then estimates V by maximizing the (unnormalized) posterior density h(V) * P(X|V). We argue that such a two-step estimation process is dangerous in principle. If the data admitted, say, one good four-class explanation and a dozen rather poor three- class ones, the Autoclass procedure could infer the presence of three classes and then be forced to infer the best of the poor models. In fact, Autoclass II, while ostensibly proceeding as outlined above, makes an approximation which causes its results to be much more similar to those of Snob2 than might be expected. The calculation of the posterior P(J|X) requires the calculation of an integral for each possible number of classes J in order to obtain the joint probability P(J,X) The integrand is proportional to the posterior density of the parameters of a J-class model

h (V) * P(X|V)

Autoclass II approximates the integral by making the assumption that most of the contribution to the integral will come from the neighbourhood of the highest peak value of the integrand. It effectively fits a Gaussian function to the integrand at this peak and uses the integral of the Gaussian as its estimate of the true integral. The estimate is very similar, both analytically and numerically, to the quantity

h (V) * P(X|V) / (sqrt Fisher determinant)
which is maximized by Snob2.

Thus, although Autoclass II is differently motivated from Snob2, and in principle aims to optimize a different (and, we argue, inferior) criterion, in practice it gives almost identical results.

6. OTHER RELATED WORK

Two further recent publications describe somewhat similar approaches. Gath and Geva (1989) describe a "fuzzy" Maximum Likelihood algorithm for continuous attributes. As in the present work, the distribution of continuous attributes within a class is modelled by a multivariate Normal density, and each class has a relative abundance. Thus for each thing, a posterior distribution q() over the classes can be computed exactly as in Snob2. Again as in Snob2, the class distribution parameters and relative abundances are then re-estimated from statistics accumulated for each class by the partial or weighted assignment of things to classes. From their equation (9), thing j contributes to the estimated covariance of class i with weight proportional to its posterior probability of being a member of class i, but from their equation (3), thing j contributes to the estimated mean of class i with weight proportional to the square of this probability. No reason is given for this choice of weight, which would lead to inconsistent estimation by a weaker version of the same effect as led to inconsistency in the original Snob. It is possible that there could be an error in the presentation of this paper: the iteration is said to optimize an objective function defined in an equation (1) for an arbitrary distance function, but when the distance defined in their equation (7) is substituted, their objective function becomes a weighted sum of the reciprocal probability densities of the things, whereas the described iteration approximately minimizes the product of these reciprocal densities. The iterative algorithm does not change the number of classes, and the objective function, however interpreted, would not show a minimum with respect to the number of classes. Instead, the algorithm is used to find classifications with various assumed numbers of classes, and auxiliary objective functions are used to select the "best" number of classes.

R.D. Wallace (1989) has described an approach which builds a binary hierarchic tree classification by a divisive process. At each step the largest leaf class is split so as to maximize an information-theoretic or entropy measure of the difference between the resulting subclass densities (assumed to be multivariate Normal). The measure used does not correspond to a message length, and the divisive process is continued till all classes are singletons. However, a Minimum Message Length approach is then used to select a pruning of the tree such that the leaf classes lead to a concise encoding of the things' attributes. The possible overlap of the multivariate Normal distributions used to model the classes is not taken into account in the message length calculation, so the method suffers exactly the same inconsistency as the original Snob. In a univariate case, classes whose means differ by less than about three standard deviations are not distinguished.

Both the above works allow for inter-attribute correlation by estimating a full covariance matrix for each class, thereby advancing on Snob2. However, in both cases the Maximum Likelihood estimate is used, which, for large attribute numbers, seriously underestimates the determinant of the covariance matrix, i.e., the hypervolume occupied by the cluster. We would expect this bias to result in a tendency to find rather too many classes in poorly-structured populations. Further, the technique used in the latter work to approximate the information needed to specify the covariance matrices of two classes, given the matrix of their parent, appears incorrect, since it at best approximates the information needed to specify merely the determinants of the matrices.

7. POSSIBLE EXTENSIONS

The distribution model used in Snob2 corresponds to a flat classification. An hierarchic message form and optimizing algorithm were derived by Boulton and Wallace (1973), and should need little alteration to meet the needs of the partial-assignment coding and attribute-significance indicators of the new message form.

We are working on the inclusion in class descriptions of a common-factor model of inter-attribute correlations within a class. For instance, if the things being classified are animals, and the attributes comprise several linear dimensions of the specimen, we would expect all such attributes to be positively correlated among the members of a single species, as all would depend to some extent on a common "size" factor. The effect of such "nuisance" correlations on the present program (as on most programs for numerical classification) is to induce a division of a single species into a set of classes more or less aligned along the direction of the "common factor". Thus a species may be divided into "small", "medium" and "large" classes, whether or not the data give any evidence of a multi-modal size distribution. The MML estimator for the common-factor model has been derived (Wallace and Freeman 1989), and leads to estimates of factor loadings superior to those of the maximum likelihood method (Harman 1967).

8. DISCUSSION

A new coding technique has been developed which overcomes the possible inconsistency of MML inference involving discrete nuisance parameters. Snob2, which applies the technique to classification, is strikingly similar to Cheeseman's Autoclass II, which is based on Bayesian rather than MML inference principles. However, the similarity is partly due to an approximation in Autoclass II which happens to remove the main distinction between these principles. Snob2 also allows for inference about which data variables are structurally significant.

Snob2 has been in use for about six years, with data from a range of problem domains. A recent application has been the classification of cloud cover using satellite image data (Chong et. al. 1989). A more detailed description of the program is given by Wallace and Patrick (1984). Snob2 is implemented in FORTRAN 77.

ACKNOWLEDGEMENTS

This paper owes much to discussions with Jon Patrick. Section 5 is based on discussions with Peter Cheeseman, made possible by travel assistance from Monash University.

REFERENCES

Boulton,D.M. & Wallace,C.S. "A Program for Numerical Classification",
    Comp.J. 13,1, pp. 63-69, 1970
Boulton,D.M. & Wallace,C.S. "An Information Measure for Hierarchic Classification",
    Comp.J. 16, 3, pp. 254-261, 1973
Chaitin,G.J. "On the Length of Programs for Computing Finite Sequences",
    J.A.C.M. 13, 4, pp. 547-549, 1966
Cheeseman,P.C. "AUTOCLASS II Conceptual Clustering System",
    Proc. Machine Learning Conference, pp. 54-64, 1988
Chong,Y.H., Pham,B., Manton,M. & Maeder,A. "Automatic Nephanalysis from
    Infrared GMS Data", Proc. Australian Joint A.I. Conf, 1989
Gath,I. & Geva,A.B. "Unsupervised Optimal Fuzzy Clustering", I.E.E.E. Trans. on
    Pattern Analysis and Machine Intelligence, 11, 7, pp. 773-781, 1989
Georgeff,M.P. & Wallace,C.S. "A General Criterion for Inductive Inference",
    Proc. 6th European Conference on Artificial Intelligence,
    Tim O'Shea (ed.). Elsevier, Amsterdam, 1984
Harman,H.H. "Modern Factor Analysis" (2nd ed.) Univ. of Chicago Press,
    Chicago, 1967
Wallace,C.S. & Boulton,D.M. "An Information Measure for Classification",
    Comp.J., 11, pp. 185-195, 1968
Wallace,C.S. "Inference and Estimation by Compact Coding",
    Monash University Computer Science Technical Report 46, 1984
Wallace,C.S. & Patrick,J. "An Improved Program for Classification",
    Monash University Computer Science Technical Report 47, 1984
Wallace,C.S. & Freeman,P.R. "Estimation and Inference by Compact Coding",
    J. R. Statist. Soc. B, 49, 3, pp. 240-265, 1987
Wallace,C.S. & Freeman,P.R. "Single Factor Analysis by MML Estimation",
    Monash University Computer Science Technical Report 89/127, 1989
Wallace,C.S. "False Oracles and SMML Estimation", Monash University
    Computer Science Technical Report 89/128, 1989
Wallace,R.D. "Finding Natural Clusters through Entropy Minimization",
    CMU-CS-89-183, Computer Science, Carnegie Mellon University, 1989

Fast Left-Linear Semi-Unification

Fritz Henglein
Department of Computer Science
Utrecht University
PO Box 80.089
3508 TB Utrecht
The Netherlands
Internet: henglein@cs.ruu.nl

Keywords: semi-unification, left-linear, P-completeness

Abstract

Semi-unification is a generalization of both unification and matching with applications in proof theory, term rewriting systems, polymorphic type inference, and natural language processing. It is the problem of solving a set of term inequalities $M_1 \leq N_1, \ldots, M_k \leq N_k$, where $\leq$ is interpreted as the subsumption preordering on (first-order) terms. Whereas the general problem has recently been shown to be undecidable, several special cases are decidable.

Kfoury, Tiuryn, and Urzyczyn proved that *left-linear semi-unification (LLSU)* is decidable by giving an exponential time decision procedure. We improve their result as follows.

1. We present a generic polynomial-time algorithm L1 for LLSU, which shows that LLSU is in P.
2. We show that L1 can be implemented in time $O(n^3)$ by using a fast dynamic transitive closure algorithm.
3. We prove that LLSU is P-complete under *log*-space reductions, thus giving evidence that there are no fast (NC-class) parallel algorithms for LLSU.

As corollaries of the proof of P-completeness we obtain that both monadic semi-unification and LLSU with only 2 term inequalities are already P-complete.

We conjecture that L1 can be implemented in time $O(n^2)$, which is the best that is possible for the solution method described by L1. The basic question as to whether another solution method may admit even faster algorithms is open. We conjecture also that LLSU with 1 inequality is P-complete.

1 Introduction

Semi-unification is a generalization of both unification and matching with applications in proof theory [Pud88], term rewriting systems [Pur87, KMNS89], polymorphic type inference [Hen88b, KTU89a, Lei89b], and natural language processing [DR89]. Because of its fundamental nature it can be expected to find even more applications.

Whereas general semi-unification was long believed to be decidable, Kfoury, Tiuryn and Urzyczyn recently gave an elegant reduction of the *boundedness* problem for deterministic Turing Machines to semi-unification [KTU89b]. By adapting a proof for a similar problem attributed to Hooper [Hoo65] they showed that boundedness is undecidable, which implies the undecidability of semi-unification.

Several special cases of semi-unification have been shown to be decidable: uniform semi-unification (solving a single term inequality) [Hen88b, Pud88, KMNS89], semi-unification over two variables [Lei89a], and left-linear semi-unification [KTU89a]. Pudlak showed that general semi-unification can be effectively reduced to semi-unification over two inequalities [Pud88]; thus bounding the number of inequalities by a number greater than one does not simplify the problem. In drastic contrast, Kapur, Musser, Narendran and Stillman gave a polynomial time procedure for uniform semi-unifiability (single inequality) [KMNS89].

In this article we investigate the special case of *left-linear semi-unification (LLSU)*. This problem was first addressed by Kfoury, Tiuryn, and Urzyczyn [KTU89a]. They were able to show that left-linear semi-unification is decidable, and a closer look at their decision procedure reveals that it takes exponential time. We improve this result by showing that left-linear semi-unification is *polynomial time* decidable. We present a generic algorithm, Algorithm L1, for LLSU that is implementable in polynomial time. An implementation based on a fast dynamic transitive closure algorithm [LPvL87, Yel88] (with only edge additions) yields an $O(n^3)$ time LLSU procedure where n is the size of a given (left-linear) semi-unification instance. Dynamic transitive closure seems too general and powerful a method for LLSU, and we conjecture that L1 can be improved to run in time $O(n^2)$. This is best possible for any method based on L1 since in L1 as many as n^2 edges are added to an initially sparse graph on n nodes. The question as to whether there is a linear-time algorithm for left-linear semi-unification or, in fact, a principally different algorithm asymptotically faster than $O(n^2)$ is left open.

We also show that, even though left-linearity is a very strong condition on input instances, it still is not strong enough to admit fast (NC-class) parallel algorithms unless NC = P. Specifically, we show that LLSU is P-complete under *log*-space reductions by adapting a well-known proof of Dwork, Kanellakis, and Mitchell for showing the P-completeness of unification [DKM84].

The outline of the rest of the paper is as follows. In section 2 we define general and left-linear semi-unification, and we present a general semi-unification algorithm, algorithm A [Hen89]. Observing the behavior of algorithm A on left-linear problem instances yields the critical insight that permits "speeding up" A to run in polynomial time. The result is Algorithm L1. In section 3 we present our polynomial time algorithm L1 for LLSU over the alphabet $\mathcal{A}_2$, which consists of a single binary function symbol, and show that a dynamic transitive closure based implementation has time complexity $O(n^3)$. In section 4 we show that left-linear semi-unification is P-complete. We conclude with some final remarks and open problems in section 5.

2 General semi-unification

In this section we present definition and properties of semi-unification and an (semi-)algorithm, Algorithm A, for solving general semi-unification problem instances. Most of this is a rehash from a previous paper [Hen89], but it is very instructive in giving insight into the correctness of our polynomial time algorithm for LLSU. For other treatments of semi-unification see also [Lei89b] and [KTU89a].

2.1 Definition and properties of semi-unification

A *ranked alphabet* $\mathcal{A} = (F, a)$ is a finite set F of *function symbols* together with an *arity* function a that maps every element in F to a natural number (including zero). A function symbol with arity 0 is also called a *constant*. The set of *variables* V is a denumerable infinite set disjoint from F. The *terms* over A and V is the set $T(\mathcal{A}, V)$ consisting of all strings generated by the grammar

$$M ::= x \,|\, c \,|\, f(\underbrace{M, \ldots, M}_{k \text{ times}})$$

where f is a function symbol from $\mathcal{A}$ with arity $k > 0$, c is a constant, and x is any variable from V. Two terms M and N are equal, written $M = N$, if and only if they are identical as strings.

A *substitution* σ is a mapping from V to $T(\mathcal{A}, V)$ that is the identity on all but a finite subset of V. The set of variables on which σ is *not* the identity is the *domain* of σ. Every substitution $\sigma : V \to T(\mathcal{A}, V)$ can be naturally extended to $\sigma : T(\mathcal{A}, V) \to T(\mathcal{A}, V)$ by defining

$$\sigma(f(M_1, \ldots, M_k)) = f(\sigma(M_1), \ldots, \sigma(M_k)).$$

A term M *subsumes* N (or N *matches* M), written $M \leq N$, if there is a substitution ρ such that $\rho(M) = N$.

Given a set of pairs of terms $S = \{(M_1, N_1), \ldots, (M_k, N_k)\}$ a substitution σ is a *semi-unifier* of S if $\sigma(M_1) \leq \sigma(N_1), \ldots, \sigma(M_k) \leq \sigma(N_k)$. S is *semi-unifiable* if it has a semi-unifier. Semi-unifiability is reminiscent of both unification (because of σ being applied to both the left- and right-hand components of S) and matching (because the resultant right-hand sides have to match their corresponding right-hand sides), but it is in fact much more general than both, as is evidenced by the recent undecidability result for semi-unifiability.

In the context of semi-unification we shall call a set of pairs of terms a *system of inequalities*. As shown in [Hen88a] (see also [Hen88b, Hen89]), every semi-unifiable system of inequalities has a most general semi-unifier if the notion of generality on substitutions is properly defined.

2.2 Algorithm A

Algorithm A is a general (semi-)algorithm for computing the most general semi-unifier of a system of inequalities. Even though it is bound not to terminate for some non-semi-unifiable inputs it "catches" many non-semi-unifiable systems of inequalities due to an *extended occurs check*, which is a generalization of the conventional occurs check in unification algorithms.

The algorithm operates on a graph-theoretic representation of systems of inequalities, both to achieve practically acceptable performance and to aid in the analysis of some combinatorial properties. Since intermediate steps of the algorithm can introduce *equations* $M \overset{?}{=} N$ between terms, not just inequalities, the representation, called an *arrow graph*, in fact encodes systems of equations and inequalities. Because a formal description of arrow graphs is notoriously cumbersome, we give a brief, but hopefully clear, informal definition below.

A *term graph* is an acyclic graph that represents sets of terms over a given alphabet $\mathcal{A} = (F, a)$ and set of variables V. It consists of a set of nodes, N, that are labeled by a function symbol from F or a variable from V or both[1]. If f is a function symbol with arity k, $k \geq 0$, every node n labeled with f has exactly k *ordered children*; i.e., there are k directed *term edges* originating in n and labeled with the numbers 1 through k. The variable labeled nodes have no children, and for every variable x there is at most one node labeled with x. The nodes together with the tree edges form a conventional directed graph, and if it is acyclic, then we say the term graph is *acyclic*.

Every node in an acyclic term graph can be interpreted as a term; for example, if n is a node labeled with function symbol f, and its children are $n_1, \ldots, n_k$ (in this order) representing terms $M_1, \ldots, M_k$, then n represents the term $f(M_1, \ldots, M_k)$. Note that for every set of terms there is an easily constructed, but generally non-unique term graph such that every term is represented in it.

In a term graph we represent all the terms occurring in a system of equations and inequalities. An *arrow graph* is a term graph with two additional kinds of edges: *Equivalence edges* encode equations, and *arrows* encode inequalities. Equivalence

---

[1] A labeling with a function symbol *and* a variable is only needed for technical reasons; see rule 4b in Algorithm A, Figure 1.

Let G be an arrow graph. Apply the following rules (depicted also in Figure 2) until convergence:

1. If there exist nodes m and n labeled with f and with children m_1, m_2 and n_1, n_2, respectively, such that $m \sim n$ then add $m_1 \sim n_1$ and $m_2 \sim n_2$.

2. If there exist nodes m and n labeled with f and with children m_1, m_2 and n_1, n_2, respectively, such that $m \overset{i}{\to} n$ then add arrows $m_1 \overset{i}{\to} n_1$ and $m_2 \overset{i}{\to} n_2$.

3. If there exist nodes m_1, m_2, n_1, and n_2 such that
   (a) $m_1 \sim n_1$, $m_1 \overset{i}{\to} m_2$ and $n_1 \overset{i}{\to} n_2$ then add $m_2 \sim n_2$;
   (b) $m_1 \sim n_1$, $m_1 \overset{i}{\to} m_2$ and $m_2 \sim n_2$ then add an arrow $n_1 \overset{i}{\to} n_2$.

4. (a) (Extended occurs check) If there is a path consisting of arrows of any color (arrow path) from n_1 to n_2 and n_2 is a proper descendant of n_1, then reduce to the improper arrow graph $\square$.[a]

   (b) If the extended occurs check is *not* applicable and there exist nodes m and n such that m is labeled with f and has children m_1, m_2, n is labeled with a variable and no function symbol, and all n' with $n \sim n'$ are variable labeled, and there is an arrow $m \overset{i}{\to} n$ then create new nodes n_1', n_2' and add f to the label of n, label n_1' and n_2' with new variables x' and x'', respectively; and make n_1', n_2' the children of n.

---

[a]Node n' is a *descendant* of node n if it there is a path from n to n' consisting of term edges (traversed in forward direction) and equivalence edges (traversed in any direction); n' is a *proper* descendant if there is a path with at least one term edge.

Figure 1: Algorithm A

edges represent an equivalence relation on the nodes of the arrow graph. They can be thought of as *undirected edges* that are kept transitively closed; that is, for every (undirected) path from node n_1 to node n_2 via equivalence edges (only) there is also an equivalence edge directly between n_1 and n_2. If there is an equivalence edge between n_1 and n_2 we write $n_1 \sim n_2$.

Arrows are directed edges labeled by natural numbers, which indicate to which inequality in a given system of equations and inequalities an arrow corresponds. We call the labels of arrows *colors*, and we write $n_1 \overset{i}{\to} n_2$ if there is an i-colored arrow pointing from n_1 to n_2.

To summarize, an arrow graph is a term graph with additional edges: undirected equivalence edges and directed arrows. Hence an arrow graph has *three* different kinds of edges: term edges, equivalence edges, and arrows.

An *arrow graph representation* of a system of inequalities

$$S = \{(M_1, N_1), \ldots, (M_k, N_k)\}$$

is a term graph G with (not necessarily distinct) nodes $m_1, \ldots, m_k, n_1, \ldots, n_k$ representing the terms in S, and arrows from m_i (representing M_i) to n_i (representing N_i) for $1 \leq i \leq k$ that have pairwise distinct colors. There are no equivalence edges. (In other formulations systems of equations and inequalities are input instances for semi-unification, in which case equivalence edges are used to represent equations in the arrow graph representation.)

Algorithm A operates on arrow graphs. It repeatedly rewrites the arrow graph representation of a system of inequalities S by nondeterministically "applying" some closure rules until no rule can be applied any more. At that point it indicates whether S is semi-unifiable and, if so, outputs a most general semi-unifier of S. The algorithm is described in detail in Figure 1 for alphabet $\mathcal{A}_2$[2], and the closure rules are also depicted graphically in Figure 2.

2.3 Left-linear semi-unification

A term is *linear* if every variable has at most one occurrence in it. For example, $f(x_1, x_2)$ is linear (assuming $x_1 \neq x_2$), but $f(x_1, x_1)$ is not. A system of inequalities S is *left-linear* if every left-hand side term in S is linear. *Left-linear semi-unification* is the problem of computing most general semi-unifiers of left-linear systems of inequalities, and *left-linear semi-unifiability (LLSU)* is the problem of deciding whether a given left-linear system of inequalities is semi-unifiable.

The correctness of Algorithm A is proved in great detail in [Hen89, chapter 6]. Actually, our presentation here differs slightly in the form of rule 4b, but it is a minor issue to verify that it is correct.

Let us consider an arrow graph representation of a left-linear system of inequalities S and one of its nodes m that represents a left-hand side. Since S is left-linear the subgraph rooted at m is a tree; that is, there is one and only one path consisting of term edges from m to any of the nodes reachable from m via term edges. Executing Algorithm A on the arrow graph representation of S_0 we see that at no point rule 3a, the only rule that could possibly introduce the first equivalence edge, is applicable. This is not just a peculiar property of the specific example, but holds for every (arrow representation of a) left-linear system of inequalities.

An *execution (of Algorithm A)* is a sequence of arrow graphs $(G_0, \ldots, G_i, \ldots)$ in which every component is derived from its predecessor by application of one of the closure rules of Algorithm A (see Figure 1 or Figure 2).

Theorem 1 *Let $(G_0, \ldots, G_i, \ldots)$ be an execution of Algorithm A. If G_0 is an arrow graph representation of a left-linear system of inequalities, then G_{i+1} is derived from G_i by rule 2 or rule 4.*

Proof: For $(G_0, \ldots, G_i, \ldots)$ we can prove by induction on i that the following properties hold for every $G_i \neq \square$:

1. Every node has at most one outarrow of any given color.

---

[2]$\mathcal{A}_2$ is the alphabet consisting of a single binary function symbol f. Semi-unifiability over any alphabet is *log*-space reducible to semi-unifiability over $\mathcal{A}_2$ [Hen89]. This reduction does not, however, preserve left-linearity.

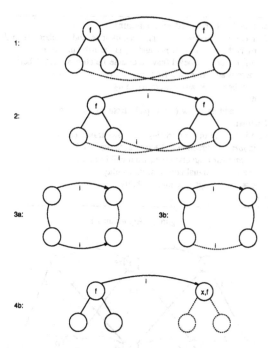

Figure 2: Closure rules

2. The subgraph rooted at any node with an outarrow (of any color) is a tree

This implies the theorem since it guarantees that neither rule 3 nor rule 1 is applicable to any of the G_i's. (End of proof) ∎

This theorem yields the critical insight for speeding up Algorithm A for the special case of solving left-linear semi-unification problems. We will give very informal considerations below that will lead us, directly from the observation of theorem 1, to the polynomial time LLSU-algorithm L1 below. L1 is presented and proved correct in the following section.

A quite immediate simplification of Algorithm A is that, for left-linear semi-unification, rules 3 and 1 are not needed. But further simplifications are possible. Note that the color maintained with every arrow is only needed as a criterion for applying rule 3. For example, if a node n has two outarrows with *equal* color to distinct nodes n' and n'' an equivalence edge $n' \sim n''$ has to be added, but if the two arrows have *different* colors no such equivalence edge has to be added. Because, by theorem 1, the first case can never happen for left-linear systems of inequalities, we can dispense with the coloring information on arrows altogether.

But without color information there is no need to distinguish between individual arrows and arrow *paths*. This is not an advantage by itself, but it does away with the need to apply rule 4b at all, if we adopt a modified extended occurs check rule (rule 4a). Basically, the only relevant effect of rule 4b on left-linear arrow graph representations is to create arrow paths between the children of f-labeled nodes that are already connected with an arrow path. This can be achieved directly, without adding new nodes, by maintaining the transitive closure of the arrows as indicated above or by generalizing rule 2 to apply arrow paths instead of only individual arrows. If there is an arrow path from a function symbol labeled node n_1 to another function symbol labeled node n_2 in the original algorithm, our strategy of maintaining an arrow for every arrow path guarantees that there is also an arrow from n_1 to n_2, and applying rule 2, which propagates arrows downwards to the children of n_1 and n_2, will guarantee that there is an arrow from any child of n_1 to the corresponding child of n_2. We call the "contraction" of arrow paths to single arrows *shortcutting* since repeated copying with rule 4b is not necessary any more — it is "cut short".

3 A polynomial time LLSU algorithm

In this section we present a generic polynomial time algorithm, Algorithm L1, for solving left-linear systems of inequalities over alphabet $\mathcal{A}_2$. In fact, the algorithm can be used to compute a most general semi-unifier, but we shall leave this aspect unexplored at this point. We show that L1 can be made to run in time $O(n^3)$ by adapting the fast dynamic transitive closure algorithm of La Poutré and van Leeuwen [LPvL87].

A *reduced arrow graph* is an arrow graph without equivalence edges and with no colors on arrows. We write $n \rightarrow n'$ for an uncolored arrow from n to n'. A reduced arrow graph representation of a system of inequalities is simply an arrow graph representation with the colors on arrows left off.

```
algorithm L1(A: reduced arrow graph)
while there exist nodes m₁, n₁ and m₂, n₂ in A and number i such that
        n₁ is the i-th child of m₁ and n₂ is the i-th child of m₂,
        m₁, m₂ are f-labeled (have the same function symbol label),
        there is an arrow path from m₁ to m₂,
        and there is no arrow from n₁ to n₂
        do
                add an arrow (arrow path) from n₁ to n₂ to A
end while;
if there is a cycle in A consisting of arrows traversed
        in forward direction and term edges traversed
        in backward direction (i.e., from child to parent)
        then        signal non-semi-unifiability
        else        signal semi-unifiability
end if;
```

Figure 3: Algorithm L1

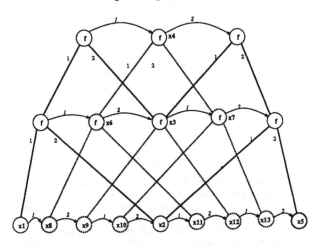

Figure 4: A final arrow graph

Algorithm L1 is described in Figure 3. Roughly, it starts with a reduced arrow graph representation of a given system of inequalities, in which the colors of arrows are ignored. It then looks for arrow paths between f-labeled nodes and adds (uncolored) arrows between their corresponding children until this entails no more changes to the reduced arrow graph. In the final stage, the resultant reduced arrow graph is checked whether it contains a cycle that is made up of arrows — traversed in forward direction — and term edges — traversed from child to parent — and contains at least one term edge. If there is such a cycle we say the final arrow graph *fails* the *acyclicity test* and the algorithm signals non-semi-unifiability; otherwise, the final arrow graph *passes* the acyclicity test, and the algorithm signals semi-unifiability.

Example: Consider the left-linear system of inequalities $S_0 =$

$$\{(f(f(x_1, x_2), x_3), x_4), x_4, f(x_3, f(x_2, x_5))\}.$$

Algorithm A of Figure 1 will produce the arrow graph depicted in Figure 4 whereas Algorithm L1 simply propagates an arrow *path* between two f-labeled nodes to *single* arrows between their corresponding children with rule 2. Thus we obtain the final arrow graph in Figure 5. (End of example) ∎

We first establish the correctness of L1 and then show that it can be implemented in polynomial time. To address correctness we need to recall some results on the structure of terms with respect to subsumption [Hue80].

Term subsumption is a preordering. The equivalence relation canonically induced by $\leq$ is defined by $M \cong N \Leftrightarrow M \leq N \wedge N \leq M$. We write $[M]$ for the $\cong$-equivalence class of term M; $T(\mathcal{A}, V)/_\cong$ for the set of equivalence classes of all terms over A and V; and $\leq$ for the partial order on $T(\mathcal{A}, V)/_\cong$ induced by the preorder $\leq$.

Theorem 2 $(T^\Omega/_\cong, \leq)$ *is a complete lattice.*

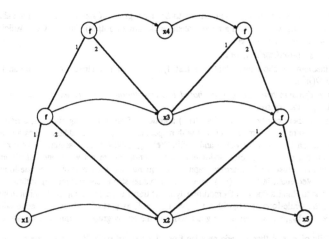

Figure 5: A final arrow graph with "shortcutting" of arrow paths

Proof: See [Hue80]. (End of proof) ■

In particular, every set of terms M has a least upper bound $\bigvee M$ w.r.t. the subsumption preordering $\leq$ that is unique modulo $\cong$. The equivalence relation $\cong$ is also sometimes informally referred to as "renaming of variables". Note that every finite set of terms has a least upper bound whose variables are disjoint from the variables occurring in *any* fixed finite set.

Theorem 3 *Let A be a reduced arrow graph representing a left-linear system of inequalities S. If A signals non-semi-unifiability then S is not semi-unifiable. If A signals semi-unifiability then S is semi-unifiable.*

Proof: We shall show that if L1 fails the acyclicity test then S has no semi-unifier, and if L1 passes the acyclicity test then it has a semi-unifier. In fact the most-general semi-unifier can be extracted from the final, acyclic reduced arrow graph.

(L1 fails the acyclicity test) Assume S has a semi-unifier σ. Then every node n in the final arrow graph represents a unique term $T(n)$ with respect to σ according to the following rule.

$$T_\sigma(n) = \begin{cases} f(T_\sigma(n_1), T_\sigma(n_2)) & \text{if } n \text{ is } f\text{-labeled with children } n_1, n_2 \\ \sigma(x) & \text{if } n \text{ is labeled with variable } x \end{cases}$$

We shall write $|M|$ for the size of M, measured in terms of the number of function symbol occurrences and variable occurrences in M. If σ is a semi-unifier of S, then it is easy to see that the final reduced arrow graph must satisfy the following relations. If $n \to n'$ then $|T_\sigma(n)| \leq |T_\sigma(n')|$, and if n is a child of n' then $|T_\sigma(n)| < |T_\sigma(n')|$. But if the final reduced arrow graph contains a cycle with at least one term edge then there is a node n with $|T_\sigma(n)| < |T_\sigma(n)|$, which is impossible. Consequently, S does not have a semi-unifier.

(L1 passes the acyclicity test) If L1 passes the acyclicity test, the final reduced arrow graph A' is acyclic in the sense that all cycles consist of arrows only. We define a term interpretation T for every node in A' as follows. Consider the strong components $C_1, \ldots, C_k$ of A' in topological order. For every node n in a strong component C_i we associate a term $T(n)$.

Let $T(n)$ be defined for all nodes in components $C_1, \ldots, C_{i-1}$. Consider the predecessors $n_1, \ldots, n_k$ of node n in component C_i where, for all $j \in \{1, \ldots, k\}$, $n_j \in C_{j'}$ for some $j' < i$, and n is labeled with variable x. If $k = 0$ then $T(n) = x$. Otherwise, define the *preliminary* term interpretation $T_{prelim}(n) = \bigvee\{T(n_1), \ldots, T(n_k)\}$. If n is f-labeled with children n_1, n_2 we define $T_{prelim}(n) = f(T(n_1), T(n_2))$.

Now, if C_i consists of the nodes $n, n', \ldots, n^{(l)}$, let

$$T = \bigvee\{T_{prelim}(n), T_{prelim}(n'), \ldots, T_{prelim}(n^{(l)})\},$$

and let $T', \ldots, T^{(l)}$ be $\cong$-equivalent to T with pairwise disjoint variables. Finally, define $T(n) = T, T(n') = T', \ldots, T(n^{(l)}) = T^{(l)}$.

Note that T is not uniquely defined, but, most importantly, it has the property that for every pair of variable labeled nodes n, n' the sets of variables in $T(n), T(n')$ are disjoint.[3]

Define substitution $\sigma = \bigcup\{x \mapsto T(n) : n$ is labeled with variable $x\}$. By construction of T we have that for every arrow $n \to n'$ in A', where n' is variable labeled, there is a substitution ρ such that $\rho(T(n)) = T(n')$; in particular, we can take $\rho = T(n')/T(n)$. By induction on the term structure in A' it follows that this holds also for an f-labeled node n'. Since it holds, in particular, for all arrows in the original arrow graph A this shows that σ is a semi-unifier. Some more analysis shows that it is a most general semi-unifier. (End of proof) ■

Theorem 4 *Algorithm L1 is implementable in polynomial time.*

---

[3] We assume that every least upper bound of a finite set of terms defined above has variables disjoint from all variables occurring in all previously defined term interpretations.

Proof: Algorithm L1 can add at most n^2 new arrows to an arrow graph of size n, and the applicability of a single arrow addition step takes time at most $O(n^3)$ (with a naive transitive closure algorithm). Finally, the acyclicity testing step can be performed in time $O(n^2)$. (End of proof) ■

Corollary 5 *Left-linear semi-unifiability is in P.*

In the following theorem we show that adapting a fast dynamic transitive closure algorithm can be used to implement Algorithm L1 in time $O(n^3)$.

Theorem 6 *There is a dynamic transitive closure based implementation of Algorithm L1 that runs in $O(n^3)$ time for a left-linear system of inequalities of size n.*

Proof: (Sketch) Since there can be as many as $O(n^2)$ additions of arrows in Algorithm A, a naive implementation that maintains the transitive closure of all arrows in $O(n^2)$ with respect to a single edge addition takes a total of $O(n^4)$ time. The algorithms of La Poutré/Van Leeuwen [LPvL87] and Yellin [Yel88], however, have accumulative cost of $O(n^3)$ and can be modified to permit finding a pair of f-labeled nodes n, n' whose children are not yet connected via arrows as a by-product of maintaining the transitive closure of the arrow graph. Consequently the total cost of the while-loop is $O(n^3)$. The final acyclicity test can be implemented in time $O(n^2)$ with a fast maximal strong components algorithm.

We give a sketch, due to Han La Poutré, of a modified dynamic transitive closure implementation that permits fast execution of the Boolean test in the while-loop of Algorithm L1 (see Figure 3) as part of updates after edge additions. Basically, we work with 5 copies, $V, V_{lc}, V_{rc}, V_{lp}, V_{rp}$, of the original nodes in the arrow graph A. Initially, we add edges as follows.

- If n_l is a left child of n in A then we add an edge from the copy of n_l in V_{lc} to the copy of n in V and an edge from the copy of n in V to the copy of n_l in V_{lp}.

- If n_r is a right child of n in A then we add an edge from the copy of n_r in V_{rc} to the copy of n in V and an edge from the copy of n in V to the copy of n_r in V_{rp}.

- If there is an arrow $n \to n'$ then we add an edge from the copy of n in V to the copy of n' in V.

Let us call the resulting directed graph G. We maintain the transitive closure of G in a bit matrix (of size $O(n^2)$). The while-loop in Algorithm L1 is executed as follows. Let S be the workset of pairs of nodes n, n' where n is a node in V_{lp} and n' in V_{lc} (or n in V_{rp} and n' in V_{rc}) and n reaches n' in G. These pairs represent the candidates for which an arrow has to be added. While there is a pair (n, n') in S, we delete it from S and, if there is no edge between the copies of n and n' in V (!) we add it, calculate the transitive closure of G, and update S accordingly; i.e., if a new node n' in V_{lc} (V_{rc}) becomes reachable from a node n in V_{lp} (V_{rp}), we add the pair (n, n') to S.

This sketch shows that finding update candidates can be performed as part of a dynamic transitive closure algorithm without additional asymptotic cost. Consequently, using the fast dynamic transitive closure algorithm for edge additions of La Poutré and van Leeuwen [LPvL87] yields an $O(n^3)$ implementation of Algorithm L1. (End of proof) ■

Since the arrow additions are predetermined by Algorithm L1 itself, we believe that there is an $O(n^2)$ implementation of L1 based on a dynamic depth-first search algorithm. Since there can be as many as $O(n^2)$ arrows added by L1, this would be the best that is possible for L1. Of course, other algorithms with even better asymptotic bounds are conceivable. We leave this as an open problem.

4 P-completeness of left-linear semi-unifiability

The existence of a polynomial time sequential algorithm raises the question as to whether there are fast (NC-class) parallel algorithms for left-linear semi-unification. We shall show that, unless NC = P, this is not the case by giving a *log*-space reduction from the circuit value problem for monotone circuits to LLSU, which establishes P-completeness of LLSU under *log*-space reductions.

A *monotone circuit* is a directed acyclic graph $C = (V, E)$ whose nodes, called *gates*, are of five different kinds:

1. *input gates* with no inedge and 1 outedge;

2. *and-gates* with 2 inedges and 1 outedge;

3. *or-gates* with 2 inedges and 1 outedge;

4. *fan-out gates* with 1 inedge and 2 outedges;

5. a single *output gate* with 1 inedge and no outedge.

Furthermore, all gates are reachable from the input gates, and the output gate is reachable from all gates.

Example: An example of a monotone circuit implementing the Boolean function $y = ((x_1 \vee x_2) \vee (x_2 \wedge x_3)) \wedge (x_3 \vee x_4)$ is shown in Figure 6. The circles represent fan-out gates. (End of example) ■

Every assignment a of truth values to the input gates of C can be extended uniquely to a truth value assignment $\bar{a}$ to all gates of C by defining

1. if n is an input gate, then $\bar{a}(n) = a(n)$;

2. if n is an and-gate with predecessors n', n'', then $\bar{a}(n) = \bar{a}(n') \wedge \bar{a}(n'')$;

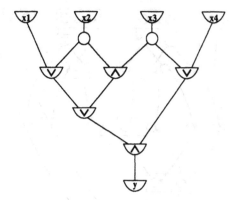

Figure 6: A monotone circuit

3. if n is an or-gate with predecessors n', n'', then $\bar{a}(n) = \bar{a}(n') \vee \bar{a}(n'')$;

4. if n is a fan-out gate with predecessor n' then $\bar{a}(n) = \bar{a}(n')$;

5. if n is the output gate with predecessor n' then $\bar{a}(n) = \bar{a}(n')$.

The *monotone circuit value problem (MCVP)* is the problem of deciding, given monotone circuit C and assignment a to the input gates of C, whether $\bar{a}(n) =$ **true** for the output gate n.

Theorem 7 *LLSU is P-complete under* log-*space reductions.*

Proof: We give a *log*-space reduction of MCVP to LLSU by adapting a proof of Dwork, Kanellakis, and Mitchell for P-completeness of unification. MCVP is known to be P-complete [Gol77]. Together with the existence of a polynomial time algorithm (see previous section) for LLSU this proves the theorem.

First we describe how we represent a circuit C by a term graph A. Then the assignment a is encoded by adding arrows to A to make it an arrow graph. The thus constructed A will be a reduced arrow graph representation of a left-linear system of inequalities. It is easy to construct the actual system of inequalities instead of its reduced arrow graph representation, but for expositional purposes it is easier to describe the construction of A.

For every kind of gate we describe a term graph "gadget" for that gate. Every one of these gadgets is actually a term graph with a pair of designated nodes for every in- and outedge of the encoded gate. These gadgets are then "glued" together at their input and output node pairs with some arrows to represent C. Additional arrows encode a.

1. An *input gadget* consists of two variable labeled nodes n, n'. It has no input node pair, and its only pair of output nodes is (n, n').

2. An *and-gadget* consists of three nodes n, n', n'' where $(n, n'), (n', n'')$ are its input node pairs and (n, n'') is its output node pair.

3. An *or-gadget* consists of two variable labeled nodes n, n'. The two identical pairs (n, n') and (n, n') are its input node pairs, and (n, n') is also its output node pair.

4. A *fan-out gadget* consists of six nodes $n, n_1, n_2, n', n_1', n_2'$, where n_1, n_2 are the variable labeled children of n and n_1', n_2' are the variable labeled children of n' (i.e., n and n' are f-labeled). The input pair is (n, n') and the output pairs are $(n_1, n_1'), (n_2, n_2')$.

5. An *output gadget* represents an output gate by three nodes n, n', n'', where n', n'' are the variable labeled children of n, and (n, n') is the designated input pair of the gadget. (It has no output pair.)

For a given combinational circuit C we use one of the gadgets above for every gate and connect the input and output node pairs with arrows whenever two gates are connected via an edge. Specifically, if there is an edge from gate g to gate g' in C, the edge corresponds to an output pair in the gadget for g and an input pair in the gadget for g'. Let (n, n') be this output pair in the gadget for g and (m, m') the corresponding input pair in the gadget for g'. We add the arrows $m \to n$ and $n' \to m$. Finally, for every input gate g that is set to **true** by a we add an arrow $n \to n'$ between the output pair (n, n') in the gadget representing g.

If we associate with every arrow in the thus constructed arrow graph A a distinct color then A is an arrow graph representation of a left-linear system of inequalities (that we can construct from A in logarithmic space). It is easy to check that after applying Algorithm L1 to A (ignoring the colors) the resultant arrow graph A' has an arrow path from n to its child n' in the output gadget of A' if and only if the value **true** is assigned to the output gate of C under a. Consequently A' fails

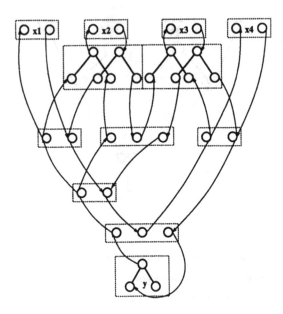

Figure 7: An arrow graph encoding of a monotone circuit

the acyclicity test if and only if $\bar{a}$ assigns **true** to the output gate in C. Since the construction of A can be implemented in logarithmic space, this proves the theorem. (End of proof) ■

Example: An arrow graph encoding of the circuit of Figure 6 is shown in Figure 7. (End of example) ■

Let kLLSU be the problem of left-linear semi-unifiability with exactly k term inequalities and *monadic semi-unification* *(MSU)* the problem of semi-unifiability for alphabet $\mathcal{A} = (F, a)$ where $a(f) \leq 1$ for all $f \in F$ (i.e., all terms contain at most one variable) and $a(f) = 1$ for at least one f. The proof of the previous theorem can be strengthened to yield the following two corollaries.

Corollary 8 *2LLSU is P-complete.*

Proof: Consider the step in the proof of Theorem 7 where a *distinct* color is associated with every arrow in the arrow graph A constructed from a monotone circuit C and assignment a. We can make do by using only two colors; in fact, only when connecting the input pairs of an or-gate g we use two distinct colors for the two outarrows from node n in the input pair (n, n') in the or-gadget. For all other arrows we can use the same color. The resulting arrow graph has two colors and represents a left-linear system of 2 inequalities that can be constructed in logarithmic space from the arrow graph. (End of proof) ■

This implies, of course, that kLLSU is P-complete for all $k \geq 2$. We conjecture that 1LLSU is also P-complete.

Corollary 9 *MSU is P-complete.*

Proof: The only two places where we use a binary function symbol in the proof of Theorem 7 is in the description of the *fan-out gadget* and of the *output gadget*.

An alternative fan-out gadget is the following arrow graph. It consists of six variable labeled nodes l, l', m, m', n, n' where (l, l') is the input pair; $(m, m'), (n, n')$ are the output pairs; and there are arrows $m \rightarrow l, l' \rightarrow m'$ and $n \rightarrow l, l' \rightarrow n'$.

An alternative output gadget consists of two nodes, n, n' where n is labeled by a function symbol f with arity 1 and n' is the variable labeled child of n; (n, n') is the designated input pair of the gadget.

The remainder of the proof of Theorem 7 goes through without a change. (End of proof) ■

5 Concluding remarks and open problems

Kfoury, Tiuryn and Urzyczyn showed that left-linear semi-unifiability (LLSU) is decidable. Their proof is essentially an exponential-time decision procedure and thus their result shows that LLSU is in DEXPTIME.

In this paper we have given a tight structural upper and lower bound for LLSU by proving that it is P-complete. As corollaries we have shown that LLSU restricted to two inequalities as well as monadic semi-unifiability are P-complete. Furthermore, we have shown that a dynamic transitive closure based implementation of a generic algorithm yields an $O(n^3)$ time decision procedure for LLSU.

Several issues and open problems remain:

- We conjecture there is an $O(n^2)$ time algorithm based on our generic Algorithm L1.

- We conjecture that LLSU restricted to a single inequality is P-complete.

- Possible applications of LLSU to proof theory remain to be explored (suggested by Hans Leiß).

- Several generalizations are not directly addressed, but do not pose any major difficulties. By adding a unification-like postprocessing phase to algorithm L1 it is possible to generalize algorithm L1 to arbitrary alphabets (instead of only A_2). A dynamic transitive closure based implementation still takes only $O(n^3)$ time. Furthermore, it is possible to extract a most general semi-unifier from the output of Algorithm L1. In particular, elementary properties regarding size of semi-unifiers appear to follow immediately from the correctness of L1. The algebraic structure of semi-unifiers of monadic semi-unification has been investigated in [Hen89].

6 Acknowledgements

I wish to thank Hans Leiß for extensive discussions on semi-unification and, in particular, for his probing questions on the correctness of Algorithm L1. I am also thankful to Han La Poutré for showing me how his and Jan van Leeuwen's dynamic transitive closure algorithm can be adapted elegantly to Algorithm L1.

References

[DKM84] C. Dwork, P. Kanellakis, and J. Mitchell. On the sequential nature of unification. *J. Logic Programming*, 1:35–50, 1984.

[DR89] J. Doerre and W. Rounds. On subsumption and semiunification in feature algebras. Manuscript, Oct. 1989.

[Gol77] L. Goldschlager. The monotone and planar circuit value problems are log-space complete for P. *SIGACT News*, 9(2):25–29, 1977.

[Hen88a] F. Henglein. Algebraic properties of semi-unification. Technical Report (SETL Newsletter) 233, New York University, November 1988.

[Hen88b] F. Henglein. Type inference and semi-unification. In *Proc. ACM Conf. on LISP and Functional Programming*. ACM, ACM Press, July 1988.

[Hen89] F. Henglein. *Polymorphic Type Inference and Semi-Unification*. PhD thesis, Rutgers University, April 1989.

[Hoo65] P. Hooper. *The Undecidability of the Turing Machine Immortality Problem*. PhD thesis, Harvard University, June 1965. Computation Laboratory Report BL-38; also in Journal of Symbolic Logic, 1966.

[Hue80] G. Huet. Confluent reductions: Abstract properties and applications to term rewriting systems. *J. Assoc. Comput. Mach.*, 27(4):797–821, Oct. 1980.

[KMNS89] D. Kapur, D. Musser, P. Narendran, and J. Stillman. Semi-unification. In *Proc. Foundations of Software Technology and Teoretical Computer Science*, Jan. 1989.

[KTU89a] A. Kfoury, J. Tiuryn, and P. Urzyczyn. Computational consequences and partial solutions of a generalized unification problem. In *Proc. 4th IEEE Symposium on Logic in Computer Science (LICS)*, June 1989.

[KTU89b] A. Kfoury, J. Tiuryn, and P. Urzyczyn. The undecidability of the semi-unification problem. Technical Report BUCS-89-010, Boston University, Oct. 1989. also in Proc. of Symp. on Theory of Computing, Baltimore, Maryland, May 1990.

[Lei89a] H. Leiß. Decidability of semi-unification in two variables. Technical Report INF-2-ASE-9-89, Siemens, July 1989.

[Lei89b] H. Leiß. Semi-unification and type inference for polymorphic recursion. Technical Report INF2-ASE-5-89, Siemens, Munich, West Germany, 1989.

[LPvL87] J. La Poutré and J. van Leeuwen. Maintenance of transitive closures and transitive reductions of graphs. In *Proc. Int'l Workshop on Graph-Theoretic Concepts in Computer Science*, pages 106–120. Springer-Verlag, June 1987. Lecture Notes in Computer Science, Vol. 314.

[Pud88] P. Pudlák. On a unification problem related to Kreisel's conjecture. *Commentationes Mathematicae Universitatis Carolinae*, 29(3):551–556, 1988.

[Pur87] P. Purdom. Detecting looping simplifications. In *Proc. 2nd Conf. on Rewrite Rule Theory and Applications (RTA)*, pages 54–62. Springer-Verlag, May 1987.

[Yel88] D. Yellin. A dynamic transitive closure algorithm. Technical Report RC 13535, IBM T.J. Watson Research Ctr., June 1988.

On the Complexity of (Off-line) 1-tape ATM's Running in Constant Reversals

Tao Jiang*

Department of Computer Science and Systems
McMaster University
Hamilton, Ontario L8S 4K1, Canada

Email: jiangs@maccs.McMaster.ca

Abstract. Yamamoto and Noguchi [YN87] raised the question of whether every recursively enumerable set can be accepted by a 1-tape or off-line 1-tape alternating Turing machine (ATM) whose (work)tape head makes only a constant number of reversals. In this paper, we answer the open question in the negative. We show that (1) constant-reversal 1-tape ATM's accept only regular languages and (2) there exists a recursive function h(k,r,n) such that for every k-state off-line 1-tape ATM M running in r reversals, the language accepted by M is in ASPACE(h(k,r,n)).

Key words: computational complexity, alternating Turing machine, 1-tape, off-line 1-tape, head reversal

1. Introduction

The complexity of reversal-bounded deterministic and nondeterministic Turing machines (TM's) and their restricted versions has been studied extensively in the literature (see, e.g., [BB74, C81, CY87, F68, GI81, G78, H68, I78, KV70]). Recently, the complexity of reversal-bounded alternating devices has attracted much attention [H85, H89, IJ88, YN87]. Some of these works considered alternating devices with only a constant number of reversals. Hromkovic [H85] showed that (1) the class of languages accepted by alternating multicounter machines running in polynomial time and constant reversals is exactly P and (2) every recursively enumerable (r.e.) set can be accepted by an alternating 4-counter machine in 1 reversal. The second result was improved by Ibarra and Jiang in [IJ88]. They showed that every r.e. set can be accepted by an alternating 2-counter machine in 1 reversal. Yamamoto and Noguchi [YN87] studied the reversal complexity of 1-tape alternating TM's (ATM's) and 1-tape-1-counter ATM's. (A 1-tape-1-counter

---
* This research was supported in part by a grant from SERB, McMaster
University and NSERC Operating Grant OGP 0046613.

TM is a 1-tape TM augmented with a counter. Note that, by definition, a multicounter machine has a separate read-only input tape while a 1-tape TM or 1-tape-1-counter TM does not have one.) They proved that (1) every r.e. set can be accepted by a 1-tape-1-counter ATM in 4 tape reversals and 1 counter reversal and (2) for functions $B(n)$ and $R(n)$ satisfying $B(n) \leq 2^{O(R(n))}$ and $B(n)R(n) \geq n$, the class of languages accepted by 1-tape ATM's running in $O(R(n))$ reversals and $O(B(n))$ leaves is $\text{NSPACE}(B(n)R(n))$. It was left as an open question whether every r.e. set can be accepted by a 1-tape ATM or an off-line 1-tape ATM (with a separate 2-way input tape) in constant reversals.

Here, we give a negative answer to this question. For any $m,n \geq 0$, let $f_m(n) = 2^{m2^{mn}}$, $g(m,n) = f_m^n(1)$, where f_m^n is the composition of n f_m's. We show that (1) every language accepted by a k-state 1-tape ATM in r reversals can be accepted by a deterministic finite-state machine (DFA) with at most $g(k+2,(r+3)/2)$ states and (2) every language accepted by an k-state off-line 1-tape ATM in r reversals is in $\text{ASPACE}(g((k+2)(n+2),(r+3)/2))$. These results show that the restriction on reversals reduces the power of 1-tape ATM's and off-line 1-tape ATM's.

Section 2 of the paper contains the basic concepts and definitions concerning an alternating computation. We assume that the reader is familiar with Turing machines and off-line Turing machines. For the formal definitions of these models, we refer to [HU79]. In Section 3, we investigate the power of 1-tape ATM's and off-line 1-tape ATM's running in constant reversals.

2. Preliminaries

An ATM [CKS81] is a generalization of a nondeterministic TM (NTM) whose state set is partitioned into "universal" and "existential" states. As with an NTM, we can view the computation of an ATM as a tree of instantaneous descriptions (ID's). An ID consists of the state of the finite-control, nonblank contents of tapes, and tape head positions. An ID is called universal (existential) if the state associated with it is universal (existential). A computation tree of an ATM M is a tree whose nodes are labled by ID's of M such that the children of any internal node labeled by a universal (existential) ID include all (one) of immediate successors of that ID. A computation tree is accepting if it is finite and all the leaves are labeled by accepting ID's. A computation tree of M is t reversal-bounded (space-bounded) if on each path from the root to a leaf, the number of times a head changes its direction of movement is at most t (each node is labeled by an ID using at most t space, respectively). An accepting computation tree of M whose root is labeled by the initial ID of M on input x is called an accepting computation tree of M on x. M accepts an input x if there exists an accepting computation tree of M on x. For a function $T(n)$, an ATM is $T(n)$ reversal-bounded (space-bounded) if for every accepted input of length n, there is a $T(n)$ reversal-bounded (space-bounded) accepting computation tree of M on x. The language accepted by M is denoted by $L(M)$.

In this paper, we are only interested in 1-tape ATM's and off-line 1-tape ATM's. For an off-line 1-tape ATM, i.e., a 1-tape ATM augmented with a two-way input tape, both space and reversal complexities are measured only on the worktape. The reversals made by the input head are not counted in the reversal complexity of the machine. In all of our results concerning off-line

ATM's, the input head is assumed to make arbitrary number of reversals.

For convenience, we will also refer to the tape of a 1-tape ATM as the worktape of the machine. The cells of a worktape are numbered 1, 2, ..., ∞ and the boundaries between the cells are numbered 0, 1, 2, ..., ∞ , from left to right. For any $0 \leq i \leq j$, let $\alpha(i,j)$ denote the segment of the worktape bounded by boundaries i and j. Thus, for any integer $i \geq 0$, $\alpha(0,i)$ is the segment consisting of all the cells to the left of boundary i and $\alpha(i,\infty)$ is the rest of the worktape. When the worktape head crosses a boundary i from right to left (from left to right), we say it *right-crosses (left-crosses*, respectively) *boundary i*.

A (off-line) 1-tape ATM M is called *normal* if it works in the following special way. Given any input, M first attaches a marker ¢ (called the left endmarker) to the symbol contained in cell 1 of its worktape. M then nondeterministically shifts the worktape head to some cell i containing a blank worktape symbol, attaches a marker $ (called the right endmarker) to the blank worktape symbol, and shifts the worktape head back to cell 1. In the subsequent steps, the worktape head never moves to the left of cell 1 or the right of cell i. M rejects by looping and accepts by shifting its worktape head to cell i and entering an accepting state. Clearly, if M a normal 1-tape ATM and τ is an accepting computation tree of M using T space, then all leaves of τ are labeled by ID's whose worktape head positions are T. It is easy to see that a t reversal-bounded k-state (off-line) 1-tape ATM can be simulated by a normal (k+2)-state (off-line) 1-tape ATM running in at most t+2 reversals.

Throughout the paper, Σ denotes the input alphabet, Δ denotes the worktape alphabet of an ATM, λ denotes the blank worktape symbol, and ϵ denotes the null string. For any integer m, m/2 means $\lceil m/2 \rceil$. The size of a set S is denoted by $|S|$. The set of equivalence classes defined by an equivalence relation R (on some set) is denoted by $<R>$. The cardinality of an equivalence relation R is the size of $<R>$. For any (computation) tree τ and a node v of τ, by *the subtree of τ rooted at v* we mean the subtree of τ consisting of v and all its descendents. From now on, we will simply call a computation tree whose root is labeled by ID β a *computation tree with root β*.

3. The Complexity of Constant-reversal 1-tape ATM's and Off-line 1-tape ATM's

We first consider 1-tape ATM's. Let M be a 1-tape ATM with state set Q, input alphabet Σ, and the worktape alphabet Δ. Note that $\Sigma \subseteq \Delta$. An ID of M is a 3-tuple (q,x,i), where $q \in Q$ indicates the current state, $x \in \Delta^*$ is the current worktape nonblank contents, and i indicates the worktape head position. For any $q \in Q$ and $x,y \in \Delta^*$, let $\pi_1(q,x,y)$ denote the set of all the possible finite computation trees corresponding to the following computation: M starts with its ID being $(q,xy,|k|)$ and stops when its worktape head left-crosses the boundary $|k|$ for the first time. Let $\pi_2(q,x,y)$ be defined the same as $\pi_1(q,x,y)$ except that now the starting ID of M is (q,xy,1) instead of $(q,xy,|k|)$. For each τ in $\pi_i(q,x,y)$, $1 \leq i \leq 2$, let $\mu(\tau) = \{ (p,z) \mid p \in Q, z \in \Delta^*,$ $|k| = |k|$, and some leaf of τ is labeled by $(p,zy,|k|+1) \}$, i.e., $\mu(\tau)$ is the set of combinations of state and $\alpha(0,|k|)$'s contents associated with the leaves of τ. Finally, let $\mu(\pi_i(q,x,y)) = \{ \mu(\tau) \mid \tau \in \pi_i(q,x,y) \}$, i = 1,2. It is easy to see that $\mu(\pi_i(q,x,y_1)) = \mu(\pi_i(q,x,y_2))$ for any $y_1,y_2 \in \Delta^*$, i = 1,2. Thus, let $\mu_i(q,x)$ stand for $\mu(\pi_i(q,x,\epsilon))$, i = 1,2. Clearly, $\mu_i(q,x) \subseteq 2^{Q \times \Delta^*}$, i = 1,2.

For any set S, let $\Phi(S)$ denote the class of equivalence relations on S. Define five mappings $D_M\colon \Phi(\Delta^*) \to \Phi(Q\times\Delta^*)$, $E_M\colon \Phi(Q\times\Delta^*) \to \Phi(2^{Q\times\Delta^*})$, $F_M\colon \Phi(2^{Q\times\Delta^*}) \to \Phi(2^{2^{Q\times\Delta^*}})$, and G_M, $H_M\colon$ $\Phi(\Delta^*) \to \Phi(\Delta^*)$ as follows:

$D_M(R) = \{ ((q,x),(q,y)) \mid q \in Q,\ (x,y) \in R \}$, for any $R \in \Phi(\Delta^*)$;

$E_M(R) = \{ (u,v) \mid u,v \in 2^{Q\times\Delta^*}$, for each $s \in u$ there is a $t \in v$ such that $(s,t) \in R$ and vice versa $\}$, for any $R \in \Phi(Q\times\Delta^*)$;

$F_M(R) = \{ (u,v) \mid u,v \in 2^{2^{Q\times\Delta^*}}$, for each $s \in u$ there is a $t \in v$ such that $(s,t) \in R$ and vice versa $\}$, for any $R \in \Phi(2^{Q\times\Delta^*})$;

$G_M(R) = \{ (x,y) \mid x,y \in \Delta^*$ and $(\mu_1(q,x),\mu_1(q,y)) \in F_M(E_M(D_M(R)))$ for all $q \in Q \}$, for any $R \in \Phi(\Delta^*)$;

$H_M(R) = \{ (x,y) \mid x,y \in \Delta^*$ and $(\mu_2(q,x),\mu_2(q,y)) \in F_M(E_M(D_M(R)))$ for all $q \in Q \}$, for any $R \in \Phi(\Delta^*)$.

Let $R_M^0 = O_M^0 = \Delta^*\times\Delta^*$ and, for each $i \geq 1$, let $R_M^i = G_M(R_M^{i-1})$ and $O_M^i = H_M(R_M^{i-1})$. Let $k = |Q|$ and functions f_k and g be as defined in Section 1. We need the following lemmas.

Lemma 1. Let x and y be two strings in Δ^* such that $(x,y) \in R_M^{i+1}$ for some $i \geq 0$. Let q be any state in Q and z be any string in Δ^*. Suppose that there is an accepting computation tree τ of M with root $(q,xz,|k|)$ such that in tree τ, the worktape head right-crosses the boundary $|k|$ at most i times and is always in segment $\alpha(|k|,\infty)$ when M accepts. Then there exists an accepting computation tree of M with root $(q,yz,|y|)$.

Proof. We prove the lemma by induction on i. Suppose $i = 0$, i.e., in tree τ, the worktape head does not return to segment $\alpha(0,|k|)$ once it leaves the segment. Let τ_1 be a subtree of τ such that the root of τ_1 is the root of τ and τ_1 is a member of $\pi_1(q,x)$. Let $Q_1 = \{ p \mid (p,x_1) \in \mu(\tau_1) \}$, i.e., the set of states associated with the leaves of τ_1. For each p in Q_1, choose a leaf v_p of τ_1 such that the state associated with v_p is p. Let σ_p be the subtree of τ rooted at v_p, for each $p \in Q_1$. Clearly, in each subtree σ_p, the worktape head position of M is always greater than $|k|$. Since $(x,y) \in R_M^1$, by the definition of R_M^1, there is a tree τ_2 in $\pi_1(q,y,z)$ such that $Q_2 = \{ p \mid (p,y_1) \in \mu(\tau_2)$ for some $y_1 \} = Q_1$. We can obtain an accepting tree of M with root $(q,yz,|y|)$ as follows. Let v be a leaf of τ_2. Suppose that $(p,y_1z,|y|+1)$ is the ID associated with v and $|y_1| = |y|$. Make a copy of subtree σ_p and modify the ID's associated with its nodes as follows: if a node is labeled by (p_1,x_1z_1,t), $|k_1| = |k|$, change it to $(p_1,y_1z_1,t+|y|-|k|)$. Identify the root of the tree just obtained with the leaf v of τ_2. Execute the above "modify-and-merge" process for each leaf of τ_2. It is easy to see that the resulting tree is an accepting tree of M with root $(q,yz,|y|)$.

Suppose that the lemma holds for all $i < j$. We prove that it also holds for $i = j$. Let τ_1 be a subtree as defined above. For each $u = (p,x_1)$ in $\mu(\tau_1)$, choose a leaf v_u of τ_1 such that the ID associated with v_u is $(p,x_1z,|k|+1)$. Let σ_u be the subtree of τ rooted at v_u and γ_u be a subtree of

σ_u rooted at v_u corresponding to the following computation: M starts with its ID being u and stops when either (1) it accepts or (2) the worktape head right-crosses the boundary $|k|$ for the first time. Let V_u be the set of leaves of γ_u corresponding to the second type of termination of M. Clearly, each w in V_u is labeled by $(q_w, x_1 z_w, |k|)$ for some $q_w \in Q$ and $z_w \in \Delta^*$. For each w in V_u, let θ_u^w denote the subtree of σ_u rooted at w. It is easy to see that in each θ_u^w, the worktape head right-crosses the boundary $|k|$ at most j−1 times.

Since $(x,y) \in R_M^{j+1}$, there must be a tree τ_2 in $\pi_1(q, yz, |y|)$ such that for each $u = (p, y_1)$ in $\mu(\tau_2)$, there is some (p, x_1) (denote it by u') in $\mu(\tau_1)$ satisfying $(x_1, y_1) \in R_M^j$. By the induction hypothesis, for each $u = (p, y_1)$ in $\mu(\tau_2)$ and w in $V_{u'}$, we can construct an accepting computation tree η_u^w of M with root $(q_w, y_1 z_w, |y|)$ from the tree $\theta_{u'}^w$. Let $Z = \{ \eta_u^w \mid u \in \mu(\tau_2)$ and $w \in V_{u'} \}$ and $\Gamma = \{ \gamma_u \mid u \in \mu(\tau_1) \}$. It is easy to see that, by using the "modify-and-merge" technique described above, we can construct an accepting computation tree of M with root $(q, yz, |y|)$ from the trees in $\{\tau_2\} \cup \Gamma \cup Z$. Only the trees in Γ need to be modified as follows: a label $(p, x_1 z_1, t)$ is replaced by $(p, y_1 z_1, t + |y| - |k|)$ for some y_1, where $|k_1| = |k|$ and $|y_1| = |y|$. Note that, Z could be empty. If Z is empty, then all the trees in Γ are accepting, i.e., the worktape head of M does not right-cross boundary $|k|$ in tree τ. Thus, the desired tree can be constructed from the trees in $\{\tau_2\} \cup \Gamma$ as in the case i = 0. □

Lemma 2 is analogous to Lemma 1 and can be proven by using Lemma 1.

Lemma 2. Let x and y be two strings in Δ^* such that $(x,y) \in O_M^{i+1}$ for some $i \geq 0$. Let q be any state in Q and z any string in Δ^*. Suppose that there is an accepting computation tree τ of M with root $(q, xz, 1)$ such that in tree τ, the worktape head right-crosses the boundary $|k|$ at most i times and is always in segment $\alpha(|k|, \infty)$ when M accepts. Then there exists an accepting computation tree of M with root $(q, yz, 1)$.

Proof. The proof for the case i = 0 is the same as in the proof of Lemma 1 except that we now choose subtrees τ_1 and τ_2 from $\pi_2(q, x, z)$ and $\pi_2(q, y, z)$ respectively. For i > 0, the proof uses the fact that Lemma 1 holds for i−1 and is very similar to the inductive step of Lemma 1. We leave the details to the reader. □

Lemma 3. $|<O_M^i>| \leq g(k,i)$, for all $i \geq 0$.

Proof. We prove $|<R_M^i>| \leq g(k,i)$ and $|<O_M^i>| \leq g(k,i+1)$, for all $i \geq 0$. The proof is done by induction on i.

Clearly, $|<R_M^0>| = |<O_M^0>| = 1 = g(k,0)$. Suppose $|<R_M^i>| \leq g(k,i)$ and $|<O_M^i>| \leq g(k,i)$, for all $i < j$. We prove $|<R_M^j>| \leq g(k,j)$ and $|<O_M^j>| \leq g(k,j)$. From the definitions of D_M, E_M, F_M, G_M, and H_M, we have:

$$|<D_M(R_M^{j-1})>| = k|<R_M^{j-1}>| \leq kg(k,j-1),$$

$$|<E_M(D_M(R_M^{j-1}))>| = 2^{|<D_M(R_M^{j-1})>|} \leq 2^{kg(k,j-1)},$$

$$|<F_M(E_M(D_M(R_M^{j-1})))>| = 2^{|<E_M(D_M(R_M^{j-1}))>|} \leq 2^{2^{kg(k,j-1)}},$$

$$|<R_M^j>| = |<G_M(R_M^{j-1})>|$$
$$\leq |<F_M(E_M(D_M(R_M^{j-1})))>|^k$$
$$\leq 2^{k2^{kg(k,j-1)}} = f_k(g(k,j-1)) = g(k,j), \text{ and}$$

$$|<O_M^j>| = |<H_M(R_M^{j-1})>|$$
$$\leq |<F_M(E_M(D_M(R_M^{j-1})))>|^k$$
$$\leq g(k,j). \qquad \square$$

Now we are ready to prove that every language accepted by a 1-tape ATM in constant reversals is regular.

Theorem 4. Every language accepted by a k-state 1-tape ATM in r reversals can be accepted by a DFA with at most $g(k+2,(r+3)/2)$ states.

Proof. It suffices to show that every language accepted by a normal k-state 1-tape ATM running in r reversals can be accepted by a DFA with at most $g(k,(r+1)/2)$ states. Let M be a normal k-state 1-tape ATM running in r reversals and Σ be the input alphabet of M. Let E be the restriction of $O_M^{(r+1)/2}$ to Σ^*, i.e., $(x,y) \in E$ iff $(x,y) \in O_M^{(r+1)/2}$, $x,y \in \Sigma^*$. Since M is normal, on any input x, the worktape head must be in segment $\alpha(k,\infty)$ when M accepts. It is easy to see that in any accepting computation tree of M, the worktape head right-crosses each boundary at most $(r-1)/2$ times. By Lemma 2, for any two strings x,y in Σ^*, if $(x,y) \in E$ then $xz \in L(M)$ iff $yz \in L(M)$ for all $z \in \Sigma^*$. From the discussion in Section 3.4 of [HU79], L(M) is accepted by a DFA with at most $|E| \leq |<O_M^{(r+1)/2}>| = g(k,(r+1)/2)$ states. $\qquad \square$

Next we consider off-line 1-tape ATM's. Let N be an off-line 1-tape ATM with state set Q, input alphabet Σ, and worktape alphabet Δ. An ID of N is a 5-tuple (q,w,i,x,j), where $q \in Q$ indicates the state, $w \in \Sigma^*$ is the input, i indicates the current input head position, $x \in \Delta^*$ is the current worktape nonblank contents, and j indicates the current worktape head position. Assume that inputs are surrounded by endmarkers $\cent$ and $. Define the object *superstate* of N as a 3-tuple (q,w,i), where q is a state, w is the input, and i is the input head position. Clearly, given input w, the number of superstates of N on w is $|Q|(|w|+2)$. It is easy to see that, all the discussions related to Lemmas 1 and 2 hold for (the off-line 1-tape ATM) N if we replace the word "state" by "superstate". For any input string w, let equivalence relation $O_{N,w}^j$ be defined as O_M^j for a 1-tape ATM M but with the state of M being replaced by the superstate of N on w, $j \geq 0$. The next two lemmas are analogs of Lemmas 2 and 3.

Lemma 5. Let w be an input and x,y be two strings in Δ^* such that $(x,y) \in O_{N,w}^{j+1}$ for some $j \geq 0$. Let (q,w,i) be any superstate of N on w, and z any string in Δ^*. Suppose that there is an accepting computation tree τ of N with root $(q,w,i,xz,1)$ such that in tree τ, the worktape head right-crosses the boundary $k|$ at most j times and is always in segment $\alpha(|w|,\infty)$ when N accepts. Then there exists an accepting computation tree of N with root $(q,w,i,yz,1)$.

Lemma 6. Let w be an input. Then $|<O_{N,w}^i>| \le g(|Q|(|w|+2),i)$, $i \ge 0$.

We prove that off-line 1-tape ATM's running in constant reversals cannot accept all r.e. sets.

Theorem 7. Every language accepted by a k-state off-line 1-tape ATM in r reversals is in ASPACE(g((k+2)(n+2),(r+3)/2)).

Proof. We only need to prove that every language accepted by a normal k-state off-line 1-tape ATM in r reversals is in ASPACE(g(k(n+2),(r+1)/2)).

Let N be a normal k-state off-line 1-tape ATM running in r reversals. Let w be a string in L(N) and n = |w|. We show that there exists a g(k(n+2),(r+1)/2))+2 space-bounded accepting computation tree of M on w.

Suppose that this is not true. Let τ be an accepting computation tree of N on w using the least space (among all accepting trees of N on w) and T be the space used in τ. Clearly, T > g(k(n+2),(r+1)/2)+2. Since N is normal, there must be an accepting subtree τ_1 of τ with root $(q,w,1,[\cent,\lambda]\lambda^{T-2}[\lambda,\$],1)$ for some state q, where $[\cent,\lambda]$ and $[\lambda,\$]$ are composite symbols. Moreover, the worktape head position is equal to T at all leaves of τ_1. Consider all strings $[\cent,\lambda]\lambda^i$, $0 \le i \le$ T−2. Since the cardinality of the equivalence relation $O_{N,w}^{(r+1)/2}$ is at most g(k(n+2),(r+1)/2)) and T−2 > g(k(n+2),(r+1)/2)), there must be i and j, such that $0 \le i < j \le$ T−2 and $([\cent,\lambda]\lambda^i,[\cent,\lambda]\lambda^j) \in O_{N,w}^{(r+1)/2}$. By Lemma 5, there exists an accepting computation tree τ' of N with root $(q,w,1,[\cent,\lambda]\lambda^{i+(T-j-2)}[\lambda,\$],1)$. It can be seen from the construction in the proof of Lemma 1 that the tree τ' is T+i−j space-bounded. Thus, there exists an accepting computation tree of N on w that is T+i−j < T space-bounded. This contradicts with the assumption that, among all accepting computation trees of N on w, τ uses the least space.

Hence, there exists a g(k(n+2),(r+1)/2)+2 space-bounded accepting computation tree of M on w. This completes the proof of Theorem 7. □

References

[BB74]   Baker, B. and R. Book, Reversal-bounded multipushdown machines, *J. of Comput. System Sci.* 8, 1974, pp. 315-332.

[C81]   Chan, T., Reversal complexity of counter machines, the *Proceedings of the 13th Annual ACM Symposium on Theory of Computing*, 1981, pp. 146-157.

[CKS81] Chandra, A., D. Kozen, and L. Stockmeyer, Alternation, *J. ACM* 28, 1981, pp. 114-133.

[CY87]   Chen, J. and C. Yap, Reversal complexity, *Proc. of 2nd IEEE Annual Conference on Structure in Complexity Theory*, 1987, pp. 14-19.

[F68]   Fisher, P., The reduction of tape reversal for off-line one-tape Turing machines, *J. of Comput. System Sci.* 2, 1968, pp. 136-147.

[GI81]   Gurari, E. and O. Ibarra, The complexity of decision problems for finite-turn multicounter machines, *J. of Comput. System Sci.* 22, 1981, pp. 220-229.

[G78]   Greibach, S., Visits, crosses and reversal for nondeterministic off-line machines, *Information and Control* 36, pp. 174-216.

[H68]   Hartmanis, J., Tape-reversal bounded Turing machine computations, *J. of Comput.
System Sci.* 2, 1968, pp. 117-135.

[HU79]   Hopcroft, J. and J. Ullman, *Introduction to automata theory, languages, and computation*, Addison-Wesley, 1979.

[H85]   Hromkovic, J., Alternating multicounter machines with constant number of reversals,
Information Processing Letters 21, 1985, pp. 7-9.

[H89]   Hromkovic, J., Tradeoffs for language recognition on alternating machines, *Theoretical
Computer Science* 63, 1989, pp. 203-221.

[I78]   Ibarra, O., Reversal-bounded multicounter machines and their decision problems, *J.
ACM* 25, 1978, pp. 116-133.

[IJ88]   Ibarra, O. and T. Jiang, The power of alternating one-reversal counters and stacks, to
appear in *SIAM J. on Computing*; also *Proc. of 3rd IEEE Annual Conference on Structure in Complexity*, 1988, pp. 70-77.

[KV70]   Kameda, T. and R. Vollmar, Note on tape reversal complexity of languages, *Information and Control* 17, 1970, pp. 203-215.

[YN87]   Yamamoto, H. and S. Noguchi, Comparison of the power between reversal-bounded
ATMs and reversal-bounded NTMs, *Information and Computation* 75, 1987, pp. 144-
161.

A Constant Update Time Finger Search Tree

Paul Dietz
Rajeev Raman

Department of Computer Science
University of Rochester
Rochester, NY 14627

Abstract

Levcopolous and Overmars [12] describe a search tree in which the time to insert or delete a key is $O(1)$ once the position of the key to be inserted or deleted was known. Their data structure does not support *fingers*, pointers to points of high access or update activity in the set such that access and update operations in the vicinity of a finger are particularly efficient [3, 8, 10, 11, 15]. Levcopolous and Overmars leave as an open question whether a data structure can be designed which allowed updates in constant time and supports fingers. We answer the question in the affirmative by giving an algorithm in the RAM with logarithmic word size model [1].

CR Classification Number: [F.2.2 - Sorting and Searching]
Keywords: Real-Time Algorithm, Search Tree, Fingers.

1 Introduction

Define the *update time* of a search tree to be the cost of an insertion/deletion once the position of the key to be inserted or deleted is known, *i.e.*, the update time is how long it takes to insert/delete a key given a pointer to it. Levcopolous and Overmars [12] describe a search tree with constant worst-case update time. However, their data structure does not support *fingers*, which are pointers to particular keys in the sorted set. A *finger search tree* supports the following operations:

- *search(x,f)* : search for key x starting at finger f,

- *insert/delete(x,f)* : insert/delete key x starting at finger f,

- *create(x)* : create a new finger at key x,

- *destroy(f)* : destroy a finger f.

The operations *search*, *insert* and *delete* should take time $O(\log d)^1$, where d is the distance of x from f and *create* and *destroy* should take $O(1)$ time. A data structure that supports finger searches and finger creation/deletion and has worst-case constant update time is superior to an ordinary finger tree, since it can clearly handle the full repertoire of finger operations, while a finger tree may not be able to guarantee constant update time. A good worst-case bound on update time also implies that the number of storage modifications made with each update to the data structure is small,

---

[1] All logarithms in this paper are to the base 2 unless otherwise stated.

which helps in making the data structure *persistent* [6], *i.e.*, to permit access and update operations on old versions of the data structure. In this paper we show good worst-case bounds on the update time of finger search trees.

In [8, 11, 15] finger tree schemes are described which have worst-case $O(\log d)$ search and update time (finger creation and deletion take $O(\log d)$ time in the latter two approaches). In [10] it is shown that 2-4 trees have constant amortized update time. By using links between all nodes at the same level (the so-called *level-links*[3]), a key can be found in $O(\log d)$ time, and thus the full set of finger operations can be realized in an amortized sense by level-linked 2-4 trees with parent pointers (figure 1 shows a level-linked 2-3 tree). Moreover, moving or creating a finger takes only constant time once the position is known, and deletion of fingers takes constant time. The best worst-case update time bound in a finger tree is by Harel [9], where a finger tree is described that allows updates in worst-case $O(\log^* n)$ time. In [6] it is shown that red-black trees can be maintained with $O(1)$ worst-case modifications per update, with the consequence that finger search trees can efficiently be made persistent. The update time in this data structure is $O(\log n)$ in the worst case, however.

In the following section we turn to the problem of constructing a data structure that can support fingers, and still perform updates in constant worst-case time. We construct such a data structure that runs on a RAM with logarithmic word size. The algorithm has very simple implementations of finger searches, creation, movement and deletion, allows finger deletion in constant time, and finger creation and movement in constant time if the position is known.

2   The Existing Algorithm

It is easy to devise a tree data structure for the sorted set problem that has $O(1)$ amortized time updates and has logarithmic search time [13]. Take any data structure for sorted sets in which one can perform updates in amortized time $O(\log n)$. Partition the elements of the set into contiguous buckets of size about $O(\log n)$. Each bucket is represented as a linear list and has a representative, its minimum element, that is stored in the overlying data structure. When a bucket doubles in size or is reduced to half its size, spend $O(\log n)$ time splitting it in two (or merging it with one of its neighbors) and a further $O(\log n)$ time inserting the new representative into (or deleting the old representative from) the top-level data structure. This is $O(1)$ work when amortized over the $O(\log n)$ updates that caused the bucket to change in size.

Levcopolous and Overmars [12] describe a worst-case analog of this method (a nearly identical approach was taken by Dietz and Sleator [5] to solve a different problem). Their solution is to perform both the bucket splitting and the insertion of the representative into the top level tree (which must now be able to support updates in *worst-case* $O(\log n)$ time) incrementally. They show how, given a data structure on N keys that is "freshly built", it is possible to perform only insertions in constant time while the size of the data structure is in the range $[N/2, 2N]$ (their approach towards handling deletions is described later). We will assume that when "freshly built" all buckets have size at most $\frac{1}{2}\log^2 N$ (figure 2). As updates progress, the bucket of largest size is repeatedly picked, and over the next $O(\log N)$ insertions into the data structure, this bucket is split and the new representative is inserted into the data structure. The buckets are organized so that splitting a bucket takes $O(\log N)$ work, and so the total work needed to perform the bucket splitting and insertion is $O(\log N)$.

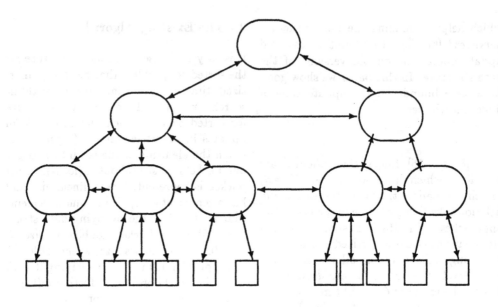

Figure 1: A 2-3 tree with level-links and parent pointers

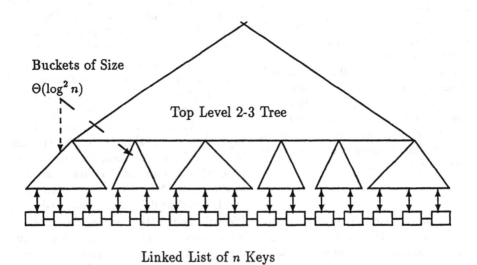

Buckets of Size
$\Theta(\log^2 n)$

Top Level 2-3 Tree

Linked List of n Keys

Figure 2: Overview of the data structure

With the right implementation, both these tasks can be performed incrementally, with $O(1)$ work per update.

Since $O(\log N)$ insertions are done to the buckets between splits, it is possible that the buckets get too large to split concurrently with the top-level insertion. As a consequence of a combinatorial lemma proved in [12] picking the largest bucket each time guarantees that each will have size $O(\log^2 N)$. In [5] a slightly stronger version of the same lemma is proved, and is formulated as the following game on an array of size n:

Lemma 1 ([5], Theorem 5)

Let $x_1, \ldots, x_n$ be n real valued variables, all initially zero. Repeatedly perform the following moves:

1. *Choose an x_i such that $x_i = max_j\{x_j\}$, and set it to zero.*

2. *Choose n nonnegative reals $a_1, \ldots, a_n$ such that $\sum_{i=1}^{n} a_i = 1$, and for all i, $1 \le i \le n$, set x_i to $x_i + a_i$.*

Then each x_i will always be less than $H_{n-1} + 1$.

Here $H_k = \sum_{i=1}^{k} 1/i$ is the kth harmonic number (it can be verified that $H_k - 1 < \ln k < H_k - 1/k$).

In the case above, $k = c \log N$ insertions occur between bucket splitting operations. Initially the data structure on N keys is constructed so that all the buckets have size less than $\frac{1}{2} \log^2 N$. Since the data structure will be maintained only while the size is less than $2N$, there will be at most $2N$ buckets. Now we apply lemma 1 to show that the buckets will never have more than $\log^2 N$ elements in them. Let the excess of the bucket size over $\frac{1}{2} \log^2 N$ (if there is no excess we define the excess to be 0) be represented by the variables x_i. Splitting the bucket will reduce the size of any bucket to below $\frac{1}{2} \log^2 N$ if no bucket ever exceeds size $\log^2 N$. By lemma 1 if $c \le 0.5/\ln 2$, the

x_i's will never grow beyond $k(H_{2N-1}+1) \le \frac{1}{2} \log^2 N$. Each bucket of size $O(\log^2 N)$ is represented by a 2-level tree with a branching factor of $O(\log N)$. Insertions necessitate controlling the branching factor at the internal nodes, which can be done in $O(1)$ time incrementally. Splitting a bucket takes $O(\log N)$ time (to partition the $O(\log N)$ children of the root) and can be done concurrently with the insertion of its representative being performed in the top level data structure.

To make the data structure valid for all values of n, their algorithm makes use of a technique called "global rebuilding" due to Overmars [14]. The idea involves maintaining two different copies of the data structure with different values of N, and "freshly building" one concurrently with updates on the other, in such a way that the new data structure is ready to take over before the old one gets out of its "operating range". Deletions can also be handled by this technique, by merely marking elements as deleted, and discarding marked elements while rebuilding the structure. While this approach is conceptually easy to describe, it leads to large increases in the running time (the particular global rebuilding algorithm described in [12] results in multiplying the run time by up to a factor of 13) and also complicates the implementation.

This data structure does not permit finger searches, however. Due to the $O(\log n)$ branching factor in the buckets, searches take $O(\log n)$ time even when fingers are provided. Another problem is the presence of the marked elements, which could increase the distance between two adjacent keys. In what follows, we will show how to overcome these problems. First we describe how to handle deletions explicitly in the above algorithm (in addition, we will avoid global rebuilding), and then we describe how to organize the buckets so that finger searches are possible.

3 An Improved Algorithm

3.1 Explicit Deletions

One problem with handling deletions explicitly is that we cannot allow the buckets to get too small. Otherwise, the deletion of the last key in a bucket would require an immediate deletion in the top-level tree, which cannot be done in constant time. We will handle deletions by operations that involve fusing small buckets. An argument similar to the one that is used to show that buckets do not grow too large can show that if the smallest underflowing bucket is chosen to rebalance each time, then the buckets do not get too small. At any point in the operation of the data structure, let $\hat{n}$ be the maximum number of keys present in the data structure at any previous time. Our buckets will always be of size $\Theta(\log^2 \hat{n})$. More precisely, if the *fullness* of a bucket b is defined to be

$$\phi(b, \hat{n}) = size(b)/\log^2 \hat{n},$$

we will ensure that $0.5 \leq \phi(b, \hat{n}) \leq 2$ unless b is the only bucket present. (We may occasionally omit the dependence of ϕ on $\hat{n}$.) As an aid to the proof, we will enforce this condition by completely restructuring the data structure whenever the bucket criticalities fall below 0.5 or exceed 2.0 (unless there is only one bucket). We will prove that such drastic measures will *never* have to be resorted to — this step merely makes it possible to assume an invariant that is true before every update and if violated during the course of an update, is restored at the end of the update.

Define the *criticality* of a bucket b to be:

$$\rho(b, \hat{n}) = \alpha \log \hat{n} \max\{0, 0.7 - \phi(b), 1.8 - \phi(b)\}$$

for an appropriately chosen constant α. A bucket is called *critical* if $\rho(b, \hat{n}) > 0$.

To maintain the sizes of the buckets in the appropriate range, we do the following: repeatedly pick the bucket b with maximum criticality and perform the appropriate rebalancing transformations, provided b is critical:

- *Split:* If $\phi(b) > 1.8$ split the bucket into two parts of approximately equal size.

- *Transfer:* If $\phi(b) < 0.7$ and one of its adjacent buckets b' has $\phi(b') \geq 1$ then transfer elements from b' to b until the sizes are approximately equal.

- *Fuse:* If $\phi(b) < 0.7$ and transferring is not possible, then fuse with an adjacent bucket b', *i.e.*, delete b and place all all the elements in b in b'.

We will show later how to organize the buckets so that all the above operations can be done in $O(\log \hat{n})$ time in such a way that for splitting and transferring, the resulting buckets have ϕ values which are equal to within an additive factor of $O(\log^{-1} \hat{n})$. Since the bucket criticalities always lie in the range $[0.5, 2.0]$, it is clear that the bucket rebalancing steps above always reduce the criticalities of a critical bucket to zero. In addition to the time required to split/fuse buckets, a bucket rebalancing step may require $O(\log \hat{n})$ time to insert/delete a bucket representative from the top-level tree. Since the total work to rebalance a bucket is $O(\log \hat{n})$, we can perform it with $O(1)$ work per update spread over no more than $\alpha \log \hat{n}$ updates.

Now we show that the buckets never get too big. Updates cause the criticalities of buckets to increase, and every $\alpha \log \hat{n}$ updates a bucket with maximum criticality is made non-critical. The criticalities of buckets can increase in two ways: by changes in bucket size and by increases in the value of $\hat{n}$ (underflowing buckets only). If $\hat{n}$ increases by 1, the criticality of an underflowing bucket b will increase by δ_b, where:

$$\delta_b \leq \frac{d\,\rho(B, \hat{n})}{d\,\hat{n}} = \frac{c_1}{\hat{n}} + \frac{c_2\,size(b)}{\hat{n}\log^2 \hat{n}} \leq \frac{c_3}{\hat{n}},$$

for some constant c_3. So the change in the criticalities of all $\Theta(\hat{n}/\log^2 \hat{n})$ buckets due to a increase in 1 in the value of $\hat{n}$ adds up to an amount that is $O(\log^{-2} \hat{n})$. Since $\hat{n}$ may change by upto $O(\log \hat{n})$ between bucket rebalancings, we see that the changes in criticalities due to the change in $\hat{n}$ between rebalancings is at most $O(\log^{-1} \hat{n})$, taken over all buckets. Updates cause the criticalities to change by values adding up to at most α between rebalancings, and thus the total change to the criticalities between bucket rebalancings is $\alpha + o(1)$. By lemma 1 at no stage can the criticality of a bucket exceed $\alpha H_{\hat{n}-1} + O(1)$, and so if α is sufficiently small, this means that all buckets will have $\rho \in [0.5, 2.0]$.

3.2 Organizing Buckets for Efficient Finger Searches

In the case of a RAM [1], a reasonable measure of the complexity of an algorithm is the *uniform cost with logarithmic word size*: if the data structure has size at most M, then the RAM can in unit time perform simple manipulations (*e.g.*, arithmetic and indexing) on $c \log M$-bit words, for some small constant c. This model is motivated by the operation of computers encountered in practice: these can perform manipulations on word-sized operands in a small (one or two) number of machine cycles, and one or two machine words usually suffice to address the entire memory into which the data structure must fit. With this model which is stronger than the "pointer machine" model, we can represent the buckets in a way that permits efficient finger searches. In this case, the permutation that represents the sorted order in sets of a sufficiently small size may be represented by bit strings that fit into a single word. Operations on these bit strings can be performed in $O(1)$ time by using the bit string to index into a precomputed table that contains the result of the operation (this paradigm also appears in other places in the literature,

such as the "four Russians" boolean matrix multiplication algorithm [1] and in the linear time union-find algorithm of Gabow and Tarjan [7]). This is the fact that we use in:

Lemma 2 *For some sufficiently small constant c, if S is a set of at most $k \leq c \log M / \log \log M$ keys, there is a data structure that permits:*

- *Updates in constant time if a pointer to the point of insertion or deletion is known.*

- *Given a pointer to an key, search for an key a distance d away in $O(\log d)$ time.*

provided certain small tables are available precomputed.

PROOF. Let $k \leq c \log M / \log \log M$ for some sufficiently small constant $c > 0$. The data structure which will contain no more than k elements consists of a record r with 2 fields: an array $A[1..k]$ that contains pointers to keys, and an array $Perm[1..k]$, which is a *representation* of the permutation of the $A[i]$'s. $Perm[i]$, $1 \leq i \leq k$, contains an integer in the range $[0, i]$, which is 0 if $A[i]$ is nil, and if not, the rank of the item stored in $A[i]$ in the subset $\{key(A[1]), \ldots, key(A[i])\}$. That is:

$$Perm[i] = 0$$

if $A[i]$=nil, and

$$Perm[i] = |\{key(A[j]) : j \leq i \wedge key(A[j]) \leq key(A[i])\}|$$

otherwise.

We will assume that the keys are actually stored in a doubly linked list L of records. Each record k in L will store in addition to a key, a pointer to a record r, as well as a number i such that $r.A[i]$ contains a pointer to k. Since the keys are stored in L, the positions for insertion/deletion are actually pointers to the appropriate place in L.

To perform an insertion, we determine j such that $A[j]$ points to the key after which the new element is to be inserted (this information is stored in L) and the rank of the new key (from our knowledge of j and $Perm$), insert the new key in L, set $A[|S| + 1]$ to point to this new key, increment the size of S and update the $Perm$ array. To perform a deletion, we determine j such that $A[j]$ points to the deleted key and the rank of the deleted key, swap $A[j]$ and $A[|S|]$, set $A[|S|]$ to nil, delete the key from L, and alter the record pointed formerly by $A[|S|]$ to record the fact that $A[j]$ now has a pointer to it, decrement the size of S and update the $Perm$ array.

The following functions are useful:

UpdatePerm(Perm, r, op):
This updates the array $Perm$ when a key with rank r is inserted or deleted (this is specified by op). Returns the updated $Perm$ array.

GetRank(Perm, i): Returns the rank of the key pointed to by $A[i]$.

GetIndex(Perm, i): Returns a number j such that the key pointed to by $A[j]$ has rank i.

These functions can easily be computed in $O(k)$ time. Since we want to do better than this, we note that the contents of the $Perm$ array can be specified by $k\lceil \log k \rceil$ bits. This is less than $\log M$ if $c < 1$, and the array can be represented by the contents of a single word of memory. We will precompute all the above functions for all possible values of their arguments, and use the arguments to index into a table to obtain the values of the function. Since k is very small, the size of this table will be small in comparison to the maximum size of the data structure. (*E.g.*, the arguments to *UpdatePerm* can take at most $2k \cdot 2^{k\lceil \log k \rceil}$ different values, which is $O(M^{c_2})$, $c_2 < 1$, if c is small enough.)

It should be clear that by using the *Index* function, in time $O(\log d)$ we can search for a key at a distance d away. □

Now we represent each bucket of size $\Theta(\log^2 \hat{n})$ by a tree of height 3, with a branching factor of $\Theta(\log^{2/3} \hat{n})$. At each internal node we will store a set that consists of the maximum elements stored in the subtrees rooted at each of its children. The sets stored at the internal nodes are represented in the manner described in lemma 2 (see figure 3). In a manner similar to [5], we will maintain the bucket so that a node at height h has between $\Theta(\log^{2/3} \hat{n})^h$ leaves under it. In the case $h = 3$, the bucket rebalancing operations described previously ensure that the buckets always have size $\Theta(\log^2 \hat{n})$. Let $\beta = \log^{2/3} \hat{n}$. We will ensure the above for nodes at height $h = 1, 2$ by ensuring they have at least $\beta/2 - 1$ and at most $2\beta + 1$ children. If after an insertion occurs beneath a node r, we detect that it has more than 2β children, we create an additional node s that is linked to r but not to r's parent. If after a deletion we detect that a node s has less than $\beta/2$ children, we take a child of an adjacent sibling node and make it s's child, provided the sibling has a little over $\beta/2$ children. If both adjacent siblings have $\beta/2$ children then we delete s from its parent and attach it as an additional node to one of its ajdacent siblings, say r (this causes a deletion in s's parent). Define the *weight* of a node r, $w(r)$, to be $nchildren(r) + nchildren(s)/2$ if it has an additional node s, and $nchildren(r)$ otherwise. Any node r with an additional node s satisfies the following invariants:

$$3\beta/4 \le w(r) \le 2\beta \qquad (1)$$

$$0 < nchildren(s) < nchildren(r)$$

If an insertion is made under either r or s children are moved from r to s or vice versa in order to maintain these invariants. If this is not possible, then either $size(r) = size(s)$ or $size(s) = 0$: in the first case, we insert s as a sibling of r (causing an

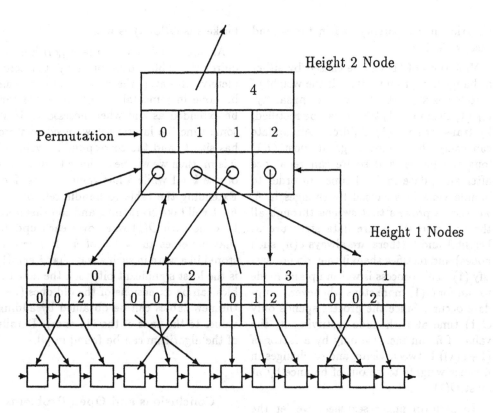

Figure 3: The Organization of Buckets

insertion in r's parent) and in the second case, we delete s.

Violations of (1) can be caused by either a change in $\hat{n}$ or an update. If the weight of a node r is at most $O(1)$ away from satisfying (1) then in $O(1)$ time it can be rectified, by transferring $O(1)$ children. An update can cause the weight to go at most $O(1)$ 'out of balance' and so we can rebalance after an update in $O(1)$ time. In order to handle violations caused by changes in $\hat{n}$, we start a process that sweeps through all the nodes in the entire data structure at height 1 and 2 (there are always $o(\hat{n})$ such nodes) and rectifies them if they do not satisfy (1). This process is woken up and made to run for $O(1)$ more steps whenever an update occurs. Since the process spends only $O(1)$ time at each node rectifying it, the value of $\hat{n}$ can increase only by a factor of $(1 + o(1))$ between visits, and so changes in $\hat{n}$ cause weights to go out of balance by at most $O(1)$.

To perform finger searches, we let the top-level data structure be a 2-3 tree with level links and parent pointers [10] (figure 1). We will assume that every node inside a bucket also has parent pointers. We can search within a bucket for a key a distance d away in several ways: for example, by finding the node that is the least common ancestor of the finger key f and the search key s in $O(1)$ time and then searching downward from this node. Let the path down to s in the bucket be s_1, s_2, s_3, and let d_1, d_2, d_3, respectively be the ranks of s_2 in s_1, s_3 in s_2 and s in s_3. The distance d between s and f must be at least $d_3 + d_2 \log^{2/3} \hat{n} + d_3 \log^{4/3} \hat{n}$. The time taken for the search is $c(\log d_1 + \log d_2 + \log d_3)$, which is no more than $c(\log(d_3 \log^{4/3} \hat{n})) \leq c \log d$, since $d_1, d_2 \leq \log^{2/3} \hat{n}$. Since we can find the bucket containing s in $O(\log b)$ time, where b is the number of buckets between the ones containing s and f (using the level-links), it is easy to show that the search time in case s and f are in different buckets is $O(\log d)$ as well.

As presented above, the algorithm requires the tables to be precomputed completely. However, the precomputation can be done incrementally, i.e., the table can be extended as and when necessary. If at some time the largest set we need to store has size k, and the corresponding value of $\hat{n}$ is m, then we will never have to store sets of size $k+1$ while $\hat{n}$ has value at most $2m$. Extending the table to handle sets of size $k+1$ will take $o(m)$ time, and can therefore be done with $O(1)$ work over each update that increases the value of $\hat{n}$. If $Perm$ is stored in a word in such a way that $Perm[1]$ is the least significant bit, then the new tables can be extensions of the old ones (i.e., the new tables can be obtained by adding values to the ends of the old ones). Details of the algorithm can be found in [4].

4 Conclusions and Open Problems

We have described a finger search tree that achieves constant update time when implemented on a RAM with logarithmic word size. This data structure is an improvement over the one of [12]: besides allowing for finger searches, it is also simpler, as it avoids having to periodically rebuild the entire data structure. We leave open the question of whether a constant update time finger search tree can be constructed on a weaker model (e.g., the pointer machine). If only *expected* time bounds are required then the randomized search trees of [2] satisfy the above requirements.

5 Acknowledgements

The work of the first author was supported by the National Science Foundation under grant CCR-8909667.

References

[1] A. V. Aho, J. E. Hopcroft, and J. D. Ullman. *The Design and Analysis of Computer Algorithms.* Addison-Wesley, 1974.

[2] C. Aragon and R. Seidel. Randomized search trees. In *Proc. 30th IEEE FOCS*, pages 540–545, 1989.

[3] M. Brown and R. Tarjan. Design and analysis of a data structure for representing sorted lists. *SIAM Journal of Computing*, 1980.

[4] P. Dietz and R. Raman. A constant update time finger search tree. Technical Report 321, University of Rochester Computer Science Department, 1989.

[5] P. Dietz and D. Sleator. Two algorithms for maintaining order in a list. In *Proc. 19th ACM STOC*, pages 365–372, 1987.

[6] J. Driscoll, N. Sarnak, D. Sleator, and R. Tarjan. Making data structures persistent. *Journal of Computer and System Science*, 38:86–124, 1989.

[7] H. N. Gabow and R. E. Tarjan. A linear-time algorithm for a special case of disjoint set union. *Journal of Computer and System Science*, 30:209–221, 1985.

[8] L. Guibas, E. McCreight, M. Plass, and J. Roberts. A new representation for sorted lists. In *Proc. 9th ACM STOC*, pages 49–60, 1977.

[9] D. Harel. Fast updates with a guaranteed time bound per update. Technical Report 154, University of California, Irvine, 1980.

[10] S. Huddleston and K. Mehlhorn. A new data structure for representing sorted lists. *Acta Informatica*, 17:157–184, 1982.

[11] S. R. Kosaraju. Localized search in sorted lists. In *Proc. 13th ACM STOC*, pages 62–69, 1981.

[12] C. Levcopolous and M. H. Overmars. A balanced search tree with O(1) worst-case update time. *Acta Informatica*, 26:269–278, 1988.

[13] M. Overmars. A $O(1)$ average time update scheme for balanced binary search trees. *Bull. EATCS*, pages 27–29, 1982.

[14] M. H. Overmars. *The design of dynamic data structures, LNCS 156.* Springer-Verlag, 1983.

[15] A. K. Tsakalidis. AVL-trees for localized search. *Information and Control*, 67:173–194, 1985.

Average Case Analysis of Algorithms using Matrix Recurrences

Ricardo A. Baeza-Yates

Depto. de Ciencias de la Computación
Universidad de Chile
Casilla 2777, Santiago, Chile
email: rbaeza@toqui.uchile.cl,
FAX: 56-2-712799

Gaston H. Gonnet

Dept. of Computer Science
University of Waterloo
Waterloo, Ontario,
Canada N2L 3G1
email: ghgonnet@dragon.uwaterloo.ca,
FAX: 1-519-888-4521 *

Abstract

We use matrix recurrences to analyze the expected behaviour of algorithms on trees. We apply this technique to the average case analysis of balanced search trees and digital trees. In particular we give the exact solution for a fringe analysis problem, a technique used for search trees, that was unknown before. This method also makes easier to solve some scalar recurrences.

Keywords: Analysis of algorithms, average case, search trees, digital trees, matrix recurrences.

1 Introduction

Solving recurrences is at the heart of analysis of algorithms. Classical introductions to the topic can be found in [12, 14, 8, 10]. However, matrix recurrences, as a topic, are only treated in differential equations books, and most of the time for very simple cases involving constant matrices (for example, see Hildebrand [11]).

There are several algorithms that naturally lead to matrix recurrences in search trees and digital trees. Also, scalar recurrences of high order, can be expressed as a matrix recurrence of lower order [11].

We propose a general method to solve matrix recurrences where all terms can be expressed as scalar functions of the independent variable and constant matrices. We also obtain the asymptotic behaviour of the solution.

We begin by giving the main ideas behind our method, followed by two applications: the solution of a fringe analysis type equation (from the expected behaviour of balanced search trees); and the expected complexity of some algorithms over tries (regular expression searching and partial match queries on a set of strings or a text).

2 Solving Matrix Recurrences

By using matrix algebra it is possible to simplify the analysis of a set of recurrence equations. For example, consider the following problem:

$$
\begin{aligned}
f_1(n) &= f_1(n/2) + f_2(n/2) + c_1 , \quad f_1(1) = 0 , \\
f_2(n) &= \alpha f_1(n/2) + f_2(n/2) + c_2 , \quad f_2(1) = 0 ,
\end{aligned}
$$

for n a power of 2 and α a real number. This recurrence looks difficult to solve.

*The work of the first author was also supported by an Ontario Graduate scholarship, and the second author by a Natural Sciences and Engineering Research Council of Canada Grant No. A-3353.

However, writing the problem as a matrix recurrence, we obtain

$$\vec{f}(n) = \mathbf{H}\vec{f}(n/2) + \vec{c}\,,$$

and this recurrence may be solved by simple iteration

$$\vec{f}(n) = \sum_{k=0}^{\log_2 n - 1} \mathbf{H}^k \vec{c}\,.$$

In many cases, this solution is not enough, and we need asymptotic results to obtain the complexity of the algorithm. Decomposing $\mathbf{H}$ in its Jordan normal form [9], namely

$$\mathbf{H} = \mathbf{P}\,\mathbf{J}\,\mathbf{P}^{-1}$$

where $\mathbf{J}$ is a block diagonal matrix of the form

$$\mathbf{J} = \begin{bmatrix} J_1 & 0 & .. & .. \\ 0 & J_2 & 0 & .. \\ .. & .. & .. & .. \\ .. & .. & 0 & J_t \end{bmatrix},$$

J_i is a $m_i \times m_i$ square matrix of the form

$$J_i = \begin{bmatrix} \lambda_i & 1 & 0 & .. \\ 0 & \lambda_i & 1 & 0 \\ .. & .. & .. & 1 \\ .. & .. & 0 & \lambda_i \end{bmatrix},$$

where each λ_i is an eigenvalue of $\mathbf{H}$ with multiplicity m_i, and $\mathbf{P}$ has as columns the respective eigenvectors. Note that λ_i may be a complex number. Hence, we have

$$\mathbf{H}^k = \mathbf{P}\mathbf{J}^k\mathbf{P}^{-1}$$

where $\mathbf{J}^k$ is the block diagonal matrix $[J_i^k]$, and each J_i^k is of the form [9]

$$J_i^k = \begin{bmatrix} \lambda_i^k & k\lambda_i^{k-1} & \frac{k(k-1)}{2}\lambda_i^{k-2} & .. & \binom{k}{m_i-1}\lambda_i^{k+1-m_i} \\ 0 & \lambda_i^k & k\lambda_i^{k-1} & .. & \binom{k}{m_i-2}\lambda_i^{k+2-m_i} \\ 0 & 0 & \lambda_i^k & .. & \binom{k}{m_i-3}\lambda_i^{k+3-m_i} \\ .. & .. & .. & .. & .. \\ .. & .. & .. & 0 & \lambda_i^k \end{bmatrix}.$$

Hence, we obtain the exact solution for $\vec{f}(n)$ as a function of the eigenvalues of $\mathbf{H}$, that is

$$\vec{f}(n) = \mathbf{P}\left(\sum_{k=0}^{\log_2 n - 1} \mathbf{J}^k\right)\mathbf{P}^{-1}\vec{c}\,.$$

Hence, we have sums of the form

$$M_j = \sum_{k=0}^{\log_2 n - 1} \binom{k}{j}\lambda^{k-j}\,.$$

In fact, we have hidden all the dependencies of the recurrences inside the matrices until this last step, where known summations that depend on the eigenvalues of $\mathbf{H}$ will have to be solved. We have

$$M_j = \begin{cases} O((\log_2 n)^j n^{\log_2 |\lambda|}) & |\lambda| > 1 \\ O((\log_2 n)^{j+1}) & |\lambda| = 1 \\ O(1) & |\lambda| < 1 \end{cases}.$$

If λ is complex, the constant of the main order term might be a periodic function with mean value and amplitude depending only on $|L|$, and with period of the form $\alpha_\lambda \log_2 n$, where α is a constant that depends on λ (this is the case in Example 3). Therefore the higher order term of $\bar{f}(n)$ is given by the eigenvalue of maximum absolute value and its multiplicity. In our example, the eigenvalues are $1 + \sqrt{\alpha}$ and $1 - \sqrt{\alpha}$. Then,

$$f_i(n) = \begin{cases} O(n^{\log_2(1+\sqrt{\alpha})}) & \alpha > 0 \\ O((\log_2 n)^2) & \alpha = 0 \\ O\left(\gamma\left(\arctan(\sqrt{|\alpha|})\log_2 n\right) n^{\log_2(1+\alpha^2)/2}\right) & \alpha < 0 \end{cases}$$

where $\gamma(x)$ is a periodic function with period 1 and constant mean value. If the exact value of the eigenvalues is unknown, we can bound them using characteristics of the matrix $\mathbf{H}$. For example, for non-negative matrices, the modulus of the maximal eigenvalue is bounded by the minimal sum of values in a row. In the example, $\min(2, 1 + \alpha)$ for $\alpha \geq 0$.

In summary, the main steps are

1. Express the set of recurrences as a matrix recurrence where all functions of the independent variable (n in the example) are scalars, and the matrices have constant entries.

2. Solve the recurrence using standard methods for scalar recurrences, but using matrix algebra (non-commutative multiplication, inverse instead of division, etc.).

3. Decompose all the matrices into their normal Jordan forms, expressing the solution as a function of the eigenvalues of the matrices.

4. Compute or bound the eigenvalues to obtain the asymptotic complexity of the solution.

3 Fringe Analysis

Fringe analysis was formally introduced by Yao in 1974 [16, 17] and was also discovered independently by Nakamura and Mizoguchi [15]. However, the first fringe type analysis was done by Knuth [13, Solution to problem 6.2.4.10, pages 679-680]. Fringe analysis is a method used to analyze search trees that considers only the bottom part or *fringe* of the tree. From the behaviour of the subtrees on the fringe, it is possible to obtain bounds on most complexity measures of the complete tree and some exact results.

Classical fringe analysis considers only insertions, and the model used is that the $n!$ possible permutations of the n keys used as input are equally likely. A search tree build under this model is called a *random* tree. This is equivalent to say that the n-th insertion has the same probability to fall in any of the $n + 1$ leaves of the tree.

The theory of fringe analysis was formalized in Eisenbarth *et al.* [6]. The fringe of the tree is defined in terms of a finite collection C of trees. A collection C is *closed* if the effect of an insertion only depends in the subtree of the fringe in where is performed, and produces one or more members of the same collection.

Type 1   Type 2

Figure 1: 2-3 tree fringe collection of height one

Example 1. Figure 1 shows a tree collection that defines a fringe of height one in a 2-3 tree, while figure 2 shows a 2-3 tree and the fringe corresponding to this collection. The composition of the fringe can be described by the number of subtrees of each type [17], or by the probability that a randomly chosen leaf belongs to each member in C [6]. An insertion in a type I subtree produces a type II subtree, while an insertion in a type II subtree produces two type I subtrees. This process defines a Markov chain

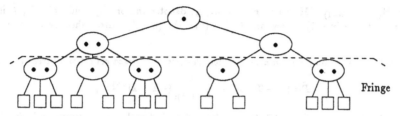

Figure 2: A 2-3 tree and its fringe of height one

[6]. Let n be the number of keys in the tree, $A_i(n)$ be the expected number of subtrees of type i in the fringe, L_i the number of leaves in type i, and

$$p_i(n) = \frac{A_i(n)L_i}{n+1}$$

be the probability of a leaf belonging to a subtree of type i in a random 2-3 tree with n keys. Then,

$$A_1(n) = A_1(n-1) - \frac{2A_1(n)}{n} + 2\frac{2A_2(n)}{n} \quad \text{and}$$
$$A_2(n) = A_2(n-1) - \frac{3A_2(n)}{n} + \frac{2A_1(n)}{n} \quad .$$

Using $p_i(n)$ and matrix notation we have

$$\vec{P}(n) = (\mathbf{I} + \frac{1}{n+1}\mathbf{H})\vec{P}(n-1) ,$$

where $\mathbf{I}$ is the identity matrix and $\mathbf{H}$ is called the *transition* matrix, given by

$$\mathbf{H} = \begin{bmatrix} -3 & 4 \\ 3 & -4 \end{bmatrix} .$$

By using the condition $p_1(n) + p_2(n) = 1$ we obtain $\vec{P}(n) = [4/7, 3/7]^T$ for $n \geq 6$. $\square$

In general, $\mathbf{H} = \mathbf{H_2} - \mathbf{H_1}$ where $\mathbf{H_2}$ represents the transitions from one type to another type, that is, h_{2ij} is the the probability that an insertion in type j produces one or more subtrees of type i times the number of leaves of type i created; and $\mathbf{H_1} = \text{diag}(L_i) + \mathbf{I}$ represents the leaves lost by each type after an insertion plus one. It is not difficult to see that $det(\mathbf{H}) = 0$.

A fringe analysis is *connected* [6], if there exist $\mathbf{H_i}$ such that $det(\mathbf{H_i}) \neq 0$, where $\mathbf{H_i}$ is the matrix $\mathbf{H}$ with the i-th row and i-th column deleted.

The solution to a connected fringe analysis is given by the following theorem:

THEOREM 3.1

$$\vec{P}(n) = \vec{x} + O(n^{Re(\lambda_2)}) ,$$

where $\vec{x}$ is the solution to $\mathbf{H}\vec{x} = 0$, normalized such that $\sum x_i = 1$, and λ_2 is the second largest eigenvalue in absolute value (the largest eigenvalue is always 0 with multiplicity 1), with $Re(\lambda_2) < 0$ [6]. ∎

In many cases, it is possible to use the structure of $\mathbf{H}$ to simplify the solution of the system of equations [4]. In the following paragraphs we give the exact solution of the recurrence for all n, and we show that the second order term also depends on the multiplicity of λ_2.

We start from the matrix recurrence equation

$$\vec{P}(n) = (\mathbf{I} + \frac{1}{n+1}\mathbf{H})\vec{P}(n-1) .$$

Let m be the dimension of the recurrence. Because the rank of $\mathbf{H}$ is $m-1$, we include the condition that $\sum_i p_i(n) = 1$, to obtain the following equation ($\vec{P}$ has now one component less)

$$\vec{P}(n) = (\mathbf{I} + \frac{1}{n+1}\mathbf{T})\vec{P}(n-1) + \frac{1}{n+1}\vec{F} ,$$

where $\mathbf{T} = \mathbf{H}_{(m-1)\times(m-1)} - \mathbf{H}'$ where $\mathbf{H}_{(m-1)\times(m-1)}$ denotes the principal minor of H, $\vec{F}$ is the last column of $\mathbf{H}$ up to the $(m-1)$-th row, and $\mathbf{H}'$ is a $(m-1)\times(m-1)$ matrix where every column is equal to $\vec{F}$.

THEOREM 3.2 *The solution for a connected fringe analysis of a closed collection of trees is given by*

$$\vec{P}(n) = -\mathbf{T}^{-1}\vec{F} + \frac{(-1)^{n+1}}{(n+1)!}(-\mathbf{T}-\mathbf{I})^{n+1}\vec{C} ,$$

where $\mathbf{T}^{\underline{n}} = (\mathbf{T}-(n-1)\mathbf{I})\cdots(\mathbf{T}-\mathbf{I})\mathbf{T}$ denotes descendent factorials over matrices, and with $\vec{C}$ obtained from the initial condition

$$\vec{P}(n_0) = [1,0,0,...,0]^T ,$$

where n_0 is the number of elements in the smallest subtree type of the fringe collection.

Proof: Introducing the generating function

$$\vec{P}(z) = \sum_{n\geq 0} \vec{P}(n)z^n ,$$

in the matrix recurrence, we obtain the following first order non-linear differential equation

$$\frac{d\vec{P}(z)}{dz} = \left(\frac{2z-1}{z(1-z)}\mathbf{I} + \frac{1}{1-z}\mathbf{T}\right)\vec{P}(z) + \frac{1}{z(1-z)^2}\vec{F} ,$$

whose solution is

$$\vec{P}(z) = \frac{1}{z}e^{-(\mathbf{T}+\mathbf{I})\ln(1-z)}\vec{C} - \frac{1}{z(1-z)}\mathbf{T}^{-1}\vec{F} ,$$

where $\vec{C}$ is obtained from the initial condition.

For $n \geq n_0$, we have

$$\vec{P}(n) = [z^n]\vec{P}(z) = -\mathbf{T}^{-1}\vec{F} + \sum_{k\geq 0}(-\mathbf{T}-\mathbf{I})^k[z^{n+1}]\frac{\ln^k(1-z)}{k!}\vec{C} ,$$

where $[z^n]P(z)$ denotes the coefficient in z^n of $P(z)$. But

$$[z^n]\frac{\ln^k(1-z)}{k!} = \frac{(-1)^n}{n!}S_n^{(k)} ,$$

for $n \geq k$ where $S_n^{(k)}$ denotes Stirling numbers of the first kind [12]. Therefore, for $n \geq n_0$

$$\vec{P}(n) = -\mathbf{T}^{-1}\vec{F} + \frac{(-1)^{n+1}}{(n+1)!}\sum_{k=0}^{n+1}S_{n+1}^{(k)}(-\mathbf{T}-\mathbf{I})^k\vec{C} ,$$

or [12]

$$\vec{P}(n) = -\mathbf{T}^{-1}\vec{F} + \frac{(-1)^{n+1}}{(n+1)!}(-\mathbf{T}-\mathbf{I})^{n+1}\vec{C} .$$

■

Example 2. In Example 1, we have $\vec{P}(1) = [1,0]$, $T = -7$, $F = 4$ and $C = 1/35$, obtaining

$$P(z) = \frac{4}{7z(1-z)} + \frac{(1-z)^6}{35z} ,$$

or

$$p_1(n) = \frac{4}{7} - \frac{(-1)^n}{35}\binom{6}{n+1} .$$

Note that the second term is 0 for $n > 5$. □

The next step is to obtain the asymptotic behaviour of the solution. Let $\mathbf{R} = -\mathbf{T} - \mathbf{I}$. We want the asymptotic value of

$$\vec{\epsilon}(n) = \frac{(-1)^{n+1}}{(n+1)!}\sum_{k=0}^{n+1}S_{n+1}^{(k)}\mathbf{R}^k\vec{C}$$

THEOREM 3.3 *Asymptotically, every component of $\bar{e}(n)$ is*

$$O(n^{Re(\lambda_1)} \log^{m-1} n) \,,$$

where λ_1 is the eigenvalue of $\mathbf{T}$ with largest real component, and m is its multiplicity. Note that λ_1 is equal to the the the second largest eigenvalue of $\mathbf{H}$ and that $Re(\lambda_1) < 0$.

Proof: We decompose $\mathbf{R}$ in its upper normal Jordan form [9]

$$\mathbf{R} = \mathbf{P} \, \mathbf{J} \, \mathbf{P}^{-1} \,.$$

Then, we obtain

$$\bar{e}(n) \; = \; \mathbf{P}\frac{(-1)^{n+1}}{(n+1)!} \sum_{k=0}^{n+1} S_{n+1}^{(k)} \mathbf{J}^k \mathbf{P}^{-1} \vec{C} \,.$$

Therefore, we have summations of the form

$$M_j \; = \; \frac{(-1)^{n+1}}{(n+1)!} \sum_{k=0}^{n+1} S_{n+1}^{(k)} \binom{k}{j} \lambda^{k-j} \,.$$

By using a well known combinatorial relation [12] we have

$$M_0 = (-1)^{n+1} \binom{\lambda}{n+1} \,.$$

From Eisenbarth *et al.* [6] we know that $Re(\lambda) > 0$ for λ an eigenvalue of $-\mathbf{T}$. If λ is an integer we have $M_0 = 0$ for $n \geq \lambda$. If λ is not an integer (that is, λ is real or complex), we have [12]

$$M_0 = (-1)^{n+1} \binom{\lambda}{n+1} = \binom{n-\lambda-1}{-\lambda-1} = \frac{\Gamma(n-\lambda)}{\Gamma(-\lambda)\Gamma(n+1)} \,.$$

Therefore, asymptotically, we have

$$M_0 = \frac{n^{-(\lambda+1)}}{\Gamma(-\lambda)} \; + \; O(n^{-\lambda-2})$$

(see [1] for details about the Γ function).

Analogously, we obtain

$$M_j = \left((\Psi(n-\lambda) - \Psi(-\lambda))^j + O(1/n)\right) M_0 = O(M_0 \log^j n) \,,$$

where $\Psi(x) = \frac{d}{dx}(\ln \Gamma(x)) = \ln n \; + \; O(1)$ [1].

But if λ is an eigenvalue of $\mathbf{T}$, then $-(\lambda+1)$ is an eigenvalue of $-\mathbf{T} - \mathbf{I}$. Then, we can state that every component of $\bar{e}(n)$ is

$$O(n^{Re(\lambda_1)} \log^{m-1} n) \,,$$

where λ_1 is the eigenvalue of $\mathbf{T}$ with largest real component, and m is its multiplicity. ∎

In all the analyses that appear in the literature, the multiplicity of the second eigenvalue is 1. However, in general this may be not true.

Example 3. For the second order analysis of 2-3 trees [17, 6] (a seven type collection), the second eigenvalue of $\mathbf{H}$ is $-6.55 + 6.25i$, and then, the order of each component in $\bar{e}(n)$ is proportional to

$$99.01 \, \cos(6.25 \ln n) n^{-6.55} \; + \; O(n^{-7.55}) \,.$$

Note that the periodic term has logarithmic period. □

4 Algorithms on Tries

The analysis of several algorithms on tries can be expressed by matrix recurrence equations. Examples are the simulation of finite automata over a binary trie [2] and partial match queries in k-d tries [7]. Here, we extend both cases to an alphabet of size σ (that is, σ-tries). A σ-trie is a σ-ary digital tree, which each node has a descendant for every symbol of a finite alphabet of size σ.

One algorithm to search what strings are members of the language defined by a given regular expression, is to simulate the corresponding deterministic finite automaton over the trie built from the set of strings. The main steps of the algorithm are [2]:

1. Convert the regular expression passed as a query into a minimized DFA without outgoing transitions from final states (see justification in step 3).

2. Simulate the DFA on the σ-trie from all strings. That is, associate the root of the tree with the initial state, and, for any internal node associated with state i, associate its k-th descendant with state $j = \delta(i, x_k)$ where δ is the transition function of the DFA and x_k is the k-th symbol of the alphabet.

3. For every node of the trie associated with a final state, accept the whole subtree and halt the search in that subtree. (For this reason, we do not need outgoing transitions in final states).

4. On reaching an external node, run the remainder of the automaton on the single string determined by this external node.

It is shown in [2] that the expected number of internal nodes visited by the automaton starting from a non-final state i, in a σ-trie of n random infinite strings can be expressed as

$$N_i(n) = 1 + \frac{1}{\sigma^n} \sum_{n_1 + \cdots + n_\sigma = n} \frac{n!}{j_1! \cdots j_\sigma!} (N_{j_1}(n_1) + \cdots + N_{j_\sigma}(n_\sigma)) \quad (n > 1)$$

where $j_k = \delta(i, x_k)$ and x_k is the k-th symbol of the alphabet. This is similar to the analysis for the expected number of nodes in σ-tries [13]. For final states we have $N_f(n) = 1$ and for undefined states we have $N_{undef}(n) = 0$ for all n. The initial conditions are $N_i(0) = N_i(1) = 0$.

Introducing exponential generating functions in the above equation, that is

$$N_i(z) = \sum_{n \geq 0} N_i(n) \frac{z^n}{n!}$$

we obtain

$$N_i(z) = e^{z/\sigma} (N_{j_1}(z/\sigma) + \cdots + N_{j_\sigma}(z/\sigma)) + e^z - 1 - z$$

Writing all the equations as a matrix functional equation, we have

$$\vec{N}(z) = e^{z/\sigma} \mathbf{H} \vec{N}(z/\sigma) + f(z) \vec{F}$$

where $f(z) = e^z - 1 - z$ and $\mathbf{H}$ is the incidence matrix of the automaton (that is, an $s \times s$ matrix where s is the number of states in the DFA and h_{ij} is the number of transitions from state i to state j, with $h_{ij} = 0$ if i is a final state) and $\vec{F}$ be a constant vector such that F_i is 1 for all i. The initial state is labelled 1.

This functional equation may be solved formally by iteration [7] obtaining

$$\vec{N}(z) = \sum_{k \geq 0} e^{z(1 - 1/\sigma^k)} f(z/\sigma^k) \mathbf{H}^k \vec{F}$$

From here, it is easy to obtain $\vec{N}(n)/n!$ by computing $[z^n]\vec{N}(z)$ using the series expansion of e^z. Then, we have

$$\vec{N}(n) = \sum_{k \geq 0} \tau_{n,k} \mathbf{H}^k \vec{F}$$

where

$$\tau_{n,k} = 1 - \left(1 - \frac{1}{\sigma^k}\right)^n - \frac{n}{\sigma^k}\left(1 - \frac{1}{\sigma^k}\right)^{n-1} .$$

The next step, it is to obtain the asymptotic value of $\vec{N}(n)$. Decomposing $\mathbf{H}$ in its upper normal Jordan form [9], and following the same steps as before, we have

$$\vec{N}(n) = \sum_{k \geq 0} \tau_{n,k} \mathbf{H}^k \vec{F} = \mathbf{P} \left(\sum_{k \geq 0} \tau_{n,k} \mathbf{J}^k\right) \mathbf{P}^{-1} \vec{F} .$$

Then, similarly to Section 2, we have summations of the form

$$M_j = \sum_{k \geq 0} \tau_{n,k} \binom{k}{j} \lambda^{k-j} .$$

The convergence of M_j is guaranteed by the fact that, for fixed n and large k we have

$$\tau_{n,k} \approx 1 - e^{-n/\sigma^k} - \frac{n}{\sigma^k} e^{-(n-1)/\sigma^k} = O\left(\frac{n^2}{\sigma^{2k}}\right) .$$

The asymptotic value of M_0 for $\sigma = 2$ has already been obtained in Flajolet and Puech [7]. In a similar manner ($\lambda > 1$) we obtain

$$M_0 = \gamma(\log_\sigma n) n^{\log_\sigma \lambda} + O(1) ,$$

where $\gamma(x)$ is a periodic function of x with period 1, mean value depending only on λ, and with small amplitude. Similarly, for $\lambda > 1$

$$M_j = \frac{\gamma(\log_\sigma n)}{j!} \left(\frac{\log_\sigma n}{\lambda}\right)^j n^{\log_\sigma \lambda} + O(M_{j-1}) .$$

If $\lambda = 1$, we have $M_j = O((\log_\sigma n)^{j+1})$. Then, for λ_i we have that the main order term of $N_i(n)$ is

$$\gamma_i(\log_\sigma n) (\log_\sigma n)^{m_i - 1} n^{\log_\sigma \lambda_i} .$$

The higher order term of $N_1(n)$ is given by $\lambda_1 = \max_i(|\lambda_i|)$. In the case that there are more than one eigenvalue with the same modulus, we select λ_1 to be the one with largest multiplicity.

In [2] is shown that $1 \leq \lambda_1 < 2$ for any regular expression when $\sigma = 2$ and there are no transitions from final states, hence the number of visited nodes is sublinear in n. Analogously, it is possible to prove that $1 \leq \lambda_1 < \sigma$ for our case. A similar analysis is done to conclude that the expected number of comparisons performed by the same DFA on a single string is bounded by a constant independent of n [2]. Therefore, the total execution time of the DFA is proportional to $N_i(n)$.

Example 4. Let A be the deterministic finite automaton of the regular expression $((0+2)(1+0))^*1((1+2)(1+0))^*0$ over a ternary alphabet (see figure 3).

The incidence matrix for A (1 is the initial state, and 5 is the final state) is

$$\mathbf{H} = \begin{bmatrix} 0 & 2 & 1 & 0 & 0 \\ 2 & 0 & 0 & 0 & 0 \\ 0 & 0 & 0 & 2 & 1 \\ 0 & 0 & 2 & 0 & 0 \\ 0 & 0 & 0 & 0 & 0 \end{bmatrix}$$

The eigenvalues of $\mathbf{H}$ are 2 and -2 (each one with multiplicity 2), and 0. Thus, the expected number of visited nodes is

$$N_1(n) = \gamma(\log_2 n) \log_2 n \, n^{\log_2 2} + O(n^{\log_2 2}) = O(\log_2 n \, n^{0.63}) .$$

$\square$

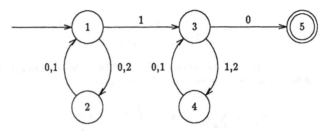

Figure 3: Minimal state deterministic finite automaton
for $((0+2)(1+0))^*1((1+2)(1+0))^*0$

In the case of partial match queries in k-d-tries of Flajolet and Puech [7], the analysis is similar to an automaton with a single cycle of length k. Namely, a partial match query over k attributes, consists in a string of length k, where some of the attributes are specified and others are unspecified. The attributes are considered to be encoded using σ symbols, and the keys stored in a σ-trie, such that the branching is decided cyclically in one of the k attributes, like in a k-d tree [5].

In this case, the recurrences can be expressed as a single one, and in [7] a scalar recurrence is solved. We use our technique to simplify the analysis. We see the partial match query as a regular expression with a single cycle where we follow one descendant if the attribute is specified, or all the descendants if the attribute is unspecified. Let u be the number of unspecified attributes. Then, the matrix $\mathbf{H}$ consists only in one upper diagonal $(H_{1,2}, \ldots, H_{k-1,k})$, plus one entry $(H_{k,1})$, where u elements have the value σ, and $k-u$ the value 1. Hence, there is a real eigenvalue λ of maximal modulus (Perron-Frobenius theorem [9]) of value $\lambda_1 = \sigma^{u/k}$ and multiplicity 1.

Using the solution given for the general automaton, with the only difference that the period of the oscillating function is divided by the number of attributes k (because we have to inspect k levels, one per attribute, to discriminate one set of keys), we have that the expected number of comparisons (visited nodes) to search the query is

$$C_n = \gamma \left(\frac{\log_\sigma n}{k} \right) n^{u/k} .$$

Therefore, the only difference between the binary case and the case $\sigma > 2$ is that the period of γ decreases when σ increases.

5 Conclusions

We have presented a solution to a class of matrix recurrences. This solution is applicable to the average case analysis of balanced search trees and digital trees. The technique used here only applies when the independent variable (for example n) appears in scalar factors, and not inside matrices. It is possible to apply this technique to other related problems, like fringe analysis with unknown probabilities of events outside the fringe (weakly closed collections), like in AVL trees [3].

References

[1] A. Apostolico and W. Szpankowski. Self-alignments in words and their applications. Technical Report CSD-TR-732, Department of Computer Science, Purdue University, West Lafayette, IN 47907, 1987.

[2] R. Baeza-Yates and G.H. Gonnet. Efficient text searching of regular expressions. In G. Ausiello, M. Dezani-Ciancaglini, and S. Ronchi Della Rocca, editors, *ICALP'89, Lecture Notes in Computer Science 372*, pages 46–62, Stresa, Italy, July 1989. Springer-Verlag. Also as UW Centre for the New OED Report, OED-89-01, Univ. of Waterloo, April, 1989.

[3] R. Baeza-Yates, G.H. Gonnet, and N. Ziviani. Expected behaviour analysis of AVL trees. Department of Computer Science, University of Waterloo, 1987.

[4] R.A. Baeza-Yates and P.V. Poblete. Reduction of the transition matrix of a fringe analysis and its application to the analysis of 2-3 trees. In *5th International Conference in Computer Science*, pages 56–82, Santiago, Chile, 1985. (in Spanish).

[5] J.L. Bentley and J.H. Friedman. Data structures for range searching. *ACM C. Surveys*, 11(4):397–409, Dec 1979.

[6] B. Eisenbarth, N. Ziviani, Gaston H. Gonnet, Kurt Mehlhorn, and Derick Wood. The theory of fringe analysis and its application to 2-3 trees and B-trees. *Information and Control*, 55(1):125–174, Oct 1982.

[7] P. Flajolet and C. Puech. Tree structures for partial match retrieval. *J.ACM*, 33:371–407, 1986.

[8] Z. Galil and K. Park. An improved algorithm for approximate string matching. In *ICALP'89*, Stressa, Italy, 1989.

[9] F.R. Gantmacher. *The Theory of Matrices (2 Vols)*. Chelsea Publishing Company, New York, 1959.

[10] R. Graham, D. Knuth, and O. Patashnik. *Concrete Mathematics*. Addison-Wesley, Reading, Mass., 1989.

[11] F Hildebrand. *Finite-Difference Equations and Simulations*. Prentice-Hall, Englewood Cliffs, New Jersey, 1968.

[12] D.E. Knuth. *The Art of Computer Programming: Fundamental Algorithms*, volume 1. Addison-Wesley, Reading, Mass., 1969.

[13] D.E. Knuth. *The Art of Computer Programming: Sorting and Searching*, volume 3. Addison-Wesley, Reading, Mass., 1973.

[14] G. Lueker. Some techniques for solving recurrences. *ACM Compuying Surveys*, 12(4):419–436, 1980.

[15] T. Nakamura and T. Mizoguchi. An analysis of storage utilization factor in block split data structuring scheme. In *VLDB*, volume 4, pages 489–495, Berlin, Sep 1978.

[16] A.C-C. Yao. On random 3-2 trees. Technical Report UIUCDCS-R-74-679, Departament of Computer Science, University of Illinois at Urbana, Oct 1974.

[17] A.C-C. Yao. On random 2-3 trees. *Acta Informatica*, 9(2):159–170, 1978.

Finding Two-Tree-Factor Elements of Tableau-Defined Monoids in Time O(n^3)

Alois P. Heinz

Institut für Informatik, Universität Freiburg
Rheinstraße 10–12, D-7800 Freiburg

Abstract

We consider the problem of finding elements in tableau-defined monoids. The solution of this problem is important to the minimization of restricted relational database queries. Although the problem has been shown to be $\mathcal{NP}$-complete in general, many polynomial-time algorithms have been proposed for some subclasses of the general problem. The contribution of this paper is a new algorithm that finds elements with two-tree-factors in time O(n^3). The number of elements that can be found in polynomial time is significantly increased by our algorithm as compared with the algorithms known so far.

Key words: relational database, relational algebra, query optimization, tableaux.

1   Introduction

Let F be a set and let $\times: F^2 \to F$ be a function. Then the pair $M = (F, \times)$ is called a monoid if $\times$ is associative and a unity element $1 \in F$ exists with $1 \times f = f = f \times 1$ for all $f \in F$. So, if $X_n = \{1, 2, \ldots, n\}$ and F_n is the set of all mappings of X_n into X_n, then $M_n = (F_n, \circ)$ is a monoid, where $\circ$ is the composition of mappings and the unity element is the identity mapping I_n. In the monoid $M_n = (F_n, \circ)$ the structure of the underlying set F_n is well-known and the number of elements in F_n is $|F_n| = n^n$.

In this paper we consider submonoids of M_n that are defined through a data structure called tableau. Tableaux give certain constraints on the elements that can belong to a submonoid of M_n. Although a tableau T for M_n can be defined in space polynomial in n, it is $\mathcal{NP}$-complete to decide whether the submonoid M_T belonging to T contains any elements other than I_n.

The main interest in most applications is to find one element $f \in M_T$ such that the image $f(X_n)$ is minimal. If an arbitrary $g \in M_T$ with $g(X_n) \neq X_n$ can be found, the problem can be reduced to the simpler problem of finding elements in a submonoid $M_{T'}$ of M_m with $m = |g(X_n)|$ by reducing the tableau T to the tableau T'. And, if a tableau can be reduced, this corresponds to an element $f \in F_n$ with $f \neq I_n$. Polynomial-time algorithms for this problem can only find elements $f \in M_T$ obeying certain restrictions, or they can find all elements in subclasses of M_n that are defined by special classes of tableaux. So they can serve as heuristics for the general problem.

Tableaux were introduced by Aho, Sagiv and Ullman [3] as a representative for restricted relational database queries. They showed that an equivalent tableau for a given query can be computed in polynomial time and that minimization of tableaux corresponds to the optimization of queries. Several algorithms for translating tableaux back to queries have been published, including a linear-time algorithm [5,6]. $\mathcal{NP}$-completeness results for tableaux were given in [3] with a reduction of the 3-satisfiability problem and by Sagiv and Yannakakis [8] with a reduction of the exact cover problem.

	A_1	A_2	A_3	A_4	A_5	A_6	A_7	A_8
w_1	a_1	·	·	·	b_1	·	·	b_4
w_2	·	a_2	·	·	b_1	b_2	·	b_4
w_3	·	·	a_3	·	·	b_2	b_3	b_4
w_4	·	·	·	a_4	·	·	b_3	b_4
w_5	a_1	a_2	·	·	·	a_6	a_7	a_8
w_6	·	a_2	a_3	·	a_5	·	a_7	a_8
w_7	·	·	a_3	a_4	a_5	a_6	·	a_8

$$(v_1, v_2) \in R \Leftrightarrow v_1 \notin \{a_1, \ldots\} \text{ or } v_2 \in \{a_1, \ldots\}$$

Figure 1: Tableau T_1

Aho, Sagiv and Ullman [2] first showed that the subclass of so-called simple tableaux can be reduced in time $O(n^4)$. We will see that this corresponds to the problem of finding one-tree-factor elements in tableau-defined monoids. Sagiv [7] later found quadratic-time algorithms for three tableau classes, including the class of simple tableaux.

The contribution of this paper is a new algorithm that works for a proper superclass of simple tableaux. And the ratio of the number of elements in M_n that are tested for membership in a tableau-defined monoid by our algorithm to the same number for the simple-tableau algorithms is exponential in n. Our algorithm runs in time $O(n^3)$, which is only a factor of n more than Sagiv's algorithm for simple tableaux.

The structure of the paper is as follows. The next section contains basic definitions and some properties of tableaux and their monoids. In section 3 we first derive some further properties of tableaux. Then we present our algorithm and prove its time complexity. Section 4 summarizes our results.

2 Basic Definitions and Properties

Tableaux can be defined in many different ways depending on the application. Informally, a tableau is a kind of matrix with some additional information. For our requirements it is sufficient to define: A *Tableau* of *degree* n, $T = \langle W, A, V, p, R \rangle$, consists of three finite sets, the *rows* $W = \{w_1, \ldots, w_n\}$, *columns* $A = \{A_1, \ldots, A_m\}$ and *variables* $V = \{a_1, \ldots, b_1, \ldots\}$ and a function p and a relation R.

The function p: $W \times A \to V$ gives the variable v at position (w_i, A_j) such that $p(w_i, A_j) = p(w_k, A_l) \Rightarrow j = l$. So, each variable must occur in only one column. The relation $R \subseteq V \times V$ is reflexive and transitive and $(a_i, b_j) \notin R$. R embodies a set of constraints, as will be described later in detail. We assume that the number of columns m is a constant and that the function p and the test of membership in the relation R can be computed in constant time. Figure 1 shows T_1 as an example of a tableau of degree 7. Variables that appear only once in the tableau and are not in the set $\{a_1, \ldots\}$ are printed just as dots.

A Tableau T of degree n defines a submonoid M_T of M_n in a very natural way. A function f: $X_n \to X_n$ is said to be *consistent* with tableau T, iff to all $w_i, w_k \in W$ and $A_j \in A$ the following rules apply:

c1) $p(w_i, A_j) R p(w_{f(i)}, A_j)$

c2) $p(w_i, A_j) = p(w_k, A_j) \Rightarrow p(w_{f(i)}, A_j) = p(w_{f(k)}, A_j)$

So, function f is consistent with T, iff f, regarded as a mapping of the set of rows into the set of rows, unambiguously induces a mapping of the set of variables into the set of variables, that meets the

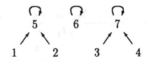

Figure 2: Function f_1, consistent with T_1

definition of R. These functions are called *containment mappings* in the literature. Figure 2 shows function f_1, the only function besides I_7 that is consistent with T_1.

Now, because the composition of containment mappings yields another containment mapping, it is easy to see that the set of functions, that are consistent with T, together with o define a submonoid of M_n, that we denote $\widetilde{M_T}$. In the next step we can realize, that it is sufficient to consider only idempotent elements, for which $f = f^2 = f^3 = \ldots$, because we are only interested in functions f with minimal $|f(X_n)|$, and for each $g \in M_n$ there is a number l_0 such that g^{l_0} is idempotent and $g^{l_0}(X_n) \subseteq g(X_n)$. The set of idempotent elements of $\widetilde{M_T}$ formes a submonoid of $\widetilde{M_T}$ that we denote M_T.

Each idempotent f is isomorphic to a forest of rooted labeled trees of height not exeeding one, where the roots are the only cyclic nodes. And it is easy to see, that the number U_n of these trees is

$$U_n = \sum_{k=0}^{n} \binom{n}{k}(n-k)^k,$$

if we consider, that each of the k nodes which are not roots, can have one of the remaining $(n-k)$ nodes as their root. Harris and Schoenfeld [4] gave an estimate for U_n,

$$U_n \approx \frac{1}{\sqrt{\log n}} \, e^{n\{\log n - \log\log n + 1/(\log n + 1)\}},$$

which shows that this number is more than exponential in n.

We shall now give another way to compute the numbers U_n, that will help us to estimate the number of elements of M_n that can possibly be found in M_T by polynomial algorithms:

Theorem 1 *The number of forests of rooted labeled trees of height not exeeding one with n nodes is*

$$U_n = \sum_{k=0}^{\lfloor n/2 \rfloor} \binom{n}{k} k! \, S_{n-k+1}^{(k+1)}$$

Proof: Consider the cases, where exacty k nodes are roots of a tree with height one. Add a special *decision element* d to the set of the remaining $(n-k)$ elements. Then $S_{n-k+1}^{(k+1)}$ is the number of partitions of this new set into the union of $(k+1)$ non-empty disjoint subsets, where the $S_i^{(j)}$ are the Stirling numbers of the second kind. Now make the nodes in the subset with the extra element d to roots of trees with only one node and make the nodes of each of the other k subsets to leaves of one tree of height one. □

For a submonoid M of M_n, we call an element $f \in M$ a *k-tree* element, if in the corresponding graph exactly k nodes are roots of trees with height greater or equal one. In this case, of course, for all numbers l, f^l is a k-tree element. And we say, an element $f \in M$ is a *k-tree-factor element*, iff exist g, $h \in M$ such that $f = g \circ h$ and g is a k'-tree element with $0 < k' \le k$. From figures 1 and 2 we derive that, in our example, f_1 is a 2-tree element and a 2-tree-factor element in M_{T_1}, but it is not a 1-tree-factor element, because in M_{T_1} it cannot be decomposed into factors, one beeing a 1-tree element.

The so-called simple tableau algorithms are able to detect all 1-tree-factor elements of tableau-defined monoids. Using the argumentation from theorem 1 and the property [1]

$$S_n^{(k)} = \frac{1}{k!} \sum_{j=1}^{k} (-1)^{k-j} \binom{k}{j} j^n,$$

we can derive the number of idempotent elements of M_n that are tested for membership in some M_T by these algorithms:

$$\mathcal{K}_n^{(1)} = \binom{n}{1} 1! \, S_n^{(2)} = n \left(2^{n-1} - 1\right)$$

Our algorithm, which is proposed in the next section, can also detect two-tree elements. Their number in M_n, according to theorem 1, is given by:

$$\mathcal{K}_n^{(2)} = \binom{n}{2} 2! \, S_{n-1}^{(3)} = \binom{n}{2} \left(3^{n-2} - 2^{n-1} + 1\right)$$

So, the total number of factors that will be tested by the new algorithm, is $\mathcal{K}_n^{(1)} + \mathcal{K}_n^{(2)}$ and the ratio of this number to $\mathcal{K}_n^{(1)}$ is exponential in n.

3 The Algorithm and its Analysis

We do not give an exact definition of a data structure for tableaux here. But we assume that the rows and the variables are stored in list-like data structures and that for each row and for each variable in these lists a constant amount of information can be stored. Further we assume that there are pointers from each occurrence of a variable in a row into the list for the variables. And for each variable in the list of variables another list can be accessed that points to the rows in which this variable occurs.

In a preprocessing step for the algorithm we build an auxiliary data structure that we call *cover table*. This is a $n \times n$ matrix that contains the values of the *cover function* $C: W \rightarrow \mathcal{P}(W)$, which is defined as follows:

$$C(w_i) = \{w_j | (\forall A_k \in A) p(w_i, A_k) Rp(w_j, A_k)\} \setminus \{w_i\}.$$

So, $C(w_i)$ contains all the rows with the exeption of w_i to which w_i could possibly be mapped according to rule c1) for consistent functions. Row w_i is said to be *covered* by $C(w_i) \cup \{w_i\}$. The cover table stores value 1 at position (i,j) if $w_j \in C(w_i)$ and value 0 otherwise. It is evident, that the cover table can be computed in time $O(n^2)$.

After building the cover table, the algorithm tests for each pair $w_j, w_k \in W$, which are not necessarily different, whether w_j and w_k are roots of a factor and eliminate the leaves of an existing factor. The algorithm so far is given below.

ALGORITHM 1, MODULE 1
procedure reduce_two_tree_factors (**var** t: tableau);
    begin
(1)   build_cover_table;
(2)   **for all** $w_j \in W$ **do**
(3)   **for all** $w_k \in W$ with $k \geq j$ **do**
(4)   reduce_trees_with_roots (w_j, w_k)
    end;

Now, for fixed w_j, $w_k \in W$ we have to find factors with w_j and w_k as roots. The first step is to find a minimal set of rows that we have to test, according to rule c2) for consistent functions, whether it can be mapped to w_j or w_k, if a given row w_i is mapped to w_j or w_k. This set is called the *closure* of w_i with respect to w_j and w_k, denoted $C_{w_j,w_k}(w_i)$. If a row is to be mapped to a second row, only a *repeated variable* from the set $\{b_1,\ldots\}$ (rep-b for short) appearing in the first row can force a third row to be mapped to that or another row. $C_{w_j,w_k}(w_i)$ will be defined later exactly.

As a preprocessing to finding the closures, we can first compute marks for rep-b variables and rows that indicate to which of the rows w_j and w_k a variable or row can be mapped. This is done in lines (1)–(11) of module 2 below. It is important here to see that a rep-b variable must be mapped to itself if it appears in one of the rows w_j and w_k. Then we can devide the set of the rows without w_j and w_k into the set Q that may be mapped to one of w_j or w_k and the complement N, lines (12)–(15). Then the set Q can be divided into closures C, lines (17)–(22). When computing a closure (18), a conflict may be detected, indicating that there is no mapping that maps the closure to the set $\{w_j, w_k\}$. If no conflict is detected, we can try to find a mapping for the closure, and if this step (20) does not produce a conflict, then the closure can be removed from the tableau. In line (16) each rep-b variable is marked "considered 0 times". With the help of the cons-tags we count how often these variables are touched, to limit computation loops.

ALGORITHM 1, MODULE 2
procedure reduce_trees_with_roots (w_j,w_k: row);
begin

```
(1)      for all b ∈ rep_b do b.mark := {w_j, w_k};
(2)      for all A_u ∈ A do begin
(3)          v := p(w_j, A_u); v' := p(w_k, A_u);
(4)          if v = v' then (* do nothing *)
             else begin
(5)              if v ∈ rep_b then v.mark := {w_j};
(6)              if v' ∈ rep_b then v'.mark := {w_k}
             end
         end;
(7)      for all w_l ∈ W \ {w_j, w_k} do begin
(8)          w_l.mark := {w_j, w_k} ∩ C(w_l);
(9)          for all A_u ∈ A do
(10)             if p(w_l, A_u) ∈ rep_b then
(11)                 w_l.mark := w_l.mark ∩ p(w_l, A_u).mark
         end;
(12)     Q := ∅; N := ∅;
(13)     for all w_l ∈ W \ {w_j, w_k} do
(14)         if w_l.mark = ∅ then N := N ∪ {w_l}
(15)         else Q := Q ∪ {w_l};
(16)     for all b ∈ rep_b do b.cons := 0
(17)     while Q ≠ ∅ do begin
(18)         C := get_a_closure;
(19)         if conflict then (* do nothing *)
(20)         else try_to_map (C);
(21)         if conflict then (* do nothing *)
(22)         else remove (C)
         end
     end;
```

We think that the best definition for the closures $C_{w_j,w_k}(w_i)$ now can be given with the help of an algorithm. Module 3 below computes one closure, starting with an arbitrary row $w_q \in Q$, so in effect it computes $C_{w_j,w_k}(w_q)$. Set H is the closure to be computed and set L is the set of rows whose rows could force other rows to be mapped to the set $\{w_j, w_k\}$. It is enough for each rep_b variable to be considered once in this procedure. And it is essential to see that the relation $\equiv_{j,k}$ with $w_i \equiv_{j,k} w_l$ iff $w_i \in C_{w_j,w_k}(w_l)$ is an equivalence relation in Q. So it is sufficient to compute each closure only once for all rows it contains. And it can be observed that, if in line (11) there is any choice, it doesn't matter whether w_j or w_k is selected.

ALGORITHM 1, MODULE 3
function get_a_closure: set_of_rows;
begin
(1) $w_q :=$ first row of Q; $Q := Q \setminus \{w_q\}$;
(2) $L := \{w_q\}$; $H := \emptyset$; conflict := false;
(3)   repeat
(4) $w_l :=$ first row of L; $L := L \setminus \{w_l\}$;
(5) $H := H \cup \{w_l\}$;
(6)   for all $A_u \in A$ do begin
(7) $b := p(w_l, A_u)$;
(8)   if $b \in$ rep_b then
(9)   if $b.\text{cons} = 0$ then begin
(10) $b.\text{cons} := 1$;
(11)   if $w_j \in b.\text{mark}$ then $t := j$ else $t := k$;
(12)   if $p(w_t, A_u) \neq b$ then
(13)   for all $w_m \in \text{rows}(b)$ do
(14)   if $w_m \in N$ then conflict := true
(15)   else if $w_m \in Q$ then begin
(16) $Q := Q \setminus \{w_m\}$;
(17) $L := L \cup \{w_m\}$
                               end
                       end
               end
       until $L = \emptyset$;
(18)
(19)   get_a_closure := H
end;

Lemma 1 *If in module 3 no conflict is derived, then the computed closure is the minimal set of rows from $W \setminus \{w_j, w_k\}$ that is to be mapped to the set $\{w_j, w_k\}$, if only one of the rows in the closure is mapped to $\{w_j, w_k\}$. If a conflict results, then none of the rows in the closure can be mapped to the set $\{w_j, w_k\}$ according to the rules for consistent functions.*

Proof: If no conflict is derived, each row of H, which is a subset of Q, may be mapped to $\{w_j, w_k\}$ and no other row can be forced to join H. A conflict results, if a row in H can force another row to join H, which is in N and therefore cannot be mapped to $\{w_j, w_k\}$. □

It is not true that every closure, computed by module 3, really can be mapped to the set $\{w_j, w_k\}$. But this is tested by module 4 below. The main idea is to devide a given closure (set S below) into groups of rows that force each other to be mapped to the *same* row, either w_j or w_k. Row w_g forces row w_m, if both have the same variable in some column and w_j and w_k have different variables in that column. In lines (4)–(19) all rows that belong to the same group are visited, if no conflict appears.

A conflict is derived, if the rows in the group cannot be mapped to the same row. This happens, if the intersection of their marks yields the empty target set. If no conflict is derived for one group, then this group may be mapped to the same row, to w_j or to w_k or to one of both. But the whole set S can only be mapped to $\{w_j, w_k\}$, if for all groups, into which it can be devided, no conflict is computed, (1)–(20). Again, it is sufficient to consider each rep_b variable only once in this procedure.

ALGORITHM 1, MODULE 4
procedure try_to_map (S: set_of_rows);
begin
(1)   while ($S \neq \emptyset$) and (not conflict) do begin
(2) $w_h :=$ first row of S; $S := S \setminus \{w_h\}$;
(3)   target $:= \{w_j, w_k\}$;
(4) $G := \{w_h\}$;
(5)   repeat
(6) $w_g :=$ first row of G; $G := G \setminus \{w_g\}$;
(7)   target $:=$ target $\cap\, w_g$.mark;
(8)   if target $= \emptyset$ then conflict $:=$ true else
(9)   for all $A_u \in A$ do begin
(10) $b :=$ p(w_g, A_u);
(11)   if $b \in$ rep_b then
(12)   if b.cons $= 1$ then begin
(13) b.cons $:= 2$;
(14)   if p(w_j, A_u) $\neq$ p(w_k, A_u) then
(15)   for all $w_m \in$ rows(b) do
(16)   if $w_m \in S$ then begin
(17) $S := S \setminus \{w_m\}$;
(18) $G := G \cup \{w_m\}$.
                                        end
                                end
                        end
(19)   until ($G = \emptyset$) or conflict
(20)   end
        end;

Theorem 2 *Algorithm 1 finds and reduces two-tree-factor elements in tableau-defined monoids.*

Proof: Follows mostly from the argumentation given above. The algorithm, as given in the descriptions above, can easily be transposed into an algorithm that uses *real* data structures. For example, the sets can be stored as lists and the marks can be derived from the cover table. □

Theorem 3 *Algorithm 1 runs in time* $O(n^3)$

Proof: We can observe that in modules 2, 3 and 4 the number of times, each variable and each row is touched, is a constant for fixed w_j and w_k, where the number of rows and variables is in $O(n)$. Together with the loops of module 1 this comes to $O(n^3)$. □

n	elements found by simple tableau algorithms $\mathcal{K}_n^{(1)}$	elements found by two-tree-factor algorithm $\mathcal{K}_n^{(1)} + \mathcal{K}_n^{(2)}$	idempotent elements $\sum_{k=1}^{\lfloor n/2 \rfloor} \mathcal{K}_n^{(k)}$
1	0	0	0
2	2	2	2
3	9	9	9
4	28	40	40
5	75	195	195
6	186	936	1,056
7	441	4,221	6,321
8	1,016	17,872	41,392
9	2,295	71,847	293,607
10	5,110	277,360	2,237,920
25	$4.19430 \cdot 10^8$	$2.82383 \cdot 10^{13}$	$1.27761 \cdot 10^{22}$

Table 1: Elements in M_n without I_n

4 Conclusion

We have presented an $O(n^3)$ run time algorithm that solves the problem of finding and reducing two-tree-factor elements in tableau-defined monoids, a problem that arises in many applications, e.g. in the optimization of relational database queries. No polynomial algorithm with the capabilities of our algorithm has been published before. Our algorithm increases the number of elements that can be found in polynomial time by a factor that is exponential in the problem size. In table 1 below, we list some values for the number of idempotent elements other than identity, found by simple-tableau algorithms, by our two-tree-factor algorithm and of the maximum number of these elements that could be found.

References

[1] M. Abramowitz and I. A. Stegun, editors. *Handbook of mathematical functions.* Dover Publications, Inc., New York, 1965.

[2] A. V. Aho, Y. Sagiv, and J. D. Ullman. Effizient optimization of a class of relational expressions. *ACM Trans. Database Syst.*, 4(4):435–454, December 1979.

[3] A. V. Aho, Y. Sagiv, and J. D. Ullman. Equivalences among relational expressions. *SIAM J. Comput.*, 8(2):218–246, May 1979.

[4] B. Harris and L. Schoenfeld. The number of idempotent elements in symmetric semigroups. *Journal of Combinatorial Theory*, 3(2):122–135, September 1967.

[5] A. P. Heinz. *Optimization of Relational Algebra Queries.* Master's thesis, Rheinisch-Westfälische Technische Hochschule Aachen, March 1984. in German.

[6] A. P. Heinz and G. Vossen. Quadratic-time optimization of SPJ-expressions including inequality selections by tableaux. *Fundamenta Informaticae VIII*, 8(3–4):397–414, 1985.

[7] Y. Sagiv. Quadratic algorithms for minimizing joins in restricted relational expressions. *SIAM J. Comput.*, 12(2):316–328, May 1983.

[8] Y. Sagiv and M. Yannakakis. Equivalences among relational expressions with the union and difference operators. *J. ACM*, 27(4):633–655, October 1980.

Toward a General Theory of Computation and Specification over Abstract Data Types

J.V. Tucker[1]

Department of Mathematics and Computer Science
University College of Swansea, Swansea SA2 8PP, Wales
csjvt@pyr.swan.ac.uk

J.I. Zucker[2]

Department of Computer Science and Systems
McMaster University, Hamilton, Ontario L8S 4K1, Canada
zucker@maccs.dcss.mcmaster.ca

Abstract. We describe an ongoing project, to develop a general theory of computation and specification over classes of structures, modelling abstract data types. Applications include logic programming module development and hardware design for synchronous concurrent algorithms.

Key words and phrases: abstract data type, computation, computability, specification.

1 Introduction

We are developing a theory of computable functions and specifiable relations over classes of many sorted algebras. Such a class K of algebras is a model of the semantics of a module defining an abstract data type. The theory of computation, specification and verification over K has many applications, thanks to the generality of K; those we have studied concern the following subjects: *program specification and verification; logic programming modules and abstract data types;* and *synchronous concurrent algorithms and their application in hardware design.* Research on these apparently disparate applications is part of a programme, based on the algebraic theory of abstract data types, that aims at a general mathematical framework for the formulation and analysis of the many interesting notions of computability, specifiability, and verifiability that exist in different areas of computer science and artificial intelligence.

2 Algebras, Modules and Abstract Data Types

Algebras and modules. A many-sorted algebraic structure A consists of a number of sets of data, operations, and relations on the data. Such a structure can be used to model semantically a concrete implementation of a software module. We concentrate

---

[1] Research supported by SERC Research Grant GR/F 59070 under the Alvey Programme (IKBS 103).
[2] Research supported by SERC Research Grant GR/F 10606 under the Alvey Programme, and by a grant from the Science & Engineering Research Board of McMaster University.

on *standard structures*, which contain sorts for the natural numbers N and booleans B, together with the standard operations on these. (This is no real restriction, since any structure can be standardised.) A class K of such structures can be used to model semantically the module abstractly as a class of implementations. We assume K is closed under isomorphism. K can then be viewed as an *abstract data type*. Among the properties of algebras that we use to characterise meaningful or useful implementations are: *minimality, initiality* and *computability*. See [5] for background material on algebra.

Higher-order computation and logic over a structure A can be represented by applying first order computation and logic to suitable extended structures. For example, we use the following *weak second order* structure over a standard structure A. Add an undefined symbol u_i to each carrier A_i and extend the operations by strictness. This forms an algebra A^u with carriers $A_i^u = A_i \cup \{u_i\}$. We model a finite array over A_i by a pair (ξ, l), where $\xi : N \to A_i^u$ and $l \in N$, such that $\xi(n) = u_i$ for all $n > l$. Let A_i^* be the set of all such pairs. We add these sets to the algebra A^u to create carriers of the array algebra A^*. The new constants and operations of A^* are: the everywhere undefined array, evaluating an array at a number address, updating an array by an element at a number address, evaluating the length, and updating the length, of an array.

3 Computability Theory

The mathematical theory is a generalisation of classical computability theory on N to any abstract algebra. Computability theory for algebras originates with work by E Engeler in 1965. For a survey of subsequent work by Friedman, Shepherdson and others, see [6] and [8, §4.10].

Computable functions on abstract data types. In [8] we examined the class IND(A) of functions over a standard algebra A that are generated from its basic operations by means of *sequential composition; parallel composition; simultaneous primitive recursion; least number (μ) operator.* If simultaneous primitive recursion is replaced by *simultaneous course-of-values recursion*, we obtain the class COVIND(A) of functions obtained is the class of *course-of-values (cov) inductively definable functions*. In either case, the functions are defined by a *parallel deterministic* model of computation, due to the simultaneous recursion. Hence we also obtain the families of functions IND(K) and COVIND(K) over the class K.

There are many models of computation equivalent with these models. This is discussed in detail in [8], where it is argued that the ideas of deterministic computation and operational semantics are meaningful and equivalent, and the following thesis is proposed.

Generalisation of the Church-Turing thesis for computation. *Consider a deterministic programming language over an abstract data type dt. The set of functions on a structure A implementing dt, that can be programmed in the language, is contained in the set COVIND(A). The class of functions over the class K of structures implementing dt, that can be programmed in the language, uniformly over all structures in K, is contained in the family COVIND(K).*

Computation on A^*. For many purposes it is convenient to present the computable functions on A using (simultaneous) primitive recursion on A^* (see §2). This is justified by the following:

THEOREM. *Let f be a function on A. Then*

$$f \in \mathrm{COVIND}(A) \iff f \in \mathrm{IND}(A^*).$$

4 Specification Theory

Paradigms for specification and computation. We use the *relational paradigm* for *specification* and the *functional paradigm* for *computation*. The connection between them is that *we can compute functions that are selection functions for certain relations.*

Given a set A and a relation $R \subseteq A^{n+m}$, a *selection function for R* is a map $f : A^n \to A^m$ such that $\forall x[\exists y R(x,y) \Rightarrow R(x, f(x))]$. In programming theory, a progam *implements a specification* over an abstract data type if it computes some selection function f for the relation R uniformly over a class K of algebras.

Now for a program to be *effectively testable* against a specification $\exists y R(x,y)$, the relation R must be computable. This leads us to study (generalisations of) the notion of r.e. set on algebras.

A relation on A is said to be *(cov) semicomputable* if it is the domain of a partial (cov) computable function on A. A relation is *projective (cov) semicomputable* if it is a *projection* of a (cov) semicomputable relation. Not every set that is projective cov semicomputable is cov semicomputable. However, in the case of *minimal structures*, the notions are equivalent.

Scope and limits of specification. According to the above, the specifiable relations are the projective cov semicomputable ones. What about the different views of specification to be found in say logic programming or the theory of stepwise program development? In [9] we formalise Horn clause definability over any structure or class of structures and show that this corresponds with projective cov definablility. Furthermore, from [8] we can characterise such sets by their definability in a specification language.

THEOREM. *A relation R on A is projective cov semicomputable over K if, and only if, either of the following holds:*
(i) R is definable by Horn clauses on A^*, uniformly over $A \in \mathsf{K}$;
(ii) R is definable by a Σ_1 formula over A^* uniformly over $A \in \mathsf{K}$.

These notions are also equivalent to several other characterisations by means of non-deterministic models for specification including *'while'-array with initialisation*; *'while'-array with random assignments*; and older notions such as *search computability* in the sense of Moschovakis. We are working on the following general kind of Church-Turing Thesis for specification to complement that for computation.

Generalisation of the Church-Turing thesis for specification. *Consider a non-deterministic programming or algorithmic specification language over an abstract data type* **dt**. *The set of relations on a structure A implementing* **dt**, *that can be specified in the language, is contained in the set of projective cov semicomputable relations on A. The class of relations over the class* K *of structures implementing* **dt**, *that can be specified in the language, uniformly over all structures in* K, *is contained in the family of relations projective cov semicomputable over* K.

This is a more complex task: for details see [9].

Provable totality of selection functions. In [10] we investigate selection functions for *existential* (Σ_1^*) *assertions* $\exists y R(x,y)$ over A, for computable predicates R. It is shown that if such an existential assertion is *provable* in a formal system which includes induction over N for Σ_1^* formulae only, then a selection function for it can be found which is *primitive cov computable*, *i.e.*, generated in COVIND(A) *without use of the μ operator*.

5 Applications

Logic programming. This work is relevant to the development of the concept of a *logic programming module* that generalises the abstract data type module. There is a close connection between logic programming modules and algebraic specification modules: see [1].

Theory of Hardware. A *synchronous concurrent algorithm* (sca) is a network of processors and channels that compute and communicate in parallel, synchronised by a global clock. Such algorithms compute on infinite streams of data. Examples of scas include: *clocked hardware; systolic algorithms; neural nets; cellular automata; and coupled map lattice dynamical systems.* This type of computation is formalised using the course-of-values inductive functions over *stream algebras* (*i.e.*, standard structures which include domains of functions from N to the various carriers). The study of such models of clocked algorithms, and their application, is a substantial task: it aims at a general mathematical theory of computation based on hardware. The special case of unit delays throughout the network corresponds with the use of primitive recursive functions and has been studied intensively in joint work with B C Thompson. Contributions to the theory and to the development of case studies have been made by K Meinke, N A Harman, S M Eker and K Hobley (see [2, 3, 4, 7] and the references therein).

Program correctness. Consider program specifications over the class K, and the validity of Hoare formulae $\{p\}S\{q\}$ over K. Our computability theory was developed originally to prove that important sets of program states, such as *weakest preconditions* and *strongest postconditions*, were expressible in a weak second order many sorted logical language. At the heart of this exercise is the theorem (ii) in §4 that characterises generalised r.e. sets in the language. The present work is a natural extension of our studies of subjects first encountered in the preparation of our book [8].

References

1. J Derrick and J V Tucker, *Logic programming and abstract data types*, in "Proceedings of 1988 UK IT Conference," held under the auspices of the Information Engineering Directorate of the Department of Trade and Industry (DTI), Institute of Electrical Engineers (IEE), 1988, pp. 217-219.

2. N A Harman and J V Tucker, *Clocks, retimings, and the formal specification of a UART*, in "The Fusion of Hardware Design and Verification," Proceedings of IFIP Working Group 10.2 Working Conference (ed. G Milne), North-Holland, 1988, pp. 375-396.

3. K M Hobley, B C Thompson, and J V Tucker, *Specification and verification of synchronous concurrent algorithms: a case study of a convolution algorithm*, in "The Fusion of Hardware Design and Verification," Proceedings of IFIP Working Group 10.2 Working Conference (ed. G Milne), North-Holland, 1988, pp. 347-374.

4. K Meinke and J V Tucker, *Specification and representation of synchronous concurrent algorithms*, in "Concurrency '88," (ed. F H Vogt), Lecture Notes in Computer Science 335, Springer-Verlag, 1988, pp. 163-180.

5. K Meinke and J V Tucker, *Universal algebra*, in "Handbook of Logic in Computer Science," (ed. S Abramsky, D Gabbay, T Maibaum), Oxford University Press (to appear).

6. J C Shepherdson, *Algorithmic procedures, generalised Turing algorithms, and elementary recursion theory*, in "Harvey Friedman's Research on the Foundations of Mathematics," (ed. L A Harrington *et al.*), North-Holland, 1985, pp. 285-308.

7. B C Thompson and J V Tucker, *A parallel deterministic language and its application to synchronous concurrent algorithms*, in "Proceedings of 1988 UK IT Conference, held under the auspices of the Information Engineering Directorate of the Department of Trade and Industry (DTI), Institute of Electrical Engineers (IEE)," 1988, pp. 228-231.

8. J V Tucker and J I Zucker, "Program correctness over abstract data types, with error state semantics," CWI Monograph 6, North Holland, 1988.

9. J V Tucker and J I Zucker, *Horn programs and semicomputable relations on abstract structures*, in "Proceedings of the 16th International Colloquium on Automata, Languages and Programming, Stresa, Italy," (ed. G Ausiello et al.) Lecture Notes in Computer Science 372, Springer-Verlag, 1989, pp. 745-760.

10. J V Tucker and J I Zucker, *Provable computable functions on abstract data types*, Department of Computer Science & Systems, McMaster University, Technical Report 90-02, 1990.

USING THE HAMILTONIAN PATH OPERATOR TO CAPTURE NP

Iain A. Stewart

Computing Laboratory, University of Newcastle upon Tyne
Claremont Tower, Claremont Road
Newcastle upon Tyne, NE1 7RU
England

Abstract : In this paper, we define the language (FO + posHP), where HP is the Hamiltonian path operator, and show that a problem can be represented by a sentence of this language if and only if the problem is in **NP**. We also show that every sentence of this language can be written in a normal form, and so establish the fact that the problem of deciding whether there is a directed Hamiltonian path between two distinguished vertices of a digraph is complete for **NP** via projection translations: as far as we know, this is the first such problem discovered. We also give a general technique for extending existing languages using operators derived from problems.

Introduction

In this paper, we pursue the characterization of complexity classes using languages (c.f. [2]), and we capture **NP** by the language (FO + posHP), where HP is the Hamiltonian path operator. We show that every sentence of this language has a normal form, so enabling us to show that the problem of deciding whether a digraph has a directed Hamiltonian path between two distinguished vertices is complete for **NP** via projection translations; these translations are apparently much weaker than logspace reductions. As far as we know, this is the first such problem discovered (although problems complete for other complexity classes via projection translations have been established c.f [2], [5]). Due to space limitations, proofs are either sketched or omitted, and the reader is referred to [4] for the full details.

1. Basic definitions

Definition 1.1. A *vocabulary* $\tau = \langle \underline{R}_1, \underline{R}_2, ..., \underline{R}_k, \underline{C}_1, \underline{C}_2, ..., \underline{C}_m \rangle$ is a tuple of *relation symbols* $\{\underline{R}_i : i = 1, 2, ..., k\}$ and *constant symbols* $\{\underline{C}_i : i = 1, 2, ..., m\}$. These relation symbols $\underline{R}_1, \underline{R}_2, ..., \underline{R}_k$ have fixed *arities* $a_1, a_2, ..., a_k$ (> 0), respectively. A *(finite) structure of size n* over the vocabulary τ is a tuple $S = \langle \{0, 1, ..., n-1\}, R_1, R_2, ..., R_k, C_1, C_2, ..., C_m \rangle$ consisting of a *universe*

$|S| = \{0,1,...,n\text{-}1\}$, *relations* $R_1, R_2, ..., R_k$ of arities $a_1, a_2, ..., a_k$, respectively, and *constants* $C_1, C_2, ..., C_m$. The size of some structure S is denoted by $|S|$. We denote the set of all structures over τ by STRUCT(τ).

Definition 1.2. A *problem of arity* $t (\geqq 0)$ over the vocabulary τ is a subset of:
$$\text{STRUCT}_t(\tau) = \{(S,u) : S \in \text{STRUCT}(\tau), u \in |S|^t\}.$$

Definition 1.3. The *first-order language FO(τ)* over the vocabulary τ has as its well-formed formulae (wffs) those formulae built, in the usual way, from the relation and constant symbols of τ, the binary relation symbols $\{=,s\}$, and the constant symbols $\{0,max\}$, using the logical connectives $\{\vee, \neg\}$, the variables $\{x,y,z_3,...\text{etc.}\}$, and the quantifier $\exists$ (we consider the logical connectives $\{\wedge, \Rightarrow, \Leftrightarrow\}$ and the quantifier $\forall$ as the usual abbreviations).

Definition 1.4. Let ϕ be some wff of some language L, and let x be a t-tuple of distinct variables, containing no bound variable of ϕ. Then we can regard ϕ as being *over* x, and in this case, we say that ϕ has *arity* t. If we regard ϕ as being over x, then we write $\phi(x)$ and regard each variable of x as being free in $\phi(x)$.

Definition 1.5. Let x be a t-tuple of distinct variables. Then a *valuation* on x from some structure S is a t-tuple $v \in |S|^t$ with the ith value of v assigned to the ith variable of x, for each $i = 1, 2, ..., t$.

Definition 1.6. Consider the wff ϕ, over the variables of the t-tuple x, of the language FO(τ), for some vocabulary τ. Then ϕ is interpreted in the set STRUCT$_t(\tau)$, and for each $S \in \text{STRUCT}(\tau)$ and $u \in |S|^t$:
$$(S,u) \models \phi(x) \text{ if and only if } \phi^S(u) \text{ holds,}$$
where $\phi^S(u)$ denotes the obvious interpretation of ϕ in S, except that the binary relation symbol $=$ is always interpreted in S as equality, the binary relation symbol s is interpreted as the successor relation on $|S|$, the constant symbol 0 is interpreted as $0 \in |S|$, the constant symbol max is interpreted as $n\text{-}1 \in |S|$, and each variable of x is given the corresponding value from u: if ϕ has free variables different from those of x, then $\phi^S(u)$ holds if and only if there is some unspecified valuation on these variables causing the interpreted formula to hold.

Definition 1.7. Let ϕ be a wff, over the t-tuple of variables x, of FO(τ), for some vocabulary τ. Then ϕ *represents* (or *specifies*) the problem:
$$\{(S,u) \in \text{STRUCT}_t(\tau) : (S,u) \models \phi(x)\},$$
of arity t.

2. Building languages

In order to ensure that our constructions have some generality, any language $L(\tau)$, over some vocabulary τ, encountered in this section is either $FO(\tau)$ or has been built from $FO(\tau)$ using Definition 2.1 and has had semantics attributed using Definition 2.4.

Definition 2.1. Let:
  (a) $L(\tau)$ be some language over some vocabulary τ, with well-defined semantics;
  (b) $\tau' = <R_1,R_2,...,R_k,C_1,C_2,...,C_m>$ be some fixed vocabulary;
  (c) Ω be some problem over τ' of arity t.
Then the *first-order extension of* $L(\tau)$ *by* (Ω,τ'), denoted $(L+(\Omega,\tau'))(\tau)$, is defined recursively as follows:
  (i) each wff of $L(\tau)$ is a wff of $(L+(\Omega,\tau'))(\tau)$;
  (ii) if ϕ and ψ are wffs of $(L+(\Omega,\tau'))(\tau)$, then so are $\neg\phi$, $\phi \vee \psi$, and $(\exists z)\phi$, where z does not occur bound in ϕ (although it is bound in $(\exists z)\phi$);
  (iii) if we are given a set of wffs:

$$\Sigma = \{\varphi_i(x_i),\psi_j(y_j) : i = 1,2,...,k; j = 1,2,...,m\} \subseteq (L+(\Omega,\tau'))(\tau),$$

with each formula ϕ_i (resp. ψ_j) over the qa_i (resp. q) distinct variables x_i (resp. y_j), for some positive integer q, such that each ψ_j has no other free variables, and such that for each $j = 1$, 2, ..., m we have that for each structure $S \in STRUCT(\tau)$:

$$S \models (\exists x_1)(\exists x_2)...(\exists x_q)[\psi_j(x_1,x_2,...,x_q) \wedge (\forall y_1)(\forall y_2)...(\forall y_q) [\psi_j(y_1,y_2,...,y_q)$$
$$\Leftrightarrow (x_1 = y_1 \wedge x_2 = y_2 \wedge ... \wedge x_q = y_q)]],$$

then the formula:
$$\Omega[\lambda x_1\phi_1,x_2\phi_2,...,x_k\phi_k,y_1\psi_1,y_2\psi_2,...,y_m\psi_m](z_1,z_2,...,z_t),$$
is a wff of $(L+(\Omega,\tau'))(\tau)$, where each z_h is a q-tuple of variables or constant symbols, and the variables of each z_h do not occur in any formula ϕ_i or ψ_j, nor tuple x_i or y_j: moreover, the variables of each tuple x_i and y_j are bound in this formula (as are the variables bound in some formula ϕ_i or ψ_j), with the variables of each tuple z_h and the other free variables occuring in each formula ϕ_i or ψ_j being free.

We do not distinguish between a problem and the operator corresponding to that problem (Ω, in Definition 2.1), and we refer to the set of formulae Σ in Definition 2.1 as τ'-*descriptive*.

Definition 2.2. Let:
  (a) $L(\tau)$ be some language over some vocabulary τ, with well-defined semantics;
  (b) $\tau' = <R_1,R_2,...,R_k,C_1,C_2,...,C_m>$ be some fixed vocabulary.
Suppose we are given a set of τ'-descriptive wffs Σ (as in rule (iii) of Definition 2.1). Consider some structure $S \in STRUCT(\tau)$. Then the τ'-*translation of* S *with respect to* Σ is the structure $S' \in STRUCT(\tau')$, defined as follows:
  S' has universe $|S|^q$,
for all $i = 1, 2, ..., k$ and for any tuples $\{u_1,u_2,...,u_{a_i}\} \subseteq |S'| = |S|^q$:

$R_iS'(u_1,u_2,...,u_{a_i})$ holds if and only if $(S,(u_1,u_2,...,u_{a_i})) \vDash \phi_i(x_i)$,

and, for all $j = 1, 2, ..., m$ and for any tuple $u \in |S'| = |S|^q$:

$C_jS' = u$ if and only if $(S,u) \vDash \psi_j(y_j)$.

Definition 2.3. Let the notation be as in Definition 2.2 and let z be a tuple of variables, where each variable of z is different from each variable in each tuple x_i or y_j, and does not occur bound in any formula ϕ_i or ψ_j. Let v be some valuation (from $|S|$) on z. Then the τ'-*translation of S with respect to Σ specified at $z = v$* is the structure $S' \in \text{STRUCT}(\tau')$, defined as follows:

S' has universe $|S|^q$,

and for all $i = 1, 2, ..., k$ and for any tuples $\{u_1,u_2,...,u_{a_i}\} \subseteq |S'| = |S|^q$:

$R_iS'(u_1,u_2,...,u_{a_i})$ holds if and only if $(S,(u_1,u_2,...,u_{a_i},v)) \vDash \phi_i(x_i,z)$,

and, for all $j = 1, 2, ..., m$ and for any tuple $u \in |S'| = |S|^q$:

$C_jS' = u$ if and only if $(S,u) \vDash \psi_j(y_j,z)$.

Definition 2.4. Consider the language $(L+(\Omega,\tau'))(\tau)$ (built from the language $L(\tau)$ as in Definition 2.1). Let ϕ be a wff of $(L+(\Omega,\tau'))(\tau)$ over the t-tuple of variables x, and let $S \in \text{STRUCT}(\tau)$ and $u \in |S|^t$.

(i) If $\phi \in L(\tau)$, then $(S,u) \vDash \phi(x)$ if and only if $(S,u) \vDash \phi(x)$ in $L(\tau)$.

(ii) If $\phi \equiv \neg\psi$, then $(S,u) \vDash \phi(x)$ if and only if it is not the case that $(S,u) \vDash \psi(x)$.

(ii) If $\phi \equiv \psi \vee \theta$, then $(S,u) \vDash \phi(x)$ if and only if either $(S,u) \vDash \psi(x)$ or $(S,u) \vDash \theta(x)$.

(iv) If $\phi \equiv (\exists z)\psi$, then $(S,u) \vDash \phi(x)$ if and only if there is some $v \in |S|$ such that $(S,u,v) \vDash \psi(x,z)$.

(v) If $\phi \equiv \Omega[\lambda x_1\phi_1,x_2\phi_2,...,x_k\phi_k,y_1\psi_1,y_2\psi_2,...,y_m\psi_m](z_1,z_2,...,z_t)$, where the notation is as in rule (iii) of Definition 2.1, then $(S,u) \vDash \phi(x)$ if and only if the τ'-translation of S with respect to Σ specified at $x = u$, that is, the structure $S' \in \text{STRUCT}(\tau')$, is such that $(S',(u_1,u_2,...,u_t)) \in \Omega$, for some tuples $\{u_1,u_2,...,u_t\} \subseteq |S|^q$, where u_h is obtained from the tuple z_h by giving:

(a) any variable of $z_h \cap x$ the corresponding value of u,

and:

(b) some unspecified value to any variable of $z_h \backslash z_h \cap x$.

Definition 2.5. Let $L(\tau)$ be some language, for any vocabulary τ. Then the wffs of the language L are $\{\phi \in L(\tau) : \tau$ is any vocabulary$\}$, with the semantics inherited from $\{L(\tau) : \tau$ is any vocabulary$\}$.

We remark that if Ω is some problem, over the vocabulary τ', and L is some language, then we often denote the language $(L+(\Omega,\tau'))$ (formed using Definitions 2.1, 2.4, and 2.5) by $(L+\Omega)$ when the vocabulary τ' is understood.

Definition 2.6. Let L be some language. Then the class of problems *represented* (or *specified*) by L (and also denoted L) consists of all those problems represented by the sentences of L.

In [2], the languages (FO+TC) and (FO+ATC) were studied, where TC is the problem of deciding whether two vertices of some digraph are joined via a directed path, and ATC is the analogue of TC applied to alternating digraphs. Immerman also studied languages related to (FO+TC), namely the languages (FO+posTC), (FO+STC), (FO+posSTC), (FO+DTC), and (FO+posDTC), where "pos" denotes that the operator may not be used within negation signs.

Theorem 2.1. ([2], [3]) *(a)* L = *(FO+DTC)* = *(FO+posDTC)*.
  (b) **NSYMLOG** = *(FO+posSTC)* ⊆ *(FO+STC)*.
  (c) **NL** = *(FO+TC)* = *(FO+posTC)*.
  (d) **P** = *(FO+ATC)*. ★

It is unknown whether (FO+posSTC) = (FO+STC). Henceforth, the vocabulary τ_0 always denotes the vocabulary $<E>$, where E is a relation symbol of arity 2.

3. The language (FO+posHP)

Let HP be the problem, of arity 2, over the vocabulary τ_0, defined as follows:
HP = {(S,(x,y)) ∈ STRUCT$_2$(τ_0) : there is a directed Hamiltonian path from x to y in the digraph S}.

Theorem 3.1. *Let ϕ ∈ (FO+posHP)(τ) be some sentence. Then the problem represented by ϕ is also represented by a sentence of the form:*
$$HP[\lambda xy\psi](0,max),$$
with ψ ∈ FO(τ), ψ quantifier-free, and ψ over the (distinct) variables of the k-tuples x and y, for some k > 0, where 0 (resp. max) is the constant symbol 0 (resp. max) repeated k times.

Proof. (Sketch) We proceed by induction on the length of ϕ.

Case (i) : ϕ ∈ FO(τ) is atomic or the negation of an atomic formula.
Let u and v be two distinct variables, not appearing in the formula ϕ. Consider the formula $\theta \equiv HP[\lambda uv\phi](0,max)$. For any structure S ∈ STRUCT(τ), let S_0 ∈ STRUCT(τ_0) be the τ_0-translation of S w.r.t. $\phi(u,v)$ (that is, regarding ϕ as being over the variables (u,v)). Then:
$$S \vDash \theta \text{ if and only if } (S_0,(0,max)) \in HP.$$
But, S_0 is either the digraph with every possible edge or the digraph with no edges, depending on whether S $\vDash \phi$ or not, respectively, and so S $\vDash \theta$ if and only if S $\vDash \phi$.

Case (ii) : $\phi \equiv HP[\lambda uv\theta](q,r)$, where q and r are k-tuples of constant symbols.

Let x_1, x_2, y_1, and y_2 be distinct variables not appearing in the formula ϕ. Define the formula ψ as follows:

$$\psi \equiv [x_1 = 0 \wedge x_2 = \max \wedge y_1 = 0 \wedge y_2 = \max \wedge \theta(u,v)]$$
$$\vee [(x_1 \neq 0 \vee x_2 \neq \max) \wedge (y_1 \neq 0 \vee y_2 \neq \max)]$$
$$\vee [x_1 = 0 \wedge x_2 = 0 \wedge y_1 = 0 \wedge y_2 = \max \wedge u = 0 \wedge v = q]$$
$$\vee [x_1 = 0 \wedge x_2 = \max \wedge y_1 = \max \wedge y_2 = 0 \wedge u = r \wedge v = 0].$$

Then, clearly, for any structure $S \in \text{STRUCT}(\tau)$:

$$S \vDash HP[\lambda uv\theta](q,r) \text{ if and only if } S \vDash HP[\lambda(u,x_1,x_2)(v,x_1,x_2)\psi](0,\max),$$

where 0 and $\max$ are $(k+2)$-tuples.

Case (iii) : $\phi \equiv HP[\lambda xy\theta](0,\max) \vee HP[\lambda uv\chi](0,\max)$, where x and y are k-tuples and u and v are k'-tuples (we may assume that $k = k'$).

Let (z,z_1,z_2,z_3) and (w,w_1,w_2,w_3) be $(k+3)$-tuples of distinct variables, none of which appears in ϕ. Define the formula ψ as follows:

$\psi_1 \equiv (z_1,z_2,z_3) = (\max,0,\max) \wedge (w_1,w_2,w_3) = (0,\max,0) \wedge z = w;$

$\psi_2 \equiv (z_1,z_2,z_3) = (0,\max,0) \wedge (w_1,w_2,w_3) = (\max,\max,0) \wedge z = w;$

$\psi_3 \equiv (z_1,z_2,z_3) = (\max,\max,0) \wedge (w_1,w_2,w_3) = (\max,0,\max) \wedge z = w;$

$\psi_4 \equiv (z_1,z_2,z_3) = (\max,\max,0) \wedge (w_1,w_2,w_3) = (0,\max,\max) \wedge z = w;$

$\psi_5 \equiv (z_1,z_2,z_3) = (0,\max,\max) \wedge (w_1,w_2,w_3) = (\max,0,0) \wedge z = w;$

$\psi_6 \equiv (z_1,z_2,z_3) = (\max,0,0) \wedge (w_1,w_2,w_3) = (\max,0,0) \wedge z = w;$

$\psi_7 \equiv (z_1,z_2,z_3) = (0,0,0) \wedge (w_1,w_2,w_3) = (\max,0,\max) \wedge z = w = 0;$

$\psi_8 \equiv (z_1,z_2,z_3) = (0,0,0) \wedge (w_1,w_2,w_3) = (0,\max,\max) \wedge z = w = 0;$

$\psi_9 \equiv (z_1,z_2,z_3) = (\max,0,0) \wedge (w_1,w_2,w_3) = (0,0,\max) \wedge z = \max \wedge w = 0;$

$\psi_{10} \equiv (z_1,z_2,z_3) = (0,\max,0) \wedge (w_1,w_2,w_3) = (0,0,\max) \wedge z = \max \wedge w = 0;$

$\psi_{11} \equiv (z_1,z_2,z_3) = (\max,0,0) \wedge (w_1,w_2,w_3) = (\max,0,\max) \wedge z \neq w \wedge \theta(z,w);$

$\psi_{12} \equiv (z_1,z_2,z_3) = (0,\max,0) \wedge (w_1,w_2,w_3) = (0,\max,\max) \wedge z \neq w \wedge \chi(z,w);$

$\psi_{13} \equiv \{(z_1,z_2,z_3),(w_1,w_2,w_3)\} \neq \{(\max,0,0),(\max,0,\max),(0,\max,0),(0,\max,\max),$
$$(\max,\max,0)\} \wedge \{(z,z_1,z_2,z_3),(w,w_1,w_2,w_3)\} \neq 0\},$$

and:

$$\psi \equiv \psi_1 \vee \psi_2 \vee \psi_3 \vee \cdots \psi_{12} \vee \psi_{13}.$$

We claim that for any structure $S \in \text{STRUCT}(\tau)$:

$$S \vDash HP[\lambda xy\theta](0,\max) \vee HP[\lambda uv\chi](0,\max) \text{ if and only if}$$
$$S \vDash HP[\lambda(z,z_1,z_2,z_3)(w,w_1,w_2,w_3)\psi](0,\max),$$

where 0 and $\max$ in the second formula are $(k+3)$-tuples.

Lemma 3.2. *Let G_1 and G_2 be digraphs on the vertices $\{0,1,...,n-1\}$, and let G be the digraph defined as follows:*

(i) G has $5n+2$ vertices, namely $\{a_{i0},a_{i1},...,a_{in-1},b_{i0},b_{i1},...,b_{in-1},c_0,c_1,..., c_{n-1},x,y : i = 1,2\}$;

(ii) G has edges $\{(a_{1j},c_j),(c_j,a_{2j}),(a_{2j},b_{1j}),(b_{1j},c_j),(c_j,b_{2j}),(b_{2j},a_{1j}) : j = 0,1,...,n-1\}$;

(iii) G has edges $\{(x,a_{20}),(x,b_{20}),(a_{1n-1},y),(b_{1n-1},y)\}$;

(iv) for each $i,j \in \{0,1,...,n-1\}$, with $i \neq j$:

G has an edge (a_{1i}, a_{2j}) if and only if (i,j) is an edge of G_1,

and:

G has an edge (b_{1i}, b_{2j}) if and only if (i,j) is an edge of G_2

(G has no other edges except those described above). Then there is a directed Hamiltonian path in G from vertex x to vertex y if and only if there is a directed Hamiltonian path in G_1 from vertex 0 to vertex n-1 or there is a directed Hamiltonian path in G_2 from vertex 0 to vertex n-1. ★

Let $S \in$ STRUCT(τ) be of size n, and let G_1 (resp. G_2) be the τ_0-translation of S w.r.t. $\theta(x,y)$ (resp. $\chi(u,v)$); that is, G_1 and G_2 are digraphs with vertices indexed by k-tuples over $\{0,1,...,n-1\}$. We can form the digraph G as in Lemma 3.2 (ordering tuples lexicographically).

Define the formula ψ' by:

$\psi' \equiv \psi_1 \vee \psi_2 \vee ... \vee \psi_{12}$.

Let the digraph H (resp. H_0) be the τ_0-translation of S w.r.t. $\psi(z,z_1,z_2,z_3,w,w_1,w_2,w_3)$ (resp. $\psi'(z,z_1,z_2,z_3, w,w_1,w_2,w_3)$). Remove all the isolated vertices from H_0 and denote the resulting digraph H_0'. Then it is easy to see that:

(i) H_0' is an induced subgraph of H;

(ii) H_0' is isomorphic to G, with the vertex $(0,0,0,0)$ (resp. $(0,0,0,max)$) of H_0' corresponding to the vertex x (resp. y) of G, where 0 is a tuple of length k;

(iii) there is a Hamiltonian path in H from vertex $(0,0,0,0)$ to vertex (max,max,max,max) if and only if there is a Hamiltonian path in G from vertex x to vertex y (with 0 and max tuples of length k). The required property of ψ follows by Lemma 3.2.

<u>Case (iv)</u> : $\phi \equiv HP[\lambda xy\theta](0,max) \wedge HP[\lambda uv\chi](0,max)$, where x and y are k-tuples and u and v are k'-tuples.

The proof is easy and proceeds similarly to Case (iii).

<u>Case (v)</u> : $\phi \equiv (\exists z)HP[\lambda xy\theta](0,max)$, where z is not bound in θ and different from any variable of the k-tuples x and y.

Lemma 3.3. Let $G_1, G_2, ..., G_m$ be digraphs on the vertices $\{0,1,...,n-1\}$, for some $m > 1$, and let G be the digraph defined as follows:

(i) G has $2n(2m-1)+2$ vertices, $\{a_{ij}, b_{ij}, c_{kj}, d_{kj}, x, y : i = 1,2,...,m; j = 0,1,...,n-1; k = 1,2,...,m-1\}$;

(ii) G has edges: $\{(b_{ji}, a_{j+1i}), (a_{ji}, d_{ji}), (d_{ji}, b_{j+1i}), (a_{j+1i}, c_{ji}), (c_{ji}, b_{ji}), (c_{ji}, d_{ji}), (d_{ji}, c_{ji}) : i = 0,1,...,n-1; j = 1,2,...,m-1\}$;

(iii) G has edges $\{(b_{mi}, a_{1i}), (a_{jn-1}, y), (x, b_{j0}) : i = 0,1,...,n-1; j = 1,2,...,m\}$;

(iv) for each $k \in \{1,2,...,m\}$, and for each $i,j \in \{0,1,...,n-1\}$, with $i \neq j$, G has an edge (a_{ki}, b_{kj}) if and only if (i,j) is an edge of G_k

(G has no other edges except those described above). Then there is a directed Hamiltonian path in G from vertex x to vertex y if and only if there is a directed Hamiltonian path in G_k from vertex 0 to vertex n-1, for some $k \in \{1,2,...,m\}$. ★

The result follows as in Case (iii).

<u>Case (vi)</u> : $\phi \equiv (\forall z)HP[\lambda xy\theta](0,max)$, where z is not bound in θ and different from any variable of the k-tuples x and y.
The proof is easy and proceeds similarly to Case (iv).

<u>Case (vii)</u> : $\phi \equiv HP[\lambda xyHP[\lambda uv\theta](0,max)](0,max)$ where x and y are k-tuples and u and v are k'-tuples.

Lemma 3.4. *Let $\{G_{ij} : i,j = 1,2,...,m\}$ be digraphs on the vertices $\{0,1,...,n-1\}$, and let G be the digraph defined as follows:*

(i) G has $4m^2n-2mn+m$ vertices, namely $\{x_i,a_{ikj},b_{ikj},c_{iqj},d_{iqj} : j = 0,1,...,n-1; i,k = 1,2,...,m; q = 1,2,...,m-1\}$;

(ii) for each $i \in \{1,2,...,m\}$, the digraph formed by the vertices $\{x_i,a_{ikj},b_{ikj},c_{iqj},d_{iqj} : j = 0,1,...,n-1; k = 1,2,...,m; q = 1,2,...,m-1\}$ is isomorphic to the digraph $G\backslash\{y\}$ formed in Lemma 4.3, where under this isomorphism:

$x_i \rightarrow x; \ a_{ikj} \rightarrow a_{kj}; \ b_{ikj} \rightarrow b_{kj}; \ c_{iqj} \rightarrow c_{qj}; \ d_{iqj} \rightarrow d_{qj};$

(iii) G also has edges $\{(a_{ikn-1},x_k) : i,k = 1,2,...,m\}$
(G has no other edges except those described above). Then there is a directed Hamiltonian path in G from vertex x_0 to vertex x_m if and only if the elements of $\{1,2,...,m\}$ can be arranged in a list:

$$1 = z_0, z_1, ..., z_{n-1} = m,$$

such that no element appears on the list twice and such that there is a directed Hamiltonian path in $G_{z_iz_{i+1}}$ from 0 to n-1, for each i = 1,2,...,m. ★

The result follows as in Case (iii). ★

In fact, the proof of Theorem 3.1 yields more information.

Definition 3.1. Let $\phi \in FO(\tau)$, for some vocabulary τ, be of the form:
$$\phi \equiv \bigvee_{i=1}^{I} \alpha_i \wedge \beta_i,$$
where:

(i) each α_i is a conjunction of the logical atomic relations, s, =, and their negations;

(ii) each β_i is atomic or negated atomic;

(iii) if $i \neq j$, then α_i and α_j are mutually exclusive.
Then ϕ is a *projective* formula.

Corollary 3.5. *Let* $\phi \in (FO+posHP)(\tau)$ *be some sentence. Then the problem represented by* ϕ *is also represented by a sentence of the form:*

$$HP[\lambda xy\psi](0,\mathbf{max}),$$

with ψ *over the (distinct) variables of the* k*-tuples* $\mathbf{x}$ *and* $\mathbf{y}$*, for some* $k > 0$*, where* 0 *(resp.* $\mathbf{max}$*) is the constant symbol* 0 *(resp.* $\mathbf{max}$*) repeated* k *times, and where* ψ *is projective.* ★

Proposition 3.6. *Let* ϕ *be some sentence of* $(FO+TC)$*, and let p be the problem represented by* ϕ*. Then there is a sentence* $\psi \in (FO+posHP)$ *representing p.*

Proof. The proof is a consequence of the following lemma.

Lemma 3.7. *Let G be some digraph on the vertices* $\{0,1,...,n\text{-}1\}$*. Let H be the digraph defined as follows:*

    (i) H has $5n+3$ *vertices, namely* $\{a_i,b_i,c_i,d_i,e_i,x,y,z : i = 0,1,...,n\text{-}1\}$*;*

    (ii) H has edges $\{(a_i,c_i),(c_i,b_i),(b_i,d_i),(d_i,c_i),(c_i,e_i),(e_i,a_i),(d_i,e_j) : i,j = 0,1,...,n\text{-}1; i \neq j\}$*;*

    (iii) H has edges $\{(x,b_0),(a_{n\text{-}1},y),(y,e_i),(y,z),(d_i,z) : i = 0,1,...,n\text{-}1\}$*;*

    (iv) for any $i,j = 0, 1, ..., n\text{-}1$*, with* $i \neq j$*:*

        H has an edge (a_i,b_j) *if and only if G has an edge* (i,j)

(H has no other edges except those described above). Then there is a directed path in G from 0 to n-1 if and only if there is a directed Hamiltonian path in H from x to z. ★

Corollary 3.8. $NL \subseteq (FO+posHP)$. ★

4. (FO+posHP) captures NP

Proposition 4.1. $(FO+posHP) \subseteq NP$.

Proof. Easy, given Theorem 3.1. ★

Definition 4.1. Let $S \in STRUCT(\tau)$, for some vocabulary $\tau = <R_1,R_2,...,R_k, C_1,C_2,...,C_m>$. Then the encoding $e_\tau(S)$ of S is defined as follows: each R_iS is encoded as a sequence of n^{a_i} 0s and 1s, denoting whether $R_iS(0,0,...,0)$ holds, whether $R_iS(0,0,...,1)$ holds, ..., and whether $R_iS(n\text{-}1,n\text{-}1,...,n\text{-}1)$ holds (with $|S| = n$); each C_jS encoded as its binary representation. If p is some problem over τ, then we define $e_\tau(p) = \{e_\tau(S) : S \in p\} \subseteq \{0,1\}^*$.

Proposition 4.2. *Let M be a logspace transducer, let* τ *be some vocabulary, and let* $k \in N$*. Then there is a formula* $\psi \in (FO+DTC)(\tau)$*, over the distinct variables of the* k*-tuple* $\mathbf{x}$*, such that for each* $S \in STRUCT(\tau)$ *and any tuple* $\mathbf{u} \in |S|^k$*:*

    $(S,\mathbf{u}) \vDash \psi(\mathbf{x})$

if and only if

the uth output of M is a 1 on input $\omega = e_\tau(S)$, where u is the usual representation of an integer in $\{0,1,...,n^k-1\}$, with $n = |S|$. ★

Theorem 4.3. NP $\subseteq (FO + posHP)$.

Proof. Follows from Proposition 4.2 and the fact that HP is complete for NP via logspace reductions (c.f. [1] and [6]). ★

Corollary 4.4. NP $= (FO + posHP)$. ★

Definition 4.2. Let p_a and p_b be problems over the vocabularies τ_a and τ_b, respectively. Let Σ be a set of τ_b-descriptive formulae of some language $L(\tau_a)$, and for each structure $S_a \in$ STRUCT(τ_a), let $\sigma(S_a) \in$ STRUCT(τ_b) denote the τ_b-translation of S_a w.r.t. Σ. Then p_b is an L-*translation* of p_a if and only if for each $S_a \in$ STRUCT(τ_a), $S_a \in p_a$ if and only if $\sigma(S_a) \in p_b$. If each formula of Σ is projective, then p_b is a *projection translation* of p_a.

Corollary 4.5. *The problem represented by the formula* $HP[\lambda xyE](0,max)$ *of* $(FO + posHP)(\tau_0)$ *is complete for* NP *via projection translations.* ★

Conclusion

In this paper, we have shown how NP can be characterized using logic and without reference to any of the usual machine models. Moreover, the problem of deciding whether there is a Hamiltonian path between two distinguished vertices of a digraph has been shown to be complete for NP via certain logical reductions, again independent of any machine. It should be clear that the first-order language can be extended by any problem(s), so defining new complexity classes, and this approach is obviously worthy of more study.

References

[1] M.R.GAREY & D.S.JOHNSON, *Computers and intractability*, W.H.Freeman and Co., San Francisco, 1979.
[2] N.IMMERMAN, *Languages that capture complexity classes*, SIAM J. Comput., Vol. 16, No. 4, 1987, pp.760-778.
[3] N.IMMERMAN, *Nondeterministic space is closed under complementation*, SIAM J. Comput., Vol. 17, No. 5, 1988, pp.935-938.
[4] I.A.STEWART, *Complete problems for symmetric logspace involving free groups*, Univ. Newcastle upon Tyne Tech. Rep., No. 300, 1989.
[5] I.A.STEWART, *Using the Hamiltonian path operator to capture NP*, Univ. Newcastle upon Tyne Tech. Rep., 1989.
[6] R.SOMMERHALDER & S.C.VAN WESTRHENEN, *The theory of computability: programs, machines, effectiveness, and feasibility*, Addison-Wesley, Wokingham, England, 1988.

Some Remarks on Polynomial Time Isomorphisms[*]

Jie Wang

Computer Science Department, CLA

Boston University

Boston, MA 02215

Internet: jwang@cs.bu.edu

Abstract

Joseph and Young [JY-85] hypothesized that the Berman-Hartmanis isomorphism conjecture fails if there exists a k-completely creative set in NP with no p-invertible p-completely productive functions. We verify this hypothesis for $DEXT$ based on new results of p-creative sets in [Wan-89]. In particular, we prove that the isomorphism conjecture for $DEXT$ fails iff there is a p-creative set for P in $DEXT$ with no p-invertible p-productive functions.

1   Introduction

Berman and Hartmanis [BH-77] observed that all of the "natural" NP-complete problems known at that time had p-honest and p-invertible padding functions, and hence that they are all polynomially isomorphic. This means that all of the "natural" NP-complete sets can be thought of as simple reencodings of the same set from the standpoint of complexity theory. Based on this result, they conjectured that all NP-complete sets are polynomially isomorphic. The conjecture remains open and is difficult since it implies $P \neq NP$. On the other hand, even if we assume $P \neq NP$, we still do not know whether or not the isomorphism conjecture holds.

The Berman-Hartmanis isomorphism conjecture has stimulated much of the recent research in structural complexity theory. In [JY-85], motivated by the fact that in recursion theory all many-one complete sets are recursively isomorphic, Joseph and Young presented some interesting evidence against the isomorphism conjecture. The classical

---

[*]This work was supported in part by NSF grant CCR-8814339 and a Boston University Presidential Fellowship.

proof from recursion theory that all many-one complete sets are recursively isomorphic breaks into three parts. First, one defines creative sets and proves that all many-one complete sets are creative. Second, one proves that all creative sets are paddable. And, finally, one easily proves that any two many-one equivalent and paddable sets are recursively isomorphic. Joseph and Young considered how much of this proof could be carried out in a polynomial setting. Clearly, the last step can, since one can prove that any two p-m-equivalent and p-paddable sets are polynomially isomorphic using the polynomial version of the Cantor-Schroeder-Bernstein construction [BH-77 and MY-85]. Two sets are said to be p-m-equivalent if they are p-m-reducible to each other. A set A is p-paddable if there is a one-one polynomial time computable and invertible function f such that for all x and y, $x \in A \Leftrightarrow p(x,y) \in A$.

To approach the first and the second steps, Joseph and Young defined and constructed k-completely creative sets [1] and proved that these sets are all p-m-complete for NP. Roughly speaking, a set $A \in NP$ is called k-completely creative if there is a total polynomial time computable function f such that for all i, if i witnesses a set L_i in $NTIME(n^k)$, then $f(i) \in L_i \Leftrightarrow f(i) \in A$. The function f is called a p-completely productive function. Joseph and Young [JY-85] constructed a class of k-completely creative sets K_f^k, where f is any one-one, p-honest, and polynomial time computable function. They observed that a k-completely creative set A does not seem to be p-paddable unless A has a p-invertible p-completely productive function. They also observed that for some one-way function f, K_f^k does not seem to have p-invertible p-completely productive functions. Joseph and Young [JY-85] therefore conjectured that if one-way functions exist, then the Berman-Hartmanis conjecture fails.

Recently, the isomorphism conjecture has been relocated to other classes such as $DEXT$ $(= \bigcup_c DTIME(2^{cn}))$, where we have access to more powerful techniques. For example, we can enumerate all polynomial time computable functions in $DEXT$. The isomorphism conjecture for $DEXT$ states that all p-m-complete sets for $DEXT$ are polynomially isomorphic. Some interesting results have been shown concerning the isomorphism conjecture for $DEXT$, for example, see Ko-Long-Du [KLD-86] and Kurtz-Mahaney-Royer [KMR-86].

In this paper we consider whether Joseph and Young's hypothesis for NP, which states that Berman-Hartmanis isomorphism conjecture fails if there is a k-completely creative set with no p-invertible p-completely productive functions, would be true for $DEXT$. We affirmatively answer this question based on new results of p-creative sets in

---

[1] Actually, [JY-85] called these sets k-creative. It was explained in [Wan-89] why these sets should be called k-completely creative in accord with the notions in recursion theory.

Wang [Wan-89]. In particular, we prove the following

Main theorem *The isomorphism conjecture for DEXT fails iff there is a p-creative set for P in DEXT with no p-invertible p-productive functions.*

We know that if the isomorphism conjecture for $DEXT$ fails, then one-way functions exist [Ber-77, BH-77]. A function f is said to be one-way if f is one-one, p-honest, polynomial time computable, but not p-invertible. From our main theorem we know that the isomorphism conjecture for $DEXT$ fails if there is a p-creative set for P in $DEXT$ with no p-invertible p-productive functions. We thereby consider and discuss what kind of one-way functions would imply the existence of such p-creative sets and so yield the failure of the isomorphism conjecture for $DEXT$.

2 Preliminaries

Languages are defined over the alphabet $\Sigma = \{0, 1\}$. Let $\omega = \{0, 1, ...\}$ be the set of all natural numbers. For each $x \in \omega$, we use $\hat{x}$ to denote the binary representation of $x + 1$ with the leading 1 omitted. This is a bijection between ω and the set of strings in Σ^*, and so enables us to disregard the distinction between strings and representations of natural numbers. For each $x \in \omega$, we use $|x|$ to denote the length of the binary representation of x. So for all $x > 0$, $x < 2^{|x|} \leq 2x$. We use multi-tape Turing machines as computation models, which can either accept languages or compute functions. A program (index) i is an integer which simply codes up the states, symbols, tuples, etc. of the ith Turing machine M_i.

Let $M_0, M_1, ...$ be a fixed enumeration of all (deterministic and nondeterministic) Turing machines. For convenience, we use DTM to denote a deterministic Turing machine and NTM a nondeterministic Turing machine. Let $L_i = L(M_i) = \{x : M_i \text{ accepts } x\}$ for all i.

Given a set A, let $\overline{A}$ denote the complement of A. Roughly speaking, a set A is called p-creative for P if there is a total polynomial time computable function f such that f provides an effective witness that $\overline{A}$ is not in P in the sense that whenever a Turing machine M_i witnesses a language in P, $L(M_i) \subseteq \overline{A} \Rightarrow \overline{A} - L(M_i)$. In particular, we consider those machines which witness languages in P in the following uniform way. Let $p_i(n) = |x|^{\sqrt[i]{|i|}} + i$. Define

$$\mathcal{PM} = \{M_i : M_i \text{ is a DTM and } (\forall x \in L(M_i))[M_i \text{ accepts } x \text{ within } p_i(|x|) \text{ steps}]\}.$$

Clearly, $P = \{L(M_i) : M_i \in \mathcal{PM}\}$. The following two definitions are from [Wan-89].

Definition 1 Say an r.e. set A is *p-creative for P* if there is a total polynomial time computable function f, which is called a p-productive function, such that

$$(\forall i)[M_i \in \mathcal{PM} \Rightarrow [L_i \subseteq \overline{A} \Rightarrow f(i) \in \overline{A} - L_i]].$$

Definition 2 Say an r.e. set A is *p-completely creative for P* if there is a total polynomial time computable function f, which is called a p-completely productive function, such that

$$(\forall i)[M_i \in \mathcal{PM} \Rightarrow [f(i) \in A \Leftrightarrow f(i) \in L_i]].$$

Define $DEXT = \bigcup_c DTIME(2^{cn})$. Wang [Wan-89] proved the following results.

Theorem 1 ([Wan-89])

1. A set A is p-creative for P iff A is p-completely creative for P.

2. A set A is p-m-complete for $DEXT$ iff A is p-creative for P in $DEXT$.

3. Every p-creative set for P in $DEXT$ has a 1-1 length increasing p-productive function.

Say a set A is polynomial time many-one reducible to a set B (in symbols, $A \leq_m^p B$) if there is a total polynomial time computable function f such that $(\forall x)[x \in A \Leftrightarrow f(x) \in B]$. A set A is p-m-complete for class $\mathcal{L}$ if $A \in \mathcal{L}$ and for each $L \in \mathcal{L}$, $L \leq_m^p A$. Say a set A is p-1-complete for class $\mathcal{L}$ if $A \in \mathcal{L}$ and each set in $\mathcal{L}$ can be polynomial time reducible to A via a 1-1 function. In this paper when we say a set is complete we mean it is p-m-complete.

Two sets A and B are said to be p-m-equivalent if $A \leq_m^p B$ and $B \leq_m^p A$. A and B are said to be p-isomorphic if $A \leq_m^p B$ via a 1-1, onto, polynomial time computable and invertible function.

Given a function f, let $f(x) \downarrow$ denote that $f(x)$ is defined and $f(x) \uparrow$ that $f(x)$ is not defined. Say a function f is p-invertible if f is 1-1 and f^{-1} is polynomial time computable.

Say a polynomial time computable function f is p-honest, if there is a polynomial p such that for all x, if $f(x) \downarrow$ then $p(|f(x)|) \geq |x|$.

Say a function f is one-way if f is 1-1, p-honest, polynomial time computable, but not p-invertible.

Say a set A is p-sparse if there is a polynomial p such that for all n, $\{x \in A : |x| \leq n\}$ has at most $p(n)$ elements.

Say a set A is p-paddable if there is a total polynomial time computable function p, p is 1-1 and polynomial time invertible, such that for all x and y, $x \in A$ iff $p(x, y) \in A$. The following result is due to [MY-85].

Theorem 2 ([MY-85]) *If sets A and B are p-paddable and p-m-equivalent, then A is p-isomorphic to B.*

Given a Turing machine M, let $T_M(x)$ denote the time bound of computation of M on input x, and $M_i(x)$ denote the output of TM M_i on input x if $M_i(x)$ halts. Without loss of generality, we assume that $T_M(x) \geq |x|$ whenever $M(x)$ halts. The following lemma is straightforward [Wan-89].

Lemma 1 (Simulation Lemma)
$\{(i, x) : M_i$ *is a DTM and accepts x within $p_i(|x|)$ steps$\}$ is acceptable by a two-tape DTM in time $O(|i|p_i^2(|x|))$.*

Consider the Kleene function $K = \lambda i x n[M_i(x)$, if M_i is a DTM and halts on input x within n steps; 0, otherwise]. Let $f_i = \lambda x[K(i, x, p_i(|x|))]$, then $f_0, f_1, \ldots$ is an enumeration of all total polynomial time computable functions. By the simulation lemma 1, the universal function $\lambda i x[f_i(x)]$ is computable in time $O(|i|[(|x|^{\sqrt[3]{|i|}} + i)]^2)$. It is easily seen that $|x|^{\sqrt[3]{|i|}} + i = 2^{\sqrt[3]{|i|} \log |x| + \log i} \leq 2^{O(|i|+|x|)}$. Therefore, $O(|i|(|x|^{\sqrt[3]{|i|}} + i)^2) \leq O(2^{2 \log |i|} \cdot 2^{O(|i|+|x|)}) = 2^{O(|i|+|x|)}$. That is, the universal function is computable in $DEXT$.

3 The Main Theorem

Theorem 3 *The isomorphism conjecture for $DEXT$ fails iff there is a p-creative set for P in $DEXT$ with no p-invertible p-productive functions.*

Proof. (Only if part) Let K be a p-m-complete set for $DEXT$ which is p-paddable (notice that such set K exists). Suppose that the isomorphism conjecture for $DEXT$ fails. This means that there is a set A in $DEXT$ which is p-m-complete for $DEXT$ and not p-isomorphic to K.

From theorem 1 (2) we know that A is p-creative for P since A is p-m-complete for $DEXT$. We will show that A does not have p-invertible p-completely productive functions. Suppose it were not true, i.e., A has a p-invertible p-productive function h. We shall show that A is p-paddable.

From the proof of theorem 1 (1) in [Wan-89], we know that there is a total polynomial time computable and p-invertible function g and a constant $N > 0$ such that for all i, when $|i| > N$, we have

$$M_i \in \mathcal{PM} \Rightarrow [hg(i) \in A \Leftrightarrow hg(i) \in L_i]. \tag{1}$$

Since h and g are total, polynomial time computable and p-invertible, so is hg.

Define a DTM M by

$$M(x, y, z) = \begin{cases} \text{``accept''}, & \text{if } x \in A, \\ \text{``reject''}, & \text{otherwise.} \end{cases}$$

Since $A \in DEXT$, there is a constant $c > 0$ such that $T_M(x, y, z) \le 2^{c|x|} + c(|y| + |z|)$. By the s-m-n theorem [2] there is a total polynomial time computable function f such that $M_{f(x,y)}(z) = M(x, y, z)$, $T_{M_{f(x,y)}}(z) = T_M(x, y, z)$, and (by suitably padding f) for every x and y, $f(x, y) \ge (2x)^c + c(|y| + 1)$ and $|f(x, y)| > N + (c+1)^3$. Since $(2x)^c \ge 2^{c|x|}$ we have for any x, y, and z that

$$\begin{aligned} T_{M_{f(x,y)}}(z) &\le 2^{c|x|} + c(|y| + |z|) \\ &\le |z| \sqrt[3]{|f(x,y)|} + f(x, y). \end{aligned}$$

Thus, for all x and y, $M_{f(x,y)} \in \mathcal{PM}$. Moreover, we can make f to be 1-1 and p-invertible. So hgf is total, 1-1, polynomial time computable, and p-invertible. Clearly,

$$L_{f(x,y)} = \begin{cases} \omega, & \text{if } x \in A, \\ \phi, & \text{otherwise.} \end{cases}$$

Since $|f(x, y)| > N$ for every x and y, from (1) we have

$$(\forall x)(\forall y)[hgf(x, y) \in A \Leftrightarrow hgf(x, y) \in L_{f(x,y)}]. \tag{2}$$

By construction, $x \in A \Rightarrow L_{f(x,y)} = \omega \Rightarrow hgf(x, y) \in L_{f(x,y)}$ and $x \notin A \Rightarrow L_{f(x,y)} = \phi \Rightarrow hgf(x, y) \notin L_{f(x,y)}$. That is, $x \in A \Leftrightarrow hgf(x, y) \in L_{f(x,y)}$. By (2) we know that $hgf(x, y) \in L_{f(x,y)} \Leftrightarrow hgf(x, y) \in A$, so $x \in A \Leftrightarrow hgf(x, y) \in A$. Hence A is p-paddable.

Since A and K are p-paddable and p-m-equivalent, A is p-isomorphic to K by theorem 2. This is a contradiction.

(If part) Suppose that there is a p-creative set for P in $DEXT$ with no p-invertible p-productive function. We shall show that the isomorphism conjecture for $DEXT$ fails.

Let B be a p-creative set for P in $DEXT$ with a p-invertible p-productive function h (notice that such sets exist). That is, $(\forall i)[M_i \in \mathcal{PM} \Rightarrow [L_x \subseteq \overline{B} \Rightarrow h(x) \in \overline{B} - L_x]]$.

---

[2] The polynomial version of the s-m-n theorem can be seen from [JY-85 or Wan-89].

From theorem 1 (2) we know that a set A is p-creative set P in $DEXT$ iff A is p-m-complete for $DEXT$. If the isomorphism conjecture for $DEXT$ holds, then for any set A, if A is p-creative for P in $DEXT$, then A is p-isomorphic to B. That is, $B \leq_m^p A$ via a total, 1-1, polynomial time computable, and p-invertible function f.

Since f is polynomial time computable, $f(y)$ is computable deterministically in time $|y|^k + k$ for some k. By the s-m-n theorem, we can have a total length increasing polynomial time computable function g such that

$$M_{g(x)}(y) = \begin{cases} \text{``accept''}, & \text{if } M_x \text{ accepts } f(y), \\ \uparrow, & \text{otherwise.} \end{cases}$$

and $M_x \in \mathcal{PM}$ implies $M_{g(x)} \in \mathcal{PM}$. This can be done by suitable padding g such that

$$\begin{aligned} T_{M_{g(x)}}(y) &\leq O(|x|T_x^2(f(y)) + |y|^k) \\ &\leq O(|x|(|f(y)|^{\sqrt[3]{|x|}} + x)^2 + |y|^k) \\ &\leq |y|^{\sqrt[3]{|g(x)|}} + g(x). \end{aligned}$$

Moreover, we can make g 1-1 and p-invertible. So fhg is total, 1-1, and polynomial time computable, and p-invertible.

Since $z \in f(L_{g(x)}) \Rightarrow (\exists y \in L_{g(x)})[f(y) = z] \Rightarrow f(y) \in L_x \Rightarrow z \in L_x$, $f(L_{g(x)}) \subseteq L_x$. So for all x, if $M_x \in \mathcal{PM}$ then $L_x \subseteq \overline{A} \Rightarrow f(L_{g(x)}) \subseteq \overline{A} \Rightarrow L_{g(x)} \subseteq \overline{B}$ (by reducibility) $\Rightarrow hg(x) \in \overline{B} - L_{g(x)}$ (by p-creativity of E) $\Rightarrow fhg(x) \in \overline{A} - L_x$ (by reducibility and the construction of $M_{g(x)}$). So A is p-creative for P with p-invertible p-productive function fhg. In other words, every p-creative set for P in $DEXT$ has a p-invertible p-productive function. This contradicts the assumption that there is a p-creative set for P in $DEXT$ which does not have p-invertible p-productive functions. ■

Definition 3 ([So-86]) A set A is said to be *weakly p-paddable* if there is a 1-1 p-honest polynomial time computable function p such that for all x and y, $x \in A$ iff $p(x, y) \in A$.

Corollary 1 (To the proof) *Every p-creative set for P in $DEXT$ is weakly p-paddable.*

Proof. The proof can be obtained from theorem 1 (3) and the proof of the only if part of theorem 3. ■

Corollary 2 ([Ga-89]) *Every p-m-complete set for $DEXT$ is weakly p-paddable.*

Proof. From theorem 1 (2) and corollary 1. ■

4 Remarks

We know that if the isomorphism conjecture for $DEXT$ fails, then one-way functions exist [Ber-77 and BH-77]. From our theorem 3 we know that if there is a p-creative set for P in $DEXT$ which does not have p-invertible p-productive functions, then the isomorphism conjecture for $DEXT$ fails. We therefore consider what kind of one-way functions would imply the existence of such p-creative sets and so fail the isomorphism conjecture for $DEXT$.

One obvious way to try it is to follow Joseph and Young's construction of K_f^k. Recall that $p_i(n) = n^{\sqrt[i]{|i|}} + i$. Given a total length increasing polynomial time computable function f, define

$$E_f = \{f(i) : M_i \text{ is a DTM and accepts } f(i) \text{ within } p_i(|f(i)|) \text{ steps}\}.$$

Theorem 4 *For every total length increasing polynomial time computable function f, E_f is p-creative for P in $DEXT$ with p-productive function f.*

Proof. We first show that $E_f \in DEXT$. Given an input x, since f is total length increasing polynomial time computable, to check whether there is an i such that $f(i) = x$ can be done in $DTIME(2^{O(|x|)})$. To check whether M_i is a DTM and accepts x within $p_i(|x|)$ steps can be done in $DTIME(2^{O(|i|+|x|)})$ as shown in section 2 when the Kleene function was defined. Since $|i| = O(|x|)$, $E_f \in DEXT$.

For all i, if $M_i \in \mathcal{PM}$, then $f(i) \in E_f \Leftrightarrow M_i$ accepts $f(i) \Leftrightarrow f(i) \in L_i$.

Therefore, E_f is p-completely creative for P in $DEXT$ with f as a p-completely productive function. So E_f is p-creative for P in $DEXT$ with f as its p-productive function. ∎

Ko, Long, and Du [KLD-86] proved that if one-way functions exist, then one-way functions that are both total and length-increasing exist. So the set E_f seems a candidate of p-creative set if f is total length increasing one-way. However, similar to the observation in [Ga-89], it is not always the case. In particular, we can show that for some total length increasing one-way function f, E_f has a p-invertible p-productive function.

Let e be an index of a Turing machine that accepts the empty set. For every x, let $\rho(x)$ be the index of the Turing machine by padding e with x. Clearly, ρ is polynomial time computable and p-invertible. For a total length increasing one-way function g, define

$$f(x) = \begin{cases} g(y)01^{|x|+1}, & \text{if } x = \rho(y) \text{ for some } y, \\ x0, & \text{otherwise.} \end{cases}$$

Then we can show that f is total length increasing one-way function and E_f has a p-productive function $h(x) = x0$ which is polynomial time invertible. Given x, suppose $M_x \in \mathcal{PM}$. If $x \notin \text{range}(\rho)$, then $f(x) = x0 = h(x)$ by the construction. It is clear that $x0 \in E_f \Leftrightarrow x0 \in L_x$ since $f(x) = x0$. If $x = \rho(y)$ for some y, then $f(x) = g(y)01^{|x|+1}$ and hence $h(x)$ is not in the range of f. Since $E_f \subseteq \text{range}(f)$, $h(x) \notin E_f$. From the definition of ρ, $L_x = \phi$. Hence $h(x) \notin L_x$. Therefore, $h(x) \in E_f \Leftrightarrow h(x) \in L_x$. This means that E_f has a p-invertible p-productive function.

From the construction of f, we can see that f is polynomial time invertible on a non-sparse set. This observation leads us to consider those one-way functions which are polynomial time invertible only on a sparse set. We call such functions "dense one-way functions". These functions were first studied by Grollmann and Selman [GS-88] as part of the study of public-key cryptosystems. Before we formally define dense one-way functions, we first notice that any one-way function can always be invertible in polynomial time on an infinite sparse set, which is shown as follows.

Theorem 5 *For any one-way function f, there is an infinite sparse set A in P and a polynomial time computable function g such that for every $x \in A$, $f^{-1}(x) = g(x)$.*

Proof. Without loss of generality, we assume that f is total. Let h be a total length increasing polynomial time computable function. Given a string x_0, let $A = \{f(x_0), fh(x_0), fh^2(x_0), \cdots\}$. Then clearly, A is infinite in P. Let

$$g(x) = \begin{cases} h^i(x_0), & \text{if } x = fh^i(x_0) \text{ for some } i, \\ x0, & \text{otherwise.} \end{cases}$$

Clearly, g is total polynomial time computable and for every $x \in A$, $f^{-1}(x) = g(x)$. ∎

Without loss of generality, we assume that all the one-way functions we shall consider are total. So $\{x : f^{-1}(x) \downarrow\}$ is not p-sparse.

Definition 4 A one-way function f is said to be *dense* if for every polynomial time computable function g, $\{x : g(x) = f^{-1}(x)\}$ is p-sparse.

Clearly, if g is a dense one-way function, then $f(x) = g(x)01^{|x|}$ is length increasing and dense one-way.

If f is length increasing and dense one-way, we know that E_f has f as its p-productive function. Does E_f have a p-invertible p-productive function? From the same observation as what Joseph and Young made in [JY-85], E_f does not seem to have a p-invertible p-productive function. If this is the case, from theorem 3, the isomorphism conjecture for *DEXT* fails.

Acknowledgments. I would like to thank Steven Homer and Alan L. Selman for their helpful comments.

References

[Ber-77] L. Berman, *Polynomial reducibilities and complete sets*, Ph.D. thesis, Cornell University, 1977.

[Ga-89] K. Ganesan, *Complete problems, creative sets and isomorphism conjectures*, Ph.D. thesis, Boston University, 1989.

[GS-88] J. Grollmann and A. Selman, *Complexity measures for public-key cryptosystems*, SIAM J. Comput., 17(1988) 309-335.

[JY-85] D. Joseph and P. Young, *Some remarks on witness functions for nonpolynomial and noncomplete sets in NP*, Theoret. Comput. Sci., 39(1985) 225-237.

[KLD-86] K. Ko, T. Long, and D. Du, *A note on one-way functions and polynomial-time isomorphisms*, Theoretical Computer Science, 47(1986) 263-276.

[KMR-86] S. Kurtz, S. Mahaney, and J. Royer, *Collapsing Degrees*, University of Chicago, TR-86-006, 1986.

[MY-85] S. Mahaney and P. Young, *Reductions among polynomial isomorphism types*, Theoretical Computer Science, 39(1985) 207-224.

[My-55] J. Myhill, *Creative Sets*, ZML 1(1955) 97-103.

[Ro-67] H. Rogers, *Theory of Recursive Functions and Effective Computability*, McGraw-Hill Book, 1967.

[Wan-89] J. Wang, *On p-creative sets and p-completely creative sets*, to appear in Theoretical Computer Science. The earlier version of this paper appeared in IEEE Proceedings of the 4th Annual Conference on Structure in Complexity Theory, June 1989, 24-33.

An Axiomatization of Wait-Freedom and Low-Atomicity

Ambuj K. Singh
Department of Computer Science
University of California at Santa Barbara
Santa Barbara, California 93106

Abstract

The concepts of *wait-freedom* and *low-atomicity* in concurrent shared-variable programs are explored in the frameworks of temporal logic and UNITY. With the help of some new primitives, axioms for these concepts are presented. Later, these axioms are used to prove the impossibility of distributed consensus.

1   Introduction

Recently there has been much interest in the concepts of low-atomicity and wait-free implementations. This interest can be mostly attributed to a seminal paper by Lamport [6] in which he defines *safe* registers, describes a hierarchy of shared registers built from safe registers, and presents wait-free implementations for some of these registers. Lamport's paper prompted two kinds of results — the first kind filled in the missing implementations in the hierarchy of shared registers [8, 9], and the second kind concentrated on impossibility results based on the concept of wait-freedom [1, 5].

All the above-mentioned papers include some definition of wait-freedom. Most of these definitions either are based on the notion of independence of execution speeds of processes (and processors) [6, 8] or rely on some syntactic means to disallow waiting [9]. In either case, they are all geared towards answering the question — is a given program wait-free? This approach works well for wait-free implementations of shared registers and other simple objects. However, it runs into difficulty when one wishes to generalize this approach to arbitrary, possibly non-terminating programs (we use the terms program and process synonymously). This is because in a more general setting one is not interested in whether a given program is wait-free, but rather in whether it meets a given progress property without waiting. As an example, consider a program F that is required to meet two progress properties, the first of them without waiting. The existing notions of wait-freedom are inadequate as F would be either required to meet both the properties *without* waiting or allowed to meet both properties *with* waiting.

In this paper we approach the requirement of wait-freedom from an axiomatic or proof-theoretic point of view. We present axioms for wait-freedom that can be applied individually to the progress properties of a program. These axioms are presented in the formal frameworks of temporal logic [3, 7] and UNITY [2] with the help of a few new operators. We chose the above two formalisms because of their different approaches towards fairness; in temporal logic one can make all the fairness assumptions explicitly while in UNITY the fairness assumptions are implicit and built into the logic. Fairness assumptions play a role when discussing wait-freedom because the set of computations that are fair only with respect to a particular process can be used to reason about the properties that are achieved by that process without waiting for rest of the system.

Closely related to the wait-freedom requirement is the requirement of low-atomicity, which states that a process can access (i.e., read or write) at most one shared variable in a single step. The relationship between these two concepts is illustrated by the fact that an arbitrary level of atomicity can be simulated by using a critical section if the processes are allowed to wait for each other. Consequently, the solutions to the atomic register construction problem become trivial if the wait-freedom condition is not enforced. The close relationship between these two conditions is also illustrated by the fact that the distributed consensus problem admits of a straightforward solution if either of these conditions is relaxed. Currently, the only mechanisms for stating the low-atomicity requirement are either syntactic [9] or operational [5, 6]. In this paper, we explore this requirement in the formalisms of temporal logic and UNITY, and present some axioms. By choosing different combinations of these axioms one obtains varying levels of atomicity. For example, by choosing just one of the axioms, one obtains *2-phase atomicity* [1] which states that a process does not both read and write shared variables in the same step.

The rest of the paper is organized as follows. In the next section, axioms for wait-freedom and low-atomicity are presented. In Section 3, these axioms are used to prove the impossibility of distributed consensus [1, 4, 5]. Concluding remarks appear in Section 4.

2 Axioms for Wait-Freedom and Low-Atomicity

We assume that the reader is familiar with branching-time temporal logic [3] and UNITY [2]; these two formalisms are recapitulated briefly in Section 2.1. In Section 2.2, the concept of program composition is discussed in the two logics and some new operators are introduced. These operators are later used to axiomatize wait-freedom and low-atomicity in Subsections 2.3 and 2.4 respectively.

2.1 A Brief Introduction to Temporal Logic and UNITY

2.1.1 Temporal Logic

We use a branching-time temporal logic similar to CTL^* [3]. We simplify our reasoning by assuming that all programs are non-terminating, in other words every computation is assumed to be infinite. The basic operators of the logic are: A (for all paths), E (for some path), $\Box$ (always), $\Diamond$ (sometime), and $\bigcirc$ (next time). Some of the rules of the logic are summarized below; p and q denote arbitrary temporal formulae.

[T0] $E\Diamond p \equiv \neg A\Box\neg p$, and $E\bigcirc p \equiv \neg A\bigcirc\neg p$.

[T1] $Ap \wedge Aq \equiv A(p \wedge q)$, $\quad Ap \wedge Eq \Rightarrow E(p \wedge q)$,
$\quad\quad \Box p \wedge \Box q \equiv \Box(p \wedge q)$, $\quad \Box p \wedge \Diamond q \Rightarrow \Diamond(p \wedge q)$,

$$A \Box A \Box p \quad \equiv \quad A \Box p, \quad \text{and} \quad E \Diamond E \Diamond p \quad \equiv \quad E \Diamond p.$$

[T2] $E \bigcirc (p \vee q) \equiv (E \bigcirc p) \vee (E \bigcirc q)$.

[T3] All the temporal operators are strict.

[T4] $(p \; \wedge \; A \Box (p \Rightarrow E \bigcirc p)) \; \Rightarrow \; E \Box p$.

2.1.2 UNITY

A program in UNITY [2] is a set of guarded assignment statements. The three basic operators for stating program properties are *unless, ensures,* and $\mapsto$ (pronounced *leads-to*). They are defined as follows. Let p and q be any predicates over program variables. Then, the property p *unless* q holds iff for all statements s in the program, the following Hoare Triple holds.

$$\{p \wedge \neg q\} \; s \; \{p \vee q\}$$

The property p *ensures* q holds iff p *unless* q holds and there exists a statement s that satisfies the following Hoare Triple.

$$\{p \wedge \neg q\} \; s \; \{q\}$$

The relation $\mapsto$ is defined to be the strongest relation satisfying the following three rules.

[U0] p ensures $q \; \Rightarrow \; p \mapsto q$,

[U1] $(p \mapsto q \; \wedge \; q \mapsto r) \; \Rightarrow \; p \mapsto r$, and

[U2] For any set W, $(\forall m : m \in W : p.m \mapsto q) \; \Rightarrow \; ((\exists m : m \in W : p.m) \mapsto q)$.

2.2 Program Composition

Both temporal logic and UNITY include mechanisms by which one can compose programs and reason about the composite programs in terms of the constituent programs. We discuss them separately in the next two subsections.

2.2.1 Temporal Logic

In temporal logic the reasoning about the composite program is carried out in terms of the (composite) computation tree that is generated as a result of the composition of the computation trees of the constituent programs. Every transition in the composite tree is obtained from a transition in one of the constituent tree and every path in the composite tree represents a possible computation of the composite program. No implicit fairness assumptions are made in generating the composite tree; specifically, from any node in this tree there exist (unfair) paths consisting of transitions of a particular constituent process only. In order to state the requirements of wait-freedom and low-atomicity, we introduce the notion of a F-path that is defined to be a path consisting of transitions of a constituent program F only. Based on this definition, we define two new temporal operators A^F and E^F as follows:

- The assertion $A^F p$ holds at a state iff formula p holds for all F-paths emanating from that state.

- The assertion $E^F p$ holds at a state iff $\neg A^F \neg p$ holds at that state.

The rules for temporal logic stated in Section 2.1.1 can be extended to these new operators. Some additional rules for these operators are stated next. Let F and G be the two constituent programs. Then,

- $E^F p \Rightarrow Ep$ and $Ap \Rightarrow A^F p$, for any temporal formula p,

- $E \bigcirc p \Rightarrow (E^F p \vee E^G p)$, for any predicate p over the program variables.

2.2.2 UNITY

The composition of two programs F and G is denoted $F \mid G$ and is obtained by the union of the sets of assignment statements of F and G. The reasoning about the composite program is done through the *Union Theorem* [2] stated as follows.

p unless q in $F \mid G \equiv$ *p unless q* in $F \wedge$ *p unless q* in G, and

p ensures q in $F \mid G \equiv$
(*p ensures q* in $F \wedge$ *p unless q* in G) $\vee$ (*p unless q* in $F \wedge$ *p ensures q* in G).

In order to state the requirements of wait-freedom and low-atomicity, we introduce two new operators — *ensures*^{F} and $\mapsto^F$, as follows.

- The assertion *p ensures*$^F q$ holds in the composite program $F \mid G$ iff
  p ensures q in $F \wedge$ *p unless q* in G.
  With this definition, the following theorem about the composite program $F \mid G$ follows immediately:
  p ensures q $\equiv$ *p ensures*$^F q \vee p$ *ensures*$^G q$.

- The relation $\mapsto^F$ is defined analogously to the relation $\mapsto$; it is defined to be the strongest relation satisfying rules $U0, U1$, and $U2$ (stated in Section 2.1.2) with *ensures*^{F} as the defining relation instead of *ensures*. Observe that $p \mapsto^F q$ implies that $p \mapsto q$.

2.3 Axiomatizing Wait-Freedom

We are given a program F and its environment G, and our aim is to axiomatize the condition that program F establishes the progress condition $A\square(p \Rightarrow A\lozenge q)$ without waiting for the environment G. (Here, p and q represent arbitrary predicates over program variables). We discuss the formal statement of the above property (henceforth called WF) in the frameworks of temporal logic and UNITY next.

Property WF is axiomatized in temporal logic by requiring that from any state satisfying predicate p, all computation paths with infinitely many transitions of F eventually establish q. In other words, from any state satisfying p, if program F is allowed to make progress infinitely often then predicate q will hold eventually. This is stated in temporal logic as $A\square(p \Rightarrow A(FAIR^F \Rightarrow \lozenge q))$, where the predicate $FAIR^F$ holds on a path iff there are infinitely many transitions of program F on that path. By ensuring fairness only with respect to F in the above formulation, we model the phenomenon that program F establishes the progress condition without relying on the environment taking any steps. If the predicate p in the above formula is true then the formula reduces to $A\square A(FAIR^F \Rightarrow \lozenge q)$. $\qquad \ldots \ldots (P)$

It follows as a special case of the above axiomatization that if the property WF holds then any path that begins in a state satisfying predicate p and consists of transitions of program F *alone* eventually establishes predicate q. In terms of the temporal operator A^F introduced in the previous section, this can be stated as $A\Box A^F \Diamond q.$ ......(P')

Property WF is formalized in UNITY by asserting that from any state satisfying predicate p, transitions of F alone will eventually establish q. In terms of the concepts introduced in the previous section, this is stated as $p \mapsto^F q$ in the composite program $F \mid G$.

2.4 Axiomatizing Low-Atomicity

The requirement of low-atomicity constrains the way a program can access shared variables; it requires that in one atomic step, a program accesses (i.e., reads or writes) at most one shared variable. For example, if programs F and G share variables x and y then all the following statements violate the low-atomicity requirement.

- $x := y$

- $b := (x = y)$ (where b is a local variable.)

- $x, y := 10, 20$

The following theorem shows that it is impossible to obtain a *complete* semantic axiomatization of low-atomicity; therefore, the best that we can hope for in the frameworks of temporal logic and UNITY is to state necessary conditions for low-atomicity and thus disallow as many instances of high-atomicity as possible.

Theorem: It is impossible to obtain a complete semantic axiomatization of low-atomicity.

Proof: The proof is by giving a counterexample. Assume such a complete semantic axiomatization exists. Consider programs F and G that share variables x and y. If program F consists of the single assignment statement $s :: x, y := x, y$, then it does not satisfy the low-atomicity requirement as the statement accesses two shared variables. On the other hand if program F consists of a single *skip* statement, then it does satisfy the low-atomicity requirements. However, the assignment statements s and *skip* are semantically equivalent and therefore, cannot be distinguished by purely axiomatic means. The theorem follows. ☐

The above theorem is not too surprising considering that low-atomicity is a syntactic requirement and two programs with different syntax may be semantically equivalent. In the remainder of this section we aim at presenting axioms that are necessary conditions for the low-atomicity constraint. We divide the constraint into three subconstraints $A0, A1$, and $A2$ and discuss their axiomatizations separately. Though these subconstraints taken together comprise low-atomicity, other combinations of the constraints are also useful. For example, by using constraint $A0$ alone one obtains *2-phase atomicity* [1] which, as shown in the next section, suffices for the proof of impossibility of distributed consensus.

[A0] In a single step, a process does not read and write shared variables; it either reads them or writes them.

[A1] In a single step, a process writes at most one shared variable.

[A2] In a single step, a process reads at most one shared variable.

For the discussion of the above three constraints in temporal logic and UNITY we assume, as before, a program of interest F and its environment G. The axiomatization of constraint $A0$ is discussed first.

From any state, let s be a single transition of program F that establishes a predicate p (over the program variables) and let t be a path consisting of transitions of program G that establishes a predicate q (also over the program variables). If step s preserves predicate q and path t preserves predicate p then in order for program F to satisfy the constraint $A0$ (note that we are stating only a necessary condition) there also exists a computation in which both predicates p and q hold. This is stated in temporal logic as follows.

$$A\square(\ (E^F(\bigcirc p \wedge (q \Rightarrow \bigcirc q)))\ \wedge\ (E^G(\Diamond q \wedge (p \Rightarrow \square p)))\ \Rightarrow\ (E\Diamond(p \wedge q))\ )\ \ldots\ldots(Q)$$

To see why the above is a necessary condition for constraint $A0$, consider separately the two cases in which program F reads and writes shared variables in step s. In the former case, the computation path t consisting of transitions of G is also feasible from the next state reached after step s of F. Furthermore, this computation path establishes predicate q and preserves predicate p; thus, there exists a path that establishes both p and q. In the latter case, F does not read any shared variables in step s and therefore, this step is also feasible at the end of the path t. Furthermore, this step establishes predicate p and preserves predicate q. Hence, there exists a path that establishes both p and q. Constraint $A0$ cannot be formalized in UNITY because there is no way to assert the existence of a particular computation path. (For the same reasons this constraint cannot be stated in a linear time temporal logic either.)

Next, we discuss necessary conditions for constraint $A1$. Let p and q be any predicates on two different shared variables and assume that both p and q hold in some state. Then, in order for program F to satisfy constraint $A1$, any *next* state that results from a transitions of F must satisfy either p or q. This is because program F can change at most one shared variable in one step. This necessary condition is stated in temporal logic as follows: $\quad A\square(p \wedge q\ \Rightarrow\ A^F \bigcirc (p \vee q))$. The formulation in UNITY is similar: $p \wedge q$ *unless* $(p \wedge \neg q) \vee (\neg p \wedge q)$ in program F.

Finally, we discuss necessary conditions for constraint $A2$. Let p be a predicate on the local variables of F and let $q.i$ be a predicate on the ith shared variable, (assuming some enumeration of the shared variables). Let s be any step of program F that is possible in a state that satisfies predicate p and all the $q.i$ predicates. Then, in order for program F to satisfy constraint $A2$, the same step s must also be possible from a state in which the predicate p and exactly one of the $q.i$ predicates hold (i.e., step s depends on at most one shared variable). This condition is best stated in terms of Hoare triples: for all statements s of F and for all predicates r over the program variables, if $\{p \wedge (\forall i :: q.i)\}\ s\ \{r\}$, then there exists an i such that $\{p \wedge q.i\}\ s\ \{r\}$. Because individual statements cannot be referenced, it is not possible to state the above requirement adequately in temporal logic and UNITY.

3 Distributed Consensus

Now we use the axiomatic definitions of low-atomicity and wait-freedom to prove the impossibility of distributed consensus [1, 4, 5]. This proof is carried out in the branching-time temporal logic discussed earlier. The specification of the distributed consensus problem is as follows.

There are two processes F and G, that have to agree on a binary value. Predicate b denotes that the processes have agreed on the value 0 while the predicate c denotes that the processes have agreed on the value 1. The constraints on the processes F and G are described in terms of the computation tree generated by the composition of the two processes as follows.

- The two outcomes of agreeing on 0 and agreeing on 1 are mutually exclusive, i.e., $A\square\neg(b \wedge c)$. $\dots\dots(S0)$

- Every outcome is possible, i.e., $E\Diamond b \;\wedge\; E\Diamond c$. $\dots\dots(S1)$

- A consesus is reached iff for all states on the computation paths leading out from the state, the same consensus is reached, i.e., $A\square(b \equiv A\square b)$ and $A\square(c \equiv A\square c)$. $\dots\dots(S2)$

  This property can be alternatively stated as $A\square(b \equiv A\bigcirc b)$ and $A\square(c \equiv A\bigcirc c)$. $\dots\dots(R0)$

- Processes F and G satisfy the low-atomicity constraint $A0$, i.e., in every step the processes either read or write shared variables. Consequently, the necessary condition (Q) stated in the previous section holds. $\dots\dots(S3)$

- Processes F and G reach a consensus without waiting for each other. Therefore, from properties (P) and (P') in the previous section,
$A\square A(FAIR^F \Rightarrow \Diamond(b \vee c))$ and $A\square A(FAIR^G \Rightarrow \Diamond(b \vee c))$, and
$A\square(A^F\Diamond(b \vee c))$ and $A\square(A^G\Diamond(b \vee c))$. $\dots\dots(S4)$

This completes the specification of distributed consensus. $\square$

Observation: From condition $S4$ stated above, it follows that
$A\square A(FAIR^F \Rightarrow \Diamond(b \vee c)) \;\wedge\; A\square A(FAIR^G \Rightarrow \Diamond(b \vee c))$.
By applying rule $T1$ for temporal logic,
$A\square A((FAIR^F \vee FAIR^G) \Rightarrow \Diamond(b \vee c))$.
Because every computation path is assumed to be infinite, $(FAIR^F \vee FAIR^G)$ is a tautology. Thus, $A\square A\Diamond(b \vee c)$. $\dots\dots(S5)$
$\square$

Next, we prove the main theorem.

Theorem: There does not exist a low-atomicity, wait-free implementation that achieves distributed consensus.

Proof: We show that the distributed consensus specification, i.e., the set of properties $S0, S1$, and $S2$, is inconsistent with the low-atomicity and wait-freedom conditions $S3$ and $S4$. In other words, we assume the above five properties and derive a contradiction.

It follows from Lemma 0 proved later that $E\Diamond(E\bigcirc b \;\wedge\; E\bigcirc c)$. Because F and G are the two constituent processes, there exist the following four possibilities.
$E\Diamond(E^F\bigcirc b \;\wedge\; E^F\bigcirc c)$, or $E\Diamond(E^G\bigcirc b \;\wedge\; E^G\bigcirc c)$, or
$E\Diamond(E^F\bigcirc b \;\wedge\; E^G\bigcirc c)$, or $E\Diamond(E^G\bigcirc b \;\wedge\; E^F\bigcirc c)$.
The first two possibilities are impossible on account of Lemma 1 (and its analogue) and the last two possibilities are impossible on account of Lemma 2 (and its analogue); this leads to a contradiction and we have the required proof. $\square$

Lemma 0: $E\Diamond(E\bigcirc b \;\wedge\; E\bigcirc c)$.
Proof: We assume that $\neg(E\Diamond(E\bigcirc b \;\wedge\; E\bigcirc c))$, i.e., $A\square\neg(E\bigcirc b \;\wedge\; E\bigcirc c)$, holds and derive a contradiction.

$$true$$
$\Rightarrow$ {fairness condition $S1$}
$$E\Diamond b \;\wedge\; E\Diamond c$$
$\Rightarrow$ {mutual exclusion condition $S0$ and
two applications of temporal logic rule $T1$}
$$E\Diamond(b \wedge \neg c) \;\wedge\; E\Diamond(c \wedge \neg b)$$
$\Rightarrow$ {predicate calculus}
$$E\Diamond\neg c \;\wedge\; E\Diamond\neg b$$
$\Rightarrow$ {temporal logic rule $T0$}
$$\neg(A\square c) \;\wedge\; \neg(A\square b)$$
$\Rightarrow$ {specification $S2$}
$$\neg c \wedge \neg b \qquad\qquad\qquad\qquad\qquad\qquad \ldots\ldots(R1)$$

Now, observe the following in the context of any state.

$$\neg c \wedge \neg b$$
$\Rightarrow$ {property $R0$}
$$\neg(A\bigcirc c) \;\wedge\; \neg(A\bigcirc b)$$
$\Rightarrow$ {temporal logic rule $T0$}
$$E\bigcirc\neg c \;\wedge\; E\bigcirc\neg b$$
$\Rightarrow$ {predicate calculus}
$$E\bigcirc((\neg b \wedge \neg c) \vee b) \;\wedge\; E\bigcirc((\neg b \wedge \neg c) \vee c)$$
$\Rightarrow$ {temporal logic rule $T2$}
$$(E\bigcirc(\neg b \wedge \neg c) \;\vee\; E\bigcirc b) \;\wedge\; (E\bigcirc(\neg b \wedge \neg c) \;\vee\; E\bigcirc c)$$
$\Rightarrow$ {predicate calculus}
$$E\bigcirc(\neg b \wedge \neg c) \;\vee\; (E\bigcirc b \;\wedge\; E\bigcirc c)$$
$\Rightarrow$ {assumption $A\square\neg(E\bigcirc b \;\wedge\; E\bigcirc c)$}
$$E\bigcirc(\neg b \wedge \neg c)$$

From property $(R1)$ and the above proof we have,
$$(\neg b \wedge \neg c) \text{ and } A\square((\neg b \wedge \neg c) \Rightarrow (E\bigcirc(\neg b \wedge \neg c))).$$
Thus, by applying rule $T4$ for temporal logic, we obtain,
$$E\square(\neg b \wedge \neg c).$$
But this violates the progress condition $S5$ and we have the needed contradiction. $\square$

Lemma 1: $\neg E\Diamond(E^F\bigcirc b \;\wedge\; E^F\bigcirc c)$.
Proof: The proof is by assuming $E\Diamond(E^F\bigcirc b \;\wedge\; E^F\bigcirc c)$ and deriving a contradiction.

$$true$$
$\Rightarrow$ {wait-freedom condition $S4$}
$$A\square A^G\Diamond(b \vee c)$$
$\Rightarrow$ {assume $E\Diamond(E^F\bigcirc b \;\wedge\; E^F\bigcirc c)$}
$$A\square A^G\Diamond(b \vee c) \;\wedge\; E\Diamond(E^F\bigcirc b \;\wedge\; E^F\bigcirc c)$$
$\Rightarrow$ {temporal logic rule $T1$}
$$E\Diamond(A^G\Diamond(b \vee c) \;\wedge\; E^F\bigcirc b \;\wedge\; E^F\bigcirc c)$$

$\Rightarrow\{$Lemma 2 and its analogue$\}$

$\quad E\Diamond(A^G\Diamond(b \vee c) \quad \wedge \quad \neg E^G\Diamond c \quad \wedge \quad \neg E^G\Diamond b)$

$\Rightarrow\{$temporal logic rule $T0\}$

$\quad E\Diamond(A^G\Diamond(b \vee c) \quad \wedge \quad A^G\Box\neg c \quad \wedge \quad A^G\Box\neg b)$

$\Rightarrow\{$temporal logic rule $T1\}$

$\quad E\Diamond(A^G\Diamond(b \vee c) \quad \wedge \quad A^G\Box(\neg c \wedge \neg b))$

$\Rightarrow\{$predicate calculus$\}$

$\quad E\Diamond(A^G\Diamond(b \vee c) \quad \wedge \quad A^G\Box\neg(c \vee b))$

$\Rightarrow\{$temporal logic rule $T1\}$

$\quad E\Diamond(A^G\Diamond false)$

$\Rightarrow\{$temporal logic rule $T3\}$

$\quad false$ $\qquad\qquad\qquad\qquad\qquad\qquad\qquad\qquad\qquad\qquad\qquad\qquad$ $\Box$

Lemma 2: $\neg E\Diamond(E^F\bigcirc b \quad \wedge \quad E^G\Diamond c)$.

Proof: The proof is by assuming $E\Diamond(E^F\bigcirc b \quad \wedge \quad E^G\Diamond c)$ and deriving a contradiction.

$\quad E\Diamond(E^F\bigcirc b \quad \wedge \quad E^G\Diamond c)$

$\Rightarrow\{$specification $S2$ and property $R0\}$

$\quad E\Diamond(E^F\bigcirc b \quad \wedge \quad E^G\Diamond c) \quad \wedge \quad A\Box(c \equiv A\bigcirc c) \quad \wedge \quad A\Box(b \equiv A\Box b)$

$\Rightarrow\{$temporal logic rule $T1$ and predicate calculus$\}$

$\quad E\Diamond(E^F\bigcirc b \quad \wedge \quad E^G\Diamond c) \quad \wedge \quad A\Box A\Box(c{\Rightarrow}A\bigcirc c) \quad \wedge \quad A\Box A\Box(b{\Rightarrow}A\Box b)$

$\Rightarrow\{$temporal logic rule $T1\}$

$\quad E\Diamond(E^F\bigcirc b \quad \wedge \quad A\Box(c{\Rightarrow}A\bigcirc c) \quad \wedge \quad E^G\Diamond c \quad \wedge \quad A\Box(b{\Rightarrow}A\Box b))$

$\Rightarrow\{$temporal logic rule $T1\}$

$\quad E\Diamond(E^F(\bigcirc b \wedge \Box(c{\Rightarrow}A\bigcirc c)) \quad \wedge \quad E^G(\Diamond c \wedge \Box(b{\Rightarrow}A\Box b)))$

$\Rightarrow\{$temporal logic$\}$

$\quad E\Diamond(E^F(\bigcirc b \wedge (c{\Rightarrow}\bigcirc c)) \quad \wedge \quad E^G(\Diamond c \wedge (b{\Rightarrow}\Box b)))$

$\Rightarrow\{$low-atomicity constraint $Q\}$

$\quad E\Diamond(E\Diamond(b \wedge c))$

$\Rightarrow\{$mutual exclusion condition $S0\}$

$\quad E\Diamond(E\Diamond false)$

$\Rightarrow\{$temporal logic rule $T3\}$

$\quad false$ $\qquad\qquad\qquad\qquad\qquad\qquad\qquad\qquad\qquad\qquad\qquad\qquad$ $\Box$

4   Discussion

In this paper we axiomatized the requirements of low-atomicity and wait-freedom in the frameworks of temporal logic and UNITY with varying degrees of success. For the wait-freedom condition, our axiomatization appears to be complete both in temporal logic and UNITY. However, for the low-atomicity condition, we proved that it is impossible to obtain a complete set of axioms. In light of this result, we presented some axioms that provided necessary conditions for low-atomicity. Later, we used these axioms to prove the impossibility of distributed consensus.

Stating requirements such as low-atomicity and wait-freedom in a formal way allows a thorough inspection of proofs that rely on these requirements. For example, we found that all the low-atomicity constraints $A0, A1$, and $A2$ do not have to be used for the proof of impossibility of distributed consensus; the 2-phase atomicity constraint $A0$ suffices for the impossibility proof. Another advantage of axiomatizing informal requirements is that a proof that relies only on these axioms holds in all systems that satisfy the axioms. For example, a close inspection of the formal statement of the wait-freedom (presented in Section 2.3) reveals that it is identical to the requirement of freedom from failure, i.e., a process satisfies some requirement in a wait-free manner if and only if the process satisfies the requirement in spite of the failures of other processes. As a result, property P (and therefore, specifications $S4$ and $S5$) also holds in a asynchronous message-passing system where processes may fail. Similarly, the necessary condition Q for low-atomicity (presented in Section 2.4) also holds for asynchronous message-passing systems in which processes do not send and receive messages in the same step. Therefore, the impossibility proof presented in the previous section also holds for such asynchronous message-passing system under the assumption of process failures. Formalizing informal requirements also permits the resulting axioms to be used as proof rules in a formal system. For example, one can appeal to the UNITY axiomatizations of the low-atomicity constraints as rules of inference in the proof of any program that uses low-atomicity.

References

[1] Anderson, J. H. , and M. G. Gouda, The Virtue of Patience: Concurrent Programming With and Without Waiting, work in progress.

[2] Chandy, K. M., and J. Misra, Parallel Program Design: A Foundation, Reading, Massachusetts: Addison-Wesley, 1988.

[3] Emerson, E. A., and J. Y. Halpern, "Sometimes" and "Not Never" Revisited: On Branching Time versus Linear Time Temporal Logic, Journal of the ACM, 33(1), January 1986, pp. 151 – 178.

[4] Fischer, M., N. Lynch, and M. Patterson, Impossibility of Distributed Consensus with One Faulty Process, Second Annual ACM Symposium on the Principles of Distributed Computing, 1983, pp. 1-7.

[5] Herlihy, M., Impossibility and Universality Results for Wait-free Synchronization, Seventh Annual ACM Symposium on the Principles of Distributed Computing, 1987, pp. 276-290.

[6] Lamport, L., On Interprocess Communication, parts I and II, Distributed Computing, 1(2), 1986, pp. 77-101.

[7] Manna, Z., and A. Pnueli, Adequate Proof Principles for Invariance and Liveness Properties of Concurrent Programs, Science of Computer Programming, 4, 1984, pp. 257-289.

[8] Peterson, G. L., and J. E. Burns, Concurrent Reading While Writing II: the Multi-writer Case, Twenty-eighth Annual Symposium on the Foundations of Computer Science, 1987, pp. 383 – 392.

[9] Singh, A. K., J. H. Anderson, and M. G. Gouda, The Elusive Atomic Register Revisited, Sixth Annual ACM Symposium on the Principles of Distributed Computing, 1987, pp. 206-221.

The Gamma Model as a Functional Programming Tool

R. HARRISON   H. GLASER
Department of Electronics and Computer Science
University of Southampton, U.K.

SUMMARY

In this paper we investigate the way in which the Gamma model, proposed by Banâtre and Le Metayer [1], might be supported in a functional language. We discuss the mechanism behind the model and examine the difficulties which arise when implementing Gamma in a functional language. We also explore its applicability as a programming paradigm by developing a library of higher order functions which can be used to facilitate the programming process.

INTRODUCTION

Banâtre and Le Metayer have proposed the Gamma model as a discipline of programming, together with an implementation technique. The mechanism of the Gamma model is analogous to the way that chemical reactions occur. Given the correct conditions for a reaction, a number of atoms or molecules may react together to form one or more new molecules.

The fundamental data type used by the Gamma model is the bag or multiset. A predicate function is used to test for a possible reaction between a subset of items, returning true if they can react and false otherwise. If the result was true, another function takes the items and performs the necessary action. These two functions will be referred to as the reaction and action functions respectively. The Gamma mechanism operates by continually using the reaction predicate on subsets taken from the multiset, followed by the action function if appropriate, until no further reactions are possible.

In this paper we are more concerned with a discussion of the use of the Gamma model as a tool to facilitate the development of higher order functions in functional languages, and with its implementation, than with the use of Gamma as a programming methodology.

The next section illustrates the action of the Gamma model using two examples taken from [1].

Example 1: Prime numbers

Suppose we wished to generate the prime numbers between 2 and 9. We choose the integers from 2 to 9 as our initial multiset. Taking two numbers at random from the set, we test them to see whether they will react. In this case the reaction function should return true if one number divides the other, i.e. if for any two numbers a and b, b mod a = 0. If they do react, then obviously b is not a prime number, so the action function must eliminate b from the set. If we call the reaction and action functions divides and remove respectively we have (using the notation of Miranda[†] [2]):

```
divides a b = b mod a = 0

remove a b = a
```

---

† Miranda (TM) is a trademark of Research Software Ltd.

The procedure described above is repeated until finally no more reactions are possible: if any two items could react, they would have already done so. For example, one possible set of reactions could be:

reacting elements	resulting set
2, 4	2,3,5,6,7,8,9
3, 6	2,3,5,7,8,9
2, 8	2,3,5,7,9
3, 9	2,3,5,7

As all the possible reactions have now taken place the result returned by Gamma is the set 2,3,5,7.

Example 2: Factorial

Consider generating factorial numbers. In particular, suppose we wish to find factorial 7. We take the integers from 1 to 7 as our initial multiset. Any two elements can react together, and when they do so they are replaced by their product. If we call the reaction and action always and times then we have:

always a b = True

times a b = a*b

and one possible set of reactions is:

reacting elements	resulting set
3,5	15,2,4,6,7,1
6,2	15,4,7,12,1
15,4	60,7,12,1
60,7	420,12,1
420,12	5040,1
5040,1	5040

Since no more reactions can take place the result returned in this case is 5040.

IMPLEMENTING GAMMA

In our first implementation we use lists to model multisets, and assume that the reaction and action are both dyadic functions, taking two items of identical type. For greater generality we permit the action function to return a list of items of the same type. With these restrictions the type of the gamma function is as shown below, using the notation of Miranda, where * denotes a type variable and brackets denote a list:

```
gamma::  (*->*->bool)->(*->*->[*])->[*]->[*]
```

One complete pass of gamma must compare all the elements in the multiset with each other. If there were no reactions whatsoever then we have finished and so we return the new set of elements:

gamma r a l = newset, ~reacted

where r, a and l denote the reaction, action and initial multiset respectively. If a reaction did occur we must call the function again, this time with the new set of elements. This new set is generated by another function, which we call delta. This takes two more parameters than gamma, one of them being a boolean which checks for the occurrence of reactions, and the other a list of elements which have been tried for reaction. This list will be returned when gamma terminates.

One procedure which is frequently employed in functional programs involves splitting a list of items into a head and tail, and testing the head against the items in the tail. Recursion is then used to repeat the action on the tail of the list, until the tail is empty. However, the function delta cannot be as simple as this, because the result of the action may be to remove an item from the tail of the list. So we must form a new tail which takes this into account. We use another function, epsilon, to find this new tail. The results of the reactions are accumulated in another list, called acc. So we have:

delta [] state r a = state
delta (h:t) (acc, reacted) r a = delta newt ((acc ++ newacc), (reacted V newreacted)) r a
                    where (newt, newacc, newreacted) = epsilon h t r a

Now consider epsilon . This function takes an element and a list and checks the element against those in the list for reaction. If there is a reaction, then epsilon returns the tail of the list, the result of the action, and a boolean set to True to indicate that a reaction has occurred. If the head of the list did not react, then it forms part of the new tail, and we must try again. So:

epsilon f [] r a = ([], [f], False)
epsilon f (h:t) r a = (t, (a f h), True), r f h
                  = (t, (a h f), True), r h f
                  = (h:newset, newacc, newbool), otherwise
                    where (newset, newacc, newbool) = epsilon f t r a

The function gamma can now be given:

gamma r a [] = []
gamma r a l = newset, ~reacted
              = gamma r a newset, otherwise
                where (newset, reacted) = delta l ([], False) r a

We now consider some of the more interesting design problems, many of which arise from the use of a strongly typed functional language. The most general definition of the Gamma model given by Banâtre and Le Meytayer [1] involved a list of reaction and action pairs which are applied to subsets of a multiset simultaneously. The types of the reaction and action functions were not defined, nor was the order in which the reaction, action pairs were to be performed. This introduces problems which are discussed in the next two subsections.

The type of the reaction and action functions

Our chosen functional language, Miranda, is a strongly typed, polymorphic language, in the sense of the Hindley-Milner type system [3]. A type inference system which is incorporated in the system is used at compile-time to infer the most general type scheme which could represent the untyped terms. This has ramifications for both the input and the output sets. We consider each set in turn, taking the former first.

Banâtre et al. imply that the Gamma model accepts reaction, action pairs which can take any number of items. However, we are forced by the Hindley-Milner type system of Miranda to fix the arity of the reaction and action functions. For example, the compiler will deduce that the type of a gamma function which has dyadic reaction and action functions is:

gamma:: (*->*->bool)->(*->*->[*])->[*]->[*]

The problem of fixed arity can be overcome by the development of a family of Gamma functions of various arities, the types of which are shown below.

monadic: gamma1:: (*->bool)->(*->[*])->[*]->[*]
dyadic: gamma2:: (*->*->bool)->(*->*->[*])->[*]->[*]
triadic: gamma3:: (*->*->*->bool)->(*->*->*->[*])->[*]->[*]   etc.

Turning to the output type, notice that the types of corresponding reaction and action functions are mutually dependent. The reaction function takes a number of items and returns a boolean. So for example, the type of a dyadic reaction function such as divides is: * -> * -> bool and this implies that the corresponding action must be of type: * -> * -> [*]. The action argument to gamma2 cannot have the type: * -> * -> [**] because the result of the action would then be of the wrong type for the reaction function to operate on a second time. However, the ability of a function to change an argument's type is so important that we felt it was necessary to incorporate this functionality. This led to the development of a family of functions called mu, the types of two of which are:

mu1:: (*->bool)->(*->[**])->[*]->[**]
mu2:: (*->*->bool)->(*->*->[**])->[*]->[**]

Of course, once an element has reacted, it cannot be tested for a further reaction. The full extent of the utility of the mu family of functions will become apparent later.

Implementation restrictions

The most general definition of the Gamma operator which is given in [1] and which is referred to above, states that Gamma takes a list of reaction, action pairs. However, throughout [1] the only examples given are of a Gamma which takes a single reaction, action pair, and we have adhered to this simplification. To generalise the family of Gamma functions further we provide a further function multi which takes a Gamma function, a list of reaction, action pairs and applies the Gamma function to each pair of functions and a set of items in turn:

multi:: (*->**->***->***)-> [(*,**)] -> *** -> ***

For example, given the functions:

limited_diff n (a,b) (c,d) = (c-a =1) & (c<n)

always a b = True

fib (a,b) (c,d) = (c,d):[(c+1, b+d)]

maximum a b = [a], a>b

= [b], otherwise

The expression: multi gamma2 [((limited_diff 10),fib),(always,maximum)] [(0,1),(1,1)]   first applies gamma2 to the list [(0,1),(1,1)], using the functions limited_diff and fib, producing the list [(9, 55), (10,89)], and then applies gamma2 to this list and the functions always and maximum, producing the list [(10,89)], indicating that fibonnacci (10) is 89.

Note that multi cannot be extended to the mu family of functions, because the consecutive pairs of reaction, action functions may have different types and hence cannot be members of a properly typed list.

Termination

When defining higher order functions using the Gamma model we must choose a pair of reaction and action functions which will guarantee the program's total correctness in that a result which is correct will be returned in a finite amount of time [5]. Each reaction between items must ensure progress towards termination. We find that a sufficient condition for termination is that the reaction, action pair must ensure that the cardinality of the multiset is strictly decreased.

The termination of Gamma functions will be examined again later.

ACCESS PROCEDURES

It was necessary to provide several procedures to support the Gamma model by enabling access or initialisation of the multiset. For example, the function singleton, given a multiset containing a single item, will return that one item. Because the implementation of the Gamma functions uses lists to simulate multisets, the implementation of singleton is as shown below:

singleton (h:t) = h

We also provided the function union, so that a Gamma function can be passed the union of two sets which have been produced by other Gamma functions. Again, due to the implementation of the Gamma model we can implement union using a built-in list function:

union s1 s2 = s1++s2

A monotonically increasing set of integers was frequently used as the initial multiset, which is provided in Miranda by the shorthand notation "..". Another multiset which we found useful consisted of the cross product of a set with itself. For example, using X to denote cross product:

{1,2,3} X {1,2,3} = {(1,1),(1,2),(1,3),(2,1),(2,2),(2,3),(3,1),(3,2),(3,3)}

We implement the cross product function, xprod, using a ZF expression: xprod s = [(a,b) | a <- s; b <- s]

USING GAMMA TO DEFINE HIGHER ORDER FUNCTIONS

The availability of a family of Gamma functions (and the mu variants) facilitates the production of other higher order functions, which are widely recognised as one of the strengths of functional languages [4].

As mentioned earlier, we must take care to choose a pair of reaction and action functions which guarantee the program's total correctness. This usually means finding a reaction, action pair which have the effect of decreasing the cardinality of the multiset.

For example, the use of the trivial reaction True with gamma2 and a dyadic action which always reduces two items to one is guaranteed to terminate, because the multiset will eventually be reduced to a singleton, at which point no more reactions are possible. This leads us to define a function (reduce) which resembles the built-in function foldr, except that it return a list:

```
reduce u f [] = [u]
reduce u f [x] = f (u:[x])
reduce u f (h:t) = gamma2 always f (h:t)        where    always a b = True
```

and we can then use this to define higher order functions. For example:

```
factorial n = reduce 1 times [1..n]        where    times a b = [a*b]
```

Similarly, we have: add_up = reduce 0 plus   where   plus a b = [a+b]

and   max_set = reduce 0 maximum   where maximum is the function given above.

The mu family of functions differs from the Gamma collection in that items are only tested once. Consequently termination need not be considered when deriving algorithms using a mu function. The reader may have recognised that mu1, combined with the trivial reaction condition True, has similar functionality to map. For example, given the functions:

```
every a = True
double a = [2*a]
maketuple first a = [(first, a)]
```

we have: mu1 every double [6,7,8] = [16,14,12]

and   mu1 every (maketuple 1) [16,14,12] = [(1,12), (1,14), (1,16)]

We formalise this by defining: map1 = mu1 every
We then have: map1 double [6,7,8] = [16,14,12]
and   map1 (maketuple 1) [16,14,12] = [(1,12), (1,14), (1,16)]

Similarly, we can define: map2 = mu2 always
For example, given a function makepairs: makepairs a b = [(a,b)]
then we have   map2 makepairs [1..6] = [(5,6),(4,5),(3,4),(2,3),(1,2)]

We can define a function select which is similar to the built-in function filter: select f = mu1 f identity
where   identity a = [a]

For example,   select (>0) [-9..5] = [5,4,3,2,1]

Similarly, we could have used a predicate which removed items of no interest. Any item which satisfies the predicate is removed, as shown below:

    sieve f = gamma1 f empty   where   empty a = [ ]

For example,   sieve (<0) [-5..6] = [0,1,2,3,4,5,6]

This function is guaranteed to terminate, since the action removes items which react until there are no more reactions.

The usual zip function which takes a function and two sets as parameters can be defined as follows. Each set contains items which are tuples, the first component of which is a unique index with an integer value between 1 and the cardinality of the set. Zip applies the function to items with equal indices. For example,

zip (+) [(4,56),(2,25),(3,39),(1,45)] [(2,23),(1,67),(3,30),(4,14)] = [(4,70),(2,48),(3,69),(1,112)]

we implement zip using gamma2. The reaction checks for items with equal indices: equal (a,b) (c,d) = a=c
and the action then applies the function to the second component of the items: apply f (a,b) (c,d) = [(a, f b d)]
Because the action combines items with equal indices, the Gamma function is bound to terminate when all items have indices which are unique. The function is given below:

    zip f set1 set2 = gamma2 equal (apply f) (union set1 set2)

We also implement the labelled union of two sets, as shown below:

    label_u n1 s1 n2 s2 = union (map1 (maketuple n1) s1) (map1 (maketuple n2) s2)

For example,   label_u True [1,2,3] False [1,2,3] = [(True,3),(True,2),(True,1),(False,3),(False,2),(False,1)]

Earlier we demonstrated the development of a fibonnacci function which uses a curried function (limited_diff) to obtain a number and its corresponding fibonnacci number:

    fibs n = multi gamma2 [((limited_diff n), fib), (always,maximum)]

We can then use a mu function to select the second component of the tuple which has n as its index, and use the access procedure singleton to return this component as an integer:

fib_num n = singleton (mu1 (eq n) second (fibs n [(0,1),(1,1)]))   where   eq n (a,b) = a = n
                                                                                  second (a,b) = [b]

For example, fib_num 10 = 89

Our final example in this section is the development of a sorting algorithm. The initial multiset consists of the integers to be sorted. Because there is no ordering associated with items in a set we must attach an index to each item, which will indicate the item's rank in the final set. Initially, we form tuples from the integers by using map1 to append the number 1 to each: map1(maketuple 1) s

We then use gamma2 to make all the indices differ by one, using two functions equal and make_differ:

    equal (a,b) (c,d) = a = c
    make_differ (a,b) (c,d) = (a,b):[(c+1,d)]

For example,   gamma2 equal make_differ [(1,78),(1,34),(1,56),(1,12),(1,54)]
gives: [(5,34),(4,56),(3,54),(2,12),(1,78)]

The reaction and action functions which perform the sort (the functions unordered and sorting respectively) simply compare the indices and values and swop them if necessary:

    unordered (a,b) (c,d) = a>c & b<d
    sorting (a,b) (c,d) = (c,b):[(a,d)]

Finally we use gamma2 and these functions to ensure that the set is sorted. Termination is guaranteed, because items only react if they are out of order, and the action always improves the ordering.

sort_set s = multi gamma2 [(equal, make_differ),(unordered, sorting)] (map1(maketuple 1) s)

For example: sort_set [78,34,56,12,54] = [(1,12),(3,54),(2,34),(5,78),(4,56)]

A FURTHER EXAMPLE

To examine the applicability of Gamma further we develop an algorithm to find the shortest paths between vertices in a weighted directed graph. The items in the multiset in this case are tuples which represent the edges of the graph. Each tuple has three fields, the first two of which are the vertices which the edge runs between and the third of which is the weight associated with the edge. For example, the graph:

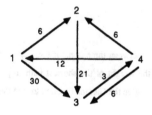

Figure 1

is denoted by: (1,2,6), (1,3,30), (2,3,21), (3,4,3), (4,1,12), (4,2,6), (4,3,6)

The aim is to develop a Gamma function which will return the shortest paths between all possible pairs of vertices in the graph. The length of a path is indicated by its weight (i.e. the third component in each tuple).

Note that the set of tuples given does not include all possible pairs of vertices. We must initialise the set by adding the pairs of vertices which do not have a direct path between them, with a weight that indicates that the direct route is not practical. This can be achieved by first forming the cross product of the set of vertices with itself, using the function xprod:

xprod[1,2,3,4] = [(1,1),(1,2),(1,3),(1,4), (2,1),(2,2),(2,3),(2,4), (3,1),(3,2),(3,3),(3,4), (4,1),(4,2),(4,3),(4,4)]

and then adding weights to each pair (in this case, a weight of 100 is sufficiently large);

    map1 addwts (xprod [1,2,3,4]) = (1,1,100),(1,2,100),(1,3,100),(1,4,100)   etc.

The initial multiset is obtained by forming the union of this set and the given set, and then removing the most expensive edges if there are any repetitions, as shown below for the digraph in Figure 1:

gamma2 equaltriples minwt (union (map1 addwts (xprod [1,2,3,4])) [(2,3,21), (1,2,6), (1,3,30),(3,4,3), (4,2,6), (4,1,12), (4,3,6)])

where   equaltriples (a,b,w1) (c,d,w2) = (a = c) & (b = d)
             minwt (a,b,w1) (c,d,w2) = [(a,b,w1)], w1<w2
                                     = [(c,d,w2)], otherwise

To solve the shortest paths problem, we note that in the digraph in Figure 2 the tuple (e,f,w3) should be replaced by (e,f,w1+w2) if and only if w1+ w2 < w3. This implies that the necessary reaction and action functions (is_shorter and shorten respectively) are given by:

    is_shorter (a,b,w1) (c,d,w2) (e,f,w3) = (b=c) & (d=f) & (a=e) & (w1+w2<w3)
    shorten (a,b,w1) (c,d,w2) (e,f,w3) = [(a,b,w1), (c,d,w2), (e,f,w1+w2)]

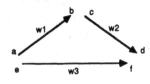

Figure 2

Notice that a reaction only takes pace between three items if there exists an indirect path which is shorter than the direct path, and that the action ensures that the weight of the shortest path replaces the previous weight, so the Gamma function is guaranteed to terminate. We can now give the Gamma function to find the shortest paths:

shortest_paths = gamma3 is_shorter shorten

For example, to find the shortest paths of the digraph in Figure 1, we evaluate the following expression:

shortest_paths (gamma2 equaltriples minwt (union (map1 addwts (xprod [1,2,3,4])) [(2,3,21),(1,2,6),(1,3,30),(3,4,3),(4,2,6),

(4,1,12),(4,3,6)]]))

which gives us the following paths:

[(4,3,6),(2,1,36),(3,4,3),(3,1,15),(1,1,42),(1,3,27),(2,4,24),(2,3,21),(4,4,9),(3,2,9),(3,3,9),(2,2,30),(4,1,12),(1,2,6),(4,2,6),
(1,4,30)]

CONCLUSIONS

The Gamma model which we have presented here has a more restricted form than that originally proposed by Banâtre et al., because of the restrictions imposed by the use of the Hindley-Milner type system. The difficulties we experienced fall into three categories:

1. Due to the implementation of multisets as lists, the multisets were restricted to be homogeneous.

2. As the arity of functions is determined at compile time we had to implement a family of Gamma functions rather than have one multi-functional Gamma operator.

3. As the reaction and action functions must be able to react on all the elements in the set it was not possible to allow an action which changed the type of its arguments.

Despite these problems we do feel that the methodology has great potential as a specification technique. The derivation of higher order functions is greatly simplified: the conventional higher order functions map and reduce could be defined immediately in terms of Gamma functions, as could a range of less familiar functions. The programmer no longer needs to consider a base case, which removes one possible area for concern.

The ease with which a more extensive problem (finding the shortest paths in a directed graph) could be solved was also demonstrated.

Since we have characterized Gamma in a functional language, the efficiency of implemented Gamma functions may be susceptible to improvement by automated transformation [6].

The lack of any explicit ordering and hierarchy implies the development of algorithms which are well suited to parallel implementations.

ACKNOWLEDGEMENTS

The authors would like to thank Pieter Hartel for his comments on an early draft of this paper.

REFERENCES

1. J.-P. Banâtre, D. Le Metayer, 'A new computational model and its discipline of programming', *INRIA Research Report*, 566, 1986.
2. D.A. Turner, 'An overview of Miranda', *ACM SIGPLAN Notices*, 21, 158-166, 1986.
3. R.J. Milner, 'A theory of type polymorphism in programming', *Journal of Computer and System Sciences*, 17, 1978.
4. R.J.M. Hughes, 'Why Functional Programming Matters', *The Computer Journal*, 32 (2), 98 - 107, 1989.
5. Z. Manna, R. Waldinger, *The Logical Basis for Computer programming, Volume 1: Deductive Reasoning*, Addison-Wesley, 1985.
6. J. Darlington, 'Program Transformation', in J. Darlington, P. Henderson, D.A. Turner (eds), *Functional Programming and its Applications:An Advanced Course*, CUP, 1982

Computing the Transitive Closure
of Symmetric Matrices

Anestis A. Toptsis [1], Clement T. Yu, and Peter C. Nelson
Dept. of Electrical Engineering
and Computer Science
University of Illinois
Chicago, IL 60680, USA

ABSTRACT

Certain real life binary relations are *symmetric* (map point connections, "iff" mathematical statements, multiprocessor links). Such relations can be represented by *symmetric* 0-1 matrices. Algorithms which take advantage of the symmetry when acting on such matrices, are more efficient than algorithms that are "good for all cases" by assuming a generic (non-symmetric) matrix. No algorithm, to our knowledge, *focusing on symmetric matrices* has been designed up to date for the computation of the transitive closure. In this paper, four algorithms - G, Symmetric, 0-1-G, 1-Symmetric - are given for computing the transitive closure of a symmetric binary relation which is represented by a 0-1 matrix. Algorithms G and 0-1-G pose no restriction on the type of the input matrix, while algorithms Symmetric and 1-Symmetric require it to be symmetric. These four algorithms are compared to Warren's algorithm in terms of the number of page faults incurred. Experimental results indicate that the new algorithms (with the exception of algorithm G) are about 2 times faster than Warren's algorithm for sparse matrices, 10 to 100 times faster for dense matrices, and about 1.4 times faster for medium dense matrices.

Keywords: Transitive closure, symmetric matrix, binary relation.

1 Introduction

Let G=(V,E) be a directed graph, where V is the set of vertices (nodes) and E is the set of edges of the graph G. The transitive closure of G is a graph G'=(V,E'), where E'=E U {e=(i,j)— there is a directed path from i to j of the form $i \rightarrow \ldots \rightarrow j$ in G}. In terms of matrices, we can represent G by its incidence matrix M, i.e. M(i,j) = 1 if there is an edge from i to j, and M(i,j) = 0 otherwise. Then the transitive closure of M is a matrix M' such that M'(i,j)=1 if there is a directed path from node i to node j in G, and M'(i,j)=0 otherwise. A matrix M is symmetric if M(i,j)=M(j,i) for all i and j. A binary relation R can be represented by a 0-1 matrix M in which M(i,j)=1 if iRj, and M(i,j)=0 otherwise. Symmetric matrices can be considered to be adjacency matrices of undirected graphs (or directed graphs where the existence of the edge $i \rightarrow j$ implies the existencee of the edge $j \rightarrow i$ and visa versa). Such graphs are used to represent symmetric binary relations.

Finding transitive closure has received considerable attention [1] [3] [2] [4] [6] [7] [8] [10] [11] [12] [13] [14] [15] [16] [17]. It appears so far in the literature, all algorithms that compute transitive closure assume the underlying binary relation to be a general (*non - symmetric*) directed graph. Although these algorithms also work for undirected graphs (since any undirected graph can be perceived as a special case of a directed graph), we maintain that algorithms especially designed for undirected graphs are better suited for applications that yield symmetric adjacency matrices, like the ones in the examples above. Algorithms that take advantage of the symmetry are presented in this paper.

It seems, so far, that two different kinds of input are the most popular, among all inputs. One is the 0-1 matrix representation described above, and the other is the successor list representation. For example, if the immediate successors of node 1 in the graph are the nodes 3, 4, 5, the successor list of 1 is the list [3,4,5]. The successor list representation is more efficient in space and time if the input graph has very few edges, while the 0-1 matrix representation is more efficient in space and time for graphs with more edges (see Appendix). So far, Warren's algorithm [16], is the best algorithm in terms of page faults, accepting as input a 0-1 matrix, and the algorithms in [8] are the best among those algorithms that accept as input successor lists. In this paper we choose to adopt the 0-1 matrix representation as the format of input to be accepted by our algorithms and compare the performance of 4 algorithms with Warren's algorithm. We assume as in [16] that only a few rows (or columns) of a matrix can be held in main memory. A major factor to be considered in the course of the computation is the number of disk access requests (page faults) incurred [11]. Experimental results indicate that the new algorithms (with the exception of algorithm G) are about 2 times faster than Warren's algorithm for sparse matrices, 10 to 100 times faster for dense matrices, and about 1.4 times faster for medium dense matrices.

In section 2, we give a short review of Warren's algorithm [16]. In section 3, algorithm G is presented. Algorithm G is applicable to any, not necessarily symmetric, matrix. However, it may not be efficient in the number of page faults. Therefore, in section 4, we introduce algorithm Symmetric which is applicable to symmetric matrices. Section 5 discusses algorithms 0-1-G and 1-Symmetric which take advantage of sparseness and denseness of matrices. Algorithm 0-1-G is applicable to any, not necessarily symmetric matrix, while algorithm 1-Symmetric is applicable to symmetric matrices. Experimental results comparing these four algorithms with Warren's algorithm, are given and analyzed in section 6. Finally, in section 7, we summarize our results, and indicate problems for further research.

---

[1] Current address: Dept. of Computer Science and Mathematics, York U., Atkinson College, Toronto, ONT, Canada, M3J-1P3

2 Warren's algorithm

Warren [16] gave an algorithm for computing the transitive closure of a binary relation R that is represented by a 0-1 n x n matrix M.

Warren's algorithm is as follows: [2]

```
1.   for i = 2 to n do          /* 1-st pass */
2.       for j = 1 to i-1 do
3.           if M(i,j) = 1 then
4.                   row(i) = row(i) V row(j);
5.   for i = 1 to n-1 do         /* 2-nd pass */
6.       for j = i+1 to n do
7.           if M(i,j) = 1 then
8.                   row(i) = row(i) V row(j);
```

Warren's algorithm makes two passes over the matrix, scans by rows and incurs fewer page faults than Warshall's algorithm [17]. In the first pass, it scans all entries below the main diagonal and updates each row using its preceding rows. In the second pass it scans all entries above the main diagonal and updates each row using its successor rows.

3 Algorithm G

Consider the following algorithm:
Algorithm G.

```
1.       for i = 2 to n do
                   /* process row i, i from 2 to n */
2.           begin
3.               for j = 1 to i-1 do /* part 1 */
4.                   if M(i,j)=1 then
5.                       row(i) = row(i) V row(j);
6.               for j = i-1 down to 1 do  /* part 2 */
7.                   if M(j,i)=1 then
8.                       row(j) = row(j) V row(i);
9.           end;
```

Algorithm G makes only one pass over the matrix. During part 1, it attempts to update row i using rows $1, 2, \ldots, i - 1$, while during part 2 it attempts to update rows $1, 2, \ldots, i - 1$ using the recently updated row i. For each $i = 2, \ldots, n$, first (part 1) it scans from left to right the entries of row i which are left of the main diagonal and secondly (part 2) it scans from bottom to top the entries of column i which are above the main diagonal. Whenever an entry M(a,b) is found to be equal to 1, the operation row(a):=row(a) V row(b) is performed.

In the remaining part of this section we illustrate how algorithm G works through an example, and then we give a proof of its correctness.

Example for algorithm G.
Let M be the input matrix as shown below.

$$M = \begin{pmatrix} 0 & 0 & 0 & 0 & 1 & 0 \\ 0 & 0 & 1 & 0 & 0 & 0 \\ 0 & 0 & 0 & 0 & 0 & 1 \\ 1 & 0 & 0 & 0 & 0 & 0 \\ 0 & 1 & 0 & 0 & 0 & 0 \\ 0 & 0 & 0 & 0 & 0 & 0 \end{pmatrix}$$

The path P: $4 \rightarrow 1 \rightarrow 5 \rightarrow 2 \rightarrow 3 \rightarrow 6$ exists. Essentially what the algorithm does is that for any path such as P, there will be an edge from the beginning vertex (4 in our example) to the end vertex (6 in our example) after the processing of the highest numbered row (5 in our example) which corresponds to the same numbered node in the path, but excluding the end node.

Proof of correctness of algorithm G.
It is essential to show that algorithm G sets M(a,b) = 1 iff there exists a directed path from a to b in the input matrix. The "if" part of the result is established by Lemma 3.3 and the "only if" part is established by Lemma 3.2. *Notation:* Given a path P: $a_1 \rightarrow \ldots \rightarrow a_n$, we will refer to the max$\{a_1, \ldots, a_{n-1}\}$ as the maxP. For example, maxP = 5 for the path P in the above example.

---

[2] In lines 4 and 8 of the algorithm, V denotes the logical "or" operation applied to each element of the rows.

Lemma 3.1

During algorithm G, if the edge $a \rightarrow b$ is added, then prior to the addition of the edge, a path P: $a \rightarrow k \rightarrow b$ is established for some k. Moreover, as soon as one such path P is established, the edge $a \rightarrow b$ is added during processing row maxP = max{a,k}.

Proof

The edge $a \rightarrow b$ can be added only if the operation (1): row(a) := row(a) V row(k) is performed for some k, and at the same time (2): M(k,b) = 1. (1) implies that the entry M(a,k)=1 was encountered, i.e. the edge $a \rightarrow k$ exists. (2) implies the existence of the edge $k \rightarrow b$. Thus, the path P exists. Moreover, note, the operation (1) is performed only during processing row maxP. In particular, if maxP = a, the entry M(a,k) is checked during processing part 1 of row a, and if maxP=k, the entry M(a,k) is checked during processing part 2 of row k. $\square$

Lemma 3.2

Suppose the edge $a_1 \rightarrow a_n$ has been added after algorithm G has processed row i, but before start processing row i+1. Then there exists a path P: $a_1 \rightarrow \ldots \rightarrow a_n$ in the input matrix, with $maxP < i+1$.

Proof

Assume that the edge $a_1 \rightarrow a_n$ is added during processing of rows $2, \ldots, i$. By Lemma 3.1, there exists a k such that the path W: $a_1 \rightarrow k \rightarrow a_n$ is first established and row maxW is processed. Since row i+1 has not been processed, $maxW < i+1$. If the path W exists in the input matrix, the statement is proved. Suppose W does not exist in the input matrix. Applying Lemma 3.1 to $a_1 \rightarrow k$ and $k \rightarrow a_n$, there exist k_1 and k_2 such that the paths $W_1: a_1 \rightarrow k_1 \rightarrow k$ and $W_2:k \rightarrow k_2 \rightarrow a_n$ are first established, and the rows $maxW_1$ and $maxW_2$ are processed respectively. Since row i+1 has not been processed, again, $maxW_1 < i+1$ and $maxW_2 < i+1$. Therefore, during processing rows $2, \ldots, i$, the path Q:$a_1 \rightarrow k_1 \rightarrow k \rightarrow k_2 \rightarrow a_n$ is established and row maxQ is processed. If Q exists in the input matrix, the statement is proved. Otherwise, iterate the above argument. Since only a finite number of iterations is possible due to the finiteness of the set $\{1, \ldots, i\}$ we get a path P from a_1 to a_n, which exists in the input matrix, and $maxP < i+1$. $\square$

Lemma 3.3

Let the path P: $a_1 \rightarrow a_2 \rightarrow \ldots \rightarrow a_n$ exist in the input matrix, and m=maxP. Then after having processed row m, using algorithm G, the edge $a_1 \rightarrow a_n$ will have been added.

Proof

By induction on the length L of the path.

If L=2, consider the path $a_1 \rightarrow a_2 \rightarrow a_3$, and let $m = max\{a_1, a_2\}$. The presence of the edges $a_1 \rightarrow a_2$, $a_2 \rightarrow a_3$ implies $M(a_1, a_2) = M(a_2, a_3) = 1$.

If $m = a_1$ (resp. $m = a_2$), during the processing of row m, part 1 (resp. part 2), since $M(a_1, a_2) = 1$, the operation $row(a_1) := row(a_1)Vrow(a_2)$ is performed. Since $M(a_2, a_3) = 1$, the entry $M(a_1, a_3)$ is updated to 1, i.e. the edge $a_1 \rightarrow a_3$ is added.

Consider the path P: $a_1 \rightarrow \ldots \rightarrow a_{L+1}$ of length L, and let $m = maxP$. If $m = a_1$ (resp. $m = a_L$), after processing row max$\{a_2, \ldots, a_L\} < m$ (resp. max$\{a_1, \ldots, a_{L-1}\} < m$) the edges $a_2 \rightarrow a_{L+1}$ (resp $a_1 \rightarrow m$) will have been added by induction hypothesis. So before start processing row m, the path $m \rightarrow a_2 \rightarrow a_{L+1}$ (resp. $a_1 \rightarrow m \rightarrow a_{L+1}$) is established, and the rest follows from the same proof as given in the induction basis.

If $m = a_k$, $1 < k < L$, then after processing row max$\{a_1, \ldots, a_{k-1}, a_{k+1}, \ldots, a_L\} < m$, the edges $a_1 \rightarrow m$ and $a_{k+1} \rightarrow a_{L+1}$ will have been added by induction hypothesis. So before start processing row m, the path $a_1 \rightarrow m \rightarrow a_{k+1} \rightarrow a_{L+1}$ is established. Then in processing part 1 of row m, the entry $M(m, a_{k+1}) = 1$ is encountered, and the operation $row(m) := row(m) Vrow(a_{k+1})$ is performed. This sets $M(m, a_{L+1}) = 1$, since $M(a_{k+1}, a_{L+1}) = 1$. In processing part 2 of row m, the entry $M(a_1, m) = 1$ is found. The resulting operation is $row(a_1) := row(a_1) Vrow(m)$, and this, due to (the recently updated) $M(m, a_{L+1}) = 1$, sets $M(a_1, a_{L+1}) = 1$. $\square$

Proposition 3.4

Algorithm G sets M(a,b)=1 iff there is a directed path P from a to b, in the input matrix.

Proof

"If": Lemma 3.3 guarantees that the entry M(a,b) will be equal to 1, after row maxP is processed.

"Only if": If M(a,b) is set to 1, the existence of a path from a to b in the input matrix, is guaranteed by Lemma 3.2. $\square$

Consider the processing of row i by algorithm G. In the first part, row i is updated by row j, $j < i$, if M(i,j)=1, and in the second part, row i updates row j, $j < i$, if M(j,i)=1. The testing of whether M(i,j)=1, $j = 1, \ldots, i-1$, can be handled by keeping row i in main memory. However, the testing of whether M(j,i)=1, $j = 1, \ldots, i-1$, requires bringing into main memory rows $1, 2, \ldots, i-1$. This incurs many page faults. However, if the matrix is symmetric, M(j,i)=M(i,j), $j = 1, \ldots, i-1$, and therefore the testing can be performed on the entries of row i which is kept in the main memory. We have to show that the symmetry property holds during the processing by algorithm G.

4 Algorithm Symmetric

Assume that the input matrix is symmetric. This assumption allows the transitive closure to be computed by the following algorithm.

Algorithm Symmetric:

```
1.    for i=2 to n do
2.       begin
3.          for j=1 to i-1 do
                        /* part 1 begins */
4.             if M(i,j)=1 then
5.                 row(i):= row(i) V row(j);
                        /* part 1 ends  */
6.          for j=i-1 downto 1 do
                        /* part 2 begins */
7.             if M(i,j)=1 then
8.                 row(j):= row(i) V row(j);
                        /* part 2 ends  */
9.       end;
```

Algorithm Symmetric is identical to Algorithm G, except that in line 7 it checks the i-th instead of the j-th row. This clearly means a substantial saving in the number of page faults since row j is accessed only if the check in line 7 succeeds. Note Algorithm Symmetric, like Algorithm G, makes only one pass over the matrix.

Notation: Given a matrix M, in the sequel, we will refer to the upper-left submatrix bounded by row i and column i of M, as the (i,i)-submatrix. For example, the(3,3)-submatrix of the matrix A below,

$$A = \begin{pmatrix} 0 & 0 & 0 & 0 & 0 \\ 0 & 0 & 0 & 1 & 0 \\ 0 & 0 & 0 & 1 & 1 \\ 0 & 1 & 1 & 0 & 0 \\ 0 & 0 & 1 & 0 & 0 \end{pmatrix}$$

is the all-zeroes 3 by 3 matrix.

Algorithm Symmetric has the following properties:
a) After processing part 1 but before start processing part 2 of row i, $M(i,j) = M(j,i)$, $j = 1, \ldots, i-1$.
b) After updating preceding rows by row i in part 2, the (i,i)-submatrix is symmetric.
Condition (a) allows us to use row i to check the values of $M(j,i)$, $j = 1, \ldots, i-1$, thus saving page faults. Condition (b) ensures that after all rows are processed, the resulting matrix is symmetric.

Example for algorithm Symmetric.
Consider the Symmetric matrix M as shown below.

$$M = \begin{pmatrix} 0 & 0 & 1 & 0 & 0 \\ 0 & 0 & 0 & 1 & 0 \\ 1 & 0 & 0 & 1 & 1 \\ 0 & 1 & 1 & 0 & 0 \\ 0 & 0 & 1 & 0 & 0 \end{pmatrix}$$

After processing rows 1 and 2, there is no change. After processing the first part of row 3 , the entry M(3,3) is set to 1, and $M(3,j) = M(j,3)$, $j = 1,2$. Scanning row 3 backwards, since M(3,1) = 1, the operation row(1) := row(1) V row(3) is performed. This sets M(1,j) = 1, j = 1,4,5. Note at this point the (3,3)-submatrix is symmetric, as shown in below.

$$(3,3) - submatrix = \begin{pmatrix} 1 & 0 & 1 \\ 0 & 0 & 0 \\ 1 & 0 & 1 \end{pmatrix}$$

After processing row 4 (both parts), the entire matrix becomes

$$\begin{pmatrix} 1 & 1 & 1 & 1 & 1 \\ 1 & 1 & 1 & 1 & 1 \\ 1 & 1 & 1 & 1 & 1 \\ 1 & 1 & 1 & 1 & 1 \\ 0 & 0 & 1 & 0 & 0 \end{pmatrix}$$

where row 4 was first updated by rows 2 and 3, and it then updated in order, rows 3, 2, and 1. Note that the (4,4)-submatrix was changed, but remained symmetric. Finally in the processing of row 5, during the first part, the entries in the entire row 5 are set to 1. The resulting transitive closure is the all-ones 5 by 5 matrix, and is thus symmetric.

We now show the properties (a) and (b).

Proof of correctness for algorithm Symmetric.

Proposition 4.1

After processing part 1 of row i, using Algorithm G, M(i,j)=1 iff M(j,i)=1, for all $j < i$. Moreover, after we finish part 2, the (i,i)-submatrix is symmetric.

Proof.

By induction on i.

When i=2, in part 1 only M(2,1) is scanned. Then clearly M(2,1)=1 iff M(1,2)=1 since the original matrix is symmetric. Also note the (2,2)-submatrix remains symmetric after part 2 is completed since the algorithm does not change any entry from 1 to 0. Consider the processing of row i. We now show:

(A) If we have $M(j, i) = 1$, $j < i$, before start processing row i, then after processing part 1 of row i we have M(i,j)=1. Note that M(j,i), $j < i$, remains unchanged during processing part 1 of row i.

(B) If after processing part 1 of row i we have M(i,j)=1, $j < i$, then we also have M(j,i)=1.

(C) After processing part 2 of row i, the (i,i)-submatrix is symmetric.

(A). If M(j,i)=1 in the input matrix, initially M(i,j)=1 by symmetry and there is no operation in algorithm G which converts "1" to "0". Suppose M(j,i) is initially 0 but is changed to 1, i.e. the edge $j \rightarrow i$ is added, during the processing of rows $2, \ldots, i - 1$. This implies by Lemma 3.2, that in the *input matrix* there is a path $P: \rightarrow m_1 \rightarrow \ldots \rightarrow m_k \rightarrow i$ with $max P < i$. The edge $m_k \rightarrow i$ in P means $M(m_k, i) = 1$ and so in the input matrix $M(i, m_k) = 1$ by symmetry. Also observe, after processing row $max\{m_1, \ldots, m_k\} < i$ the edge $m_k \rightarrow j$ is added by Lemma 3.3, since the path $m_k \rightarrow \ldots \rightarrow m_1 \rightarrow j$ also exists in the input graph by symmetry. Thus, $M(i, m_k) = M(m_k, j) = 1$ before start processing row i. Then, in processing part 1 of row i, when the entry $M(i, m_k) = 1$ is encountered, the operation $row(i) := row(i) V row(m_k)$ is performed. This sets M(i,j)=1.

(B). Again we assume M(i,j) is not 1 in the input matrix, for else the proof is trivial. Since M(i,j)=1 after processing part 1 of row i, it will also be M(i,j)=1 after processing part 2 of row i and before start processing row i+1. This is because algorithm G does not convert any "1" to "0". Therefore, by Lemma 3.2 there exists a path $P: i \rightarrow m_1 \rightarrow \ldots \rightarrow m_k \rightarrow j$ in the input matrix, with $max P < i + 1$. Since the highest numbered processed row is row i, maxP=i. So $m_1, \ldots, m_k < i$. Observe also the path $P' : j \rightarrow m_k \rightarrow \ldots \rightarrow m_1 \rightarrow i$ exists, since the input matrix is symmetric. Therefore, after algorithm G processed row $max P' < i$, the edge $j \rightarrow i$ was added according to Lemma 3.3, i.e. M(j,i) was set to 1.

(C). By induction hypothesis before start processing part 1 of row i, the (i-1,i-1)-submatrix is symmetric. Also, during processing part 1 of row i, the (i-1, i-1) - submatrix does not change, and at the end of part 1 of row i the segments of row i and column i which are included in the (i,i)-submatrix are identical, by (A) and (B). Moreover, these segments do not change during processing part 2 of row i. This is because, on the one hand, the entire row i is not modified and on the other hand the only updates that may occur in the segment of column i, are overwrites caused by operations of the form row(j):=row(j) V row(i), whose triggering requires M(j,i) to be already 1. So the only changes that may occur in the (i,i)-submatrix are those made during processing part 2 of row i, and such changes may occur only inside the (i-1,i-1)-submatrix. Suppose during processing part 2 of row i, the entries $M(j_m, i) = 1$, $m = 1, \ldots, k$, $j_m < i$, are encountered, and so the operations (*): $row(j_m) := row(j_m) V row(i)$ are performed. By (A), $M(i, j_m) = 1$. Therefore, after the completion of the operations (*), the entries

$$\begin{matrix} (j_1, j_1) & (j_1, j_2) & \cdots & (j_1, j_k) \\ (j_2, j_1) & (j_2, j_2) & \cdots & (j_2, j_k) \\ \vdots & \vdots & \vdots & \vdots \\ (j_k, j_1) & (j_k, j_2) & \cdots & (j_k, j_k) \end{matrix}$$

have been set to 1, inside the (i-1, i-1)-submatrix. Clearly, the symmetry of the (i,i)-submatrix has been preserved.□
There are three situations in which algorithm Symmetric may save in the number of page faults.

- First, during processing part 2 of row i, the checking of M(j,i), $j < i$, can be replaced by that of M(i,j). Since row i can be kept in main memory in processing part 2 of row i, the checking is free. This was reported earlier.

- Second, suppose rows i_1, i_2, ..., i_k were brought into main memory during processing part 1 of row i. This implies $M(i, i_j) = 1$, j = 1, ..., k.

  Thus, these rows will also be needed into main memory during processing part 2. If the main memory can hold m rows and $k > m$ rows are accessed in the first part and then m of these rows are kept in the main memory at the end of the first part, then these m rows need not be paged in during part 2. To ensure that these m page faults will be saved, observe that the last accessed row in part 1 is the first accessed row in part 2. If this row is kept in main memory at the end of part 1, it will not incur any page fault in part 2. As soon as the row is processed, it will not be needed in the remaining part of part 2 and can be replaced by another row. Thus, if the highest numbered row is replaced during part 2, no useful row is discarded and the m rows of page faults are guaranteed to be saved.

- Third, in starting the processing of part 1 of row j, if $M(j, j_t) = 1, j_t < j, t = 1, \ldots, w$, for some w, and these rows are in main memory, then try to preserve them in main memory by marking them as "useful" rows until they are processed. As soon as a row is processed in part 1, it is not needed for the rest of part 1, and can be replaced by another row. In general, the lowest numbered row is replaced unless a row not marked as "useful" is found.

5 Algorithms 0-1-G and 1-Symmetric

We consider cases where the input matrix or some intermediate matrix is very sparse (i.e. small percentage of 1's), or very dense (i.e. high percentage of 1's). All of these cases have the characteristic that many rows of the matrix will be all-zeroes or all-ones. In all of the above algorithms (G, Warren's, Symmetric), we do not distinguish any such case from other cases. On the other hand, if we know in advance that a row contains only zeroes or only ones, then there would be no reason to access it, since the outcome of any such access is known and well-defined, as is explained below. The above considerations lead us to introduce the following utility.

Keep permanently two linear arrays Q0 and Q1 in Main Memory, consisting of n bits each. Denote by $Qm(i)$ the i-th bit of array Qm, where m = 1 or 2. Then,

$Q0(i) = 1$ if row i has been found to be an all-zeroes row, 0 otherwise.
$Q1(i) = 1$ if row i has been found to be an all-ones row, 0 otherwise.

There are three situations in which algorithms G and Symmetric can save in the number of page faults, by using the arrays Q0 and Q1.

- First, when an operation (*): row(i) := row(i) V row(k) is to be performed, if $Q0(k)=1$ then there is no need to perform (*) since row i will not be changed if it is "or"ed with an all-zeroes row. On the other hand, if $Q1(k)=1$, then again there is no need to perform (*). It only suffices to set $Q1(i)=1$. In either case, row k is not accessed and therefore no page fault is incurred. Note, however, $Q0(k)$ cannot be 1 if the input matrix is symmetric. This is because execution of the operation (*) implies that the entry $M(i,k)=1$ was found. In such a case, $M(k,i)=1$ according to Proposition 4.1.

- Second, if prior to processing row i, it is found $Q1(i)=1$, then part 1 of row i need not be executed, since row i can not be changed during part 1. Since the entries $M(i,j)=1$, $j = 1,\ldots,i-1$ are not scanned, the rows $1,\ldots,i-1$ are not accessed, and therefore no page fault is incurred. Moreover, if the input matrix is symmetric, algorithm Symmetric obtains further benefits. Specifically, since $Q1(i)=1$, $M(i,j)=1$, $j = 1,\ldots,i-1$, and according to Proposition 4.1, $M(j,i)=1$ as well. Therefore, part 2 of row i need not be performed either. It only suffices to set $Q1(j)=1$, $j = 1,\ldots,i-1$. So, again the rows $1,\ldots,i-1$ are not accessed and no page fault is incurred.

- Third, if during processing part 1 of row i, an entry $M(i,j) = 1, j < i$, is encountered with $Q1(j)=1$, $Q1(i)$ is set to be 1. Then, similar to the second case, the entries $M(i,t)$, $t = j+1,\ldots,i-1$, need not be scanned. So none of the rows t will be accessed and thus no page fault is incurred. Moreover, for symmetric matrices, similar to the second case, part 2 of row i need not be executed, thus saving even more page faults.

In the above three situations, algorithm G can save in the number of page faults by utilizing both arrays Q0 and Q1, and algorithm Symmetric can save in the number of page faults by utilizing the array Q1. We incorporate the above concepts into algorithms G and Symmetric, thus getting the algorithms 0-1-G and 1-Symmetric respectively. The main drawback of 0-1-G and 1-Symmetric is the additional space required to store the two arrays Q0 and Q1. This space is equivalent to k rows, where k = 2 for 0-1-G, and k = 1 for 1-Symmetric.

6 Experimental Results

We compared the four algorithms described above with Warren's algorithm, in terms of the number of page faults incurred during the computation of the transitive closure. We measure their performance for sparse, medium dense, and dense matrices. We define the *critical percentage* (CP) to be the least percentage of 1's in the input matrix which makes the transitive closure to be the all-ones matrix. Clearly, if the input matrix contains the path $1 \rightarrow 2 \rightarrow \ldots \rightarrow n \rightarrow 1$, the resulting transitive closure will be all 1's. The path has n edges and therefore it is sufficient to have n 1's in the input matrix. Thus $CP = \frac{100 \cdot n}{n^2} = \frac{100}{n}$. A sparse matrix is defined to be a matrix having the percentage of 1's no more than CP. A dense matrix is arbitrarily defined to be a matrix having the percentage of 1's between 25% and 100%. A medium dense matrix is neither sparse nor dense. The positions of the 1's within each matrix were generated randomly in our experiments. An important component of the experimental setup is the page replacement simulating routines. For Warren's algorithm, the LRU (Least Recently Used) replacement policy is used — Warren himself assumes LRU in [16]. For the four algorithms presented in this paper, the page replacement methods used are LRU and MRU (Most Recently Used). Specifically, during part 1 of all four algorithms, LRU is used. During part 2, MRU is used. The reason MRU is chosen for part 2, is that after row k, $1 \leq k \leq i-1$, is used, this row becomes useless at least until the end of the current iteration. Therefore, it can be replaced by another row if the space is needed without having to be concerned that a potentially useful row is thrown out of the main memory. Also, in case that during iteration i of any of the four algorithms, a decision should be made to replace either row i or some other row z with a row w, then row i is always kept in memory, and row z is replaced.

The results presented in the Figures 6.1 to 6.9 below, are results averaged over 10 readings per point. S stands for Symmetric. We present results with matrix sizes N x N, with N = 40,50,100, i.e. the CP's are k%, with k = 2.5, 2, 1 respectively. In the experiments it is assumed that one page holds exactly one row, and the matrix is stored in row-major order. In the figures, N stands for N x N matrix and $|MM| = t\%$ means that t% of the matrix can reside in main memory at any time. Of course, for the algorithms 0-1-G and 1-S, the number of rows of the matrix can reside in main memory, is 2 less and 1 less respectively, since 2 and 1 additional pages are required for the algorithms in order to store the arrays Q0 and Q1. It is assumed that at least 10% of the matrix can reside in main memory. (It was observed that algorithm S is slightly inferior to Warren's algorithm for range of sparseness 2% to 4%, if less than 10% of the matrix resides in main memory. Specifically, for 100 x 100 matrices, algorithm S incurs 1.010 times the page faults incurred by Warren's algorithm for 2% sparseness, and 1.028 times the page faults incurred by Warren's algorithm for 4%, when the main memory holds less than 10% of the matrix.)

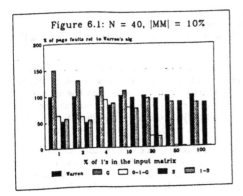

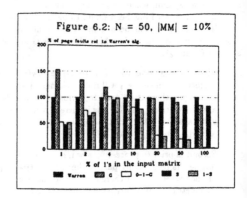

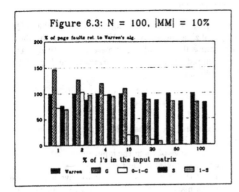

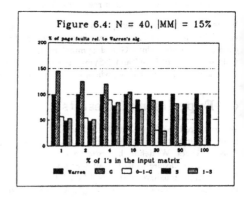

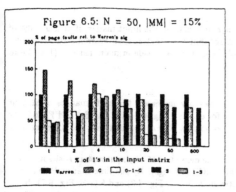

Figure 6.5: N = 50, |MM| = 15%

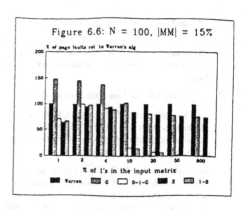

Figure 6.6: N = 100, |MM| = 15%

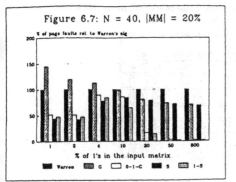

Figure 6.7: N = 40, |MM| = 20%

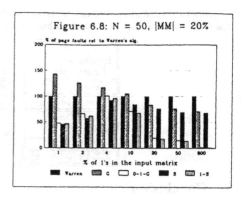

Figure 6.8: N = 50, |MM| = 20%

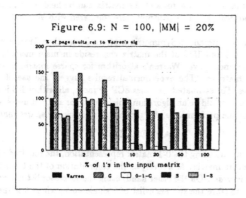

Figure 6.9: N = 100, |MM| = 20%

From the Figures we draw the following conclusions.

1. Algorithm S is better than Warren's algorithm, *for any range of density* of the input matrix, if at least 10% of the matrix can reside in main memory (all Figures), and Algorithm 1-S is better than Warren's algorithm, *for any range of density* of the input matrix, if at least 15% of the matrix can reside in main memory (Figs 6.4 to 6.9).

2. Algorithm S is the best algorithm for sparse matrices (all Figs).

3. As the percentage of the matrix that can be held in main memory increases, the performances of *all* four algorithms relative to Warren's algorithm improve. Compare for example Fig. 6.1 with Fig. 6.4 and Fig 6.7. As main memory sizes of systems continue to increase rapidly, we expect the requirement that the main memory holds at least 10% of the matrix to be satisfied.

4. Algorithms 1-S and 0-1-G outperform algorithm S, as soon as the denseness of the input matrix is slightly more that 2CP (all Figs). Moreover, they improve very rapidly after 4CP (all Figs). By the time that 8CP denseness is reached, the speedup over Warren's algorithm ranges between 2 (0-1-G, Fig. 6.3) and 5 (1-S, Fig. 6.7). Note, as the size of the matrix increases, a matrix with 8CP denseness is still quite sparse. For example, 8CP=8% for 100X100 matrices. Furthermore, algorithms 1-S and 0-1-G perform extremely well when the percentage of 1's in the input matrix is 20% or more. Specifically, the speedup over Warren's algorithm is between 4 (0-1-G, Fig. 6.2) and 100 (1-S, Fig. 6.9).

5. Algorithm G improves as the input matrix becomes more dense, and is better than Warren's for denseness 20% 1's or more (all Figs).

Following the definitions of sparse, dense, and medium dense matrices, the overall improvements achieved with the new four algorithms, over Warren's algorithm, are summarized in the following table. [3]

Sparseness of input matrix	Speedup over Warren		Algorithm (Fig.#)	
	min	max	for min	for max
Sparse (S)	1.4	2.1	S (6.3)	S (6.7)
Dense (0-1-G,1-S)	5.5	100	0-1-G (6.2)	1-S (6.9)
Medium Dense:				
4CP (1-S)	1.05	1.54	1-S (6.3)	1-S (6.7)
8CP (0-1-G,1-S)	1.5	6.7	0-1-G (6.3)	1-S (6.7)
20% 1's (0-1-S,1-S)	3.9	16.7	0-1-G (6.2)	1-S (6.9)

7 Conclusion

We have presented four algorithms to compute the transitive closure of a symmetric binary relation which is represented by a 0-1 matrix. It was assumed that only a few rows of the matrix can be held in main memory, and therefore the disk I/O cost was the main issue addressed. The algorithms were compared with Warren's algorithm, as it is given in [16].

As we expected, algorithms Symmetric and 1-Symmetric perform better than Warren's algorithm for any range of density, provided that at least 10% and 15% of the matrix can reside in main memory respectively. Algorithm Symmetric yields significant improvements over Warren's algorithm for sparse matrices, and algorithms 1-S, 0-1-G perform extremely well for dense matrices. The experimental results suggest the use of algorithm Symmetric for symmetric and very sparse matrices. For estimated densities 8CP or more, algorithm 1-S is the best choice.

An interesting problem for research would be an algorithm which works for any, not necessarily symmetric, matrices, yet maintaining and / or improving the performance of algorithm Symmetric for sparse matrices.

APPENDIX

Given a graph G=(V,E), $|V| = n$, and using the 0-1 matrix representation, the required amount of storage for each row is n bits, i.e. n^2 bits for the entire matrix. Moreover, as the computation of the transitive closure proceeds, the initially allocated storage *does not increase*. On the other hand, using the successor list representation, it can be shown that $k(1 + log_2 n)$ bits are required to store the successor list of a single node, where k is the number of successors of that node ($k < n$). As the computation of the transitive closure proceeds, the successor lists grow significantly in size. The 0-1 representation can be used to find the successors and the predecessors of a given element, while the successor list representation is inefficient in the computation of predecessors of a given list, if the immediate predecessor list of each element is not stored. Thus, there are advantages and disadvantages of using either representation.

Acknowledgment: We are grateful to ideas contributed by T. Chiu and S. Park.

---

[3] The algorithm(s) names in parenthesis in the first column of the table, indicate the best algorithm(s) for the specified range of density.

References

[1] Arlazarov, V. L., Dinic, E. A., Kronrod, M. A., and Faradzev, I. A. "On Economical Construction of the Transitive Closure of an Oriented Graph", *Soviet Math. Doklady 11*, 1970, 1209-1210.

[2] Agrawal, R., Borgida A., and Jagadish, H., "Efficient management of transitive relationships in large data and knowledge bases", *ACM SIGMOD 1989*, 253-262.

[3] Agrawal, R. and Jagadish, H.V. "Direct Algorithms For Computing the transitive closure Of Database Relations", *Proc. 13-th VLDB*, Brighton, England, Sept. 1987.

[4] Baker, J.J. "A note on Multiplying Boolean Matrices", *CACM*, 1962, 102.

[5] Bancilhon, F. "Naive Evaluation of Recursively Defined Relations", *On Knowledge Based Management Systems - Integrating Database and AI Systems*, M. Brodie and J. Mylopoulos, eds., Springer-Verlag, 1985.

[6] Bancilhon, F. and Ramakrishnan, R. "An Amateur's Introduction to Recursive Query Processing Strategies" *ACM SIGMOD 1986*, 16-52.

[7] Ioannidis, Y.E.. "On the Computation of the transitive closure of Relational Operators", *Proc. 12-th VLDB*, Kyoto, Japan, 1986, 403-411.

[8] Ioannidis, Y.E. and Ramakrishnan, R., "Efficient Transitive Closure of Relational Operators", *Proc. 14-th VLDB*, Los Angeles, California, 1988, 382-394.

[9] Jagadish, H.V., Agrawal, R., and Ness, L. "A Study of transitive closure as a Recursion Mechanism", *ACM SIGMOD 1987*, 331-344.

[10] Lu, H., "New Strategies for Computing the Transitive Closure of a Database Relation", *Proc. 13-th VLDB*, Brighton, England, 1987, 267-247.

[11] Lu, H., Mikkilineni, K., and Richrardson, J.P. "Design and Evaluation of Algorithms to Compute the transitive closure of a Database Relation" *Proc. IEEE 3-rd Inter. Conf. Data Engineering*, Los Angeles, Feb. 1987, 112-119.

[12] Naughton, J.F., Ramakrishnan, R., Sagiv, Y., and Ullman, J.D., "Efficient evaluation of right-, left-, and multi-linear rules", *ACM SIGMOD 1989*, 235-242.

[13] Schmitz, L., "An Improved Transitive Closure Algorithm", *Computing 30*, 1983, 359-371.

[14] Schnorr, C.P. "An Algorithm for transitive closure with Linear Expected Time", *SIAM J. Computing 7*, 1978, 127-133.

[15] Valduriez, P. and Boral, H. "Evaluation of Recursive Queries Using Join Indices" *Proc. 1-st Inter. Conf. on Expert Database Systems*, Charleston, 1986, 197-208.

[16] Warren, H., Jr. "A Modification of Warshall's Algorithm for the transitive closure of Binary Relations". *CACM 18*, 1975, 218-220.

[17] Warshall, S., "A Theorem on Boolean Matrices", *Journal of the ACM 9*, 1962, 11-12.

3. Data and Software Engineering

An Environment for Information System Prototyping: A System Simulation Approach

Kung-Chao Liu
Department of Management Information Systems, The University of Arizona
Tucson, Arizona 85721 U.S.A.

ABSTRACT

A system entity structure represents the decompositions and taxonomies of a system. DEVS-Scheme is an object-oriented implementation of the DEVS formalism for hierarchical, modular discrete-event system simulation. This paper describes using both instruments to establish an integrated environment for building prototypes of information systems modeled in data flow model. Also presented is the strategy for administering the prototyping process and some preliminary evaluations of the proposed framework.

INTRODUCTION

Prototyping Paradigm and Data Flow Model

Prototyping is an information system development paradigm [1] which emphasizes building an executable prototype of the whole or part of an information system. In other words, the objective of prototyping is to clarify the characteristics and operation of an information system by constructing a working model that can be exercised.

The *data flow model* represents a system as a connected directed graph: the components of the system are nodes and the data "flowing" between the components are the edges. Data flow diagram (DFD) [2], a graphical representation of the data flow model, has four kinds of elements: *external entity*, which is the ultimate source or sink of data; *data flow*, which is the data in action; *data store*, which is the data at rest; and *process*, which receives data, transforms it, and releases the transformed data. It is implied that a process executes only when all its inputs are available, but it does not necessarily produce all its outputs simultaneously.

Figure 1 shows an example DFD: a square is an external entity, an arc is a data flow (its accompanying arrow indicates the direction), an open rectangle is a data store, and a circle is a process.

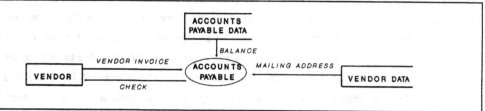

Figure 1. An example data flow diagram

Integrated Environment for Prototyping in Data Flow Model

Considering the characteristics of the prototyping paradigm and the data flow model, the requirements for an integrated environment for information system prototyping in data flow model should include the following:

* A user can define the structure of the system to be built. The environment should provide means for describing the elements of DFDs, the interconnections between the elements, and the *leveling* [2] between DFDs.

* A user can choose a suitable configuration for the system according to certain criteria. The environment should have facilities that help the user to determine the configuration.

* A user can derive an executable prototype with respect to the chosen configuration. The environment should supply building blocks for composing the prototype.

* A user can experiment on the prototype to observe its behavior and gather essential statistics (for example, the performance of the whole or some components of the prototype). The environment should provide mechanisms for collecting statistics and should permit the user to run a prototype in different settings.

* A user can prototype a partial system. The environment should enable the user to select the scope of a partial system and build its prototype. The environment should also make sure that the partial prototype is valid within the context of the whole system.

System Entity Structure and DEVS-Scheme Approach

System entity structure (SES) [6, 8] is a tree-like graph for representing the elements of a system and their decompositions and taxonomies. Shown in Figure 2 are two simple SESs: each named item is an entity type; a single-bar under an entity is a *decomposition*, which depicts the constituents of the entity; a double-bar under an entity is a *taxonomy*, which shows the allowable variants of the entity. Decomposition and taxonomy can be nested alternately to form large SESs. *DEVS* is a discrete-event system simulation formalism that models systems in hierarchical, modular manner. The details of DEVS can be found in [8].

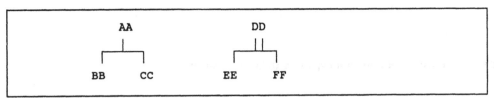

Figure 2. Two simple system entity structures

It has been shown that SES and DEVS form a sound conceptual basis for integrated, model-based system development [6]. The objective of this paper is to describe an integrated environment, that is based on SES and *DEVS-Scheme*--an object-oriented implementation of DEVS [9, 10], for fabricating prototypes of information systems formulated in data flow model. The process of using the integrated environment is introduced in the next section.

PROTOTYPING PROCESS

The process of prototyping in the integrated environment consists of three phases [3]: *decomposition, composition,* and *evaluation* (Figure 3). During the decomposition phase, a user fits the set of DFDs that represent an information system into an SES and selects a configuration for the information system according to certain criteria. During the composition phase, the user composes an executable prototype in DEVS-Scheme. During the evaluation phase, the user runs the prototype and analyzes the information gathered. Afterwards, the user may decide to return to the decomposition phase or exit from the iteration of prototyping process. Procedures of the three phases are summarized in the following:

Decomposition

The goal of the decomposition phase is to derive an SES that represents a configuration of an information system that fulfills given requirements. A user first builds the generic SES for the data flow model (Figure 4, where a triple-bar indicates that the entity above consists of a number of instances of the entity below). An information system is represented by a DFD which comprises a number of external entities, data stores, and processes. An external entity is composed of some sources and/or sinks. A process is either an elementary one or a complex one; in the latter case, it is decomposed into another DFD. The user then expands the generic SES into a specific one by adding decompositions of data store and process, such as those in Figure 5.

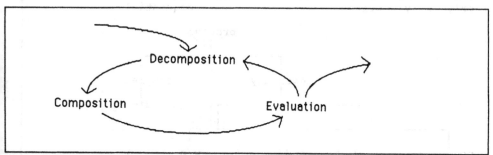

Figure 3. Phases of the prototyping process

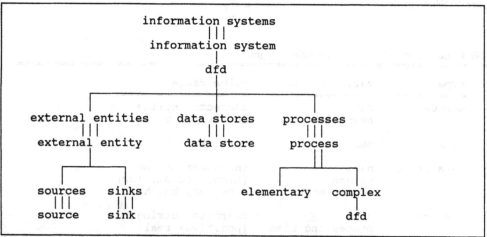

Figure 4. Generic system entity structure for data flow modeling

Next, the user attaches variables to information system, external entity, source, sink, data store, and process types, and specifies rules that use the values of the variables to select appropriate entities. The rules and value ranges of the variables reflect the given criteria of the system under study. Some example variables are listed in Table 1; two sample rules for selecting a data store are shown in Figure 6.

Finally, the user feeds the variables and rules into an expert system and has it work out the best configuration. An expert system specialized for the process of *pruning* SESs has been implemented [5]. The pruned SES is the blueprint for the next phase.

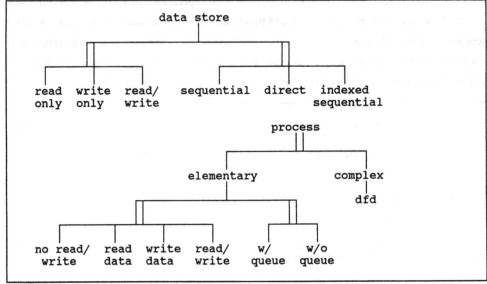

Figure 5. Example decompositions of data store and process

Table 1. Sample variables and their value ranges

type	variable name	value range
source	name mean_time	character string (positive) real
sink	name	character string
data store	name volume access_mode	character string {high, medium, low} {on-line, batch}
process	name processing_time frequency	character string (positive) real integer

```
If    access_mode = on-line and
      (volume = high or volume = medium)
Then  organization = indexed_sequential

If    access_mode = on-line and volume = low
Then  organization = sequential
```

Figure 6. Sample rules for selecting a data store

Composition

The first step in the composition phase is to prepare generic DEVS-Scheme program templates (called *models*) for external entity, source, sink, data store, and elementary process types. Because of the object-oriented implementation of DEVS-Scheme, each model is an autonomous, executable unit. Moreover, the hierarchical modular nature of DEVS makes it easy to compile models into larger models. For example, an external entity model is made up of a source model and/or a sink model.

In the same way, the user can then synthesize an executable prototype from the set of available DEVS-Scheme models in accordance with the pruned SES obtained in the decomposition phase. This prototype is in fact an instance of information system model. Data flows, which are the couplings between other entity types, are added into the executable prototype by matching the appropriate output and input *ports* between the concerned information system, external entity, data store, and process models. The resultant DEVS-Scheme program is ready for use in the evaluation phase.

Evaluation

The user interactively exercises the information system prototype obtained in the composition phase in different circumstances. This is done by setting variables in the DEVS-Scheme environment to different values before each execution. The statistics and other information captured in the DEVS-Scheme environment help the user to determine the quality of the prototype, validate the specifications of the information system being modeled, and so on. Based on the result, the user may go back to the decomposition phase or exit from the prototyping process.

ADMINISTRATION OF THE PROTOTYPING ENVIRONMENT

The prototyping process discussed above is a "one-shot" approach. It is suitable for a single project situation. However, an organization usually handles several projects at the same time. In order for an organization to adopt the proposed prototyping environment for all or most of its projects without replicating similar tasks, the prototyping process has to be modified.

This modified prototyping process has five phases: *generic installation, specific installation, decomposition, composition,* and *evaluation*. The SESs, variables, rules for pruning SESs, and

DEVS-Scheme models that are invariant across projects are installed in the generic installation phase. While the SESs, variables, rules for pruning SESs, and DEVS-Scheme models that are specifically related to a project are installed in the specific installation phase. During the remaining three phases, a user performs the tasks described in the previous section, except those absorbed into the generic and specific installation phases.

Figure 7 shows the sequence of the five phases. The generic installation phase is performed when the prototyping environment is first instituted in an organization. After that, the specific installation phase is performed whenever a project is initiated. A user then goes through the decomposition, composition, and evaluation phases to choose a configuration for an information system, build its prototype, and exercise the prototype. At the completion of the evaluation phase, the user may iterate to the decomposition phase or go back to the specific installation phase. In the latter case, the user might have found some parameter of the project needs adjustment. For example, the specific decomposition of data store is not quite relevant to the problem on hand. After making the necessary change, the user enters the inner cycle again.

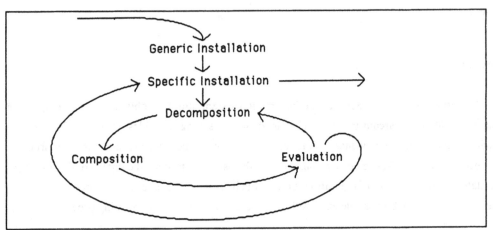

Figure 7. Phases of the enhanced prototyping process

A successful completion at the evaluation phase also sends the user back to the specific installation phase. In this situation, the specific installation for a new project is inaugurated.

SOME OBSERVATIONS ABOUT THE PROTOTYPING ENVIRONMENT

To measure the effectiveness of the proposed prototyping environment, it is necessary to evaluate it against the requirements for an ideal environment, as asserted earlier in this paper. The comparison is tabulated in Table 2.

Table 2. Comparison of the ideal and the proposed prototyping environments

Ideal Environment	Proposed Environment
Provides means for describing elements of DFDs, interconnections between the elements, and leveling between DFDs.	SES can represent elements of DFDs and leveling between DFDs. Interconnections between the elements of DFDs are achieved by coupling input/output ports of DEVS-Scheme models.
Provides facilities to help choosing a configuration.	An expert system helps a user to select a configuration.
Supplies building blocks for composing prototype.	Each DEVS-Scheme model is a building block. A comprehensive library of models could be accumulated.
Provides means for experimenting on prototype and provides mechanisms for collecting statistics.	DEVS-Scheme environment allows a user to run a prototype in various settings and collects statistics for the user. The user can step the run and change the state of the environment.
Supports partial system prototyping.	Each entity on SES (without respect to partial system or component) is mapped to a DEVS-Scheme model that can be run separately.

The proposed environment is also compared to the system by Tate and Docker [7]. They tend to advocate the operating system approach instead of the simulation system approach in implementing the executor of their prototyping system because "the application model [can be] implemented more directly on a suitable distributed system including multiple processors." This argument is not sound since a hierarchical DEVS-Scheme model can be straightforwardly realized in a distributed environment [9, 10].

Tate and Docker's approach has a number of deficiencies. First, a user can observe the behavior of a prototype but can not gather numerical information about its performance, and the like. Second, since they assume that only the lowest-level processes are executable, their system does not support leveling between DFDs. Third, prototyping for a partial system is not provided, nor can a component be evaluated alone. The up side is that their system does support prototyping of input screens and output reports.

CONCLUDING REMARKS

Some possible extensions to the prototyping environment have been envisioned in the process of this research. They are briefed in the following:

* Incorporating a graphical data flow diagramming tool to serve as a front-end facility to the prototyping environment. This tool should help a user to draw and edit DFDs and transform the user's DFDs into SESs.

* Adding the capabilities of user-interface prototyping to the environment.

* Installing other models, in addition to the data flow model, as the underlying model for conceptualizing information systems. It is possible to realize a versatile information system prototyping environment by installing a number of complementary models. This can be done at the generic installation phase. The arrow leaving the specific installation phase in Figure 7 will loop back to the generic installation phase and a new arrow will emit from it.

* Consolidating the administration strategy of the prototyping environment with other information system development paradigms to achieve a combined paradigm [4].

Acknowledgments. I am grateful to Dr. B. P. Zeigler and Dr. J. W. Rozenblit for their continuous support. The Department of Management Information Systems at The University of Arizona provided the resources for conducting this research.

REFERENCES

1. Agresti, W. W. *New Paradigms for Software Development*. IEEE Computer Society Press, Washington, DC, 1986.

2. DeMarco, T. *Structured Analysis and System Specification*. Yourdon, New York, 1978.

3. Herniter, B. C., Liu, K. C., and Pendergast, M. O. Using artificial intelligence based system simulation in management information systems research: Three cases studies. In R. Uttamsingh and A. M. Wildberger, Eds., *Advances in AI and Simulation: Proceedings of the Society for Computer Simulation Multiconference on AI and Simulation*, pp. 147-152. The Society for Computer Simulation International, San Diego, CA, 1989.

4. Pressman, R. S. *Software Engineering: A Practitioner's Approach, 2nd. Ed.* McGraw-Hill, New York, 1987.

5. Rozenblit, J. W., and Huang, Y. M. Constraint-driven generation of model structures. In *Proceedings of the 1987 Winter Simulation Conference*, pp. 604-611.

6. Rozenblit, J. W., and Zeigler, B. P. Design and modeling concepts. In *International Encyclopedia of Robotics Applications and Automation*, pp. 308-322. Wiley, New York, 1988.

7. Tate, G, and Docker, T. W. G. A rapid prototyping system based on data flow principles. *Software Engineering Notes 10*, 2 (1985), 28-34.

8. Zeigler, B. P. *Multifacetted Modelling and Discrete Event Simulation.* Academic, New York, 1984.

9. Zeigler, B. P. DEVS-Scheme: A Lisp-based environment for hierarchical, modular discrete event models. Tech. Rep. No. AIS-2, Department of Electrical and Computer Engineering, University of Arizona, 1986.

10. Zeigler, B. P. Hierarchical, modular discrete-event modelling in an object-oriented environment. *Simulation 49*, 5 (1987), 219-230.

A logic-free method for modular composition of specifications

Victor Yodaiken

Department of Computer Science

University of Massachusetts (Amherst)

yodaiken@cs.umass.edu

Abstract

Clear mathematical description of large scale digital systems is not possible without extensive use of encapsulation. We argue that standard models of concurrency and composition are too unstructured to support modular composition and verification of systems. We offer an alternative model based on algebraic feedback products of finite state machines. We also describe a technique for concisely specifying complex state machines in terms of state dependent (modal) functions. The product automata model provides a precise interpretation for the formal expressions, and the formal expressions provide an intuitive language for describing multi-layer concurrent digital systems. We develop several examples, showing how specifications of varying levels of abstractness can be composed to specify rather complex systems.

1. Introduction

Modular techniques for the design and implementation of concurrent digital systems are far in advance of the techniques for specifying and verifying concurrent digital systems. Surveys of the current literature [4, 1] demonstrate that, despite some highly sophisticated mathematical approaches, the goal of modular composition of specifications remains very much unattained. The obstacle seems to be inherent in the standard models of concurrency. While there are deep and significant differences among the various trace, net, and logic based computational formalisms, we find that composition of concurrent systems is invariably described in one of two ways. Either the composite system *interleaves* state transitions of the component systems (e.g. [8]), or each composite state transition is associated with an element of the power set of possible component state changes (e.g., [13]). Neither paradigm places much of a restriction on how concurrent components interact. To specify a concrete example of a concurrent system in terms of interleaving or transition power-sets, we must develop a host of supplementary constraints on the nature of the units of computation, on scheduling and on communication. The very generality of these paradigms entails lengthy axiomatization of what would be intuitive and obvious in a more faithful model (c.f., [2]).

In this paper we present a language of formal expressions based on an alternative model of concurrency and composition. We represent composite systems as finite state automata in algebraic *feedback product* form, and specify automata via state dependent (modal) functions. We claim the following:

- A natural, functional style for describing finite state digital systems, for parameterizing specifications, and for modular composition of specifications.

- A precise mathematical interpretation for multi-level specifications in terms of automata and automata products.

- An "open", semantically derived, proof system.

Automata corresponding to substantive systems will tend to be large and complex, and, as we will see in section 3, the algebraic product that we use is not as elementary as string interleavings. For this reason, we have developed a modal (context dependent) arithmetic that provides both a concise notation for specifying and composing automata, and an intuitive proof system for verifying the behavior of automata. Arithmetic expressions are implicitly evaluated in the *context* of the current state of a digital system. The context is represented by a state machine and a sequence of transition symbols we call the *trace*. Traces are sequences of transition symbols which drive the state machine from its initial state without causing an undefined transition. Expressions may be evaluated in the current context; in the context of a future state obtained by appending additional transition symbols to the trace; or in the context of a component sub-system obtained by replacing the current context with a factor state machine and a "factor" trace.

The formal system is called the *modal primitive recursive* (m.p.r.) arithmetic to denote both its modal (state dependent) nature, and its basis in the primitive recursive arithmetic [6]. The primitive recursive arithmetic is a logic-free formalization of a significant part of integer mathematics [12], containing functions which range over non-negative integers and sequences[1]. We summarize the m.p.r functions below.

- *Component selection.* For each function f, the function $(\text{in } c)f$ computes f within the context of a component sub-system c. That is $(\text{in } c)f(\vec{x})$ is evaluated by evaluating $f(\vec{x})$ in the context corresponding to factor c of the current state machine.

- *Path offset.* For any sequence of state transitions u, and any function f, the function $(\text{after } u)f$ computes f in the state reached by following u from the current state. That is $(\text{after } u)f(\vec{x})$ is evaluated by appending u to the current trace, and evaluating $f(\vec{x})$ in the resulting context.

- *Enabled transitions.* The m.p.r. boolean function Enable tests paths to see if they lead to a undefined state. If u labels a defined path originating at the current state, then $\text{Enable}(u) = 1$; If not, $\text{Enable}(u) = 0$.

- *Feedback.* Each state change of a composite system induces state transitions in all of the components. The value of $f\_effect(u, c)$ is the (possibly empty) path induced in component c if the composite system traverses the path u. If $v = f\_effect(u, c)$, then v is a sequence of transition symbols over the alphabet of factor c; when the composite system follows u to a new state, c will, in parallel, follow v to a new state. Since $f\_effect(u, c)$ may be the empty path, $\langle\rangle$, or a multiple element path, we do not need to require components to change state in lock step. We call f_effect a *feedback* function, because the value of $f\_effect(u, c)$ may depend on the value of the outputs from one or more of the components: the output of components, thus, influences the input. Because of the way f_effect is interpreted, $f\_effect(u \cdot z, c) = f\_effect(u, c) \cdot (\text{after } u) f\_effect(v, c)$.

---

[1]Formally, some form of *encoding* is used to represent sequences, but this has little practical effect.

- *The precedence function.* The left-right ordering of the trace describes the relative order in which state transitions have happened, with the rightmost symbol in the trace representing the most recent state transition. If the current trace contains at least i a symbols, then a pair (a, i) refers to the "i^{th} most recent a" symbol in the trace. If the current trace contains fewer than i a symbols, then (a, i) refers to the null transition. The infix boolean function precedes compares the relative order of two such pairs. The value of (a, i) precedes (b, j) is 1 iff either (a, i) is more recent than (b, j), or (a, i) refers to the null event and (b, j) does not refer to the null event.

- *Everything else.* The primitive recursive functions, and the functions defined by composition and primitive recursion from any m.p.r. functions are also m.p.r. functions.

We will consider an expression to be *true* when it takes on a non-zero value, and *false* otherwise. We say a state machine *satisfies* a specification iff the specification is true in the context of every trace belonging to the state machine. Thus, each n-ary function f, and each appropriate n-vector of constant arguments $\vec{m}$ defines the class of state machines which satisfy $f(\vec{m})$. A detailed specification $f(\vec{m})$ is said to *implement* a more abstract specification $g(\vec{k})$ iff every state machines that satisfies $f(\vec{m})$ also satisfies $g(\vec{k})$.

More abstract (high level) specifications will define large, possibly infinite, classes of satisfying automata. It is often important, however, to describe an algorithm or design in a detailed fashion, and to determine whether or not the design or algorithm is finitely realizable. For example, the specification $enable(a) \bigwedge (after\ a)f() = f() + 1$ defines an unbounded counter that cannot be realized by any finite state machine. A specification $f(\vec{m})$ is called a *modal grammar* if f is defined without use of $after$, and if f is defined as a conjunction of clauses which describe a finite alphabet, a finite component set, a specification for each element of the component set, and the operation of Enable and f_effect. A modal grammar is *exact* if it defines an empty set of components, or if every component specification is an exact modal grammar. Exact modal grammars are satisfied by exactly one (minimal) finite automaton. Thus, if we can describe a design or algorithm with a modal grammar, we have proved that the algorithm is finitely realizable. A proof of this result, and a formal definition of modal grammars can be found in [14]. There are several examples of modal grammars in the next section.

The remainder of this paper is in three sections: illustrative examples are developed in section 2, the formal semantics is sketched in section 3, and the final section concludes with a summary and comparison to related work.

2. The examples

We introduce the modal arithmetic and style of specification by developing a rather simple example involving shift registers, fifo queues, and latches. The example illustrates our treatment of concurrency and encapsulation: we will show how latches can be used to construct shift registers, and how shift registers can be used as components of larger shift registers and fifos.

2.1. A latch

We begin with a specification of a single bit latch. The alphabet of the latch should be load.0 and load.1, its output function should be $Data() \in \{0, 1\}$ and should obey (after load.x)Data() = x, and the cell should always be able to load either value. A specification for such a cell is given in figure 1.

Figure 1: Specification of a single bit storage cell.

$$\text{cell}() \overset{\text{def}}{=} \{ \qquad\qquad\qquad\qquad\qquad\qquad \}$$

$\qquad\qquad$ **Alphabet** $= \{\text{load.x} : x \in \{0, 1\}\}$
$\qquad\qquad \wedge$ **Outputs** $= \{\text{Data} : \emptyset \rightarrow \{0, 1\}\}$
$\qquad\qquad \wedge (\text{after load.x})\text{Data}() = x$
$\qquad\qquad \wedge \text{Enable}(\text{load.x}) = 1$

In the sequel we will omit the $\wedge$ symbols connecting clauses of a specification, leaving the conjunction to be implicit. The enabling rules of this system are particularly simple: both possible state transitions are enabled at all times.

To assert that the system obeys $\text{cell}()$ in all states, we assert that in the initial state every enabled path leads to a state where $\text{cell}() > 0$. We therefore, take a short digression to define a function $\text{Initial}()$ which is true only in the initial state, and an operator $\square$ (always), so that $\square f(x)$ is non-zero iff $f(x)$ is non-zero in the current state and all future states.

In the initial state, the trace is the empty trace $\langle\rangle$. Thus, in the initial state $(a, 1)$ precedes $(b, 1) = 0$ for every a and b.

$$\text{Initial}() \overset{\text{def}}{=} (\forall a, b)\big((a, 1) \text{ precedes } (b, 1) = 0\big).$$

If $f(\vec{m})$ ever becomes false, then there must be an enabled path u which leads to the state where $f(\vec{m})$ is false. We define $\square f(\vec{x})$ as follows.

$$\square f(\vec{x}) \overset{\text{def}}{=} (\forall u)(\text{enable}(u) \rightarrow (\text{after } u)f(\vec{x}) > 0).$$

The operator (functional) $\square$ is inspired by a similar operator found in modal and temporal logics [9].

Thus, $\text{Initial}() \wedge \square\text{cell}()$ specifies that $\text{cell}()$ is true in all states.

2.2. A shift register

We turn now to the specification of a shift register. We begin with an abstract specification of the interface and output of such a device, and then define an implementation constructed from latches.

The output of a n bit shift register will be an integer value between 0 and $2^n - 1$. It is sometimes advantageous to be a little more careful in distinguishing between bits and integers, we could define the output to be a vector of binary values, but there is no need for such care here. The alphabet of such a device will consist of symbols Left.0, and Left.1, which represent a single bit shift left, and symbols Right.0, and Right.1, representing single shifts to the right. The high order bits are the rightmost bits, so left.x should divide the current output by 2, and then add $2^{n-1} * x$. Similarly, right.x should multiply the current output by 2, add x and then mod the result by 2^n. We will use the same name for the output function of the shift register as we used for the latch — Data. The desired operation and interface of an n bit shift register is given by the specification in figure 2

Figure 2: Specification of a n bit Shifter.

$$\text{Shifter}(n) \stackrel{\text{def}}{=} \Box \left(\begin{array}{l} \textbf{Alphabet} \subset \{\text{Left}.x, \text{Right}.x \,:\, x \in \{0, 1\}\} \\ \wedge \textbf{Output} \subset \{\text{Data}()\} \\ \wedge (\text{after Left}.x)\text{Data}() = (\text{Data}() \textbf{ div } 2) + 2^{n-1} * x \\ \wedge (\text{after Right}.x)\text{Data}() = ((\text{Data}() * 2) + x) \textbf{ mod } 2^n) \end{array} \right)$$

2.3. A grammar for a shift register

There are any number of possible ways to build a system which implements a shift register. We will develop a straightforward implementation based on n components, latch.0, ..., latch.$(n-1)$, where each component satisfies cell(). The value of Data() will depend on the values of the outputs of the components:

$$\text{Data}() = \sum_{i=0}^{n-1} 2^i * (\text{in latch.i})\text{Data}().$$

Note that (in latch.i)Data is the name of a function defined within sub-system latch.i, while Data is the name of a function in the current context. The expression (in latch.i)($\Box$cell)() is true iff the expression ($\Box$cell)() is true in the component latch.i. Thus, we specify the behavior of the components, by writing:

$$(\text{in latch.i})(\Box\text{cell})().$$

We consider latch.0 to be the leftmost latch. When the shift register computes Right.x we want latch.0 to load x, and for each $0 < i < n$, we want latch.i to load the current output of its neighbor to the left. When the shift register computes Left.x, we want latch.$(n-1)$ to load.x and each latch.i, $i < n-1$ to load the current contents of its neighbor to the right. The complete specification appears in figure 3

Figure 3: Grammar for a n bit shift register.

$\text{ShiftRegister}(n) \stackrel{\text{def}}{=} \{$
Alphabet $= \{\text{Left}.x, \text{Right}.x : x \in \{0, 1\}\}$
Components $= \{\text{latch}.i : i \in \{0, ..., n-1\}\}$
$(\forall i)(\text{in latch.i})(\Box\text{cell})()$
Outputs $= \{\text{Data}() \in \{0, ...2^n - 1\}\}$
$\text{cdata}(i) = (\text{in latch.i})\text{Data}()$
$\text{Data}() = \sum_{i=0}^{n-1} 2^i * \text{cdata}(i)$

$$\text{f\_effect}(a.x, \text{latch}.i) = \left\{ \begin{array}{ll} \langle \text{load}.x \rangle & \text{if } i = 0 \wedge a = \text{Right}.x; \\ & \text{or if } i = n \wedge a = \text{Left}.x; \\ \langle \text{load.cdata}(i-1) \rangle & \text{else if } (\exists x)a = \text{Right}.x; \\ \langle \text{load.cdata}(i+1) \rangle & \text{otherwise.} \end{array} \right.$$

$\text{Enable}(\text{Left}.x) = 1$
$\text{Enable}(\text{Right}.x) = 1\}$

ShiftRegister(n) is correct iff:

$$(\text{Initial}() \bigwedge \Box\text{ShiftRegister}(n)) \rightarrow \Box\text{Shifter}(n).$$

In this paper we will not offer a proof system, but we will mention the two proof rules that are central to the verification of this property. First, we note that in and after only matter to state dependent functions, purely arithmetic functions and function modifiers do not depend on state or context. In particular:

$$(\text{after } u)(\sum f(\vec{x})) = (\sum (\text{after } u)f(\vec{x})).$$

We call this rule *invariance*. The second rule, called *modal inversion*, allows us to invert expressions of the form $(\text{after } u)(\text{in } c)f(\vec{x})$. Note that the value of $(\text{in } c)f(\vec{x})$ in the state reached after u, depends on the path that u induces for component c. This path is given by $f\_\text{effect}(u, c)$. Thus, the *inversion* rule is as follows:

$$f\_\text{effect}(u, c) = v \rightarrow (\text{after } u)(\text{in } c)f(\vec{x}) = (\text{in } c)(\text{after } v)f(\vec{x}).$$

More details of the proof system can be found in [14]. In this paper we are more concerned with illustrating composition than with illustrating proof techniques. In the next subsection we describe a "big" shift register composed of serially connected ShiftRegisterss.

2.4. A composite shift register

Suppose that we want to construct a larger shift register from n bit shift registers. Clearly we can connect the component registers in series as shown in figure 4.

Figure 4: Grammar for a $m * n$ bit shift register, constructed from m serially connected shift registers.

$$\text{BigRegister}(m, n) \overset{\text{def}}{=} \{$$

Alphabet $= \{\text{Left.x}, \text{Right.x} : x \in \{0, 1\}\}$
Components $= \{\text{Reg.i} : i \in \{0, ..., m-1\}\}$
$(\forall i)(\text{in Reg.i})(\Box\text{ShiftRegister})(n)$
Outputs $= \{\text{Data}() \in \{0, ...2^{m+n+1} - 1\}\}$
$\text{rdata}(i) = (\text{in Reg.i})\text{Data}()$
$\text{Data}() = \sum_{i=0}^{m-1} 2^i * \text{rdata}(i)$

$$f\_\text{effect}(a.x, \text{Reg.i}) = \begin{cases} \langle\text{Right.x}\rangle & \text{if } i = 0 \wedge a = \text{Right.x}; \\ \langle\text{Left.x}\rangle & \text{if } i = m - 1 \wedge a = \text{Left.x}; \\ \langle\text{Right.rdata}(i-1)\rangle & \text{else if } (\exists x)a = \text{Right.x}; \\ \langle\text{Left.rdata}(i+1)\rangle & \text{otherwise.} \end{cases}$$

$\text{Enable}(\langle\text{Left.x}\rangle) = 1$
$\text{Enable}(\langle\text{Right.x}\rangle) = 1\}$

The correctness property of interest for the big shift register will be:

$$(\text{Initial}() \bigwedge \Box\text{BigRegister}(n, m)) \rightarrow \Box\text{Shifter}(m * n).$$

2.5. A fifo queue

Finally, let's construct a first in first out queue (fifo) by connecting shift registers in parallel. Suppose we want to be able to enqueue integers in the range $X = \{0, ..., 2^m - 1\}$ on a queue with maximum length n. The alphabet of the queue should contain symbols enq.x and deq.x for $x \in X$. The output of the queue should include two boolean signals, Empty(), and Full(), and a data value Front() $\in X$ which reflects the value of the element at the head of the queue.

We construct the fifo from m *data* shift registers which hold the enqueued words, and an additional *control* shift register which keeps track of the head of the queue. Any element of X can be represented as a m length binary string, and we will store each of these bits in a *data* shift register. Let $\text{Bit}(i, k)$ denote the ith bit of the binary representation of k, i.e.,

$$\text{Bit}(i, k) \stackrel{\text{def}}{=} \begin{cases} 1 & \text{if } k \bmod 2^{i+1} \geq 2^i; \\ 0 & \text{otherwise.} \end{cases}$$

The data registers will be named $\text{reg}.0, ..., \text{reg}.(m - 1)$. When we enqueue x, data register Reg.i will compute Right.Bit(i, x), storing the ith bit of x. The control register will compute Right.1 at the same time. When we dequeue the head element, the control register will compute Left.0. Thus, the position of the rightmost 1 bit in the control register marks the position of the head of the queue. This position is given by the following function.

$$\text{RightBit}(x) \stackrel{\text{def}}{=} (\max i \leq x)\text{Bit}(i, x) > 0.$$

Let l be the value of the control register data output. When $l = 0$ no elements belong to the queue. If $l > 0$ then the element at the head of the queue is given by: $\sum_{i=0}^{m-1} 2^i * \text{Bit}(l, (\text{in Reg.i})\text{Data}())$. The full fifo specification is given in figure 5.

Figure 5: Specification of a m bit wide, n bit deep fifo.

$\text{fifo}(m, n) \stackrel{\text{def}}{=} \{\textbf{Alphabet} = \{\text{deq}, \text{enq.x}, x \in \{0, ...2^m - 1\}\}$

Components $= \{\text{control}, \text{Reg.i} : i \in \{0, ..., m - 1\}\}$

$(\text{in control})(\square\text{Shifter})(n)$

$(\forall i)(\text{in Reg.i})(\square\text{Shifter})(n)$

Outputs $= \{\text{Empty}(), \text{Full}() \in \{0, 1\}, \text{Front}() \in \{0, ..., 2^m - 1\}\}$

$\text{rdata}(i) \stackrel{\text{def}}{=} (\text{in Reg.i})\text{Data}()$

$\text{Level}() \stackrel{\text{def}}{=} \text{RightBit}((\text{in control})\text{Data}())$

$\text{Full}() = ((\text{in control})\text{Data}() = 0)$

$\text{Empty}() = (\text{Level}() = n - 1)$

$\text{Front}() = \sum_{i=0}^{m-1} 2^i * \text{Bit}(\text{Level}(), \text{rdata}(i))$

$\text{f\_effect}(a, c) = \begin{cases} \langle \text{Left}.0 \rangle & \text{if } c = \text{control} \wedge a = \text{dequeue}; \\ \langle \text{Right}.1 \rangle & \text{if } c = \text{control} \wedge (\exists x)a = \text{enq.x}; \\ \langle \text{Right}.x \rangle & \text{if } c \neq \text{control} \wedge a = \text{enqueue.x}; \\ \langle \rangle & \text{otherwise.} \end{cases}$

$\text{Enable}(\text{enqueue.x}) = \neg\text{Full}()$

$\text{Enable}(\text{dequeue}) = \neg\text{Empty}()\}$

We can transform fifo into an exact modal grammar quite easily. Basically, we need to define a modal grammar version of Cell(), and then substitute this definition for the one used in the specification of ShiftRegister(n). Showing that $\square$ShiftRegister$(n) \rightarrow$ $\square$Shifter(n) is quite simple. It follows that $\square$fifo$'(n) \rightarrow \square$fifo(n).

3. Semantics

In this section we associate m.p.r. expressions with precise mathematical semantics in terms of finite state machines. We will define a class of product form automata, so that if P is a product form automaton, and if w is a trace of P, then (P, w) confers a unique integer value on each closed (no-free variables) m.p.r. expression.

A *Moore machine* [10] is a finite state machine with output. The Moore machine consists of a finite alphabet A, a state set Q, a finite output alphabet Y, a transition function $\delta : Q \times A \rightarrow Q$, and an output function $\lambda : Q \rightarrow X$.

$$\mathcal{M} = (A, Q, Y, \delta, \lambda).$$

By convention a *state set* is a finite set Q with a distinguished element $s \in Q$ called the *start state*.

The *traces* of a Moore machine are defined by extending δ to strings. Let $\Delta(q, \langle\rangle) = q$ and let $\Delta(q, \langle a\rangle \cdot u) = \Delta(\delta(q, a), u)$. In the sequel, we abuse notation and write δ for Δ. We write $\delta(q, w) = \bot$ when δ is otherwise undefined on q and w. Thus, w is a trace of M iff $\delta(s, w) \neq \bot$.

We now define a *feedback product* of Moore machines. This product is, essentially, the *general product* described in [5], modified to more closely represent our model of composition of systems. In particular, we have taken care to make sure that only the output of the components is visible to the product. Suppose that $M = (M_1, ... M_n)$, where each $M_i = (A_i, Q_i, Y_i, \delta_i, \lambda_i)$, is a Moore machine with start state $s_i \in Q_i$. Let A be an alphabet, let Q_{sync} be a state set with start state $s_{sync} \in Q_{sync}$, and let Y be an output alphabet. We can construct a product from M, Q_{sync}, and Y given the following synchronization functions described in figure 6

Figure 6: Synchronization functions.

Feedback. $\Phi : Q_{sync} \times Y_1 \times ... \times Y_n \rightarrow (A_1^* \times A_n^*)$,
Synchronizer output. $\lambda_{sync} : Q_{sync} \times Y_1 \times ... \times Y_n \rightarrow X$,
Synchronizer transition. $\delta_{sync} : Q_{sync} \times Y_1 \times ... \times Y_n \rightarrow Q_{sync}$,
Encapsulation.
$\psi((q_{sync}, q_1, ..., q_n) = (q_{sync}, \lambda_1(q_1), ..., \lambda_n(q_n))$.

We denote the feedback product of these elements as follows:

$$M = \prod_{i=1}^{n} M_i [A, Q_{sync}, Y, \Phi, \lambda_{sync}, \delta_{sync}].$$

The product state machine will have: alphabet A, state set $Q = Q_{sync} \times Q_1 ... \times Q_n$ with start state $s = (s_{sync}, s_1, ..., s_n)$, and output alphabet Y. Let $q = (q_{sync}, q_1, ..., q_n) \in$ Q, The output function is defined as follows:

$$\lambda(q) = \lambda_{sync}(\psi(q)).$$

Let $\Phi(q, a) = (w_1, ..., w_n)$. Then the transition function is defined in figure 7

> **Figure 7:** The transition function of a product machine.
> Let $q = (q_{sync}, q_1, ..., q_n) \in Q$.
>
> $$\delta(q, a) = \begin{cases} \bot & \text{if } (\exists i \leqslant n)\delta_i(q_i, w_i) = \bot; \\ & \text{or if } \delta_{sync}(\psi(q), a) = \bot; \\ (\delta_{sync}(\psi(q), a), q_1' ..., q_n') & \text{otherwise.} \\ & \text{where } q_i' = \delta_i(q_i, w_i) \end{cases}$$

Let $\Phi_i(q, a) = w_i$ when $\Phi(q, a) = (w_1, ..., w_i, ..., w_n)$. As with δ we will want to identify Φ with its natural (homomorphic) extension to strings: $\Phi_i(q, \langle\rangle) = \langle\rangle$ and $\Phi_i(q, \langle a\rangle \cdot u) = \langle\Phi_i(q, a)\rangle \cdot \Phi(\delta(q, a), u)$. Because of the way we have defined δ, each state transition induced for each component must be enabled. More formally:

$$\delta(s, u) \neq \bot \rightarrow \delta_i(s_i, \Phi_i(s, u)) \neq \bot.$$

Intuitively, we guarantee that state transitions of the product state machine will respect the rules of the factor state machines.

The *semantic structures* for m.p.r. arithmetic are triples $P = (M, C, P)$, where M is a Moore machine, and either $C = P = ()$, or M is a product over C, and P is a tuple containing the semantic structures of the factors of M. When $P = (M, (), ())$, we say that P is an atomic semantic structure: there are no components. Otherwise $P = (M, C, P)$ where: $P = (P_1, ..., P_n)$, each $P_i = (M_i, C_i, P_i)$ is a semantic structure, $C = [(M_1, ... M_n), A, Q_{sync}, Y, \Phi, \lambda_{sync}, \delta_{sync}]$, and $M = \prod_{i=1}^n M_i[A, Q_{sync}, Y, \Phi, \lambda_{sync}, \delta_{sync}]$,

We can now sketch m.p.r. interpretation. Let P be a product form state machine:

$$P = \big(M, (M, A, Q_{sync}, Y, \Phi, \lambda_{sync}, \delta_{sync}), (P_1, ..., P_n)\big).$$

We write $P, w \models f(\vec{m})$ to denote the value of formal expression $f(\vec{m})$ in the context of P and w. The value of $(P, w \models (a, i) \text{ precedes } (b, j))$ depends only on w, and should be obvious. Similarly $(P, w \models \text{Enable}(u)) = 1$ iff $\delta(s, w \cdot u) \neq \bot$. If f is a primitive recursive function, then $(P, w \models f(\vec{m}) = f(\vec{m})$, the context is ignored. The critical fragments of the interpretation are for *after* and *in*: these are given in figure 8.

> **Figure 8:** Interpretation of *after* and *in*.
>
> $$(P, w \models (\text{after } u)f(\vec{m})) = (P, w \cdot u \models f(\vec{m}))$$
> $$(P, w \models (\text{in } c)f(\vec{m})) = (P_c, \text{trace}_c(u) \models f(\vec{m}))$$

4. Conclusion

As far as we know our work is unique among computational formalisms in: use of the feedback product of automata to represent composition and concurrency, primitive recursive basis, and notion of state predicates as assertions about the reverse relative order of transitions. As a consequence, we believe that m.p.r. arithmetic provides a uniquely modular approach to specification and verification. Given the graphical or explicit automata based specification of a 2 element shift register, it is unclear how one would obtain the corresponding specification of a 3 element register. On the other hand, the more abstract formal methods, such as the temporal logics or the dynamic logics [7] seem better suited to description of "programs" written in high level languages, than to investigation of operating systems or computer architectures. The purpose of a programming language is to substitute a generic, uniform computational environment for the machine dependent, irregular "low level" environment provided by the operating system. But when we design an operating system or computer architecture, we are designing the underlying machine environment, we cannot assume its previous existence. Thus, a formal notion of composition of "low level" components cannot be based on some single communication paradigm or concurrency construct. We suggest that the absence of such paradigms or underlying conventions about storage, processes, scheduling, and communication is a critical advantage for m.pr. arithmetic.

In some respects, our work is closest to that of Clarke *et al* [3] and Ostroff [11], who have employed temporal logic to describe finite automata. As m.p.r. arithmetic permits definition of analogs of the temporal operators, one could consider m.p.r. arithmetic to simply provide an alternate semantic basis for temporal logic, and thus integrate m.p.r. arithmetic into the large body of temporal logic based research. In particular, there is no obvious barrier to the extension of model checking methods to product form automata and precedence relations.

References

[1] K. Apt, editor. *Logics and Models of Concurrent Systems*. Springer-Verlag, 1985.

[2] R. T. Boute. On the shortcomings of the axiomatic approach as presently used in computer science. In *Compeuro 88 Systems Design: Concepts Methods, and Tools*, 1988.

[3] E. M. Clarke, Emerson A., and A.P. Sistla. Automatic verification of finite-state concurrent systems using temporal logic specifications: A practical approach. In *Proceedings of the 10th Annual Symposium on Principles of Programming Languages*, pages 117–119, 1983.

[4] J.W. de Bakker, editor. *Current Trends in Concurrency*. Number 224 in Lecture Notes in Computer Science. Springer-Verlag, 1985.

[5] Ferenc Gecseg. *Products of Automata*. Monographs in Theoretical Computer Science. Springer Verlag, 1986.

[6] R. L. Goodstein. *Recursive Number Theory*. North Holland, Amsterdam, 1957.

[7] D. Harel. Logics of programs: Axiomatics and descriptive powers. Technical Report TR-200, MIT/LCS, 1978.

[8] C. A. R. Hoare. *Communicating Sequential Processes*. Prentice-Hall, 1985.

[9] S. Kripke. Semantical considerations on modal logic. *Acta Philosophica Fennica*, 16:83–94, 1963.

[10] E.F. Moore, editor. *Sequential Machines: Selected Papers*. Addison-Welsey, Reading MA, 1964.

[11] J.S. Ostroff and W.M. Wonham. Modelling, specifying, and verifying real-time embedded computer systems. In *Symposium on Real-Time Systems*, Dec 1987.

[12] Rozsa Peter. *Recursive functions*. Academic Press, 1967.

[13] K. Voss, H.J. Genrich, and G Rozenberg, editors. *Concurrency and Nets: Advances in Petri Nets*. Springer-Verlag, 1987.

[14] V. Yodaiken and K. Ramamritham. Axiomatic specification of automata. Technical Report in preparation, University of Massachusetts, 1990.

On Real-Time Program Specification Description with a Data Model-Based Language

Katsumi OKAMOTO   Masaaki HASHIMOTO

ATR Communication Systems Research Laboratories

Sanpeidani, Inuidani, Seika-cho, Soraku-gun, Kyoto 619-02, Japan

E-mail: okamoto@atr-sw.atr.co.jp

Key Words—Program specification description language, nonprocedural language, conceptual data model, entity-relationship model, constraint, real-time software, timing.

Abstract—This article discusses a real-time software specification description using a nonprocedural conceptual data model-based language. In the past several years, extensive studies have been carried out on real-time software specification description languages based on the dynamic aspect of real-time systems: timing and state transition, but few are based on the structural aspect. The control information of real-time systems has been more complicated. Therefore, it is also important to describe the structural aspect in a more comprehensible manner. The authors have been studying a nonprocedural conceptual data model-based language, which helps to describe the structural aspect. The language enables automatic program generation and software reusability. This paper describes how to treat the characteristics of real-time software: state transition, timing and external I/O, in the nonprocedural conceptual data model-based language.

1   Introduction

Databases have been increasingly used in the field of real-time software such as communication software and process control software. Therefore, data models which have been developed in the field of databases have been introduced into the studies of real-time software specification description. For example, the relational data model and the relational database query language SQL2 have been applied to network service description [1]. Most real-time software specification description languages, such as PAISLey [2] and LOTOS [3], are based on the dynamic aspect of real-time systems: timing and state transition. However, such languages are not always adapted to the specification description of real-time software with complex control information. On the other hand, the specification description languages based on data models are beneficial to describing the structural aspect of a universe of discourse. Therefore, even a method to treat complex control information can be specified in a more comprehensible manner, if the real-time system structure and the attributes of the system components are represented using a data model. In real-time software specification description, it is of course important to describe the dynamic aspect. It is also important to describe the structural aspect more comprehensibly, as the real-time systems have come to be more complicated and include more complex control information.

The authors have been studying the nonprocedural conceptual data model-based language *PSDL (Program Specification Description Language)* [4], and real-time software specification description. In PSDL, the structural aspect is described using the ER (Entity-Relationship) model

[5] which is a conceptual data model, and the dynamic aspect is described using constraints on the model. Thus, the structural aspect and the dynamic aspect are harmoniously described in PSDL. At present, PSDL describes the specification of individual program modules in real-time software. PSDL is an executable formal language. The authors are implementing a program generator to convert a PSDL program specification to a C program. Furthermore, PSDL improves comprehensibility leading the authors to also study software reusability in PSDL.

This paper discusses how to treat the characteristics of real-time software: state transition, timing and external I/O , in the nonprocedural conceptual data model-based language PSDL. Section 2 explains PSDL through the elevator problem [6]. Section 3 describes how to treat real-time software in PSDL, and compares related works.

2 PSDL

A PSDL program specification is composed of three layers: *the information layer* for framing the information represented by the program I/O data, *the data layer* for specifying the I/O data structures, and *the access layer* for determining the method of accessing the I/O data files and devices. Moreover, the three layers are described through the structure and constraints, and the description of *the information layer* is based on the ER model and constraints.

2.1 Example

The example of real-time software in this paper is the modified elevator control software used in [6]. The example is described as follows.

An elevator system serves each floor of a six-story building. With the exception of the top floor, there is a button on each floor which users can press to summon the elevator to take them to an upper floor. Except for the ground floor, there is a similar button for downward travel. Inside the elevator there are six buttons marked with the floor numbers. The elevator is raised and lowered by a cable which is wound and unwound by a motor positioned above the top floor. At each floor, in the elevator shaft, there is a sensor operated by a small wheel attached to the elevator. When the elevator is within 15 cm of the home position at that floor, the sensor is depressed by the wheel, an electrical switch is closed, and the elevator position (floor number) is sent to the elevator control system.

The motor commands are:

- STOP: causes the motor to stop.
- START_UP: sets the motor polarity for upward travel, and causes the motor to start.
- START_DOWN: sets the motor polarity for downward travel, and causes the motor to start.

The elevator ordinarily waits at a floor with the door open. If there is a request for service, the door is closed and the elevator commences operation. The elevator control system determines the direction of travel and whether to stop at a floor or not by taking into account the direction of travel, floor number, and user request. The elevator control system then sends the appropriate command to the motor.

The authors assume that when there are no requests, the elevator waits at the floor at which all requests were satisfied with the door open, and that when the elevator arrives at each floor to satisfy a request, the door is opened and then automatically closed. The authors do not treat opening and closing the door in the example.

```
00: INFORMATION
01: E request
02: ED post.request_renewal.pre.request
        ON post.request_renewal.pre.request.outstanding = "NO"
03: A floor    NUM
04:   = post.request_renewal.pre.request.floor
05: A direction    STR
06:   = post.request_renewal.pre.request.direction
07: A outstanding STR
08:   = IF (.request_satisfaction..elevator.floor = floor
        && (.request_satisfaction..elevator.direction = direction || direction = "EL"))
09:   "YES"
10:   ELSE
11:   "NO"
12: E elevator
13: ED post.state_transition.pre.elevator
        ON post.state_transition.pre.elevator.next_action = "STOP"
14: A floor    NUM
15:   = IF (post.state_transition.pre.elevator.next_action = "STOP")
16:     post.state_transition.pre.elevator.floor
17: A direction    STR
18:   = IF (post.state_transition.pre.elevator.next_action = "START_UP")
19:   "UP"
20:   ELSE IF (post.state_transition.pre.elevator.next_action = "START_DOWN")
21:   "DOWN"
22:   ELSE
23:     post.state_transition.pre.elevator.direction
24: A next_action STR
25:   = IF ("YES" IN SET(.request_satisfaction..request.outstanding))
26:   "STOP"
27:   ELSE IF (("YES" NOT IN SET(.request_satisfaction..request.outstanding))
        && post.state_transition.pre.elevator.next_action = "STOP")
28:   "PASS"
29:   ELSE IF (direction = "UP"
        && TRUE INCLUDE SET(.request_satisfaction..request.floor > floor))
30:   "START_UP"
31:   ELSE IF (direction = "DOWN"
        && TRUE INCLUDE SET(.request_satisfaction..request.floor < floor))
32:   "START_DOWN"
33:   ELSE IF (TRUE INCLUDE SET(.request_satisfaction..request.floor > floor))
34:   "START_UP"
35:   ELSE IF (TRUE INCLUDE SET(.request_satisfaction..request.floor < floor))
36:   "START_DOWN"
37: E motor
38: ED .motor_command..elevator ON .motor_command..elevator.next_action != "PASS"
39: A command STR
40:   = .motor_command..elevator.next_action
41: R request_renewal

42: C pre.request
43: C post.request
44: R request_satisfaction
45: C .request
46: C .elevator
47: RC .elevator.post.state_transition.pre.elevator..request_satisfaction..
        request.pre.request_renewal.post.request.
48: R state_transition
49: C pre.elevator
50: C post.elevator
51: RC post.elevator.post.state_transition.pre.elevator.
        pre.state_transition.post.elevator.pre
        && post.elevator.post.state_transition.pre.elevator.next_action = "STOP"
52: R motor_command
53: C .elevator
54: C .motor
55: DATA
56: O request_record
57:   = request
58:   = IF (NEXT) request_satisfaction..request
59: IX request.index
60: {
61:   %1d request.floor
62:     = request.floor
63:   %4s request.direction
64:     = request.direction
65: }
66: O elevator_record
67:   = elevator
68:   = IF (PRIOR) request_satisfaction..elevator
69:   = IF (PRIOR) state_transition.pre.elevator
70:   = IF (NEXT) state_transition.post.elevator
71: IX elevator.index
72: {
73:   %1d elevator.floor
74:     = elevator.floor
75: }
76: O motor_record
77:   = motor
78: IX motor.index
79: {
80:   %10s motor.action
81:     = motor.action
82: }
83: ACCESS
84: D request.d INPUT    8 request_record
85: D elevator.d INPUT   1 elevator_record
86: D motor.d OUTPUT 10 motor_record
```

Fig.1. PSDL program specification

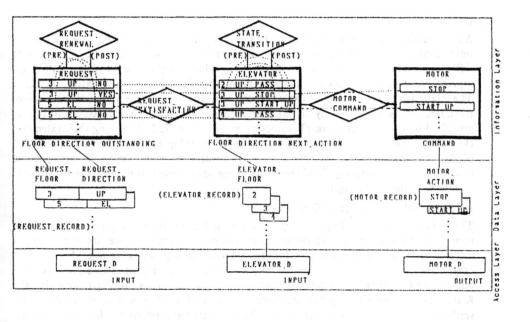

Fig.2. Program specification illustration

2.2 PSDL Statements

PSDL statements are outlined with reference to Figures 1 and 2. Fig.1 presents the PSDL program specification of the above example. Fig.2 illustrates the specification. The program inputs the requests for services and the sensor data, and outputs motor commands.

2.2.1 The Information Layer

In Fig.1, the statements between the INFORMATION and DATA statements on lines 00 and 55 specify the information layer. This layer is illustrated at the top of Fig.2.

1. Entity Type

   A thing existing, or an event which happened in a universe of discourse is called *an entity.*
   An entity type is a set of entities. Entities, such as REQUEST "3 UP YES" (A user has pressed a button on the third floor for upward travel.), ELEVATOR "3 UP STOP" (The elevator must stop at the third floor on its upward travel.), and MOTOR "STOP" (The motor has received a command to stop.), are represented in I/O data as shown in Fig.2. The entity types REQUEST, ELEVATOR, and MOTOR including the entities "3 UP YES", "3 UP STOP" and "STOP" are marked by the heavily outlined rectangles. Each entity type is described by the E (Entity) statement on line 01.

2. Attribute

   Properties of each entity are expressed by the collection of *attribute values.* Each attribute of the entity type is described by the A (Attribute) statement on line 03. STR (STRing) on line 05 specifies the attribute value set of character strings, and NUM (NUMber) on line 03 indicates that of numbers.

3. Relationship Type

An association among the entities is called *a relationship*. *A relationship type* is a set of relationships. Relationships, such as "A REQUEST '3 UP' is satisfied by the ELEVATOR '3 UP'." and "The 'STOP' MOTOR command is decided using the ELEVATOR '3 UP'.", are represented in the I/O data as shown by the broken lines between the entities in Fig.2. The relationship types REQUEST_SATISFACTION and MOTOR_COMMAND including the above relationships are illustrated by the heavily outlined diamonds. Each relationship type is described by the R (Relationship) statement on line 41 in Fig.1. Following this statement, the entity types related to each other by the relationship type are described by the C (Collection) statements on lines 42 and 43. The entity types and their roles are specified in the form "role.entity_type". If the entity types are different, the roles may be dropped as shown on line 45 in Fig.1.

4. Attribute Value Dependency Constraint

The AD (*Attribute value Dependency constraint*) is the constraint for gaining the values of non-primary key attributes. In the example illustrated in Fig.2, the REQUEST OUTSTANDING is derived by determining the REQUEST FLOOR, the ELEVATOR FLOOR, the REQUEST DIRECTION, and the ELEVATOR DIRECTION, where the entities REQUEST and ELEVATOR are related to each other by the relationship REQUEST_SATISFACTION. In Fig.1, following the A statement of non-primary key attribute, the value of which is computed, an AD is described by the = (equal) statement on line 08. The attributes referred to by the AD are described in the form "attribute" or "role_1.relationship_type.role_2.entity_type.attribute". The former indicates the attributes of the same entity whose attribute value is obtained, and the latter refers to the attributes of other entities via relationships. Role_1 and role_2 are, respectively, the roles of the entity whose attribute value is obtained, and other entities.

5. Entity Existence Dependency Constraint

The ED (*Entity existence Dependency constraint*) is the constraint for deriving new entities. In Fig.2, if the ELEVATOR NEXT_ACTION is not "PASS", the entity MOTOR related to the entity ELEVATOR exists, and the relationship MOTOR_COMMAND is obtained. Whether the ELEVATOR NEXT_ACTION is "PASS" or not is described as the ON phrase in the ED statement. In Fig.1, following the E statement of entity, the ED is described by the ED statement on line 38.

6. Relationship Existence Dependency Constraint

The RD (*Relationship existence Dependency constraint*) is the constraint for obtaining new relationships, illustrated by the broken lines in Fig.2. A new relationship exists when the RD is satisfied. Otherwise, the relationship does not exist. In the succession of R and C statements, the condition expression for specifying the relationship existence is described by the RC (Relationship existence Condition) statement. The RC statements are described in the form "P(role.entity_type.attribute, ···)" or "role_1.entity_type_1.role_2.relationship_type_1. ··· .role_3.entity_type_2.role_4". The former is used when the condition for a new relationship to exist is decided by P, where P is the predicate name. If P is simple, the logic expression meaning P may be described directly. The latter expresses *the path* between two entities related to each other by a new relationship. For example, the RD of the relationship STATE_TRANSITION is described as "POST.ELEVATOR.POST.STATE_TRANSITION.PRE.ELEVATOR.PRE.STATE_TRANSITION.POST. ELEVATOR.PRE" on line 51 in Fig.1, and illustrated in Fig.3. Thus means that the entity '4 UP PASS' is POST.ELEVATOR, the entity '3 UP START_UP' is PRE.ELEVATOR, r_1 and r_2 are the relationships STATE_TRANSITION, and the path is " '4 UP PASS' → r_1 → '3 UP STOP' → r_2 → '3 UP START_UP' ". This is the path between '4 UP PASS' and '3 UP START_UP' which are related to each other by a new relationship STATE_TRANSITION.

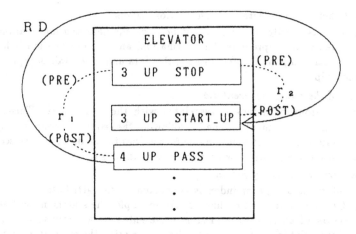

r_1, r_2 : relationship STATE_TRANSITION

Fig.3. *Path* form in RC

2.2.2 The Data Layer

The data layer statements are described between the DATA and ACCESS statements on lines 55 and 83 in Fig.1. This layer is illustrated in the middle of Fig.2. The I/O data structures are hierarchically determined by the *elementary, sequence group, iteration group,* and *selection group data types.* The associations between the information and data layer specification are also described.

1. Elementary Data Type

   The elementary data type is described by the % statement on line 61 in Fig.1. The % statements specify the datum forms, such as %1d, in the same manner as in programming language C. In the data layer part of Fig.2, the data types are shaped into tree structures. The elementary data types are arranged like leaves on a tree.

2. Sequence Group Data Type

   The sequence group data type is described by the O (sequence Order) statement on line 56 in Fig.1. This type's datum is composed of several data arranged in a line. The latter data are taken one by one from each data type enclosed by brackets, { }, on lines 60 and 65 following the O statement.

3. Iteration Group Data Type

   The iteration group data type is described by the IX (IndeX) statement following the description of other data types, and this is presented on line 59 in Fig.1. The former type's datum is composed of the latter type's data. The IX statement is described as "IX index_name [iteration termination condition]". The iteration termination condition is specified by the IF phrase. If the latter type's data iterates an infinite number of times, the iteration termination condition is dropped as can be seen from line 59, Fig.1.

4. Selection Group Data Type

   The selection group data type is described by the S (Selection) statement. No example of this data type is presented in Fig.1. This type's datum is composed of only one datum taken from one of the data types enclosed by brackets following the S statement. The selection condition of data types is specified by the IF-ELSE phrase.

5. Constraints between the Data and Information Layers

These constraints specify the associations between the data and information layers. The data and index values represents the information, and the information is framed by the entity and relationship types. Accordingly, the data and index values express the entities and relationships.

- In the case of *the entity representation*:

  The sequence group data type is associated with the entity type. This association is described by the = statement on line 57, following the sequence group data type O statement. For example, the statement on line 57 specifies that a datum of the sequence group data type REQUEST_RECORD represents an entity REQUEST.

- With *the attribute value expression*:

  The elementary data type or index is connected to the attribute. This connection is described by the = statement on line 62. For example, the statement on line 62 specifies that the FLOOR of an entity REQUEST is represented by a REQUEST_FLOOR datum. In Fig.2, this constraint is illustrated by the line associating the elementary data type in the data layer with the attribute in the information layer.

- For *the relationship representation*:

  The sequence group data types are associated with the entity types which are related to each other by the relationship type. These associations are described by the = statements on lines 69 and 70. For example, the statements on lines 69 and 70 specify that the PRIOR and NEXT ELEVATOR_RECORDS represent the relationship STATE_TRANSITION.

2.2.3　The Access Layer

The access layer statements for specifying the data access are described following the ACCESS statement on line 83 in Fig.1. Each I/O file and device is called *a dataset*. In PSDL, I/O data of devices such as ELEVATOR_D on line 85 in Fig.1 are regarded as sequential access files. Each of the datasets is described by the D (Dataset) statement on line 84, 85, or 86. In the statement, the file or device name, the random access key (if the file is a random access file), the input or output usage which is described by INPUT or OUTPUT, the record length and the association with the data structure are specified. This layer is illustrated at the bottom of Fig.2.

3　Discussion

3.1　How to Treat Characteristics of Real-Time Software

This section describes how to treat the characteristics of real-time software: state transition, timing and external I/O, with PSDL.

3.1.1　State Transition

When a thing has a state transition, the entity having an attribute value representing pre-state and the entity having an attribute value representing post-state are represented by different entities. A state transition is described by an ED, and an attribute value representing a new state is obtained by an AD. That ED specifies that a new entity representing a post-state exists, if the attribute of an entity representing a pre-state has a special value. Those entities are elements of the same entity type, and distinguished by roles. An example is illustrated in Fig.2. The STATE_TRANSITION is the association between the PRE.ELEVATOR and the POST.ELEVATOR. Both "PRE" and "POST" are roles of the entities. The ED on line 13 in Fig.1 specifies the state transition. If the PRE.ELEVATOR NEXT_ACTION is "STOP", the POST.ELEVATOR exists by the ED.

3.1.2 Timing Constraints

The concept of time in PSDL—the time that an event happens or ends, the running time of an event, and the association between the events—is described by entity types, attributes, relationship types and three constraints (AD, RD, and ED). Thus, in the information layer, all concepts of time are described. However, there are devices in the data layer and the access layer to describe these characteristics.

- *The input-output timing constraint*

  If the input data include input times, the association of before and after between entities is described by the relationship type in the information layer. However, when treating real-time software, that association can be known through input timing, even if the input data do not include input times. The input-output timing constraint describes the association of before and after between I/O data structures in the data layer, as illustrated on lines 58 and 68 in Fig.1. This means that the relationship REQUEST_SATISFACTION is always associated with two entities ELEVATOR and REQUEST which arrives after the entity ELEVATOR has arrived. If ELEVATOR has arrived but REQUEST has not, the relationship is not yet obtained. When REQUEST arrives, the relationship is obtained.

- *The system clock constraint*

  The system clock constraint is described when getting the input data from the system clock. The clock is treated as a device, so the constraint is described by the D statement in the access layer.

- *The response time constraint*

  Real-time software must run along the axis of time in a universe of discourse, thus the response time constraint is described. However, it is difficult to automatically generate a real-time program which always satisfies that constraint. Accordingly, the response time constraint is described as a comment in the access layer.

3.1.3 External Input-Output

Real-time software has external input-output such as control signals, interruptions to inform the state change of external devices, and interactions among other processes. The control signal, the external interruption and the interaction are all regarded as one kind of data. Accordingly, there is no description device in the information layer and the data layer. However, their methods of access are different from file's. Thus, that the data is a control signal, or an external interruption or an interaction between other processes, as well as the method of access, must be indicated.

When adapting various applications, an entity type sometimes has two or more input data. In such cases, it is necessary to have a group of indispensable attributes to identify each entity in an entity type, in PSDL program specification. Those attributes are called *primary key attributes*. Each primary key attribute of the entity type is described by the K (Key) statement.

Although the entities are provided from different input data, the several entities are the same entity. Therefore, the set union operation must be applied to the entity sets obtained from each of the input data. For the operation, the primary key attribute values are compared among the entity sets.

An example is illustrated in Fig.4. The arrows A_1 and A_2 are input data of the entity type E. The entities $e_{11}, e_{12}, \cdots, e_{1n}$ are the inflow from A_1, and the entities $e_{21}, e_{22}, \cdots, e_{2n}$ are the inflow from A_2. If the primary key attribute value of e_{12} and e_{21} are the same, e_{12} and e_{21} are the same entity. Therefore, the entity set of E is $\{e_{11}, e_{12}(= e_{21}), e_{22}, \cdots, e_{1n}, \cdots, e_{2n}\}$.

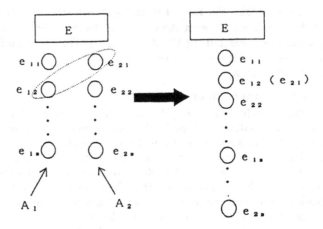

Fig.4. Entity set union

3.2 Comparisons to Related Works

The features of PSDL are compared to related works.

3.2.1 Description of a Universe of Discourse

Concepts in a universe of discourse are represented by a framework composed of entity and relationship types. According to this commonly accepted viewpoint, PSDL directly describes a universe of discourse using the ER model with constraints. Therefore, the PSDL improves comprehensibility, extensibility and constructibility. There are several approaches to representing the universe of discourse of real-time software.

PAISLey and LOTOS are software specification description languages based on the dynamic aspect of software. The approach in PSDL and MODEL [7] is to treat real-time software using the program specification description language for data processing. G. Gopal's approach is to describe real-time software with data processing in the relational database language SQL2. PSDL, MODEL and G. Gopal's are based on the structural aspect. Therefore, the approach in PAISLey and LOTOS is different from the approach in PSDL.

In MODEL, both the program I/O data and intermediate data are described by arrays. The arrays of I/O data are meaningful for determining the I/O data structures in the manner of high level languages such as COBOL. However, it is uncertain that the arrays are even used for the intermediate data, as the arrays are not necessarily suitable for representing the entity and relationship types. It was pointed out that the use of subscripts might be the most difficult aspect of MODEL.

SQL2 is a database query language based on the relational data model. In the relational data model, a universe of discourse is described by "sets" and "relations". However, in the relational data model there is no concept of entity existence as there is in the ER model. Therefore, the ER model is better suited to expressing a universe of discourse than the relational data model.

Thus, PSDL is adapted to expressing a universe of discourse. Therefore, a PSDL program specification can be reused. The authors call this technique *the specification parts technique*. In this technique, the prototypes of entity types, relationship types and constraints are stored in a dictionary. Entity types, relationship types and constraints are components of concepts in a universe of discourse. Accordingly, the authors call that dictionary *the concept database*. Thus, PSDL is also beneficial to reusability.

3.2.2 How to Treat Real-Time Software

As discussed in Section 2, PSDL treats real-time software in the same way as data processing software, describing the state transition, the timing, and the external I/O by the entity types, attributes, relationship types, and constraints. Therefore, PSDL readily describes real-time software with complex control information. The data store treated in SQL2 can also be described by the ER model in PSDL.

Moreover, PSDL can treat *the timing constraint* described in Section 3. However, in both PAISLey and MODEL, each process and its interface is described but *the input-output timing constraint* is not explicitly described.

4 Conclusion and Further Work

A nonprocedural conceptual data model-based program specification description language, PSDL, directly describes the entity types, relationship types, and constraints that are components of concepts in a universe of discourse, and adapted to the way a programmer understands a universe of discourse. Moreover, in PSDL, the characteristics of real-time software: state transition, timing and external I/O, can be described. Thus, PSDL readily describes real-time software with complex control information. Furthermore, PSDL can treat *the input-output timing constraint* that is the association of before and after between I/O data, which is important for real-time software.

The authors are implementing a program generator which converts a PSDL program specification to a C program. Moreover, the authors plan to design a diagram editor to edit illustrations such as Fig.2, in order to improve describability, comprehensibility, and maintainability in PSDL. Furthermore, the authors are studying a software reusability technique which they call *the specification parts technique*.

Acknowledgements

The authors are grateful to K.Habara and K.Yamashita for their suggestions. The authors also wish to thank T.Takenaka and other colleagues in the ATR Communication Systems Research Laboratories for their helpful discussions.

References

[1] G. Gopal, G. Herman, W. Mansfield Jr. "A Data Base Model For Network Services", *Proceedings of IEE Software Engineering for Telecommunication Switching Systems 89*, pp. 154-157, 1989.

[2] P. Zave, "An Operational Approach to Requirements Specification for Embedded Systems", *IEEE Trans. Software Eng.*, Vol. SE-8, No. 3, 1982.

[3] Ed Brinksma, "A tutorial on LOTOS", *Protocol Specification, Testing, and Verification, IFIP 85*, North Holland Publishing Company, pp. 171-194, 1986.

[4] M. Hashimoto, K. Ibuki, "Program Specification Description Method Using Data Model-based Information Structure Description", *Review of the Electrical Communications Laboratories*, Vol. 35, No. 4, pp. 409-416, 1987.

[5] P.P. Chen, "The Entity-Relationship Model — Toward a Unified View of Data", *ACM Trans. Database Syst.*, Vol. 1, No. 1, pp. 9-36, 1976.

[6] M.A. Jackson, "System Development", *Prentice-Hall*, Englewood Cliffs, N.J., 1983.

[7] J.S. Tseng, B. Szymanski, Y. Shi, N.S. Prywes, "Real-Time Software Life Cycle with the Model System", *IEEE Trans. Software Eng.*, Vol. SE-12, No. 2, 1986.

DINAS: COMPUTER-ASSISTED SYSTEM FOR MULTI-CRITERIA TRANSPORTATION AND LOCATION ANALYSES

Wlodzimierz Ogryczak
Marshall University
Computer & Information Sciences
Huntington, WV 25755, USA

Krzysztof Studzinski and **Krystian Zorychta**
Warsaw University, Institute of Informatics
Warsaw, Poland

Abstract

DINAS (Dynamic Interactive Network Analysis System) is an interactive system to aid in the solution of various multiobjective transportation problems with facility location. DINAS utilizes an extension of the reference point approach for interactive handling multiple objectives. In this approach the decision-maker forms his requirements in terms of aspiration and reservation levels, i.e., he specifies acceptable and required values for given objectives. A special solver was developed to provide DINAS with solutions to single-objective problems. It is based on the branch and bound scheme with a pioneering implementation of the simplex special ordered network (SON) algorithm with implicit representation of the simple and variable upper bounds (SUB & VUB). DINAS is prepared for IBM-PC XT/AT or compatibles as a menu-driven and easy in usage system equipped with a special network editor which reduces to minimum effort associated with data input for real-life problems.

1. The problem

The distribution-location type problems belong to the class of the most significant real-life decision problems based on mathematical programming. They are usually formalized as the so-called transportation problems with facility location. A network model of the transportation problem with facility location consists of nodes connected by a set of direct flow arcs.

The set of nodes is partitioned into two subsets: the set of fixed nodes and the set of potential nodes. The fixed nodes represent "fixed points" of the transportation network, i.e., points which cannot be changed whereas the potential nodes are introduced to represent possible locations of new points in the network. Some groups of the potential nodes represent different versions of the same facility to be located (e.g., different sizes of warehouse etc.). For this reason, potential nodes are organized in the so-called selections, i.e., sets of nodes with the multiple choice requirement. Each selection is defined by the list of included potential nodes as well as by a lower and upper number of nodes which have to be selected (located).

A homogeneous good is distributed along the arcs among the nodes. Each fixed node is characterized by two quantities: supply and demand on the good, but for mathematical statement of the problem only the difference supply-demand (the so-called balance) is used. Each potential node is characterized by a capacity which bounds maximal flow of the good through the node. The capacities are also given for all the arcs but not for the fixed nodes.

A few linear objective functions are considered in the problem. The objective functions are introduced into the model by given coefficients associated with several arcs and potential nodes. They will be called cost coefficients independently of their real character. The cost coefficients for potential nodes are, however, understood in a different way than those for arcs. The cost coefficient connected to an arc is treated as the unit cost of the flow along the arc whereas the cost coefficient connected to a potential node is considered as the fixed cost associated with activity (locating) of the node rather than the unit cost.

Summarizing, the following groups of input data define the transportation problem under consideration:
- objectives,
- fixed nodes with their balances,
- potential nodes with their capacities and (fixed) cost coefficients,
- selections with their lower and upper limits on number of active potential nodes,
- arcs with their capacities and cost coefficients.

The problem is to determine the number and locations of active potential nodes and to find the good flows (along arcs) so as to satisfy the balance and capacity restrictions and, simultaneously, optimize the given objective functions. A mathematical model of the problem is described in details by Ogryczak et al. [4].

2. Overview of the system

DINAS (Dynamic Interactive Network Analysis System) enables a solution to the above problems using an IBM-PC XT/AT or compatibles. It requires 640K RAM and a hard disk or at least one floppy disk. The basic version of the DINAS system can process problems consisted of:
- up to seven objective functions,

- a transportation network with up to one hundred of fixed nodes and three hundred of arcs,
- up to fifteen potential locations.

DINAS consists of three programs prepared in the C programming language:
- an interactive procedure for efficient solutions generation,
- a solver for single-objective problems,
- a network editor for input data and results examination.

For handling multiple objectives DINAS utilizes an extension of the reference point approach proposed by Wierzbicki [6]. The basic concept of the interactive scheme is as follows:
- the DM forms his requirements in terms of aspiration and reservation levels, i.e., he specifies acceptable and required values for given objectives, respectively;
- the DM works with the system in an interactive way so that he can change his aspiration and reservation levels in any direction;
- after editing the aspiration and reservation levels, the system computes a new efficient solution by solving a corresponding single-objective problem;
- each computed efficient solution is put into a special solution base and presented to the DM as the current solution in the form of tables and bars which allow him to analyze performances of the current solution in comparison with the previous ones.

A special TRANSLOC solver has been prepared to provide the multiobjective analysis procedure with solutions to single-objective problems. The solver is hidden from the user but it is the most important part of the DINAS system. It is a numerical kernel which generates efficient solutions. The concept of TRANSLOC is based on the branch and bound scheme with a pioneering implementation of the simplex special ordered network (SON) algorithm proposed by Glover and Klingman [1] with implicit representation of the simple and variable upper bounds (VUB & SUB) suggested by Schrage [5]. The mathematical background of the TRANSLOC solver was given in details by Ogryczak et al. [3].

DINAS is equipped with the built-in network editor EDINET. It is a full-screen editor specifically designed for input and edit data of the network model of the transportation problems with facility location. The general concept of EDINET is to edit the data while defining the logical structure of the network. More precisely, the essence of the EDINET concept is a dynamic movement from some current node to its neighboring nodes, and vice versa, according to the network structure. The numerical data (in fact, attributes to the nodes and arcs) are inserted by a special mechanism of windows, while visiting several nodes (see Fig. 1). At any time only one of the windows representing different kinds of the data is active. The corresponding part of the data can be inserted then. While working with the editor the DM activates several windows. Apart from the windows with local information some special windows containing a list of nodes and a graphic scheme of the network (see Fig. 2) are available at any moment to ease movement across the network.

The interactive analysis of the multiobjective problem can be performed with DINAS by the DM who is not familiar with neither computer techniques nor mathematical programming. DINAS is a menu-driven system with very simple commands. Operations available in the DINAS interactive procedure are partitioned into three groups and corresponding three branches of the main menu (see Table 1): PROCESS, SOLUTION and ANALYSIS.

Table 1. DINAS Main Menu

PROCESS	SOLUTION	ANALYSIS
Problem	Summary	Compare
Convert	Browse	Previous
Pay-Off	Save	Next
Efficient	Delete	Last
Quit		Restore

The PROCESS branch contains basic operations connected with processing the multiobjective problem and generation of several efficient solutions. There are included problem definition operations such as calling the network editor for input or modification of the problem (PROBLEM) and converting of the edited problem with error checking (CONVERT). Further, in this branch the basic optimization operations are available: PAY-OFF and EFFICIENT. As the last command in this branch is placed the QUIT operation which allows the DM to finish work with the system.

The PAY-OFF command must be executed as the first step of the multiobjective analysis. It performs optimization of each objective function separately. In effect, one gets the so-called pay-off matrix. The pay-off matrix is a well-known device in MCDM. It is displayed as a table containing values of all the objective functions (columns) obtained while solving several single-objective problems (rows) and thereby it helps to understand the conflicts between different objectives.

The execution of the PAY-OFF command provides also the DM with two reference vectors: the utopia vector and the nadir vector. The utopia vector represents the best values of each objective considered

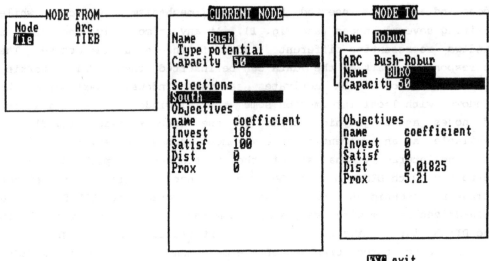

Figure 1

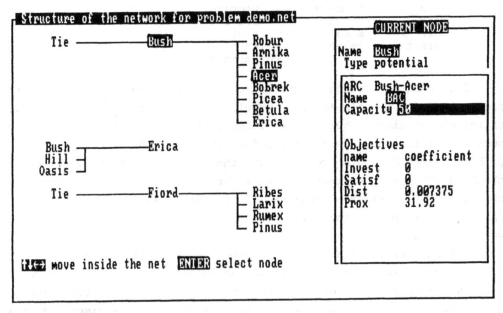

Figure 2

separately, and the nadir vector expresses the worst values of each objective noticed during several single-objective optimizations. The utopia vector is, usually, not attainable, i.e., there are no feasible solutions with such objective values. Coefficients of the nadir vector cannot be considered as the worst values of the objectives over the whole efficient (Pareto-optimal) set. They usually estimate these values but they express only the worst values of each objective noticed during optimization of another objective function.

Due to a special regularization technique used while computing the pay-off matrix (see [2]) each generated single-objective optimal solution is also an efficient solution to the multiobjective problem. So, after the calculation of the pay-off matrix there is already available a number of efficient solutions connected with several rows of the pay-off matrix. The pay-off matrix calculation is, usually, the most time-consuming operation of the multiobjective analysis. Therefore DINAS automatically saves the computed pay-off matrix on the problem file.

Having executed the PAY-OFF command one can start the interactive search for a satisfying efficient solution. DINAS utilizes aspiration and reservation levels to control the interactive analysis. More precisely, the DM specifies acceptable values for several objectives as the aspiration levels, and necessary values as the reservation levels. All the operations connected with editing the aspiration and reservation levels as well as with computation of a new efficient solution are performed within the EFFICIENT command.

The system searches for a satisfying efficient solution using an achievement scalarizing function as a criterion in the single-objective optimization. Namely, DINAS searches the feasible solution to minimize the following objective function:

$$\underset{i=1,\cdots,p}{\operatorname{maximum}} u_i(\mathbf{q},\mathbf{a},\mathbf{r}) + s/p \sum_{i=1}^{p} u_i(\mathbf{q},\mathbf{a},\mathbf{r})$$

where s is an arbitrarily small number, p denotes number of the objectives, $\mathbf{q}$ represents the objective vector, and u_i is a function which measures the deviation of results from the DM's expectations with respect to the i-th objective depending on a given aspiration level $\mathbf{a}$ and reservation level $\mathbf{r}$. The function u_i is a strictly monotone function of the objective vector $\mathbf{q}$ with value 0 if $\mathbf{q}=\mathbf{a}$ and value 1 if $\mathbf{q}=\mathbf{r}$. In our system, we use a piece-wise linear function u_i (see [2] for details). The computed solution is always an efficient solution to the original multiobjective model (even if the given aspiration levels are attainable).

Figure 3

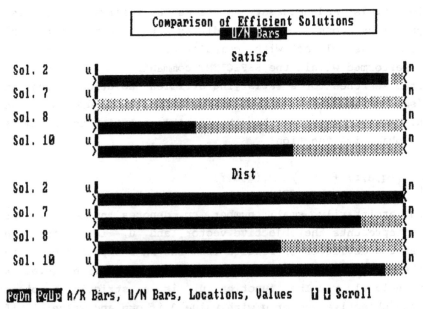

Figure 4

DINAS stores the efficient solutions in a special solution base. All the efficient solutions generated (or input from a file) during a session get consecutive numbers and are automatically put into the solution base. However at most nine efficient solution can be stored in the solution base. When the tenth solution is put into the base then the oldest solution is automatically dropped from it. On the other hand any efficient solution can be saved on a separate file and restored during the same or a subsequent session with the problem.

DINAS is armed with many operations which help to manage the solution base. There are two kinds of operations connected with the solution base: operations on a single efficient solution, and operations on the whole solution base. Operations addressed to a single solution are connected with the current solution. The newest generated efficient solution is automatically assumed to be the current solution but any efficient solution from the solution base can be manually assigned as the current solution.

The SOLUTION branch of the main menu contains additional operations connected with the current solution. You can examine in details the current solution using the Network Editor (BROWSE) or analyze only short characteristics such as objective values and selected locations (SUMMARY). Values of the objective functions are presented in three ways: as a standard table, as bars in the aspiration/reservation scale and as bars in the utopia/nadir scale. The bars show percentage level of each objective value with respect to the corresponding scale (see Fig. 3). One may also save the current solution on a separate file in order to use it during next runs of the system with the same problem (SAVE). There is also available a special command to delete the current solution from the solution base if one finds it as quite useless (DELETE).

The ANALYSIS branch of the main menu contains commands connected with operations on the solution base. The main command COMPARE allows the DM to perform a comparison between all the efficient solutions included in the solution base or in some subset of the base. In the comparison only short characteristics of the solutions are used, i.e., objective values in the form of tables and bars (see Fig. 4) as well as tables of selected locations. Moreover, some commands included in this branch (PREVIOUS, NEXT and LAST) allow to select any efficient solution from the solution base as the current solution. One can also restore some efficient solution (saved earlier on a separate file) to the solution base (RESTORE).

3. Final comments

DINAS has been already successfully used while analyzing two real-life problems: routes optimization for building materials transportation and location of new children clinics. The former one was a three-objective transportation problem without facility location. It was originally a two-commodity transportation problem but we managed to model it as a single-commodity one. The latter problem was more complex location-allocation one. It contained 5 objective functions, nearly 300 arcs and nearly 100 nodes including 8 potential ones.

Initial experiences with the DINAS system confirm appropriateness of the used methodology for solving multiobjective transportation problems with facility location. The interactive scheme is very easy and supported by many analysis tools. Thereby, a satisfactory solution can be usually reached in a few interactive steps.

When real-life problems are solved with DINAS on IBM-PC XT/AT microcomputers the single-objective computations take, obviously, much more time than while using some standard optimization tools (like the MPSX/370 package) on a mainframe. However, our experiences with both these approaches allow us to trust that DINAS, in general, will take much less time for performing the whole multiobjective analysis.

4. References

[1] F.Glover and D.Klingman, "The simplex SON method for LP/embedded network problems". Mathematical Programming Study 15 (1981) 148-176.
[2] W.Ogryczak, K.Studzinski and K.Zorychta, "Dynamic Interactive Network Analysis System DINAS Version 2.1 (1988): User's Manual". WP-88-114, IIASA, Laxenburg 1988.
[3] W.Ogryczak, K.Studzinski and K.Zorychta, "A solver for the multiobjective transshipment problem with facility location". European Journal of Operational Research, 43 (1989) 53-64.
[4] W.Ogryczak, K.Studzinski, K.Zorychta: A Generalized Reference Point Approach to Multiobjective Transshipment Problem with Facility Location, in: Aspiration Based Decision Support Systems - Theory, Software and Applications, A.Lewandowski and A.Wierzbicki (eds.), Lecture Notes in Economics and Mathematical Systems 331, Springer Verlag, Berlin, New York 1989, pp.t213-229.
[5] L.Schrage, "Implicit representation of variable upper bounds in linear programming". Mathematical Programming Study 4 (1975) 118-132.
[6] A.P.Wierzbicki, "A mathematical basis for satisficing decision making". Math. Modelling 3 (1987) 391-405.

LOGIC PROGRAMMING FOR SOFTWARE TESTING

Sanjay Khanna
Dept. of Electrical and Computer Engineering
Syracuse University
P.O. Box 574, Syracuse NY 13210, USA
skhanna@zookeeper.cns.syr.edu

Abstract

We propose a methodology for using logic programming to software testing. The methodology is based on logic programming applications for the formation of decision-to-decision graph, path predicate evaluation and symbolic evaluation of output variables. We mention an efficient software testing scheme which utilizes multiple theories in logic, organized as a tree structure. An Algol-like language is used to present our approach.

1 Introduction

The application of logic programming to the areas of expert systems design [9] and compiler design [10] has been investigated by several researchers. We feel that logic programming can have abundant applications in the area of software testing.

It is essential to establish that a computer program meets its specifications. Since program proving is not well established, we must rely on various testing strategies to gain confidence in a program's correctness. References on software testing can be found in [3],[7] and [8]. Software testing schemes involving numeric test cases are usually not thorough and use excessive amount of computer and programmer time. An alternative, that we discuss in this paper, is a symbolic testing scheme utilizing logic programming. Specifically, we propose the application of logic programming to the following.

1. Determination of the path of execution through a program on a given set of input values.
2. Symbolic evaluation of the output and intermediate variables of a program.
3. Evaluation of the path predicates of the program.

Before we elaborate on our testing scheme, we would like to review some definitions.

Definition 1: A *program block* is a list of one or more statements such that if the first statement is executed, then all others are also executed. A block is also referred to as a node.

Definition 2: A *path* is a sequence of nodes (blocks) $n_1, ..., n_k$ traversed during the program execution, such that n_1 is the first node and n_k is the last node. Most programs have a large number of paths because of loop structures.

Definition 3: In the *path testing* strategy, each path in the program is traversed at least once. The logical conditions which the set of input variables must satisfy for a path to be traversed are called the *path predicate*.

We illustrate how a combination of path testing strategy and logic programming can be applied to program testing. The program is first converted to a decision-to-decision graph and then the different path predicates are evaluated using logic programming. The output variables are symbolically expressed in terms of input variables and numeric values. Symbolic evaluation is a useful aid for verifying a program's functional specifications. Determining the path predicates and the symbolic values of the variables which they produce can help verify whether or not a program meets its intended specifications. We also mention how symbolic testing can be performed with the help of multiple theories where the theories are organized in a tree structure.

2 Logic Programming for Program Testing

Our methodology for program testing involves performing lexical analysis on the source program to produce a list of tokens, parsing the tokens to form a decision-to-decision graph (dd-graph), and utilizing this graph to perform path testing and symbolic evaluation. The parsing task is easily achieved using Definite Clause Grammar which is standard with any logic programming language. A detailed discussion of parsing with definite clause grammars can be found in [2], [6].

2.1 Formation of Decision-To-Decision Graph

We discuss how a *decision-to-decision graph* (dd-graph) can be formed for a given program. When we convert the program to its internal form during parsing, the program statements are stored as a list. Markers in the form of $N (N=0,1,2...) are placed at the beginning of each program block. Thus, for the *if* statement, a marker is inserted in each of the *then* and *else* parts. For the *while* statement, markers are put at the beginning of the *while* loop body and after the end of the loop. Markers are also inserted at the beginning and end of the program. The dd-graph also contains a list of all the variable-value pairs in the program. Each element of the list has the variable name and an initial value *nil*.

        [(var1,nil), (var2,nil), ... , (varn,nil)]

The *nil* values are substituted by numeric or symbolic values during the execution of the dd-graph. This representation of the *decision-to-decision graph* aids in determining the path of execution on given input values, as well as in program testing using symbolic evaluation, as will be discussed in the next section.

We use the following representation for the *if* and *while* statements in the decision-to-decision graph.

        * if statement *
            [if,COND,[$Ni|THEN],[$Nj|ELSE]]

where COND specifies the conditional predicate of the *if* statement and $THEN$ and $ELSE$ consist of the list of statements in the *then* and *else* parts respectively.

        * while statement *
            [while, COND , [$Ni| LOS] , $Nj]

where COND is the conditional predicate of the *while* statement, and LOS is the list of statements in the body of the *while* loop.

As an example, let us consider a program which performs integer division by successive subtractions. The reference branches in the program are illustrated with three markers.

```
/* PROGRAM 1 */
begin integer x, y, div, mod;
$0
div := 0;
mod := x;
while (mod >= y) do
  begin
  $1 mod := mod - y ;
      div := div + 1 ;
  end;
$2
end.
```

The *decision-to-decision graph* for the above program is as follows:

```
graph([(x,nil),(y,nil),(div,nil),(mod,nil)],
   [$,0,[div,:=,[0]],[mod,:=,[x]],
   [while,[mod,>,=,y],
     [$,1,[mod,:=,[mod,-,y]],[div,:=,[div,+,1]]]],$,2]).
```

2.2 Use of Decision-To-Decision Graph For Path Testing

The user specifies the list of input values to the program. This forms the current environment of the variables. The conditional predicates in an *if* or *while* statement are evaluated using an *expression evaluator (expr)*. Based on the evaluation of the conditional predicate to *true* or *false*, the set of statements in one of the two possible branches is executed. The environment is changed appropriately for variables to which a new value is assigned. The branches executed in this process from the beginning to the end are recorded in the form of nodes traversed during execution and the user is informed of the path taken by the program. The above concepts have been incorporated in the predicate *path_eval* in Prolog.

```
Explanation of Variables
OE        Present Numeric Environment of Variables.
NE        New Numeric Environment of Variables.
IE        Intermediate Numeric Environment of Varibales.
NO        The node number in the dd-graph.
SLIST     List of Statements.
COND      The conditional expression in the If or While
          statement.

path_eval([], [], OE, OE).

path_eval([while, COND, SLIST], NO, OE, NE) :-
   expr(Result, OE, COND, []),
   ((Result= false -> NO = [] , NE = OE);
   Result= true, path_eval(SLIST, NO1, OE, IE),
   path_eval([while, COND, SLIST], NO2, IE, NE),
   append(NO1, NO2, NO)).

path_eval([if, COND, THEN, ELSE], NO, OE, NE) :-
   expr(Result, OE, COND, []),
   ((Result = true -> path_eval(THEN, NO, OE, NE));
   Result = false, path_eval(ELSE, NO, OE, NE)).

path_eval([VAR, ':=', EXP], [], OE, NE) :-
   expr(VAL, OE, EXP , []), change_environ(OE, [VAR, VAL], NE).

path_eval([H | T], NO, OE, NE) :- path_eval(H, NO1, OE, IE),
```

```
        path_eval(T, NO2, IE, NE), append(NO1, NO2, NO).

path_eval([$, NO | SLIST], [NO | RemNO], OE, NE):-
    path_eval(SLIST, RemNO, OE, NE).

change_environ([[VAR,_] | REST],[VAR, VAL], [[VAR,VAL]|REST]):-!.

change_environ([H | T], VARVAL, [H | NEWT]) :-
    change_environ(T, VARVAL, NEWT).
```

The predicate *expr* evaluates the value of an arithmetic or boolean expression (EXP), given the current numeric environment. The predicate *change_environ* updates the numeric (OE) or symbolic (OSE) environment given a variable and its current value.

The clauses for *path_eval* can be understood declaratively, and have the following meaning, in the order of their appearance above.

1. If the statement list is empty, then the list of nodes traversed in the dd-graph, is also empty and the numeric environment does not get changed.

2. For the *while* statement, we evaluate the conditional expression (COND) with the current numeric environment (OE). If the result is false, then no additional nodes have been traversed. In the otherwise case we evaluate the list of statements (SLIST) in the body of *while* statement to obtain the intermediate numeric environment (IE) and the nodes (NO1) traversed in the body. Now the *while* statement is recursively evaluated in the context of IE, to give us the final numeric environment (NE) and the remaining list of nodes (NO2) traversed. To obtain the complete list of nodes (NO) traversed, we append NO1 and NO2.

3. For the *if* statement, if the evaluation of the conditional expression (COND) with the current numeric environment (OE) comes out to be *true*, then we perform path evaluation for statements in the *then* body (THEN) to obtain the new numeric environment (NE) and the nodes (NO) traversed. If the result of conditional expression evaluation is *false* then we do a similar path evaluation in the *else* body.

4. For the assignment statement, we evaluate the expression on the RHS to obtain the value VAL. We then change the numeric environment to reflect the new value (VAL) of the variable (VAR).

5. To accomplish path evaluation for a list of statements, we first evaluate the head statement with the current numeric environment (OE) to give us the nodes (NO1) traversed and the intermediate numeric environment (IE). We then evaluate the remaining statements in the context of IE to obtain the remaining nodes (NO2) and the new numeric environment (NE). The complete list of nodes is obtained by catenating NO1 and NO2.

6. When we observe a marker in the list of statements, we include the marker number in the list of nodes. We evaluate the statements (SLIST), to obtain the other nodes (RemNO).

A minimal testing requirement for a program should be that all *simple paths* in the dd-graph be executed at least once. A *simple path* is defined to be a path such that all nodes in decision-to-decision graph are traversed at most once. This is equivalent to executing the body of a *while statement* in a program zero or one time. We may also wish to check that the input and intermediate variables are adequately used in the program during execution. If an input or intermediate variable does not appear on the right hand side of an assignment statement for the paths selected, we have either not tested the program adequately, or there are redundant variables in the program. In our dd-graph, checking to see whether or not the concerned variable appears on the right of the assignment symbol (':=') in a STMTLIST associated with the branches that are traversed, will ensure that the input values as well as the results of intermediate computation are used.

2.3 Symbolic Evaluation of Programs

Path predicate evaluation proceeds along a tree structure where the symbolic environments form the nodes and the conditional statements (branch predicates) form the edges between nodes. A branch predicate is evaluated in a current environment and leads to one or two new environments along a true branch, a false branch, or both. Both branches are followed if the result of the evaluation is not specific enough to yield true or false. Each node in the tree is tagged with the node number of the dd-graph which will be executed if that branch is followed. We start building the tree with the root node containing an empty path predicate. The path predicate corresponding to the left child of a node is obtained by a conjunction of the path predicate of the parent node and the branch predicate obtained by substituting the variables in the next condition (COND) of the dd-graph with their values in the symbolic environment represented by the parent node. The path predicate corresponding to the right child is similarly obtained except that the condition is replaced by its negation. The new symbolic environment for a child node is obtained by acquiring the symbolic environment of the parent node, then making the modifications according to the statements in the block following the conditional statement. A leaf node is reached when the node is tagged with the highest numbered node of the dd-graph. As an example, the *symbolic environments tree structure* for Program 2 below is illustrated in Figure 1.

```
/*  PROGRAM  2  */
/*  INPUT VARIABLES  X, Y, Z  */
      begin  integer P, Q, R, X, Y, Z ;
      $0 R := X ; P := Y ; Q := Z + 1;
      while  R < P do
        begin
        $1  R := R + 1 ;
            if  P > Q then  $2  P := P - Q
            else  $3  Q := Q - 1
        end;
      $4
      end.
```

The conjunction of branch predicates from the root node to a leaf node form a path predicate. The tags on the nodes from the root to a leaf node show the path executed by the program for the evaluated path predicate. As an example, we have the following path predicate (before simplification) corresponding to LEAF 2.

$$(X < Y) \text{ and } (Y < Z+1) \text{ and } (X+1 > Y)$$
$$\text{Path: } 0 \to 1 \to 3 \to 4$$

Symbolic execution has been investigated by several researchers [1] [4] [5]. The proposed methodologies evaluate the symbolic value of output variables along the corresponding path

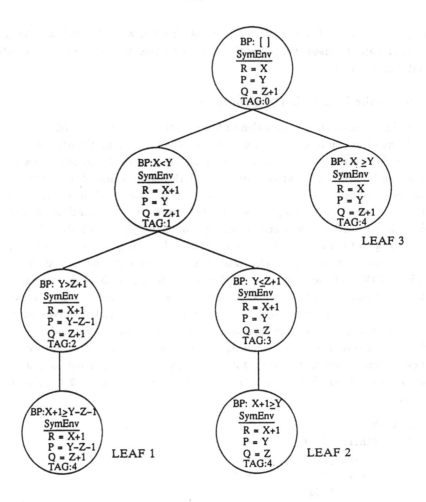

Figure 1: Symbolic Environments Tree Structure for Program 2

predicates. However, the techniques used suffer from the disadvantage that the values in the symbolic environments have to be passed along every branch of the program.

2.4 Symbolic Evaluation Using Logic Programming

Symbolic evaluation with the aid of logic programming can be performed by maintaining all the variable-value pairs in a substitution list.

    [(Name1,Sym1), (Name2,Sym2), ..., (NameN,SymN)]

Each element of the substitution list has the variable name followed by its current symbolic value. Initially, the symbolic value of an input variable is the input variable itself, and the symbolic value of other variables is *nil*. When an assignment statement is encountered, the symbolic value of the variable on the left hand side of the assignment is updated in terms of the symbolic value of the variables on the right side. This involves a lookup of the variable in the substitution list, and the replacement of its value by the new one. A portion of the old substitution list is duplicated during this process which results in the creation of a new substitution list. The substitution lists corresponding to each environment have to be passed down to the new environments created as the execution of the dd-graph proceeds. The variables in the conditional expression of the *if* and *while* statements, (COND in our dd-graph), are updated using the substitution list. The conditional expression then produces the branch predicate. In the *while* loop, variables in COND are symbolically updated every time around the loop. The new path predicates are just the conjunction of the old path predicates and the branch predicate before each node. To evaluate a procedure call, we symbolically substitute the actual parameters for the formal parameters. The body of the procedure may consist of *while*, *if* or assignment statements. The procedure body is symbolically evaluated in terms of these statements, as discussed above, and the symbolic value of the variables in the formal parameter list is passed back to the calling procedure.

We illustrate the above concepts with the predicate *symbolic_evaluate* in Prolog. The integration of numeric and symbolic execution is of valuable aid here. The numeric execution helps us decide the path of execution and the symbolic evaluation computes the path predicate and the symbolic output values. Thus even though the user only specifies the numeric values of the input variables, we evaluate for him the symbolic values of variables and the corresponding path predicate as output.

```
Explanation of Variables
OSE        Present Symbolic Environment of Variables.
NSE        New Symbolic Environment of Variables.
ISE        Intermediate Symbolic Environment of Variables.
OCOND      The path predicate prior to the execution
           of current statement.
NCOND      The path predicate after the execution of
           current statement.
ICOND      Intermediate path predicate.
COND       The conditional expression in the If or While
           statement. (The branch predicate)
SCOND      The branch predicate with variables replaced by
           their symbolic values (OSE).
```

```
symbolic_evaluate([while, COND, SLIST], OE, NE, OSE, NSE, OCOND, NCOND):-
  expr(Result, OE, COND, []),
  ((Result= false -> NE = OE, NSE = OSE,
    symbolic_negated_branch_predicate(COND, OSE, SCOND),
    conjunct_predicate(OCOND, SCOND, NCOND)) ;
  Result = true, symbolic_branch_predicate(COND, OSE, SCOND),
  conjunct_predicate(OCOND, SCOND, ICOND1),
  symbolic_evaluate(SLIST,OE,IE,OSE,ISE,ICOND1,ICOND2),
  symbolic_evaluate([while,COND,SLIST], IE,NE,ISE, NSE,ICOND2,NCOND)).

symbolic_evaluate([if, COND, THEN, ELSE], OE, NE, OSE,
                      NSE, OCOND, NCOND):-
  expr(Result, OE, COND, []),
  ((Result = true -> symbolic_branch_predicate(COND, OSE, SCOND),
    conjunct_predicate(OCOND, SCOND, ICOND),
    symbolic_evaluate(THEN, OE,NE,OSE,NSE,ICOND,NCOND));
  Result = false, symbolic_negated_branch_predicate(COND, OSE, SCOND),
  conjunct_predicate(OCOND, SCOND, ICOND),
  symbolic_evaluate(ELSE, OE, NE, OSE, NSE, ICOND, NCOND)).
```

```
symbolic_evaluate([VAR,':=',EXP], OE, NE, OSE, NSE, OCOND, OCOND) :-
  expr(Value, OE, EXP,[]),change_environ(OE,[VAR,Value],NE),
  symbolic_expr(SymbolicValue, OSE, EXP , []),
  change_environ(OSE, [VAR,SymbolicValue], NSE).

symbolic_evaluate([H|T], OE, NE, OSE, NSE, OCOND, NCOND):-
  symbolic_evaluate(H, OE, IE, OSE, ISE, OCOND, ICOND),
  symbolic_evaluate(T, IE, NE, ISE, NSE, ICOND, NCOND).

symbolic_evaluate([], OE, OE, OSE, OSE, OCOND, OCOND).

symbolic_evaluate([$,NO|SLIST],OE,NE,OSE,NSE,OCOND,NCOND):-
  symbolic_evaluate(SLIST, OE, NE, OSE, NSE, OCOND, NCOND).

conjunct_predicate([], SCOND, SCOND).

conjunct_predicate(OCOND, [], OCOND).

conjunct_predicate(OCOND, SCOND, NCOND) :-
  append(OCOND, [and], T), append(T, SCOND, NCOND).

symbolic_branch_predicate([VarCOND |RestCOND], OSE, [SymVal |RestSCOND]):-
  symbolic_branch_predicate(VarCOND, OSE, SymVal),
  symbolic_branch_predicate(RestCOND, OSE, RestSCOND).

symbolic_branch_predicate(Var,[[Var,SymVal]|TailOSE], SymVal) :-!.

symbolic_branch_predicate(Var,[[VAR1,_],TailOSE ],SymVAL):-
  symbolic_branch_predicate(Var, TailOSE, SymVAL).

symbolic_branch_predicate(Var, [], Var) :- !.

symbolic_branch_predicate([], OSE, []).

symbolic_expr(SymVal,SymEnv)-->symbolic_expr2(Val1,SymEnv),
  (symbolic_expr1(Val1,SymVal,SymEnv); empty,{SymVal=Val1}).

symbolic_expr1(Val1,SymVal,SymEnv) --> addop(A),
  symbolic_expr2(Val2,SymEnv), {SymVal2 = [Val1, A, Val2]},
  (symbolic_expr1(SymVal2,SymVal,SymEnv) ; empty, {SymVal = SymVal2}).

symbolic_expr2(SymVal,SymEnv)-->symbolic_expr4(Val1,SymEnv),
  (symbolic_expr3(Val1,SymVal,SymEnv); empty,{SymVal=Val1}).

symbolic_expr3(Val1,SymVal,SymEnv) --> mulop(M),
  symbolic_expr4(Val2, SymEnv), {SymVal2 = [Val1, M, Val2]},
  (symbolic_expr3(SymVal2,SymVal,SymEnv) ; empty, {SymVal = SymVal2}).

symbolic_expr4(Lit,SymEnv) --> literal(Lit).

symbolic_expr4(Val,SymEnv) --> identifier(Iden),
                              {lookValue(Iden,Val,SymEnv)}.

symbolic_expr4(Val,SymEnv) --> leftpar(L),
                        symbolic_expr(Val,SymEnv),rtpar(R).
empty(E,E).
```

The predicate *symbolic_evaluate* takes the decision-to-decision graph and the current numeric and symbolic environments of the variables. Every conditional predicate in an *if* or *while* statement is evaluated using the *expression evaluator*, and the set of statements of the corresponding reference branch are symbolically evaluated. The symbolic and numeric environments are changed for variables to which a new value is assigned. The predicate *expr* evaluates the numeric value of an arithmetic or boolean expression, given the current numeric environment (OE). The predicate *symbolic_expr* evaluates the symbolic value of an arithmetic expression on the right hand side of the assignment statement with the help of the current symbolic environment. The predicate *symbolic_branch_predicate* substitutes the present symbolic environment (OSE) in the conditional expression (COND) of the *if* or *while* statement, to obtain the symbolic branch predicate (SCOND). The predicate *symbolic_negated_branch_predicate* substitutes the current symbolic environment (OSE) in the negated conditional expression, to obtain the symbolic branch predicate (SCOND). This predicate is used when the result of the evaluation of the conditional expression in the *if* or *while* statement with the present numeric environment (OE) yields a *false* boolean value. The predicate *conjunct_predicate* performs a conjunction of the current path predicate (OCOND) and the symbolic branch predicate (SCOND) obtained from the conditional expression as discussed above. If the current path predicate (OCOND) is empty, then the new path predicate is the same as SCOND.

The results of a symbolic evaluation of program 2 from the previous section is shown below. The path predicates are shown on the left, while the symbolic values of the output variables for each possible path are depicted on the right. The symbolic output values for a given path predicate can now be matched against the functional specifications of the program to establish its correctness.

PATH PREDICATE	SYMBOLIC	VALUE	OF
	r	p	q
$(x < y)$ and $(y > z+1)$ and $(x+1 > y-z-1)$	x+1	y-z-1	z+1
$(x < y)$ and $(y < z+1)$ and $(x+1 > y)$	x+1	y	z
$(x > y)$	x	y	z+1

Nonexecutable paths can be detected with the help of the *symbolic environments tree structure*. If the addition of a child node to an existing tree structure introduces a branch predicate, such that the conjunction of branch predicates from the root to the newly introduced node is logically *false*, then the path from the root to this child node represents an *infeasible path*. Once an *infeasible path* is found, expansion of the tree structure and symbolic evaluation along this path is discontinued. However, other nodes in the tree, not producing an *infeasible path*, are explored.

3 Conclusion

We have illustrated how the path predicates and the symbolic values of the output variables can be evaluated for each path in the program using the substitution list. However, this technique is not very efficient for programs with a large number of variables. Whenever the value of a variable needs to be updated (as a result of an assignment, for example) during the symbolic evaluation, the entire list may have to be scanned and a large portion of it duplicated. This process is repeated for every variable in every environment. To get around the inefficiency of the list searchings and duplications, we are currently working on a technique that uses multiple theories to store the values currently held in the substitution list. We organize the theories as a tree structure and establish a one to one mapping between them and the nodes of the tree structure for symbolic environments. The conditional expressions in the *if* and *while* statements can produce a *true* or *false* value, and two child theories are created for each case. These theories do not store a complete symbolic environment or a path predicate at each node, since such a scheme will consume excessive memory space. Instead, we utilize an inheritance mechanism to pass the symbolic values from the parent theory to the descendent theories.

Symbolic evaluation with multiple theories can be accomplished in parallel. For a node in the tree structure where two alternatives along two child theories are possible, symbolic execution can fork into two parallel executions: one following the alternative along the left child theory and the other along the right child theory. The state of symbolic computation and the path constraints at the parent theory are inherited by the two child theories. The two child theories proceed independently from this stage, building on the computation state which exists at the parent theory.

To summarize, we have illustrated how one could use logic programming to perform decision-to-decision graph formation, determination of the path taken for specified input values, detection of infeasible paths, path predicate evaluation and symbolic execution.

Acknowledgement

The author would like to thank Dr Hamid Bacha for his suggestions regarding the improvement of the presentation of the paper.

References

[1] L.A. Clarke, "A system to generate test data and symbolically execute programs", IEEE Trans. Software Eng., vol SE-2, pp 215-222, Sept. 1976.

[2] W. F. Clocksin and C.S. Mellish, "Programming in Prolog", Springer-Verlag, 1981.

[3] William Howden, "Reliability of the path analysis testing strategy", IEEE Transactions on Software Engineering, pp 208-215, September 1976, vol. SE-2, No. 3,

[4] William Howden, "Symbolic Testing and the DISSECT Symbolic Evaluation System", IEEE Transactions on Software Engineering, pp 266-278, July 1977, vol. SE-3, No. 4.

[5] J.C. King, "Symbolic execution and program testing", Comm. of the ACM, vol 19, pp 385-394, July 1976.

[6] L. Sterling and E. Shapiro, "The Art of Prolog", Chapter 16, MIT Press, 1986.

[7] E.J. Weyuker and T.J. Ostrand, "Theories of program testing and the applications of revealing subdomains", IEEE Transactions on Software Engineering, pp 236-246, May 1980, vol. SE-6, No. 3.

[8] L.J. White and E.I. Cohen, "A Domain Strategy for Computer Program Testing", IEEE Trans. on Software Engineering, pp 247-257, May 1980.

[9] Clark and McCabe, "Prolog: A language for implementing Expert Systems", Machine Intelligence 10, John-Wiley and Sons Publishers, New York. 1980.

[10] D. H. D. Warren, "Logic Programming and Compiler Writing", Software - Practice and Experience 10, Number II, 1980.

Block Concatenated Code Word Surrogate File for Partial Match Retrieval

Soon Myoung Chung

Dept. of Computer Science and Engineering
Wright State University
Dayton, Ohio 45435
U. S. A.

Abstract

In this paper, a block concatenated code word (BCCW) surrogate file scheme is developed to speed up partial match retrieval operations. A BCCW is generated for each block of the data file by hashing the attribute values in the data block. Then the BCCWs forms a surrogate file which is used as an index to the data file. For a partial match retrieval query, a block query code word (BQCW) is generated and compared with the BCCWs. Only those data blocks whose corresponding BCCWs match the BQCW are retrieved from secondary storage and compared with the actual query. The size of the BCCWs is usually less than 10% of the size of the data file and only a subset of each BCCW is accessed. Thus, we can obtain considerable speed up in partial match retrieval by using the BCCW surrogate file. The storage requirement and the performance of the BCCW surrogate file are evaluated and compared with those of other schemes.

Key Words: database, partial match retrieval, code words.

1. Introduction

In the context of very large relational databases, a major problem is how to obtain the records satisfying a query in the minimum amount of time. Two reasonable choices of indexing schemes for partial match retrieval are concatenated code word (CCW) and superimposed code word (SCW) surrogate file techniques discussed in [BER87, CHU88]. A surrogate file consists of binary codes which are transformed from the records by using well chosen hashing functions. A partial match retrieval query is transformed to a query code word (QCW) by the same hashing functions used to generated the code words. Then, the surrogate file is searched to find the matching code words. The records corresponding to the matching code words are retrieved and compared with the actual query. If the retrieved record satisfies the query, it is called a matching record, otherwise it is called a false matching record. The false matching records are caused by the non-ideal property of hashing functions.

Compared with other full indexing schemes such as inverted lists [CAR75], SCW and CCW surrogate file techniques require much smaller storage space; usually less than 20% of the size of the EDB [BER87] while the inverted lists may be as large as the EDB. In terms of maintenance, the surrogate file shows considerable advantages. When a new record is added to a relation the SCW or CCW is generated and added to the surrogate file. In the case of inverted lists, each list must be processed. If file updates are frequent, the costs associated with updating, sorting, and garbage collection of inverted lists can be significant [ROB79].

In [CHU88], CCW and SCW surrogate file techniques were analyzed on the basis of storage space required for the surrogate file and time needed to answer partial match queries. It is shown that the storage overhead and the query processing time of the CCW surrogate file are smaller than those of the SCW surrogate file when the average number of attributes specified in a query is small. However, the analysis shows that most of the query processing time is used for surrogate file processing when the relation is large (10^9 bytes). This is due to the sequential searching of all surrogate file code words.

The SCW and CCW surrogate files are composed of code words corresponding to the records in the data file, so that the entire surrogate file must be read into main memory and searched to retrieve the desired records. To reduce the surrogate file searching time, one can produce a block code word for each block of the data file and use the block code words as an index for the data blocks. A given block query code word (BQCW) is compared with the block code words first and only those data blocks whose corresponding block code words match the BQCW are retrieved and searched with the actual query. The performance of the block code word surrogate file will depend on the following factors:

1) Type of hashing functions used for code generation.
2) Algorithm for generating the block code words.
3) Blocking factor which represents the number of records in a data block.
4) Requirement for updating the block code word surrogate file for changes in the data file.

To speed up the partial match retrieval, a block CCW (BCCW) surrogate file scheme is developed in this paper. In Section 2, the structure of BCCW surrogate file is introduced. We compare the BCCW surrogate file with other surrogate files in terms of size in Section 3, and in terms of performance in Section 4.

2. Structure of the Block CCW Surrogate File

The procedure for generating a BCCW for a data block of m records having n attributes is shown in Figure 1. To generate a BCCW, for each record r_i, $1 \leq i \leq m$, attribute a_{ij}, $1 \leq j \leq n$, is transformed to an extended binary representation, EBR_{ij}. For each attribute position j, the EBR_{ij}, $1 \leq i \leq m$, has the same length and weight, which are pre-determined based on the factors affecting the performance of the BCCW surrogate file. A code word constructed by concatenating the EBR_{ij}, $1 \leq j \leq n$, will be called an extended CCW_i ($ECCW_i$).

$$r_1 : (a_{11}, a_{12}, \quad \cdots \quad , a_{1n})$$
$$r_2 : (a_{21}, a_{22}, \quad \cdots \quad , a_{2n})$$
$$\vdots$$
$$r_m : (a_{m1}, a_{m2}, \quad \cdots \quad , a_{mn})$$

$$H_1(a_{i1}) \qquad H_2(a_{i2}) \qquad \cdots \qquad H_n(a_{in})$$
$$\downarrow \qquad\qquad \downarrow \qquad\qquad\qquad \downarrow$$
$$EBR_{i1} \qquad\quad EBR_{i2} \qquad\qquad\qquad EBR_{in}$$

$ECCW_1$:	EBR_{11} |	EBR_{12} |	...	EBR_{1n}
$ECCW_2$:	EBR_{21} |	EBR_{22} |	...	EBR_{2n}

$$\vdots$$

$$ECCW_m : \quad EBR_{m1} \mid \quad EBR_{m2} \mid \quad \cdots \quad \mid EBR_{mn}$$

$$BCCW : \quad BBR_1 \mid \quad BBR_2 \mid \quad \cdots \quad \mid BBR_n$$

$$\text{where,} \quad BBR_j = \bigcup_{i=1}^{m} EBR_{ij}, \quad \text{for} \quad 1 \leq j \leq n$$

Figure 1. Procedure of Generating a Block CCW (BCCW)

Then, the $ECCW_i$, $1 \leq i \leq m$, of the m records in the data block are bitwise logically ORed together to form the BCCW of the data block. A BCCW is a concatenation of n block BRs (BBRs), where BBR_j is generated by logically ORing the EBR_{ij}, $1 \leq i \leq m$. A BCCW surrogate file of a data file is a set of the BCCWs corresponding to the data blocks within the data file.

When a query is given, we apply the same hashing functions used to generate the EBRs to the attribute values specified in the query. A block query code word (BQCW) is then obtained by concatenating the EBRs corresponding to the query attribute values. The bit positions of the BQCW for the attributes which are not specified in the query are filled with 0's. The BCCWs are searched against the BQCW, and the data blocks corresponding to the matched BCCWs will be retrieved and searched with the actual query to find the desired records. The matching between a BCCW and the BQCW is an inclusive matching. In other words, if a BCCW has 1's in all the bit positions where the BQCW has 1's, then the BCCW matches the BQCW.

The proposed BCCW structure is a modification of the block descriptor proposed in [PFA80]. In [PFA80], a record descriptor is a bit-string of width W which is the sum of the widths w_j, $1{\leq}j{\leq}n$, where n is the number of attributes of the record and w_j is the width of the bit-string corresponding to the value of the j-th attribute of the record. Transformation from the j-th attribute value to a bit-string of width w_j is such that, only one of the w_j bits is set to 1 and remaining $w_j{-}1$ bits are set to 0. Thus, to represent the j-th attribute which may have D_j distinct values, ideally we need a bit-string of width D_j, which results in an inefficient storage utilization when D_j is very large. If we limit the w_j to save storage space, D_j distinct values are mapped into w_j ranges, and we may have many false matching records when the record descriptors are used to index the corresponding records.

In [PFA80], a block descriptor is generated by bitwise logically ORing the record descriptors of the records within a block, and the block descriptor is used to index the block. When a query is given, the query descriptor is generated as the record descriptor while the portions of the bit-string corresponding to the unspecified attribute positions are filled with 0's. Then the block descriptors are searched with the query descriptor to find the matching blocks. Since the weight of the bit-strings for each attribute is 1, when only one attribute is specified in the query there is no false matching block caused by the logical OR operation used to generate a block descriptor. However, the transformations of attribute values to limited ranges, w_j, $1{\leq}j{\leq}n$, may cause many false matching blocks especially for very large data files.

On the other hand, a BCCW is generated by logically ORing the ECCWs of optimal width and weight. Thus, we can reduce the number of false matching blocks while maintaining small storage space for the BCCW surrogate file.

[SAC83] developed a two level superimposed coding scheme, where the lower level index is the SCW file which consists of SCWs corresponding to the records within the data file, and the upper level index consists of SCWs corresponding to the blocks of records within the data file. The SCW corresponding to a block of records will be called a block SCW (BSCW).

To generate a BSCW, all the attribute values of the records within a block are transformed to binary code words (BCWs), and then the BCWs are bitwise logically ORed together to form a BSCW. Thus, if a block has m records and each record has n attributes, m × n BCWs are ORed to form the BSCW of the block. Since a BSCW is a SCW, a BSCW surrogate file has all the characteristics of the SCW surrogate file. A given query is transformed to a block query code word (BQCW) by the same transformations used for the BSCWs. If there is any BSCW matching the BQCW inclusively, the corresponding data block is retrieved and searched against the actual query to find the matching records within that block.

3. Storage Requirement for the BCCW Surrogate File

In this section we develop the equations for the optimal size of the BCCW surrogate file under the assumption that the hashing functions used to transform the attribute values to bit-strings are ideal.

The BCCW of m records with n attributes is a concatenation of the BBR_j, $1{\leq}j{\leq}n$, where BBR_j is formed by superimposing the EBR_{ij}, $1{\leq}i{\leq}m$. Thus, the width of a BCCW is the sum of the width of the EBR_{ij}, $1{\leq}j{\leq}n$, and the optimal width and weight of the EBR_{ij}, $1{\leq}j{\leq}n$, can be obtained by modifying the equations developed for SCW surrogate file in [ROB79]. The equation for the optimal width of the EBR_{ij} which is equal to the optimal width of the BBR_j (b_{BBRj}) is

$$b_{BBRj} = \left\lceil m{\times} \frac{\log_2 \left[(N/m)/(FDB_j + GDB_j) \right]}{\ln 2} \right\rceil \tag{1}$$

where

m : number of records in a data block (blocking factor)
FDB_j : number of false matching data blocks caused by the logical OR operation for the j-th attribute
GDB_j : number of matching data blocks for the j-th attribute.

The optimal weight of the EBR_{ij} (k_{BCCWj}) for all i is

$$k_{BCCWj} = b_{BBRj} (1 - 2^{-1/m}) .$$ (2)

In Equation 1, GDB_j represents the average number of matching data blocks when the j-th attribute alone is specified in a query. If C_j denotes the average redundancy of the data file at the j-th attribute, i.e., the average number of records having the same j-th attribute value, then there are C_j matching records in the data file when the j-th attribute is specified in a query. Thus the GDB_j can be approximated as

$$GDB_j = \left\lceil \frac{N}{m} \right\rceil \times \left[1 - (1 - \frac{1}{\left\lceil \dfrac{N}{m} \right\rceil})^{C_j} \right] .$$ (3)

From Equations 1 and 3 we can obtain the optimal width of the BBRs. The optimal width of a BCCW (b_{BCCW}) of a record with n attributes is

$$b_{BCCW} = \sum_{j=1}^{n} b_{BBRj} .$$ (4)

Since there are $\left\lceil \dfrac{N}{m} \right\rceil$ blocks in the data file, the size of the BCCW file (S_{BCCW}) is

$$S_{BCCW} = \left\lceil \frac{N}{m} \right\rceil (b_{BCCW} + \text{size of a block pointer}) .$$ (5)

We compare the size of the BCCW surrogate file with the size of the BSCW and the CCW surrogate files. For the size of BSCW and CCW surrogate files, we used the equations developed in [CHU90]. In evaluating the size of the BCCW and CCW surrogate files, we assumed that each attribute of the relation has the same average redundancy value, C_g .

In Figure 2 we plot the size of the BCCW, BSCW, and CCW surrogate files as functions of the average redundancy, when

number of records in the data file (N) = 10^6
number of attributes in a record (n) = 6
number of records in a data block (m) = 40
number of false matching blocks for each attribute with BCCW (FDB_j)=10
number of false matching blocks with BSCW (FDB_{BSCW}) = 10
size of a block pointer = 4 bytes

The size of the BCCW surrogate file (S_{BCCW}) and the size of the CCW surrogate file (S_{CCW}) decrease as the average redundancy (C_g) increases, because a smaller number of bits can be used for the code words as C_g increases. However, the size of the BSCW surrogate file (S_{BSCW}) is not dependent on C_g since the average number of matching blocks is not considered in estimating the width a BSCW [CHU90]. Therefore, S_{BCCW} is smaller than S_{BSCW} for all C_g values and S_{CCW} becomes smaller than S_{BSCW} when C_g is larger than a certain value.

S_{BCCW} is smaller than S_{CCW} for two reasons. First, we assume that there are FDB_j false matching blocks caused by the logical OR operation for each attribute with the BCCW scheme, and the width of a BCCW becomes smaller with larger FDB_j. Secondly, the total storage space for the pointers of the BCCW surrogate file is smaller than that of the CCW surrogate file, because the unique identifier associated with each CCW is a record pointer while the pointer associated with a BCCW is a block pointer.

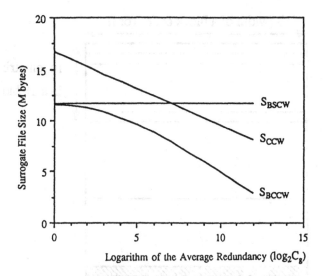

Figure 2. Surrogate File Size Comparison

If we assume that the size of a record is about 100 bytes, which is reasonable for a record with 6 attributes, the size of the BCCW surrogate file is less than 10% of the size of the data file when the number of records in the data file is 10^6. As the data file increases, the size of the BCCW surrogate file increases almost linearly due to the increase in the number of data blocks. Thus, the ratio of the size of the BCCW surrogate file to that of the data file will be almost constant.

4. Performance of the BCCW Surrogate File

Performance of block code word surrogate files can be evaluated by estimating the number of surrogate file blocks and data blocks retrieved to answer partial match queries. To reduce the number of surrogate file blocks retrieved, we assume that the BCCW and BSCW surrogate files are structured in bit-sliced organizations. We assume that a surrogate file is composed of N_B block code words of width b, and there are m_s bit-strings in a surrogate file block.

If a BCCW or BSCW surrogate file is stored in a bit-string organization as shown in Figure 3.(a), then a block code word is a bit-string of b bits. Thus, to find the matching block code words, we need to retrieve and compare all the N_B bit-strings with the block query code word.

On the other hand, if a BCCW or BSCW surrogate file is stored in a bit-sliced organization as shown in Figure 3.(b), then a block code word is a bit-slice of b bits. Thus, a bit-slice is a matching code word if it has 1's in all the k bit positions where the block query code has 1's. Since the i-th bit-string contains all the i-th bits of the N_B code words, to find all the matching code words, we need to retrieve the k bit-strings corresponding to the k bit positions where the block query code word has 1's, and then bitwise logically ANDing the k bit-strings. The i-th bit position of the resultant bit-string contains 1 if and only if the i-th block code is a matching code word. The block pointers associated with the block code words are stored separately from the block code word surrogate file for fast accessing. The sequence of the block pointers corresponds to the sequence of the block code words. If the i-th block code word is a matching code word, then we read the i-th block pointer from the block pointer store, which is a linear array of block pointers, retrieve the data block pointed to by the i-th block pointer, and search the block with the actual query.

Therefore, in the case of the bit-sliced organization the number of bits to be retrieved is $(k \times N_B)$ to answer a query, while it is $(b \times N_B)$ in the bit-string organization. The weight of a block query code word is much smaller than the width of a block code word. Therefore, the bit-sliced organization is much better than the bit-string organization in terms of the number of surrogate file code word bits to be retrieved to answer a query. However, a bit-string organization is suitable for the CCW surrogate file because the width of a CCW is not large and the matching condition between a CCW and a QCW is an exact match.

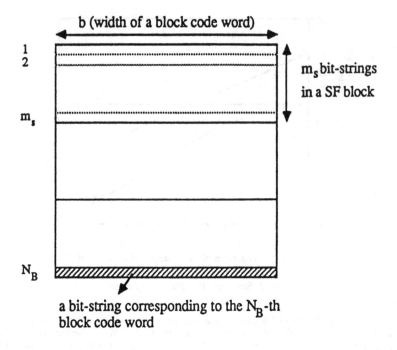

b (width of a block code word)

1
2

m_s

m_s bit-strings
in a SF block

N_B

a bit-string corresponding to the N_B-th
block code word

(a) A Bit-String Organization

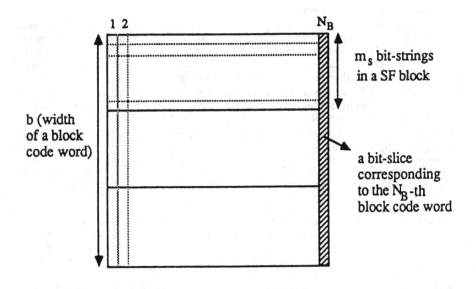

1 2

N_B

m_s bit-strings
in a SF block

b (width
of a block
code word)

a bit-slice
corresponding
to the N_B-th
block code word

(b) A Bit-Sliced Organization

Figure 3. Organization of a Block Code Word Surrogate File

4.1. Number of Blocks Retrieved to Answer a Query with the BCCW Scheme

With a BCCW file, if Aq attributes are specified in a query then the weight of the BQCW (k_{BCCW}) is

$$k_{BCCW} = \sum_{j \in Q} k_{BCCWj} \tag{6}$$

where Q denotes the set of Aq attribute positions specified in the query and k_{BCCWj} is the weight of the extended binary representation for the j-th attribute and is given in Equation 2. Thus we need to check k_{BCCW} bit positions for each BCCW. If k_{BCCWj} 1's are distributed uniformly over the b_{BBRj}, $j \in Q$, and a BCCW surrogate file block has m_s bit-strings of N1 bits, then the number of BCCW surrogate file blocks to be retrieved to check k_{BCCW} bit positions of the N1 BCCWs is approximately

$$NSB_{N1} = \sum_{j \in Q} \frac{b_{BBRj}}{m_s} \left[1 - (1 - \frac{1}{\frac{b_{BBRj}}{m_s}})^{k_{BCCWj}} \right] \quad \text{if } m_s > 1, \text{ and} \tag{7}$$

$$NSB_{N1} = \sum_{j \in Q} k_{BCCWj} \quad \text{if } m_s = 1. \tag{8}$$

Since there are $N_B = \left\lceil \dfrac{N}{m} \right\rceil$ block code words when N is the number of the records in the data file and m is the data file blocking factor, the average number of BCCW surrogate file blocks to be retrieved to check k_{BCCW} bit positions of the N_B block code words is approximately

$$NSB_{BCCW} = \left\lceil \frac{N_B}{N1} \right\rceil \sum_{j \in Q} \frac{b_{BBRj}}{m_s} \left[1 - (1 - \frac{1}{\frac{b_{BBRj}}{m_s}})^{k_{BCCWj}} \right] \quad \text{if } m_s > 1, \text{ and} \tag{9}$$

$$NSB_{BCCW} = \left\lceil \frac{N_B}{N1} \right\rceil \sum_{j \in Q} k_{BCCWj} \quad \text{if } m_s = 1. \tag{10}$$

We estimate the number of data blocks to be retrieved with BCCW surrogate file under the assumption that the hashing functions used to generate the code words are ideal, so there are no false matching block caused by the non-ideal hashing functions. With the BCCW surrogate file scheme, if we assume that the attributes are independent within a relation, the number of data blocks to be retrieved to answer a query can be approximated as

$$NDB_{BCCW} = N_B \prod_{j \in Q} (\frac{GDB_j + FDB_j}{N_B}) \tag{11}$$

where N_B is the number of data blocks, GDB_j is the number of matching data blocks when only the j-th attribute is specified in the query, and FDB_j is the expected number of false matching data blocks caused by the logical OR operation on the j-th attribute. Therefore, when only the j-th attribute is specified in the query, there are FDB_j false matching blocks.

4.2. Comparison of Retrieval Performance

Retrieval performance of the surrogate file schemes can be compared in terms of the number of surrogate file blocks and data blocks to be retrieved to answer partial match queries. Here we assume that the BCCW and BSCW surrogate files are stored in bit-sliced organizations and the CCW surrogate file is stored in a bit-string organization. BCCW and BSCW surrogate files can take advantage of the bit-sliced organization because the width of a block code word is very large and the matching condition between a block code word and a block query code word (BQCW) is an inclusive matching. However, a bit-string organization is suitable for the CCW surrogate file because the width of a CCW is not large and the matching condition between a CCW and a QCW is an exact match.

By using the equations developed above for the BCCW surrogate file and the equations developed in [CHU90] for the BSCW and CCW surrogate files, we evaluate the number of the surrogate file blocks and data blocks to be retrieved when

number of records in the data file (N) = 10^6
number of attributes in a record (n) = 6
number of attributes specified in the query (Aq) = 2
number of records in a data block (m) = 40
number of bit-strings in a BCCW and BSCW block (m_s) = 1
size of a CCW block = 4 Kbytes
number of false matching blocks for each attribute with BCCW (FDB_j)=10
number of false matching blocks with BSCW (FDB_{BSCW}) = 10
number of false matching records with CCW (FD_{CCW}) = 0
size of a block pointer = 4 bytes.

When the number of records in the data file is 10^6 and the data blocking factor (m) is 40, the number block code words is 25000. Thus, if we assume that m_s is 1, then a reasonable choice for the size of the BCCW and BSCW surrogate file block is 4 Kbytes, which can store one bit-string of 25000 bits. For fair comparison, we select 4 Kbytes for the size of the CCW surrogate file block.

Since we assumed that the hashing functions used to generate the code words were ideal in estimating the size and the number of surrogate file blocks and data blocks to be retrieved, the CCW scheme does not have false matching records, i.e. FD_{CCW} is 0, and the BCCW and BSCW schemes have false matching blocks, FDB_j and FDB_{BSCW}, respectively, which are caused only by the logical OR operations. In actual cases, there are false matching records and false matching blocks caused by the non-ideal hashing functions. However, we can reduce the false matches to a negligible level by increasing the width of the code words [CHU88].

Figure 4 shows the number of blocks to be retrieved with the BCCW surrogate file scheme. As the average redundancy (C_g) increases the number of the BCCW surrogate file blocks retrieved (NSB_{BCCW}) decreases, because as C_g increases the width of a BCCW decreases and consequently the weight of a block query code word (BQCW), which is the number of BCCW surrogate file bit-strings to be retrieved, decreases. On the other hand, the number of the data blocks retrieved (NDB_{BCCW}) becomes large when C_g is large due to the increased number of matching and false matching blocks. NTB_{BCCW} denotes the total number of blocks retrieved, i.e. the sum of NSB_{BCCW} and NDB_{BCCW}.

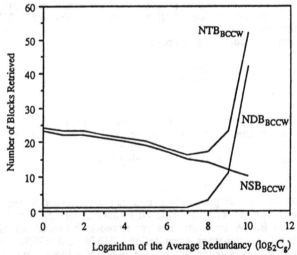

Figure 4. Performance of the BCCW Surrogate File

The BCCW and BSCW surrogate file schemes are compared in Figure 5 in terms of the number of blocks to be retrieved to answer a query. The number of the surrogate file and data blocks to be retrieved with the BCCW scheme (NTB_{BCCW}) is smaller than that of the BSCW scheme (NTB_{BSCW}) for two reasons. First, the number of the BCCW surrogate file blocks to be retrieved (NSB_{BCCW}) is smaller than the number of the BSCW surrogate file blocks to be retrieved (NSB_{BSCW}). Secondly, we use an expected number of false matching blocks for all possible queries with the BSCW scheme, so even though C_g is small there are at least FDB_{BSCW} false matching blocks to be retrieved. On the other hand, the false matching blocks considered for each attribute with the BCCW scheme (FDB_j) will not result in as many false matching blocks when the number of attributes specified in the query (Aq) is more than one, as can be seen from Equation 11.

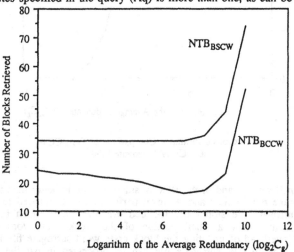

Figure 5. Performance Comparison of the BCCW
and BSCW Surrogate Files

In Figure 6, we compare the retrieval performance of the BCCW and CCW surrogate file schemes by plotting (NTB_{CCW} / NTB_{BCCW}), i.e. the ratio of the number of blocks to be retrieved with the CCW surrogate file scheme to that with the BCCW surrogate file scheme. When C_g is small, NTB_{BCCW} is much smaller than NTB_{CCW} because the number of BCCW surrogate file bit-strings to be checked is much smaller than the total number of CCW surrogate file blocks. However, the number of data blocks retrieved with the BCCW scheme becomes large when C_g is large. Therefore, the speedup of the BCCW surrogate file scheme over the CCW surrogate file scheme is small when C_g is large. As C_g increases the number of matching records with the CCW surrogate file increases also. But the increasing rate of the number of data blocks retrieved with the BCCW surrogate file is much higher because a data block, which stores m (data file blocking factor) times more attribute values than a record, becomes a false matching block if it stores the attribute values specified in the query even though no one record in that block is a matching record.

5. Updating of Block Code Word Surrogate Files

Generally, the width of a block code word is about m (data file blocking factor) times larger than the width of a CCW. Therefore, we need to read and write back many more surrogate file blocks to add or change a block code word. Moreover, if a block code word surrogate file is stored in a bit-sliced organization, where the number of bit-strings in the surrogate file block is m_s, then we need to access (width of a block code word / m_s) surrogate file blocks to add a block code word.

The BCCW surrogate file is better than the BSCW surrogate file in terms of updating. If an attribute value is changed, we need to access the bit-strings corresponding to the changed attribute value to update the BCCW, while we need to access all the bit-strings storing the BSCW to be changed.

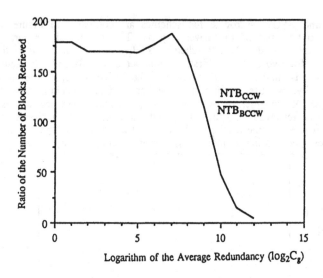

Figure 6. Performance Comparison of the BCCW
and CCW Surrogate Files

6. Conclusion

As we can see from Figures 2 and 5, the BCCW surrogate file is better than the BSCW surrogate file in terms of storage requirement and retrieval performance. Compared to the CCW surrogate file, the BCCW surrogate file stored in bit-sliced organization is much better in terms of retrieval performance because only a small portion of the block code word surrogate file is searched. However, the overhead of updating the block code word surrogate file is a disadvantage for dynamic databases. The BCCW surrogate file can be processed in parallel. If the BCCWs (bit-slices) are distributed over the disks and a processor is assigned to each disk, then multiple processors can process the block code words of a surrogate file simultaneously.

References

[BER87] P. B. Berra, S. M. Chung, N. I. Hachem, " Computer Architecture for a Surrogate File to a Very Large Data/Knowledge Base," IEEE Computer Vol. 20, No. 3, 1987, pp. 25-32.

[CAR75] A. F. Cardenas, " Analysis and Performance of Inverted Data Base Structures," Communications of the ACM, Vol. 18, No. 5, 1975, pp. 253-263.

[CHU88] S. M. Chung, P. B. Berra, " A Comparison of Concatenated and Superimposed Code Word Surrogate Files for Very Large Data/Knowledge Bases," Advances in Database Technology - EDBT'88, Proc. Int'l Conf. on Extending Database Technology, Springer-Verlag, 1988, pp. 364-387.

[CHU90] S. M. Chung, " Block Code Words for Partial Match Retrieval in Very Large Databases," Technical Report WSU-CS-90-10, Dept. of Computer Science and Engineering, Wright State University, 1990.

[PFA80] J. L. Pfaltz, W. J. Berman, and E. M. Cagley, " Partial-Match Retrieval Using Indexed Descriptor Files," Communications of the ACM, Vol. 23, No. 9, 1980, pp. 522-528.

[ROB79] C. S. Roberts, " Partial Match Retrieval via the Method of Superimposed Codes," Proceedings of the IEEE, Vol. 67, No. 12, 1979, pp. 1624-1642.

[SAC83] R. Sacks-Davis, K. Ramamohanarao, " A Two level Superimposed Coding Scheme for Partial Match Retrieval," Information Systems Vol. 8, No. 4, 1983, pp. 273-280.

APPLICATIONS DEVELOPMENT TOOLKITS FOR ENVIRONMENTAL MODELLING AND MONITORING

D. A. Swayne[1,2], John Storey[2]
D. C.-L. Lam[3], Isaac Wong[3] and A. S. Fraser[3]
[1]University of Guelph, [2]ES Aquatic Inc. and
[3]National Water Research Institute

ABSTRACT

Experience gained in developing models for the LRTAP (Long-Range Transport of Atmospheric Pollutants) project at the National Water Research Institute has led to a number of development tools for modelling, data fitting, and simulation studies in environmental policy decision-support. The mechanisms for developing the initial models on personal workstations carry directly into prototype/demonstration systems which are then connected to production support databases.

KEYWORDS: Applications development, scientific computing, microcomputer applications, software engineering.

INTRODUCTION

Large-scale environmental models require corroborating data collected in the regions under study [1]. However, it is usually not possible to collect data expressly for the purpose intended. There are of course large monitoring collections and also occasional landmark studies (such as the MISA - for Municipal and Industrial Strategies for Abatement - project). Geochemical and hydrological models are on the other hand often local, specific, and connected with a particular data set from which they are individually derived.

Models which have been developed for local effects have to compete among each other in order to be chosen the most relevant to explain a local environmental effect. Larger-scale predictions then require a geographic information systems component with the capability of mapping the regional picture of the phenomena under investigation (such as sources, transport and effects of water pollution). Spatial and temporal scale variations require interpolation or extrapolation to supply missing data for models [2,3,5]. Modelling in an interactive mode using subsets of the data is a frequent component of environmental research. These prototypical models are then "scaled up" to accommodate full data sets and larger regions. The "rules" by which the prototypical models are chosen, together with the basic assumptions of the theoretical are also part of the knowledge base for larger scale models.

The RAISON project at the National Water Research Institute of Environment Canada has been involved heavily with the monitoring and modelling of the aquatic effects of acid rain. This effort has used salient features of spreadsheet, geographic information system, database and expert system shell, integrated with the use of a procedural programming language interpreter.

SYSTEM DESCRIPTION

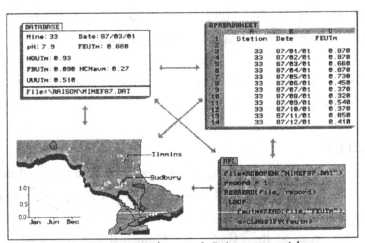

Figure 1 System Overview and Interconnection

The RAISON system, the computer software system designed to support the modelling research, has been described in the literature previously [6]. It consists of the necessary features for database modelling of: a spreadsheet, a database system, an expert system shell, and a map editing/GIS system of limited capability (together with an assemblage of graphics primitives for construction of map and display graphics). The system is held together by a programming system (called RPL for RAISON Programming Language and RAS for RAISON Shell) which is a combination of procedural language and shell for construction of production systems.

The spreadsheet structure and operation form an essential programming environment, with a rich assembly of operations and effects. Spreadsheet structures which have been created by autonomous program execution are accessible from the spreadsheet sub-system. Most of the interactive data exploration, the graphics subsystem, and execution of RPL code is controlled from a "pretty-print" spreadsheet layout on screen. Character, numeric, executable statement functions, and units of measure (either SI or gram-molecular with conversion tables in the kernel of the system) are all attributes attachable to a spreadsheet cell.

The database interface has the characteristic feel of typical commercial products, with some particular differences. Layouts are centralized rather than, say, resident with the datasets, since scientific data collections are repetitious in their format (or nearly so). Narratives to describe the purpose of the data are required and form part of layout selection during database creation. Text files, map files, layout files, and programming language source code are all maintainable through the database system. RPL primitives support database creation and access.

The map/graphics system is controllable from spreadsheet sub-menus and from RPL. Vector drawing and raster image files are both available and can be intermixed (vector overlaid on raster image background) for modelling and also for report generation. Figure 1 is an example of a "mixed screen". Input from various graphical scanners and interactive tablets are supported. Output options include painting, filling, polygonal overlays, titles and a rich assortment of visualization tools for data manipulation. Interaction includes database access through map location, regional access through polygon encircling, area calculation, and query of contour map values point-by-point. Hierarchies of maps may be defined, and accessed by graphical means. Actions may be associated with map points through the programming shell, in a very general framework.

Expert system prototyping is supported, using a number of commercially available software products such as 1stClass from AICorp. Character data derived from expert system interaction or other external means, which is recognizable as RPL code is directly executable. Early development has begun to compare prototype with production output, to provide a measure of reliability in performance.

PROTOTYPING

The environmental researcher has at his disposal, initially, a spreadsheet with which direct communication to the current graphics screen (with operators such as drawbox, fill, point, etc. included in the vocabulary of spreadsheet cell commands). Marked screen positions or shapes (whose locations in a current icon file) may be selected as icons or act as objects for "fill", etc., when the operational menu commands are invoked in the spreadsheet command menu. Qualitative movement of plumes, similarly enacted is another example of the degree of control of the graphics system from the spreadsheet [7].

Simple "if-then" statement functions can be executed in normal spreadsheet calculation mode, e.g.:

+if pH < 4.0 then "red" else if pH < 6 then "yellow" else "green"

Surprisingly complex interactive systems can be created in this way. Sometimes, however this simple subsystem is insufficient. RPL code is written to accommodate larger models or missing features. When data collections are particularly large, the spreadsheet is used only for summary (by watershed or sampling station), and the database subsystem RDBS is used directly in RPL. found in modelling.

Typically, the spreadsheet-map combination permits single model construction. When a reasonably complete suite of models has been built and converted to RPL, a prototype structure for execution is developed, using the commercial package 1stClass. RAISON RPL can use the 1stClass layout to order execution of the models according to rules or matching criteria specified during development. Tasks of central importance or with long execution times are written in C, using a RAISON function library.

RATIONALE FOR DEVELOPMENT

We are asked frequently why we did not just use commercial products in the application. There are several reasons. The costs of these products together are in excess of what might be considered a reasonable software budget. Their interconnections are often clumsy and unpredictable. When the project was begun, many commercial systems were not sufficiently comprehensive or reliable. It has remained economical to continue upgrading and tuning to support an expanding model base. Utility is being expanded with faster CPU and larger memory.

RAISON functions as a development toolkit for a number of other applications: state-of-environment reporting by several national and international agencies, safety of public water supplies in developing countries [4], spill and accident management, real estate sales and tourist information. The development has been conditioned by the need to answer important environmental questions quickly and with certainty that the contribution of the computer system is timely, accurate, has significant visual impact, and is achieved at modest cost.

ACKNOWLEDGEMENTS

Support from Environment Canada in the form of research contracts gratefully acknowledged, for Swayne and Storey. Other participants, particularly Yoko Ando and Jane Kerby have also made significant contributions.

REFERENCES

[1]. Fraser, A. S., 1986. Aquatic characterization for resources at risk in Eastern Canada. Water Air and Soil Pollution, 1986

[2]. Lam, D.C.L., D.A. Swayne, John Storey, and A.S. Fraser. 1989. Regional Acidification Models using the Expert Systems Approach. J. Eco. Model. 47:131-152.

[3]. Lam, D.C.L., D.A. Swayne, John Storey, A.S. Fraser and I. Wong. 1988. Regional analysis of watershed acidification using the expert systems approach. Environmental Software 3(3):127-134.

[4]. Lam, D.C.L., D.A. Swayne, A. El-Shaarawi and John Storey. 1989. "Water Quality Data Management (Malaysia/Canada): From RAISON/Acid Rain to RAISON/Water Quality", Interim Report to International Development Research Centre Coliphage Meeting, Banff, Alberta, September 5-7, 1988. (IDRC File No. 3-P-86-1051-01)

[5]. Swayne, D.A., D.C.L. Lam, A.S. Fraser, and John Storey. 1988. Regional Acidification Models using the Expert Systems Approach", Expert Systems Theory and Applications IASTED International Conference, Geneva :19-22.

[6]. Swayne, D.A., John Storey, A.S. Fraser and D.C.L. Lam. 1989. A microcomputer-based system for environmental modelling. J. Microcomputer Appl. 8(2):35-38.

[7]. Swayne, D.A. and A.S. Fraser. 1986. Development of an expert system/intelligent interface for acid rain analysis", Microcomputers in Civil Engineering, 1(1):181-185.

A Hypertext for Literate Programming

M. Brown
Department of Computer Science
University of Alabama
Box 870290, Tuscaloosa, AL 35487-0290
(205) 348-6363
marcus@fred.cs.ua.edu

B. Czejdo
Department of Mathematical Sciences
Loyola University
New Orleans, Louisiana 77004

Abstract

In this paper we describe a hypertext presentation for the WEB system for literate programming. The requirements for an environment for modern literate programming are analyzed and the WEB hypertext system is proposed. Different types of windows for displaying text, indices and graphical representations are discussed. All semantic links and operators using them are analyzed. The proposed architecture of the WEB hypertext system includes a general purpose relational database management system. Mapping between hypertext queries and relational database queries is provided. The system allows the user to define new hypertext operations by providing the corresponding SQL queries for the underlying relational database. The described system can be easily extended by many other types of queries and applications.

Keywords: Literate Programming, Hypertext, Database

I. INTRODUCTION

One current research topic in the area of information systems is concentrated on devising mechanisms to extend the traditional notion of "flat" text to a hypertext presentation [10]. As a result of this extension the text is treated as a structure with complex organizational links allowing direct references from one part of the text to another. While many texts do not have such links as a natural part of their presentation, computer source programs have a structure which often allows for relatively straightforward division into fragments with connecting semantic links. In particular, the WEB [5] approach to literate programming requires extensive usage of semantic links. An experimental environment for browsing and editing WEB computer source programs has been proposed [3]. In this paper we present a WEB Hypertext System (WHS) with extendible database and user defined operations.

The paper is organized as follows. In the next section, we describe the concept of literate programming together with the requirements for an environment for modern literate programming. Section 3 presents a WEB hypertext environment for literate programming while the operators for the environment are discussed in Section 4. The architecture of a WHS with the underlying database is described in Section 5. Mapping between hypertext queries and relational database queries is also provided in this section. The Summary presents some conclusions and directions for further work.

II. THE WEB SYSTEM FOR LITERATE PROGRAMMING

Donald E. Knuth coined the term *Literate Programming* to describe his concept that programming should produce *works of literature*. Literate programming should concentrate on explaining to the human reader/programmer what the computer is supposed to do, rather than concentrating our effort on simply writing instructions for the computer [5]. Knuth insists that the format and structure of a literate program should be designed to communicate primarily with the humans who read the source program rather than the computers which perform the program. Programming in this way should produce better programs with better documentation of those programs.

Knuth created the WEB system in 1981 in order to rewrite his TeX program in the most portable and understandable manner possible [6], the basic concept behind literate programming. WEB allows a single source program to produce two different results. a running program on a computer and a typeset document which defines and describes that program for human readers. WEB consists of a combination of a high level programming language and a typesetting language (TeX) with additional commands to control the relationship between the two languages and to allow for modularization: The WEB system applies two preprocessors to the source. TANGLE creates programming code suitable for the compiler, while WEAVE creates TeX code which produces the typeset documentation, as is shown in Figure 1.

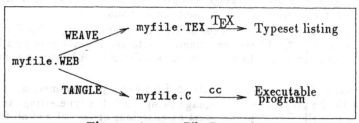

Figure 1. WEB File Processing
(Using CWEB, a WEB for C)

A WEB source program contains WEB modules. Each module contains up to three parts: documentation, macro definitions, and programming code. The documentation section may include any relevant commentary. The macro definitions are similar to the #define statement in C, but are programming language independent. The programming code may be in any high-level language for which WEB has been implemented (currently Pascal[5], C[8], Modula-2[11] and Ada[9].) For the purposes of this discussion the terms "function," "procedure" and "subroutine" will be used interchangeably to refer to a syntactically complete subprogram as defined by the programming language. "Module" on the other hand, refers to a section of WEB code which may or may not be functionally equivalent to a "subroutine."

The listing of a WEB source program provides a full index of all the variable names, module names, functions, and procedures in the source program. This is not a new feature, but it is usually not an integral part of the source program listing. One new aspect of the WEB index is that the programmer can include strings in the index as he chooses. These selected strings or "topics" (also called "control texts") are used to indicate some special feature or problem of the current module.

Literate programming in WEB provides important advantages over traditional programming in four different ways:

1) WEB *encourages organization of code based on psychological rather than syntactic divisions.* The code can be modularized as the programmer chooses by separating

a group of statements which he considers as a single logical unit into a named module. The name of the module is then inserted in the code where that group of statements should be. This allows for conceptual abstraction of the code on whatever basis the programmer feels is logical. The division into modules and the presentation of the modules can be made independent of any syntactic considerations of the high level programming language.

2) WEB *makes the program structure more easily visible.* The conceptual abstraction mentioned above enables increased clarity in presenting the structure, whether of the entire program or of a procedure, no matter how complex, in a flexible modular structure. For example, if a procedure has three major parts, they can be represented within a single WEB module embedded in the control structure while the details of each part can be hidden inside separate sub-modules.

3) WEB *encourages an expository style of writing, which leads to more careful consideration of the details of the program.* In discussing the "expository" style of writing, Knuth [5] claims that WEB encourages the discipline of explaining and hence clarifying one's thoughts about a module as the code is written. He claims this leads to better code and less errors.

4) WEB*'s index provides the programmer direct access to portions of the code relevant to the problem at hand.* The index often allows the programmer to go directly to the module where an error message was produced, or to the group of modules listed under a topic appropriate to the problem at hand.

Jon Bentley addressed the concept of literate programming in his *Programming Pearls* columns in [1], [2]. These two columns contained literate programs by Knuth using WEB. Other examples of literate programs written in WEB may be found in [4] and [7].

Knuth states [5] that WEB is not intended for every programmer, since it requires familiarity with the programming language being used, the typesetting language rules, and WEB rules as well. The WEB user must be conscious of the rules of all three languages at once and be able to switch contexts from documentation to programming code and back again easily. This additional complexity is one of the major barriers to wider use of WEB, and forms the motivation for development of an improved interface to WEB.

III.   THE WEB HYPERTEXT SYSTEM

The WEB Hypertext System (WHS) should adopt an approach to the display and editing of the WEB source code which is entirely different from typical text editors. This new approach stems from the fact that WEB source code is inherently non-sequential. Module n may have a relationship with module $n+1$ which is strong, weak, or even effectively absent. Modules are self-contained units, having explicit links to other modules. As such, WEB code is a natural candidate for a hypertext presentation. However, it should not be thought that the links between modules proliferate in an uncontrolled manner. Currently, the links in a WEB source program are limited to the five types discussed below. They allow the exhaustive search of all the modules in the WEB. Later we will discuss the possibility of allowing the programmer to create new types of links.

The nodes of the hypertext are the WEB modules, where each module forms a separate piece of text. The links between the modules are based on their relationships, where those relationships are of five different types.

1) *Module n is the parent of module m.* Module n may contain three logical parts. Each part can be abstracted into a separate module. This would mean that n is the parent of m_1, m_2 and m_3.

2) *Module n is an addition to module m.* WEB allows the programmer to add to a module later in the text of the source program. One common example of this is later additions to the module <Global variables m>. This is typically used when the programmer, perhaps pages deep into the program, decides to declare another global variable. It is a simple matter to add an additional module, <Global variables n>, which is to be added to the <Global variables m> module, even though it is actually module number n. These two modules use the same name.

3) *Modules n and m are both flagged in the index under the same topic.* As an example, suppose both modules contain code sensitive to changes in the underlying computer word size. Typical usage would call for both to be listed in the index under a topic such as "word size dependencies."

4) *Modules n and m both use the same variable.* This case is similar to the previous case. The difference is that one module, say n, may define the variable in question, while m references or modifies it. This means that a given identifier may have three different types of relationships to modules: some modules may define it, some reference it, and some modify its value.

5) *Modules n, n+1, n+2, ..., n+m are all contained in the same section.* Typical WEB programs texts are broken into several sections, from **Introduction** to **Index**. In between are various sections, each containing several modules which all relate together. Examples of such sections include **Input and output**, **String handling**, and **Reporting errors**. Sections provide a good overview to the program text, and form the table of contents to the printed listing.

The rest of this section describes the major types of windows used in the WHS. The operations will be discussed later.

A. *The* WHS *Module Window*

When the WHS displays a module on the screen, the module will be shown in a window. This window will have four subwindows. The three parts of the WEB module (documentation, definitions and code) will occupy the first three subwindows. The fourth subwindow will present the topics in the module. If one part is empty, that subwindow will be collapsed to its smallest reasonable size while still allowing the programmer to enter text there if desired.

B. WHS *Indexing*

The printed WEB listing contains a complete index to all the variables in the code and all the topics (or "control texts") designated by the programmer, and an alphabetic list of all the modules. This functionality must be available in the WHS, and additional functionality is also needed. The preceding section describes how topics and variables will be displayed in module window. These will allow the programmer to request a small index containing the information indexed under a specific variable or topic. There should also be the option to bring up a complete index similar to that found in the printed listing. However there should be at least four indices, and perhaps two others. Each index window will include scrollbars, since the complete index typically will not fit in a window.

The index will use module numbers to indicate specific modules. While module names might be more intuitive, not all WEB modules have names, and the numbers are much easier to handle in an index format.

The first index window can provide a view of the identifiers used in the WEB source program. For each identifier, a list of module numbers should be provided designating each module which uses that identifier. Modules which define the identifier and modules which modify its value will be specially designated.

The second index can list the topics which are put in the WEB code by the programmer. These topics are not *defined* in the same sense as an identifier, nor are they modified, so a simple listing of which modules reference them is sufficient.

The third index can provide a list of the modules by name and number. This index window will show when a module is a add-on to an earlier module, and when a module has other modules added to it.

The fourth index can provide a list of the major sections in the WEB source program, with the numbers of the module which make up that section.

Additional index windows could show the parent/child relationships between the modules, but a better option, a graphical view, is discussed below.

C. The WHS *Graphical Representation*

The WHS provides a graphical representation of some of the relationships of the WEB. A graphical view of the code provides the ability to see the WEB in terms of module dependencies. If module n is the parent of module m, this should be demonstrated by a line from a graphical symbol representing n down (or across) to a symbol for m. This view should make the "parent/child" relationships between modules obvious to the viewer. There are several other graphical presentations which could be shown for the code, but additional presentation fall outside the scope of this paper.

IV. WHS OPERATORS

The user interface displays the program text, graphs, and indices as described earlier. These different ways of showing the program text demand a set of operations in order to allow the user to move intuitively between display methods. Operations should allow simple navigation of the WEB hypertext space, and bind the different display methods into a single integrated view of the WEB program text.

These functions or *operations* are associated with the different types of semantic links and allow the user to retrieve and display referenced modules. According to the operation the referenced module can contain the next usage of the selected variable, the definition of the selected variable, the next occurrence of the selected topic etc. These operations are described below.

A. *Operators Presenting Modules*

Some operations cause a new module to be presented in a window. The first set of operators relates to new modules on the basis of the module name. Since there can be several modules with the same name, we need special operators to locate one of the other modules with the same name as the specified module. Some operations relate to modules on the basis of number. Module number is a unique value: no two modules can have the same number. It is occasionally useful to check modules contiguous to the specified module.

The WEB programmer will often want to move from the specified module to related modules in the parent/child hierarchy. Operators must be provided to move from parent to child and vice versa.

The WEB programmer will often be interested in checking on other modules which use an identifier found in the current module. The identifier can be selected and related modules can be opened. Similar to checking identifiers, the WEB programmer may want to look at other modules mentioned in the index under the same topic.

B. Operators Presenting Indices and Graphs

Some operations open a window showing the index of identifiers. The user may select a particular identifier and show it in the identifier index. A similar operation applies to opening the topical index.

While working with a particular module, the WEB programmer will sometimes want to review the major sections, particularly to look at other modules within the same section. The programmer will also want to examine the parent/child hierarchy as presented in the graphics window.

We must provide the programmer an initial avenue for inquiry into the WEB source program. The most common ways of initial entry into a WEB source program are to use one of the indices, such as the sections (which make up the table of contents of the printed listing) or the topical index. We must also provide the ability to look at the complete parent/child hierarchy of the source program.

C. Miscellaneous Operators

Several other operations must be supplied for a complete environment. Some of the operators listed above return more than one result. An operation to provide the second, third, etc. of those results can be defined. This is particularly useful when the user wants to see the *next* object which also fits the last query.

As the WEB programmer uses the system, new operations may suggest themselves. The hypertext environment should allow for these to be added into the system. This operation allows the user to define a new semantic link type. Once defined, the new link must be available for use *via* an operator.

Finally, when a particular window is no longer needed, it can be closed.

D. WHS Options

There are two sets of options which will influence how some of the operations behave:

1. When opening a new module window, it may be desirable to replace a window currently on the screen rather than put an additional window on the screen. The default would be to create a new window, but the programmer could set an option to replace the contents of a selected window.

2. Several of the operators take some type of argument: a module name or number, an identifier, etc. This can usually be specified by using the context (i.e. selecting or highlighting with a mouse) but in some cases it would be appropriate to allow the programmer to specify the argument by typing it directly.

This set of operations will allow the programmer to navigate the WEB hypertext. Their implementation is described in the following section.

V. WEB HYPERTEXT SYSTEM ARCHITECTURE

In the previous sections requirements for the WHS were described. In this section the system architecture for implementation of WHS is presented. We briefly describe the functions of each component and the typical flow of information and control among the various components as shown in figure 2.

The WEB hypertext database contains information about all semantic links of the program texts in the form of relations. The DBMS is a relational database management system accepting requests (database queries) in SQL language and returning the results in the form of a table. Considerations such as performance may lead to the use of an alternative system, such as a network DBMS, but with the relational interface.

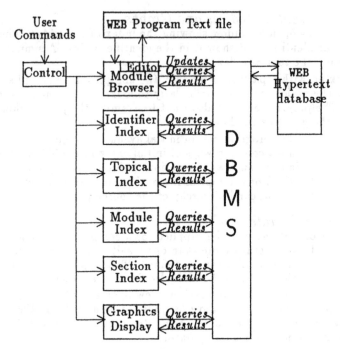

Figure 2. The major components of the WEB Hypertext System

The Module Browser performs the most important functions of the WEB hypertext. It accepts browsing requests, converts them into database queries, receives the information about position of the module (and possibly position of the identifier within the module) and displays the appropriate text in the module window. The Module Editor contained within the Module Browser allows for standard screen text editing and upon termination of the edit mode generates appropriate database updates. Identifier, Topic, Module and Section Index components accept the requests, translate them into database queries, receive the resulting tables from the DBMS and display them in the appropriate format. The Graph Display is very similar to the above components. The only difference is in the way the database tables are presented. The Control interface accepts the user's commands and directs them to the appropriate component of the system.

Under the proposed structure, the modification of the text structure and the resulting changes in the indexes and graphs are easy implemented by updating the WEB hypertext database using the Module Editor. It gives the user the capability to add new fragments to the text. New semantic links between the elements of the text can be easily supported by adding new operators defined in terms of SQL language. These functions along with table sharing, locking and security are implemented by a typical SQL DBMS kernel.

A. WEB *Hypertext Database*

Modules are the most often used or referenced components of the WEB source program therefore **module** is the central relation in the WEB hypertext database schema. Each module must have a number and most modules have a name. Hence *module_number* and *module_name* are important attributes of the relation **module**. Each module begins at some particular offset in a file and is contained entirely and completely in that one file therefore *file_name* and *displacement* are other attributes of the **module** relation. A section can group several of modules and therefore *section_name* is also included in the **module** attribute set. Values of *module_numbers* are unique; values of other attributes are not. Hence, the primary key of the **module** relation is *module_number*.

Modules can be parents or children of other modules. This is reflected in the **parent_child** relation. A single module may have several modules which are children, and a single child module may have several parent modules. The primary key of the **parent_child** relation is the *parent_number* and the *child_number*.

Module_Number	module_name	displacement	file_name	section_name

Module

parent_number	child_number	line_number

Parent_Child

identifier_name	module_number	line_number	type_of_usage

Identifier_Used_In_Module

topic_name	module_number

Topic_Referenced_In_Module

Figure 3. WEB Hypertext Database Schema.

Identifier_used_in_module is a relation with the attributes *identifier_name* and *module_number*. An identifier can be used several different ways in each module that it is in. It can be defined, referenced or modified. Each of this functions correspond to different value of the attribute *type_of_usage*. The *type_of_usage* attribute can have three values: modified, referenced, and defined. *Line_number* is an attribute of each relationship. All attributes are included in the key.

Topic_referenced_in_module is a relation with attributes *topic_name* and *module_number*. The same topic may be in several modules and each module can contain several topics. Both attributes compose the primary key.

B. Semantics of WHS Operators

Users queries for the WEB hypertext defined in Section 3 can be mapped into database queries expressed in SQL language by Module Browser, Graphics Display and Index components. For the sake of brevity, we will give only a few examples.

The operator "show module with selected name" has as an argument the module name $M (e.g. 'Global Variables'). It can be translated to the following SQL query:

```
SELECT file_name, displacement
FROM MODULE
WHERE module_name = $M
ORDER BY module_number
```

The result of this query contains *file_name* and *displacement* and therefore provides all the necessary information for the execution of this function. This operator (and several to follow) can return a table of several entries, though only the first entry is immediately used. Successive entries in the table can be accessed by use of the "Repeat" operator.

The operator "show parent module of the specified module" has as an argument the module number $N. It can be translated to the following SQL query:

```
SELECT file_name, displacement, line_number
FROM PARENT_CHILD, MODULE
WHERE child_number = $N AND parent_number = module_number
```

The result of this query contains *file_name, displacement* and *line_number* and therefore provides all the necessary information for the execution of this function. By including the *line_number* it is possible not only to display the requested module but also to display the place in the parent module where the module $N is referenced.

The result of this query contains *file_name, displacement* and *line_number* and therefore it is possible not only to display the requested module but also to display the place where the identifier $I is defined.

The queries for the operators: "show module where selected identifier is used," "show module where selected identifier is modified" and "show module where selected topic is used" as well as many others, can be represented by very similar SQL expressions.

C. Index for WHS

Now we address the question of how to create the indexes mentioned in the previous section. The method presented here is to use simple database queries to gather the necessary information into the relational tables and rearrange them if necessary to resemble indexes in a book. The necessary SQL query for "Open the complete Identifier index" operator is as follow.

```
SELECT identifier_name, module_number, type
FROM IDENTIFIER_USED_IN_MODULE
ORDER BY identifier_name, module_number
```

The operator "show the identifier index, displaying where the identifier is defined" has as an argument the identifier name $I and displays only the partial identifier index. It can be translated to the following SQL query:

```
SELECT identifier_name, module_number, type
FROM IDENTIFIER_USED_IN_MODULE
WHERE identifier_name = $I AND type = "DEFINED"
ORDER BY identifier_name, module_number
```

The complete and partial index for the topics, sections, and module names can be generated using similar queries.

D. GRAPH for WHS

The information necessary to create the graphs mentioned in the last section is readily available in the NAMES_USED_IN_MODULE table. For the first layer the modules with no name are retrieved by a simple query:

```
SELECT module_number
FROM MODULE
WHERE module_name = "no_name"
```

Then, for each module number the next layers are constructed by recursively invoking "show child module of the specified module." Partial diagrams can also be easily constructed by restricting the first layer to the specified module and/or restricting the number of layers.

VI. SUMMARY

In this paper we have described requirements for a WEB Hypertext System (WHS). The architecture of a hypertext system for WEB allows use of a general purpose relational database management system. Considerations such as performance may lead to the use of an alternative system, such as a network DBMS, but with the relational interface. Mapping between hypertext queries and relational database queries is provided. The system allows the user to define new hypertext operations by providing the corresponding SQL queries for the underlying relational database. The described system can be easily extended by many other types of queries and the basic principles could be extended to programming systems other than WEB.

The first prototype of WHS using only a single window has been implemented on an IBM PC at the University of Alabama.

REFERENCES

[1] J. Bentley, "Programming Pearls: Literate Programming," *Commun. ACM*, vol. 29, no. 5, pp. 364-369, April 1986.

[2] J. Bentley, "Programming Pearls: A Literate Program," *Commun. ACM*, vol. 29, no. 6, pp. 471-483, May 1986.

[3] M. Brown, "An Interactive Environment for Literate Program," *Structured Programming*, vol. 11, pp 11-25, 1990.

[4] M. Brown, "The Literate Programming Tool," Texas A&M Computer Science Dept., Tech. Rep. TR-88-012, Aug. 1988.

[5] D. E. Knuth, "Literate Programming," *Computer J.*, vol. 27, no. 2, pp. 97-111, 1984.

[6] D. E. Knuth, "Stanford Instructinal Television Network, Stanford Univ., California," CS 349 TEX: The Program: A Case study in software design Video-taped Lectures.

[7] D. E. Knuth, *Computers and Typesetting*, Addison-Wesley, Reading, MA (1986).

[8] S. Levy, "WEB adapted to C, another approach," *TUGboat*, vol. 8, no. 1, pp. 12-14, April 1987.

[9] Norman Ramsey, "Weaving a Language-Independent WEB," *Commun. ACM*, vol 32, no.9, pp. 1051-1055, September 1989.

[10] Darrell R. Raymond and Frank W. Tompa, "Hypertext and the Oxford English Dictionary," *Commun. ACM*, vol. 31, no. 7, pp. 871-879, July 1988.

[11] E. W. Sewell, "How to MANGLE your software: the WEB system for Modula-2," *TUGboat*, vol. 8, no. 2, pp. 118-122, July 1987.

Ethics and Computers: Can Universities Set the Standards?

Gerhard Steinke
University of Passau
D-8390 Passau, F. R. Germany
steinke@unipas.fmi.uni-passau.de

Gilbert Hamann
University of Toronto
Toronto, Canada
unido!ecf.toronto.edu!hamann

Abstract

The increasing use of computers in universities raises ethical issues which must be addressed. These ethical implications will impact and affect society as a whole. Educational institutions should act not only according to the requirements of the law but also be subject to higher ethical standards. Two areas where computers and ethics intersect are dealt with in this paper, namely data protection and privacy policies with regard to student information and the acquisition of "illegal" software.

Introduction

The impact of computers in the educational environment during the last few decades has been significant. One could hardly imagine a university, or any institution of higher learning, without computers. Computers are used for administrative tasks as well as in many aspects within the academic and research functions of a university. Computers have in fact, become essential, and the application of computers and information technology continues to increase. Along with this increased use of computers come questions of an ethical nature which each institution must deal with--each in the setting of their own country, their laws, expectations and culture. The impact of the universities decisions will be felt in the rest of society.

This paper attempts to highlight and, perhaps, jog our consciences with some of these ethical implications brought about by the use of computers at universities. After discussing why universities should be concerned with high ethical standards, two specific areas are dealt with, namely the issue of privacy and protection of student information and the issue of using "illegal" computer hardware and software. Preliminary results from questionnaires dealing with computers and ethics which were completed by students at a number of universities around the world are presented. The paper concludes by providing further areas within a university that are related to computers and which have ethical implications. While this paper concentrates on universities, many of the issues similarly affect other public and private organizations as well as individuals.

There is no doubt that a university, whether publicly or privately sponsored, is required to act according to the laws of the country in which it is situated. But in addition, there are further expectations and standards which go beyond that which is legal or illegal. These ethical standards, as we shall call them, are expected from a university because of its role, nature and function in society. There is, therefore, an expectation as well as a requirement for the educational institution to provide an example to society by acting not only according to what is legal under existing laws, but also by striving to act according to higher standards. Universities create a moral tone that powerfully influences the thinking, conduct, values and even personalities of its students and staff as well as the society as a whole.

There would seem to be two main difficulties for universities in the quest to function beyond the legal requirements to a higher ethical level. First there is the problem of money, since it is usually more expensive to uphold a high ethical standard rather than to act strictly by what is legal. While there is a world-wide demand for increased funding and expansion of universities, at the same time, many universities are experiencing economic uncertainty and governmental funding cutbacks. Does the university not have the goal to provide the best education for the lowest possible cost? While that which is clearly illegal is usually not tolerated, there is often the temptation to achieve the goal of providing the best education in a manner which may be unethical, or perhaps in the gray area bordering on the illegal. For example, one may be tempted to acquire a "questionable" copy of a software program when the higher cost may make acquisition of an "original" copy impossible. Does the end, providing a good education, justify the means, which may be unethical or bordering on the illegal?

A second difficulty in functioning at high ethical standards has to do with the ability of the educational institution to influence and control its staff as well as its students. How can the institution require the highest ethical standard of its many constituents? Can the educational institution hold accountable, and be held accountable for the actions of its staff and students? What level of security does a university need to implement in order to provide adequate protection of its information? One must remember to keep in mind that ethical standards are not absolute and even when they are written, usually leave more room for interpretation then legal standards.

Protection of Student Information

One area where ethical considerations play an important role at a university is in dealing with the privacy and protection of student information. While the concept of privacy is held high, particularly in free societies throughout the world, privacy is not an easy term to define, especially in the legal sense. (That is one reason why the more technical term, data protection, is often used.) Privacy entails the right to withhold aspects of our lives from others--be they individual or government. Yet government, for example, has legitimate claims for information from its citizens--how could a government otherwise function? Today, large amounts of personal data can be collected, processed, integrated with data from other sources and stored--with the result that often more data than is necessary is kept. Inaccuracies become difficult to discover and correct. While the concern for privacy is not new, the increased use of computers has raised the anxiety and concern for privacy.

The United States was one of the first countries to enact legislation defining privacy and the required data protection methods with The Privacy Act of 1974. But this act was limited to information systems maintained by federal government agencies. West Germany's Federal Data Act (Bundesdatenschutzgesetz) of 1978 is applicable to both government and the private sector. Great

Britain did not pass legislation in this area until 1984 with the Data Protection Act and in Japan data protection legislation was not submitted to their parliament until 1988. Hong Kong is an example of a country which still does not have data protection legislation. There will, therefore, be a difference in the requirements and guidelines for universities in terms of privacy and data protection depending on the country in which they exist.

Universities initially ask for, as well as continually collect information on their students. Some of this information is sensitive and may have significant impact on the life of the students. Consider rather harmless situations such as the following:

a) A company requests and may even be willing to pay a substantial amount of money for the names and addresses of students. The reason may be to mail credit card applications, send advertising, sell insurance, etc.

b) A private evening school may request the names of students who are failing, in order to promote itself.

c) A student may wish to see the comments made about himself or herself by an instructor.

Such situations indicate that an educational institution must have a clear policy on releasing student information which often goes beyond the legal requirements which may or may not exist for such situations. What information may be released, to whom, and must students be informed and give their prior permission? Should each request be evaluated independently, and if so, how and by whom? Should students be allowed to view all information concerning themselves, for example, evaluations by teachers--or is that the property of the evaluator? How do students ask for clarification or correction of information?

Students in different countries regard the release of their information differently. This was clear from a questionnaire given to students at a university in Canada, two universities in the United States, one university in West Germany and one in Hong Kong. While 69 percent of the American students thought it was ethical for the university to give an external organization their names and addresses, only 49 percent of the students in Canada, 38 percent of the students in Hong Kong and 16 percent of the respondents in Germany were of a similar opinion. In Germany the release of stduent information is strictly prohibited, although only 39 percent of the students thought it was illegal. Only 3 percent of the American students thought that the release of their names and addresses by the university was illegal.

Universities must implement significant security measures to ensure adequate protection of their data. One should not rely on the "high ethics" of the staff and students who have access to the university computer system and hope that they will access only information they have a right and a need to see. In Germany, all organizations employing more than a certain number of staff, require the appointment of a person who is responsible for data protection. In June 1988 a new data protection law was enacted in Bremen in Germany dealing with data protection in educational institutions. One of the regulations stipulates that sensitive data may not be processed outside of the educational institution. The use of private personal computers is prohibited--perhaps so there is less chance of taking information home.

In most universities the decison on what measures are to be implemented to protect student information is left to the institution. Since protection costs money, security measures are seldom given the needed priority.

A high ethical standard for the protection and privacy of data would include informing students as to what information is being held and making them aware of the degree of confidentiality of the information collected. Students should give their consent before any information is released to outside organizations. The university has the ethical, if not legal requirement to take reasonable and significant precautions and to implement sufficient security procedures to hinder unauthorized access to student information and ensure that those who have access to information are aware of and abide by the legal requirements and institutional policies.

Acquisition of Software

A second area where ethical considerations play an important part at the university is in the acquisition of computing software. Issues such as the following face the university: Does one have to buy "original" software, or can one buy goods that are described by terms such as "copy", "look-a-like", "compatible", "fake", "pirated" or "counterfeit"? (Maybe the question is, which of these terms is really applicable and correct.) Can one let the responsibility for the legality of the desired product rest with the supplier? Why should we buy one software package for each student or terminal when we can easily make our own copies? How does one prevent illegal copying of software by individuals using university computer facilities?

There is a substantial gray area, both legally as well as ethically. The legal questions relating to computer products are uncertain as technology is developing so rapidly that laws are usually only written or amended after serious misuse of new developments is noticed. Many laws that have been passed in recent years dealing with computers still need to be tested before the courts. In the area of software protection there has been a worldwide trend, perhaps because of strong lobbying by software developers, for countries to modify their copyright legislation to specifically include computer programs under literary works. ADAPSO, an American organization representing more than 750 computer service companies published the following statement in order to inform people of the seriousness of copying software:

> Reproducing computer software without authorization violates the U.S. Copyright Law. It is a Federal offense. The money paid for a software product represents a license fee for the use of one copy. It does not represent an authorization to copy. Civil damages for unauthorized software copying can be as much as $50,000 or more and criminal penalties include fines and imprisonment. Bills have been introduced in Congress to strengthen the law and increase penalties.

An industry practice is to rely on protection by means of licensing agreements which are included as part of the software package. A license allows one to use a software package subject to certain conditions, but ownership remains with the company. For example, the Lotus License Agreement as found on the Lotus 1-2-3 manual implies that by buying a Lotus software package you do not own but are only purchasing a license to use their software. "Each Lotus product sold at retail is licensed by Lotus Development Corp. to the original purchaser and any subsequent owner of the product... Opening the diskette package indicates your acceptance of these terms." One of the restrictions then listed is that one may not make copies of the system diskettes. Backup copies are not mentioned--yet who does not make at least a backup copy?

Copyright laws and licensing agreements are easily and often broken--even at universities. The questionnaire mentioned earlier showed that only 20 to 29 percent of the students responding to the questionnaire indicated that it was illegal to give a copy of a program to someone else. The existence of illegal software is common. Just as photocopy machines have resulted in the copying of books, so computers have made it possible to copy programs and data -- except that it is much easier, less expensive and faster to copy a computer diskette than a book. The price differential between buying an original and the cost of making a copy is great. (The issue is often turned around and the question asked: Is it ethically acceptable for a company to charge such high prices for its software? One may try to rationalize one's actions by claiming that one is "justified" in buying a counterfeit copy because the company is charging unethically high prices. But how can two wrong actions result in a correct or good result?) It is reported that outside of the United States a piracy ratio of 250 pirated copies of a software program to one legitimate copy exists. But relatively few cases have been taken to court because of the expense, time requirements and the possible bad public relations that a software developer may endure as a result. Since violations of software copyright and licensing laws are seldom prosecuted and "everyone does it", the practice continues.

Educational institutions need multiple copies of a software package so that a number of students can use the software at the same time. Software firms have been rather reluctant and unwilling to provide site licenses, which would let the institution make as many copies as needed, but usually insist that original copies of the software be purchased for each terminal. Yet it seems that such an expense for buying a large number of identical software packages is extravagant and should not be necessary.

A common practice today is to link microcomputers together into networks. A number of microcomputers sharing a disk unit could then share one copy of the software. How can a software developer discover or prevent one from installing their software onto a network where it may be used by many users simultaneously? Lotus includes the following statement in their license agreement in the Lotus 1-2-3 manual: "You may not provide use of the software in a computer service business, network, timesharing, interactive cable television, multiple CPU or multiple user arrangement to users who are not individually licensed by Lotus."

One solution to this issue of software on networks is to buy the number of software packages equal to the number of terminals on the network. Even though these additional software packages are not used, one package or license then exists for each terminal. Some universities try to determine the average number of terminals which use a particular software package at any one point in time and then buy that number of software packages. While technically this solution borders on the illegal, the intent is to be fair. There are firms which are seeking to provide special licenses for the educational environment.

Other Ethical Issues

These are only two areas at a university involving ethical considerations. There are other areas involving computers where responsible decisions must be taken. The existence of illegal hardware seems to be declining since such products are prohibited from being imported into many western countries. If most computers are indeed legal, then the issue of whether to buy a name brand or a non-name brand can be determined purely on business and economic terms rather than ethical and legal considerations. But in some countries in the Far East the issue is not quite so clear since "illegal" hardware is available on the market, at prices significantly below the legal products. The question arises whether it should even be possible for a company to prevent others from manufacturing a similar computer.

The increased emphasis on CAI (Computer Assisted Instruction) where students have less and less interaction with instructors must be carefully evaluated to determine if the decrease in human interaction affects the transfer of ethics and values. There are research areas that raise ethical questions. In the artificial intelligence field, computers are being developed to think and act like humans--no doubt there are significant ethical issues to be considered. Research on military products as well as in fields such as genetic engineering involve computers heavily--but the related ethical issues are often left in the shadows. Curricula at the university are ammended to include computers, but often the ethical issues that arise from the use of computers are forgotten. In the study mentioned earlier 36 percent of the respondents from the Canadian, American and Hong Kong instutitions indicated that they had never heard ethical issues related to computers discussed in their classes, while 59 percent of the German students said they had never heard ethical issues mentioned in their lectures.

Computers have raised many ethical and legal issues which universities must address. While there are no set solutions or fixed standards, to ignore these issues is both unacceptable and irresponsible--and yet that is so often done. How then, can the university develop a respect for the law in their students and in society as a whole? One must conclude that the process for providing a good education and the example that is set by the process is as important as the education itself--and may in fact, ultimately, have the more lasting effect on the students. Regardless of the cost and the consequences, it is our opinion, that the highest ethical standards must be strived for by educational institutions. Only then will students and society see by example and also consider following the path of higher standards of ethical conduct.

Alternatives to the B$^+$- tree

William Boswell
Intergraph Corporation
One Madison Industrial Park
Huntsville, Alabama 35824 USA

Alan L. Tharp
Computer Science Department
North Carolina State University
Raleigh, North Carolina 27695-8206 USA
email: tharp@cscadm.ncsu.edu

ABSTRACT

For many years, the **b+ tree** has been the file structure of choice for applications requiring both sequential and direct access. But two file structures developed recently for similar applications, **bounded disorder file organization** and **adaptive hashing**, may offer improvements. Are they better? In what ways? When should they be used? To answer these and related questions, this paper summarizes the performance characteristics, implementation aspects, and use considerations for these three file structures. The primary variation among the three techniques is the form of the index structure. Results from an investigation comparing the three methods are presented; parameters varied in the study were the distribution of the record keys, file size, and data node size. For many circumstances, one of the newer techniques *is* preferable to the b$^+$-tree.

Key words: index structures, b$^+$-tree, hashing, bounded disorder, adaptive hashing.

1. INTRODUCTION

In many data storage applications, a versatile file structure is needed to provide efficient direct *and* sequential access. For many years, the index-based b$^+$-tree [1,2,3,4] has been a standard for such situations. Recently two techniques which provide improvements over the venerable b$^+$-tree, bounded disorder file organization [5] and adaptive hashing [6], have been introduced. These techniques are similar in that they reduce the height of the index by integrating the direct access technique of hashing into the index traversal process. When a technique has been a standard for as long as the b$^+$-tree has, people may assume that there is no better method and fail to seek alternatives. The purpose of this paper is to remind researchers and developers that improvements do exist and to provide them with comparison data and insights to assist them in making an informed selection.

1.1 B⁺ TREES

A b⁺-tree consists of an **index** of nonterminal nodes referencing terminal nodes of data[1] linked together into a **sequence set** as illustrated in Figure 1. The b⁺-tree is balanced in that all terminal nodes are on the same level, and all direct retrievals require the same number of probes; hence there is no best or worst case retrieval. A disadvantage of the b⁺-tree is its low storage utilization, which is often in the range of 50 to 65 percent because the splitting operation required to handle overflow situations at a node during insertion may create nodes with as low as 50 percent storage utilization. An improvement in storage utilization can be realized by implementing the index as a b* or b#-tree [1-4]. When inserting a record into b⁺-tree file, the algorithm relies completely on the current contents of the file to decide where to store the record while retaining the con-

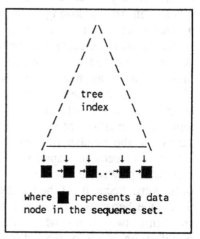

Figure 1 B+-tree Structure

sistency of the entire file. Therefore, the storage structure of the file is not *directly* dependent on the keys of the records and the only way to retrieve a particular record in the file is to descend through the entire tree-like index structure to a data node. It is impossible to calculate the stored location of a record in the file by its key. Maintaining the tree-like index structure introduces storage overhead and traversing it degrades the retrieval performance as the index grows and more of it must be stored in auxiliary memory.

1.2 BOUNDED DISORDER ORGANIZATION

The bounded disorder file organization [5] reduces the size of the index (so that it will fit into primary memory) by increasing the size of the data nodes. To accomplish this increase, each data node is subdivided into data buckets which are individually accessed within the data node through hashing as illustrated in Figure 2. A data bucket may contain one or more records. The form of the index is independent of the bounded disorder concept but here we assume a b⁺-tree structure. Then the bounded disorder organization is simply a b⁺-tree with a special sequence set. Instead of pointing to a data node, a pointer in the b⁺-tree index points to an *index* of pointers into the data buckets. If a suitable hashing scheme is employed, storage utilization in the data nodes is better than that of a b⁺-tree, but index requirements are greater (see Table I).

A limitation of the bounded disorder concept is that perfect sequential order is lost. Within the sequence set, records are in order between data nodes, but are stored randomly across the buckets within a node due to the operation of the hashing function;

---

[1] In this discussion, the smallest unit of information is the record. Records are grouped into data nodes (also referred to as data pages). An intermediate unit of grouping, the bucket, is used with bounded disorder.

each record within a particular data node has a smaller key value than the keys of the records in the following data node and a greater value than those in the preceding data node. Bounded disorder does provide sequential access, but the records within a data node must be sorted as they are retrieved.

As the file grows, it may be necessary to adjust the index structure to reduce the number of overflow records which are necessary when the number of records mapping to a bucket exceeds its capacity. First, a node may be expanded to contain a larger number of buckets. Secondly, if the number of buckets in a node becomes too large, a node may be split into two nodes which then causes a modification of the b-tree index.

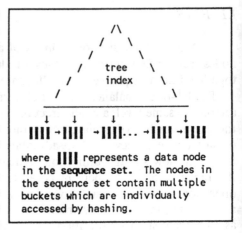

where **||||** represents a data node in the **sequence** set. The nodes in the sequence set contain multiple buckets which are individually accessed by hashing.

Figure 2   Bounded   Disorder   File Organization

1.3 ADAPTIVE HASHING

Adaptive hashing [6] organizes a file as a sequentially ordered linked list of data nodes. Like the b^+-tree and bounded disorder, an index structure is used to point to the data nodes. However, unlike the other two, the index is a single-level hash table and *not* a tree-like structure. The index contains data page pointers (DP) into evenly-spaced intervals of the file and index pointers (IP) into the index itself. A DP points to a segment of the ordered linked data pages, and, like the pointers from the b^+-tree index, is not related to the records stored in the segment of the file it points to. Adaptive hashing uses a form of linear hashing [7] to decide the initial index location to examine. However, since the DP in the initial index entry may not always point to the exact part of the file where a record is stored because the index (hash table) expands as the file grows. Therefore an IP contains the index location whose DP points to the beginning of the portion in a file where a specific record *is* stored. This scheme represents a compromise between the speed of hashed addressing and the flexibility of indirect addressing. Since many records can be hashed to the same entry in the index, the IP in the entry only indicates another entry whose DP points to the *beginning* of the segment of a file in which that class of records is stored. It may be necessary to search several data pages of the file to locate the proper data page for accessing a particular record. To retrieve a record, its key is hashed into the index, the index pointer for that entry is followed to an index entry (possibly different) and its data page pointer indicates the data page where the search is to begin. Figure 3 illustrates the file organization of adaptive hashing.

After many records have been inserted, some data pages may overflow causing additional ones to be created. Since these newly created data pages are not referenced by a data page pointer, they can not be retrieved directly and several file accesses may be needed to fetch them. Such a situation degrades performance. In addition, if the keys of the inserted records are unevenly distributed, these newly created data pages will be clustered in some segments of the file which will cause uneven performance in retrieving records in different portions of the file. In order to keep the performance of adaptive hashing *efficient* and *stable*, the hash table is reorganized and its number of entries increased. The parameter to control the timing of the hash table reorganization is the average number of data pages that each data page pointer points to (ANDPP), that is, the ratio of total number of data pages in the file to the number of entries in the hash table. When the value

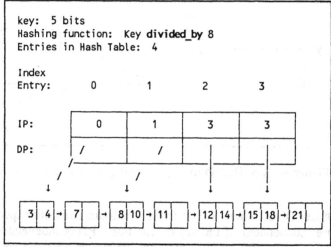

Figure 3 File Organization of Adaptive Hashing

of ANDPP is greater than a predefined threshold, a hash table reorganization occurs. When the hash table is reorganized, it is necessary to double the size of the index and change the two hashing functions (as in linear hashing) to accommodate the new index size (as in linear hashing). Then the ordered linked list of data pages is divided into as many equal intervals, of possibly multiple data pages, as there are index entries; however, if the ratio for reorganization is two, each interval can contain a single data page. Then the DP of each entry in the hash table is set to point sequentially to each interval, that is, entry 0 points to interval 0, entry 1 points to interval 1, etc. For each entry in the index, the IP field is set to point to that index entry for the beginning of the segment in the file that can store the records which map to that home (initial) entry.

Adaptive hashing provides practical direct and sequential access. Even with large files, the index remains small enough to be kept in primary memory. If the ratio for reorganization, which approximates the upper bound on average retrieval probes, is kept small, performance is excellent but reorganization is more frequent. A ratio smaller than two complicates implementing the reorganization process since multiple pointers would point to a single page.

2. ANALYSIS

One purpose of this study was to compare these three file structures for direct and sequential access. Direct access retrieval performance was examined with a variety of representative distributions for the record keys, file sizes, and data node sizes. For each method, the four disparate key distributions shown in Figure 4, data nodes (or buckets for bounded disorder) of 8, 32, and 64 records, and file sizes of 1,000 and 10,000 records were tested in all combinations. For the bounded disorder method, 5, 11, and 17 buckets were combined to form a data node. A typical run consisted of a particular data node and file size, while varying the number of buckets per node for bounded disorder. After each 10 percent of the records of a test run were inserted, direct retrievals were made for the records inserted thus far and the results stored. The effect of the various factors are analyzed individually. The unexpected or noteworthy outcomes are highlighted.

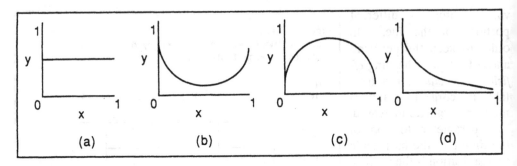

Figure 4 Key Distributions; x = range of data; y = number of data (normalized)

■ **Key Distribution** The test results substantiated our expectation that all three methods are independent of the key distribution. Being independent of key distribution is thus an advantage for all three methods. However, adaptive hashing is sensitive to insertions made in key order. In that case, the records mass in one segment of the file creating a chain of data buckets between index pointers (see Figure 5). Retrieving the records in such a segment requires significantly more probes until the index is reorganized; ten retrieval probes were required compared with the typical two or fewer for the other distributions. The other methods did not exhibit any variation resulting from the input in key order. Key distribution did have an effect on storage utilization for bounded disorder as noted subsequently.

■ **Data Node Size**
Varying the data node size also gave predictable results. With larger capacity nodes, fewer were needed to store an equivalent number of records. As a result, the indexes for the tree methods were smaller which meant fewer retrieval probes. A larger node size did not have a discernible effect on adaptive hashing because its index

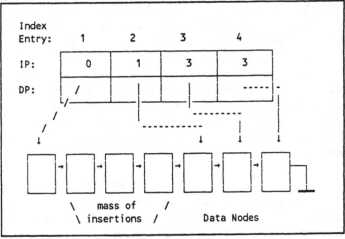

Figure 5 Ordered Insertions Using Adaptive Hashing

structure does not grow in height as the number of data nodes increases. When system or application constraints require a small node size, adaptive hashing is thus preferable to the other methods. Bucket size combined with data node size did affect the performance of the bounded disorder method. For the larger data node size, the results indicated that bounded disorder is superior to the b$^+$-tree for direct access retrieval. The added index level of bounded disorder enables the tree index to store more records,

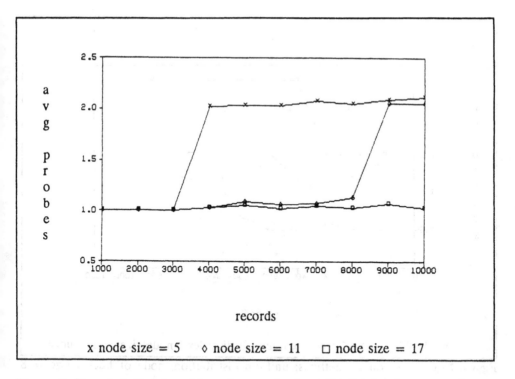

Figure 6 Bounded disorder with various node sizes; distribution b;
bucket size = 32 records

and tree growth (and retrieval probes) is decreased significantly. Figure 6 displays the performance of bounded disorder for three data node sizes. For this and the subsequent graphs, and for all methods, one level of the index is assumed to be kept in primary memory; the average probes plotted then are the accesses of auxiliary storage. One can see from the graph how performance degrades when another level must be added to the index. The larger the node size, the greater the number of records that can be added before it is necessary to add another level.

■ Performance Results

Figure 7 gives typical results comparing the three methods. A small data node size and relatively few records are used to demonstrate more clearly how the methods compare as records are added.

The results are similar for larger node sizes and more records, but the results are shifted to the right; that is, it takes more records to effect a change, see Figure 8. The results for adaptive hashing are not monotonic because as the file size increases, ANDPP increases until it exceeds the predefined threshold which triggers a reorganization, which in turn *reduces* the average number of retrieval probes. Adaptive hashing has the advantage with larger files since its index height is *not* a function of the file size; it has an upper bound of approximately 2 probes (reorganization threshold) independent of the file size. The performance of a b$^+$-tree and bounded disorder can be enhanced if more levels of the index can be stored in primary memory. With a large data node size, bounded disorder performs the best.

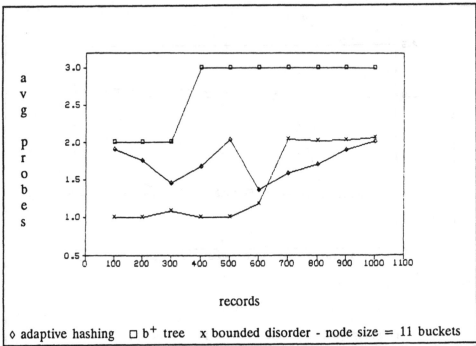

◊ adaptive hashing   □ b$^+$ tree   x bounded disorder - node size = 11 buckets

Figure 7   Comparison of methods; uniform distribution; node or bucket size = 8 records

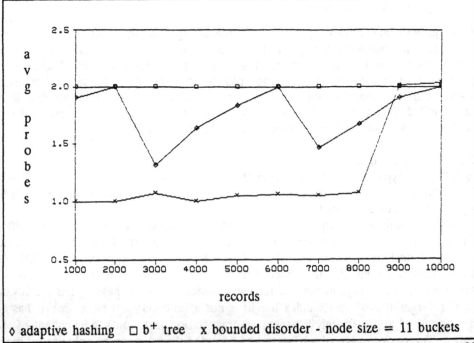

◊ adaptive hashing   □ b$^+$ tree   x bounded disorder - node size = 11 buckets

Figure 8   Comparison of methods; uniform distribution; node or bucket size = 32 records

■ Storage Requirements

Storage utilization for adaptive hashing ranged from 76% to 81%, the best among the methods. Utilization for the b$^+$-tree averaged from 69% to 72%, which is respectable for a b$^+$-tree. Key distributions affected storage utilization for the bounded disorder method. Utilization varied widely - averaging lower than the b$^+$-tree, but sometimes outperforming adaptive hashing. An explanation is that the hashing function $f(key) = key \bmod number\text{-}of\text{-}buckets\text{-}per\text{-}node$ produced primary clustering for some key distributions resulting in more overflow records and therefore lower storage utilization. Table I gives typical index storage requirements (in bytes) for the three methods. The record keys for this experiment were four byte integers. In practice, the keys would likely be much longer character fields. For longer keys, adaptive hashing has an advantage over the B+-tree and to a lessor extent bounded disorder, because, the other methods require the key values (or several characters of them) to be stored in the index whereas adaptive hashing only requires two integer (pointer) values which would require four bytes per index entry at most [8].

■ Sequential Retrieval

Sequential retrieval performance was measured by the time required to list the file in sequential order. Sequential retrieval for bounded disorder was much slower than for the other methods because the contents of each node had to be sorted as it was retrieved. Adaptive hashing and b$^+$-tree performed almost identically, with adaptive hashing having a slight edge perhaps because of its higher storage utilization.

■ Other Considerations

With B+-trees and bounded disorder, reorganization of the index occurs steadily during the insertion process whereas with adaptive hashing it occurs infrequently but at a greater one-time cost. Since the index structure is modified infrequently for adaptive hashing, performance during insertions is faster and more consistent than for the other methods. Adaptive hashing would have a definite advantage if its reorganizations could be performed during a time when the application in which it was used was not in production. If that were not the case, the reorganization time could be a disadvantage for adaptive hashing.

Table I Comparison of index storage requirements (in bytes) for the data with a uniform key distribution and a node or bucket size of 32.

	1,000 records	10,000 records
B+-tree	591	3,940
bounded disorder buckets/node = 5	462	1,386
bounded disorder buckets/node = 11	859	2,577
bounded disorder buckets/node = 17	1,255	1,256
adaptive hashing	128	1,024

Adaptive hashing also was the easiest to implement; it took approximately a quarter of the time to implement and about one fifth the number of programming statements compared with the other two methods.

3. CONCLUSIONS

For each method, there are situations in which it should be the method of choice. Rather than always using just one structure, the b^+-tree, for all situations requiring both sequential and direct access, we now can use any of three structures. With three structures instead of one, we can do a better job of matching the solution to the demands and constraints of the problem.

Adaptive hashing requires less memory for its index so it is preferable when the amount of primary memory for storing the index is limited. Direct access retrievals are bounded by the ratio for reorganizing, which can be set as low as two. An additional and unique bonus is that its performance can be controlled easily by the programmer simply by changing the ratio. Since its index is reordered infrequently, its normal insertion time is faster and more consistent. Its implementation is easier since its algorithm is simpler. When inserting data, it is important that the data not be inserted in key order.

Since bounded disorder needs to sort the records within a data node for sequential processing, it is not appropriate when both types of access are needed regularly. If either the amount of primary memory for storing the index is not limited or the data node size is very large, which in turn causes the index to become small, bounded disorder can provide the best direct access performance. Key distributions may affect storage utilization.

A b^+-tree is preferable when there is not a limit on the amount of primary memory for storing the index and both sequential and direct access are equally important.

REFERENCES

1. Bayer, R. and C. McCreight, "Organization and Maintenance of Large Ordered Indexes," *Acta Informatica*, Vol. 1, No. 3 (1972), pp. 173-189.

2. Knuth, D.E., *Sorting and Searching*, Addison-Wesley, Reading, MA, 1973, p. 477.

3. Comer, D., "The Ubiquitous B-Tree", *Computing Surveys*, Vol. 11, No. 2 (June 1979), pp. 121-137.

4. Tharp, A.L., *File Organization and Processing*, John Wiley & Sons, New York, NY, 1988, pp. 243-253.

5. Litwin, Witold and David B. Lomet, "A New Method for Fast Data Searches with Keys", *IEEE SOFTWARE*, March 1987, pp 16-24.

6. Hsiao, Yeong-Shiou, and Alan L. Tharp, "Adaptive Hashing," *Information Systems*, Vol. 13, No. 1, 1988, pp. 111-127.

7. Litwin, Witold, "Linear Hashing: A New Tool for File and Table Addressing", *Proceedings of the Sixth International Conference on Very Large Data Bases*, pp.212-213, October 1980.

8. Anderson, Alan, Personal Communication, 1989.

Minimal Perfect Hashing For Large Sets of Data

Vincent G. Winters

Department of Computer Science, University of Cincinnati
Cincinnati, Ohio

Abstract

We present and analyze a method that permits the efficient application of minimal perfect hashing functions to much larger sets of data than previously possible. The method employs a probabilistic algorithm to obtain a separation of legal key values into disjoint subsets. The cardinality of each subset is small enough so that it can be efficiently minimally perfectly hashed. In the retrieval phase, the subset to which an input key belongs is determined and the hashing function for that subset is applied. The time complexity of locating the data associated with a given input key value is $O(LogLogN)$. The space complexity of the algorithm is $O(N\,LogLogN)$. Construction time for the necessary data structures is $O(N^2\,LogLogN)$.

Keywords: Search and Retrieval, Algorithms, Hashing, Complexity

1   Introduction

There have been published a number of algorithms ([1],[2],[3],[5],[9]) for generating perfect (collision free) hashing functions and minimal (having no unused space in the data storage area) perfect hashing functions. These generating algorithms can be employed if the set of all active keys (those associated with stored data) is known at the time parameters for the hashing function are being computed. However, such systems have been computationally practical only for active keys sets of small cardinality. The breakdown in computational feasibility is most frequently due to rapid growth in the magnitudes of the parameters associated with the generated hashing functions. One possible solution to the problem is to obtain a mutually exclusive and exhaustive subsetting of the active (valid) keys such that no subset has cardinality greater than the maximum that is computationally acceptable for the type of (minimal) perfect hashing functions being generated. Subsequently, when given a key whose associated data is to be located, the key's subset is determined and the appropriate hashing function is applied. The usefulness of such a method hinges on the efficiency of the algorithm that locates the proper subset. Previous work utilizing subsetting for minimal perfect hashing functions [5], [7], [8], has been limited by the exponential complexity of the algorithms. To date, there has been no efficient algorithm (with respect to worst case performance) usable in conjunction with available minimal perfect hashing function generators. The following presentation provides a probabilistic algorithm for accomplishing such subsetting and for efficiently locating the proper subset at retrieval time.

This paper is organized into 5 parts. In section 2 we describe the algorithm and its associated data structures. In section 3 the time and space complexities of the algorithm in both subset construction and location are derived. Section 4 gives a small example of the method applied to the 256 most common English words. The conclusion is given in section 5.

2   The Method

2.1   Key Magnitude Reduction

In the following we assume the static type situation in which minimal perfect hashing functions are applicable. That is, the set of active keys (those associated with data stored in the data base) is known at the time the subsetting algorithm and hash function generators are applied.

To apply the method it is necessary that the values of active keys (considered as binary integers) be reduced such that they are bounded above by N^2 (N is the cardinality of the set of active keys). This reduction can be accomplished by either of two methods. First, it can be done probabilistically. It has been shown [9] to be highly likely that there exists an integer less than N^2 such that each element of the input set gives a unique value modulo that integer.

(i.e. treating current active keys as random variables their first differences are from a uniform distribution), there is very high probability that there is a $Z < N^2$ such that the active keys are incongruent $\bmod Z$. Letting $Pr(Z \leq N^2)$ represent the probability that there exists such a Z less than N^2 we have that

$$Pr(Z \leq N^2) \geq 1 - (1 - (\frac{(N^2 - N - 2)}{N^2 - N})^{\frac{N^2 - N}{2}})^{\frac{N^2 + N + 2}{2}} \tag{1}$$

Since for $N = 10$ $Pr(Z \leq N^2) \geq (1.0 - 10^{-10})$ and because this is an increasing function of N, the probability of being able to reduce the values to the desired level is very high.

A second method for magnitude reduction, which is deterministic given that $N^2 > (1 + \log M)$, utilizes the fact (proven by Fredman et al [3]), that for any input set there exists an $R < (N^2 \times \log M)$ such that elements of the set are incongruent $\bmod R$ (where M is the maximum magnitude over the set of active keys). Using this result, the input can be treated as consisting of at most $(1 + \log M)$ subsets each consisting of elements less than N^2. The determination of which of the $(1 + \log M)$ subsets a modified input key $(K' = K \bmod R)$ belongs to is made based on the integer portion of the quotient obtained from $K'/(1 + \log M)$. Our algorithm then processes each subset separately. Each value to be processed by the algorithm is then the remainder after the modified input key is divided by N^2. Thus, we can bound the magnitudes of the active key values by N^2.

2.2   Creating Data Structures For Splitting The Active Key Set

In general, the separation of a given set of keys is accomplished by dividing each key value by N (the cardinality of the set). Each division generates an integral quotient, Q_i, and an integral remainder, R_i. The determination of the subset into which a key will be placed is based on its Q_i value or its R_i value. If the number of keys having a given Q_i value is small enough, then that Q_i value is used to define a subset - i.e. all keys giving that quotient comprise one subset. If the number of elements having a given Q_i value is not small enough, that Q_i value is not used to define a subset. In the latter case, the subset placement of keys having that Q_i is based on those keys' R_i values. A Q_i or R_i value that is used to define a subset is called a *subset generator*.

The first step in the method is to divide each of the active key values, k_i by N. The system retains both the quotient, Q_i, and the integral remainder, R_i, from each of these divisions. Each quotient/remainder pair has the following properties:

- $Q_i \in [0..N - 1]$

- $R_i \in [0..N - 1]$

- (Q_i, R_i) is unique within the set.

Any Q_i value having at least one but no more than $\sqrt{N}$ keys mapping to it (by virtue of generating it as a quotient) is used as a subset generator - i.e., the keys mapping to it form one subset. Those keys not placed into a subset by their Q_i value are placed into a subset based on their R_i value. That is, all such keys with the same R_i value are in the same subset. Since no Q_i generated subset can have more than $\sqrt{N}$ keys, we have by Theorem 2.1 that no subset can have more than $\sqrt{N}$ keys. At this point, some subsets may have cardinality small enough to allow (minimal) perfect hashing while others may require further subsetting.

Theorem 2.1 *Let $\{w_i\}$ be the input elements (less than N^2) such that, when any one is divided by N, it gives an integer quotient having more than than $\sqrt{N}$ elements mapping to it. Let $\{R_i\}$ be the set of integral remainders generated by $\{w_i\}$ mod N. No $\{R_i\}$ can have more than $\sqrt{N}$ elements mapping to it.*

PROOF:

Assume there exists an $\{R_i\}$ with more than $\sqrt{N}$ elements mapping to it.

Clearly, no two elements which generated this R_i value could have generated the same quotient value. This means that each of the elements mapping to $\{R_i\}$ had a different quotient value. Therefore, more than $\sqrt{N}$ quotient groups, each with more than $\sqrt{N}$ elements mapping to it, have contributed elements to this $\{R_i\}$ subset. This implies that there were more than N original input elements.

Since each Q_i and R_i value produced at level 1 was obtained via division by N, its magnitude is bounded above by N. Now, take as the elements of any subset generated by a Q_i value the R_i values resulting from the division (at level one). Similarly, take as the elements of any subset generated by an R_i value the Q_i values resulting from the division at level one. Then we have not only that every subset consists of no more than $\sqrt{N}$ elements but also that each element is less than N. Therefore, each generated subset created at level one can be further split (if necessary) using the same process employed at level one with the modification that the divisor used is $\sqrt{N}$ rather than N. By the reasoning employed above, subsets produced at the second level have no more than $\sqrt[4]{N}$ elements with each element less than $\sqrt{N}$. The process can be repeated similarly, at subsequently higher levels with appropriate divisors, until every subset

As each (sub)set is split, the system creates a table of pointers in contiguous storage locations. Each created pointer corresponds to one of the *possible* subset generator values Q_i or R_i. Each pointer is set to one of three values depending on the subset generated by the (Q_i or R_i) associated with it. If the Q_i or R_i does not generate a subset (i.e. too many elements map to it or no elements map to it) the pointer is set to zero. If the subset generated by the associated generator value is small enough to be hashed, the pointer addresses the parameters of the hashing function (obtained by invoking the hashing function generator). If the associated subset is too large to be hashed, the pointer addresses another pointer table. In this latter case, the pointer gives the address of the start of a pointer table at the next higher level. This next level table is used with subset generators obtained when the subset associated with this current level pointer is further split (by division) at the next higher level. Thus, we have subsets being iteratively split, with pointers (indexed by Q_i or R_i values) indicating what further processing the new subset should undergo, until all subsets have become small enough to be minimally perfectly hashed.

2.3 Locating Data Associated With A Key

In the retieval phase the system divides the input key value (treated as a binary integer) by N. It then uses the quotient to index the proper pointer in the level one table. If the indexed pointer contains a zero, then the integer value of the remainder plus $(N - 1)$ (to get past the pointers associated with quotients) is used as an index into the pointer table. The indexed pointer will give either the address of the table to be used at the next level or the address of the hashing function parameters. Now the remainder or quotient value (whichever was *not* used to access the pointer in the level 1 table) is divided by the second level divisor, $\sqrt{N}$. The quotient or remainder from this operation is used to index a pointer (in the table pointed to by the pointer obtained at level one) giving the address of either the level three table to be used or hashing function parameters. At each level, the system makes use of the pointer value indexed by the subset generator obtained from the division. It uses the pointer value obtained at level i as the base address for the pointer table to be used at level $i + 1$. The location of the pointer to be used at level $i + 1$ will be given by the sum of the base address (for remainders base address plus divisor value) and the subset generator obtained by the division at level $i + 1$. Thus the quotients and/or remainders generated by the sequence of divisions define a path through the tables of pointers. The path ends when a pointer is obtained giving the address of (minimal) perfect hashing function parameters that will be used with the input key to locate the data. An example of how the method functions is given in section 4.

3 Time And Space Complexities Of The System

3.1 Time Complexity Of Retrieval

At each level of retrieval processing, the calculations require only one division, no more than 3 comparisons (to determine whether Q_i or R_i should be used and whether the pointer is to hashing parameters or a higher level pointer table). Therefore, the time complexity of locating data will be determined by the number of levels of processing and the complexity of the associated hashing function. Assuming that subsets containing only two elements can be minimally perfectly hashed, we have, from Theorem 3.1, that the number of levels of processing is $O(LogLogN)$. Thus, retrieval time complexity is $O(LogLogN) + hash\ function\ time\ complexity$. Since perfect hash function complexity is $O(1)$, the over all complexity of the system is $O(LogLogN)$. The constants associated with this complexity are small.

Theorem 3.1 *There will be no more than* $1 + LogLogN$ *levels in the subsetting structure.*

PROOF:

From Theorem 2.1 and the fact that $N, \sqrt{N}, \sqrt[4]{N}, \ldots$ are used as divisors, it follows that no table at level i will contain more than $N^{(1/2)^{i-1}}$ elements. A minimal perfect hashing function with acceptable parameter size can be found for any subset consisting of two elements. Because of this the structure will never have more than X levels, where $N^{(1/2)^{X-1}} = 2$ or, equivalently, $N = 2^{2^{X-1}}$. Thus we have that $X - 1 = LogLogN$.

3.2 Space Complexity Of Retrieval

We are now interested in the largest possible amount of storage overhead that could be required. That is, the amount of storage beyond that needed for storing all of the original data. Again, we make the conservative assumption that acceptable minimal perfect hashing functions can be obtained only for subsets with no more than two elements. Now, the number of pointers in one pointer table at any given level is determined by the divisor used at that level and by the maximum possible magnitude of elements entering that level. Since the divisor and the maximum possible element magnitude at any given level are fixed, the most costly situation arises when the maximum possible number of tables occurs at each level. The number of tables at a level (higher than the first) is determined by the cardinalities of the subsets created at the previous level. Therefore, the maximum number of tables occur if the first level splits the level. We have then, counting the $2 \times N$ pointers needed in the level 1 table, that the total number of pointers in all levels is no more than $2 \times N + 2 \times N/3 \times (\sqrt{N} + \sqrt[4]{N} + \ldots + {}^{LogLog}\sqrt[N]{N})$ - that is the sum, over all levels, of the product of the number of tables at a level and the maximum possible number of pointers per table at that level. From Theorem 3.2, we have that, since hashing parameter space is $O(N)$, the overall space complexity is $O(N^{3/2})$ in units of words.

Theorem 3.2 $\sum_{i=1}^{LogLogN} N^{1/2^i} \leq 2 \times \sqrt{N}$

PROOF:

For $\lceil LogLogN \rceil = 2$ (meaning $2 < N \leq 16$) we have that the value of this sum is $\sqrt{N} + \sqrt[4]{N}$ which is less than $2 \times \sqrt{N}$. Now, assume the proposition is true for all values of N for which $\lceil LogLogN \rceil = X$, where X is some fixed value no less than 2. Consider the two sides of the Theorem's equation for any N' such that $\lceil LogLogN' \rceil = X + 1$. The second term of the series being summed (i.e. $\sqrt[4]{N'}$) is less than or equal to $\sqrt{N}$, for some N such that $LogLogN = X$. This means that this term is greater than the sum of all terms subsequent to it in the series. Now, if it can be shown that $\sqrt{N'} \geq 2 \times \sqrt[4]{N'}$ the proof will be complete. However, we know that $N' > 2^4$ since $\lceil LogLogN' \rceil > 2$. This gives that $\sqrt{N'} \geq 2 \times \sqrt[4]{N'}$.

With modifications to the construction phase and the retrieval phase, we can probabilistically reduce space complexity to $O(N \, LogLogN)$ without increasing the time complexity of the system. The technique used to accomplish this reduction is to effect a lower bound on the cardinality of subsets generated at each level. This lower bound, which is a function of the level at which the subset is generated, places an upper bound on the number of tables that can occur at the next level. In this way, the storage complexity is improved.

The lower bound on cardinality is achieved by combining small subsets that are generated at one level into one large subset before their elements are processed at the next higher level. Recall that each generated subset has an associated pointer. If not pointing to hashing function parameters, this pointer identifies that table of pointers to be used in processing elements of the subset at the next level. Small subsets can be combined by setting their associated pointer values to address the same table at the next level. Our original subsetting scheme depends on the existence of an upper bound on the cardinality of subsets entering a given level, L - i.e. for $L = 1, 2, \ldots (1 + LogLogN)$ cardinality is bounded above by $N^{1/2^{(L-1)}}$. The combining of subsets will be limited by this upper bound.

The determination of the new maximum number of tables occurring at a given level, L, can be made if the average cardinality of subsets entering that level is known. If, at level $(L-1)$, subsets are combined until any further combining would result in violating the upper bound for subsets entering level L, then there can be at most one subset having fewer than $\frac{N^{1/2^{(L-1)}}}{2}$ elements. Further, every subset other than the smallest must be too large to be combined with the smallest. Therefore, the average size of subsets entering level L must be greater than $\frac{N^{1/2^{(L-1)}}}{2}$. Because the number of tables at level L cannot exceed the total number of active keys, N, divided by the lower bound on average table size, we have $2 \times N^{1-1/2^{(L-1)}}$ as an upper bound on the number of tables at level L. We can now bound the total number of pointers needed for level L. This bound on pointers is obtained from the product of the maximum possible number of tables and the pointers per table at level L. The number of pointers per table will be twice the divisor used at level L - corresponding to the number of possible quotients and remainders that can be generated. Since the divisor at level L is $N^{1/2^{(L-1)}}$, we have that there can be no more than $4 \times N$ pointers at any level. Thus we have that storage complexity is $O(N \, LogLog \, N)$ words. We will now see that this storage complexity is achieved probabilistically.

In the above derivation we have, for pedagogical reasons, ignored a potential difficulty. Recall that in the original scheme if an element is placed into a subset based on the quotient generated by dividing the element then the value carried on to be processed at the next higher level is the remainder that was generated by the division. Conversely, an element belonging to a remainder generated subset has its quotient carried on for processing at the next level. However, in combining subsets it is quite possible that two or more identical values can be placed into the same (combined) subset for processing at the next level. Such duplicates result in the method functioning incorrectly. A solution to this problem is to carry to the next level not quotients or remainders but rather the original key values from which the quotients or remainders have been derived. However, in order to limit the size of tables generated at a given level, it is also necessary to ensure a level dependent bound on element magnitude - i.e. elements entering level L must be no larger than $N^{1/2^{L-2}}$. This bound was met naturally when quotients and remainders were carried on. To ensure that it is met when original keys are carried on, some extra processing is necessary. Specifically, each subset that has been combined and contains values exeeceding the limit at level L must have its elements mapped to unique values that are no larger than $N^{1/2^{L-2}}$. This mapping will be acheived by the same probabilistic method [7] used earlier to ensure that each key value processed at level one was less than N^2. That is, we can with extremely high probability find for each subset, $\{s_i\}$, an integer that will reduce every element of the set to a value no greater than $N^{1/2^{L-2}}$ (the square of the maximum possible number of elements in that set).

3.3 Time Complexity Of The Construction Phase

The cost of creating the the data structures used in the retrieval phase can be considered in three parts. These are:

- generating the hash function parameters for sets of acceptable size,

- determining and storing the reducer values associated with the tables,

- setting up the pointers in the tables at all levels.

Since the method is usable in conjunction with any minimal perfect hashing function generator, the cost of the first component will vary. It has been shown [9] that a minimal perfect hashing function can always be constructed in polynomial time. The second component (finding reducer values) involves dividing each element of a table containing C elements by values starting at C and going no further than C^2. These divisions take place at each level 2 through $Log\,Log\,N$. At any level, there cannot be a need to divide into more than N elements (the maximum possible number in all tables). Also, the largest divisor occurs at level 1 and is N. Thus, the total cost of finding all reducers is $O(N^2\,Log\,Log\,N)$.

The final component (setting pointers) requires determining subset generators, allocating pointer table space and storing pointer values for each subset. This requires at most N divisions and $O(N)$ allocation/setting operations at each level. Thus, the overall complexity of the construction phase is $O(N^2\,Log\,Log\,N)$.

4 An Example With The 256 Most Common Words

The following example (detailed in Figures 1, 2, 3 and 4) illustrates the process. The active keys here are the first 256 most common english words. In the two instances in which a word's length exceeded 8 characters we have used only the first 8 characters of the word. This was done only for the convenience of working with variables that do not exceed 8 bytes (a doubleword). Using the untruncated version of the long english words would have no significant effect on the results.

In Figure 1 we have the reduced values (each made less than 256^2) of the EBCDIC encodings of the 256 most common english words. The reduced values were obtained from the remainders after division by 4895. In Figure 2 we have the level 1 pointer table. For readability quotient and remainder values that did not generate subsets are not shown. Non-zero values identify the level 2 table to be used for elements in the subset corresponding to this quotient or remainder value after division by 256. Figure 3 contains the first 6 of the 16 level 2 pointer tables. Indicated at the start of each table is the reducer value to be used on elements mapping to that table. The entries in these tables correspond to quotients and remainders from division by 16 into the reduced values. An entry of 'P' indicates that a single value maps to this pointer and so the pointer gives the address of the data associated with that key. An entry of 'H' indicates that exactly two values map to this pointer and so the pointer gives the address of hashing parameters to be used in obtaining the addresses of the data associated with these keys. A '$T_{3,x}$' indicates that table 'x' at level 3 is to be used for further subsetting of the more than two values that map to this pointer. Figure 4 gives the first 6 of the 12 level 3 tables.

As an example of retrieval, consider locating the data associated with the keyword 'SOON'. The value of the EBCDIC encoding of 'SOON' is 3,805,730,517. The reduced value (mod4895) is 182. Dividing this value by 256 places it in the subset generated by quotient zero at level 1. Items in this subset are processed next by table 1 at level 2. Here 182 is reduced to 41 (mod47) which is then divided by 16. This would place it into the subset generated by quotient value 2. However, the pointer value associated with quotient 2 is zero. This is because the group would have contained 7 elements and exceeded the upper limit of 4 on the cardinality of subsets generated at this level. Therefore, the element is placed into the subset generated by the remainder value of 9. This subset contains only 2 elements and so has been hashed. The value in the pointer field gives the address of the hashing parameters. The actual amount of storage required for the structures of this example was 874 words plus storage for hashing parameters. The storage requirement is substantially reduced if we allow that minimal perfect hashing functions can be obtained for sets of cardinality greater than 2.

5 Conclusion

We have presented an efficient method that can be used in conjunction with currently available minimal perfect hashing functions. The method greatly extends the range of data base sizes for which these types of functions can be applied. Thus, due to the elimination of both the possibility of collisions and wasted space in the storage allocated to the data, significantly improved performance in both space and time are obtained.

241	242	193	1301	1527	1797	3869	2491	150	1188
2930	3294	4615	671	647	4009	2531	683	1672	2026
684	2412	685	1613	2347	911	3625	676	3547	626
4639	4356	640	4374	1500	2840	2806	1524	946	2068
3842	4241	2935	4603	3499	631	1266	1252	3278	1632
1440	2843	3240	1488	3595	44	3356	3406	4026	4030
3962	4847	158	2007	3999	1195	983	2829	2397	1477
639	2261	2989	187	2301	3093	2236	2208	1906	3528
2550	258	3939	4562	3969	3764	2447	2151	1883	89
3401	1505	1108	1122	173	4005	4454	201	2704	352
2719	4180	2732	2733	4784	4805	4124	1120	4642	2648
1157	1112	1548	1430	4227	3213	2404	3172	2229	2373
3412	3679	502	348	3932	2293	4735	2312	624	3317
4504	1590	3924	917	644	2995	1168	659	1600	468
4893	340	4308	900	897	4689	4692	3826	1137	2465
4429	896	1152	3054	1409	2290	1156	2795	374	384
4632	882	2374	2117	3728	1769	1415	1486	2285	2753
1169	971	3788	4449	4451	2090	3936	545	575	1313
4350	2955	215	3827	2268	4225	4549	420	226	182
4872	4186	1086	2744	2339	432	3411	4508	4522	3214
3577	636	637	2758	167	656	2506	4456	1674	3114
2250	1393	2885	1467	3758	4481	408	1920	2230	1121
4131	445	4738	4749	1981	3147	4175	2488	2259	149
2265	337	4669	302	1296	885	1895	1736	3711	2909
2110	4039	4057	2483	1673	312	4242	4383	4256	3298
4629	2712	4169	380	1649	1391				

Figure 1: Reduced values of 256 most common words

quots		remdrs		remdrs	
0	$T_{2,1}$	16	$T_{2,12}$	182	$T_{2,11}$
1	$T_{2,2}$	20	$T_{2,5}$	187	$T_{2,11}$
3	$T_{2,3}$	21	$T_{2,3}$	188	$T_{2,6}$
4	$T_{2,4}$	33	$T_{2,15}$	197	$T_{2,6}$
6	$T_{2,5}$	42	$T_{2,10}$	202	$T_{2,14}$
7	$T_{2,6}$	62	$T_{2,13}$	206	$T_{2,10}$
9	$T_{2,7}$	63	$T_{2,10}$	208	$T_{2,6}$
10	$T_{2,8}$	69	$T_{2,9}$	211	$T_{2,11}$
11	$T_{2,9}$	103	$T_{2,6}$	213	$T_{2,16}$
12	$T_{2,10}$	111	$T_{2,15}$	217	$T_{2,12}$
13	$T_{2,11}$	112	$T_{2,8}$	220	$T_{2,12}$
14	$T_{2,12}$	113	$T_{2,11}$	225	$T_{2,8}$
15	$T_{2,13}$	114	$T_{2,5}$	237	$T_{2,10}$
16	$T_{2,14}$	119	$T_{2,6}$	242	$T_{2,9}$
17	$T_{2,15}$	124	$T_{2,10}$	244	$T_{2,5}$
18	$T_{2,16}$	125	$T_{2,10}$	245	$T_{2,8}$
19	$T_{2,11}$	127	$T_{2,6}$	247	$T_{2,3}$
-	-	128	$T_{2,5}$	253	$T_{2,6}$
-	-	129	$T_{2,9}$		
-	-	132	$T_{2,9}$		
-	-	135	$T_{2,16}$		
-	-	144	$T_{2,1}$		
-	-	147	$T_{2,9}$		
-	-	150	$T_{2,8}$		
-	-	159	$T_{2,3}$		
-	-	160	$T_{2,12}$		
-	-	164	$T_{2,5}$		
-	-	171	$T_{2,3}$		
-	-	172	$T_{2,3}$		
-	-	173	$T_{2,3}$		
-	-	181	$T_{2,8}$		

Figure 2: Level 1 Tables (unspecified entries contain zeros)

$T_{2,1}$ (reducer=47)

Q/R	Qptrs	Rptrs
0	0	P
1	$T_{3,1}$	0
2	0	0
3	0	0
4	0	0
5	0	P
6	0	H_1
7	0	P
8	0	P
9	0	H_2
10	0	P
11	0	0
12	0	P
13	0	H_3
14	0	P
15	0	0

$T_{2,2}$ (reducer=49)

Q/R	Qptrs	Rptrs
0	0	P
1	0	0
2	0	P
3	0	0
4	0	P
5	0	H_4
6	0	0
7	0	0
8	0	H_5
9	0	H_6
10	0	0
11	0	H_7
12	0	H_8
13	0	P
14	0	P
15	0	P

$T_{2,3}$ (reducer=47)

Q/R	Qptrs	Rptrs
0	0	0
1	0	0
2	$T_{3,2}$	P
3	0	P
4	0	P
5	0	0
6	0	0
7	0	H_9
8	0	P
9	0	P
10	0	P
11	0	P
12	0	0
13	0	P
14	0	0
15	0	P

$T_{2,4}$ (reducer=52)

Q/R	Qptrs	Rptrs
0	0	P
1	0	0
2	$T_{3,3}$	P
3	0	P
4	0	H_{10}
5	0	0
6	0	0
7	0	0
8	0	H_{11}
9	0	P
10	0	0
11	0	0
12	0	H_{12}
13	0	H_{13}
14	0	P
15	0	0

$T_{2,5}$ (reducer=45)

Q/R	Qptrs	Rptrs
0	0	0
1	$T_{3,4}$	0
2	$T_{3,5}$	0
3	0	0
4	0	0
5	0	0
6	0	0
7	0	P
8	P	0
9	P	0
10	0	P
11	0	0
12	P	0
13	0	0
14	0	P
15	0	P

$T_{2,6}$ (reducer=52)

Q/R	Qptrs	Rptrs
0	0	P
1	0	0
2	$T_{3,6}$	0
3	0	P
4	0	0
5	0	H_{14}
6	0	0
7	0	H_{15}
8	0	0
9	0	P
10	0	0
11	0	P
12	0	0
13	0	H_{16}
14	0	0
15	0	P

Figure 3: First 6 tables of level 2

$T_{3,1}$ (reducer=5)		
Q/R	Qptrs	Rptrs
0	0	P
1	0	0
2	0	P
3	0	P

$T_{3,2}$ (reducer=5)		
Q/R	Qptrs	Rptrs
0	0	P
1	0	P
2	0	P
3	0	P

$T_{3,3}$ (reducer=5)		
Q/R	Qptrs	Rptrs
0	0	0
1	0	P
2		P
3	0	P

$T_{3,4}$ (reducer=5)		
Q/R	Qptrs	Rptrs
0	P	P
1	0	P
2	0	0
3	0	P

$T_{3,5}$ (reducer=6)		
Q/R	Qptrs	Rptrs
	H_{19}	0
1	H_{20}	0
0	0	0
0	0	0

$T_{3,6}$ (reducer=7)		
Q/R	Qptrs	Rptrs
0	H_{17}	P
1	H_{18}	0
2	0	0
3	0	0

Figure 4: First 6 tables of level 3

References

[1] Chang, C. C. *The Study of an Ordered Minimal Perfect Hashing Scheme*. Communications ACM 27, 4 (1984) 384-387.

[2] Cichelli, R.J. *Minimum Perfect Hashing Functions Made Simple*. Communications ACM 23, 1 (1980), 17-19.

[3] Fredman, M., Komlos, J. and Szemeredi, E. *Storing a Sparse Table with O(1) Worst Case Access Time*. JACM 31, 3 (1984) 538-544

[4] Hogg, R. and Craig, A. *Introduction To Mathematical Statistics*. Macmillan, New York, 1970.

[5] Jaeschke, G. *Reciprocal Hashing - A Method For Generating Minimal Perfect Hashing Functions*. Communications ACM 24, 12 (1981) 829-833.

[6] Mitronovic, D.S. *Analytic Inequalities*. Springer-Verlag, Berlin 1970

[7] Sager, T.J. *A Polynomial Time Generator for Minimal Perfect Hash Functions*. Communications ACM 28, 5 (1985) 523-532.

[8] Sprugnol1, R., *Perfect Hashing Functions: A Single Probe Retrieval Method for Static Sets*. Communications ACM 20, 11 (1977) 841-850.

[9] Winters, V., *Minimal Perfect Hashing In Polynomial Time*. BIT (to appear, 1990).

Architectural Classification and Transaction Execution Models of Multidatabase Systems*

M. Tamer Özsu
Ken Barker

Laboratory for Database Systems Research
Department of Computing Science
University of Alberta
Edmonton, Canada T6G 2H1
{ozsu,barker}@cs.ualberta.ca

Abstract

A multidatabase system is constructed from autonomous and independent database managers. There is considerable confusion of terminology related to multidatabase systems and their difference from distributed databases, heterogeneous systems, etc. In this paper, we discuss a basic taxonomy for these systems highlighting their fundamental features. We then present a computational model that describes the operational characteristics of multidatabase systems. This model is used in our research on transaction management in such systems.

1 Introduction

The development and maturity of distributed database technology [11] within the last decade has brought to the forefront the issue of the appropriate architectural models for building these systems. One popular alternative is to build distributed systems in a top-down fashion, by distributing data across sites to be managed by data managers that are specifically designed to handle distributed data management. An alternative methodology is to build the system bottom-up by using single-machine, autonomous database managers (DBMSs) which cannot individually manage distributed data. Systems built in a top-down fashion are commonly known as *distributed database system* [11]. Bottom-up designed databases are referred to by many names such as *heterogeneous distributed database systems* [13], *federated database systems* [8] and *heterogeneous multidatabases* [12]. In this paper we will call them *multidatabase systems*.

There is significant debate regarding the nature of these alternative architectures accompanied with significant confusion in the terminology related to them. In this paper, we discuss a taxonomy of database systems that highlights the differences of multidatabases and distributed databases. This taxonomy enables precise definition of the commonly used, but ill-defined terms. We also present a computational model for multidatabase systems that concentrates on the execution of user transactions. The subject matter of this paper forms the basis of our studies on transaction management protocols in multidatabase systems.

---

*This research has been supported in part by the Natural Sciences and Engineering Research Council (NSERC) of Canada under grant OGP-0951.

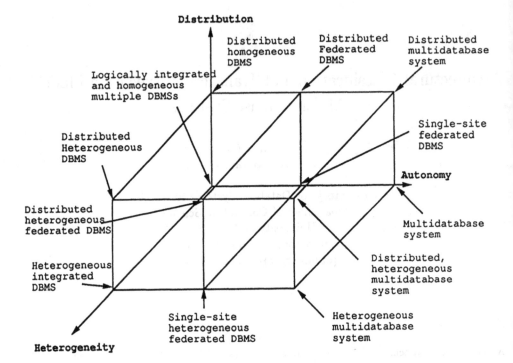

Figure 1: DBMS Implementation Alternatives

2 A Taxonomy

We use a classification (Figure 1) which characterizes the systems with respect to (1) the auton-omy of local systems (2) their distribution, and (3) their heterogeneity. We consider autonomy as the more important of these characteristics. Therefore, in the following presentation, we will emphasize the autonomy dimension.

Autonomy refers to the distribution of control. It indicates the degree to which individual DBMSs can operate independently. Autonomy is a function of a number of factors such as whether the component systems exchange information, whether they can independently execute transactions and whether one is allowed to modify them. Requirements of an autonomous system have been specified in a variety of ways. For example, [7] lists these requirements as follows:

1. The local operations of the individual DBMSs are not affected by their participation in the multidatabase system.

2. The manner in which the individual DBMSs process queries and optimize them should not be affected by the execution of global queries that access multiple databases.

3. System consistency or operation should not be compromised when individual DBMSs join or leave the multidatabase confederation.

On the other hand, [5] specifies the dimensions of autonomy as consisting of three issues:

1. Design autonomy: Individual DBMSs are free to use the data models and transaction management techniques that they prefer.

2. Communication autonomy: Each of the individual DBMSs is free to make its own decision as to what type of information it wants to provide to the other DBMSs or to the software that controls their global execution.

3. Execution autonomy: Each DBMS can execute the transactions that are submitted to it in any way that it wants to.

In the taxonomy that we consider in this paper, we will use a classification that covers the important aspects of these features. One alternative that we consider is *tight-integration* where a single-image of the entire database is available to any user who wants to share the information which may reside in multiple databases. From the users' perspective, the data is logically centralized in one database. In these tightly-integrated systems, the data managers are implemented so that one of them is in control of the processing of each user request even if that request is serviced by more than one data manager. The data managers do not typically operate as independent DBMSs even though they usually have the functionality to do so.

Next we identify *semi-autonomous* systems which consist of DBMSs which can (and usually do) operate independently, but have decided to participate in a federation to make their local data sharable. Each of these DBMSs determine what parts of their own database they will make accessible to users of other DBMSs. They are not full-autonomous systems because they need to be modified to enable them to exchange information with one another.

The last alternative that we consider is *total isolation*, where the individual systems are stand-alone DBMSs, which know neither of the existence of other DBMSs nor how to communicate with them. In such systems the processing of user transactions that access multiple databases is especially difficult since there is no global control over the execution of individual DBMSs.

It is important to note at this point that the three alternatives that we consider for autonomous systems are not the only possibilities. We simply highlight the three most popular alternatives.

Whereas autonomy refers to the distribution of control, the distribution dimension of the taxonomy deals with data. We consider two cases, namely, either the data is physically distributed over multiple sites that communicate with each other over some form of communication medium or it is stored at only one site.

Heterogeneity may occur in various forms in distributed systems, ranging from hardware heterogeneity and differences in networking protocols, to variations in data managers. The important ones from the perspective of this paper relate to data models, query languages and transaction management protocols. Representing data with different modeling tools creates heterogeneity because of the inherent expressive powers and limitations of individual data models. Heterogeneity in query languages not only involves the use of completely different data access paradigms in different data models (e.g., set-at-a-time access in relational systems versus record-at-a-time access in network and hierarchical systems), but also covers differences in languages even when the individual systems use the same data model. Different query languages that use the same data model often select very different methods for expressing identical requests.

Let us consider the architectural alternatives in turn. We start at the origin in Figure 1 and moving along the autonomy dimension. The first class of systems are those which are logically integrated. Such systems can be given the generic name *composite systems* [8]. If there is no distribution or heterogeneity, then the system is a set of multiple DBMSs which are logically integrated. There are not many examples of such systems, but they may be suitable for shared-everything multiprocessor systems. If heterogeneity is introduced, then one has multiple data managers which are heterogeneous but provide an integrated view to the user. In the past, some work was done in this class where systems were designed to provide integrated access to network, hierarchical, and relational databases residing on a single machine. The more interesting case is where the database is physically distributed even though a logically integrated view of the data is provided to users. This is what is known as a *distributed DBMS* [11]. A distributed DBMS can be homogeneous or heterogeneous.

Next in the autonomy dimension are semi-autonomous systems which are commonly called as *federated DBMS* [8]. As specified before, the component systems in a federated environment have significant autonomy in their execution, but their participation in a federation indicate that they are willing to cooperate with others in executing user requests that access multiple databases. Similar to logically integrated systems discussed above, federated systems can be distributed or single-site, homogeneous or heterogeneous.

If one moves to full autonomy, then we get what we call *multidatabase system* (MDS) architectures. Without heterogeneity or distribution, an MDS is an interconnected collection of autonomous databases. A multidatabase management system (MDMS) is the software that provides for the management of this collection of autonomous databases and transparent access to them. If the individual databases that make up the MDS are distributed over a number of sites, then we have a *distributed MDS*. The organization of a distributed MDS as well as its management is quite different from that of a distributed DBMS. We discuss this issue in more detail in the upcoming sections. At this point, it suffices to point out that the fundamental difference is one of the level of autonomy of the local data managers. Centralized or distributed multidatabase systems can be homogeneous or heterogeneous.

The fundamental point of the foregoing discussion is that the distribution of databases, their possible heterogeneity, and their autonomy are orthogonal issues. It is fair to claim that the fundamental issues related to multidatabase systems can be investigated without reference to their distribution or heterogeneity. The additional considerations that distribution brings, in this case, are no different than those of logically integrated distributed database systems for which solutions have been developed [11]. Furthermore, if the issues related to the design of a distributed multidatabase are resolved, introducing heterogeneity may not involve significant additional difficulty. This, of course, is true only from the perspective of database management; there may still be significant heterogeneity problems from the perspective of the operating system and the underlying hardware. In that sense, the more important issue is the autonomy of the databases rather than their heterogeneity.

3 MDS Architecture

The fundamental architectural model that has been used in describing database management systems is the well known ANSI/SPARC framework [14] which specifies the layers of abstraction of data in a database. Accordingly, the ANSI/SPARC model specifies a *conceptual schema* which defines the logical organization of all the data entities in the database. The physical storage specification of these data entities are defined by the *internal schema*. The users' view of the database is specified by various *external schema* definitions. This model is also extended to distributed and multidatabase systems by the definition of a *global conceptual schema* (GCS) (Figure 2) in addition to the local schemas.

The differences in the level of autonomy between the multidatabase systems and distributed DBMSs is also reflected in their architectural models. In a distributed DBMS, the GCS defines the logical structure of all the data in all of the individual DBMSs. Thus, it is equal to the union of the local conceptual schemas. In a MDS, however, it is not even clear that the global conceptual schema is necessary. This question forms the basis of one dimension of our architectural discussions in this section. Even if one exists, it only defines the data that each DBMS is willing to make globally accessible. Thus, the GCS is only a subset of the union of the local conceptual schemas.

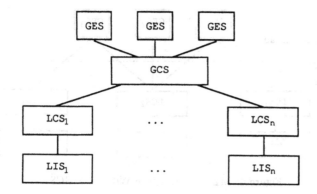

Figure 2: ANSI/SPARC Extension to Distributed DBMS

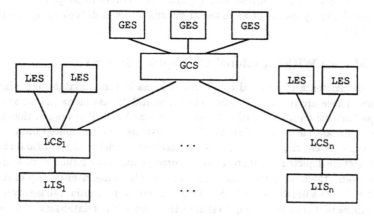

Figure 3: MDS Architecture with a GCS

3.1 MDS Models with Global Conceptual Schema

MDBS architecture that defines a global conceptual schema is depicted in Figure 3. Comparison of this figure with Figure 2 shows that they differ only in the definition of the local external schemas (LES) in addition to global external schemas. However, in addition to this, global conceptual schema design in multidatabase systems is significantly different than in the distributed database case. In the latter the mapping is from the global conceptual schema to the local onces. In the former, however, the mapping is in the reverse direction. As mentioned before, this is because the design in distributed database systems is usually a top-down process, whereas in multidatabase systems it is usually a bottom-up procedure. Furthermore, the GCS design in multidatabase systems involves the integration of either the local conceptual schemas or the local external schemas.

To access data from another database, there are two possible modes of operation, which we call *unilingual approach* and *multilingual approach*. The terms unilingual and multilingual are from the perspective of the MDMS, not the user. Unilingual systems (e.g., MULTIBASE [9]) require the user of one DBMS to define a global external view to a access another database. All of the global view definitions use a specific language supported by the MDMS for this purpose.

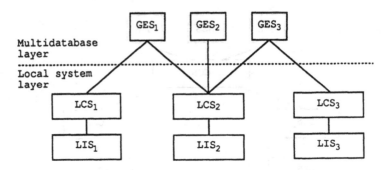

Figure 4: MDS Architecture Without a GCS

Multilingual architectures (e.g., Sirius-Delta [6] and the HD-DBMS project [4]) permit access to indicidual databases by means of an external schema which is defined using the language of the user's local DBMS.

3.2   MDS Models Without Global Conceptual Schema

The need for the existence of a global conceptual schema in a multidatabase system is a controversial issue. There are researchers who define a multidatabase management system as one which manages "several databases without a global schema" [10]. It is argued that the absence of a GCS is a significant advantage of multidatabase systems over distributed database systems.

One prototype system that has used this architectural model is the Multidatabase project [10]. The architecture depicted in Figure 4, which corresponds to the structure of Multidatabase, identifies two layers: the local system layer and the multidatabase layer on top of it. The local system layer consists of a number of DBMSs. They present to the multidatabase layer the part of their local database that they are willing to share with users of other databases. Above this layer, external views are constructed where each view may be defined on one local conceptual schema or on multiple conceptual schemas. Thus, the responsibility of providing access to multiple (and maybe heterogeneous) databases is delegated to the mapping between the external schemas and the local conceptual schemas. This is fundamentally different from architectural models that use a global conceptual schema, where this responsibility is taken over by the mapping between the global conceptual schema and the local ones.

This difference in responsibility has a practical consequence. If a global conceptual schema is defined, then the consistency rules of the global database can be specified according to this single definition. If a global conceptual schema does not exist, however, dependencies have to be defined between the various local conceptual schemas.

Federated database architectures do not use a global conceptual schema either. In the specific system described in [8], each local DBMS defines an *export schema*, which describes the data it is willing to make available to a specific user. Each application that accesses the global database does so by the definition of an *import schema*, which is simply a global external view.

3.3   Component Architecture

The fundamental feature of a MDMS design is the existence of full-fledged DBMSs, each of which manage a different database. The MDMS provides a layer of software that runs on top of these individual DBMSs and provides users with the facilities of accessing various databases (Figure 5). Depending upon the existence (or lack) of the global conceptual schema or the existence of heterogeneity (or lack of it), the contents of this layer of software would change significantly. In

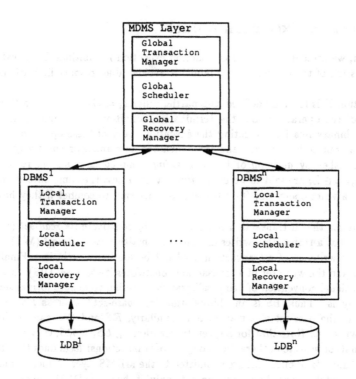

Figure 5: MDS Architecture

Figure 5, we concentrate only on those components that are necessary to execute transactions since that is our major emphasis in this paper. Note that Figure 5 represents a non-distributed MDMS. If the system is distributed, one would need to replicate the multidatabase layer to each site where there is a local DBMS that participates in the system.

Each of the DBMSs making up such a system has the functionality to receive user transactions, execute them to termination (either commit or abort) and then report the result to the user. In this context, the term "user" generically refers to interactive user requests as well as application programs issuing database access commands. Each DBMS has its own transaction processing components. These components consist of a transaction manager (called the *local transaction manager* or LTM), a *local scheduler* (LS) and a *local recovery manager* (LRM). This structure is quite common for centralized DBMSs (see, for example, [3]). The function of the LTM is to interface with the user and coordinate the atomic execution of the transactions. The local scheduler is responsible for ensuring the correct execution and interleaving of all transactions presented to the LTM. Finally, the local recovery manager ensures that the *local database* (LDB) contains all of the effects of committed transactions and none of the effects of uncommitted ones. Note that, without loss of generality, we assume that each autonomous DBMS manages a single database.

From the perspective of each DBMS, the MDMS layer is simply another "user" from which they receive transactions and present results. In fact, the only type of communication among the autonomous DBMSs is via the MDMS layer. The scheduling of global transactions, however, is done by the MDMS layer. The transaction manager of the MDMS layer is called the *global transaction manager* (GTM) since it manages the execution of global transactions.

4 Transaction Execution Model

In this section, we present a model of transaction execution in multidatabase systems. A more detailed discussion of the computational model is avoided due to space limitations, but can be found in [2].

A transaction T_i is formally defined as a partial order $T_i = \{\Sigma_i, \prec_i\}$ where Σ_i is the domain and consists of the operations and the termination condition of T_i, and $\prec_i$ is an irreflexive and transitive binary relation indicating the execution order of these operations. The possible operations of a transaction are *read* and *write*, denoted as r and w, respectively. A transaction can terminate either by *aborting* or by *committing*, denoted as a and c, respectively. Two operations $o_{ij}, o_{ik} \in \Sigma_i$ are said to be *conflicting* if they access the same data item and at least one of them is a write operation. Two transactions are said to conflict if they have conflicting operations.

The data items that a transaction reads are said to constitute its *read-set* (RS). Similarly, the data items that a transaction writes are said to constitute its *write-set* (WS). Note that the read-set and the write-set of a transaction need not be mutually exclusive. Finally, the union of the read-set and the write-set of a transaction constitutes its *base-set* (BS). In this paper, we adopt the notational convention of using calligraphic lettering to denote formal sets and roman fonts for acronyms. Thus, BS is an abbreviation for "base-set" whereas BS denotes the set of data items in the base-set of a transaction. Similarly, RS and WS can be defined for the read-set and write-set. Note that for a given transaction T_i, $BS_i = RS_i \cup WS_i$.

In a multidatabase system, there are two types of transactions: *local* ones that are submitted to each DBMS and *global* ones that are submitted to the MDMS layer. A local transaction is one that can be completely serviced by accessing data only at the single DBMS where the transaction is posed. Global transactions, on the other hand, are those that require access to more than one local database or need to be serviced by a DBMS which is not the same as the one where the transaction is posed. A local transaction is always submitted to one DBMS and is completely executed by that DBMS. Global and local transactions can be formally defined with respect to the data items that they access as well as their mode of operation.

Definition 1 *(Local transaction):* A transaction T_i submitted to DBMS j (denoted $DBMS^j$) is a *local transaction* (denoted LT_i^j) on $DBMS^j$ iff $BS_i \subseteq LDB^j$ where LDB^j is the local database managed by $DBMS^j$. □

We denote the set of all local transactions at $DBMS^j$ by $LT^j = \bigcup_i LT_i^j$. The set of all local transactions in a multidatabase system is $LT = \bigcup_j LT^j$.

Definition 2 *(Global transaction):* A transaction is a *global transaction* (GT_i) iff:

(i) $\nexists LDB^j$ such that $BS_i \subseteq LDB^j$ or

(ii) GT_i is submitted to $DBMS^k$ but $BS_i \subseteq LDB^r$ $(k \neq r)$. □

Item (i) states that global transactions submitted to the MDMS access data items stored in more than one database. Item (ii) represents the case where a user working on one DBMS requires access to the data stored and managed by another DBMS. We will also let GT be the set of all global transactions, i.e. $GT = \bigcup_i GT_i$.

A global transaction is parsed into set of *global subtransactions* which are subsequently submitted to the local DBMSs for execution. Thus, a global transaction is executed as a set of subtransactions that execute on a number of local DBMSs. We will define global subtransactions in terms of the data items that they reference (i.e. their base-set) with respect to the global transaction creating the subtransaction.

Definition 3 *(Global Subtransaction)* A global subtransaction submitted to $DBMS^j$ on behalf of a global transaction GT_i (denoted GST_i^j) is a transaction where:

(i) $\Sigma_i^j \subseteq \Sigma_i$, and

(ii) $BS_i^j \subseteq \mathcal{L}DB^j$ where BS_i^j is the base-set for GST_i^j. $\square$

Definition 3 implies that each global subtransaction executes at only one DBMS. Therefore, a global subtransaction can be seen as a local transaction by the DBMS to which it is submitted. To simplify the computational model, we further make the assumption that a global transaction may not submit more than one subtransaction to any single DBMS.

The set of all global subtransactions produced by a global transaction GT_i is denoted as $\mathcal{G}ST_i$. The set of all global subtransactions submitted to a particular local database $DBMS^k$ is denoted $\mathcal{G}ST^k$. Therefore, the set of all global subtransactions in a multidatabase system is $\mathcal{G}ST = \bigcup_i \mathcal{G}ST_i = \bigcup_k \mathcal{G}ST^k$.

The computational model can be summarized as follows. A global transaction that accesses non-local data is handled by the MDMS layer which partitions it into a set of global subtransactions. Each subtransaction is submitted to a local DBMS. Local DBMSs are responsible for the concurrent execution of both the global subtransactions and the local subtransactions submitted to them. The synchronization of the concurrent execution of the global transactions is the responsibility of the MDMS layer.

5 Conclusion

We have defined a classification scheme that has been found to be useful for the precise definition of concepts and terms related to multidatabase systems. We have also discussed the different architectural models that are possible within this classification scheme. Finally, we discussed a quite general computational model for multidatabase systems which emphasizes the execution of user transactions.

Implicit in this architecture and the accompanying computational model are certain assumptions about the system architecture and how users interact with the MDS. The following is a summary of these assumptions.

1. *Local Autonomy.* The individual DBMSs are assumed to be fully autonomous as defined in Section 1.

2. *Heterogeneity.* This model makes no assumptions about heterogeneity of the data models, user interfaces or the transaction management policies of the individual DBMSs. Heterogeneity is orthogonal to local autonomy which is the central aspect of our study.

3. *Subtransaction Decomposition.* The model assumes that a number of subtransactions execute on various databases on behalf of a global transaction. This raises the question about the feasibility of such a decomposition. Even though this is a legitimate and interesting research question, it is not one that we address in this research. Our position is that either such decomposition algorithms are available, or the global transaction model readily lends itself to the identification of individual subtransactions (e.g. the nested transaction model.)

4. *Data Replication.* The model does not consider data replication across multiple databases. This is a corollary of the way global subtransactions are defined (i.e. they execute at only one site).

5. *Value Dependence.* It is assumed that there are no value dependencies between data items that are stored in different databases. Integrity and consistency constraints are defined locally on each database. This is a direct consequence of the full local autonomy of individual DBMSs.

6. *Multiple Subtransactions.* A global transaction can not submit multiple global subtransactions to a single DBMS. This restriction should not be too confining since the global subtransactions can, in general, be created so that only one subtransaction is required per local DBMS.

We have used the computational model discussed here in developing global scheduling algorithms [2]. The model has also been extended to include reliability and recoverability of multidatabase systems [1].

References

[1] K. Barker and M.T. Özsu. Reliability and recoverability of transactions in multidatabase systems. Technical Report TR90-10, Department of Computing Science, University of Alberta, Edmonton, Canada, April 1990.

[2] K. Barker and M.T. Özsu. Concurrent transaction execution in multidatabase systems. In *Proc. COMPSAC90 - The 14th. Annual Int. Computer Software and Applications Conference*, October 1990 (in print).

[3] P.A. Bernstein, V. Hadzilacos, and N. Goodman. *Concurrency Control and Recovery in Database Systems*. Addison Wesley, Reading, MA, 1987.

[4] A.F. Cardenas. Heterogeneous distributed database management: HD-DBMS. *Proceedings of the IEEE*, 75(5):588–600, May 1987.

[5] W. Du and A.K. Elmagarmid. Quasi serializability: a correctness criterion for global concurrency control in InterBase. *Proc. 15th International Conference on Very Large Databases*, pages 347–355, August 1989.

[6] A. Ferrier and C. Stangret. Heterogeneity in the distributed data management system SIRIUS-DELTA. In *Proc. 8th International Conference on Very Large Databases*, pages 45–53, 1982.

[7] V. Gligor and R. Popescu-Zeletin. Transaction management in distributed heterogeneous database management systems. *Information Systems*, 11(4):287–297, 1986.

[8] D. Heimbigner and D. McLeod. A federated architecture for information systems. *ACM Transactions on Office Information Systems*, 3(3):253–278, July 1985.

[9] T. Landers and R.L. Rosenberg. An overview of MULTIBASE. In H.-J. Schneider, editor, *Distributed Data Bases*, pages 153–184. North-Holland, 1982.

[10] W. Litwin. From database systems to multidatabase systems: Why and how. In *Proc. British National Conference on Databases (BNCOD)*, pages 161–188, 1988.

[11] M.T. Özsu and P. Valduriez. *Principles of Distributed Database Systems*. Prentice-Hall, 1990 (in print).

[12] M. Rusinkiewicz, R. Elmasri, B. Czejdo, D. Georgakopulos, G. Karabatis, A. Jamoussi, K. Loa, and Y. Li. Query processing in a heterogeneous multidatabase environment. In *Proc. 1st Annual Symp. Parallel and Dist. Comp.*, pages 162–169, 1989.

[13] J.M. Smith, P.A. Bernstein, U. Dayal, N. Goodman, T. Landers, K. Lin, and E. Wong. MULTIBASE – Integrating heterogeneous distributed database systems. In *Proc. National Computer Conference*, pages 487–499, 1981.

[14] D. Tsichritzis and A. Klug. The ANSI/X3/SPARC DBMS framework report of the study group on database management systems. *Information Systems*, 1:173–191, 1978.

Semantic Query Optimization in Distributed Databases

H.J.A. van Kuijk   F.H.E. Pijpers   P.M.G. Apers

University of Twente
P.O. Box 217, 7500 AE Enschede
The Netherlands
E-mail : vankuyk@cs.utwente.nl

Abstract

In this paper, semantic query optimization in distributed database systems is
translated into a multilevel search process. The overall search process is decomposed
in two main stages: (1) guided by the syntactic complexity of a query expression,
search for an appropriate optimization strategy, (2) given this strategy, transform
the query expression into an efficient distributed query evaluation plan. During the
second stage, properties of the application being modeled are used to attack a number of problems: detecting inconsistent and redundant selection and join conditions,
estimating intermediate and final results, defining and using fragmentation knowledge. An extensible knowledge-based architecture is described to accommodate a
variety of existing and future optimization techniques.

1   Introduction

The last decade has shown a rapid development of both computer hardware and database
technology that have imposed new dimensions to the problem of query optimization
in database systems. In this paper, the impact on query optimization of distributed
databases, semantic transformation techniques, and extensible databases is considered.

Informally, query optimization is defined as the problem of finding the most efficient
query evaluation plan (QEP) for a query expression. Because this search problem is
NP-hard [Hevn 79], an exhaustive search is impossible or undesirable. To keep the costs
of query optimization within limits, the search process should be guided by powerful
heuristics. As a consequence, the resulting QEP is not guaranteed the most efficient one.

A survey of query optimization problems and techniques can be found in [Grae 89].
Although there are earlier papers, Hammer [Hamm 80] and King [King 81] are considered
to have introduced a technique called *semantic query optimization*. The fundamental idea
is to use properties of the application being modeled to guide the search for efficient QEPs.
The trend towards the distribution of computing power over the sites of a computer
network has resulted in distributed database systems. The need for communication
among sites to complete the evaluation of distributed queries imposes another dimension
to the problem of query optimization [Ceri 84]. Future database applications will require
extensible database systems. The possibility and necessity to define new operators and

access mechanisms requires *extensible* query optimizers [Osbo 88]. Rule-based techniques are recognized to allow the realization of flexible extensible query optimizers [Frey 87].

Our approach to a potentially large and complex search space is a decomposition of the problem into a number of smaller subproblems. This has resulted in an extensible set of basic query optimization techniques. Upon receiving a query, the query optimizer must search for an appropriate combination of some of these basic techniques to arrive at an efficient distributed schedule.

It is important to keep a sound balance between the optimization costs and the expected resulting improvement in evaluation costs [Shek 88]. We have divided the overall problem of query optimization in two main stages. During the classification stage, a query is analyzed and classified according to its syntactic complexity. The properties of the query are used to generate a set of candidate optimization *strategies*. During the transformation stage, the most promising strategy is used to transform the query into an efficient distributed schedule. Our classification schema produces optimization strategies that are tuned to the syntactic complexity of the queries. During query transformation, application knowledge in the form of a hierarchy of state constraints and functional dependencies is used to attack a number of problems: detecting unsatisfiable and redundant selection and join conditions, estimating intermediate and final results, defining and using fragmentation knowledge.

In our research we kept a strict separation between the optimization techniques and the knowledge-based realization of the query optimizer. Most query optimization knowledge translates quite naturally into a rule-based paradigm [Frey 87]. Our extensible set of basic optimization techniques allows a potentially large and growing set of rules to be partitioned into a number of well-defined modules. Instead of searching a large rule base, the query optimizer can concentrate upon a single module containing a relatively small set of rules relevant to the problem to be solved. We have adopted an extensible, knowledge-based architecture with an object-oriented flavor to accommodate a variety of existing and future query optimization techniques.

The rest of this paper is organized as follows. In Section 2, our approach to semantic query optimization in distributed database systems is presented. In Section 3, the architecture of our knowledge-based query optimizer is discussed. Finally, in Section 4 some conclusions and extensions are given.

2 Multilevel Query Optimization

A database system consists of a *database* and a *database management system* (DBMS). A database is a collection of logically coherent data with an intended meaning. The DBMS provides an interface between the users of the system and the stored database. The users communicate with the DBMS in some formal query language.

The DBMS is responsible for the efficient evaluation of queries against the stored database. The problem of query processing is divided into three phases.

Phase 1 : query parsing.

Phase 2 : query optimization.

Phase 3 : query evaluation.

The *query optimizer* is a component of the DBMS that is responsible for the transformation of queries into efficient schedules. Within this context, the rest of this section is organized as follows. In Subsection 2.1, our approach to query optimization is presented. In Subsection 2.2, the classification of algebraic query expressions is explained. Finally, in Subsection 2.3, the process of query transformation is described.

2.1 Query Optimization

For each query, there exists a set of semantically equivalent, but syntactically different expressions. The query optimizer should be able to find the expression that is expected to result in the most efficient schedule. The overall problem of query optimization is defined as the following search problem.

> *Given a query expression, a database state, and the database system characteristics, search for the most efficient schedule.*

Query optimization is known to be NP-hard [Hevn 79]. The search process should therefore be guided by powerful heuristics. The search problem is hampered further by the lack of a well-defined goal state. This means that weak search methods like the A^*-algorithm are useless. A consequence of the fact that most of the heuristics that are used during query optimization are non-admissible is that the resulting schedules are not guaranteed the most efficient ones [Pearl 84].

We think it is important to keep a sound balance between the costs of query optimization and the expected improvement in evaluation costs. An exhaustive search for the most efficient schedule is impossible or undesirable. Our approach to attack a large and complex search space is twofold. First, we have assembled a set of basic query optimization techniques. This allows a particular optimization problem to be decomposed into basic subproblems. Second, we distinguish a number of stages in the overall search problem.

Stage 1 : preprocessing query expressions.

Stage 2 : classifying query expressions.

Stage 3 : transforming query expressions.

Upon receiving a query from one of the parsers, during Stage 1 this query is transformed into an equivalent algebraic expression without views. During Stage 2, the algebraic expression is analyzed and classified according to its syntactic complexity. The syntactic properties are used to generate a set of candidate query optimization strategies, one of which is selected. A strategy is tuned to a particular class of expressions. Depending on this class, only a relevant subset of basic techniques is needed to solve the optimization problem at hand. For example, it is useless to address the problem of determining an efficient join sequence in case of a selection operation on a single operand relation. During Stage 3, the selected optimization strategy is used to transform the query into an efficient distributed schedule. Our three stages are shown in Figure 1.

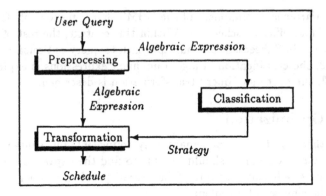

Figure 1: Our approach to query optimization

2.2 Classifying Query Expressions

The starting point of the classification process is an algebraic expression involving only
(global) relations. The algebraic expression is analyzed to obtain a number of syntactic
properties that can be used to guide the search for an efficient schedule.

The following syntactic properties are important: the number of (global) operand
relations, the set of relational operators appearing in the algebraic expression, and the
type of fragmentation in case of distributed relations. Our main classification criterion
is the number of (global) operand relations.

Class 1 : expressions with one relation.

Class 2 : expressions with two relations.

Class 3 : expressions with more than two relations.

Our classification schema is motivated by the fact that we expect the majority of the
algebraic expressions to be of Class 1 or Class 2. In the context of a sound balance between
optimization costs and benefits, we think it is appropriate to pay some extra attention
to these two classes. However, the classification schema could be made application-
dependent.

Given the syntactic properties of an algebraic expression, the query optimizer generates an appropriate optimization strategy. Because of the classification data, only
relevant optimization techniques are considered. An optimization strategy covers an entire class of algebraic expressions. During the transformation stage, the strategy is used
to guide the transformation process resulting in an efficient schedule.

2.3 Transforming Query Expressions

Having generated an optimization strategy, the actual query transformation process can
be done. In our approach, properties of the application being modeled are used to attack
the following problems that must be solved during query optimization [Kuijk 89]:

- detecting unsatisfiable and redundant selection and join conditions;

$$
\begin{aligned}
TC_{\sigma_F(r(R))} &= TC_R \wedge F. \\
TC_{\pi_A(r(R))} &= TC_R[A]. \\
TC_{r(R) \cup r(S)} &= TC_R \vee TC_S. \\
TC_{r(R) - r(S)} &= TC_R. \\
TC_{r(R) \cap r(S)} &= TC_R \wedge TC_S. \\
TC_{r(R) \times r(S)} &= DC[R, S]. \\
TC_{r(R) \bowtie_F r(S)} &= DC[R, S] \wedge F.
\end{aligned}
$$

Table 1: Constraints and operators

- estimating intermediate and final results;

- defining and using fragmentation knowledge.

During database design, application knowledge in the form of state constraints is used to define a universe of legal database states. For this knowledge to be applicable, the query optimizer uses a suitable representation and application formalism based on a hierarchy of state constraints: attribute constraints (AC), tuple constraints (TC), relation constraints (RC), and database constraints (DC) [Kuijk 88]. Given a relational operation and the state constraints on its operand relation(s), the state constraints on the relation resulting from this operation can be derived (see Table 1). As an example, consider a Join operation. The tuple constraint on the result relation consists of the the the conjunction of the database constraint projected on the attributes of schemas of the operands and the join condition, $TC_{R \times S} = TC_R \wedge TC_S \wedge DC_{R,S}$.

State constraints can only influence a query by manipulating its selection and join conditions (if it has any). State constraints must be satisified by every database state (in fact they are used in defining the set of permissible database states). They can therefore be used to expand selection and join conditions. Because of our hierarchy, the relevant state constraints are retrieved from the data dictionary of the database system without the need for an expensive inference process. The constraint formalism allows the detection of unsatisfiable and redundant selection and join conditions. Because unsatisfiable conditions define empty relations, the search for efficient schedules can be simplified. Selection and join conditions are minimized to avoid unnecessary test during query evaluation.

Example 1 Given the small example database of Appendix A, consider a selection operation on the global relation E.

$Q_0 = \sigma_F(E)$.

$Q_1 = \sigma_F(E_1 \cup E_2 \cup E_3)$.

$Q_2 = \sigma_F(E_1) \cup \sigma_F(E_2) \cup \sigma_F(E_3)$.

$Q_3 = \sigma_{F \wedge TC_{E_1}}(E_1) \cup \sigma_{F \wedge TC_{E_2}}(E_2) \cup \sigma_{F \wedge TC_{E_3}}(E_3)$.

Suppose we need all employees with a number less than 1500. This translates into the selection condition: $F = (enum < 1500)$. Because $TC_{E_1} \rightarrow F$, all tuples of E_1 will satisfy F. Because $TC_{E_3} \wedge F \equiv \square$, none of the tuples of E_3 will satisfy F. The original query is thus transformed into $Q_4 = E_1 \cup \sigma_F(E_2)$. □

Traditional estimation techniques are hampered by the assumptions of independent attributes and a uniform distribution of attribute values. In our approach, state constraints are used to arrive at more accurate estimates of intermediate and final results. Tuple constraints define a restriction on the Cartesian product of attribute values. They can therefore be used to arrive at more accurate estimates [Kuijk 89]. Functional dependencies are used to arrive at more accurate estimates of selectivities. Histogram-based techniques can be used to alleviate the restriction of uniform distributions of attribute values.

In our approach, fragments are defined by algebraic expressions involving a number of unary operations on a single global relation (horizontal, vertical, and mixed fragmentation). Given the state constraints on the global relation, the rules of Table 1, and the algebraic expressions defining the fragments, the state constraints on the individual fragments are constructed. These state constraints are again used to arrive at more efficient schedules. Given the state constraints on the global global relation and the state constraints on its fragments, the constraint facility can validate the fragmentation design (completeness and disjointness) [Ceri 84].

Example 2 Given the database of Appendix A, consider a request for the cities of the departments having employees with a number less that 1500 and earning more than \$40.000.

$$Q_0 = \pi_A(\sigma_F(E \bowtie_G D)).$$
$$A = city.$$
$$F = ((enum < 1500) \wedge (sal > 40.000)).$$
$$G = (dept = dnum).$$

Q_0 is an expression of Class 2 involving the set $\{\pi, \sigma, \bowtie\}$ of relational operators and two horizontally fragmented relations the reconstruction of which results in a number of additional union operations.

$$Q_1 = \pi_A (\sigma_F(E_1 \cup E_2 \cup E_3) \bowtie_G$$
$$(D_1 \cup D_2 \cup D_3)).$$
$$Q_2 = \pi_A ((\sigma_F(E_1) \cup \sigma_F(E_2) \cup \sigma_F(E_3)) \bowtie_G$$
$$(D_1 \cup D_2 \cup D_3)).$$

Combining selection conditions and tuple constraints indicates that only E_2 can have tuples that may satisfy the selection condition F.

$$Q_3 = \pi_A(\sigma_F(E_2) \bowtie_G (D_1 \cup D_2 \cup D_3))$$

Our constraint facility enables the query optimizer to derive the tuple constraint on the relation schema of the relation resulting from Q_3.

$$TC_{Q_3} = F \wedge G \wedge TC_{E_2} \wedge (TC_{D_1} \vee TC_{D_2} \vee TC_{D_3}).$$
$$= ((enum > 1000) \wedge (enum < 1500) \wedge$$
$$(dept = 2) \wedge (dept = dnum) \wedge (dnum = 2)$$
$$\wedge(sal > 20.000) \wedge (sal < 40.000)).$$

The constraint facility generates the condition $(dnum = 2)$ (transitivity). This new selection condition allows Q_3 to be simplified because only fragment D_2 is useful.

$$Q_4 = \pi_A(\sigma_F(E_2) \bowtie_G D_2).$$

The fragment E_2, and thereby the join operation, has become superfluous because none of its attributes contribute to the result relation.

$$E_5 = \pi_A(D_2).$$

Because $TC_{Q_3} = (dnum = 2)$, and $dnum$ functionally determines $city$, the cardinality of the relation resulting from the original query Q_0 is 1. □

3 A Knowledge-Based Approach

In this section, the architecture of our knowledge-based query optimizer is described. We have adopted a rule-based paradigm to represent our query optimization techniques. Basically, there are three problems with rule-based query optimizers. First, searching a large rule base for the tranformation rules that are appropriate to a particular situation may cause the optimizer to be unaccepatbly slow. Second, the necessity to handle *commutative* rules, such as $\sigma_F(R \cup S) \leftrightarrow \sigma_F(R) \cup \sigma_F(S)$, causes additional overhead to prevent the system from looping. Third, although a rule-based paradigm is advertized to be highly modular the modification of the rule base may cause unexpected side-effects.

We have assembled an extensible set of basic query optimization techniques. Each technique is represented by a relatively small well-defined module of rules. As a result of a classification process, an optimization strategy specifies *when* to use *what* basic optimization technique. Instead of searching a large rule base, the strategy identifies a relatively small module of rules to solve a particular optimization problem. We solved the problem of commutative rules by not allowing them within the same module. The effect of modifying optimization techniques is limited to their particular modules of rules.

We have adopted an extensible architecture with an object-oriented flavor. The query optimizer consists of a system of instances (objects) of a class *rule-based system*. An instance of this class is a small rule-based system the main components of which are an interface, an inference mechanism, and a relatively small rule base. The rule base of an individual object represents a module of rules that is tuned to solve a well-defined subproblem. The individual objects communicate by means of a collection of predefined messages (methods). The implementation details of the objects are invisible to the outside world (encapsulation).

Upon receiving a query from one of the parsers, a master object initiates the optimization process. As described in Section 2, a strategy represents a decomposition of an optimization problem into a number of well-defined subproblems. The dedicated objects are then requested to solve such a subproblem. At the end of the optimization process, the master object delivers an efficient distributed schedule. A distributed environment provides the possibility of exploiting *horizontal* and *vertical parallelism*.

4 Conclusions and Extensions

This paper describes our approach to semantic query optimization in in distributed database systems. We identify query optimization as a search problem. Our approach to this search problem is twofold. First, we assembled an extensible set of basic optimization techniques. Each of these techniques is tuned to solve a particular subproblem. Second, we developed a multilevel search method to attack the potentially large and complex search spaces.

Upon receiving a query, the expression is analyzed and classified according to its syntactic properties. Given these properties, the optimizer searches for an efficient optimization strategy in terms of our basic optimization techniques. This strategy is used to transform the query into an efficient distributed schedule. During the transformation stage, properties of the application in the form of a hierarchy of state constraints and functional dependencies is used to attack a number of problems: detecting unsatisfiable and redundant selection and join conditions, estimating intermediate and final results, defining and using fragmentation knowledge.

We have developed an extensible knowledge-based query optimizer with an object-oriented flavor. The knowledge representation paradigm consists of a combination of production rules and frames. The extensible set of basic optimization techniques enables a partitioning of the large and growing knowledge base into a number of modules. Our query optimizer consists of a number of objects each of which represents a small rule-based system. Each object has the tranformation rules to solve a particular subproblem.

We are inverstigating a number of extensions. New optimization techniques should be characterized and added to the existing repertoire. An interesting extensions concerns the incorporation of techniques to optimize recursive queries. Our classification schema is being adjusted to enable a discrimination between recursive queries and nonrecursive queries.

A   Example Database

In this appendix, a relational database is defined. Let $RS = \{DEPT,\ EMP\}$ be a set of relation schemas where the relation schemas $DEPT$ and EMP are defined as follows:

$DEPT$ (_dnum_, _dname_, _city_)
EMP (_enum_, _ename_, _dept_, _sal_)

In the examples of Section 2, the relation names are abbreviated. A relational database schema is defined as a 2-tuple $DBS = \langle RS, IC \rangle$, where RS is the set of relation schemas and IC is a finite set of integrity constraints:

$TC_{DEPT} = ((dnum > 0) \wedge (dnum \leq 3))$.
$TC_{EMP} = ((enum > 0) \wedge (enum \leq 3000) \wedge (dept > 0) \wedge (dept \leq 3) \wedge$
$\qquad (sal > 0) \wedge (sal \leq 75.000))$.

The relations defined by $DEPT$ and EMP are both partitioned into three horizontal fragments:

$DEPT = DEPT_1 \cup DEPT_2 \cup DEPT_3$.
$EMP\ = EMP_1 \cup EMP_2 \cup EMP_3$.

The tuple constraints defining the fragments are derived from the tuple constraints TC_{DEPT} and TC_{EMP}:

$TC_{DEPT_1} = (dnum = 1)$.
$TC_{DEPT_2} = (dnum = 2)$.
$TC_{DEPT_3} = (dnum = 3)$.

$TC_{EMP_1}\ = ((enum > 0) \wedge (enum \leq 1000) \wedge (dept = 1) \wedge$
$\qquad (sal > 0) \wedge (sal \leq 25.000))$.
$TC_{EMP_2}\ = ((enum > 1000) \wedge (enum \leq 2000) \wedge (dept = 2) \wedge$
$\qquad (sal > 20.000) \wedge (sal \leq 50.000))$.
$TC_{EMP_3}\ = ((enum > 2000) \wedge (enum \leq 3000) \wedge (dept = 3) \wedge$
$\qquad (sal > 40.000) \wedge (sal \leq 75.000))$.

References

[Ceri 84]   S. Ceri and G. Pelagatti, *Distributed Databases: Principles and Systems*, McGraw-Hill, Inc., New York, (1984).

[Chak 88]   U.S. Chakravarthy, J. Grant, and J. Minker, "Foundations of Semantic Query Optimizations for Deductive Databases," *Foundations of Deductive Databases and Logic Programming*, pp. 243-273, Morgan-Kaufman, Los Altos, California, (1988).

[Frey 87]   J.C. Freytag, "A Rule-Based View of Query Optimization," *Proceedings of the ACM-SIGMOD Conference*, pp. 172-180, (1987).

[Grae 89]   G. Graefe, "Research Problems in Database Query Optimization," *Proceedings of the ODBF Workshop on Database Query Optimization*, pp. 1-11, May, (1989).

[Hamm 80] M. Hammer and S.B. Zdonik, "Knowledge-Based Query Processing," *Proceedings of the 6th International Conference on Very Large Databases*, pp. 137-146, (1980).

[Hevn 79]   A.R. Hevner, "The Optimization of Query Processing on Distributed Database Systems," PhD Thesis, Purdue University, (1979).

[King 81]   J.J. King, "QUIST: A System for Semantic Query Optimization in Relational Databases," *Proceedings of the 7th International Conference on Very Large Databases*, pp. 510-517, (1981).

[Kuijk 88] H.J.A. van Kuijk and P.M.G. Apers, "The application of Constraints in Query Optimization," Internal Report INF 88-55, University of Twente.

[Kuijk 89] H.J.A. van Kuijk and P.M.G. Apers, "Semantic Query Optimization in Distributed Database: A Knowledge-Based Approach," *Proceedings of the ODBF Workshop on Database Query Optimization*, pp. 53-58, May, (1989).

[Morg 84]   M. Morgenstern, "The Role of Constraints in Databases, Expert Systems, and Knowledge Representation," *Proceedings of the 1st International Workshop on Expert Database Systems*, pp. 207-223, (1984).

[Osbo 88]   S. Osborn, "Identity, Equality, and Query Optimization," *Advances in Object-Oriented Database Systems*, pp. 346-351, Springer-Verlag, New York, (1988).

[Pearl 84] J. Pearl, *Heuristics: Intelligent Search Strategies for Computer Problem Solving*, Addison-Wesley, Inc., Reading, Massachusetts, (1984).

[Shek 88]   S. Shekhar, J. Srivastava, and S. Dutta, "A Formal Model of Trade-off between Optimization and Execution Costs in Semantic Query Optimization," *Proceedings of the 14th International Conference on Very Large Databases*, pp. 457-467, (1988).

[Shen 87]   S.T. Shenoy and Z.M. Ozsoyoglu, "A System for Semantic Query Optimization," *Proceedings of the ACM-SIGMOD Conference*, pp. 181-195, (1987).

An Architecture for a Multimedia Database Management System Supporting Content Search

Vincent Y. Lum
Naval Postgraduate School
Department of Computer Science
Monterey, CA 93943, U.S.A.

Klaus Meyer-Wegener
Universitaet Erlangen-Nuernberg
IMMD VI
Martensstr. 3, 8520 Erlangen, West Germany

Abstract

Advanced applications frequently require the management of multimedia data like text, images, graphics, sound, etc. While it is practical for today's computers to store these types of data, managing them requires the search of them based on their contents. Database management systems should be extended to organize these new types of data and to enable content search. However, the complexity of the contents and their semantics makes content search of these data a very difficult problem. This paper proposes to have multimedia data accompanied by natural language descriptions that will be used for content search of these data. A parser is used to interpret the descriptions and to later match them semantically with queries. Implications and difficulties of such an approach are discussed.

1. Introduction

Many advanced applications like simulators, office automation, classroom teaching, etc. require the use of multimedia or media data such as text, images, graphics, sounds, videos, etc. To be effective, content search of these data must be available. Lack of such capability frequently forces the users to rely on the use of hard copies as an alternative. Such is the case, for example, when a police department keeps hard copy photos or mugshots for witnesses to browse through when a crime has been committed. Current technology allows us to store the images in the computer. However, without an effective means to perform content search, hardly any advantage can be gained from that.

Content search of the traditional alphanumerical data is taken for granted; content search of multimedia data is not only difficult, but has hardly been discussed anywhere. The difficulty lies in the complexity of the contents and the semantics associated with any media data. Whereas in the alphanumerical data, the semantics is very restricted, in the media data the semantics is almost unbounded.

Proposals to extend the database management systems (DBMS) to handle media data are not new. As early as the 70s, proposals were made to include pictures in databases [CK81].

This research was supported by Direct Funding with external sponsor NOSC

Broader recognition of the need of media data came later in the early 80s when office automation became a prime target [Ch86, BRG88]. All these works, however, were designed for specific application areas and are not generally extensible. In recent years, development of systems to support media data became more intensive. For example, MUSE (MUlti SEnsory Information Management System) [WK87] is designed to provide operations on multimedia data as well as the traditional data. Their approach is to have an object-oriented system for this purpose [WK87, BKK88]. In a different environment, multimedia data is handled in hypertext and hypermedia systems. Here, however, the data is not stored in a DBMS environment. In all of the above works, none addresses the problem of content search of the media data.

The old saying of "a picture is worth a thousand words" provides us a hint how to do content search in media data. It is strongly believed that automatic recognition of the contents of media data is not only impossible in today's state of the art, but quite possibly remains the same for the foreseeable future. Recognition of contents of media data requires a very sophisticated knowledge and frequently the experiences of the individuals. Moreover, often contents of media data are not explicitly included in the data itself. For example, in a book a picture containing mainly a gun turret being fired is described with the caption "The USS Enterprise firing at enemy aircraft off the coast of Saigon during the Vietnam War in 1959". It is not possible at all to know that the guns are firing at aircrafts as the picture contains no aircraft. Nor can the location be determined although there is water around.

We dismiss the approach of using keywords for the description of media data contents as done in library information retrieval systems, because it is too imprecise. Instead, we need a method to link the keywords in a complex manner as in prose for the users to state the contents of a media object and to specify their intentions in queries.

It is understood that *natural language descriptions* are also imprecise and their understanding is difficult. However, it is believed that descriptions can be given in caption form, as normally done with pictures and illustrations in books. A restriction of the natural language to a small subset is thought to be quite sufficient. Moreover, applications themselves automatically restrict the domain of discourse, which provides further relief. Studies in natural language understanding have a long history and have demonstrated sufficient success to make the proposed technique workable [Al87, Mi75, Sc75, SR81].

We therefore propose that media data with content descriptions is to be incorporated into a DBMS as abstract data types. We define operations on these data which are incorporated into an existing high-level query language. We shall call systems with such an interface *multimedia database management systems* (MDBMS). In the following sections, we shall discuss how to manage the media data, how to make use of natural language for the descriptions of the media data contents and the implications that come with such an approach, what new data structures are needed to manage the description information for efficient retrieval, and what to do for the architecture of such a system.

2. Multimedia Data Object Management

Media data, as in alphanumeric data, in itself is a bit string which we call the *raw data*. However, unlike alphanumeric data, media data invariably comes with *registration data* that is required for the interpretation of the raw data. For example, the raw data of an image cannot be displayed without knowing the registration data like pixel depth (bits per pixel), height, width, colormap, etc. Similarly, the raw data of a sound recording cannot be interpreted without knowing the sampling rate and compression method used in the input process.

Registration data can also include additional information that is needed to identify media data, e.g. date and time of capture.

In addition to raw data and registration data, we propose to include *description data* with each instance of media data. As said before, the description data is a text in natural language, although a subset of it. The triplet of raw data, registration data, and description data as a whole will be treated as an instance of media data as shown in Figure 1. Although each instance of a media data is composed of three parts, this fact is transparent to the users.

At this time it is appropriate to examine how media data is to be fitted into a data model. The best approach seems to be treating media data as different types as in the concept of abstract data types (ADT) [LM88, MLW89], a method also given in [Ta80] and [Gr84]. Thus the data like IMAGE, SOUND, GRAPHICS, SIGNAL, etc. would each be a different type and have different operations associated with them. For example, operations for the IMAGE data type may include enlarging and shrinking of the images, subsetting a section, retrieving, editing or entering the description data or the registration data, etc. A set of these operations on IMAGE data has been defined [LM88, MLW89]; a similar set for SOUND has been defined, too [Sa88]. It is believed that a certain set of operations would be adequate only when substantial experience of using that data type has been acquired. Even then one is expected to add new operations from time to time as the need arises.

Before we proceed to illustrate how the media data operations are to be used, let us illustrate how the data type IMAGE can be used in an MDBMS. Without loss of generality, we shall use image data for illustration purpose. Further, we shall use the relational data model for embedding the ADT concepts, although any data model would do.

The new data types can be used as attribute domains. The simple case of having an attribute of IMAGE data type is a relation OBJECT (e.g. PERSON) with an attribute O_IMAGE (the PHOTO of a person) in the schema OBJECT (O_ID, ..., O_IMAGE). In the case where multiple images exists for a given object, the schema would become

OBJECT (O_ID, ...)
OBJECT_IMAGE (O_ID, O_IMAGE)

The most general kind would be the case in which, for a given object, there are many images, and a particular image may show several objects. Such is the case that a car may appear in many pictures and a given picture may have many cars. In this case, the schema would have to be something like:

OBJECT (O_ID, ...)
IMAGE_OBJECT (I_ID, I_IMAGE)
IS_SHOWN_ON (O_ID, I_ID, ...)

Figure 2 illustrates these three schemas.

To use such a system, the operations for the ADT must be included in the query language of the system. Again without loss of generality, we consider as an example the way the relational query language SQL is being extended.

First we observe that abstract data type operations are functions. The function

CONSTRUCT_IMAGE (height, width, pixel-depth, encoding, colormap length,
colormap-depth, colormap, pixel-matrix)

produces a transient value of type IMAGE that cannot be assigned to a program variable, but can only be used in INSERT and UPDATE statements of the query language. Thus we can have, for instance,

```
INSERT (2233, CONSTRUCT_IMAGE ($ht, $wd, 24, IHS_NO_COLORMAP, 0, ...)
INTO IMAGE_OBJECT;

UPDATE IMAGE_OBJECT
SET I_IMAGE = CONSTRUCT_IMAGE ($height, $width, $depth,
                               RGB_COLORMAP, 256, ...)
WHERE I_ID = 1122;
```

where $ represents program variables and parameters with only capital letters indicate named constants. Retrieving attribute values of type IMAGE from the database into program variables uses another set of functions like

```
HEIGHT (IMAGE attribute) : integer;
WIDTH (IMAGE attribute) : integer;
ENCODING (IMAGE attribute) : encoding-type;
     etc.
```

Each function naturally has a specific output type and different functions can be defined to produce different output types for an IMAGE attribute. A query using these functions may look like

```
SELECT HEIGHT (I_IMAGE), WIDTH (I_IMAGE), DEPTH (I_IMAGE)
INTO $yrange, $xrange, $dep
FROM IMAGE_OBJECT
WHERE I_ID = 3344;
```

Consider the case of a PERSON relation with attribute PHOTO of type IMAGE. The query

```
SELECT P_ID
FROM PERSON
WHERE CONTAINS (PHOTO, "large, beady eyes and banana nose with
                       a big scar on the left chin")
```

will retrieve all the tuples in the PERSON relation where the descriptions of the PHOTO media instances match the specified description in the query. Again, as before, CONTAINS is an operation defined for the ADT for processing descriptions. It will return a boolean value indicating whether the stored description matches the query phrase or not. A more detailed description of the ADT and its operations is given in [MLW89].

3. Structures to Support Content Search

As stated earlier, we propose to perform content search on media data by matching the natural language descriptions with the query specifications. However, if a string-match of the query specification and the natural language descriptions is used, hardly any media data would satisfy any query, regardless of what is stored. This happens because in natural language there are many words with the same meaning and there are many ways to say the same thing. Different users will describe and query information differently. In fact, even the same user is likely to describe things differently at different times. We must find ways to solve this problem. We observe that a description data satisfies a query specification when the former logically implies the latter. The system must process data in this manner.

To be able to understand natural language descriptions, whether in the description data or in the queries, a *parser* is needed. The parser uses a *dictionary* or lexicon to perform parsing which holds a vocabulary along with the parts of speech information. Synonymous information also is defined there. Later we will see that other kind of information is included as well. We regard the dictionary to be the place where all knowledge is deposited for the system.

Although it is suggested that descriptions are to be defined with the use of a natural language, we do not intend to use the natural language descriptions themselves for query processing. From the different ways of representing their semantics, we have chosen *first order predicate calculus* to be the formal representation of the descriptions. This selection is preferred because of the broad capability of predicate calculus and because other methods, when enhanced to become more formal, tend to be similar to logic [So88]. Further, predicates can be processed with logic programming languages like Prolog, which we shall use for processing queries.

Thus, the parser translates the text descriptions into a set of predicates. It uses the dictionary extensively to select the appropriate set of predicates on the basis of the syntax and the semantics in the descriptions as generally done in any natural language understanding [Al87]. As a word in English can be in more than one part of the speech, such as the case of the word "can", the parser must attempt to select the most appropriate interpretation for any given sentence. In other cases, several words may have the same meaning and they may be represented in a canonical form. For example, area, territory, region, section, etc. may all be translated into area in the predicates if these words take on the same meaning.

It is proper at this time for us to illustrate how predicates are derived. Consider the sentence "a car manufactured by Horch in 1922". The predicates derived from this are: car(x), manufacturer(x,Horch), year-built(x,1922). The parser uses an artificial name, x, to connect different predicates that state the properties of the same object. This is exactly what is needed by Prolog to process predicates to qualify objects. Query phrases are translated in the same way, only that variables are used instead of artificial names. If a binding of those variables to object names can be found by Prolog, the descriptions logically imply the query and thus the media object contents matches.

With synonymous definitions in the dictionary, certain variances of natural language descriptions can be transformed into the same set of predicates. However, because there is a great variety of ways a user can describe the same thing, more information would be needed for different descriptions to be considered synonymous. For example, one person may enter into a description "a red car" and another user may ask for "a car with a red body". By most standards, these two ways of specification should be considered the same. But it would be very difficult for the parser to recognize this without additional help.

To overcome problems of this kind, *rules* can be included in the dictionary. Thus, in our example, the rule would be included as follows:

if car(A), component (A,B), body (B), color (B,C)
then color (A,C);

The parser can use this rule to detect the matching. Other uses of the rules include the specification of default options. For example, one may want to tell the parser that French always drink wine with dinner. The parser can use this knowledge even when no explicit description is given on this topic for matching queries and descriptions. This use of rules is similar to the use of S-rules in the START system [Ka88].

Another way of using the dictionary is to define hierarchy of information. It is frequently the case that certain things can be inherited from others in a generic way. For example, one may describe the cars with certain characteristics like "it runs on wheels; it is powered by engines; it can be steered; it runs on land." Subcategories of cars can be passenger-cars, trucks, tractors, armor-cars, etc. and they automatically or selectively inherit descriptions of their parents. With each subcategory additional information can be described and part of all the information of the parent (or ancestor) category inherited. This indeed is very much similar to the way people do.

As stated before, representing the descriptions by predicates allows the system to use Prolog to process queries with the descriptions. This is not efficient for large databases. Research is continuing to find better methods for searching predicates.

As discussed above the purpose of the existence of the dictionary is for the depository of information for the parser to have information to resolve all semantics, ambiguities, imprecisions, etc. As such, the dictionary must be compiled by the database administrator for the application. We must first decide whether to have one dictionary for the whole database, one dictionary for each application, one dictionary for each media type (e.g. IMAGE, SOUND, etc.), one dictionary for each media attribute, or any other way.

The first solution leads to problems if the same word has different meanings in different contexts. It also slows down the parsing process, because the parser always searches the whole dictionary, although it is using only a subset. Having as many dictionaries as there are attributes will on the other hand introduce a significant amount of redundancy, because common words like "the", "and" and "not" have to be defined in all of them. The best approach would be to use several dictionaries: a common dictionary for the whole database with words like "the", "and", "not", etc., a more specific dictionary for each of the different applications, an IMAGE dictionary with words like "foreground", "background", "behind", "left", "right", etc., and an X_RAY_PHOTO dictionary with predicates for "skull", "bone", etc. In this scenario, the parser uses a combination of four dictionaries to translate a specific description.

The dictionary caters mainly to the parser and hence should be optimized to support the parser's information needs. Right now, the parser searches for natural-language words and retrieves the grammatical class and the predicate templates. Tree structures or hashing schemes could be used to support this search. In designing a storage structure, one can make use of the fact that the dictionaries are hardly ever modified. It is our belief that access organization in this part is not a major problem, although different organizations will influence the parser's performance. Investigation into this part's data organization for optimal performance is left for solution at a later date.

As stated before, rules are associated with the dictionary. They could be used to extend all the descriptions in the database by additional predicates that can be inferred, but that would lead to large storage consumption. They could also be used "backwards" to modify the query, which seems to be more appropriate. The details of the data structure for the rules are yet to be worked out. We should note, however, that rules are used in many expert systems, and we believe that we can find one of their organizations to be satisfactory for our use as well. In fact, if our experience shows that there are not many rules for any given application, a purely sequential search of the rules may be quite satisfactory, as we see that rules are application dependent and each application will have its own set of rules.

4. Architecture

In this section we shall identify the components of an MDBMS that actually deal with the data structures introduced in the previous section. From what we have mentioned so far it is clear that we need building blocks like: conventional data management, media object management, description management, parser, language generator, matcher, and query processing. The description management could be integrated with the conventional data management (e.g. in extensible database management systems like EXODUS [Ca86], Genesis [Ba86], or Starburst [Ha88]), but for now we keep them apart to point out their specific roles. Both rely on a lower level storage manager that takes care of things like file allocation and buffer management. The description management organizes the descriptions by relation (or object class) and attribute (or instance variable), and each description will be linked to its media object by means of tuple identifier (TID), surrogate, or object identifier.

The way how these building blocks interact is depicted in Figure 3. Query processing accepts queries from the users (sometimes represented by programs) and executes them by calling the other components. The task of each component is demonstrated best by sketching the processing of different types of queries:

- Insert and Update

Query processing calls the conventional data management that takes care of the attributes with standard types, and the media object management components for all the media objects that are affected. Conventional data management selects an identifier for the new object or retrieves the identifier of an existing one. For every new description entered, query processing calls the parser. The parser uses the dictionary to produce the predicates and returns them to the query processing. Query processing finally hands the predicates over to the description management, specifying relation name (object class), attribute name, and identifier.

- Query

Query processing decomposes a query into subqueries to be handled by conventional data management, media object manager, or description management separately. For the subqueries that only use text descriptions, query management calls the parser to obtain the query predicates. They are then passed to the matcher. The matcher calls description management and uses the rules. It returns a (possibly empty) list of identifiers to query processing.

- Output

Query processing provides identifiers of tuples (objects) to be presented. These identifiers are handed to the language generator which calls description management to get the predicates. It uses the dictionary to generate natural language phrases, which it returns to query processing for output. Naturally, query processing also engages conventional data management and media object management to retrieve raw data and registration data for output.

The primary *user interface* we have in mind for the system is based on natural language for descriptions. However, it might be useful to offer an additional interface for the expert to work with the predicates directly, bypassing the parser in insert and update as well as in queries. But we may also build applications on top of the predicate-oriented interface that again provide a different view to the end user. A complete architecture would then require adding a block, interface management, on top of the query proc block in Figure 3.

5. Conclusion

Handling multimedia data imposes a new challenge on database management systems. Despite many differences in data model and implementation aspects, all the research projects on Multimedia Database Management Systems (MDBMS) have decided to organize media data in new (abstract) data types. This is generally accepted as the adequate approach. However, none of the other projects have addressed the problem of content description and search of media data. We viewed this to be of prime importance for the widespread use of MDBMS and therefore concentrated on this aspect.

Our proposal is to attach text descriptions in natural language form to media data instances to capture their contents. This is very convenient for users, because the descriptions are easy to enter and easy to understand. However, they are not as easy to handle by the MDBMS. To reduce the vagueness and ambiguity involved with natural language, a parser is used to reduce the noun phrases and sentences to predicate lists; one might say, to condense and to give focus to the meaning of the text descriptions. Queries are entered as text phrases and are translated into predicate lists, too. A binding of variables must be found so that the description predicates of a media object logically imply the query predicates. If it can be found, the media object satisfies the query.

The requirements of managing contents information in addition to the media data leads to a new architecture for MDBMS. It consists of basic building blocks for conventional data management, media data management, description (predicate list) management, parser, language generator, matcher, and query processing. We have defined the task of each building block and the ways how they interact with each other. This architecture provides a framework for the development of MDBMS that enables content search on multimedia data. The paper also indicates that to support the kind of processing needed, additional data structures must be constructed.

Although a complete system has not been built, some major concepts have been explored and parts of the system have been implemented. The system can now store and retrieve image data in the manner as stated. Prolog is used to process the queries and the description predicates. At this time, we are studying the structure of captions entered with the pictures from books to learn how people naturally describe the contents of these images. In any case, what capability we have in our system for processing media data and their contents already far exceeds the capability of any system today.

To be sure, there are many other open problems, including data structure and database problems, as already stated in the paper. The overall concept and architecture, however, are believed to be sound.

Acknowledgement

The authors are indebted to Neil Rowe for the design and implementation of the parser.

References

Al87   Allen, J., *Natural Language Understanding*, Benjamin/Cummings Publ. Co., Menlo Park, CA, 1987.

Ba86   Batory, D.S., Barnett, J.R., Garza, J.F., Smith, K.P., Tsukuda, K., Twichell, B.C., and Wise, T.E., "Genesis: A Reconfigurable Database Management System," University of Austin at Texas, Technical Report TR-86-07, March 1986.

BKK88   Banerjee, J., Kim, W. and Kim, K.C., "Queries in Object-Oriented Databases," in *Proc. 4th Int. Conf. on Data Engineering* (Los Angeles, Feb. 1988), pp. 31-38.

BRG88   Bertino, E., Rabitti, F., and Gibbs, S., "Query Processing in a Multimedia Document System," *ACM Trans. on Office Information Systems,* vol. 6, no. 1, Jan. 1988, pp. 1-41.

Ca86   Carey, M.J., DeWitt, D.J., Frank, D., Graefe, G., Richardson, J.E., Shekita, E.J., and Muralikrishna, M., "The Architecture of the EXODUS Extensible DBMS," in *Proc. Int. Workshop on Object-Oriented Database Systems* (Pacific Grove, CA, Sept. 1986).

Ch86   Christodoulakis, S., Theodoridou, M., Ho, F., Papa, M., and Pathria, A., "Multimedia Document Presentation, Information Extraction, and Document Formation in MINOS: A Model and a System," *ACM Trans. on Office Information Systems,* vol. 4, no. 4, Oct. 1986, pp. 345-383.

CK81   Chang, S.K., and Kunii, T.K., "Pictorial Data-Base System," *IEEE Computer,* vol. 14, no. 11, Nov. 1981, pp. 13-19.

Gr84   Grosky, W.I., "Toward a Data Model for Integrated Pictorial Databases," *Computer Vision, Graphics, and Image Processing,* vol. 25, no. 3, March 1984, pp. 371-382.

Ha88   Haas, L.M., Cody, W.F., Freytag, J.C., Lapis, G., Lindsay, B.G., Lohman, G.M., Ono, K., and Pirahesh, H., "An Extensible Processor for an Extended Relational Query Language," IBM Research Report RJ6182, San Jose, April 1988.

Ka88   Katz, B., "Using English for Indexing and Retrieval," in *Proc. RIAO 88* (Cambridge, MA, March 1988), pp. 314-332.

LM88   Lum, V.Y., and Meyer-Wegener, K., "A Conceptual Design for a Multimedia DBMS for Advanced Applications," report no. NPS52-88-025, Naval Postgraduate School, Monterey, CA, August 1988, also in *Proc. 4th National Encounter on Cooperative Processing* (Medellin, Colombia, July 24-30, 1988), pp. AC2-1 to AC2-22.

Mi75   Minsky, M., "A Framework for Representing Knowledge," in *The Psychology of Computer Vision,* Winston (ed.), McGraw Hill, N.Y., 1975, pp. 211-277.

MLW89   Meyer-Wegener, K., Lum, V.Y., and Wu, C.T., "Image Database Management in a Multimedia System," in *Visual Database Systems,* IFIP TC 2/WG 2.6 Working Conf. (Tokyo, Japan, April 3-7, 1989), ed. T.L. Kunii, North-Holland, Amsterdam 1989, pp. 497-523.

Sa88   Sawyer, G.R., "Managing Sound in Relational Multimedia Database System," Master Thesis, Computer Science, Naval Postgraduate School, Dec. 1988.

Sc75   Schank, R.C., *Conceptual Information Processing,* North Holland, N.Y., 1975.

So88   Sowa, J.F., "Knowledge Representation in Databases, Expert Systems, and Natural Language," in *Proc. IFIP WG2.6/WG2.8 Working Conf. on the Role of Artificial Intelligence in Databases and Information Systems* (Guangzhou, China, July 1988), eds. C.-H. Kung and R.A. Meersman, North-Holland Publishing Co., Amsterdam.

SR81   Schank, R.C., and Riesbeck, C.K., *Inside Computer Understanding,* Lawrence Erlbaum, N.J., 1981.

Ta80   Tang, G.Y., "A Logical Data Organization for the Integrated Database of Pictures and Alphanumerical Data," in *Proc. IEEE Workshop on Picture Data Description and Management,* (Asilomar, CA, Aug. 1980), pp. 158-166.

WK87   Woelk, D., and Kim, W., "Multimedia Information Management in an Object-Oriented Database System," in *Proc. 13th Int. Conf. on VLDB* (Brighton, England, Sept. 1987), eds. P.M. Stocker and W. Kent, Morgan Kaufmann Publishers, Los Altos, CA, 1987, pp. 319-329.

WLK87   Woelk, D., Luther, W., and Kim, W., "Multimedia Applications and Database Requirements," in *Proc. IEEE CS Office Automation Symposium* (Gaithersburg, MD, Apr. 1987), pp. 180-189.

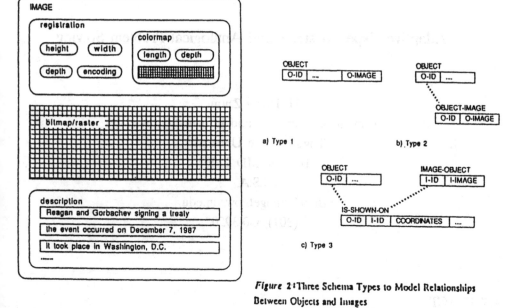

a) Type 1

b) Type 2

c) Type 3

Figure 2: Three Schema Types to Model Relationships Between Objects and Images

Figure 1: Internal Structure of a Media Object (using image as an example)

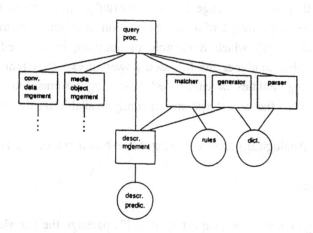

Figure 3: Proposed Architecture of an MDBMS: Building Blocks and Their Interaction

Adaptive Expert Systems and Analogical Problem Solving

H. Harry Zhou
Department of Computer and Information Sciences
Towson State University
Towson, MD 21204
U.S.A.
zhou@midget.towson.edu
(301) 830-3950

ABSTRACT

Conventional expert systems are "brittle" in the sense that they require substantial human intervention to compensate for even slight variations in descriptions, and break easily when they reach the edge of their knowledge. In response to this problem, this paper describes a prototype of a new generation of expert systems, called an adaptive expert system (AES), which is capable of adapting its knowledge dynamically and analogically. AES combines the focussed power of expert systems with the analogical problem solving abilities of case-based reasoning systems, and demonstrates much higher "IQs" than the expert systems currently available on the market.

Key Words: Analogical problem solving, Case-based reasoning, Expert systems.

1. Introduction

Although conventional expert systems [2] package the knowledge of one or more domain experts into their knowledge bases, they do not possess the experts' analogical problem solving ability which is an important aspect of human intelligence as well as an effective approach in AI systems. Without reasoning by analogy, these expert systems would break easily when they reach the edge of their knowledge [3]. That is, they respond appropriately only in the narrow areas of knowledge defined by knowledge engineers, but require substantial human intervention to compensate for even slight variations in representations or descriptions.

Another problem with conventional expert systems is that it is almost impossible to keep the reasoning and problem solving capabilities consistent when frequent changes occur in the external environment. They lack the ability to draw inductive inferences from observations, they do not know how to improve their performance over time (that is, learn from experience), nor can they develop new strategies for unexpected events, no matter how similar the current problem is to past experience.

In response to these problems, analogical expert systems can offer assistance by benefiting from its past experience and adapting the recalled knowledge appropriately with respect to the current problem.

2. The Basic Approach and Algorithm

In this section, the basic approach employed in AES is outlined. AES consists of two parts: an expert system and a case-based reasoning system. Initially, AES works with the input data supplied by the user, and searches its knowledge base for a solution to a given problem. If a solution is available in the knowledge base, an answer is generated. Up to this point, AES acts just like a conventional expert system. However, if no solution is found, AES does not give up like conventional expert systems, instead it employs a heuristic approach in which reasoning can be guided, past experiences can be recalled, and solutions to new but similar problems can be constructed [6].

AES requires a more sophisticated knowledge representation than the ones commonly used in conventional expert systems. The knowledge representation employed in AES has two levels: a lower level and a higher level. The lower level contains IF-THEN rules and the higher level is the case representation. A case consists of a problem description and a set of rules applicable in the situation described by the problem description. Formally, the case representation can be described as follows:

$$\text{Case Base } \{C\} := <C_1><C_2> ... <C_i> ... <C_p>$$
$$\text{Case } C_i := <D_i> <R_i>$$
$$\text{Rule Set } R_i := <r_{i1}><r_{i2}> ... <r_{ij}> ... <r_{im}>$$
$$\text{Description } D_i := <d_{i1}><d_{i2}> ... <d_{ij}> ... <d_{ik}>$$

where R_i is a set of rules

C_i is a case consisting of a description and a set of rules

D_i is a description consisting of k descriptors

r_{ij} is a rule represented in IF-THEN form

d_{ij} is a descriptor

Let C_n be a new case. The basic analogical problem solving algorithm used in AES can then be described as follows:

. Interpret D_n of C_n and classify it in terms of the descriptors
   d_{ij}, where $1 <= i <= p$, D_i associates with C_i, and C_i is a case in $\{C\}$
. Compute the similarity score, $S(D_n,D_i)$, and find a case with the highest
   $S(D_n, D_h)$
. Select and modify the relevant rules r_{hj} in R_h associated with D_h to r_{hj}',
   with respect to D_n
. Inject the rule set R_h' into the working memory
. Determine the acceptability of R_h' by trying to solve the given problem
. If accepted, construct a new case C_n which consists of R_h' and D_n
. If rejected, store the reason and choose an alternative case from $\{C\}$
   if possible, and repeat the process.

Generally speaking, analogical problem solving consists of three major steps [1,7]:

1) recollection of past experience, given the current situation,
2) establishment of correspondence between past experience and the
   current situation, and
3) transformation of related experience to a form applicable to the current
   situation.

Given a known problem, AES acts exactly the same way as most expert systems. Given an unknown problem, unlike conventional expert systems which simply respond with an "I don't know", AES uses the algorithm and the three steps described above to conduct analogical problem solving. It approaches the problem by quickly recalling a set of prior rules from $\{C\}$ with certain similarities, and adapting the associated rules with respect to the current problem. In the process of analogical problem solving, the similarity evaluation algorithm of AES evaluates past experience and the current situation, and locates the most similar experience available in the knowledge base. The built-in background knowledge is referenced to provide information and explanation necessary to measure similarities and establish correspondence between the current problem and past experience. Finally, the knowledge transformation operations are performed to make similar past experience applicable to the current problem. To provide rational justifications for its behavior, AES comments and explains every decision it makes. It explains why a set of rules is considered similar and by what criteria; why a piece of knowledge is selected as a basis for knowledge transformation; how old solutions to similar problems are modified, and how a final answer is generated.

There are four research issues in the development of AES:

1) since the number of rules in the knowledge base is usually very large, one concern is how to economically organize the rules and efficiently retrieve them,

2) how to design an evaluation function to measure the similarity, $S(D_a, D_j)$, during recall of past experience,

3) how to adapt accumulated knowledge and make it suitable in the current situation, and

4) how to generalize specific rules to construct "meta" knowledge applicable in a wide range of situations.

In the next few paragraphs, these issues will be addressed in the context of vehicle troubleshooting.

2.1. Dynamic Index Generation

In order to efficiently retrieve relevant experience, similar problem descriptions should be placed in adjacent locations in memory. Furthermore, they should be differentially retrieved, and quickly located when needed [4]. To facilitate this process, AES uses conceptual hierarchies to organize cases (rule sets). As described above, rules are grouped together into cases based on the contexts their problem descriptions represent. Each case consists of a problem description and a rule set. In a hierarchy, problem descriptions are organized into conceptual hierarchies. Components of a lower order are brought together to form a super-component of a higher conceptual order, which may in turn be brought together to form a component of a still higher order. Thus, the most specific problem descriptions are at the bottom and the most general problem descriptions are at the top. For each component of the hierarchy, there is a scheme (a descriptive format) which consists of one or more statements and a set of indices. The statements characterize the events being covered, while the indices connect other schemata and differentiate the problems contained. The problem description expresses the main properties of the problem and the rule set contains the rules applicable for the problem.

The advantages of such a hierarchy are: for evenly distributed N indices the system needs to compare at most log(N) indices, which cuts down the work significantly. In contrast to the hierarchical model in databases, the most striking difference is how an index scheme is constructed and who is responsible for doing it. In a database, human programmers design and implement a hierarchy step by step, specifying and determining every index needed and every piece of information involved. As an intelligent decision making system, AES is designed to construct the index hierarchies dynamically during storage. Based on similar features and properties, AES generates and selects schemata to characterize relatively specific instances which may themselves be schemata at the more specific levels. For example, suppose that AES has two sets of rules which can recognize and diagnose the problem of "Engine won't start" for GM and Ford cars respectively. Some standard procedures and common symptoms can be indexed by a scheme, called "domestic cars." With the expertise about Toyota and Honda added to the system, AES will need to introduce a new, general scheme, called "cars", in order to conceptualize the troubleshooting expertise for engine problems common to all types of cars, such as "no gas in tank," "bad battery," "bad connection," and "starter malfunction." For model-dependent problems, however, the diagnostic process could be directed to an individual electronic diagnostic procedure using the index associated with the model. As more and more cases accumulate, some more general schemata may be needed and constructed, such as "automobiles" and "motor-powered vehicles". In short, a scheme implements the idea of association by which relevant events or problems are grouped together and stored in nearby locations, while an index represents discrimination by which similar concepts can be further differentiated by their specific characteristics. It is worth repeating that, based on the common properties shared by similar events, AES is able to adaptively select appropriate indices and dynamically construct hierarchies without any assistance from humans. In the design of AES, a cross-index technique may be needed. That is, a case may be indexed by more than one way: its model, the symptoms, the troubleshooting history, and the parts. In searching for a similar case, it is often necessary to traverse several hierarchies to compute the similarity score. The organization of index hierarchies in AES makes it possible to quickly recall similar expertise even when the number of cases in memory grows considerably.

2.2. Similarity Evaluation

The similarity evaluation algorithm of AES evaluates past experience and the current situation in terms of conceptual and feature similarities. Conceptual similarity is concerned with how two set of rules should be measured in the context of a given domain, not simply counting the number of common properties shared. The following five relationships are used in classifying a new problem, N, and an old problem, O [5]:

. N and O are concerned with the same concept (conceptual identity)
. N is more specific than O (conceptual subclass)
. N is more general than O (conceptual superclass)
. N and O share a common parent (conceptual siblings)
. N and O have no relationship with each other (conceptual irrelevancy).

In light of the above measurements, a new problem can be conceptually measured and identified in terms of past experience stored in the knowledge base. For example, assume that AES has obtained a set of rules from an experienced mechanic regarding how to fix the problem of "The key is turned on, but the engine doesn't start" on most GM cars. Some probable causes are: the battery is too weak; the starter does not function properly; and the gas tank is empty. Even though AES was never told how to diagnose Honda motorcycles and Dodge trucks, it is able to conclude that Honda motorcycles and Dodge trucks are similar since both of them are the siblings of GM cars indexed by the scheme "motor-powered vehicles." As a result, some standard procedures obtained from the GM mechanic can then be applied in the diagnosis of automotive problems for trucks and motorcycles. To measure similarities a step further, the feature matching operation is applied which counts the common features shared by two chunks of knowledge. The basic idea behind feature matching is the prototypicality which assumes the problems in the same class would approximately share same features. Given the symptoms, the model, and the year of a car, AES may find two cases with the same similar score. The feature matching process may be able to select, for example, the most similar experience in terms of the total mileage or the car repair record. A survey of cognitive literature suggests that humans do not often use all data in memory when faced with a problem. Rather, they recognize, extract, and compile from the data a limited set of features, and use it to recall relevant experience. The feature measurement is a computational implementation of this aspect of human analogical problem solving.

Overall, the combination of conceptual evaluation and feature measurement makes this similarity evaluation function promising and powerful for exploration of the computational aspects of analogical reasoning in expert systems.

2.3. Knowledge Transformation

Having located the most similar experience in the knowledge base, the next step is to decide how the components of past experience may match the current situation. The system can use built-in background knowledge to make its own judgement regarding various components. The main idea is the automated knowledge transfer from an old set of rules to a new set of rules by means of analogy. The basic knowledge transformation operator applied in AES is the substitution operation, which replaces some phrases, words, or segments of old rules with the terms more appropriate to the current situation. A difficult task is to locate corresponding replacing and replaced terms, and to determine their relationships. There are three kinds of relationships: situational correspondence, conceptual correspondence, and structural correspondence.

Situational correspondence refers to the relations between the problem description of a new case and that of a recalled case. In the domain of vehicle troubleshooting, the maker, the model, and the year of a vehicle described in the recalled case can be substituted by that in the description of a new case, forming new rules for the new case. A rule concerning with the problem "If the transmission of a 1985 Ford Taurus sticks to gear, check the mainshaft pilot bearing and, if necessary, replace it," for instance, can be modified to a rule concerning a 1986 Ford Escort by changing the year and the model of the car involved.

Conceptual correspondence refers to terms with similar meanings or relations in a given context. Searching for causally equivalent terms is often guided by certain conceptual relations. This process was implemented by a recursive function which traverses along the conceptual relations connecting the substituting terms and the substituted terms. Assume that the system has the following rule provided by a GM mechanic: "If an Oldsmobile Cutlass Supreme hesitates on acceleration, one possible defective part is the accelerator pump. Replace it with an inspected GM part if necessary." Assume that the current problem is a Honda Suzuki, which is a motorcycle, with similar symptoms. From a conceptual correspondence point of view, the term "Honda Suzuki" of the current problem is considered a counterpart of the term "GM Oldsmobile Cutlass Supreme" in the matched experience, because both of them can be characterized as motor-powered vehicles. Therefore, a correspondence is found between them and a link is established. In the transformation phase, past experience is made applicable to the current problem by means of substitution. The substitution operator substitutes the linked words with their counterparts. Having substituted "GM Oldsmobile Cutlass Supreme" with "Honda Suzuki", and "GM part" with "Honda part," the above rule would become one applicable to Honda Suzuki motorcycles.

It is worth pointing out that sometimes the above process is done interactively. That is, whenever the system needs more information about certain aspects of the current problem, it can ask specific questions and then utilize the response from the user to direct its analogical problem solving activities.

Structural correspondence refers to the similarity in the structures of two situations, even though the counterparts may not have any conceptual relations. The challenge is to consistently decompose rules into basic components and structurally interpret the relations among them. A global view of the rules being interpreted is needed to separate a rule into parts, which can then be replaced and combined. Structural correspondence provides a supplementary means, not a major role, in the knowledge transformation process.

2.4. Knowledge Generalization and Specialization

In this paper knowledge generalization refers to a general rule generation process in which case-independent or domain-independent rules are constructed. Storing every rule and every solution in a large AI system usually is impractical. Hence, storing accumulated knowledge both efficiently and economically is vital to the design of an AI system. The goal of the knowledge generalization is to construct "meta-rules" applicable to many situations. By means of inheritance, one copy of such general knowledge may be sufficient for many similar situations. It is suggested that the individual rules which share common elements, and which are totally subsumed, should be permanently masked or deleted. The basic method of knowledge generation is the intersection operation. That is, locating and abstracting common terms from "conceptual siblings" cases. For concreteness, consider the following condition parts of two hypothetical vehicle troubleshooting rules: "If the engine of a Dodge Aries doesn't start after the key is turned .....," and "If the engine of a Dodge Aspen doesn't start after the key is turned ...... ". A meta-rule constructed by the intersection operator would look like this: "If the engine of a Dodge <compact car> doesn't start after the key is turned .....". Combining with another rule "If the engine of a GM <compact car> doesn't start after the key is turned .....," a more general rule can be constructed as follows: "If the engine of a <domestic> <compact car> doesn't start after the key is turned .....". In the process of knowledge abstraction, specific terms are replaced by more general vocabularies, forming an abstract rule applicable to a wider range of problems.

As a counterpart, knowledge specialization makes meta-rules suitable for a particular situation. The basic approach employed in knowledge specialization in AES is to replace general terms with case-dependent vocabularies. This operation implements the idea of specializing general knowledge for a particular situation. Humans tend to apply general knowledge to a specific task at will. They usually have no difficulties in employing both common sense and abstract concepts in the process of solving a specific problem. The challenge for AI systems is to incorporate and utilize general knowledge in the context of a particular problem. By replacing general terms with domain-specific vocabularies, a general rule could be tailored to fit in a particular situation. For concreteness, let us assume a "meta" rule concerning with the problem of front brakes: "If the front brakes heat up during driving and fail to release, one possible replacement is to change the proportioning valve." To make this rule applicable to a Dodge Aspen, the term "Dodge Aspen" can be added to this rule. If this specialized rule has been triggered and fired many times by the 1978 Dodge Aspen cars during the diagnostic process, the system may be able to conclude that, whenever examining the brake problem of the 1978 Dodge Aspen cars, the brake proportioning valve should be inspected first. The rule would be modified to the following: "If the car is a 1978 Dodge Aspen and the front brakes heat up during driving and fail to release, it frequently needs to have its proportioning valve replaced."

In short, AES generalizes knowledge obtained at the end of problem solving and specializes relevant general knowledge at the outset of rule modification and construction.

3. Conclusion

With a research area as new as analogical expert systems, it often raises more questions than answers. In what follows, some research topics are summarized:

. A weight could be assigned to each feature of a set of related rules. The weight could be adjustable and used to reflect the relative importance of a feature. Thus, by modifying the weights, an appropriate index scheme may be created without physically having stored many pointers.

. In the current implementation, indexing is done by similarity. The combination of indexing by similarity and by difference may provide a powerful and flexible way to organize knowledge.

. A domain model provides background knowledge necessary to understand certain vocabularies and concepts. It is usually designed and constructed in advance. It would be more flexible and adaptive if the domain model could be changed and enhanced during execution.

. During storage, the derivational steps by which a feasible set of rules was constructed may be stored, not only the rules. This information may be used in constructing new rules in the future.

. Analogical problem solving is only one of many heuristics used by humans in creative endeavors. An interesting research question is: how may analogical reasoning be combined with other heuristics to form a more robust cognitive model?

The development of AES demonstrates the effectiveness and potential values of the use of analogy in expert systems, particularly in the situation of imprecision, dynamics, or lack of initial knowledge. Both as a cognitive simulation and as an intelligent decision-making system, AES shows its ability to manipulate two kinds of knowledge over time: episodic information and evolving experience. As part of this research, a class of automotive troubleshooting problems are utilized as an example domain. The ultimate niche for this work is, however, much broader than this diagnostic domain. It represents a new generation of expert systems with analogical problem solving abilities and with much higher "IQs" than the expert systems currently available on the market.

Reference

[1] J.G. Carbonell, "Learning by Analogy: Formulating and Generalizing Plans from Past Experience", Machine Learning (I): pp 137-162, 1983.

[2] F. Hayes-Roth, Waterman, D.A. & Lenat, D.B., "Principles of Pattern-Directed Inference Systems", Pattern-Directed Inference Systems, Academic Press, 1978.

[3] J. H. Holland, "Escaping Brittleness: The possibilities of general purpose learning algorithms applied to parallel rule-based systems", Machine Learning (II): pp. 593-623, Morgan Kaufmann, 1986.

[4] J. Kolodner, "Retrieval and Organizational Strategies in Conceptual Memory", Ph.D. Thesis, Yale University, 1980.

[5] R. L. Simpson, Jr. "A computer model of case-based reasoning in problem solving: an investigation in the domain of dispute mediation", Ph.D. thesis, Georgia Tech., 1985.

[6] H. H. Zhou, "A Computational Model of Cumulative Learning", to appear in Machine Learning.

[7] H. H. Zhou, "CSM: A Genetic Classifier System with Memory for Learning by Analogy", Ph.D. thesis, Computer Science Department, Vanderbilt University, Dec. 1987.

The Behavior of Database Concurrency Control Mechanisms under Bursty Arrivals

Jerry Place, Vijay Kumar and Appie van de Liefvoort
Computer Science Telecommunications Program
University of Missouri - Kansas City
5100 Rockhill Road
Kansas City, MO 64110

place@vax2.cstp.umkc.edu
Tel: (816) 235-2359

Abstract. The robustness and sensitivity of four two-phase databases concurrency control mechanisms are studied under a dynamically changing workload due to the bursty arrival of transactions. The concurrency control mechanisms are studied under closely controlled conditions in which the only variable is the coefficient of variance of the arrival rate distribution. This paper shows that bursty traffic does impact the performance of the concurrency control mechanisms at both high and low loads, and that the degree of this impact is different for the different mechanisms investigated. We also show that the behavior of some CCMs change significantly under such environment.

1. Introduction

Database Management systems execute transactions concurrently for optimal resource utilization. Concurrent execution, however, threatens database consistency, therefore, such execution is managed by Concurrency Control Mechanisms (CCMs). The performance of CCMs has been an area of active research and there is common agreement that CCMs based on a *two-phase* locking policy [ESW76], outperforms other non-two phase CCMs [e.g., AGR87, KUM87, KUM89, TAY85]. These studies used simulation and/or analytical modeling to describe the behavior of CCMs. However, these did not consider the case of "bursty traffic", i.e. non-exponential transaction arrival rates.

The rate of transaction processing has increased dramatically in the last several years. Also the way that transactions interact with the database and with themselves has also changed dramatically. Transaction rates of 800-1000 per second are now possible and applications will require increasing transaction rates. Also, the traditional view of exponential arrival rates are no longer sufficient to describe the way that transactions arrive at the transaction server. For example, in television shopping, the arrival of orders increases significantly when a new product is introduced. Examples of bursty arrival traffic can be found in distributed systems where the failure of one nodes causes the workload to be diverted to other nodes, thus causing a sudden increase in transaction arrivals at these nodes.

We believe that these variations in the workload arrival rate effect the performance of the system significantly and, further, we believe that different CCMs have differ in their sensitivity to the changes in the arrival rate distribution.. We, therefore, have tried in this work to measure the sensitivity of four commonly used concurrency control mechanisms. Our main objective was to show that the dynamics of the data processing environment may be a limiting factor in designing a universally efficient CCM. In this work we investigated the effect of bursty traffic on the behavior of the CCMs. The bursty traffic, to some extent, can be generated by varying the second moment (with a fixed first moment) of the arrival rate distribution. The arrival rate distribution can be identified as *non-dense* when transactions arrive at perfectly spaced intervals, and *bursty*, when a large number of transactions arrive with very small inter-arrival time. The non-dense traffic creates conceivably the best environment as the system has maximal time between successive transactions to complete a transaction and avoid possible conflicts. This is not the case in a bursty environment, where there are many conflicts during a burst and the system has a chance to catch up only between bursts. We identify the volume of the bursty traffic as the parameter of practical significance. Under this scenario, an unpredictable variation in the traffic volume may cause a CCM to be unable to adjust itself to keep up with the work load. The system may go into an unstable state and the duration of the unstable state could depend solely upon the underlying CCM. We have not encountered a study of this kind in the literature, apparently because this situation was thought to be rare or, if it existed, it had an insignificant effect on the behavior of CCMs. This thinking may not be valid any more due to the emergence of new transaction processing environments. Motivated by the lack of such study, we investigated the effect of bursty traffic on the behavior of CCMs. We believe that the effect of changes in the transaction arrival rate may be more noticeable in some CCMs than in others. Also, systems with bursty traffic may temporarily go into an unstable state and the duration of the unstable state could depend upon the underlying CCM. Finally, some CCMs may never recover from the unstable state while others do recover.

The rest of the paper is organized as follows: Section 2 introduces the four CCMs that we have investigated. The expected behavior of these CCMs under the dynamic environment is discussed in section 3. The simulation model is presented in section 4, and results of the model are discussed in section 5. The paper is concluded in section 6.

2. Concurrency Control Mechanisms Investigated

We have investigated the behavior of four well known two-phase locking CCMs. They are Cautious Waiting (CW) [HSU, KUM90], General Waiting (GW) [TAY85b], Wound-Wait (WW), and Wait-Die (WD) [ROS78]. We selected these algorithms because their performance has been studied extensively and they use different combinations of transaction roll-back and blocking, effecting the behavior of a system in a various ways. The GW has been selected to investigate the effect of bursty traffic on deadlocks, WD for uniform selection policy (it treats older and younger transactions equal), WW for its favored policy (it favors older transactions over younger) and CW for its "intelligent" selection (it selects transactions to roll-back or block cautiously). We give a brief description of these algorithm, a detailed description can be found in [KUM87,KUM90, ROS78]. A conflict over a data item in GW is resolved by blocking the requestor (transaction requesting the data item). The policy of blocking the requestor creates the possibility of deadlock and is resolved by rolling-back one of the transactions involved in a deadlock. In CW, when a requestor conflicts with a holder, the requestor is rolled-back only if the holder is in a blocked state (waiting for an page, not for CPU). If the holder is in execution, i.e. not blocked due to a lock conflict, then the requestor is blocked and resumes its execution when the holder finishes. If the holder is subsequently blocked, the previously blocked transaction remains blocked. In WD, action is taken only on the requestor. A requestor is rolled-back if it is younger than the holder, otherwise it is blocked. WD avoids deadlock since it rolls-back only the younger requestor capable of precipitating a deadlock. In WW, if the requestor is older it rolls-back the holder, otherwise the requestor waits for the older holder to release the desired data item. WW avoids deadlock by not blocking the older requestor.

We studied the impact of bursty arrivals on the performance of CW, GW, WD and WW by changing the coefficient of variation (noted Cx) of the arrival distribution. We use Erlang's method of stages to generate inter-arrival times for transactions. By using hyper-exponential inter-arrival times, the actual arrivals will be clustered, as the infrequent lapses in arrivals will cause the inter-arrival time for most of the customers to be considerably shorter than the average inter-arrival time. Other methods that are sometimes used to attain burstiness were deemed either unrealistic (grouped arrivals, batched arrivals) or could not regenerate themselves, i.e. Poisson arrivals with a rate exceeding the maximal throughput, thus making some of the statistical analysis impossible. Our method has the added advantage that the influence of both the first as well as the second moment can be studied independently.

For each of the four CCMs, we studied both the build-up time at the onset of bursty arrival, as well as the relaxation time at the end. Studies were conducted by generating a stream of arrivals with exponential inter-arrival times and mean transaction response times were recorded. When the system stabilized, the Cx of the arrival rate distribution was increased to the target for that particular study and mean transaction response times were again recorded. Finally, the Cx of the arrival distribution was reset to one and mean transaction response times were recorded. Note that an exponential stream has a coefficient of variance of 1 for event inter-arrival times. The mean of the arrival rate distribution remained constant over the entire simulation. The only variable was the Cx of the inter-arrival times.

3. Expected Behavior

In this section we speculate on the behavior of the CCMs when the second moment of the arrival rate distribution increases. In GW, a sudden burst of transactions is likely to increase the number of blockings. A higher number of blocking may increase the number of deadlocks consequently requiring increased deadlock resolution. Bursty arrival under GW would probably force the system to spend more time dealing with deadlocks. If a second burst of transactions arrived before the system had completed a previous burst, the system may never regain its stability. It is likely that the frequency of deadlock occurrence will increase with higher arrival rates [KUM87] and because deadlocks are resolved by rolling-back victims, we believe that the system will experience heavy stress, and will regain stability slowly, if at all.

In the case of CW, WD and WW mechanisms, no deadlock detection is required, however, transaction roll-backs do occur. On the basis of other performance studies, a deadlock detection and resolution policy is more expensive than a transaction roll-back. It may be the case then that the replacement of deadlock detection and resolution by transaction roll-backs will enhance the restabilizing capability of the system. The system may regain stability sooner compared to the time required to regain stability under GW.

We believe that under CW the system would regain its stability faster than under WD or WW. This is because under CW, unnecessary roll-backs are reduced by applying an "intelligent" conflict resolution policy. This should keep the number of roll-backs to a minimum thus spending the system resources in forward processing of transactions. CW should also have a favorable effect on the restabilizing of the system.

The behavior of WD and WW is difficult to speculate. It appears that lower transaction arrival rates will allow the system to regain its stability sooner under WD than under WW. This conjecture is based on the fact that under WW a blocked transaction may be rolled-back before getting rescheduled for execution. So the progress of a transaction during its life time may be affected by blocking and then subsequently rolling-back the transaction. WD does not exhibit this behavior - a transaction is either blocked or rolled-back, but never both. This may help the system to regain stability sooner. Other performance studies have shown that WW outperforms WD in certain environment [AGA, KUM87]. In summary we believe that CW will perform best when the transaction arrival rate Cx increases and GW will perform the worst. Transaction performance will be measured as mean transaction response time, i.e. the average time required to complete a transaction.

4. Simulation Model

The general model for all CCMs is shown in Figure 1. It is an open ended model and it is based on the following assumptions:

1. There is one CPU and one I/O.

2. A transaction size is measured as the total number of pages required by the transaction. We assume that the model makes use of main memory buffers such that any number of required pages may be in the main memory.

3. The database is updated in-place.

4. A roll-back operation has the highest priority.

5. All transactions in the workload are write-only transactions. We are interested in CCM performance in the face of a large number of conflicts.

6. Lock table resides in the main memory.

The simulation model maintains a CPQ, an IOQ, a BQ (Blocked Queue), and a DQ (Delay Queue). The BQ holds blocked transactions and the DQ holds rolled-back transactions. During its lifetime, a transaction may visit a subset of these queues. The progress of a transaction through the model is managed with the help of a set of priorities, 1 (highest) through 4 (lowest). A priority is (re-)assigned to a transaction depending upon its status. Priorities have the following interpretation:

Priority 1:   Transactions to be rolled-back.

Priority 2:   Normal transactions. A transaction is normal if it is ready for execution.

Priority 3:   Transactions that have made at least one lock request.

Priority 4:   Transactions that have not made any lock request (new transactions) but are prepared to do so and rolled-back transactions coming from DQ.

Figure 1 describes the simulation model and the flow of transactions through this model is as follows. For clarity we explain the flow of transaction starting from priority 3 or 4 and go up.

1. New transactions arrive and are assigned an ID number. Transaction identity is a unique integer that determines the age of a transaction. Under this scheme, the *larger* the identity value the *younger* the transaction. Transactions then join the CPQ with a priority of 4.

2. Initially there will be transactions in the CPQ with priority 4 only. A transaction is selected and its lock request is analyzed. If the request is granted, then its priority is upgraded to 2 and it joins the IOQ. If the lock request is denied, then the transaction undergoes the conflict resolution process. The conflict is resolved under the CCMs being simulated as follows:

GW: We apply continuous deadlock detection policy, i.e. at every transaction conflict deadlock detection is activated. If a deadlock is detected then a victim (transaction to be rolled-back) is selected, whose priority is upgraded to 1 and passed on the IOQ. If there is no deadlock then the requestor joins the BQ.

CW: If the holder is waiting for a data item in the BQ, then the requester becomes the victim. The requestor's priority is upgraded to 1 and it joins the IOQ. If the holder is not in the BQ then the requestor joins the BQ.

WD: If the requestor is older then it joins the BQ but if the requestor is younger then it becomes a victim, and its priority is upgraded to 1, and it joins the IOQ.

WW: If the requestor is younger then it is blocked and joins the BQ. If the holder is younger then it becomes the victim, its priority is upgraded to 1, and it joins the IOQ. (The younger holder may be active or blocked and can be in CPQ, IOQ or in BQ.)

4. A transaction from the BQ is moved to the CPQ with a priority 3 when the lock it was waiting for is released by the holder.

5. A priority 1 transaction is picked up from the IOQ and its IO request is processed. It then joins the CPQ with the same priority. In the absence of priority 1 transactions, priority 2 transaction is picked up and after processing its IO request it joins CPQ with priority 2.

6. A priority 1 transaction is picked up from the CPQ for processing. A victim (priority 1 transaction) is rolled-back and joins the Delay Queue (DQ) where it encounters an average transaction execution delay. From DQ, the transaction joins CPQ with priority 4. In the absence of priority 1 transactions, a priority 2 transaction is picked up from CPQ and executed until it requires the next item or it commits. When the transaction requires the next item, its priority is changed to 3 from 2 and joins CPQ as priority 3 transactions.

When a transaction is rolled-back, it is re-scheduled as a new transaction but its previous resource (CPU, IO etc.) utilization is not erased. A transaction may suffer several roll-backs during its life time and when it eventually completes, its entire history is used to compute its response time.

5. Simulation Results and Discussion

Our aim in this experiment has been to study the comparative behavior of General Waiting (GW), Cautious Waiting (CW), Wound-Wait (WW) and Wait-Die (WD) mechanisms under bursty traffic via simulation modeling. In particular the departure from their normal behavior when traffic suddenly becomes bursty. For a meaningful comparison we have used parameter values similar to those used in most of the earlier studies. The database size was 10,000 pages with equal probability of access. Write-only transactions are used to generate the worst case scenario, i.e., a highly conflict producing workload. The arrival rates varied from 1 to 16 transactions per second. Each transaction required between 10 and 20 pages.

A simulation run goes through three phases. In the first phase 1,800 transactions are executed and the arrival traffic has normal variability, i.e. the $Cx = 1$ for the arrival distribution. In the second phase, the Cx is changed to 7, 13 or 19. This produces various levels of bursty traffic. 3,600 transactions are executed in the lifetime of this phase. The final phase is a replication of the first phase and the value of Cx is reset to 1. Simulation experiments were completed for each of the four CCMs at transaction arrival rates of 1, 4.5 and 8 transactions per second and at an inter-arrival time Cx=1, 7, 13 and 19. Thus a total of 12 simulation studies were completed for each CCM.

Figure 2 shows the relationship between the response time and the arrival rate for Cx = 1 (no bursty traffic). As expected, we do not observe any transient effect. As the load increases, the response time of WD is the first to be affected significantly followed by GW and WW (virtually equal), and CW being very close. Similar behavior has been observed in the earlier experiments [KUM87, AGA].

Figures 3, 4, 5 and 6 summarize the transient behavior of these CCMs. These figures show the relationship among the response times (Z-axis), cumulative number of transactions (X-axis) and the coefficient of variation for Cx=7 and Cx=19(Y-axis). The figures depict the results for arrival rate $\lambda=1$, $\lambda=4.5$ and for $\lambda=8$ respectively. These plots are smoothed so the dramatic increases in transaction response time that occur when the Cx of the inter-arrival time is increased appear to come before 1,800, however, the charts clearly illustrate that the four CCMs departure significantly from their normal behavior. The charts clearly indicate the dependency of response time on the workload and the degree of variability (Cx) of the workload. Under light traffic, the variability has little or no impact, even though WD is affected the most, GW the least, and CW and WW fall somewhere in between. When the traffic is heavy, the variability causes the response time to grow substantially. In this case, all CCMs show an increase in the response time as soon as the bursty phase begins. The first and the second moments determine the growth rate and the maximal values of the mean response times. The maximal response time is different for CCMs for higher values of Cx. All CCMs show excessive response times but only WD fails to recover. \These conclusions are verified with a 1-tail test (significance level of 0.95). All computed z-statistics exceed the critical value (1.645). The behavior of CW is surprisingly different. CW performs best under normal arrival, but under bursty traffic it is unable to regain stability after a high-variability traffic burst.

We look at the number of roll-backs and blockings to partly explain the departure of the CCMs from their normal behavior. The number of blocks and roll-backs (tables 1 and 2) explodes for CW and WD compared to GW and WW. In WD, the younger requestors are rolled-back and the older requestors are blocked. Every transaction, here, may suffer two obstacles: a younger transaction is rolled-back and when rescheduled, it may be older than most of the transactions in the system, so it is blocked when it conflicts with a younger holder. If it conflicts with an older transaction, it suffers another roll-back. It seems that in WD, a transaction's age has no influence on its execution, i.e. it being younger or older does not have any advantage when a conflict arises. The situation is different in WW, an older requestor is never rolled-back. If a transaction is younger, it gets blocked, otherwise it wounds. It is possible that a blocked transaction may get rolled back, but our results indicate that this does not happen often.

In GW, a transaction is always blocked when a conflict arises. It is well-known that at lower arrival rates the frequency of deadlock occurrence is very low, consequently the roll-backs remains low. At higher arrival rates with bursty traffic, more deadlocks occur, but as soon as the inter-arrival Cx is reset to 1, GW manages to clear the deadlocks before the arrival of the next burst. CW and WD also try to clear the large number of roll-backs and blockings when the inter-arrival Cx is reset to 1, but this backlog was so high that the system became unable to process them before the arrival of the next burst, thus these two CCMs fell into a prolonged unstable state.

6. Conclusions

In this work we have demonstrated the effect of "bursty traffic" on the behavior of four commonly used two-phase locking concurrency control mechanisms. Under bursty traffic, a system experiences random changes in the volume of workload. We found GW (General Waiting) followed by WW (Wound Wait) to be the most robust, and CW (Cautious Waiting) and WD (Wait-Die) to be the least. The last two do not seem to regain stability even after inter-arrival time Cx is reset to 1. We found this very surprizing since under normal arrival, CW offers the best performance. We plan to explore further the sudden change in its behavior. We believe that the results of this study expose some limitations of commonly used concurrency control mechanisms for further improvement in their performance. This study may also lead us to investigate other environments such as the distribution of work in gracefully slowing down distributed systems where bursts of work exist. We plan to investigate the behavior of some non two-phase, as well as some other two-phase CCMs under a bursty environment.

References

[AGA87]   R. Agrawal, et al., "Concurrency Control Performance Modeling: Alternative and Implications", ACM TODS, 12, 4, December 1987.

[ESW76]   Eswaran, K. P., Gray, J. N., Lorie, R. A., and Traiger, I. L., "The Notions of Consistency and Predicate Locks in a Database System", CACM, 19, 11, Nov. 1976, pp 623 - 633.

[KUM87]   Kumar, V. An Analysis of the Roll-Back and Blocking Operations of Three Concurrency Control Mechanisms, NCC '87, Chicago, 1987.

[KUM89]   Kumar, V. "A Study of the behavior of the Read:Write ratio under two-phase locking schemes", Info Sys, 14, 1, pp. 1-12, 1989.

[KUM90]   Kumar Vijay and Meichun Hsu, "A Superior Two-Phase Locking Algorithm and its Performance", Info Sci, Accepted for publication, 1990.

[LIN82] Lin, W. K. and Nolte, J., "Read only Transactions and Two-Phase Locking", Proc. of 2nd Symp on Rel in Distributed Software and Database Systems, Pittsburg, July 1982 pp 85 - 93.

[ROS78]   Rosencrantz, D.J., et al. System Level Concurrency Control for Distributed Database Systems. ACM Trans. on Database Systems, 3, 2, (July 1978), 178-198.

[TAY85a]   Tay, Y.C., Suri, R., and Goodman, N. A Mean Value Performance Model for Locking in Databases: The No waiting case. JACM, 32, 3 (July 1985), 618-651.

[TAY85b]   Tay, Y.C., Suri, R., and Goodman, N. Locking Performance in Centralized Systems. ACM Trans. on Database Syst, 10, 4 (December 1985), 415-462

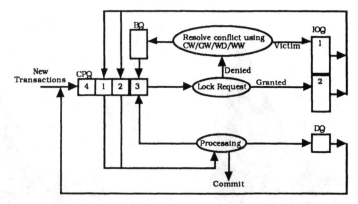

Figure 1: Simulation Model of CCM's

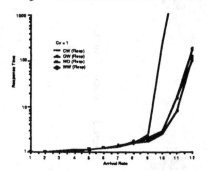

Figure 2: Response times for the four CCMs under Poisson arrivals

	GW	WW	CW	WD
Cx = 1	0.052	0.045	0.057	0.039
Cx = 7	0.618	0.352	0.585	0.270
Cx = 13	1.198	1.254	1.093	13.467
Cx = 19	3.305	2.417	6.149	12.083

Table 1: Number of times a transaction is blocked, l=8.

	GW	WW	CW	WD
Cx = 1	0.000	0.000	0.000	0.021
Cx = 7	0.009	0.009	0.007	0.251
Cx = 13	0.055	0.105	0.032	28.718
Cx = 19	0.403	0.430	2.233	25.540

Table 2: Number of of times a transaction is rolled back, λ=8.

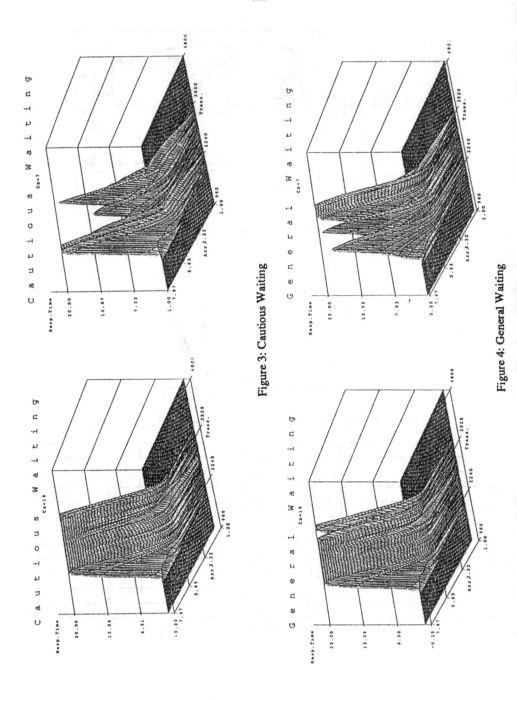

Figure 3: Cautious Waiting

Figure 4: General Waiting

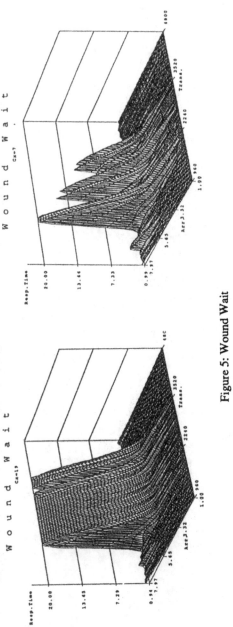

Figure 5: Wound Wait

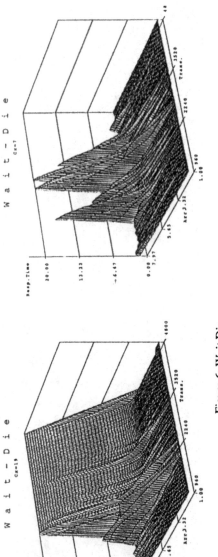

Figure 6: Wait Die

4. Computer Architecture, Concurrency, Parallelism, Communication and Networking

THE CORE CONCURRENCY
(Revised Version)

Piotr W. Proszynski
Jodrey School of Computer Science
Acadia University
Wolfville, Nova Scotia, Canada B0P 1X0
e-mail: Piotr@AcadiaU.CA

Keywords: Concurrency, Nonsequential systems, COSY, nets.

Abstract
The paper presents a unique net semantics of regular and concurrent regular expressions. The resulting nets are 1-save, unlabelled nets with silent actions. We argue that in this way a highly *structural* and independent from concurrent context representation of systems can be obtained. Interestingly enough, nonsequential representation of sequential behaviours has been found to be an alternative for *symbolic* representation.

Introduction

There are many formal models of concurrent and nonsequential systems and there have been numerous attempts to provide descriptions of such systems' behaviours. We assume that the reader has some knowledge of Petri Nets [Rei85], COSY [Lau79], CSP [Hoa85] and CCS [Mil80], and recall only basic definitions. We feel free to borrow from these models what we find the best, without confining ourselves to any single formalism. One of our goals is to demonstrate that concurrency is not just a feature to-be-achieved to improve performance of some, essentially sequential systems; instead it is the very *primitive* concept without which non-trivial systems are unthinkable. Unfortunately, we all are trained to percept phenomena and organize our understanding of them in a language-based, sequential manner. As a result, we generally reveal a tendency to replace *true concurrency* (that we observe) by an *inadequate description* before any study starts; a sort of "cognitive dissonance" is resolved in this way, but we never can get close enough to the problem.

In more radical words, one may say that analysing a *description* of a system's behaviour is common approach, while an analysis of the *behaviour itself* is intended. Since the description is often inadequate, a number of essential problems cannot be captured, in spite of additional rules of interpretation added. Particular approaches aim at providing suitable tools to deal with selected problems - but generally, handling properly both non-determinism and concurrecy at the same time is troublesome. Let us recall two major views on representation of behaviours:

• "linguistic" (*symbolic representations* of behaviours interpreted as subsets of free partially commutative monoids) ; string/trace/subset languages, (vector) firing sequences are in this class,

• "operational" (*symbolic representations* of behaviours interpreted as congruence classes of certain *observation congruence* relation) ; any CCS-related studies use this idea; the approach formalized in [Mil82&89]

It is well-known that the first of the above classes fails to capture fully non-determinism, and the second is not capable to express true concurrency. Seemingly, there is no obvious way to improve any of the above approaches, for the changes to-be-made are contradicting the ideas already implemented - but we feel that the accepted behaviours' representation itself is to be blame.

Hence, we postulate a shift from *describing, then analysing* to *structural explanation* of behaviours. To make it possible, one has to be concerned with certain abstract *objects revealing behaviours* in question - rather than with sequential, *subjective* records of execution histories. In this paper simple, Petri Net-like objects are accepted as the generators of behaviours. We want our generators to be self-contained and free from any unnecessary interpretation rules, with possibly many information encoded into "topological" structure.

Finally, non-sequential systems should be fully characterized through an equivalence relation over static structures of their abstract representations. Equivalence classes of such a relation can be seen as <u>canonical generators</u> of corresponding systems behaviours.

1. Notations: Cosy and Nets

In this section, we deal with relationships between COSY-like specifications and nets. [Best86] is an excellent reference on the topic and we admit a substantial impact of that paper on the presented ideas.

Let us start recalling some fairly standard notations used in this paper. If Σ is an arbitrary alphabet, the elements of Σ are denoted by a,b,c (with indices, if necessary.) By Σ^* we denote the set of all strings over A, including the empty string ε. For every regular expression R, let L(R) denote the language defined by R, and Σ_R denote the alphabet of R.

We define regular expressions using COSY syntax:

Definition 1.1
Regular expressions over Σ are of the form:
$$R ::= a \mid R; R \mid R, R \mid R^* \quad \text{where } a \in \Sigma .$$
Elements of Σ are interpreted as **atomic** actions names. ";" denotes *concatenation*, "," denotes (exclusive) *choice*, and "*" denotes *iteration*. Unlike the traditional notation we assume that "," has higher precedence than ";" ; "*" has the lowest priority. ∎

Regular expressions represent sequential specifications and to represent nonsequential specifications, the following definition has been introduced in [Jan85]:

Definition 1.2
A **concurrent regular expression** is of the form CR: $R_1 \mid \mid ... \mid \mid R_n$ where R_i for i = 1,...,n, are regular expressions. We often write Σ_i instead of Σ_{R_i}. Let also $\Sigma_{CR} = \bigcup_i \Sigma_i$ denote the alphabet of CR. ∎

The interpretation of the above purely syntactic inscription is crucial:

We impose over CR all the COSY program structure, although, unlike in COSY, we do not assume that the star operator is implicitly applied to regular expressions representing sequential components of (concurrent) systems. The remaining features of COSY are preserved. In particular, identical action names appearing in *different* regular expressions are *are considered the same*. and the whole concurrent regular expression is to represent a system, whose components are synchronized through <u>any</u> common action names (hand-shake synchronization) . Concurrent systems like these are said to be **loosely cooperating** - and we will restrict our attention to those systems only, accepting the above synchronization as a primitive in any more sophisticated constructs. Readers familiar with results of [Ziel87] may be disappointed now, because loosely cooperating automata were proven there to be incapable to generate an arbitrary regular trace language - but, as we shall explain later, that statement is inadequate in our case.

We can define semantics of concurrent regular expressions formally in linguistic terms (we follow [Shi79] and [JLKD85]). Let Σ be an alphabet. For every subset $A \subseteq \Sigma$ let $h_A : \Sigma^* \to \Sigma^*$ be an **erasing homomorphism** based on A defined as follows:

$$h_A(a) = \begin{cases} a \text{ if } a \in A \\ \varepsilon \text{ if } a \notin A \text{ or } a = \varepsilon \end{cases}$$

and $h_A(xa) = h_A(x)\, h_A(a)$ if $x \in \Sigma^*$, $a \in \Sigma$.

Definition 1.3

The **language generated** by a concurrent regular expression CR: $R_1 | | ... | | R_n$ is defined as

$$L(CR) = \{x \in \Sigma_{CR}^*\colon (\forall i)\ h_{\Sigma_{R_i}}(x) \in L(R_i)\}.\ \blacksquare$$

Note that the language L(CR) contains all the *possible* interleaving of sequences in $\cup L(R_i)$.

In the above semantics concurrency is not represented directly, but knowing all the alphabets Σ_{R_i} and the synchronization rule one may easily construct traces, [Maz86] or vector firing sequences, [Shi79] to have concurrent aspects of the system behaviour sufficiently exposed. Nevertheless, even then, one is not able to distinguish between such expressions as e.g. a^* ;a;b and a;a*;b - which *are different* from the operational point of view and a number of reasons may be given in the favour of such a distinction.

On the other hand, sophisticated usage of the operational approach may be quite tricky: an operational semantics for COSY was first defined in [Lau85] , but no advantage of this step could be found in that paper; however, in [Sob86] nonstandard semantics for COSY and its comparison with ASCCS [Mil82] follows. In the latter work the distinction between a* ;a;b and a;a*;b or (a;b) , (a;c) and a; b,c is evident.

Several authors, [Best86] , [Lau75], and others were interested in defining the *net semantics* of concurrent regular expressions. In some aspects this is exactly our goal stated in Introduction, although we shall have quite specific, additional criteria to be met. Although we recall rarely used net formalism, due to Janicki [Jan84], comparison with the other results is straightforward.

Let X be a set; denote by $\pi_1: X \times X \to X$, $\pi_2: X \times X \to X$ projections defined as follows: $\pi_1((x,y)) = x$, $\pi_2((x,y)) = y$.

Definition 1.4

An **unmarked net** (net *static structure)* is a pair N = (T,P), where:

T is a set (of *transitions)*,

$P \subseteq 2^T \times 2^T$ is a relation (interpreted as *places)* such that:

$\forall t \in T\ \exists p,q \in P\ (t \in \pi_1(p) \cap \pi_2(q)).\ \blacksquare$

Note that the **flow relation** F, usually defined for nets can be derived from our places as :

$\forall x,y \in T \cup P,\ (x,y) \in F \Leftrightarrow x \in \pi_1(y)\ \vee\ y \in \pi_2(x).$

Note also that:

1. Every place can be understood as a pair of sets: the set of its input transitions and the set of its output transitions.

2. $\{\pi_1(p) \mid p \in P\}$ and $\{\pi_2(p) \mid p \in P\}$ are coverings of T ; if these coverings are *minimal* the net is called **atomic**.

3. $\{\pi_1(p) \mid p \in P\}$ and $\{\pi_2(p) \mid p \in P\}$ are coverings by pairwise disjoint sets (they are partitions) iff the net is a **state machine net.**

4. The whole net structure can be derived from full description of places - which are pairs of sets (of *preceding* and *following* transitions).

Definition 1.6

A **marked net** is a pair MN:(N,M),where N is a net; $M \subseteq P$ is called an **initial marking** . $\blacksquare$

Let $A \subseteq T$; denote: $\quad \cdot A = \{\ p \in P \mid\ \exists a \in A\colon\ a \in \pi_2(p)\ \}$

$\qquad\qquad\qquad\qquad A\cdot = \{\ p \in P \mid\ \exists a \in A\colon\ a \in \pi_1(p)\ \}$

Definition 1.7

A subset $A \subseteq T$ of transitions is said to be **enabled under marking** M iff

1) $\forall a,b \in A\ \forall p \in P\colon\ a \in \pi_1(p) \cup \pi_2(p) \Rightarrow\ b \notin \pi_1(p) \cup \pi_2(p)\quad$ or $\quad a=b$

2) $\cdot A \subseteq M\ \&\ (A\cdot - \cdot A) \cap M = \varnothing$

Moreover, **firing** A transforms M into M' , such that $M' = M - \cdot A \cup A\cdot\ \blacksquare$

A *net's behaviour* can be defined in terms of a (firing sequence) language or a subset language generated by this net, or in terms of marking graph (also called *reachability tree*). We do not provide any definitions here, and refer the reader to [Pet81] or [Rei85]. Let us remark, however, that typically strings of symbols associated with transitions are considered. In the simplest case T is taken for an alphabet, but many authors study **labelled nets**, that is nets together with a mapping $\lambda{:}T{\rightarrow}\Sigma$, which attaches a label from Σ to any transition of the net. As the *labelling* mapping is arbitrary, an *increase* of complexity of the language generated may be expected. Indeed, labelled nets may reveal (concurrent) behaviours substantially different from those described by any concurrent regular expression interpreted as above. A standard example can be found again in [Zie87]. This paper provides also elegant theoretical results of general nature: *loosely cooperating finite asynchronous automata* (and our expressions can be classified as such) are shown to be incapable to recognize (or generate) some regular trace languages - on the other hand, **labelled** nets can do the job easily. The example is very simple: (((a;a;b;b;) , (a;b);)c)* - where a and b are mutually independent. We shall discuss this example in the following chapters.

Accepting labelled nets is not the *only* way to solve the problem: Lauer and Campbell, [Lau74], described a formal semantics of a *subset* of COSY systems, using unlabelled nets with silent transitions. We are thankful to an anonymous referee for pointing out connections of our work with that paper.

Best in [Best86] provided a net semantics of *control programs*, limited forms of COSY programs. His nets are unlabelled , and he does not admit silent transitions - but there is a price also - a number of restrictions on the form of (concurrent) expression:

• any action symbol occurs within any regular expression at most once; this is referred to as *regular naming*;

• by definition, any iteration is of the form: $(S|x)^*$, where S is a sequence (regular expression) and x is an *exit* action; hence $(S|x)^*$ can be seen as equivalent to $(S)^*;x;$ in our notation.

• there are no "unguarded" loops (*regular forming*): every loop is preceded (sequentially) by an action symbol.

Hence, to proceed, one has to transform an arbitrary expression into regularly named, regularly formed one and ensure that every loop has a definite exit.

Taking a formal stand-point one may say that in this paper we postulate a method of constructing a net semantics for regular (concurrent) expressions. The method imposes one-to-one correspondence between symbols used within expression and transitions of the resulting net,what is a central idea of [Best86] - but, unlike in that paper, direct relabelling as a tool for ensuring regular naming is rejected. A solution accepted in place is quite close to that of [Lau74] - at least with respect to the final output: finite-state decomposable nets with silent transitions are created. However, we should like to convey a far more important message, addressing the issue of very general representation of concurrent behaviours - a message that could not have been formulated as early as 1974.

2. Semantics of Concurrent Expressions

We have already presented a possible formal semantics of concurrent regular expressions - Definition 1.3 describes how the language generated by such an expression can be constructed. Now however, we should focus our attention on almost common-sense understanding of our specifications, as one is not able to find limitations of any formal method without leaving its boundaries.

Let us start with sequential specifications: regular expressions in the sense of Definition 1.1.

Observation 2.1.

We talk about *specifications* by means of *regular expression*. If we understand the word literally, as a specification of an abstract system given through its behaviour description - is such a specification always precise enough to have the system *built?*

One should expect an affirmative answer to this question - or reject the method; and in absence of a reasonable criterion *any* system revealing described behaviour should be accepted.

Unfortunately, rather narrow subclass of all regular expressions seems to be satisfactory as so understood specifications. The class of <u>regularly named expressions, with every iteration preceded by an *entry* (so, guarded) and followed by an *exit* symbol</u> - in line with [Best86] .

If the above conjecture is correct, then the expressions **a; b, c** and **(a;b) , (a;c)** are different - and the latter is in a sense *worse*. Note these expressions are equivalent from linguistic point of view - but interpretation of connectors given in Definition 1.1. does not anticipate the ordinary distributiveness of ; over , . In fact, the opposite may be deduced : if " , " is interpreted as *choice* we observe two different choices, indeed (c.f. [Mil80], [Mil82]).

Equally *bad* are expressions:

a* ; b (unguarded iteration) and **b; a*** (lack of exit symbol).

Observations 2.2.

1. The synchronization rule accepted is not precise enough for irregularly named expressions. What is the meaning of: **(a;b) , (a;c) || (a;b) , (a;c)** ? (c.f. [Bes86])

2. *Choice* cannot be realized directly in the absence of *guards* or *exits*. Consider : g ; **(a* ; b) , c** or **(b; a*) , c ; x** .

Note that just distributing ; over , results in the previous problem.

The above observations lead us to the following conclusion:

<u>if specified behaviours can really be observed for some systems, then at least part of these systems' structure is concealed (some actions are *internal* and not observable)</u>

Hence, building an abstract system that reveals specified behaviour may require initial augmenting of the specification with *silent* (internal) actions. Such a solution not only results in homogeneous approach to both problems communicated in Observations 2.2, but is consistent with the method of transforming traces into concurrent regular expressions described in [JM89], as well. The latter method is beyond the scope of this paper - our specifications are already of the form of concurrent expression - and the reader is advised to refer to [JM89]. Exceptionally, the following example starts the process *ab ovo* and is intended to work out proper intuitions.

Example 2.3

Let us consider Zielonka's construction (see [Ziel87]) of an automaton accepting the trace language:

T: $(((a;a;b;b) , (a;b) ;)c)^*$ (a,b - mutually independent);

(more formally: $[((a;a;b;b),(a;b); c)^*]_I$ - a trace represented by the sequence given above with fixed independency relation I , $[]_I$ denotes an equivalence class of I).

What anyway mean that we expect concurrent execution of **a** and **b** exactly once, followed by **c** or exactly twice, also followed by **c** - and so on.

Trivialized a bit, the construction can be seen then as a sophisticated realization of the idea "have enough different places to *remember*" and one may describe it informally as follows:

Feel free to transform the language description using rules valid for regular expressions (we deal here with languages rather than behaviours in the sense of [Mil82]); so we have:

T: $(a;b; (a;b;c) , c)^*$ (a,b - independent).

Then, *distinguish* between *different* occurrences of the same action :

T": $(a1;b1; (a2;b2;c1) , c2)^*$; (independency is retained).

Now, *split* the above into two sequences (justification of this step can be found in [[JM89] - this is in fact a projection onto cliques of dependency relation):

SA": $(a1;(a2;c1) , c2)^*$,   SB": $(b1;(b2;c1) , c2)^*$,

Of course, SA" || SB" is a concurrent specification - and both components of the expression are regularly named.

Relatively easy construction of the corresponding net is given in the next chapter and the resulting (labelled net) is of the form:

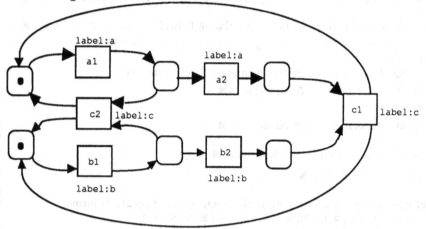

The above net is a structural image of T' not T , and this is our major stricture against such an approach resulting in **labelled** nets: <u>most of the essential features of the represented behaviour are not reflected in the net's *structure*.</u>. Consecutively, if the above net is to be composed with any other *requesting synchronization* on some of the action symbols a complete modification of the structure may be (and will be) necessary.

On the other hand dealing with unmodified T is much more complicated from the very beginning; *splitting* (projection) yields an incorrect concurrent specification. A remedy suggested in [JM89] is to insert a silent action (called *synchronization guard*) ; In this way we obtain:

T1: $(((a;a;b;b) , (G;a;b) ;)c)^*$ (a,b - mutually independent);

and , after projection:

S1A: $(((a;a) , (G;a) ;)c)^*$ S1B: $(((b;b) , (G;b) ;)c)^*$

The new concurrent specification, S1A || S1B , must be further augmented, since none of the components is regularly named, ∎

3. Cosy, Nets and Memorising

Observe that the problem of limited expressive power of concurrent expressions built of loosely cooperating components is generally of the following nature: we have no means to *remember* how many times a particular action has been executed, which decisions have been made, or, taking some specifications literally, we cannot tell "which **a** is which"

Seemingly, the absence of *places* is the problem - but essentially the comparison of concurrent expressions with loosely cooperating automata follows from an observation made in [Pro89] that <u>the lack of places in COSY is equivalent to the assumption that places (states) are derivable from the sets of their *input* and *output action symbols*.</u> The idea of places defined through sets of their input/output transitions is due to Janicki [Jan84] and related definitions has been already recalled in Section 1. Hence, we may expect that - at least for regularly named regular expressions - the construction of a net revealing specified (sequential) behaviour is very natural, if not trivial.

Definition 3.1

Let R be a regular expression over Σ. The **successor** function
$f_R : \Sigma \to 2^\Sigma$ is defined as follows:

$$f_R(a) = \{ b \in \Sigma \mid (\exists x \in L_R)(\exists y \in \Sigma^*) : x=yab \} \blacksquare$$

Definition 3.2

The successor function $f_R : \Sigma \to 2^\Sigma$ is said to be **consistent** iff

$$(\forall a,b \in \Sigma) : \quad f_R(a) = f_R(b) \quad \text{or} \quad f_R(a) \cap f_R(b) = \varnothing \quad \blacksquare$$

Proposition 3.3

Let R be a regularly named ; then the net N simulating R is of the form $N = (\Sigma_R, P)$,
where: $P = \{ (f^{-1}(f(x)), f(x)) \mid x \in \Sigma_S \} \cup \{ (\varnothing, \Sigma_S - \cup(f(\Sigma_S))) \}$
(set of places, $(f = f_R)$)

The initial marking M is an arbitrary one-element subset of the set:

$$\{ p \in P \mid \exists a \in \Sigma)(\exists y \in \Sigma^*) : ay \in L_R \ \& \ a \in \pi_2(p) \} \blacksquare$$

Proposition 3.4

The mapping f_R in Proposition 3.3 is consistent. $\blacksquare$

Corollary 3.5

$\{ \pi_1(p) \mid p \in P \}$ and $\{ \pi_2(p) \mid p \in P \}$ are partitions of Σ_S

- hence, N is a state machine net. $\blacksquare$

Example 3.6

Construct a net simulating the expression: (a*;b),c which is not regularly formed.
$\Sigma = \{ a, b, c \}$ and $f(a) = \{ a, b \}$ $(b) = f(c) = \varnothing$ (f is consistent)
Hence, we have the following places:

$(\{ a \}, \{ a,b \})$, $(\{ b, c \}, \varnothing)$ and $(\varnothing, \{ c \})$) Note, a difference with
approaches in [Best86, Lau75], where a definite composition rule is suggested to represent
the exclusive choice. Note that the initial choice in our net is made in some way "from
the outside" (marking selection). $\blacksquare$

Nets built for inconsistent successor function are, in an obvious way, always different
from state-machine nets, although they are atomic. It can be shown that such nets are
either unsafe or some of their transitions are never enabled.
Fortunately, expressions yielding inconsistent successor functions may be easily
improved by introducing new (silent) actions.

Algorithm 3.7

Input: An inconsistent successor function f_R

Output: A consistent function over augmented alphabet R' .

Construction: Repeat until successor function consistent:
If , for some a and b , $f_R(a) \cap f_R(b) = H \neq \varnothing$ and, say, $f_R(a) \neq H$ then:
$\Sigma_{R'} = \Sigma_R \cup \{ \delta_a \}$ (where δ_a is not in Σ_R)
$f_{R'}(\delta_a) = H$
$f_{R'}(a) = f_R(a) - H \cup \{ \delta_a \}$

$f_{R'} = f_R$ - otherwise. $\blacksquare$

4. Concurrency of Sequential Systems

The problem of translating irregularly named programs into (unlabelled) nets is still to
be solve, although the reader might already have guessed the very simple solution
following intuitions built in the previous chapters.
Note that the net representing (an ordinary, sequential) expression R not necessarily has
to be sequential. Note also that we aim at observational equivalence of behaviours in the
sense of [Mil82] - much finer than usual language-based criteria - we would like, for
example, to distinguish between a; b,c and (a;b) , (a;c) or a;a* and a*;a
The reader is advised to refer to [Pro89] for some general intuitions and motivations.

Definition 4.1. (*informal*)

An expression R is said to be a **perfect context** iff *every decision anticipated* within R can be seen as a choice between unique action symbols. ∎

Hint: Syntactic structure of perfect context should be recognizable even, after removing all the repeating action symbols (c.f. the role of *guards* in [JM89]) .

Note that creating a perfect context by inserting silent actions is not too difficult - but in practice we would like to have *a method ensuring* that the result is *minimal*.

Construction:

Input: A perfect context expression.

Output: Net structure representing the expression.

Build the net's places according to Proposition 3.3 - ensure consistent successor function using Algorithm 3.7.

Find a *derived* expression removing all repeated action symbols from the most enhanced version of the expression given. Build places of the second net, using Proposition 3.3 again. ∎

Example 4.4

Return to the final specification of Example 2.3.:

S1A: $(((a;a) , (G;a) ;)c)^*$ S1B: $(((b;b) , (G;b) ;)c)^*$

We are now able to construct two, topologically identical structures representing both components, each composed of two finite-state machine nets. The following figure shows an image of S1A:

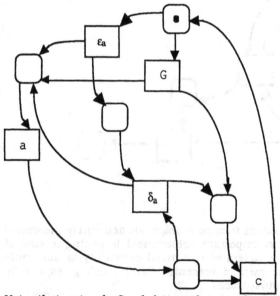

Note, that not only Greek letters denote silent transitions - the capital G is also silent, but unlike the others the latter will engage in synchronization with S1B. ∎

Example 4.5

Finally let us construct nets simulating expressions A: $a;a^*;b$ and B: $a^*; a;b$ respectively. Note that $a; a^*; b$ and $a^*; a ; b$ - although equivalent from the linguistic point of view - should be represented in essentially different ways in our approach.

A is not perfect context - so, we shall insert ε to create it .

344

Seemingly, just one new symbol separating a and a* is necessary - but the successor function is inconsistent then, and also δ shall be inserted. Finally the enhanced expression: A': a;ε ; (a; δ)*; b .
This will lead directly to the following net:

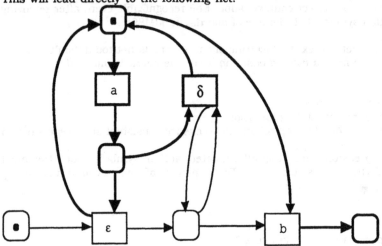

Similar considerations will give us : B': (v; a)* ; μ ; a; b

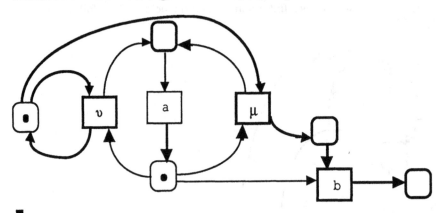

■

Final comment
The results presented seem to be important from both pragmatic and purely theoretical point of view. We believe that the most important achievement is getting a kind of justification for the statement that any system of non-trivial complexity is inherently concurrent. Not less important is the method presented here, which gives a fully structural representation of arbitrary regular traces.

Acknowledgements
I would like to thank Dr. Tomasz Müldner, for many valuable discussions and his sound criticism of the ideas presented here.
This work was partially supported by the NSERC General Grant, Acadia University, 1989/90.

References.

[Bes86] Best, E., COSY: Its relation to Nets and to CSP, LNCS 225, 1986

[Hoa85] Hoare, C.A.R: Communicating Sequential Processes, Prentice Hall, 1985

[JLKD85] R. Janicki, P.E. Lauer, M. Koutny, and R.Devillers. *Concurrent and Maximally Concurrent Evolution of Non-Sequential Systems.* Theoretical Comp. Science 43 (1985).

[Jan84] Janicki, R.: Nets, Sequential Components and Concurrency Relations, TCS 29, 1984. pp. 87-121.

[JM89] Janicki, R., Müldner, T.: On Algebraic Transformations of Sequential Specifications, AMAST, Iowa City, May 22-24, 1989

[Lau75] Lauer, P. E. and R.H. Campbell: Formal Semantics of a Class of High-Level Primitives for Coordinating Concurrent Processes. Acta Informatica 5, (1975) pp. 297-332.

[Lau79] Lauer, P. E. et al.: COSY: a System Specification Language Based on Path Expressions, Acta Informatica 12, 1979

[Lau80] Lauer, P. E. et al.: Design and Analysis of Highly Parallel and Distributed Systems, LNCS 86, 1980

[Maz86] Mazurkiewicz, A.: Trace Theory, LNCS 255, pp. 297-324

[Mil89] Milner, R.: A Complete Axiomatization for Observatoinal Congruence of Finite-State Behaviours, Inf. and Computing, 81, 1989), no.2

[Mil82] Milner, R.: A Complete Inference System for a Class of Regular Behaviors, Report CSR-111-82, Dept. of Comp. Sci., Univ. of Edinburgh, 1982

[Mil80] Milner, R.: A Calculus for Communicating Systems, LNCS 92, 1980

[Pet81] Peterson, J.L. Petri Net Theory and the Modeling of Systems. Prentice Hall 1981.

[Pro89] Proszynski, P.W.: Concurrency: Free Choice vs. Synchronization, in Computing and Information, North-Holland 1989, pp 213-219.

[Rei85] Reisig, W.: Petri Nets, Springer-Verlag, 1985.

[Shi79] M.W. Shields. Adequate Path Expressions. *Lecture Notes in Comp.Sci.* 70. Springer 1979.

[Sob86] Soborg, Ole: Transforming COSY into ASCCS, M.Sc. Thesis, Aalborg Univ.,1986

[Zie87] Zielonka, W.: Notes on Finite Asynchronous Automata. Theoretical Informatics and Applications, vol. 21, no. 2, 1987.

Concurrent Data Structures

Adrian Colbrook Colin Smythe

Department of Electronic & Electrical Engineering

& D.H. Pitt

Department of Mathematics & Computer Science

University of Surrey, Guildford, Surrey, GU2 5XH, UK

Summary

Several techniques for the storage of large data structures in main memory have been proposed and, although none is optimal in every situation, tree structures have become a commonly adopted algorithm. A scheme for maintaining a balanced search tree on a distributed memory parallel architecture is described. A general 2^{P-2}–2^P (for integer $P \geq 3$) search tree is introduced with a linear array of up to $[\log_2 N/(P-2)]+1$ processors being used to implement such a search tree. As many as $([\log_2 N/(P-2)]+1)/2$ operations can execute concurrently. Several examples of 2^{P-2}–2^P search trees have been implemented on an array of transputer processors.

The search structures developed were highly flexible allowing variations in the throughput and response time to be achieved by simple changes to the transputer architecture or the value of P. Applications of these search structures presently in use or under consideration include neural networks, parallel simulation systems, distributed database applications and the migration of sequential systems onto parallel architectures.

1. Introduction

Data structures are conventionally implemented as passive programming objects (collections of units which have some access structure). An alternative representation is as a collection of processes, each process representing a unit or part of the structure [1]. Such structures may be accessed concurrently, subject to internal synchronisation constraints. A scheme is presented herein for the efficient implementation of a variety of data structures on a distributed memory multiprocessor architecture. A general $2^{P-2}–2^P$ (P≥3) search tree structure [2] is introduced which utilises an array of up to $[\log_2 N/(P-2)]+1$ processors to store N data elements. This search tree structure is shown to be capable of implementing a set data structure with support for higher order operations such as iterative constructs.

Quinn's study of dictionary style search operations [3] gave guidance as to how increases in the throughput of data structure queries can be achieved on a parallel architecture. The sequential algorithm for a single search operation on a balanced B–tree [4] has logarithmic complexity [5]. If an N–element table is to be searched then the worst case for the sequential binary search is $\log_2 N+1$ comparisons. The improvement in the response time which may be achieved by a parallel algorithm for a single search can be logarithmic only in the number of processors used (for p processors the improvement in response time is $\log_2 p+1$) [3]. Therefore, the strategy suggested by Quinn is to seek increases in throughput for a series of searches, insertions and deletions operating in parallel.

Historically, much of the interest in parallel data structures has centred around shared memory multiprocessor systems due to their earlier development and commercial availability. In these architectures, the data structure is held in global memory for each processor to access. In the case of distributed memory architectures, the data structure is partitioned between the local memory of the processing elements. For such architectures, the increasing speed and density of very large scale integrated (VLSI) circuits has led to the development of several customised designs for database machines based upon tree structures [6–12]. These architectures all utilise O(N) processing elements to form a tree of N entries. Carey and Thompson [13] proposed a pipeline architecture using $O(\log_2 N)$ processing elements to implement a 2–3–4 tree. This was a similar architecture to that used by Tanaka, Nozaka and Masuyama [14] in their pipelined binary tree system. Fisher [15] also proposed a pipeline system which used a pipeline length proportional to the length of a key. He demonstrated that the processor–profligate VLSI architectures are not always the best route to a high performance system. In his concluding remarks, Fisher noted that Carey and Thompson's design may be preferred in systems with relatively short keys and that tree machines can be expected to be of more value in applications where a query or update requires O(N) time on a uniprocessor. Walden and Sere [16] presented a survey of distributed memory processor architectures based upon transputers [17] for the implementation of a document retrieval system. This was a distributed search based upon the processor farm paradigm in which each processor executes the same program on different data. They compared array, ring and tree structures and concluded that the tree was a superior search structure, a result supported by Green and Paddon [18]. A general $2^{P-2}-2^P$ (P≥3) search tree structure was introduced in [2] based upon the work presented by Carey and Thompson [13].

In Section 2 the general $2^{P-2}-2^P$ tree structure is introduced. The implementation of a concurrent $2^{P-2}-2^P$ tree is demonstrated in Section 3.

2. A Concurrent $2^{P-2}-2^P$ Search Tree Implementation

There are several techniques for the storage of data structures in main memory [5] and though none is optimal in every situation [20], tree structures have been widely used [4].

A $2^{P-2}-2^P$ tree (integer P≥3) is a tree in which every vertex which is not the root or a leaf has between 2^{P-2} and 2^P sons and every path from the root to a leaf is of the same length. If the root is not empty or a singleton tree then it has between 2 and 2^P sons. A $2^{P-2}-2^P$ search tree is a $2^{P-2}-2^P$ tree where associated with a node n is a value V(n) such that all the values at the same level in the tree are distinct. In addition, for all nodes (expect the root):

$$V(n) \geq V(fatherof(n))$$

where the function fatherof(n) returns the father of node n in the tree. Also, if n1 and n2 are any two nodes then:

$$((depth(fatherof(n1)) = depth(n2)) \wedge$$
$$(V(fatherof(n1)) < V(n2))) => (V(n1) < V(n2))$$

where the function depth(n) returns the level of node n in the tree. Data elements are represented by data values stored at the leaf nodes. Each leaf node stores between 2^{P-2} and 2^P data values (except in the case of the singleton tree which stores up to 2^P data values).

A $2^{P-2}-2^P$ search tree may be implemented as a linear array of processes, where each process holds a level of the tree structure and the last process stored the actual data items. The tree grows in an upwards direction.

It is possible to place bounds upon the maximum size of the data structure, S_{MAX}, which may be stored in a tree of L levels (L processes):

$$2^{L(P-2)} \leq S_{MAX} \leq 2^{LP} \quad (1)$$

Therefore, for a tree of N data elements, the number of levels L required in the tree (and the number of processes) is given by:

$$L = \frac{\log_2 N}{P - 2} \quad (2)$$

The searching operation is a simple pipeline version of the normal B+ tree search [4] and the insert and delete operations are based upon the top–down node–splitting scheme presented by Guibas and Sedgewick [19]. In this scheme transformations are applied during a single traversal of the tree for an update operation. There is no need to maintain a record of the tree structure during the traversal since no portion of the search path need be traversed again to restore the balancing condition. The insertion transformation is applied when an insertion operation encounters a node, other than the root, with 2^P branches. The node is split to form two nodes each with 2^{P-1} branches, as depicted in Figure 1. In this diagram, the optional pointers are represented by the dashed lines and the search path pointer is indicated by the small filled circle. This transformation ensured that any future node splitting does not cause upward propagation in the tree structure. When a deletion operation encounters a node, other than the root, with 2^{P-2} branches one of two general deletion transformation is applied. If the neighbouring node has less than or equal to 2^{P-1} branches then the transformation depicted in Figure 2a is applied, otherwise the transformation of Figure 2b is used. (Note, that the neighbour relationship used in the deletion algorithms relates a node to its left brother in the subtree or in the case of the leftmost node, to the right brother.) When the transformations are applied to a root node, the insertion transformation converts a root node with 2^P descendants into a twin 2^{P-1} node configuration and a new root node, increasing the height of the tree. The deletion transformation (I) converts a root node with 2 descendants into a new root node formed by the merging of the root's offspring.

The array of processes operates on a request/reply paradigm, half of the processes can be processing requests at any given time. The scheme requires $O(\log_2 N)$ time per tree operation, but allows $O(\log_2 N)$ concurrency on the operations; one operation completes every $O(1)$ time. As queries enter the pipeline at the top and replies leave at the bottom the root bottleneck problem [16] normally encountered in tree architectures is removed. The protocol between processes is simple and

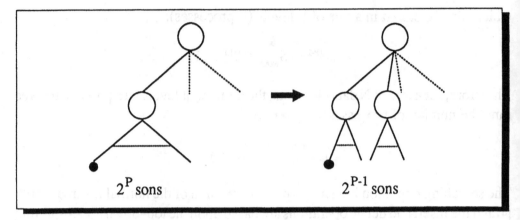

Figure 1 The insertion transformation

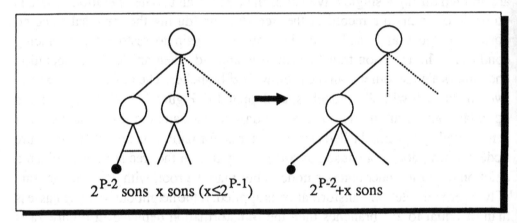

Figure 2 The deletion transformation I

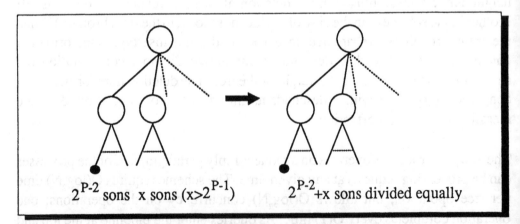

Figure 3 The deletion transformation II

each process needs only to communicate with its two neighbouring processes. Changes in the structure of a tree level are restricted to a pair of processes and are simply implemented as part of the protocol. Since both the number of processors allocated to the array and the value of P may be varied, the flexibility of this search structure make it a strong candidate for the solution of data processing problems on a variety of parallel architectures.

3.　A Concurrent Set Implementation

A variety of $2^{P-2}-2^P$ search tree structures have been implemented [2] on an array of transputer processors [17] using the Supernode architecture developed under Esprit Project 1085 [20–22]. The basic single Supernode architecture consists of sixteen T800 worker transputers each with 256Kb SRAM or 4Mb DRAM local memory, a controller transputer, one or two T800 processors acting as disc servers and caches, a link switching network and a number of external links and devices. A complete supercomputer may be formed by combining up to sixty four Supernodes with an appropriate outer switching network, controllers and devices [22]. The structures presented here were developed on a Supernode consisting of sixteen T800 worker transputers each with 4Mb DRAM.

Six tree structures were implemented:

(1) 6 level 2-3-4 tree	(3) 3 level 4-16 tree	(5) 2 level 16-64 tree
(2) 4 level 2-8 tree	(4) 2 level 8-32 tree	(6) 1 level 4096 tree

Note that the 2-3-4 tree was not a $2^{P-2}-2^P$ tree but will be assumed to have a value of P=2 in the results given herein. Each structure was implemented on a linear array of transputers and the length of the array was varied for each case. For example, for the six level 2-3-4 tree arrays lengths of one, two, three and six processors were used. This allowed the effect of assigning several levels of the tree structure to a single processor to be determined. Measurements were made for one hundred queries to the tree structures using random data keys, generated by the linear congruential method. The keys were five digit integer values. The measured values of the throughput and response time were normalised for each case. Since the search time for a given tree structure was proportional to $\log_2 N$, a normalising coefficient for each case was calculated as $[\log_2 N/\log_2 N_{2-3-4}]$, where N is the number of elements in the tree prior to the one hundred queries being applied and N_{2-3-4} is this value for the 2-3-4 tree. Normalisation allows comparisons between the values of throughput and response time for differing tree structures to be made without the need to consider the number of elements stored in each structure.

The throughputs and response times are shown in Figures 4 and 5. The value of L for a given search tree was the maximum array length used in the implementation of that tree. The throughput for the single processor case improved with increasing P as far as P=5, the 8-32 tree. This was due to the reduction in context switching between processes on a single processor. The results for the 16-64 tree (P=6) demonstrated the effect of increasing the size of the data structure allocated to each process so that the correspondingly long processing times caused a degradation in throughput. When the array length was increased to L processors an increase in throughput was seen on changing from a 2-3-4 (P=2) to a 2-8 (P=3) tree and then to a 4-16 (P=4) tree. The change to a 8-32 (P=5) and then to a 16-64 (P=6) tree resulted in a decrease in throughput. The response time followed a similar pattern with improvements being seen for increasing values of P until the 16-64 (P=6) tree was reached. Note that the response time decreased as additional processors were added for the 2-4 (P=2), 2-8 (P=3) and 4-16 (P=4) trees. However, for the 8-32 (P=5) and 16-64 (P=6) trees the response time increased as additional processors were used since very little of the processing for a single query ran concurrently in these cases. When the 4096 tree with a single processor was considered, the burden of the single computational intensive process was clearly demonstrated by poor values for throughput and response time.

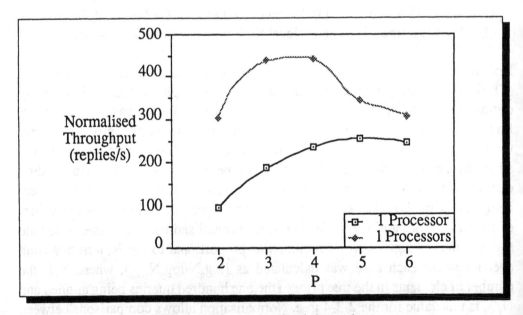

Figure 4 The normalised throughput

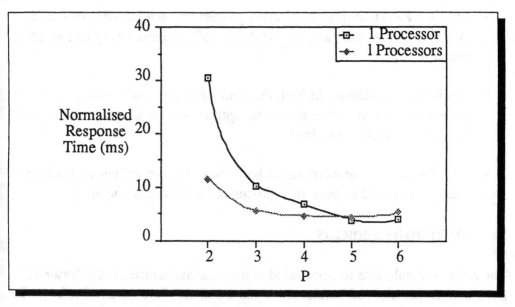

Figure 5 The normalised response time

4. Conclusion

A top–down node–splitting scheme may be generally applied to a linear array of processes implementing a 2^{P-2}–2^P search tree structure (P≥3). In such a structure, an insertion transformation is applied when a node with 2^P branches is encountered by an insert operation. Similarly, a deletion transformation is applied a node with 2^{P-2} branches is encountered by a delete operation. A reconfigurable system of Transputer processors provides an architecture on which 2^{P-2}–2^P search tree structures may be implemented.

The 2^{P-2}–2^P tree search structures has been shown to support the implementation of set data structures which may be accessed concurrently [2]. This implementation is hidden from the programming environment, allowing similar data structure to be used for a variety of environments through only minor changes to the interface.

For other distributed memory systems based upon either differing processing elements and/or architectures the optimal search tree structure will vary and is largely dependent upon the speeds of the processor and the communication links between processors. However, these underlying properties of the 2^{P-2}–2^P tree search structure remain:

- Efficiency – at most $[\log_2 N/(P-2)]+1$ processors are required to store N data elements and as many as $([\log_2 N/(P-2)]+1)/2$ operations may be executing concurrently;

- Flexibility – variations in both the number of processors allocated to the array and the value of P allow the optimal search structure for a given architecture to be determined;

- Performance – improvements in both the query throughput and response time are achieved as additional processors are added to the array.

5. Acknowledgements

The authors should like to acknowledge the kind assistance of Professor S.A. Schuman, Department of Mathematics and Computer Science and Professor B. Cohen, Department of Electronic and Electrical Engineering, University of Surrey. This work was completed under a Science and Engineering Research Council Studentship and was undertaken during a period spent at Thorn EMI Central Research Laboratories, Hayes, Middlesex.

6. References

[1] Dowsing R.D., "Introduction to Concurrency using Occam", Van Nostrand Reinhold, 1988.

[2] Colbrook A., Smythe C., "Efficient Implementation of Search Trees on Parallel Distributed Memory Architectures", to appear IEE Proceedings Part E.

[3] Quinn M.J., "Designing Efficient Algorithms for Parallel Computers" McGraw–Hill, New York, 1987.

[4] Comer D., "The Ubiquitous B–Tree", Computer Surveys, 11(2), pp121–137, 1979.

[5] Knuth D.E., "The Art of Computer Programming vol III : Searching and Sorting", Addison–Wesley, Reading, MA, 1969.

[6] Bentley J.L., Kung H.T., "A Tree Machine for Searching Problems", Proceedings of the International Conference on Parallel Processing, , IEEE, New York, 1979.

[7] Song S.W., "A Highly Concurrent Tree Machine for Database Applications", Proceeding of the International Conference on Parallel Processing, IEEE, New York, 1980.

[8] Ottman T.A., Rosenberg A.L., Stockmeyer L.J., "A Dictionary Machine (for VLSI)", IEEE Transactions on Computers, C–31(9), pp892–897, 1984.

[9] Bonuccelli M.A., Lodi E., Luccio F., Maestrini P., Pagli L., "A VLSI Tree Machine for Relational Data Bases", Proceeding of the 10th ACM International Symposium on Computer Architecture, pp67–73, IEEE, 1983.

[10] Atallah M.J., Kosaraju S.R., "A Generalized Dictionary Machine for VLSI", IEEE Transactions on Computers, C–34(2), pp151–155, 1985.

[11] Somani A., Agarwal V., "An Efficient Unsorted VLSI Dictionary Machine", IEEE Transactions on Computers, C–34(9), pp841–852, 1985

[12] Chang J.H., Ibarra O.H., Chung M.J., Rao K.K., "Systolic Tree Implementation of Data Structures", IEEE Transactions on Computers, C–37(6), pp727–735, 1988.

[13] Carey M.J., Thompson C.D., "An Efficient Implementation of Search Trees on [LgN+1] Processors", IEEE Transactions on Computers, C–33(11), pp1038–1041, 1984.

[14] Tanaka Y., Nozaka Y., Masuyama A., "Pipeline Searching and Sorting Modules as Components of a Data Flow Database Computer", Proceedings of the International Federation for Information Processing, pp427–432, North–Holland, Amsterdam, 1980.

[15] Fisher A.L., "Dictionary Machines With a Small Number of Processors", Proceedings of the 11th Annual International Symposium on Computer Architecture, pp151–156, IEEE, New York, 1984.

[16] Walden M., Sere K., "Free Text Retrieval on Transputer Networks", Microprocessors & Microsystems 13(3), pp.179–187, 1989.

[17] Inmos Ltd, "Transputer Reference Manual", Prentice Hall, London, 1986.

[18] Green S.A., Paddon D.J., "An Extension of the Processor Farm Using a Tree Architecture", Proceedings of 9th Occam User Group Technical Meeting, pp53–69, IOS, Amsterdam, 1988.

[19] Guibas L.J., Sedgewick R., "A Dichromatic Framework for Balanced Trees", Proceedings 19th Annual IEEE Computer Society Symposium of the Foundations of Computer Science, pp8–21, 1978.

[20] Harp J.G., "Phase 2 of the Reconfigurable Transputer Project – PT85", Proceedings of Esprit'87–Achievements and Impact, pp583–591, 1987.

[21] Hey A.J.G., Pritchard D.J., "Parallel Applications on the RTP Supernode Machine", Proceedings of the International Conference on Supercomputers 2, pp264–270, Supercomputing Institute, Florida, 1988.

[22] Nicole D.A., "Reconfigurable Transputer Processor Architectures", Proceedings 22nd Annual Hawaii Conference on Systems Sciences, 1, pp365-374, IEEE, Washington DC, 1989.

ASYNCHRONOUS FUNCTIONAL PARALLEL PROGRAMS

Jacques Julliand, Guy-René Perrin

Laboratoire d'Informatique, URA CNRS 822,
and Centre de Recherche en Informatique de Nancy
Université de Franche-Comté
25030 Besançon cédex   France
e-mail : julliand@loria.crin.fr, perrin@loria.crin.fr

ABSTRACT

Our purpose is to make a contribution to parallel programming in an asynchronous context, according to distributed architectures. The main difficulty in inventing parallel programs is to specify the way parallel components do cooperate. These features have to be progressively derived as systematically as possible from abstract specifications. The challenge is then to introduce relevant expression tools and a convenient parallel modeling for such developments. Programming with equations seems to be a very convenient way for that purpose. The aim of this paper is to associate an asynchronous parallel interpretation with fix-point systems, in which communications are defined.

KEYWORDS

Parallelism, Equations, Functional Language, Natural Semantics, Asynchronous Communications.

INTRODUCTION

Our purpose is to make a contribution to parallel programming in an asynchronous context, according to distributed architectures. The main difficulty in inventing parallel programs is to specify the way parallel components do cooperate. These features have to be progressively derived as systematically as possible from abstract specifications. The challenge is then to introduce relevant expression tools and a convenient parallel modeling for such developments.

The first point we put forward here is the interest of a functional language for such expressions, in which programs are sets of recurrence equations such as:
$$x[z] = f (..., x[\rho(z)], ...).$$

The second point is the problem of a parallel interpretation for such fix-point systems. Some proposals exist in the literature, either for synchronous parallelism models (as the language Lustre [9]), or for asynchronous ones (see for example [14], or [3]). Our point of view is to express time dependencies of algorithms behaviour, because time is an actual parameter in computing parallel algorithms on distributed machines. In some sense, for this target domain, these time dependencies are the least operationnal aspect to be expressed in any parallel language semantics.

The way time dependencies are expressed has to be discussed. For example, Ruth [10] makes time explicit : a program is a function updating temporal data structures. On the contrary, imperative languages such as CSP [11] or Ada [12] express time through non deterministic instructions and synchronization rules. Our approach considers an implicit time expression, by composing functions in a non deterministic way. In an operationnal point of view, this functional composition expresses relations between value sequences. Intuitively it means communications between machines that compute the functions, and define consumed value sequences depending on some produced ones and on the time where each element of these consumed sequences are requested. The figure hereunder shows an asynchronous parallel system. It is described by processes, whose calculations are models of some equation system, and by message passing operations which define non deterministic behaviours of this system.

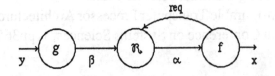

More formally, if a process f defines a variable x from a variable α, and g defines a variable β from a variable y, the relation between x and y is expressed as a parallel composition of f and g through a communication $\mathcal{R}$, defined by the λ-expression : $\lambda y . f \|_{\mathcal{R}} (g\ y)$.

After a first section devoted to programming with equations, we introduce our functional language in the section 2 and an example in section 3. In the section 4 we define the semantics of this language.

1. PROGRAMMING WITH EQUATIONS

1.1. Objects and functions

A program is an equation set of the form $x = f(..., u, ...)$, where x and u denote variable instances, and f denotes a function.

The semantics of a variable is a mapping which defines a possible infinite set of values, in a domain specified by the variable type. Each element of this set, a variable instance (or still an unknown), can be selected by an index which runs over a domain $\mathbb{D}$ of $\mathbb{Z}^p$.

The symbol "=" links two identical instances, which may be substituted one for the other. A function is a composition of operations, which are defined in its argument types.

Then we can define a recurrence equation as an equation in which the same variable name occurs each side of the symbol "=". We note :

$$x[z] = f(..., x[\rho(z)], ...)$$

such equations, where ρ is a function mapping over $\mathbb{Z}^p$. The "..." mark some other arguments (variables, constants or other instances of x).

A program is then expressed as a recurrence equation system, each of them being defined over a sub-domain of the indices set :

$$x_u[z] = f_u(..., x_r[\rho_{u,r}(z)], ...)\quad u \in \mathcal{U}, r \in \mathcal{U}_u, \mathcal{U}_u \subset \mathcal{U}$$

1.2. Computing equations

Some synchronous interpretations can be defined for a few target architectures, as systolic arrays [18] or more general processor arrays. Such architectures are characterized by a regular structure, local connections and a global external clock. In an abstract programming point of view we could say that they are infinitely fast machines, running deterministic calculations.

In the particular domain of systolic arrays and efficient mappings, the literature is rich about architecture synthesis ([7],[19],[5],[20], etc.). The implementation of the calculations defined by recurrence equations supposed to be linear ones over convex domains, that is the array and the data stream definitions, consists in transforming the system to obtain uniform recurrence equations [16], in which the affine mapping is a translation. Classical synthesis techniques process in three steps : define a dependence graph, derive a convenient time ordering, by defining a linear timing function, and then allocate computations to a set of cells.

The interpretation we are concerned with here is an asynchronous one, which could model non deterministic temporal behaviours of algorithms running on distributed architectures (MIMD machines). Such an interpretation may be presented as a straightforward generalization of the preceeding equation systems, such as :

$$x_u[z] = f_u(..., x_r[z_{u,r}], ...)\quad u \in \mathcal{U}, r \in \mathcal{U}_u, \mathcal{U}_u \subset \mathcal{U}$$

where z and $z_{u,r}$ satisfy some relation $\mathcal{R}$.

Suppose you apply the substitution rule, you may rename arguments by introducing new variables, as following :

$$x_u[z] = f_u(..., y_r[z], ...)\quad u \in \mathcal{U}, r \in \mathcal{U}_u, \mathcal{U}_u \subset \mathcal{U}$$

$$y_r[z] = x_r[z_{u,r}]\quad \text{where z and } z_{u,r} \text{ satisfy some relation } \mathcal{R}.$$

If the occurrence indices run over an inductive domain and the functions f_u and the relations $\mathcal{R}$ (in some sense) are monotonic, such fix-point equation system have a minimal solution, which can be computed by a recurrence path. The language we present in the next section expresses such convenient objects, functions and compositions, whose semantics will be defined by introducing timestamped sequences.

2. A PRESENTATION OF THE LANGUAGE

We propose then a functional language, in which each process defines the infinite value sequence of a variable. Its definition is given as an equation, the right side of which is a functional expression. Functions can be composed by a parallel application.

2.1. Expressions of sequences

Each expression name denotes an infinite sequence of values. For example, A denotes the sequence $(a_0, a_1, a_2, \ldots, a_n, \ldots)$. The result sequence of a function is expressed by operations on parameter sequences and constant sequences. The arithmetic, boolean and conditional operations are extended to operate on sequences element by element. For example, the expression A+B denotes the following sequence : $(a_0+b_0, a_1+b_1, a_2+b_2, \ldots, a_n+b_n, \ldots)$.

The following operators of Lucid [1] and Lustre [9] are defined in this language to construct recurrence sequences:
- operator pre :
    let be $(a_0, a_1, a_2, \ldots, a_n, \ldots)$ the value of A, then $(nil, a_0, a_1, a_2, \ldots, a_{n-1}, \ldots)$ is the value of pre A, where nil is an undefined value,
- operator $\rightarrow$: let the sequences of same sorts of values
    $A = (a_0, a_1, a_2, \ldots, a_n, \ldots)$ and $B = (b_0, b_1, b_2, \ldots, b_n, \ldots)$ then
    $A \rightarrow B = (a_0, b_1, b_2, \ldots, b_n, \ldots)$.

2.2. Processes

A process defines an infinite sequence as the result of some function on arguments. Its definition can use local definitions.

Example 1 : A process which defines the integer sequence is expressed as :
    process x == $1 \rightarrow$ (pre x) + 1
Note that this expression should be presented in an equational style as :
    x[0] = 1
    x[i] = x[i-1] + 1 in the integer domain i > 0

Example 2 : A process which calculates the factorial sequence is expressed as:
    process fact == $1 \rightarrow$ (pre fact) * x where x == $0 \rightarrow$ (pre x) + 1

Example 3 : A process which calculates the parity of an integer sequence is expressed as :
process even == λ n . ((n mod 2) = 0)

Note that the operators pre and $\rightarrow$ are polymorphic. The processes are defined by functions whose the sort of co-domain is infered, as in the ML language ([6], [4]).

2.3. The communication concept

While processes are functions on sequences of values, communications are defined in an operational style by a state transitions system on a data structure. This dynamic characteristic of communication satisfies some temporal properties of the consumed sequences relatively to that of the produced ones and the request times.

The communication operation "consume" is defined by axiomatic pre-post conditions. The state of communication is composed of three files which are intuitively the following :
- a file of produced values denoted sp,
- a file of available values denoted a,
- a file of consumed values denoted sc.

An unique "produce" operation is defined for any communication : it adds a given value to the head of sp and a. On the other hand, different communications are defined by various "consume" operations which add an available value of the file a to the consumed values sc.

Example 1 : The communication "equality" is such that the consumed file is equal to the produced one. This communication is defined as :
    - the consummation operation is defined on a non empty file a,
    - the consumed value is the oldest of a,
    - the new file a is the previous one without the consumed value.
        communication equality ::
                pre_cons == not empty? a
                val_cons == first a
                post_cons == tail a
where empty?, first, last, tail and [] are the operations of the file data structure. [] denotes the empty file.

Example 2 : The communication "refresh" consumes the last produced value at most once. It is defined as :

```
communication refresh ::
        pre_cons == not empty? a
        val_cons == last a
        post_cons == []
```

These two styles of expression are chosen for their adequacy for parallel system:
- the result values of the parallel system are result of function applications,
- the temporal behaviours of parallel calculation compositions are easier expressed in an operational style.

Such an idea is also presented in Turner [21], Kröger [17] and Wing [2] propositions which compose algebraic specifications and path expressions or temporal logic.

2.4. Parallel application

The semantics of a communication is a function connecting a produced timestamped sequence and a request time sequence with a consumed timestamped sequence. The operational expression hides clock calculations. Then asynchronous parallel systems may be described as transformational systems shown on this figure. The producer-consumer system schematized by :

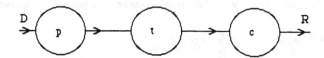

is a process which defines the result sequence R from the data sequence D. If c and p are processes and t is a communication it is expressed as :

$$\text{process prod\_cons} \quad == \quad \lambda\,D.\,c \parallel_t (p\ D)$$

In a semantical point of view, R may be regarded as the result sequence of the function c applied to the consumed timestamped sequence sc' which is itself the result of a communication function t applied to the produced timestamped sequence sp' (whose value sequence is defined by the application of p on D) and to some request sequence Req. This interpretation is that of a reactive system schematized by the same figure completed by the timestamped sequences sp' and sc' and by the clock Req as :

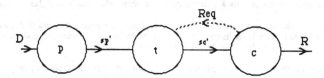

In section 4.2 we show that the clocks of timestamped sequences sp' and sc' depend on the computer architecture. As the clock Req, they are defined by the dynamic semantics.

3. AN EXAMPLE : COMPUTING FACTORIAL IN PARALLEL

The solutions are based on a decomposition of the product $1*2*3...*n$ in two products as :
- a product of the growing integers : $1*2*...*m$, denoted gp
- a product of the descreasing integers from n : $n*n-1*...*m+1$, denoted dp.

Then fact(n) is defined as the product of gp and dp. The number m may be defined according to the parity of n as : if n is even then m is equal to n divided by two else m is equal to n+1 divided by two.

We obtain the following specification (for a n given value) :

. fact = gp * dp

$$\text{. gp} = \prod_{j=1}^{m} j \quad , \qquad \qquad \text{. dp} = \prod_{j=m+1}^{n} j$$

m = if (even n) then n / 2 else (n+1) / 2 fi

From this specification, we derive many parallel solutions which calculate the three following sequences of integers :

- gp : the sequence of growing products : 1, 2, 6, 24, ..., m!,
- dp : the sequence of decreasing ones : n, n∗n-1, n∗n-1∗n-2, ..., n∗n-1∗...∗m+1,
- fact : a sequence of products of an item of gp and an item of dp.This sequence ends towards the value of factorial n.

These three sequences are calculated by the three following processes :

process gp == λ m . 1 → if gnat ≤ m then (pre gp m) ∗ gnat else (pre gp m) fi
     where gnat == 1 → (pre gnat) + 1   {growing integers}

process dp == λ n . λ m . n → if (dnat n) ≥ m then (pre dp n m) ∗ (dnat n) else (pre dp n m) fi
     where dnat == λ n . n → (pre dnat n) - 1{descreasing integers from n}

process times == λ n . λ m . n ∗ m {product of two sequences of integers}

The first asynchronous solution calculates the same sequence than a sequential one or a parallel synchronous one. That is the following :
          (n) ∗ (1), (n∗n-1) ∗ (1∗2), (n∗n-1∗n-2) ∗ (1∗2∗3), ...

This sequence becomes stable towards the value of factorial n.

The introduction of the communication "equality" allows an asynchronous interpretation of that system. This program is expressed as :

process fact == λ n.times ||$_{equality}$ (gp (m n))||$_{equality}$ (dp n ((m n)+1))
     where m == λ n.if (even n) then n div 2 else (n+1) div 2 fi
          where even == λ n . ((n mod 2) = 0)

We can observe that the result of this asynchronous system does not depend on the running times for each process gp, dp, times. Other solutions may depend on the running time. In these cases the sequence result converges towards the same value than the previous one but it may be different of it. These solutions are expressed by the same process fact in which the communications "equality" are replaced by "refresh" or "at_once" communications.

This last communication is defined as :
communication at_once::{consummation of the last available value}
     pre_cons == not empty? a
     val_cons == last a
     post_cons == clear_except_last a
       where clear_except_last == λ a . if empty? (tail a) then a else clear_except_last (tail a) fi

The second solution with the communication "refresh" uses at most once the last values of the sequences gp and dp at the date where the process "times" is ready for its computation. For example this following sequence may be a result :
     (n)∗(1∗2), (n∗n-1∗n-2)∗(1∗2∗3), (n∗n-1∗n-2∗n-3)∗(1∗2∗3∗4∗5), ...

The third solution is such that at any computation time the last values are used, but they may be used several times. For example this following sequence may be a result :   (n)∗(1), (n)∗(1), (n∗n-1)∗(1), (n∗n-1)∗(1∗2), ...

4. THE LANGUAGE SEMANTICS

4.1. Syntax

We define now the semantics of a fragment of the language. The syntax of this fragment is given using a BNF-like notation in which the bold symbols are the terminal symbols :

progr	::=	**progr decl ;** | **nil** {nil is the empty derivation}
decl	::=	**process ident == lambda** | {identifiers are considered as terminal symbols}
		communication ident :: pre_cons == exprs
		val_cons == exprs post_cons == exprs
lambda	::=	**λ ident . lambda** | exprs {lambda expression}
exprs	::=	exprs expr | expr {function application or simple expression}
expr	::=	**ident** | **constant** | {identifier and constant}
		exprs ||$_{ident}$ expr | {parallel application}
		pre exprs | exprs → expr | {operator pre and →}
		if exprs **then** exprs **else** exprs **fi** | (exprs)

Notes : infix operations and the "where" construction used in the previous examples are not described in this part of syntax. It does not describe the main expression from which an execution runs.

The domains *progr, expr, lambda , name, constants* of the abstract syntax are respectively associated with the following set of domains of the concrete syntax : {progr, decl}, {exprs, expr}, lambda, ident and constant.

Note that, for instance, this syntax allows a parallel application in a communication expression. An inference system defined in [13] which defines the welltyped expressions make a such an expression impossible.

4.2. Dynamic Semantics

The semantics value of a parallel system is a timestamped sequence of values. Intuitively, such a sequence is a sequence of pairs : value, time. Thus, with each value is associated its calculation time. Projections of such a sequence are a sequence of values called "value" and a sequence of times called "clock". This domain allows us to give an asynchronous interpretation of a parallel system defining a denotational semantics of parallelism by function application on timestamped sequences.

We define the dynamic semantics by a formal system in the natural semantics style [15], [8]. A semantics definition is an unordered collection of rules. A rule has basically two parts : a numerator and a denominator. Variables may occur both in the numerator and the denominator of a rule. These variables allow a rule to be instanciated. Usually, typographical conventions are used to indicate that the variables in the rule must have a given type (see notations in section 4.2.2) in the abstract syntax.

The numerator of a rule is again an unordered collection of formulaes, called the premises of the rule. Formulaes are divided into two kinds : sequents and conditions. The denominator is a single sequent. In the numerator, sequents are distinguished from conditions, that are placed slightly to the right of the inference rule. Sequents have several forms depending on the syntactic nature of their subject. In general conditions convey a restriction on the applicability of the rule : some relation must hold between two variables.

In the rules below, a condition is a property between the clock of the semantics value v of an expression E and the clocks of the semantics values of its subexpressions. This predicate defines the set of possible clocks which defines the set of semantics value v.

Intuitively, if all premises hold, then the denominator holds. More formally, from proof-trees yielding the premises, we can obtain a new proof-tree yielding the denominator, or conclusion, of the rule.

A sequent has two parts, an antecedent (on the left) and a consequent (on the right), and we use the turnstyle symbol "⊢" to separate these parts. The consequent is a predicate. Predicates come in several forms, indicated by various infix symbols. For example a predicate denoted "E ⇒ v" expresses the correct association between a well-formed and well-typed expression E of the abstract syntax and a semantics value v. The antecedent is generally a context. A context is a set of hypotheses necessary to assume a sequent.

In our language, there are declarations and expressions. The dynamic semantics will contains sequents of two following forms :
- for the elaboration of declarations : ⊢ *progr* ≈ context`. For example, the formulae ⊢ P ≈ ρ is read as : the declarations list P defines the context ρ.
- to state that an expression e has a set of semantics values v in a context ρ, the sequent has the following form :

context ⊢ *expr* ⇒ V   (example : ρ ⊢ e ⇒ v)

4.2.1. Semantics domain

As shown in [3], the denotational semantics of communicating processes networks require time to distinguish the functions associated with some parallel system. For that, we propose the timestamped sequence notion which is isomorphic to the "history" proposed in [3].

The timestamped sequences allow an asynchronous interpretation for our language, meaning that our abstract machine is not infinitely rapid. The domain of semantics values V is defined as :

$$V = S + C + TS + [V \rightarrow V].$$

It is the sum of the four following sets which are domains in the sense of SCOTT :

- S : set of finite or denumerably infinite sequences of integer or boolean values. S is defined as : $S == S_{integer} + S_{boolean}$ where S_T is defined below in 4.2.1.2.,
- C : set of clocks (consummation request times),
- TS : set of timestamped sequences (parameter and result of communications),
- [V → V] : set of continuous functions on this domain (value of processes and communications),

This sum is such that each domains of V have a common least element denoted ⊥ which is the empty sequence. Each domain of V is a complete partial order. S, C, TS are c.p.o. for the prefix relation and the least element ⊥.

4.2.1.1. We call "clock" an element of the inductive set C. C is the set of no descreasing mappings from $\mathbb{N}$ to $\mathbb{N}$. It is provided by a "cons" operation (add at the head of a sequence) denoted @> and by the following continuous functions :
- interleave : $C \times C \to C$ *{strict sorted interleaving of two clocks}*
- $C\geq$: $C^1 \times C^2 \to$ boolean *{each element of the result sequence is true if and only if the element of C^1 is greater than or equal to the corresponding element of C^2}*.

As in [3] we allow identical consecutive instants. That allows us to deal with a discrete time model instead of a continuous one.

In order to avoid making presentation heavy only intuitive definitions and some examples are given.

4.2.1.2. We call infinite sequence of type T any element of the inductive set S_T of mappings : $\mathbb{N} \to T \cup \{ \omega \}$. It is provided by a "cons" operation denoted @ and by the following continuous functions :
- K : $T \cup \{ \omega \} \to S_T$ *{constant sequence}*
- FBY : $S_T^1 \times S_T^2 \to S_T$ *{sequence composed of the first element of S_T^1 followed by S_T^2 without its first element}*
- PRE : $S_T \to S_T${sequence with the element ω followed by the data sequence}
- BEFORE : $S_T \to S_{file(T)}$ *{infinite sequence of files}* defined as :
$$BEFORE(s) = FBY([], push(PRE \; s, PRE(BEFORE(s))))$$
where push(x, f) is the classical operation extended to infinite sequences.

example : BEFORE $(a_0, a_1, a_2, ..., a_n, ...) =$
$[], [a_0], [a_0, a_1], [a_0, a_1, a_2], ..., [a_0, a_1, a_2, ..., a_n], ...$

4.2.1.3. We call timestamped sequence of type T any element of the inductive set ST_T. They are mappings of $\mathbb{N} \to T \cup \{ \omega \} \times \mathbb{N}$ such that their two projections are the followings :
- $\mathbb{N} \to T \cup \{\omega\}$ is an infinite sequence of element of type T,
- $\mathbb{N} \to \mathbb{N}$ is a clock.

We note trans (s, c) a timestamped sequence ts composed of an infinite sequence of values s and of a clock c. ts is a pair (value, time) sequence. For example :
$$trans[(a_0, a_1, a_2, ...), (i, j, k, ...)] = ((a_0, i), (a_1, j), (a_2, k), ...)$$
The projections s $(a_0, a_1, a_2, ...)$ and c $(i, j, k, ...)$ are respectively denoted val(ts) and clk(ts).

The set TS is defined as : $TS = TS_{integer} \cup TS_{boolean}$. It is provided from the following continuous functions :
- when : $TS_{boolean} \times TS \to TS$
{extracts the elements of the sequence TS corresponding to a boolean value true. For example when ((true, false, true, ...), $(a_0, a_1, a_2, ...)) = (a_0, a_2, ...)$}
- current : $C \times TS \to TS$ *{sequence of current values of TS at times of C}*
- incr : $TS \to TS$ *{same temporal sequence in which the clock is incremented}*
$$incr(ts) = trans(val(ts), clk(ts)+1)$$

4.2.2. Declaration semantics

Notations :
- ρ and [ident i $\Leftarrow$ v].ρ are contexts. They are stacks of pairs (name, semantics value). The top of the stack denoted [ident i $\Leftarrow$ v] is an association between the identifier i and the semantics value v. The point denotes the push operation.
- v, vE, vE1, vi are semantics values in V,
- c, c' are clocks in C,
- fpre_cons, fval_cons, fpost_cons, Φ are semantics values in $[V \to V]$
- E, E1, E2, E3 are expressions of abstract syntax domain *expr*,
- P is a program of abstract syntax domain *progr*,
- A is a lambda expression of abstract syntax domain *lambda*,
- i, x are *names*, b and n are respectively boolean and integer *constants*.

Rules :
1 <u>Process</u>

$$\frac{\vdash P \approx \rho, \; \rho \vdash A \Rightarrow v}{\vdash P; \; process \; i == A \approx [ident \; i \Leftarrow \mu(\lambda i . v)].\rho}$$

where $\mu(\lambda\ i\ .\ v)$ is the least fix-point of the functional $\lambda\ i\ .\ v$

2 Communication

{a:file sequence of available values} {fsc : file sequence of consumed values}

$\vdash P \approx \rho,$ $\rho \vdash \lambda\ a.\ \lambda\ fsc.\ E1 \Rightarrow$ fpre_cons,

                 $\rho \vdash \lambda\ a.\ \lambda\ fsc.\ E2 \Rightarrow$ fval_cons,

                 $\rho \vdash \lambda\ a.\ \lambda\ fsc.\ E3 \Rightarrow$ fpost_cons

----

     $\vdash P$; communication i :: pre_cons == E1 val_cons == E2

          post_cons == E3 $\approx$ [ident i $\Leftarrow \lambda$sp. λreq. trans(VSC, HSC)].

where VSC and HSC are intermediate sequences defined below from sp and req.

A communication is a function which defines a timestamped sequence sc of consumed values from a timestamped sequence of produced values sp and a clock req. The definition given below for the intermediaries VSC and HSC assumes that communication operations do not take time. The times of result sequence are :
- either equal to the times of request if the consummation operation is applicable at this time, i.e pre_cons is true,
- or greater than the time of request if the consummation operation is not applicable at this time. In this case, the time of the consumed value is equal to the first time of a production operation greater than the request time, such that pre_cons is satisfied. Any imperative language treats this waiting case by a synchronisation : guarded commands and handshake.

This semantics gives priority to the producer on the consumer and secures the mutual exclusion.

We note app the functional application to an infinite sequence which applies functions pointwise.

Let be: - cons_clk is the consummation clock,
            - a is the sequence of available element file at production and consummation request times,
            - a' is the sequence of available element file at consummation times,
then VSC and HSC are defined as :
            VSC = (app ((app fval_cons) val(a'))) BEFORE (VSC)
            HSC = clk(a')

where : a' = current(cons_clk, a)
          a = trans (VA, HA)
          cons_clk = ...{define from req and PRE_CONS}
          PRE_CONS =(app((app fpre_cons) val(a))) BEFORE(VSC)

Let be :   POST_CONS = (app ((app fpost_cons) val(a))) BEFORE(VSC)
         h = interleave (req, clk(sp))
         {request times of consummation and production operations}
         V_SP = val(current (h, sp)) {produced values at times of h}
         H_SP = val(current (h, trans (clk(sp), clk(sp))))
              {times of the last production operation at times of h}
         H_SC = val(current (h, trans (HSC, HSC)))
              {times of last consummation operation at times of h}

we define HA and VA as :
         HA = @> (0, h)   {times of available file sequence}
         VA = FBY ([],   {at time 0 the available file is empty}
              case h = H_SP and PRE(h) = H_SC :
                       push(PRE(val(POST_CONS)), V_SP)
{production after consummation operation : the produced value is added to the available file modified by the previous consummation operation}
              case h = H_SP and PRE(h) ≠ H_SC : push (PRE(VA), V_SP)
{production operation after a consummation operation request or a production operation : the produced value is added to the previous available file}
              case h ≠ H_SP and PRE(h) = H_SC : PRE(val(POST_CONS))
{consummation request after a consummation operation : value of available file modified by consummation operation}
              case h ≠ H_SP and PRE(h) ≠ H_SC : PRE (VA)
{consummation request after a production operation}   )

Note that :   - =, ≠ are the classical comparison predicates extended to infinite sequences,
                - [], push are respectively the constructors empty file and adds at the top of file.

4.2.3. Semantics of expressions

The semantics value of an expression is a set of timestamped sequences defined by a value sequence and a set of clocks. The clocks are defined by minimal properties that the interpretations must satisfy on any architecture.

4.2.3.1. Axioms

Let n be an integer, and b a boolean. The constants are self notations in the syntactic and the semantics domains. The following axioms indicate that the semantics value is a constant timestamped sequence defined by any clock c :

$$\rho \vdash \text{const } n \Rightarrow \text{trans}(K(n), c)$$
$$\rho \vdash \text{const } b \Rightarrow \text{trans}(K(b), c)$$

The value of a name is its value in the context : [ident i $\Leftarrow$ v].$\rho \vdash$ ident i $\Rightarrow$ v

The value of a lambda expression is a semantics lambda expr. in $[V \rightarrow V]$:
$$\rho \vdash \lambda i . E \Rightarrow \Phi \text{ in } V$$
where $\Phi(vi)$ is such that [ident i $\Leftarrow$ vi]. $\rho \vdash E \Rightarrow \Phi(vi)$

Note that for the evaluation of the abstraction body E we use the environment in which the abstraction expression is defined (rather than the operator-operand combination that caused the activation). The scope of identifiers is then always statically determined, as in ML language.

4.2.3.2. Rules

1/ The value of a name is its value in the context .

$$\frac{\rho \vdash \text{ident i} \Rightarrow v}{[\text{ident } x \Leftarrow v'].\rho \vdash \text{ident i} \Rightarrow v} \quad x \neq i$$

2/ The value of function E1 applied to the value of E is a timestamped sequence such that :
- its value sequence is the result of semantics function Φ applied to vE (the semantics value of E),
- its clock c is such that each time is greater than or equal to the clock time of c' (the clock of the semantics value of E). For an infinitely rapid abstract machine, c' = c.

$$\frac{\rho \vdash E1 \Rightarrow \Phi, \quad \rho \vdash E \Rightarrow \text{trans}(vE, c')}{\rho \vdash E1\, E \Rightarrow \text{trans}(\Phi(vE), c)} \quad C \geq (c, c')$$

3/ The function E1 applied to the value of E via communication i is a timestamped sequence composed of :
- an infinite sequence of values which is the result of function Φ applied to the value of the infinite sequence val_sc, where sc is the result of the communication function vi applied to the timestamped sequence vE and a clock of requests @(1, c),
- a clock c such that each time is greater than or equal to the times of the timestamped sequence sc.

We note sc the consumed timestamped sequence trans(val_sc, clk_sc) where val_sc and clk_sc are values of semantics values VSC and HSC in which we are substitued sp and req :

val_sc = VSC[vE/sp] [@(1, c)/req] ,
       {@(1, c) is the clock Req on the second figure in section 2.4}
clk_sc = HSC[vE/sp] [@(1, c)/req].

$$\frac{\rho \vdash E1 \Rightarrow \phi, \ \rho \vdash E \Rightarrow vE,}{\rho \vdash i \Rightarrow \lambda \text{ sp} . \lambda \text{ req} . \text{trans (VSC, HSC)}} \quad C \geq (c, \text{clk\_sc})$$
$$\rho \vdash E1 \parallel i\, E \Rightarrow \text{trans}(\phi(\text{val\_sc}), c)$$

The request clock @(1, c) is such that the consumer makes its first request at the first time of the basic clock. After that, the consumer makes each request when it terminates the calculation of the consumed value associated with the previous request.

The consumed sequence defined by (app((app λ sp . λ req . trans (VSC, HSC)) vE)) @(1, c) is the result of the communication function applied to the produced sequence vE and the request clock.

4/ Other rules are of the same form. For example, the rule of the pre operator is the following :

$$\frac{\rho \vdash E \Rightarrow \text{trans}(vE, c')}{\rho \vdash \text{pre } E \Rightarrow \text{trans}(\text{PRE } vE, c)} \quad C \geq (c, c')$$

5. CONCLUSION

Programming with equations seems to be a very convenient way to rationalize parallel program developments. The aim of this paper was to associate an asynchronous parallel interpretation with fix-point systems, in which communications are defined. This was made through a fragment of a functional language. The main ideas of this language are :
- to model parallelism as a function application on timestamped sequences,
- to separate the expression into a functional part and into an operational part in order to avoid time expression,
- to propose a communication intuitive concept expressed by operations on a predefined data structure.

The functional expressions on sequences have three advantages :
- they support a design program method based on decompositions and transformations,
- they allow the proof yielding of a specification in the timestamped sequence model,
- they allow transformation of systems by vectorization of processes or by modification of communication strategies.

REFERENCES

[1]   E.A. Ascroft, W.W. Wadge. LUCID : a non procedural language with iteration. CACM vol 20 n° 7, 07 / 77

[2]   M.R. Barbacci, J. Wing. Specifing functional andtiming behavior for real-time applications.
      L.N.C.S.n° 258, Spring-Verlag, PARLE, Eindhoven, 06/87.

[3]   F. Boussinot. Réseaux de processus avec mélange équitable : une approche du temps récl. Thèse d'état, PARIS 7, 1981.

[4]   L. Cardelli. Basic polymorphic typechecking. Polymorphism, January 85.

[5]   Ph. Clauss, G. Perrin. Synthesis of process arrays. CONPAR'88, Manchester.

[6]   L. Damas, R. Milner. Principal type-schemes for functional programs. 1st ACM conf. P.O.P.L. 82, pp 207.

[7]   J.M. Delosme, I.C.F. Ipsen. An illustration of a methodology for the construction of efficient systolic
      architectures in VLSI. Sd Inter. Symposium on VLSI technology systems and applications, 1985.

[8]   T. Despeyroux. TYPOL : A formalism to implement natural semantics. R.T. INRIA n°94, 03/88

[9]   N.Halbwachs, P. Caspi, D. Pilaud, J.A. Plaice. LUSTRE : A declarative language for programming
      synchronous systems. P.O.P.L. 1987, München, L.N.C.S n° 215, pp 178.

[10] D. Harrison. RUTH : A functional language for real-time programming.
      L.N.C.S. n° 258, Springer-Verlag, PARLE, Eindhoven, 06/87, p 297, vol II.

[11] C.A.R. Hoare. Communicating Sequential Processes. Com. ACM 21, 8, 1978.

[12] J.D. Ichbiah and all. Preliminary ADA reference manual and rationale for the design of the ADA prog. language.
      SIGPLAN Notices, vol 14, n° 16, 1979.

[13] J. Julliand. Expression fonctionnelle de systèmes de processus communicants. Rap. L.I.B. n° 48, Univ. de Besançon.

[14] G. Kahn. The semantics of a simple language for parallel programming. I.F.I.P. 74. North Holland.

[15] G. Kahn. Natural semantics. Rapport INRIA n° 601.

[16] R.Karp, R.Miller, S.Winograd. The organization of computations for uniform recurrence equations. J. of ACM, 14/3/67.

[17] F. Kröger. Abstract modules : combining algebraic and temporal logic specification means. T.S.I.87, vol. 6,n°6

[18] H.T. Kung. The structure of parallel algorithms.Advances in Comput.,15,1,79.

[19] C. Mongenet, G.R. Perrin. Synthesis of systolic arrays for inductive problems. PARLE, Eindhoven, LNCS 259, 87.

[20] P. Quinton, V. Van Dongen. The mapping of linear recurrence equations on regular arrays.
      Submitted to The Journal of VLSI Signal processing, 1988.

[21] D. Turner. Functional programming and communicating processes. L.N.C.S. n° 258, Spr.-Ver., PARLE, Eindhoven,
      06/87, p 54.

Symbolic Configuration for SuperNode Multiprocessors

Jean-Marc ADAMO Christophe BONELLO

Laboratoire LIP-IMAG, Projet C_NET
Ecole Normale Supérieure de Lyon
46, Allée d'Italie, 69364 LYON cedex 07 FRANCE

Abstract: As symbolic tools are not yet available on the SuperNode reconfigurable multiprocessor, the user is required to carry out manually a number of tasks which are highly minute, time-consuming and quite irrelevant to the distributed program he is developing. Needless to say, this makes the SuperNode machines highly unworkable. Fortunately, all these tasks can be automated. To this end, we designed a configurer : TéNOR, which makes it possible to describe network configurations at a purely symbolic level.

Introduction

Programming the SuperNode reconfigurable multiprocessor is at present a painstaking and time-consuming job. As symbolic tools are not yet available, the user is required to carry out manually a number of tasks which are quite irrelevant to the distributed program it is developing: making the configuration-setting program corresponding to the interprocessor communication graph, assigning appropriate physical links addresses to the interprocessor communication channels, building a loading tree and composing the file intended to the network loader, etc... These tasks are low level, highly minute, take an enormous amount of time, and in short make the SuperNode machine currently unworkable.

Fortunately most of these tasks can be automated. This is what the TéNOR software presented here aims at. TéNOR is a symbolic network configurer composed of a language, a compiler and a library of specific functions. The language is an algorithmic language that makes it possible to describe network topologies, at a complete symbolic level. The TéNOR compiler aims at examining network descriptions and checks them against the SuperNode architecture features. It issues a C program whose execution automatically produces what is required for setting the SuperNode switch, for assigning link addresses to communication channels and for loading the distributed program onto the SuperNode multiprocessor.

The paper is subdivided into five sections. We first give a brief presentation of the SuperNode architecture. Next, the need of a symbolic network configurer is discussed. In the third section we present the TéNOR language and give a few examples of symbolic network description. The TéNOR compiler needs to use an algorithm capable of mapping the communication channels of the distributed program at hand onto the physical connections.

Such an algorithm will be given in the fourth section and will be proved to be correct. Finally, the last section contains a few details on current implementation.

1. SuperNode Architecture

SuperNode is a reconfigurable transputer-based MIMD multiprocessor which was designed within the P1085 ESPRIT project [Ni]. The machine can contain from 16 to 1024 transputers. The basic SuperNode architecture is composed of a set of 16 or 32 worker transputers (T800) with their private memory, and a controller transputer (T414). Workers and controller are connected through a couple of communication media: a programmable switching device that connects the workers to one another, and a bus that connects workers to controller. Larger machines can be generated by recursively reusing the basic architecture. SuperNode is intended to be used throughout a front end computer which runs the programming environment.

1.1. Switching network

As far as the worker connection is concerned, the switching device can be considered as functionally equivalent to a pair of 32x32 crossbars. Let us label the four links of transputers north, south, east, and west (from now referred to as link labels). One of the crossbars allows the north link of any worker to be connected to the south link of any other workers (including itself). The second crossbar does the same thing with east and west links. It has been proved [Ni, NL] that this architecture is sufficiently flexible to allow for the implemention of any graph whose degree is less than or equal to four. The switching device is programmable and exclusively mastered by the controller.

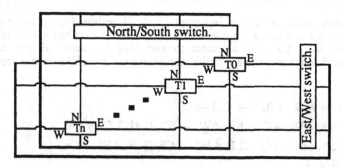

Fig. 1: Switching network

1.2. Control bus

Workers are connected to the controller via a second communication medium called a control bus. This bus works in a master-slave mode and provides a convenient support for system and debugging functionalities such as: fast worker-synchronisation, dynamic reconfiguration, local-timer synchronisation, non-interfering extraction of debugging observations.

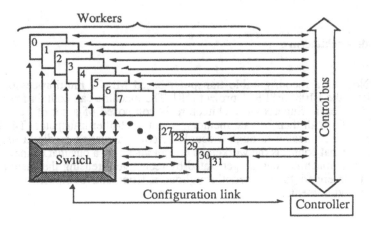

Fig. 2: Control bus

2. Need for a configuration tool

Let us take any distributed application, that is a set of component programs connected to one another by a set of communication channels. Let us assume that the corresponding connection graph has a degree less than or equal to four, so as to meet the four links limitation of transputers. Here is the task sequence the user has to complete, in order to implement the distributed application on the SuperNode machine:

(1) assign a transputer to each component of the distributed program and a physical connection to each communication channel. As physical connections are actually couples of link labels, the last operation amounts to assigning a couple of link labels to any communication channel. Here is a possible assignement for the illustration provided by Fig. 3:

$$1 \to A, 2 \to B, 3 \to C, 4 \to D,$$
$$(1.S, 2.N) \to C1, (1.E, 2.W) \to C2, (1.N, 3.S) \to C3,$$
$$(2.S, 4.N) \to C4, (2.E, 4.W) \to C5, (3.W, 4.E) \to C6,$$
$$(3.N, 4.S) \to C7.$$

(2) use the assignment completed in **(1)** to:

- provide each communication channel with a link label in each component. For the same example, C1 to C7 have to be manually relabelled:

C1 in A as 1.S, C1 in B as 2.N, C2 in A as 1.E, C2 in B as 2.W, etc

- write down a configuration setting program that will ultimately be executed by the controller so as to set up the SuperNode switch appropriately. For instance, in the illustration provided by Fig. 3, this program is the sequence of instructions that allows the T.node switch to be set as displayed in (b).

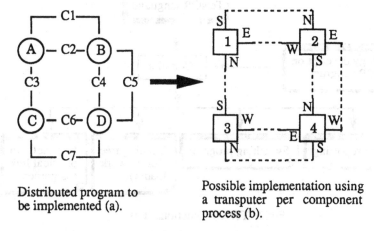

Distributed program to be implemented (a).

Possible implementation using a transputer per component process (b).

Fig. 3: Implementing a network of components

(3) find a covering binary tree in the graph of the application program so as to compose the description file required by the network loader. Such a tree is displayed in Fig. 4.

Logical number	Loading unit	Predecessor	Connected processors			
			link 0	link 1	link 2	link 3
1	unit_1	R0	3	2		0
2	unit_2	R1				1
3	unit_3	S1			1	4
4	unit_4	R3		3		

Fig. 4: Binary covering tree and loading file for the above illustration

(4) load and execute the configuration-setting program on the controller transputer.

(5) Finally, load and execute the application program.

Some of these tasks are low-level, all of them are highly minute and time-consuming so that developing application programs (even very small ones) on the SuperNode machine requires an enormous amount of time. Needless to say, this makes the SuperNode machines highly unworkable. Fortunately, all these operations can be automated, and this is what TéNOR aims to do. TéNOR makes it possible to describe network configurations at a purely symbolic level. The user is only required to describe the topology his application program has to run on, in a given high-level language . Then, TéNOR automatically checks whether the described topology meets the architectural constraints of the SuperNode machine, and automatically produces: a configuration-setting program, a file for the network loader, and a set of data that dispenses the user from providing each component program with a mapping that assigns a link label to any communication channel. This is illustrated in the following simplified diagram that describes the TéNOR functionalities (a more detailled diagram can be found in [B]).

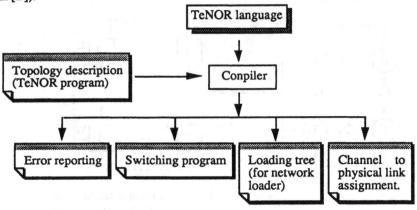

Fig. 5: TéNOR functionalities

The fourth generated file in Fig. 5 contains declarations that must be included in the components. They allow physical link references (so far named north, ...) to be substitued to channel identifiers in each component.

3. The TéNOR language

The TéNOR language aims at describing network topologies. For this purpose, the language needs to contain both algorithmic structures and specific network-describing oriented declarations. It was quite unnecessary to design the TéNOR language from scratch, so we decided to build it as an extension of C. A small number of declarations have been introduced in this language which are described below.

3.1. Network-describing oriented declarations

The *transputer* declaration.

transputer (node-identifier, component-name);

This declaration identifies a node within a network description and relates the node to the component the node is assigned to. The node identifier is simply a number.

The *connect* declaration.

connect node-identifier-1 **to** node-identifier-2;

This declaration specifies a connection between two nodes which have been previously defined using the **tranputer** declaration.

The *disconnect* declaration.

disconnect node-identifier-1 **from** node-identifier-2;

It is sometimes avantageous to define an irregular network as a partial network of a regular one. The **disconnect** declaration aims at providing such a facility (see Fig. 8).

The *remove* declaration.

remove (node-identifier);

This statement makes it possible to derive a network from another as one of its subnetworks (see Fig. 8).

The *root* declaration.

root (node-identifier) ;

The SuperNode machine is used as a slave machine driven by a front end computer. The **root** declaration identifies the particular transputer in the network which is responsible for communicating with the front end.

3.2. Topology description: a few examples

Grid.

```
void grid (int rn, int cn)
{
  int r, c, t_nb ;

  for (r = 0; r < rn; r++)
    for (c = 0; c < cn; c++)
    {
      t_nb = r * cn + c ;
      transputer (t_nb, "component", t_nb) ;
      if (r > 0)
        connect (r - 1) * cn + c to t_nb ;
      if (c > 0)
        connect t_nb - 1 to t_nb ;
    }
}

// An example of grid instanciation.
main ()
{
  grid (3, 4) ;
  root (0) ;
}
```

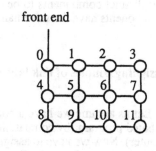

Fig. 6: Grid description

Hypercube.

```
void hypercube (int degree, int n)
{
    int i ;

    if (degree == 0)
        transputer (n, "hypercube", n) ;
    else {
            hypercube (degree - 1, n) ;
            hypercube (degree - 1, n + pow (2, (degree - 1))) ;
            for (i = n; i < n + pow (2, (degree - 1)); i++)
                connect i to i + pow (2, (degree - 1)) ;
        }
}

// An example of hypercube instanciation.
main ()
{
    hypercube (3, 0) ;
    root (0) ;
}
```

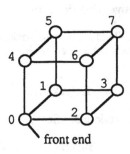

Fig. 7: Hypercube description

Deriving an irregular network from a regular one.

```
main ()
{
    hypercube (3, 0) ;

    disconnect 4 from 5 ;
    remove (2) ;
    root (0) ;
}
```

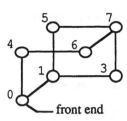

Fig. 8: An irregular network

Notice that the component name (in the "transputer" declaration) is generally given as a couple of arguments. The first is a simple label and the second is an expression whose value allows distinct components to be differentiated. This expression is simply missing when all the components have the same name.

4. Assigning couples of link labels to the edges of a network

Let us assume we have a compatible TéNOR description of the network attached to a distributed program (by compatible we mean compatible with the four links limitation of the transputer). Now we have to assign a couple of link labels to any communication channel, so as to be able to configure the SuperNode switch appropriately. Of course, the assignment has to meet the property that any couple of distinct communication channels attached to a same node is assigned a couple of distinct link labels.

The problem amounts to finding a partition of the network into coloured cycles (say black and white) so that any node in the network belongs both to a white and a black cycle. When this has been done, it is easy to assign north-south labels to the edges of white cycles, and east-west labels to the edges of the black ones, so that each node in the network receives four distinct link labels. This is illustrated in the network below.

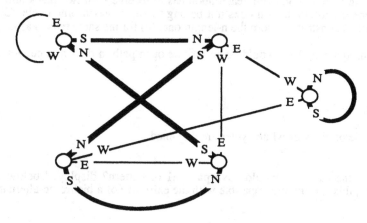

Fig. 9: Network labelling

Algorithm.

(1) construct a bichrome-alternate eulerian cycle in the network,

(2) take a node whose white and/or black edges have not yet been labelled,

    (2.1) if the white edges have not yet been labelled,
        - go along the white cycle containing the node,
        - for each edge, label the first end with north and the second end with south,

    (2.2) if the black edges have not yet been labelled,
        - go along the black cycle containing the node,
        - for each edge, label the first end with east and the second end with west,

(3) reexecute (2) until all the nodes have their four links labelled.

This algorithm will be justified by the following three propositions.

proposition1.

Each graph whose degree is equal to 4 contains a bichrome-alternate eulerian cycle.

Proof. It is a well-known result of the graph theory that 4-degree graphs have eulerian cycles [GM]. Besides, as the length of the eulerian cycle has to be even, the cycle admits an alternate bicoloration.

Proposition2.

The bichrome-alternate eulerian cycle allows the finite 4-degree network to be subdivided into a set of monochrome cycles.

Proof. Let us assume that the result is not true. In this case, there is a open monochrome path that is not embedded in any monochrome cycle. If we suppose that n is the length of the path, then we can prove that there is a path: which is (1)monochrome and (2)open, (3)whose length is n+1 having the n-length open path as an initial part, and (4)which is not embedded in any monochrome cycle.

1) since, in the eulerian cycle, each node has to receive both two black and two white edges. (2) since the n-length path does not belong to any monochrome cycle. (3) since the n+1-length path is constructed from the n-length one. (4) for the same reason as in (2).

As a consequence, there would be an infinite open path in the finite network, which is impossible.

Proposition3.

Any couple of black or white cycles are disjoined.

proof.
If this was not the case, we would have pattern1 or pattern2 displayed below within the Network. Now, this is quite incompatible with the existence of a bichrome-alternate eulerian cycle.

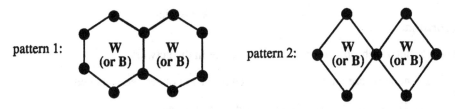

Fig. 10: Patterns

The algorithm we have proposed in this section only works for SuperNodes with at most 64 transputers. Indeed, this algorithm assumes that the north (east) link of any transputer can be connected to any south (west) link of other transputers. For machines with more than 64 transputers this property is no more satisfied.

5. TéNOR Implementation

Current implementation.

The current version of theTéNOR software has been developed on top of the Logical-Systems toolset [LST]. The software is essentially composed of a compiler and a library of functions. The compiler analyses any network description and checks it against the SuperNode architectural features. It produces a C program whose execution issues a set of files that contain: the switching program, the network loading-description given in a format that can be accepted by the standard network loader *ld-net*, and the assignment of a physical-link address to any communication channel for each component in the distributed program. Each communication channel is implemented as a variable that contains the pointer to a link control word.

The future.

The TéNOR software is part of the C_NET project [A89b], which is currently under development and aims at providing an integrated high-level programming environment for the SuperNode machine. TéNOR is currently being tightly coupled with the C_NET distributed language [A89a] in order to allow for the development of distributed programs capable of exploiting the reconfiguration features of the SuperNode architecture.

References

[A89a] J.M. Adamo, "C_NET: a C++ Based Language fot Distributed and Real-Time Programming", 11 OUG meeting Edinburg, Sept 89.

[A89b] J.M. Adamo, "The C_NET Project: An overview", rapport de recherche du LIP à paraître.

[B] Ch. Bonello, "TéNOR: un configurateur symbolique pour l'architecture T.node, manuel de référence", rapport technique du LIP numéro 90-01.

[GM] M. Gondrand, M. Minoux, "Graphes et algorithmes", Eyrolles 1979.

[Je] C. Jesshope, "Transputers and switches as objets in OCCAM", Parallel Computing 8, (1988), 19-30.

[Jo] A. Joubert, "SIGLe: Description et simulation d'algorithmes et d'architectures distribuées", Thèse de Docteur-Ingénieur, université de Rennes 1, Oct. 1988.

[L] W. Y-P. Lim, "HIDSL: A structure description language.", Communication of the ACM, 25(11): 820-830, Nov. 1982.

[LST] Logical Systems Transputer Toolset, Version 88.4, 2/20/89, Copyright 1989 by Logical- Systems.

[Ni] D.A. Nicole, "Esprit project 1085: Reconfigurable Transputer Processor Architecture", Dept. of Electronics and Computer Science, Univ. Southampton, Sept. 1988, and COMPAR88, 81-89.

[NL] D.A. Nicole, K. Lloyd, "Switching Networks for Transputers Links", Dept. of Electronics and Computer Science, Univ. Southampton, Feb. 1988.

A MODEL OF EXECUTION TIME ESTIMATING FOR RPC-ORIENTED PROGRAMS

Wanlei Zhou

Brian Molinari

Department of Computer Science
The Australian National University
Canberra, ACT 2601, Australia

e-mail: zhou@anucsd.anu.oz.au

ABSTRACT

This paper describes an execution time estimating model for programs which use Remote Procedure Calls (RPCs) as the tool for distributed computing. At first a general model with no closed-form solution is developed and a nondeterministic algorithm for its solution is given. Then the closed-form solution for a special case of the general model is derived. After using some approximate methods, the lower and upper bounds of the general form solution are described. The last section of this paper presents two examples of the application of the model.

Key Words: Concurrency, Distributed computing, Remote procedure call, Performance evaluation.

1. INTRODUCTION

The Remote Procedure Call (RPC) is a powerful primitive for distributed programming[5, 10], and the growing interest in its use demands tools for modeling and analysing the performance of such programs. Because a remote procedure call blocks the calling process until the call is completed and a reply has been received, a concurrency primitive such as **COBEGIN** or **FORK** is usually used to introduce the parallelism into the program. In this article, we consider the **COBEGIN-COEND** primitive with the usual semantics. We term an RPC-oriented program (in short, an RPC program) as one which executes on a local host and which calls, both separately and concurrently, remote procedures located on other hosts.

One of the successful commercial RPC-oriented distributed computing tools is the Network Computing System[1, 13] (NCS) (NCS and Network Computing System are trademarks of Apollo Computer Inc.). In this system, an RPC program consists of two kinds of programs: the server program and the client program. Usually server programs reside on remote hosts, while the client program resides on the local host (relative to the user). The user uses the client program to access the functions provided by the server programs. Also, a program must register all of its services (remote procedures) with Location Brokers. The client program can then find the service by interrogating the Location Brokers. After the client finds the location of the service, it then calls the service directly.

Usually a client program knows nothing about the location of the RPCs, and the only way to get them is through the Location Brokers during program execution. Also, the location of a remote procedure may be changed by its server or by some application programs during the execution. So, without lost of generality, we will assume that no locations of remote procedures are known by an RPC program before its execution. In that case, all remote procedure calls within an RPC program are channeled through Location Brokers. The operational semantics of an RPC program is indicated in the following figure.

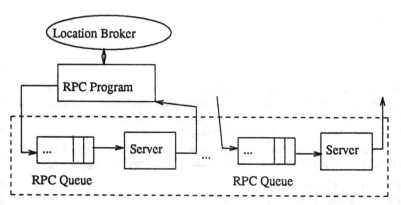

Fig. 1 The relationship among program, location broker, and servers

The program interrogates the location broker for the identify of the server for a remote procedure call. The call is then placed on a queue associated with the server.

One of the important performance metrics for a concurrent program is the execution time. Many existing articles discussing the execution time estimation of concurrent programs are based on queueing theory[8]. Heidelberg and Trivedi[6] discussed analytic queueing models for programs with internal concurrency. Thomasian and Bay[12] presented several queuing network models which may be used to analyse parallel processing of task systems. The queueing network model given by Almeida and Dowdy[2] can be used to analyse the performance of programs with concurrency / synchronisation schemes.

Although queueing theory is a powerful tool in the analysis of concurrent models, queueing network models with closed form solution are not directly applicable to these systems[4] because of the internal program concurrency. Also, because of the huge number of status, models with non-closed form solution are often not feasible. Another thing is, the queueing models obtain the execution time from the system's viewpoint by estimating all the possible jobs. While a user is often interested in the execution time of his / her own job, that is, from the user's viewpoint[11, 13]. Based on the user's viewpoint, we present in this article an execution time evaluation model which has closed form solution for simple RPC programs and nondeterministic algorithm as well as upper and lower bounds for complex RPC programs.

2. A MODEL OF RPC PROGRAMS

2.1. Syntax Issues

An RPC program executing on the local host may do several things: At first, it may execute program segments which are completely located on the local host; secondly, it may call several remote procedures in sequence; thirdly, it may call several remote procedures in parallel. Generally speaking, the execution time of a remote procedure call is much longer than the execution time of a local procedure call because the RPC will involve some remote communications. To analyse an RPC program, we will omit the program segments executed on the local host except for the segments which may be related to the concurrent control of RPCs. That is, we idealise RPC programs to contain only RPCs and some necessary control stuff, and consider all local execution of the program as zero time. The motivation for that is the fact we want to study programs that are dominated by the time spent in RPCs.

A sequential RPC program block is indicated by

```
BEGIN
  a; b; c                                    (2.1)
END
```

where a, b, and c are *atomic remote procedures* (or simply, *atoms*). That is, no remote procedures are called again from these procedures. Sequential RPC program blocks offer no speedup in a distributed system, because of the remote procedure call semantics. The execution time of a sequential program block is the sum of the execution times of a, b and c. Our model allows remote procedure calls to be made concurrently, as indicated by

```
COBEGIN
  d; e; f                                        (2.2)
COEND
```

If the atomic procedures `d`, `e`, and `f` are supported on different server hosts then they can be executed in parallel and the execution time of the `COBEGIN ... COEND` block is simply that of the largest component. But usually these remote procedures are allocated by the location broker to a set of available hosts. This means the evaluation of execution time will not be as such simple.

Our model is concerned with programs constructed from a set of atomic remote procedures by the repeated application of the above two operators. The abstract syntax of these programs is quite simple.

```
prog ::= seq_block | par_block | atom
seq_block ::= BEGIN { prog } END            (2.3)
par_block ::= COBEGIN { prog} COEND
```

Next is an example of RPC program (where A_i and A_{ij} are atoms). Its motivation is given in section 4.2.

```
BEGIN
  A₁
  COBEGIN
    BEGIN A₂ ; COBEGIN A₂₁; A₂₂ COEND END;
    A₃;
    BEGIN A₄; COBEGIN A₄₁;A₄₂;A₄₃;A₄₄ COEND END
  COEND
  A₅
END
```

Equivalently we can associate each program with a flowgraph[9]. It is built up from its atomic remote procedure calls, with edges denote the atomic procedures and the nodes denote the begin and end of sequential atoms and `COBEGIN-COEND` operations. Two special nodes s and f denote the begin and end of the program, respectively. The flowgraph of the previous RPC program is given in figure 3. It is easy to see that the flowgraph of an RPC program is acyclic.

2.2. Semantics Issues

First we shall formalise the situation indicated in figure 1. If we denote P as the set of remote procedure atoms and N as the set of server hosts, then we can represent the location broker by a function $m : P \to N$. Further, let us model the execution time of a remote procedure by a function $t : P \to reals$. Given a remote procedure $p : P$, the location broker tells us the host $m(p)$, and the execution of p will take time $t(p)$.

The operational semantics of figure 1 shall be made precise by describing an algorithm which determines the execution time of an RPC program. This algorithm consists of a "colouring game" on the associated flowgraph g. We use the following colour scheme for flowgraph arcs:

white	initial condition
blue	in RPC queue
red	executing
black	completed

and all arcs progress through the colours in this order. The game has the invariant: *All red arcs are associated with a different server.* Further, we say that a blue arc can *execute* if no red arc is associated with the same server.

The game involves assigning a value to an attribute *CompletionTime* for each node and each arc of the flowgraph. It also involves a single global variable, denoted *CurrentTime* (with initial value 0).

```
WHILE red arcs remain DO
```

```
select red arc x with minimum completion time;
colour x black;
CurrentTime := x.CompletionTime;
denote target node of x by n;
IF all arcs y entering n are black THEN
   n.CompletionTime := max(y.CompletionTime);          (2.4)
   colour blue all the arcs leaving n;
ENDIF
WHILE there exist blue arcs which can execute DO
   select a blue arc v which can execute;
   colour v red;
   v.CompletionTime := CurrentTime + v.ExecutionTime;
ENDWHILE
ENDWHILE
```

The initialisation includes assigning *CompletionTime* = 0 at the start node and colouring blue all arcs leaving it. These blue arcs are then processed according to the last statement of the algorithm loop.

There are two sources of nondeterminism in the algorithm, corresponding to the selection operations. The second of these is the most significant, corresponding to the scheduling of the queues in figure 1. That the execution time depends on the selection strategy is easy to see. A simple example is provided by the following flowgraph

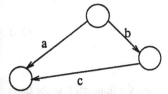

where *a*, *b*, and *c* are atomic remote procedures with unit execution time. Consider *a* and *b* to be mapped to host 1 and *c* to be mapped to host 2. If procedure *a* is selected first the overall execution time is 3 units, while if procedure *b* is selected first the overall execution time is 2 units (*a* and *c* can execute in parallel).

2.3. Performance Measures

Given a location broker map *m*, an RPC program *g* will execute (according to our model) in a time denoted $T_m(g)$. This time depends on the topology of the flowgraph of *g*, and the scheduling of the atoms over hosts. Our problem interest is that repeated executions may take place, with a different location broker map each time. If we denote by *M* the set of maps of interest, then the standard metrics are

$$T_{min}(g) = \min_{m:M} T_m(g); \quad T_{max}(g) = \max_{m:M} T_m(g);$$

$$T_{av}(g) = exp\,(T_m(g)) = \sum_{m:M} T_m(g)pr\,(m).\qquad(2.5)$$

where *pr* is a probability function defined over the set of maps *M*. We are only interested in the equiprobable case, namely,

$$pr\,(m) = \frac{1}{S}; \quad where\ S = card\,(M).$$

3. PARALLEL BLOCK SPECIAL CASE

3.1. Analysis

In this section we consider the special case of programs involving the parallel execution of atomic procedure calls. These programs have the structure indicated in equation (2.2), and equivalently have a flowgraph of the following form (where p_i are atoms).

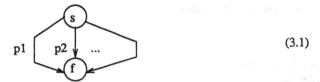

$$(3.1)$$

Now given $n : N$, we denote by $m^{-1}(n)$ the set of remote procedures that execute on the host n. If we denote by P the set of all remote procedures involved in the graph (3.1), then $A_n = P \cap m^{-1}(n)$ is the subset of P that will execute on n. In Fig. 1 these are the remote procedures that will be placed on the queue of the server n. To get a closed-form solution we need to make a further assumption, namely, that all procedures execute in a standard time.

$$t(p) = 1 \quad \text{for all } p : P \tag{3.2}$$

The analysis is now simple. The time needed to execute the queue on node n is the sum of the queue components

$$T_m(A_n) = \sum_{p : A_n} t(p). \tag{3.3}$$

while the time needed to execute all queues is the time of the largest queue.

$$T_m(g) = \max_{n : N} T_m(A_n). \tag{3.4}$$

Because of (3.2), (3.3) can be written as

$$T_m(A_n) = card(A_n). \tag{3.5}$$

3.2. Closed Form Solution

We characterise the set M of maps as follows. Each $m : M$ is a map from the finite set P to the finite set N where we denote

$$k = card(N) ; \quad L = card(P). \tag{3.6}$$

When maps are being set up in the location broker the procedures themselves are not distinguished. It is their allocation to a host that is of interest. Hence we identify a distinct map with the allocation of k identical "balls" to L different "boxes". This is a standard problem in combinatorics and its solution is well-known[3,7]. The maximum and minimum measures are easy:

$$T_{max}(g) = k ; \quad T_{min}(g) = \lceil \frac{k}{L} \rceil. \tag{3.7}$$

The first formula assumes to the case where all procedures are mapped to a single host, while the second corresponds to the case where the procedures are distributed as evenly as possible. Here $\lceil x \rceil$ denotes the integer least upper bound.

The average measure is harder. First we compute S, the total number of maps. From combinatorics results[3,7] we know this is a type-2 distribution problem and

$$S = d_k^{(2)}(L, [0, \infty)) = \begin{bmatrix} L+k-1 \\ L-1 \end{bmatrix} \tag{3.8}$$

where $[0, \infty)$ is the restrict condition of balls in a single box. But from the problem we know the maximum balls within a single box can not be more than k So here the restrict condition can be changed to $[0, k]$.

If we denote by $Q_i^{k/L}$ the number of maps with $\max_{n : N} card(A_n) = i$, then

$$T_{av}(a) = \frac{1}{S}(1 \times Q_1^{k/L} + 2 \times Q_2^{k/L} + \cdots + k \times Q_k^{k/L}) \tag{3.9}$$

$$= \frac{1}{S} \sum_{i=1}^{i=k} i \times Q_i^{k/L}$$

The combinatorial meaning of $Q_i^{k/L}$ is: k identical balls are to be distributed to L different boxes and the maximum number of balls within a single box is exactly equal to i and at least one box has this number of balls. If the maximum number of balls within a single box is less than or equal to i, then[7]

$$d_k^{(2)}(L,[0,i]) = \sum_{0 \le j \le L} (-1)^j \binom{L}{j}\left[\begin{array}{c} L+k-(i+1)j-1 \\ L-1 \end{array}\right] \tag{3.10}$$

So,

$$Q_i^{k/L} = d_k^{(2)}(L,[0,i]) - d_k^{(2)}(L,[0,i-1]), \tag{3.11}$$

$$i = 1,2,\cdots,k, \text{ and } d_0^{(2)}(L,[0,0]) = 0.$$

It is evident that $S = \sum_{i=1}^{i=k} Q_i^{k/L}$.

4. LOWER AND UPPER BOUNDS ESTIMATION

4.1. Lower Bound

At first we define an *extended parallel block* as

```
COBEGIN
  B₁ ; B₂ ;   · · ·   ; B_k                    (4.1)
COEND
```

where B_i is a parallel block (as in (2.2)) or an extended parallel block. This is a recursive definition. If there are L hosts, the average execution time of an extended parallel block A is defined as:

$$T_{Lav}(A) = \max\left(\frac{\sum_{i=1}^{k} T_{Lav}(B_i)}{L}, \max(T_{Lav}(B_i))\right) \tag{4.2}$$

If B_i is a parallel block, then $T_{Lav}(B_i)$ is calculated by using the formula in section 3. That is, in that case we have $T_{Lav}(B_i) = T_{av}(B_i)$. If g is an RPC program, then the calculation can be carried out from the inner parallel blocks of g to the out, and we have,

$$T_{min}(g) \le T_{Lav}(g) \le T_{av}(g) \tag{4.3}$$

where $T_{min}(g)$ is defined in (3.7).

The left part of (4.3) is evident because $T_{Lav}(g)$ considers some sequential allocation of atoms in parallel blocks of program g while $T_{min}(g)$ only considers the even allocation of atoms. The right part of (4.3) is also true because: (1) In (4.1), if $k = 1$, then $T_{Lav}(A) = T_{av}(A)$. (2) If $k > 1$ and B_i and B_j are two parallel blocks, then the calculation of (4.2) considers them independently, while in fact they may execute concurrently. In that case we have $T_{Lav}(A) \le T_{av}(A)$. (3) The meaning of (4.3) is to consider k sub-extended parallel blocks as being allocated on L hosts as evenly as possible, while it is not always the case. So we still have $T_{Lav}(A) \le T_{av}(A)$. This proves that (4.3) holds.

4.2. Upper Bound

If g is an RPC program and G is its flowgraph, we define the *level* of an atom $p : g$ as the length of the path from node s to the end node of p and denote it as $p.level$. Now the upper bound of g's average execution time $T_{Uav}(g)$ can be calculated as follows:

(1) Construct parallel block A_i such that if $p : A_i$, then $p.level = i$, $i = 1, ..., M$ and M is the maximum level of G;

(2) Calculate $T_{av}(A_i)$ by using formula in section 3;

(3) $T_{Uav}(g) = \sum_{i=1}^{M} T_{av}(A_i).$

It is not difficult to see that

$$T_{av}(g) \le T_{Uav}(g) \le T_{max}(g) \tag{4.4}$$

The right part of (4.4) is evident because $T_{max}(g)$ views all atoms as sequentially executed, while $T_{Uav}(g)$ considers some degree of parallelism. The left part is also true because atoms in different levels may execute concurrently, while $T_{Uav}(g)$ views them as strictly sequential execution. So (4.4) holds.

5. APPLICATIONS OF THE MODEL

5.1. A Simple Example: The Seller-Buyer System

Suppose there is one Seller and several Buyers. The Seller at first sends a message to each Buyer by using a remote procedure provided by the Buyer, describing the price, amount and performance of some goods. After a Buyer receives the message, he will decide whether or not to buy the goods and what are the amount and bid price he is going to offer. When the Seller receives the bids from the return values of the remote procedure, he will send out goods to the Buyer with the best offer, again using a remote procedure provided by the Buyer. The Seller resides on the main host, while the buyers are allocated on the distributed system (which consists of 5 hosts). The structure of the RPC program g corresponds to the flowgraph of figure 2, where A_2 to A_6 are remote procedures provided by Buyer 1 to 5 which can be used by the Seller to send out the message and get the return bids, and A_7 is the remote procedure call the Seller sends out goods to the best Buyer. Remote procedure call A_1 is used by the Seller to do some preparation before issuing the message.

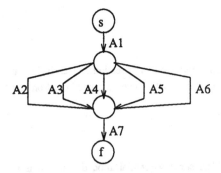

Fig. 2. Flowgraph of the Simple Example

Suppose all of the A_i's (i=1 to 7) are atomic remote procedure calls and the execution times for A_1 to A_7 are all 1. For convenience, we denote the parallel block of the program as C. We have

$$T_{av}(C) = \frac{1}{S} \sum_{i=1}^{i=5} i \times Q_i^{5/5}$$

$$= \frac{1}{126} \times (1\times1 + 2\times50 + 3\times50 + 4\times20 + 5\times5) = \frac{356}{126} \approx 2.8.$$

That is, the execution time for C is 2.8 time unit. So the evaluation time of this RPC program is $T_{av}(g) = 1 + 2.8 + 1 = 4.8$ time units.

Now, if we assume the distributed system has only 3 hosts instead of 5, then

$$T_{av}(C) = \frac{1}{S} \sum_{i=1}^{i=5} i \times Q_i^{5/3}$$

$$= \frac{1}{21} \times (1\times0 + 2\times3 + 3\times9 + 4\times6 + 5\times3) = \frac{72}{21} \approx 3.4.$$

So the estimated execution time of this RPC program will be 5.4 time units. In each case the lower bound and upper bound of the average execution time is the same as the average execution time.

5.2. A More Complex Example: Extended Seller-Buyer System

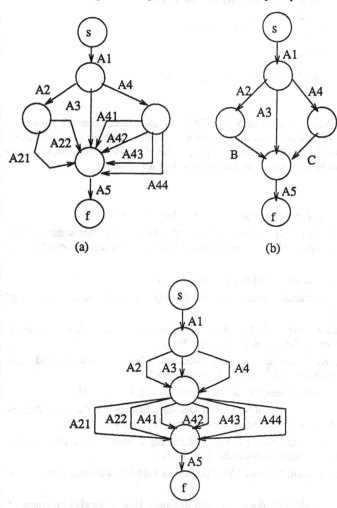

Fig. 3. Structure of the Complex Example

Next we extend the above Seller-Buyer system by adding two wholesalers. That is, the Seller concurrently sends out the goods information to some Buyers and two wholesale-persons. These two persons then send the information to their own customers (Buyers) with their own comments which may influence these Buyers, All the bids return to the Seller. At last, the Seller will send the goods to the Buyer with the best offer. The structure of RPC program g corresponds to the flowgraph of figure 3(a). Here A_1 and A_5 are the same as the A_1 and A_7 of the last example, respectively. A_2 is the remote procedure of the first wholeseller, while A_{21} and A_{22} are its customers' remote procedure calls. A_4 is the RPC of another wholeseller and A_{4i} are the RPCs of the customers. A_3 is the Seller's customer. Here A_i and A_{ij} are atoms and their completion time are all 1 unit.

To this time the derivation of a closed form solution to $T_{av}(g)$ for this program is intractable. Instead we shall indicate the use of lower and upper bounds to estimate the average execution time of g.

Fig. 3(b) is the restructuring of Fig.3(a) using extended parallel blocks, and Fig. 3(c) is the restructuring of Fig. 3(c) using levels. If we assume that there are 5 hosts, then we have

$$T_{Lav}(g) = 1 + max\left(\frac{(1+1.3)+1+(1+2.4)}{5}, 3.4\right) + 1 = 5.4,$$

$$T_{Uav}(g) = 1 + 1.9 + 3.3 + 1 = 7.2.$$

So, $5.4 \leq T_{av}(g) \leq 7.2$. If there are 3 hosts, then we have $5.8 \leq T_{av}(g) \leq 8.2$.

6. CONCLUSIONS

We have presented a performance evaluation model for RPC programs. Then we mentioned a non-deterministic algorithm for general case solution. The closed-form solution of the general case is infeasible, instead, we present a closed-form solution for a special case -- the parallel blocks. Based on this, the lower and upper bounds of the general form solution are given and two examples are described.

References

1. *Network Computing System (NCS) Reference*, Apollo Computer Inc., June 1987.

2. Almeida, V. A. and Dowdy, L. W., "Performance Analysis of a Scheme for Concurrency / Synchronisation Using Queueing Network Models," *International Journal of Parallel Processing*, vol. 15, no. 6, 1986.

3. Bogart, P. K., *Introductory Combinatorics*, Pitman Publishing Inc., 1983.

4. Chandy, K. and Martin, A., "A Characterisation of Product-form Queueing Networks," *Journal of ACM*, vol. 30, no. 2, April 1983.

5. Gifford, G. K., "Communication Models for Distributed Computation," in *Distributed Operating Systems, Theory and Practice*, ed. Y. Paker, vol. 28, Springer-Verlag, 1986.

6. Heidelberg, P. and Trivedi, K., "Analytic Queueing Model for Programs with internal concurrency," *IEEE Trans. on Computers*, vol. C-32, no. 1, January 1983.

7. Ke, Z. and Wei, W. D., *Combinatorial Theory (I)*, Science Press, Beijing, China, 1981.

8. Lavenberg, S. S. and Sauer, C. H., "Analytical Results for Queueing Models," in *Computer Performance Modeling Handbook*, ed. S. S. Lavenberg, Academic Press, Inc., New York, 1983.

9. Marcotty, M. and Ledgard, H. E., *Programming Language Landscape: Syntax / Semantics / Implementation (2nd Edition)*, Science Research Association, Inc., 1986.

10. Nelson, B. J., "Remote Procedure Call," Report CSL-81-9, Xerox Palo Alto Research Centre, May 1981.

11. Qin, B. and Ammar, R. A., "A Model to Estimate Average Response Time of Parallel Programs," *Proceedings of the IEEE 13th Annual International Computer Software & Applications Conference*, pp. 67-74, Orlando, Florida, September 1989.

12. Thomasian, A. and Bay, P., "Queueing Network Models for Parallel Processing," in *Proceedings of the International Conference on Parallel Processing, IEEE*, 1983.

13. Zhou, W. and Molinari, B., "A Performance Evaluation Model for Programs Using Remote Procedure Calls," *Australian Computer Science Communications*, vol. 11, no. 1, pp. 98-109, February 1989.

Parallel Computation of Longest-Common-Subsequence [†]

Mi Lu

Electrical Engineering Department

Texas A&M University

College Station, TX 77843

Abstract

A parallel algorithm for finding the longest common subsequence of two strings is presented. Our algorithm is executed on r processors, with r equal to the total number of pairs of positions at which two symbols match. Given two strings of length m and n respectively, $m \leq n$, with preprocessing allowed, our algorithm achieves $O(\log \rho \log^2 n)$ time complexity where ρ is the longest common subsequence. Fast computing of Longest-Common-Subsequence is made possible due to the exploiting of the parallelism.

I. Introduction

A *string* is a sequence of symbols. The recognition of two information-bearing strings that are related, even though not identical, is requested very often in visual pattern matching, speech recognition, editing error correction, bird song classification, artificial intelligence, data retrieval and genetics [1].

Given a string, a *subsequence* of the string can be obtained from the string by deleting none or some symbols (not necessarily consecutive ones). If string C is a subsequence of both string A, and string B, then C is a *common subsequence* (CS) of A and B. String C is a *longest common subsequence* (LCS) of string A and B if C is a common subsequence of A and B with maximal length. For example, if *"development"* and *"depend"* are the two input strings, then *"dee"* is a CS of the strings, and *"depen"* is a LCS of them. The LCS problem was first studied in molecular biology where similar sequences in the analysis of amino acids and nucleic acid involve hundreds of symbols [2]. For example, ARV-2DNA, the human retrovirus associated with AIDS disease, consists of about 10,000 symbols. Manual analysis is not promising due to the massive time needed and the limitation in the human recognition ability. A special application of the LCS problem is the pattern-matching problem, where a string A of m symbols is a substring of a string B of n symbols, $m \leq n$. In syntactic pattern recognition, a pattern is usually represented by a string, or a graph of pattern primitives. The processes on the strings are usually slow due to the large amount of data to be processed. Efficient algorithms need to be generated [3] for the pattern-matching recognition.

The string-to-string correction (or string-editing) problem is a generalization of the LCS problem. In the editing error analysis, one string is needed to be transformed/corrected to others, say, some given keywords. The "distance" of the edited string away from the given string can be a function of the cost of different operations such as deletion, insertion and substitution. Also, it can be a function of the possibilities of different characters to be mistyped/misspelled for another. For example, because of the conventional keyboard arrangement, it may be far more likely that a character *"j"* be mistyped as an *"h"* than as a *"r"*. Thus preference should be given to correcting the word *"jail"* to *"hail"* rather than to *"rail"*.

Hirschberg [4] solved the LCS problem in quadratic time and linear space first, and proved with others that the bounds on the complexity of LCS problem is $O(mn)$ for two strings with length m and n respectively if the comparisons of two symbols provides only "equal-not equal" information [5]. He later on developed two algorithms with time performance $O(\rho n + n \log n)$ and

[†] This research is partially supported by the National Science Foundation under Grant No. MIP-8809328.

$O(\rho(m+1-\rho)\log n)$ respectively, where ρ is the longest common subsequence. Hunt presented an algorithm for this problem which needs $O((r+n)\log n)$ running time and $O(r+n)$ space, where r is the total number of ordered pairs of positions at which the two sequences match [6]. In [7], Hsu and Du presented their new results for the LCS problem. With $O(n\log n)$ preprocessing time, their algorithms improved the time complexity to $O(\rho m\log(n/m)+\rho m)$ and $O(\rho m\log(n/\rho)+\rho m)$ respectively. They also gave a method in [8] to compute a longest common subsequence for a set of strings. All the previous algorithms are sequential. Although some parallel arrays are proposed as the special-purpose hardware to perform sequence comparison, or to be programmed to solve more general problems, very few parallel algorithms have been designed for solving the LCS problem on parallel machines [9].

Our algorithm is based on the divide-and-conquer strategy which allows concurrency and hence improved efficiency. Better time performance has been achieved by exploiting the parallelism in the current work. With preprocessing allowed, our algorithm is run on r processors of CREW PRAM, and needs $O(\log\rho\log^2 n)$ time, where r is the total number of pairs of positions at which two strings match, ρ is the longest common subsequence, and n is the length of the longer string out of the two.

In the next section, we give the preliminaries of the algorithm design. Our algorithm for finding LCS is presented in section III along with the analysis of the time performance of our solution. Section IV includes the discussion on preprocessing. Concluding remarks and related research problems are given in section V.

II. Preliminaries

Let string $A = a_1a_2\cdots a_i\cdots a_m$ and $B = b_1b_2\cdots b_j\cdots b_n$ be two input strings, and the length of the string $|A| = m$ and $|B| = n$ respectively. Assume $m \leq n$ without loss of generality. Let $L(i,j)$ be the length of the LCS of $a_1a_2\cdots a_i$ and $b_1b_2\cdots b_j$, and $L(i,j)$ can be determined as follows [4]:

Compute L

1. $L(i,0) \leftarrow 0$ for $i = 0, 1, \cdots, m$; /* Initialization */
2. $L(0,j) \leftarrow 0$ for $j = 0, 1, \cdots, n$;
3. **for** $i = 1$ to m **do**
   begin
4. **for** $j = 1$ to n **do**
5. **if** $a_i = b_j$ **then** $L(i,j) \leftarrow L(i-1,j-1)+1$
6.   **else** $L(i,j) \leftarrow max\{L(i,j-1), L(i-1,j)\}$

   end

An $m \times n$ matrix, L, is constructed for computing $L(i,j)$ [10] such that the entry of row i and column j indicates $L(i,j)$. The $L(i,j)$'s are computed row by row with the above method and the length of LCS is given by $L(m,n)$ when the computation is completed. Figure 1 shows an L matrix of an example with $m = 6$ and $n = 9$. Further observation is made to reduce the entries to be considered in the L matrix [7]. Since only matched symbols will constitute an LCS, $L(i,j)$ is

			B								
			c	b	a	c	b	a	a	b	a
		0	1	2	3	4	5	6	7	8	9
		0	0	0	0	0	0	0	0	0	0
A	a 1	0	0	0	1*	1	1	1*	1*	1	1*
	b 2	0	0	1*	1	1	2*	2	2	2*	2
	c 3	0	1*	1	1	2*	2	2	2	2	2
	d 4	0	1	1	1	2	2	2	2	2	2
	b 5	0	1	2*	2	2	3*	3	3	3*	3
	b 6	0	1	2*	2	2	3*	3	3	4*	4

Figure 1

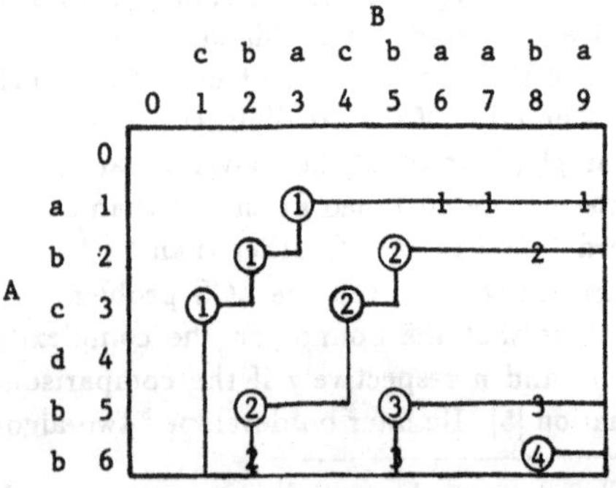

Figure 2

selected (indicated by "$*$" in Fig. 1) only if $a_i = b_j$.

The selected entries (i, j) are now referred to as "points", and the value of the corresponding $L(i, j)$ is called the *class* of that point, say p, denoted as $class(p)$. The left most point of a row in a class is denoted as the *break point* if it is the top point of its column in the class (see the circled ones in Figure 2). The horizontal and vertical lines connecting the points in the same class form the outline of the class. Point $q(i_q, j_q)$ is said to be dominated by point $p(i_p, j_p)$ *iff* $i_p < i_q$ and $j_p < j_q$. The definition of "dominate" is slightly different from the conventional one.

Instead of considering class 1, then class 2, class 3, $\cdots\cdots$, as is done sequentially in the previous results, our algorithm employs the divide-and-conquer strategy and runs faster. Assume that the total number of given points is r, then r processors will be operated under the PRAM model with each processor maintaining the record for one point.

Divide the given set of points by a horizontal line into two halves, the lower half and the upper half, such that the points in the lower half have i values greater than that of the points in the upper half. Recursively solve the problem for each half concurrently, and then merge the subresults. Before the merge, each PE containing a point is aware of the class of that point in its own half. (For simplicity, we hereafter say that the point, instead of the PE containing the point, is aware of certain information.) After the merge, the class of the points in the upper half will remain the same as before, but the points in the lower half need to recompute their classes.

Project the left most point of each class, say class k, in the upper half onto the horizontal dividing line. Denote the projection as *joint* (indicating by ϕ in Fig. 3), and index it by k. Locate a dummy joint at the left boundary of the plane with index 0.

For the example shown in Figure 3, the class outlines in the upper and lower halves before the merge are drawn in the solid lines. The indices of the joints projected from the upper half and the class number for the class outlines in the lower half are indicated. The dash lines show the new class outlines after the merge. Let a point $f(i_f, j_f)$ be point $s(i_s, j_s)$'s *father* if point f dominates point s and $class(f) = class(s) - 1$. Point $s(i_s, j_s)$ is the *son* of point $f(i_f, j_f)$. Initially, we choose for each point its father in the class above it and with j_f closest to j_s than any other points in $class(f)$. Refer to Figure 3, point F's son is point S, and point S's father is point F. Note that one point may have more than one sons, but a son has only one father. Each arrow in Figure 3 points from a son to its father, and two trees are hence formed with joint 0 and joint 2 as their roots respectively. We can find that after the merge, the class numbers of point A, B, and C are different from the ones before the merge. They are updated to those in the parentheses. This type of the update is due to the insertion of joint 1 and 2 with the smaller j than that of the points. Such kind of update will be taken care of by the "Update with Joint" included in the merge algorithm.

On the other hand, we can find in Figure 3 that point D changed its class number to 5 (marked by an asterisk) after the merge. A dashed arrow points from D to C which is a point in another tree such that C dominates D and with the maximal class number. Since B has a new class number 4, D updated its class number to 5. Such kind of update is referred to as "Update between Trees" which is included in the merge algorithm.

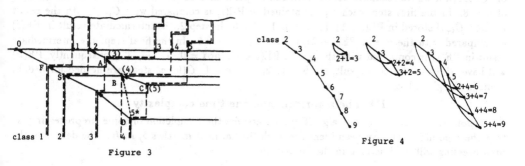

Figure 3

Figure 4

In a word, the merge step includes two phases in which the class of a point will be updated. When executing the first phase of the update, "Update with Joint", each point in the lower half is to find its father in the class above it. A point in class 1 is to find its father among the joints. A tree is hence formed by connecting consecutive fathers and sons, as is indicated by directed bold lines in Figure 3. A joint is the root of a tree, and is to notify its descendants of its index. A point receiving information from its ancestor can decide its new class by computing its depth from the root.

The second phase of the merge step, "Update between Trees". is conducted in a binary tree fashion, that is, in iteration i, 2^i trees should be merged together. Denote the left 2^{i-1} trees to be merged as *left trees*, and the right 2^{i-1} trees as *right trees*. Each point, say $p(i_p, j_p)$, is to find in the right trees the point $t(i_t, j_t)$ such that point t dominates point p and $class(t)$ is the maximum. If $class(t) + 1 > class(p)$, then $class(p)$ should be updated to $class(t) + 1$. Otherwise, it remains the same. If there are in total ρ trees in the lower half of the plane, then $\log\rho$ iterations are needed to complete the "Update between Trees".

The notification of the root of the tree to its descendants is performed in a "data compression" fashion. First, a point communicates with its son, and then with its son's son, that is the grandson, and then its grandsons's grandson, and so on. Following is the approach to complete the propagation.

Propagation

Figure 4 shows a propagation along a tree of 8 nodes, with the root indexed by 2. First, the root transferred its index, 2, to its son, and the son updated its class by increasing 1 on the received data, i.e. $2 + 1 = 3$. Then, the root and its son transferred their classes, 2 and 3 respectively, to their grandsons. Their grandsons updated their classes by increasing 2 on the received data, i.e. $2 + 2 = 4$ and $3 + 2 = 5$ respectively. Finally, the root, and its son, and their grandsons transferred their classes to their grandson's grandsons respectively. Their grandson's grandsons updated their classes by increasing 4 on the received data. This type of propagation is referred to as *Propagation 1*. Another type of propagation, *Propagation 2*, differs from it in that there may be multiple sources from which datum are propagated. In addition, a PE compares the received data with the one it contains before determining whether accepts the data or not.

In the detailed algorithm, instead of considering that the ancestors transfer the data to the descendants, we let the descendants to make requests of the data from the ancestors. Suppose originally, each point keeps the address of the PE maintaining its father. When making the request of the data from the father, the address of the PE maintaining the father's father can also be obtained. Now since each point has the address of the PE maintaining its grandfather, it is not difficult to obtain the address of the PE maintaining its grandfather's grandfather by similarly performing the described operation. For both of the two types of propagation, $\log\rho$ iterations are needed to complete the propagation along a tree of depth ρ.

Premax

Let $C_0, C_1, \cdots, C_n$ be the n data items in a list, $M(k) = max_{i=0}^{k}(C_i)$, for $k = 0, 1, \cdots, n-1$. We have $M(0) = C_0$, and $M(k) = max[M(k-1), C_k]$, for $k = 0, 1, \cdots, n-1$. Distribute the data on n PE's, the above recursive comparison can be performed as shown in Figure 5 for an example of $n = 8$. In the first step, each C_i maintained in PE(i) is compared with C_{i+1}, with the result $max[C_i, C_{i+1}]$ stored in PE($i+1$), for $i = 0, 1, \cdots, 6$. In step 2, the intermediate result in PE(i) is compared with the one in PE($i + 2$), for $i = 0, 1, \cdots, 5$. In the final step, the intermediate result in PE(i) is compared with the one in PE($i + 4$), for $i = 0, 1, \cdots, 3$. Consequently, PE(k) will have $M(k)$ as the final result, for $k = 1, 2, \cdots, n-1$. $O(\log n)$ steps are needed for n data items in the given list.

III. The algorithm and the time complexity

Before the execution of our algorithm, we assume the completion of some preprocessing, so that the r points (i, j) have been identified such that a_i in A matches b_j in B. The details of the preprocessing will be described in the next section.

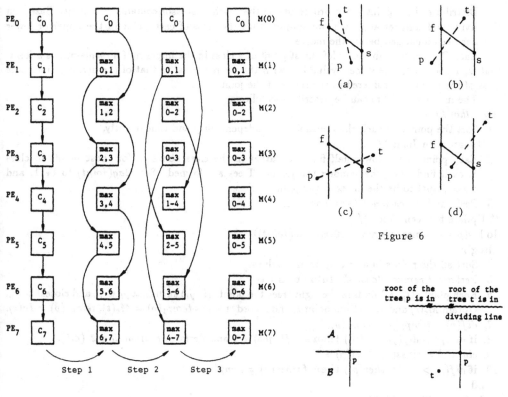

Figure 5

Figure 6

Figure 7

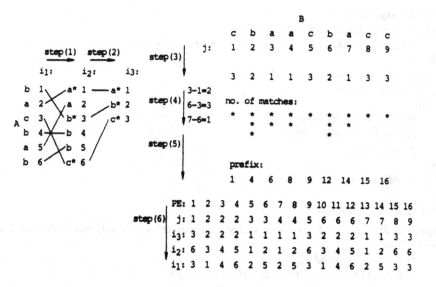

Figure 8

Distribute the r points on r processors so that each processor contains one point. Based on the divide-and-conquer approach, we suppose that the class of each point in the upper or lower half has been identified before the merge.

Each PE which maintains a left most point of a class in the upper half now maintains a joint, that is, a point with the same j value but with the i value equal to that of the dividing line. The class of the point is considered as the index of the joint.

The merge algorithm can be described as follows.

Algorithm LCS

1. Sort the points on each class outline by j independently and concurrently.

/* Update with Joint */

2. Each point in the lower half finds its father in the class above it; for those points in class 1, each finds its father among the joints. Trees are formed. Set $flag(joint)$ to be 1, and $class(joint)$ to be the index of the joint.

3. Perform *Propagation 1 (class)* on each tree.

/* Update between Trees */

do $\log(\rho+1)$ times (with $\rho = max(class(joint))$)

   begin

4. Sort all the points in a tree by their j values.

5. Perform *Premax(class, M_c, Id)* in each tree.

6. Each point $p(i_p, j_p)$ finds in the right trees the point $t(i_t, j_t)$ such that $j_t < j_p$ and closest to j_p. Obtain $M_c(t)$ and $Id(t)$ from point t, and record them as $temp_1(p) = M_c(t)$, $temp_2(p) = Id(t)$.

7. $dif(p) = temp_1(p) - class(p)$.

8. **if** $dif(p) > dif(father(p))$ **then** set $flag(p) = 1$ and Perform *Propagation 2 (dif)*.

9. $class(p) = class(p) + dif(p) + 1$.

10. **if** $dif(p) > dif(father(p))$ **then** $father(p) = temp_2(p)$;

   end

end /* *Algorithm LCS* */

The subroutine *Propagation* is presented below.

Algorithm Propagation 1 (class)

1. Each point p performs $addr = father(p)$.

for $i = 1$ to $\log\rho$ **do** (with ρ being the maximum depth of the tree)

   begin

2. Each point makes a request from PE($addr$).

   if $flag(addr) = 1$ **then**

   begin

3. $\quad temp(p) = class(addr)$;

4. $\quad class(p) = temp(p) + 2^{i-1}$;

5. $\quad flag(p) = 1$.

   end

6. $addr = addr(addr)$

   end

end /* *Algorithm Propagation 1* */

Algorithm *Propagation 2 (value)* is similar to *Propagation 1 (class)* but with Step 3 and 4 modified as follows.

3'. $\quad temp(p) = value(addr)$;

4'. $\quad$ **if** $temp(p) > value(p)$ **then** $value(p) = temp(p)$;

Following is the algorithm *Premax*.

Algorithm Premax (class, M_c, Id)

1. Each PE(i) performs $M_c(i) = class(i)$.

for $k = 0$, **to** $\log k - 1$, **do**

    begin

2. All the PE(i)'s route $M_c(i)$ and i to PE($i + 2^k$). All the PE(i)'s record the received data in $temp_1(i)$ and $temp_2(i)$ respectively.

3. PE(i)'s with $i > 2^k - 1$ perform

    if $temp_1(i) > M_c(i)$, **then**

      begin

4. $M_c(i) = temp_1(i)$;

5. $Id(i) = temp_2(i)$.

      end

    end

end /* *Algorithm Premax* */

    We now prove that *Algorithm LCS* can find the correct class number for each point.

Lemma 1:

    If a point q is dominated by a point p, then $class(q) > class(p)$.

    This is from line 5 in *Compute L*, and the definition of "dominate".

    Obviously, if $P\{p_i\}$ is a set of the points such that p_i dominates point q, then $class(q) > max[class(p_i)]$, $\forall i \in \{i | p_i$ dominates $q\}$.

Lemma 2:

    A point q in class k is dominated by at least one point in class $k - 1$.

    This is true because if no point in class $k - 1$ dominates point q, then point q could have been in class $k - 1$ instead of class k, contradiction.

Lemma 3:

    The class outlines are numbered by consecutive integers.

    This is from line 5 and line 6 in *Compute L*.

Lemma 4:

    Let $P\{p_i\}$ be the set of all the points p_i dominating point q, then $class(q) < max[class(p_i)] + 2$, $\forall i \in \{i | p_i$ dominates $q\}$.

Proof:

    Let $max[class(p_i)] = M$. From Lemma 1, if $class(q) \geq M + 2$, then q does not dominate any point on the class outline of $M + 2$. Then, either (i) q is on the class outline of $M + 2$, or (ii) q is dominated by a point, say q', on this outline.

    According to Lemma 2, there is at least one point in class $M + 1$ which either dominates point q for case (i), or dominates point q' for case (ii) and hence dominates point q. Since M is the maximum class number of the points dominating point q, the above described point in class $M + 1$ contradicts the assumption.

Theorem 1:

    Let $P\{p_i\}$ be the set of all the points p_i dominating point q, then

$$class(q) = max[class(p_i)] + 1, \forall i \in \{i | p_i \text{ dominates } q\}.$$

    From Lemma 1, we have $class(q) > max[class(p_i)]$. From Lemma 4, we have $class(q) < max[class(p_i)] + 2$. Since the class numbers are integers (Lemma 3), so $class(q) = max[class(p_i)] + 1, \forall i \in \{i | p_i$ dominates $q\}$.

Lemma 5:

    The left tree(s) and the right tree(s) formed in *Algorithm LCS* do not intersect.

Proof:

    In the execution of *Algorithm LCS*, suppose $\overline{fs}$ is an edge of a tree generated in Step 2 of *Algorithm LCS*, and point f is the father of point s. Suppose $\overline{tp}$ is an edge of another tree, with point t being the father of point p.

    If $\overline{tp}$ intersects the edge $\overline{fs}$, then there must be $j_t > j_f$ and $j_p < j_s$, as is the case shown in Figure 6(a). The other cases shown in Figure 6(b), (c) and (d) are not realistic because t can not be point p's farther with $j_t > j_p$. Investigate the class numbers of point p and point t for the case in Figure 6(a). Following are the three possibilities:

(i) $class(p) = class(s)$.

Then $class(f) = class(t) = class(s) - 1$. Point s should have chosen point t as its father since j_t is closer to j_s. Otherwise it contradicts the way that the tree is generated as is indicated in Step 2 of *Algorithm LCS*.

(ii) $class(p) > class(s)$.

Then $class(t) \geq class(s)$. According to Lemma 1, point t does not dominate point s. This contradicts the existence of the case in Figure 6(a).

(iii) $class(p) < class(s)$.

Then $class(p) \leq class(f)$. According to Lemma 1, point f does not dominate point p. This contradicts the existence of the case in Figure 6(a).

Thus, any two edges with one in a tree and the other in another tree can not intersect, therefore the trees formed in Step 2 of *Algorithm LCS* do not intersect. Since the initially generated trees do not intersect, the left trees and the right trees formed by merging some of them, as is done in the later steps of *Algorithm LCS*, do not intersect neither.

Lemma 6:

The point t found in the right trees by point p in Step 6 of *Algorithm LCS* dominates point p.

Proof:

Since $j_t < j_p$, so t must locate in area $\mathcal{A}$ or area $\mathcal{B}$ (see Figure 7(a). If t is located in area $\mathcal{A}$, then t dominates p.

If t is located in area $\mathcal{B}$, and t is in a right tree, then we have t on the left of p, and the root of the tree that t is in on the right of the root of the tree that p is in, then there must be some edge in one tree which intersects the edge in another tree, this contradicts Lemma 5. So, point t found in Step 6 can not be in area $\mathcal{B}$. It must be in area $\mathcal{A}$ and thus dominates point p.

Theorem 2:

Algorithm LCS finds for point q the point p_m among all the points p_i's such that p_i dominates q and $class(p_m) = max[class(p_i)], \forall i \in \{i | p_i$ dominates $q\}$. Thus $class(q)$ is correctly computed as $class(q) = max[class(p_i)] + 1, \forall i \in \{i | p_i$ dominates $q\}$.

Proof:

(i) In the execution of "Update with Joint", each point in class 1 in the lower half found the point p_m in the upper half such that p_m dominates q and $class(p_m)$ is the maximum.

From Step 2 in *Algorithm LCS*, each point in class 1 found its father among the joints. According to the definition of *father*, the joint chosen to be point $q(i_q, j_q)$'s father, say $f(i_f, j_f)$, must dominate point q and have j_f closest to j_q. Since joint $(f + 1)$ has $j_{(f+1)} > j_q$ (otherwise q would have chosen joint $(f + 1)$ as its father), and a *joint* is projected from the left most point in its class, all the points within class $(f + 1)$ must lie on the right of point q, and thus f must be the maximum class number of those points dominating point q.

(ii) In the execution of "Update between Trees", each point q with $class(q) > 1$ in the lower half found the point p_m such that $class(p_m)$ is the maximum among the points which dominate point q.

From Lemma 6, the point t found in Step 6 of *Algorithm LCS* by p dominates point p. Any point t' in the same tree that t is in and with $j_{t'} < j_t$ should dominate p either. After executing Step 5 in *Algorithm LCS*, the maximum class number of point t and all the points t' is known, as $M_c(t)$. By step 7, $M_c(t) = class(p) + dif(p)$. Thus if the condition in step 8 does not hold, after step 9, point p will have updated its class number as $M_c(t) + 1$ where t is recognized as the point in the right tree with maximum class number dominating p. If the condition in step 8 holds, then $class(p) + dif(father(p)) > class(p) + dif(p)$. That means $class(father(p)) + 1 + dif(father(p)) > M_c(t)$, and $father(p)$ will have a greater class number, than t, assuming updated in the above way. In this case, p updates its class number based on its father's new class number, as $class(p) + dif(p) + 1$ with $class(p) = class(father(p)) + 1$ as was before and $dif(p) = dif(father(p))$ after performing *Propagation 2 (dif)*. According to Theorem 1, the class of p is correctly computed.

Executing on r processors, with r equal to the total number of pairs of positions at which two symbols match, our algorithm is with the time complexity analyzed as follows. The maximal number of points on a outline is $m + n$, with $n \geq m$. Hence the sorting in step 1 takes $O(\log n)$ time [11]. Step 2 involves a binary search on the class outline, hence $O(\log n)$ is required in the worst case. *Propagation* includes $O(\log \rho_1)$ iterations in step 3 and for the worst case in step 8, if ρ_1 is the total number of classes in the lower half to be merged. Step 4 to step 10 need to be repeated $\log(\rho_2 + 1)$ times with ρ_2 equal to the total number of classes in the upper half to be merged. In Step 4, sorting of k points in the trees requires $O(\log k)$ time. *Premax* involved in Step 5 needs $\log k$ steps to find the desired maximal data for the k given data items. A point is to search in Step 6 for the point with the smaller and closest j in the right trees, which needs $O(\log k)$ time given k points in the trees. For each of these steps, $k = n$ is the worst case, thus $O(\log n)$ will be the time bound. Step 7, 9 and 10 involve constant time computation only. The whole merge algorithm needs to be executed $O(\log n)$ times to complete the divide-and-conquer operation, thus, the total time needed is $O(\log \rho \log^2 n)$ with ρ being the longest common subsequence.

IV. Discussion of preprocessing

At the beginning of the algorithm presented in the previous section, we assumed that all the pairs of the positions on which the two strings match have been determined. This is completed by preprocessing which we have not discussed yet. Given two strings with length m and n respectively, let the pair (i, j) indicate the match of two symbols at position i in string A and position j in string B. To find (i, j) pairs, we need m processors to maintain symbols in A and n for B. Distribute the symbols on the $m + n$ PE's, with one symbol per PE. Assume that the symbols have some order. Each PE containing a symbol in A generates a record with two fields: $< i, order >$ and those containing a symbol in B generate records $< j, order >$'s. i, j indicate the position of the symbol in string A and B respectively. *order* indicates the order of the symbol contained in the PE. Following are the operations to be performed in the preprocessing.

Preprocessing

(1) Sort the m symbols in A by *order* on m PE's. Ties are broken by i.
(2) Select the distinct symbols each with a smallest rank in the sorted sequence to form a "concentrated sequence" (see Figure 8 as a reference). Assume that there are in total t distinct symbols.
(3) Each PE maintaining a symbol in B performs a binary search on the t records to find an *order* which matches the *order* maintained in its record for a point.
(4) Compute for the two adjacent distinct symbols in the concentrated sequence generated in step (2), the difference of their ranks in the sequence generated in step (1). Each symbol in string B now knows the total number of the positions in A at which the symbol can be found.
(5) Perform a parallel prefix computation, each symbol in B, say in position j, obtains the total number, say c_j, of matches found for all the symbols prior to it. Prepare r PE's to execute the *Algorithm LCS* if r matches are found in total. Each PE maintaining a symbol in B notifies the c_jth PE among r PE's the position j in B, the symbol it is assigned and the position of the symbol in the sorted sequence of B.
(6) By reverse tracing (say $i_3 \rightarrow i_2 \rightarrow i_1$ in Fig. 8), each of the r PE's can get the information about the position i in A at which the symbol lies.

We next compute the running time to accomplish the preprocessing. In step (1), sorting m elements on m processors needs $O(\log m)$ time. Step (2) requires $O(\log m)$ time in the worst case. The binary search performed on m items in step (3) is running on $O(\log m)$ time. Step (4) needs only constant time. In step (5), the parallel prefix computation is performed on n PE's each containing a symbol in string B. The time complexity of parallel prefix computing for n data items is $O(\log n)$ [12], therefore the time needed in step (6) is no greater than $O(\log n)$.

Thus, distributing the symbols on $m + n$ processors, the preprocessing time to find the matches for two strings with length m and n is bounded by $O(\log m + \log n)$, including the assigning of the matched pairs to r PE's to execute the LCS algorithm.

V. Conclusion and related research

A parallel algorithm for computing the longest common string has been presented. The described algorithm suggested the employment of a divide-and-conquer approach which exploited the concurrency in solving LCS problems and hence achieved efficient results, compared with existing algorithms of which most are sequential.

A related research problem which can be solved is the maxima problem occurred very often in computational geometry. Given a set S of n points in the plane, a point p in S is a *maximal element* (or, briefly *maxima*) of S if there does not exist q other than p in S such that $x_q \geq x_p$ and $y_q \geq y_p$. As an example, the maxima of a given set of points shown in Figure 9 have been connected by dash lines. In addition, excluding the maxima on the dash lines, we can find the second layer maxima and so on. This problem can be solved by extending the algorithm presented in the earlier sections.

Let the four extreme points N, S, E and W define the four quadrants, assign different signs + and − to the coordinates of the points. It can be observed that the problem of determining the maxima in a quadrant is similar to the problem of determining the points with smallest class number in the L matrix. Furthermore, the layers of maxima can be found in parallel, based on the approach of divide-and-conquer, and the methods we provided in the LCS algorithm design. Distributing n points on n PE's with one point per PE, the layers of the maxima in a given set can be determined in $O(\log \rho \log^2 n)$ time, where ρ is the number of the layers. We believe that the importance of the generated idea lies not only in the solutions of these problems, but also in that they provided valuable insight into the difficulty of parallelism exploiting.

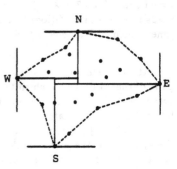

Figure 9

References

[1] D. Sankoff and J. B. Kruskal, editors, *Time warps, string edits, and macromolecules: the theory and practice of sequence comparison*, Reading, MA: The MIT Press, 1985.

[2] J. L. Modelevsky, "Computer applications in applied genetic engineering," *Advances in Applied Microbiology* Vol. 30, 1984, pp. 169-195.

[3] Y. Chiang and K. S. Fu, "Parallel processing for distance computation in syntactic pattern recognition," *Proceedings of IEEE Computer Society Workshop on Computer Architecture for Pattern Analysis and Image Database Management*, Nov. 1981.

[4] D. S. Hirschberg, "A linear space algorithm for computing maximal common subsequences," *Communications of the ACM*, Vol. 18, No. 6, June 1975, pp. 341-343.

[5] A. V. Aho, D. S. Hirschberg and J. D. Ullman, "Bounds on the complexity of the maximal common subsequence problem," *Proceedings of 15th Annual IEEE Symposium on Switching and Automata Theory*, 1974, pp. 104-109.

[6] D. S. Hirschberg, "Algorithms for the longest common subsequence problem," *Journal of the ACM*, Vol. 24, no. 4, Oct. 1977, pp. 664-675.

[7] W. J. Hsu and M. W. Du, "New algorithms for the LCS problem," *Journal of Computer and System Sciences*, 29, 1984, pp. 133-152.

[8] W. J. Hsu and M. W. Du, "Computing a longest common subsequence for a set of strings," *Bit*, 24, 1984, pp. 45-59.

[9] D. P. Lopresti and R. Hughey, "The B-SYS programmable systolic array", Technical Report CS-89-32, Department of Computer Science, Brown University, Providence, June 1989.

[10] P. A. Wagner and M. J. Fischer, "The string-to-string correction problem," *Journal of ACM*, 21 (1), 1974, pp. 168-173.

[11] R. Cole, "Parallel Merge Sort," *SIAM J. on Comp.*, Vol. 17, No. 4, Aug. 1988, pp. 770-785.

[12] A. Gibbons and W. Rytter, "Efficient Parallel Algorithms", Cambridge University Press, Cambridge, 1988, pp. 13-18.

PARALLEL BREADTH-FIRST AND BREADTH-DEPTH TRAVERSALS OF GENERAL TREES[1]

Calvin C. -Y. Chen   Sajal K. Das
Department of Computer Science
University of North Texas
Denton, TX 76203-3886
U. S. A.

ABSTRACT

Two adaptive, level-order tree traversal algorithms are proposed for an exclusive-read and exclusive-write (EREW), parallel random access machine (PRAM) model of computation. Our breadth-first traversal algorithm for a general tree with n nodes achieves $O((n/p)*\log n /\log(n/p))$ time complexity using p processors on the EREW model, and hence it attains optimal speedup for $p \leq n^{1-e}$, where $0 < e \leq 1$. This algorithm performs better (in terms of processor-time product) than an existing algorithm [12] which has $O(k \log n)$ time complexity using $O(n^{1+1/k})$ processors on a concurrent-read and exclusive-write (CREW), PRAM model. The proposed breadth-depth algorithm for traversing a general tree requires $O(n/p + \log n)$ time on the EREW model, and thus it achieves optimal speedup for $p \leq n/\log n$. This algorithm provides a significant improvement over an existing parallel breadth-depth algorithm [4] which requires $O(\log n)$ time with $O(n^2)$ processors on CREW model. Our breadth-first traversal algorithm uses an Euler tour technique [20], and a list construction technique which is similar to the one used in [18] for solving the adjacency list construction problem for graphs. The breadth-depth traversal algorithm, on the other hand, is based on a special characterization which enables the reduction of this problem into a variety of list ranking problems.

KEY WORDS: Tree traversal, Linked list ranking, Breadth-first search, Breadth-depth search, Parallel algorithm, Optimal speedup.

1. INTRODUCTION

The tree is a widely used data structure in computer science [1,14,17], and traversal of trees is a fundamental operation in manipulating them. The three commonly-used traversal techniques for binary trees are pre-order, in-order, and post-order. In addition, there are other techniques such as breadth-first and breadth-depth (also called *level-order*) tree traversals which fit the needs of various applications. Berztiss [2] is a good reference for a survey of such applications, where binary tree traversals are categorized into seven classes. There are optimal sequential algorithms for implementing these traversals, which require $O(n)$ time where n is the number of nodes in the tree [14,17]. It is obvious that each node of the tree has to be visited at least once and thus an $O(n)$ time algorithm is optimal.

With the advent of parallel processing, a number of parallel tree-traversal algorithms have been proposed. Wyllie [21] proposed an $O(\log n)$ time parallel algorithm for (pre-, in-, and post-order) traversing binary trees using $O(n)$ processors on the CREW PRAM model. Ghosh and Bhattacharjee [12] provided an $O(k \log n)$ time algorithm for breadth-first tree traversal using $O(n^{1+1/k})$ processors on the CREW model, where k > 0. Their algorithms for pre-order and post-order traversals also have the same time- and processor-complexities but run on the EREW PRAM model [13]. Kalra and Bhatt [15] presented an $O(\log n)$ time algorithm using n processors on an EREW model for pre-order and post-order tree (and forest) traversals. Based on the Euler tour technique, Tarjan and Vishkin [20] developed an $O(\log n)$ time algorithm for pre-order and post-order tree traversals using $O(n)$ processors on an EREW model. Kruskal, Rudolph, and Snir [18] presented $O((n/p)(\log n)/\log(n/p))$ time algorithms for pre-order and post-order traversals of both general and binary trees, which achieve optimal speedup (or efficiency) using $p \leq n^{1-e}$ processors, for $0 < e \leq 1$, on the EREW PRAM model. Chaudhuri [4] proposed an $O(\log n)$ time breadth-depth traversal algorithm using $O(n^2)$ processors on the CREW PRAM model. A systematic survey of several parallel algorithms for traversing trees is presented in [6]. Chen, Das, and Akl [7] have also proposed a unified characterization for tree-traversal techniques followed by new parallel algorithms for pre-, in-, and post-order traversals. The purpose of the present paper is to design new, adaptive parallel algorithms for level-order traversals of general trees on the EREW model.

In particular, we provide a breadth-first (general) tree traversal algorithm which requires $O((n/p)*(\log n /\log(n/p)))$ time using p processors on the EREW PRAM model. In comparison with the result in [12] for the CREW model, this algorithm is adaptive and it achieves optimal speedup on the EREW model for $p \leq n^{1-e}$, where $0 < e \leq 1$. We also present a breadth-depth (general) tree traversal algorithm which has $O(n/p + \log n)$ time complexity using p processors on the EREW PRAM model. This performance is better than the algorithm in [4] on the CREW model, which uses a larger number of processors. Our approach to breadth-first traversal uses the Euler tour technique [20], and a list construction technique similar to the one used in [18] for solving the adjacency list construction problem for graphs. On the other hand, our approach to the breadth-depth traversal algorithm is based on a special characterization which allows us to reduce this problem into a variety of list ranking problems.

The rest of the paper is organized as follows. In Section 2, we review some basic terminology and Section 3 discusses the linked list ranking problem. In Sections 4 and 5, respectively, we present the breadth-first and breadth-depth algorithms. Section 6 concludes the paper.

---

[1]This work was in part supported by a faculty research grant from the University of North Texas.

2. BASIC TERMINOLOGY AND DEFINITIONS

Definition 1: Given a general tree T rooted at node r having k subtrees, T_1, T_2, ..., T_k, we define *pre-order traversal* as a list consisting of the node r, followed by nodes of T_1 in pre-order, followed by nodes of T_2 in pre-order, ..., followed by nodes of T_k in pre-order. The *breadth-first tree traversal* is a list consisting of the root r (considered to be at level 0), followed by all nodes in level 1 from left to right, followed by nodes in level 2 from left to right, and so on. And the *breadth-depth tree traversal* is a list consisting of the root node r, followed by r's children from left to right, followed by nodes of T_k in breadth-depth order (excluding the root of T_k), followed by nodes of T_{k-1} in breadth-depth order (excluding the root of T_{k-1}), ..., and followed by nodes of T_1 in breadth-depth order (excluding the root of T_1).

Definition 2: *Rightmost (leftmost)-sibling* is defined as
(i) If node u is the rightmost (leftmost) child of its parent, the rightmost (leftmost)-sibling of u is u itself.
(ii) If a node u is not a rightmost (leftmost) child of its parent, the rightmost (leftmost)-sibling of u is defined recursively as the rightmost (leftmost)-sibling of u's right (left) sibling.

Definition 3 (*Optimal speedup*) : Let Seq(n) be the fastest known worst-case running time of a sequential algorithm for a problem of size n. A parallel algorithm for the same size problem using p processors is said to achieve optimal speedup if its parallel time complexity is O(Seq(n)/p).

The model on which the algorithms in this paper are designed, belongs to the parallel random access machine (PRAM) family. We consider two variants of this family, namely exclusive-read and exclusive write (EREW) and concurrent-read and exclusive-write (CREW). An EREW PRAM model does not allow simultaneous reading from or writing into a memory cell of a global shared memory. On the other hand, a CREW PRAM allows concurrent reading by more than one processor but exclusive writing into a cell. For details on various classes of the PRAM family, see [16].

3. LINKED LIST RANKING PROBLEM

The linked list ranking problem often exists as a subproblem of many important problems including tree-traversals. Let us have a linked list of length n implemented as an array. Each of the n elements is associated with a weight and each (except the last) has the array index of its successor in the linked list. *The linked list ranking* problem is defined as follows: For each element, compute the sum of the weights of the elements following it in the list. This problem can also be extended to the *general linked list* ranking problem, which is defined in the same way but with multiple linked lists implemented as an array of total length n. Each of the n elements (except each of the terminal elements) has the array index of its successor in its list.

A parallel algorithm for the linked list ranking problem is originally developed by Wyllie [21], which requires O(log n) time using O(n) processors on the EREW model. Subsequently, a few other algorithms have been proposed [9, 10, 18, 19]. Karp and Ramachandran [16] give a brief survey of parallel algorithms for this problem. Kruskal et al. [18] developed an O((n/p)(log n)/log(n/p)) time algorithm on the EREW model. This is the first optimal parallel algorithm for linked list ranking problem using p ≤ n^{1-e} processors, for 0 < e ≤ 1. Cole and Vishkin [8] also presented an optimal algorithm requiring O(log n) time using O(n/log n) processors on the EREW model.

The approach due to Cole and Vishkin to the linked list ranking problem is based on an algorithm for the duration-unknown task scheduling problem . The general list ranking algorithm used here is from Chen and Das [5,6], which is a modification of the one presented in [8]. The complexities of these two algorithms are summarized as follows.

Theorem 3.0 (Brent [3]). Any synchronous parallel algorithm taking time t that consists of a total of x elementary operations can be implemented by p processors within a time of x/p + t.

Theorem 3.1 [5,8]. There exist algorithms for the linked list ranking problem and general linked list ranking problem, each requiring O(n) total number of operations and O(log n) time complexity using O(n/log n) processors on the EREW model.

Corollary 3.1. The (general) linked list ranking problem of size n can be solved using p processors and requiring O(n/p + log n) time complexity on EREW PRAM model.
Proof: Use Brent's Theorem on the result of Theorem 3.1.

Since both of the linked list ranking and the general linked list ranking algorithms have the same parallel time complexity, we will use the notation LINKDED-LIST-RANKING (NEXT, rank, n) to denote either algorithm, where the input parameter NEXT and the output parameter *rank* are each implemented as an array of integers and n is the total size (i.e. number of elements) of the list.

4. BREADTH-FIRST TREE TRAVERSAL

Our algorithm starts with ordering the nodes on the same level of the input tree. The concatenation of the orderings from the lowest level (the root is at this level) through the highest level produces the breadth-first traversal for the given tree. To compute the ordering of nodes on the same level, we need to make use of each node's level number and its pre-order rank. Therefore, the proposed breadth-first algorithm has three phases. In Phase 1, it computes level numbers of nodes in the given input tree. Phase 2 computes the pre-order list of nodes. In Phase 3, the breadth-first ranks are determined. Example 1 illustrates the overview of the execution of our algorithm.

Example 1

Given a general tree as in Fig. 1, the level numbers for nodes in the tree are shown as

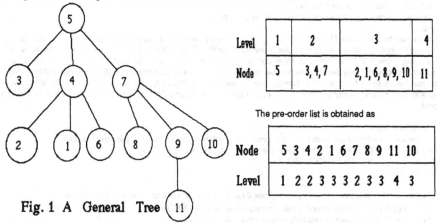

Level	1	2	3	4
Node	5	3, 4, 7	2, 1, 6, 8, 9, 10	11

The pre-order list is obtained as

Node	5 3 4 2 1 6 7 8 9 11 10
Level	1 2 2 3 3 3 2 3 3 4 3

Fig. 1 A General Tree

The breadth-first ranks can be determined by bucket-sorting the pre-order list

Node	5	3	4	7	2	1	6	8	9	10	11
Level	1	2	2	2	3	3	3	3	3	3	4

The computations of level number and pre-order rank are greatly facilitated by the use of a linked list which determines the ordering of nodes to be visited in an Euler tour [19]. The linked list implements the following NEXT function. We consider that each node of the given input tree consists of a varying number of fields. For example, if a node has i children, this node will have $(i + 1)$ fields. The notation x_i denotes node x's i-th field. The linked list starts with r_1, where r is the root node. An *Euler tour* starts at a field of a node, travels to fields of other nodes, and returns to the starting field by using the tree edges in both directions exactly once. The function $NEXT[x_i]$ gives the successor of a field x_i of node x in the Euler tour. It is defined as

$$NEXT[x_i] = \begin{cases} f_{k+1} & \text{if } i = \text{no-of-children}[x] + 1 \text{ and } x \text{ is the k-th child of its parent f, where f is not the root.} \\ c_1 & \text{if } i \neq \text{no-of-children}[x] + 1 \text{ and c is the i-th child of x.} \end{cases}$$

Figure 2 illustrates the use of the Euler tour for the tree in Fig. 1 and shows the linked list defined by the tour.

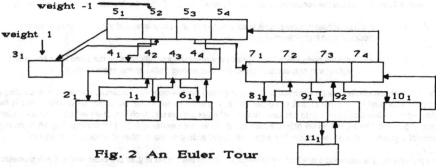

Fig. 2 An Euler Tour

Note that this NEXT function does not give the successor of the last field of the root node in the tour. This is because we break the tour into a linked list such that r_1 is the starting field and r_m is the terminal field, where r is the root and m = (number of children of r) + 1. The linked list can be represented as an array [1 .. 2n - 1] of SNODEREC :

record
   node   : integer;
   subscript : integer; /* field number */
   nxt-idx   : integer; /* the array index of its successor */
end.

This data structure can be constructed from the input tree which is represented by a "parent-of" relation with explicit ordering of children and "no-of-children" relation by applying the following algorithm GEN-COMP-NEXT. The input tree is represented by three arrays, namely parent-of, childrank, and no-of-children, where parent-of [i] denotes i's parent; childrank[i] is i's rank among siblings; and no-of-children[i] denotes the number of children the node i has. Note that in [6, 7], we have shown that this representation can be obtained from the other two commonly-used representations, namely, "right-sibling and leftmost-child" and "parent-of with artificial ordering of children" in a total of $O(n)$ operations and $O(\log n)$ time using $O(n/\log n)$ processors on an EREW model.

Algorithm GEN-COMP-NEXT
/* This algorithm generates a linked list from the given input tree which is represented as a "parent-of" relation with explicit ordering of children. Each field of a tree-node is a record of typw SNODEREC. */
   SUPERNODE : array [1 .. 2n - 1] of SNODEREC;
for all P_i, $1 \le i \le n$, **do**
  parbegin
  Step 1.   Processor P_i builds j-th field of i's parent node if node i is the j-th child of its parent. The j-th field
               (if it is not the last field) is stored in the i-th index of array SUPERNODE.
  Step 2.   Processor P_i builds node i's last field whose array index is $(n + i)$.
  parend.

Clearly, there are $O(n)$ operations; and using p processors, we obtain $O(n/p)$ parallel time for this algorithm on EREW PRAM model.

To compute the level number for each tree-node without read-conflicts, we assign a weight of -1 to each element x_i, where $i \ne 1$, and assign a weight of +1 to each x_1, where $i = 1$. The prefix sum of the fields from r_1 to x_1, where r is the root, gives the level number of the node x. For example, in Fig. 2, field 6_1 has prefix sum 3 which implies that node 6 is at the level 3. We implement this idea by an algorithm COMP-LEVEL (supernode, level), where *supernode* is an input parameter and *level* is an output parameter. The array, level, is indexed by node numbers. It can be shown that this algorithm requires $O(n)$ assignment operations and makes use of LINKED-LIST-RANKING algorithm for computing prefix sum on list [5]. This leads to Theorem 4.1. The computation of the ordering of nodes on the same level is based on Theorem 4.2.

Theorem 4.1: The level numbers of all nodes in a given tree of size n can be computed in $O(n/p + \log n)$ time using p processors on an EREW PRAM model.

Theorem 4.2: If node x and node y are on the same level, and preorder-rank [x] < preorder-rank[y], then level-order-rank [x] < level-order-rank [y].

Theorem 4.3 [6,7]: The pre-order ranks of nodes of a given tree having n nodes can be obtained in $O(\log n)$ time using $O(n/\log n)$ processors on the EREW model.
Corollary 4.3. The pre-order ranks of nodes of a given tree having n nodes can be obtained in $O(n/p + \log n)$ time using p processors on the EREW PRAM model.
Proof: From Theorem 4.3 and Brent's Theorem.

Based on Theorem 4.2, we can define the successor of node u (denoted by NEXT[u]) in the breadth-first tree traversal as

$$
NEXT[u] = \begin{cases}
v, & \text{if u has highest pre-order rank among nodes on the same level and v has lowest rank among nodes in next higher level of u.} \\
\\
w, & \text{if u is not the node which has highest pre-order rank among nodes on the same level and w has next higher (with respect to u) pre-order rank among nodes on the same level.}
\end{cases}
$$

Since we are able to obtain efficiently a list of nodes in pre-order (called the pre-order list) traversal, we next aim at building a list of nodes on the same level in the order of their pre-order ranks. The difficulty lies in that we do not know which node is the leftmost or rightmost on its level, and that we do not know how to schedule processors such that there will be no read-conflicts when processing in parallel. The technique we propose here is similar to that discussed in [18] for constructing an adjacency list representation of a graph. There are two cases to be discussed, depending on the number of processors available.
Case I: if $p^2 \le n$
(1) Each of the p processors is assigned a block of n/p tree-nodes, which are sorted in their pre-order ranks. Each processor builds linked lists (called partial lists) for the nodes in that block, where each list consists of nodes on the same level and they are in the order of their pre-order ranks. The headers and tailers of lists in block i form two arrays, which are denoted by hd[*,i] and tl[*,i], respectively. The array hdflag[i] is used to indicate whether the i-th element of the pre-order list is the first element in its partial list or not. The array level[*] contains the level number of each node. Since there are p blocks and each block may have n lists, it is costly to initialize the n entries in hd[*,i] and tl[*,i] for each i. We initialize only the entries that are going to be

used. This is done in the first phase in which the initialization process simply scans over the pre-order list. In the second phase, the linking is actually built and hdflag is updated whenever the first node on a level is attached to its header. Hdflag is to be used later in the second step. A node linked to its list is attached at the tail of the list. In this way, nodes on the same level are linked in the order of their pre-order ranks.

(2) All partial lists are linked to obtain global lists by assigning p processors to one block. The headers and tailers of these global lists are stored in the arrays head[*] and tail[*], respectively. There are two phases in this step also. In the first phase, each of the processors picks a node from the same block, initializes the arrays head[*] and tail[*] to zeros. In the second phase, the linking is actually done. The hdflag is checked again and the array hd[*,i] and tl[*,i] are used for linking. If a node is the first node on its partial list, then it is linked at the end of the list which is pointed to by the entry in the array tail[*]; and tail[*] is updated to point to the node pointed by the entry in tl[*,i].

Case II : If $p^2 > n$

(1a) The pre-order list is divided into n/p blocks, each of size p. Then (p^2/n) processors are assigned to work on a block. Therefore, we have n/p subproblems, each of size p and to be solved using (p^2/n) processors. The solutions to these subproblems will be partial lists of nodes stored in the array list[*]. The headers and tailers of the partial lists of subproblem i are stored in the array hd[*,i] and tl[*,i], respectively, $1 \leq i \leq n/p$. In the same manner as in Case I, hdflag[k] is set if the k-th input element is the header node of a partial list. All partial lists are then linked to obtain global lists using the same procedure as in Step (2) of Case I. Note that we may need to partition a subproblem recursively such that the size of a subproblem is no less than the square of the number of processors allocated to it. At that point, the procedure involving Steps 1 and 2 of Case I can be called to solve the subproblem.

Step 3, described below, is common for both range of processors in Cases I and II.

(3) A linked list implementing the NEXT function is created by linking the last node of a level to the first node of its next higher level. Once the NEXT function is obtained, the linked list ranking algorithm can be applied to obtain the ranks of nodes.

Algorithm BF-TRAVERSAL given below implements the preceding ideas. For brevity, we restrict to the case when $p^2 \leq n$. The detailed implementation and illustrations are given in [5].

Algorithm BF-TRAVERSAL (bfrank, level, preorder-list)
 /* bfrank : output parameter, array [1 .. n] of integer;
  level : input parameter, array [1 .. n] of integer;
  preorder-list : input parameter, array [1 .. n] of integer */
Step 1. Divide the preorder-list into p blocks. Each processor builds partial lists from the nodes in a block. The header
    and the tailer arrays for the lists built by processor i are denoted by hd[*,i] and tl[*,i], respectively.
 for all P_i, $1 \leq i \leq p$, **do**
  parbegin
   P_i works on nodes pre-order-list[k], where $(i - 1)*(n/p) \leq k < (i*n/p)$.
   P_i initializes list[k] to zero. /* the successor of k-th input in a partial list */
   /* Phase 1. P_i initializes entries in hd[*,i] and tl[*,i] that are to be used and entries in hdflag */
   hd [level [preorder-list[k]], i] := 0; tl [level [preorder-list[k]], i] := 0; hdflag[k] := 0;
   /* Phase 2. Build partial lists */
   P_i adds each of the n/p nodes to the partial list for the level of that node
   and updates hd[*,i], tl[*,i], and list[*] accordingly.
  parend;
Step 2. Link up partial lists.
  /* Phase 1. Initialize header and tailer for the global lists. */
 for all P_i, $1 \leq i \leq p$, **do**
  Initialize head[k] and tail[k] to zero, for $(i - 1)*n/p \leq k < (i*n/p)$.
  P_1 sets head[n+1] and tail[n+1] to zero;
  /* Phase 2. Link partial lists to form a list for each level */
 for each of the p blocks **do**
 for all P_i, $1 \leq i \leq p$, **do** /* all processors work on the same block */
  parbegin
  for l := 1 to (n/p^2) **do**
  begin
  P_i is given at most a node m_i in each iteration.
  If hdflag[m_i] = 1 /* The first element in its partial list */
  then
   If the global list for the level of node m_i is empty
   then let head [level [m_i]] and tail [level[m_i]] point to m_i.
   else list[tail [level [mi]]] := m_i and
    update tail [level [m_i]] to be the tail of the partial list for m_i.
  end;
  parend;

Step 3. Create a linked list to implement the NEXT function.
  for all P_i, $1 \le i \le p$, **do**
    parbegin
      for k:= (i-1)*(n/p) + 1 to (i*n/p) **do**
      If (head[k] ≠ 0 and head [k+1] ≠ 0) **then** list [tail[k]] := head [k+1];
    parend;
Step 4. Obtain ranking.
  LINKED-LIST-RANKING (list, tmp-rank, n);
Step 5. Output the result.
  for all P_i, $1 \le i \le p$, **do**
    parbegin
      for k:= (i-1)*(n/p) + 1 to (i*n/p) **do** bfrank[preorder-list[k]] := tmp-rank[k];
    parend;

Example 2
  This algorithm for the case of $p^2 \le n$ is illustrated in the following. Given the pre-order list and level numbers of nodes of the tree in Example 1, the pre-order list is divided into p blocks. (Let us consider the case when p = 3.) Each processor builds partial lists by bucket-sorting nodes in its block according to level numbers. The partial lists are built as follows.

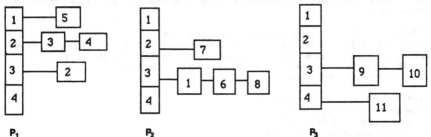

  The global lists are obtained by letting p processors work on the same block and link partial lists. In the following, the partial lists of block 2 are linked to those of block 1. Note that only the processors assigned to the head nodes of lists perform the linking; all others remain inactive.

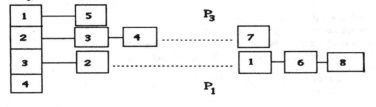

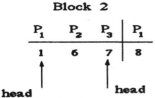

Block 2

Theorem 4.4: The breadth-first tree (of size n) traversal can be obtained in $O((n/p)*(\log n /\log(n/p)))$ time using p processors on an EREW PRAM model.

Proof: Let $T_p(n)$ be the running time of Steps 1 and 2 of algorithm BF-TRAVERSAL. In the case of $p^2 \le n$, we note that p blocks are processed sequentially and each block is processed in $O(n/p^2 + c)$ time, where c is a constant. Therefore, $T_p(n) = O((n/p^2 + c)*p) = O(n/p + p) = O(n/p)$, since $p \le n^{1/2}$. In the case of $p^2 > n$, the time $T_p(n) = T_{p*p/n}(p) + O(n/p)$, where the term $O(n/p)$ is due to linking partial lists [5]. Solving this recursion, we obtain $T_p(n) = O((n/p)*(\log n /\log(n/p)))$. In Steps 3 and 5 of algorithm BF-TRAVERSAL, since p processors work in parallel and each processor works on n/p nodes, we require $O(n/p)$ time. Step 4 requires $O(n/p + \log n)$ time by Corollary 3.1. Also the level numbers and pre-order list can be obtained in $O(n/p + \log n)$ time using p processors on the EREW model by Theorem 4.1 and Corollary 4.3. Therefore, the overall time complexity of algorithm BF-TRAVERSAL is $O(n/p + (n/p)*(\log n /\log(n/p)) + \log n)$ using p processors. Since $(n/p)*(\log n /\log(n/p))$ is the dominating term when p < n, the time complexity can be simplified as O((n/p)*(log n /log(n/p))).

It is easy to show that that this algorithm achieves optimal speedup for p ≤ n^{1-e}, where 0 < e ≤ 1. It is worth pointing out that the algorithm for breadth-first tree traversal in [12] does not use linked list ranking approach for computing level numbers of tree-nodes. Also it calls a non-adaptive sorting algorithm to sort on values which is computed for each node as [(level number of the node) * (size of the input) + (pre-order rank of that node)]. Furthermore, the algorithm in [12] is not optimal, and runs on the CREW model instead of the EREW model.

5. BREADTH-DEPTH TRAVERSAL OF GENERAL TREES

Our breadth-depth tree traversal algorithm is based on the observation that if node i is the root of a subtree and node j is its closest right sibling who has at least a child, the nodes except the root of the subtree rooted at node i will be visited after the rightmost node at the highest level of the subtree rooted at node j is visited. Before proceeding further, we need the following definitions.

Let *yawlshc[u]* be node u's youngest ancestor one of whose left siblings has at least a child. Define *closest-lf-s-h-c[u]* to be u's closest left sibling who has (a) child(ren). The characterization of the NEXT function for breadth-depth (general) tree traversal is defined as follows, where NEXT[u] denotes the successor of node u in the breadth-depth traversal.

$$NEXT[u] = \begin{cases} \text{right-sibling}[u], & \text{if u has a right sibling,} \\ \text{leftmost-child}[u], & \text{if u has no right sibling and u has a child,} \\ \text{leftmost-child [closest-lf-s-h-c [yawlshc[u]]], if u has no right sibling and no children.} \end{cases}$$

Example 3

The definitions of closest-lf-s-h-c , yawlshc, and NEXT are illustrated in the following.

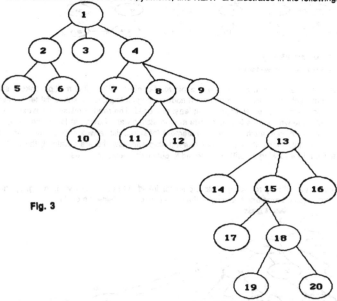

Fig. 3

Closest-lf-s-h-c [16] = 15, closest-lf-s-h-c [4] = 2; yawlshc [20] = 9, yawlshc [16] = 16; NEXT[8] = 9, NEXT[9] = 13, and NEXT[20] = 11.

To come up with a linked list implementing the NEXT function, we need to compute the values of yawlshc and closest-lf-s-h-c for each node. We first compute the number of left siblings who have at least a child. This is implemented by recording 1 in LSHC-flag[i], where LSHC-flag is an array, if node i's immediate left sibling has at least a child; otherwise a zero is recorded. The summation of LSHC-flag[k], for all k, is the number of i's left siblings having at least a child; where k is node i's left sibling including k itself. This is actually a general linked list ranking problem of size n. Let COMP-LSHC denote the algorithm implementing this idea, which has O(n/p + log n) parallel time complexity using p processors on EREW model. The details are presented in [5].

To compute, for each node, the closest left sibling who has at least a child, we define multiple linked lists on the input array consisting of n nodes. The head element of each linked list is a tree-node which has at least one child or is the rightmost node among siblings; and the tail (terminal element) is a node whose immediate left sibling has at least one child. Each of the elements (except the terminal elements) in the list holds the index of its left sibling, and is assigned a weight of 0. Each terminal element is assigned a weight of y, where y is the index of its left sibling. The purpose of this formulation is to relay (using the linked list ranking algorithm) the index of a node having at least one child to its closest right sibling who also has at least one child, or who is the rightmost node among siblings. Again, this is a general linked list ranking problem of size n and if we use an algorithm CLOSEST(closest-lf-s-h-c) to implement this idea as in [5], the output parameter closest-lf-s-h-c can be computed in O(n/p + log n) time using p processors on the EREW model. Example 4 illustrates the reduction of the computation of closest-lf-s-h-c into a general linked list ranking problem. In Fig. 4, a solid line between two sibling nodes represents a pointer and a broken line between sibling nodes is used to indicate that the processor associated with the left sibling passes the node's index to the processor associated with the right sibling node.

Example 4

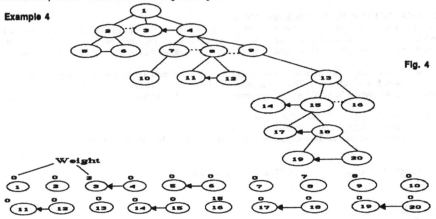

Fig. 4

(General) linked list ranking problem.

Rank of node u gives closest-lf-s-h-c[u]

The computation of yawlshc can be formulated similarly, but with care to avoid read-conflicts. We define multiple linked lists based on the "parent-of" relation. The head of each linked list is the rightmost node among siblings. Each linked list terminates at a node which has a left sibling (may not be the closest left sibling) with at least one child. The read-conflicts are avoided as follows. Only the processor assigned to that node which is its leftmost node among siblings and having at least one child, is allowed to read information from its parent node. Assign each nonterminal element (of linked list) a weight of 0, and terminal element a weight of y where y is the index of this element. Once the closest-lf-sh-c and yawlshc are obtained, the NEXT function can be defined. Then the general linked list ranking algorithm is applied to obtain the ranks of nodes.

Example 5

This example illustrates the computation of yawlshc by reducing it into a general linked list ranking problem. In Fig. 5, the linked lists are represented by a sequence of directed arcs and the weight of a node is shown outside the circle.

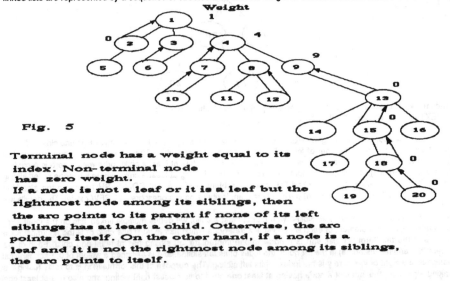

Fig. 5

Terminal node has a weight equal to its index. Non-terminal node has zero weight. If a node is not a leaf or it is a leaf but the rightmost node among its siblings, then the arc points to its parent if none of its left siblings has at least a child. Otherwise, the arc points to itself. On the other hand, if a node is a leaf and it is not the rightmost node among its siblings, the arc points to itself.

The parallel algorithm for computing yawlshc is formally described here, followed by a parallel algorithm for breadth-depth traversal. For details of this algorithm and illustrations, refer to [5].

Algorithm YAWLSHC(yawlshc[u])
/* This algorithm computes the youngest ancestor one of whose left siblings has at least one child. */
Step 1. /*Set up a multiple-linked-list array *t-parent-of* and initialize the array *yawlshc*. The element *yawlshc*[u] holds the index of the youngest anscestor of node u, who has a left sibling having at least a child. A node is identified as a terminal element of a linked list if it has a left sibling with (a) child(ren). */
   for all P_i, $1 \le i \le n$, **do**
     parbegin
      t-parent-of[i] := parent-of[i];   yawlshc [i] := 0;
       /* for leaf but not rightmost child */
     If (no-of-children[i] = 0 and rightmost-sibling[i] ≠ i)
     then begin
        t-parent-of[i] := -1; /*terminal node */
        yawlshc [i] := i;   /*i is the number to be broadcasted */
        end
     else   /* for the node which has a left sibling with child(ren) */
     If LSHC-flag[i] > 0 **then**
     begin
      t-parent-of[i] := -1;   /* terminal element */
      yawlshc[i] := i;   /* i is the number to be broadcasted */
     end;
     If i = root **then**
     begin
      yawlshc[root] := root; t-parent-of[root] := -1;
     end
     parend
Step 2. /* Broadcast the index of yawlshc to its descendants */
    LINKED-LIST-RANKING(t-parent-of, yawlshc, n);

Algorithm BREADTH-DEPTH (bd-traversal)
/* This algorithm computes breadth-depth tree-traversal */
Step 1. /* Define the NEXT function */
   for all P_i, $1 \le i \le n$, **do**
     parbegin
     If right-sibling[i] ≠ i   /* If a rightmost sibling */
     then NEXT[i] := right-sibling[i]
     else If no-of-children[i] ≠ 0 /* i has no right sibling and i has at least a child*/
        then NEXT[i] := leftmost-child[i]
        else NEXT[i] := leftmost-child [closest-lf-s-h-c[yawlshc[i]]];
     tmp-rank[i] := 1;
     parend
Step 2. /* Set up a linked list , pred, and initialize an array tmp-rank to hold ranks of nodes */
   for all P_i, $1 \le i \le n$, **do**
     parbegin
     If i = root
     then begin
        pred[root] := -1; tmp-rank[root] := 0;
        end
     else pred[NEXT[i]] := i;
     parend
Step 3. LINKED-LIST-RANKING(pred, tmp-rank, n);
Step 4. /* put the result onto the output parameter */
   for all P_i, $1 \le i \le n$, **do** bd-traversal[tmp-rank[i]] := i;

Using p processors on the EREW model, Step 1 of algorithm YAWLSHC requires O(n/p) time and Step 2 requires O(n/p + log n) time, by Corollary 3.1. Furthermore, Steps 1, 2, and 4 of algorithm BREAD-DEPTH require O(n/p) time, whereas Step 3 requires O(n/p + log n) time, by Corollary 3.1.

Theorem 5.1: The breadth-depth traversal for a general tree of size n can be computed in O(n/p + log n) time using p processors on the EREW PRAM model.
Proof: Follows from the complexity analyses of algorithms COMP-LSHC, CLOSEST, and YAWLSHC. For details, see [5].

6. CONCLUSIONS

We have presented two adaptive parallel algorithms for level-order traversals of general trees. The breadth-first algorithm requires $O((n/p)^e(\log n /\log(n/p)))$ time using p processors on the EREW PRAM model, and it is cost-optimal for $p \leq n^{1-e}$, where $0 < e \leq 1$. Hence it requires $O(\log^2 n/ \log \log n)$ time using $n/\log n$ processors. The performance of this algorithm can be compared with a non-optimal parallel breadth-first algorithm for the CREW model [12]. Our breadth-depth tree traversal algorithm achieves $O(n/p + \log n)$ time complexity on the EREW model, and hence it attains optimal speedup for $p \leq n/\log n$. It is an improvement over an exisitng algorithm [4], having $O(\log n)$ time complexity using $O(n^2)$ processors on the CREW model. The proposed algorithms can be used as subalgorithms in graph traversal algorithms as observed in [4, 11, 12]. As part of our future work, we intend to investigate level-order tree-traversal algorithms on fixed-connection parallel machine models without shared memory. We would also attempt to come up with a unified approach for traversing graphs in general.

Acknowledgement: We are grateful to the anonymous referees for helpful suggestions which improved the quality of the paper.

REFERENCES

[1] A.V. Aho, J.E. Hopcroft and J.D. Ullman, *Data Structures and Algorithms*(Addison-Wesley, Reading, Mass.,1983).

[2] A. Berztiss, "A Taxononmy of Binary Tree Traversals", *BIT*, Vol. 20, 1986, pp. 266-276.

[3] R.P. Brent, "The Parallel Evaluation of General Arithmetic Expressions", *J. ACM*, Vol. 21, No. 2, Apr. 1974, pp. 201-206.

[4] P. Chaudhuri, "Fast Parallel Graph Searching with Applications", *BIT*, Vol. 28, 1988, pp. 2-18.

[5] C. C-Y. Chen and S. K. Das, "Parallel Algorithms for Level-Order Traversals in General Trees",Tech. Rep., #N-89-005, Dept. Computer Science, Univ. North Texas, Denton, TX, Aug. 1989.

[6] C. C-Y. Chen and S. K. Das, "On Traversing Trees in Parallel", Tech. Rep., #N-89-006, Dept. Computer Science, Univ. North Texas, Denton, TX, Sep. 1989.

[7] C. C-Y. Chen , S. K. Das, and S. G. Akl, "A Unified Approach to Parallel Depth-First Traversals of General Trees", Tech. Rep., #N-90-004, Dept. Computer Science, Univ. North Texas, Denton, TX, Mar. 1990.

[8] R. Cole and U. Vishkin, "Approximate Parallel Scheduling. Part I: The Basic Technique With Applications To Optimal Parallel List Ranking in Logarithmic Time", *SIAM J. Comput.*, Vol. 17, No. 1, Feb. 1988, pp. 128-142.

[9] R. Cole and U. Vishkin, "The Accelerated Centroid Decomposition Technique for Optimal Parallel Tree Evaluation in Logarithmic Time", Courant Institute Tech. Rep. 242, New York University, New York,1986.

[10] R. Cole and U. Vishkin, "Deterministic Coin Tossing with Applications to Optimal Parallel List Ranking", *Information and Control*, Vol. 70, 1986, pp. 32-53.

[11] S. K. Das and N. Deo, "Divide-and-Conquer-Based Optimal Parallel Algorithms for Some Graph Problems on EREW PRAM model", *IEEE Transactions on Circuits and Systems*, Vol.35, No. 3, Mar. 1988, pp. 312-322.

[12] R. K. Ghosh and G.P. Bhattacharjee, "Parallel Breadth-First Search Algorithms for Trees and Graphs", *Intern. J. Computer Math.*, Vol. 15, 1984, pp. 255-268.

[13] R.K. Ghosh and G.P. Bhattacharjee, "A Parallel Search Algorithm for Directed Acyclic Graphs", *BIT*, Vol. 24, 1984, pp. 134-150.

[14] E. Horowitz and S. Sahni, *Fundamentals of Data Structures* (Computer Science Press., Rockville, Maryland, 1977).

[15] N.C. Kalra and P.C.P. Bhatt, "Parallel Algorithms for Tree Traversals", *Parallel Computing*, Vol. 2, 1985, pp. 163-171.

[16] R. M. Karp and V. Ramachandran, " A Survey of Parallel Algorithms for Shared-Memory Machines", Computer Science Division (EECS) Rep. UCB/CSD 88/408, Mar. 1988, University of California, Berkeley, CA.

[17] D.E. Knuth, *The Art of Computer Programming. Vol. 1, Fundamental Algorithms* (Addison Wesley, Reading, Mass. 1973).

[18] C.P. Kruskal, L. Rudolph, and M. Snir, " Efficient Parallel Algorithms for Graph Problems", *Proc. International Conference on Parallel Processing*, 1986, pp. 869-876.

[19] G. Miller and J. H. Reif, "Parallel Tree Contraction and Its Application", *Proc. 26th Annual IEEE Symposium on Foundations of ComputerScience*, 1985, pp. 478-489.

[20] R. E. Tarjan and U. Vishkin, "An Efficient Parallel Biconnectivity Algorithm", *SIAM J. Comput.*, Vol. 14, Nov. 1985, pp. 862-874.

[21] J. Wyllie, "The Complexity of Parallel Computations", *Ph.D. Thesis*, Cornell University, Ithaca, NY, 1979.

Parallelism via Speculation in Pure Prolog

Benjamin Yu

Department of Computer Science
University of Toronto
Toronto, Ontario, Canada M5S 1A4

byu@csri.toronto.edu

Abstract: A parallel execution model of Prolog programs based on speculative computation is presented. The model relies on three simple rules: unfolding, unrecursing and partial unrecursing. Speculative computation results by "guessing" to certain depth N where clauses should be unfolded. We show how this framework can be implemented efficiently by proposing an extension to the WAM architecture.

1 Introduction

Much research have been concentrated on program development in the sequential uniprocessor machine. As hardware becomes more and more readily available, parallel processing on multi-processor machines and distributed environments becomes more and more attractive. It is unfortunate, however, that methodology in parallel program development has not kept pace with hardware development. On the one hand, programmers would like to move away from the imperative paradigm of programming, but current parallel implementations of declarative languages have their shortcomings and limitations. In this paper, we propose the idea of using speculation as a tool for parallel execution in the logic programming paradigm. We feel that logic programming affords the programmer a better approach in program development than imperative programming since most of the control issues can be left to the executing engine. It is the purpose of this paper to show how the executing engine can be adapted to parallel execution of logic programs.

Logic programming is concerned with the expression and execution of programs based on first order logic. However logic programming as in traditional Prolog programming on a uniprocessor is limited in its speed and functionality. It is limited in its speed because of its sequential nature of execution and it is limited in its functionality because of its use of depth-first left-to-right computation rule resulting in its incompleteness. Yet Prolog programming has gained much acceptance and popularity in its application in many areas since its inception around 1970. With the advent of parallel computer architecture, a natural extension of logic programming languages is to allow logic programs to be executed in parallel. It is, in fact, a 'natural' extension because logic inherently has a parallel computation model [16]. Moreover, a carefully constructed parallel computation model can remove the incompleteness due to the depth first search strategy of sequential Prolog [14]. This paper proposes a strategy to enhance the performance of parallel execution of a Prolog program. A number of research proposals have been made in this area along the lines of And, Or, and And/Or parallelism. Section 2 briefly discusses some features and limitations of these systems. We note that although linear speedup was reported for a class of programs, this class imposes too much of a restriction in the form of Prolog programs for it to be useful in real applications. We therefore propose a new model for the parallel execution of Prolog programs on top of And parallelism based on speculative computation. We give a brief summary of the subject in section 3. Section 4 shows how speculative programming can be incorporated in a framework for parallel Prolog execution. In addition we will show how this can be implemented efficiently by extending the WAM abstract machine to support such a framework.

2 Current Models for Parallel Interpretation of Logic Programs

Among the different methods of executing a Prolog program in parallel that have been proposed in the literature, the three most widely studied are: And parallelism, Or parallelism, And/Or parallelism (and variants of above). The two major obstacles in executing efficiently logic programs in parallel are the control of the proliferation of processes and the consistent binding of variables in each process. And parallelism seeks to evaluate conjunction of goals in parallel. Annotated variables and Data Dependency Graph have been used to specify which variables are "producers" and which are "consumers" [22,3,5]. Degroot proposed a method called Restricted And Parallelism (or RAP) shifting more of the work of monitoring to the compiler and thus reducing the amount of run-time support [7]. Hermenegildo & Nasr extends Degroot's model to incorporate backtracking [11]. Or parallelism of logic programs seeks to execute clauses whose head unifies with a subgoal in parallel. Since the parallel processes involved are independent, implementation is relatively straightforward, at least in principle. However, since each process is independent from each other, a separate environment has to be maintained for each process. [2] proposes an Or parallel system that manage variable bindings in a similar way as demand paging. Other systems such as [29,6] uses copying of previous variables binding for new processes while [4,23] uses recomputation to construct new variable bindings. Much research has been directed to ways of managing bindings to allow fast access from each process [26,27,10,6].

In [5], Conery proposed the And/Or process model. Biswas et al. proposed a scheme that combines Degroot's restricted And parallelism (RAP) with a limited Or parallelism in [1]. The Sync model proposed by Li and Martin [18] attempts to extract both And and Or parallelism by creating an Or process for each literal being evaluated by the parent And process. Although both Conery's AND/OR process model and Li & Martin's Sync model can generate correct solutions in most situations, they are shown to be incomplete [14]. Kalé proposed the Reduce-Or process model [15] which is complete and recent results show linear speedup for strictly independent Prolog subgoals is achieved runing under the Reduce-Or model [21]. This subclass of Prolog programs limits severely the subgoals that can be expressed since no dependencies must exist between subgoals. There are many more proposed parallel systems which space will not allow inclusion of a more complete list.

2.1 Summary of Past Work

Much work has been done in the areas of And, Or, And/Or, and related schemes. Resolving of binding conflicts seem to dominate the overhead cost of these parallel system. In this paper, we do not propose a new strategy to improve resolution of binding conflicts but rather, we propose a scheme where binding conflicts may be avoided during execution. We turn to speculative computation on top of And/Or parallelism for performance speedup.

3 Speculative Computation

The idea of speculation is that it is a form of eager evaluation where the results computed may be unnecessary. In the case where the result is useful, it is hoped that it has been computed already when it is needed. Speculative computation has been used to achieve speedup in parallel execution of processes in other systems. Osborne in [20] proposed a scheme to support speculative computation in Multilisp. Multilisp [9] features the use of the **future** construct where (*future X*) (*X* is an arbitrary expression) creates a task to evaluate *X* and also creates an object which will eventually hold the value of *X* which is called a future. Parallelism using the **future** construct is possible by allowing processes to return a future as its value without waiting for it to resolve to the final value. This is implemented in the Mul-T parallel lisp system [17].

4 Speculative Parallelism in Prolog

In the area of logic programming, particularly in the execution of Prolog programs, a form of speculative execution called Randomized Parallel Backtracking has been proposed [12]. Performance of this model was studied by Lin [19]. Basically, the method is to let a number of processors work simultaneously and independently, on a given query. No interprocessor communication is necessary. Alternative clauses are chosen at random during forward execution and backtracking is performed when the path is blocked. Test results show no significant speed-up in most of the test programs compared to a typical divide-and-conquer parallel backtracking algorithm. However, for special types of program which have a full backtracking tree and solutions lie evenly in the leaves, it is shown that a randomized scheme will always be better than the typical divide-and-conquer scheme (even when communication overhead which always exist in divide-and-conquer is not included in the cost comparison).

In this section, we propose a framework for speculative computation in Prolog. The tool we use is a form of the unfolding rule proposed in [24] and an *unrecursing* rule which will be described in the next section.

4.1 Unfolding, Unrecursing and Partial Unrecursing

The unfolding rule basically consists of performing a computation step by applying the SLD-resolution to a clause with respect to a selected atom of its body. Transformation always preserves equivalence of programs in the least Herbrand model semantics. We define *unfolding-to-depth-N* as unfolding a clause with respect to the same atom N times or less. The *unrecursing-to-depth-N* rule uses the unfolding rule to unfold a recursive predicate to depth N resulting in a clause without the recursive predicate. Formally:

Unrecursing-To-Depth-N Rule

Let C be a clause in a program P where C_h is the head of C and $B_1, ..., B_n$ are the predicates in the body of C (i.e. $C : C_h :- B_1, ..., B_n$.) Given a B_i $\{1 <= i <= n\}$ which has the same functor as C_h, (ie a recursive call) and B_i unifies with the heads of $D_1, ..., D_m$ where $D_1, ..., D_m$ are clauses in P where the body of each of the clauses $D_1, ..., D_m$ have a predicate whose functor is the same as B_i, and B_i unifies with the heads of $E_1, ..., E_p$ where $E_1, ..., E_p$ are clauses in P where the body of each of the clauses $E_1, ..., E_p$ have no predicate whose functor is the same as B_i, then let C_k be the result of resolving C with any one of $D_1, ..., D_m$ upon B_i $k-1$ times followed by resolving C with one of $E_1, ..., E_p$ upon B_i. C_N is then the result of apply the *unrecursing-to-depth-N* rule to C.

Partial-Unrecursing-To-Depth-N Rule

The *partial-unrecursing-to-depth-N* rule is the same as *unrecursing-to-depth-N* rule except the recursive predicate is not unfolded away. The basic idea of the unrecursing-to-depth-N rule is to unfold the recursive predicate in a clause $N - 1$ times making sure that after each unfolding the recursive predicate is still in the clause. The last unfold gets rid of the recursive predicate by unfolding using a "base" clause. On the other hand, the partial-unrecursing-to-depth-N rule unfolds the recursive predicate in a clause N times and leaving the recursive predicate in the unfolded clause. The use of unrecursing has similar effects as generating **futures**. Placeholders are created but they are not executed as processes as in the case of [20]. As an example, consider the clauses for *append*:

$$append([], X, X).$$
$$append([X|X0], Y, [X|Z]) :- append(X0, Y, Z).$$

Unrecursing-to-depth-3 for the second clause results in:

$$append([X, X1, X2], Y, [X, X1, X2|Y]).$$

whereas partial-unrecursing-to-depth-3 results in:

$$append([X, X1, X2|X3], Y, [X, X1, X2|Z]) :- append(X3, Y, Z)$$

4.2 Model of Computation

The underlying computation model is And parallelism where goal predicates are executed in parallel. Prolog programs are compiled into a set of partial-unrecursed-to-depth-N, unrecursed-to-depth-N and unfolded-to-depth-N clauses before being executed.

Speculative computation results during execution when clauses are continually being unfolded and unrecursed. On one hand, we speculate that the clauses being unfolded will be used eventually. On the other hand, we "hope" that the unfolded clauses will not generate binding conflicts among the subgoals by continually unfolding and merging sibling subgoals. And parallel processes are created to solve conjunction of clauses. It will be seen that data dependency among the subgoals can be eliminated or reduced in the unfolded clauses. Or parallel processes can be created for each alternative clause but fully unfolded and unrecursed clauses are usually mutually exclusive to each other. Thus efficient implementation and compilation of unfolded clauses may benefit more from the overhead cost incurred by Or parallelism. We will expand on this in section 5.

4.3 Use of Unfolding and Unrecursing Rules

The unrecursing rule is used to unfold predicates defined with one recursive clause. The partial-unrecursing rule is used to unfold predicates defined with more than one recursive clause. An example of the latter is the $split(H, L, U, B)$ predicate where the list L is split into two lists U and B such that all elements in U are greater than H and all elements in B are less than H.

$$split(H, [H1|T1], [H1|U1], U2) :-$$
$$H1 < H, \ split(H, T1, U1, U2).$$
$$split(H, [H1|T1], U1, [H1|U2]) :-$$
$$H1 > H, \ split(H, T1, U1, U2).$$
$$split(\_, [], [], []).$$

The two unrecursing rules are invoked to generate clauses unrecursed from depth 1 to depth N where N can be determined during the execution or specified by the user. See Appendix 1 for program listing. The unfolding rule unfolds each predicate in the body by resolving each predicate and then unifying arguments with adjacent predicates and generates clauses with sometimes fewer predicates and less data dependency among them. See examples later in this section. Arithmetic and system predicates are not unfolded away.

The distinction in using the unrecursed and partial unrecursed rule is that unfolding a recursive predicate which is defined by more than one recursive clause can result in exponential number of clauses due to the explosive combination of the choices of clause to be unfolded. To generate the clause that may be needed to solve a goal predicate may require a long time. The partial unrecursed rule alleviates this problem by keeping the recursive predicate in the generated clause. This allows the process which succeeds in unifying with the generated clause to continue executing with the recursive predicate until the goal clause is solved. Clauses generated by the partial unrecursed rule are more efficient than the original clauses since they are partially unfolded and thus avoid additional clause invocation. It should be noted that unfolding a recursive predicate defined by only one recursive clause results in N clauses if the unrecursed rule is invoked for depth N. Hence, for predicates defined with more than one recursive clause, partial-unrecursed rule is used. Speed up will not be as significant as that results from using the unrecursed rule. However, in terms of space allocation and other implementation details, this may turn out to be more efficient for parallel execution.

It should be noted that unfolded and unrecursed clauses do not replace the original clauses since, unless extra information is provided, it is unknown whether the unfolded and unrecursed clauses are "expanded" to the required depth for the entire duration of the execution of the program. We give here a few examples to illustrate the use of the unfolding and unrecursing rule.

Example 1

The append/3 predicate is unfolded into the following clauses:

$$append([X], Y, [X|Y]).$$
$$append([X, X0], Y, [X, X0|Y]).$$
$$append([X, X0, X1], Y, [X, X0, X1|Y]).$$
$$....$$

Example 2

The predicate a checks if X is a member in the list Y, and if so, the list is processed by the predicate c.

$$a(X, Y) :- member(X, Y), c(Y).$$

$$member(X, [X|Y]).$$
$$member(X, [Y|Z]) :- member(X, Z).$$

The *member* predicate is first unfolded into the following clauses:

$$a(X, Y) :- member(X, Y), c(Y).$$

$$member(X, [X|Y]).$$
$$member(X, [X1, X|Y]).$$
$$member(X, [X1, X2, X|Y]).$$
$$....$$

and then to:

$$a(X, [X|Y]) :- c([X|Y]).$$
$$a(X, [X1, X|Y]) :- c([X1, X|Y]).$$
$$a(X, [X1, X2, X|Y]) :- c([X1, X2, X|Y]).$$
$$....$$

Example 3

$$m(X, Z) :- double(X, Y), reverse(Y, Z).$$

$$double([], []).$$
$$double([X|Y], [Z|Z1]) :- Z \ is \ X * 2, \ double(Y, Z1).$$

$$reverse([], []).$$
$$reverse([X|Xs], Z) :- reverse(Xs, Ys),$$
$$append(Ys, [X], Z).$$

The *double* and *reverse* predicates are unfolded first to:

$$m(X, Z) :- double(X, Y), reverse(Y, Z).$$

$$double([], []).$$
$$double([X1], [X2]) :- X2 \ is \ X1 * 2.$$
$$double([X1, X2], [X3, X4]) :- X3 \ is \ X1 * 2,$$
$$X4 \ is \ X2 * 2.$$
$$....$$

$$reverse([], []).$$
$$reverse([X1], [X1]).$$
$$reverse([X1, X2], [X2, X1]).$$
$$reverse([X1, X2, X3], [X3, X2, X1]).$$
$$....$$

and then m is unfolded to:

$$m([],[]).$$
$$m([X1],[X2]) :- X2 \ is \ X1 * 2.$$
$$m([X1,X2],[X4,X3]) :- X4 \ is \ X2 * 2,$$
$$X3 \ is \ X1 * 2.$$
....

Example 4

The *split* predicate defined earlier is partial-unrecursed to the following clauses:

$$split(H,[H1,H2|T1],[H1,H2|U1],U2) :-$$
$$H1 < H, \ H2 < H, split(H,T1,U1,U2).$$
$$split(H,[H1,H2|T1],U1,[H1,H2|U2]) :-$$
$$H1 > H, \ H2 > H, split(H,T1,U1,U2).$$
$$split(H,[H1,H2|T1],[H1|U1],[H2|U2]) :-$$
$$H1 < H, \ H2 > H, split(H,T1,U1,U2).$$
$$split(H,[H1,H2|T1],[H2|U1],[H1|U2]) :-$$
$$H1 > H, \ H2 < H, split(H,T1,U1,U2).$$
$$split(H,[H1,H2,H3|T1],[H1,H2,H3|U1],U2) :-$$
$$H1 < H, \ H2 < H, H3 < H, split(H,T1,U1,U2).$$
$$split(H,[H1,H2,H3|T1],U1,[H1,H2,H3|U2]) :-$$
$$H1 > H, \ H2 > H, H3 > H, split(H,T1,U1,U2).$$
....

The use of unrecursing rule eliminates the recursive call in *append* in Example 1, *member* in Example 2, *double* and *reverse* in Example 3. The unfolding rule unfolds *member* and unifies its arguments with c in Example 2. In example 3, arguments from the unfolded *double* and *reverse* are unified. Example 2 also shows that dependency between the predicate *member* and c is unfolded away.

5 Implementation

Though we propose the use of speculative computation in the parallel execution of Prolog programs with the goal of improving performance, without proper supporting architecture, we are not too optimistic about the performance speedup. The reason is that with optimized tail recursion, unfolding may not contribute much to the overall performance. Another reason is that unfolding will create a larger number of clauses which may also delay in finding the clause with the appropriate argument structure. Hence, our model calls for efficient implementation to support the framework.

Much work has been done in mapping a Prolog engine to a Von Neuman machine. Perhaps the most widely used and studied is the WAM abstract machine model proposed by David H. Warren [25]. Recently, David S. Warren extended the WAM model to include extension table [8] which supports the memo function [28]. The extension table facilities aids in the generation of unfolded and unrecursed clauses. However, fast indexing to clauses and also on the length of arguments are required to sift through the numerous clauses that may be generated. We shall discuss only one major aspect of our extension to the WAM model here, due to shortage of space, leaving other issues aside. Interested readers are referred to [30].

We propose the addition of two new instructions to the WAM model. The first instruction **switch_on_length A0 L0** allows fast branching to unfolded predicates labeled at **L0** by indexing on the length of a list or structure **A0**. If the list has a variable tail, its length is defined to be the number of items in the head. This is meant to complement the **switch_on_...** instructions of the original WAM model. The second instruction **match A0 A1** allows testing of input arguments **A0** and **A1** to check that their use of variables is consistent with the expected use when unified with a predicate. The arguments may be indexed {eg. A0.i A1.j} if A0 and A1 are lists. The idea is not to check for successful unification of the input argument with the expected argument in the predicate (like get_term, get_constant, etc.) but rather, a check for consistent use of variables among the input arguments themselves. The reason for this instruction is that unfolded clauses will have eliminated many of its predicates in the bodies, shifting much of the specification of variable bindings among the terms in the head. We demonstrate the use of the two instructions by compiling the unfolded clause:

$$member(X, [A, B, C, D, E, X|Y])$$

to our extended WAM machine.

$$switch\_on\_length \quad A1, Lmember$$

$$....$$

$$Lmember.1: \quad ...$$

$$....$$

$$Lmember.6: \quad match\,A0, A1.6$$

$$proceed$$

Details of compilation and other supporting architecture can be found in [30].

6 Conclusion

In order to improve the performance of parallel execution of Prolog programs, it seems that additional strategies need to be devised on top of the traditional parallel models. We have proposed in this paper that perhaps making each process do extra work, be it speculative, and whether they may be useful and necessary or not, may improve the performance. Coupled with supporting execution architecture, performance improvement may be obtained.

Acknowledgement

The author would like to thank Charles Elkan for interesting discussion about the paper and David Wortman for reviewing an earlier draft of this paper. Funding from the Natural Science and Engineering Research Council of Canada is gratefully appreciated.

References

[1] Biswas, P. and Su, S.C. and Yun, D.Y.Y.; A Scalable Abstract Machine Model to Support Limited-OR (LOR)/Restricted-AND Parallelism (RAP) in Logic Programs; Proceeding of the 5th International Conference on Logic Programming; 1988.

[2] Ciepielewski, A. and Haridi, S.; A Formal Model For Or-Parallel Execution of Logic Programs; IFIP 83.

[3] Clark, K.L. and Gregory, S.; PARLOG: Parallel programming in logic; ACM Trans. Prog. Lang. Syst. 8,1; Jan 1986.

[4] Clocksin, W.F. and Alshawi, H.; A Method for Efficiently Executing Horn Clause Programs Using Multiple Processors; Technical Report, Computer Laboratory; University of Cambridge; 1986.

[5] Conery, J; The AND/OR Process Model for Parallel Interpretation of Logic Programs; PhD thesis; University of California, Irvine; 1983. Revised version appears in: Parallel Execution Of Logic Programs; Kluwer Academic Publishers; Boston; 1987

[6] Conery, J.; Binding Environments for Parallel Logic Programs in Non-Shared Memory Multiprocessors; Proceeding of 1987 Symposium on Logic Programming; San Francisco, California; 1987.

[7] Degroot, D.; Restricted And-Parallelism; Proceeding of the International Conference on Fifth Generation Computer Systems; 1984.

[8] Dietrich, Suzanne Wagner; Extension Tables: Memo Relations in Logic Programming; IEEE Symposium on Logic Programming, 1987.

[9] Halstead, R.; Parallel Symbolic Computing; IEEE Computer 19:8; August 1986.

[10] Hausman, B. and Ciepielewski, A. and Haridi, S.; OR-parallel Prolog Made Efficient on Shared Memory Multiprocessors; Proceeding of 1987 Symposium on Logic Programming; San Francisco, California; 1987.

[11] Hermenegildo, M. and Nasr, R; Efficient Management of Backtracking in AND-Parallelism; Proceedings of the Third International Conference on Logic Programming; London, England; 1986.

[12] Janakiram, V., Agrawal, D., and Mehrotra, R.; A Randomized Parallel Backtracking Algorithm; IEEE Transaction on Computers; Vol 37, No 12; December 1988.

[13] Jefferson D. Virtual Time; TOPLAS; July 1985.

[14] Kalé, L.V.; 'Completeness' and 'Full Parallelism' of Parallel Logic Programming Schemes; Proceeding of 1987 Symposium on Logic Programming; San Francisco, California; 1987.

[15] Kalé, L.; The Reduce-Or Process Model for Parallel Evaluation of Logic Programs; Proceeding of the 4th International Conference on Logic Programming; 1987.

[16] Kowalski, Robert; Logic For Problem Solving; North-Holland, New York; 1979.

[17] Kranz, David and Halstead, Robert and Mohr, Eric; Mul-T: A High Performance Parallel Lisp; SigPlan 1989 Conference on Programming Language Design and Implementation.

[18] Li, P and Martin, A; The Sync Model: A Parallel Execution Method for Logic Programming; Proceedings of the 1986 Symposium of Logic Programming; Salt Lake City; Utah 1986.

[19] Lin, Zheng; Expected Performance of the Randomized Parallel Backtracking Method; North American Conference on Logic Programming; 1989.

[20] Osborne, Randy; Speculative Computation in Multilisp; Proceedings of U.S./Japan Workshop on Parallel Lisp; Sendai, Japan; June 5-8 1989.

[21] Ramkumar, Balkrishna and Kalé, Laxmikant; Compiled Execution of the Reduce-Or Process Model on Multiprocessors; North American Conference on Logic Programming; Cleveland, Ohio; 1989.

[22] Shapiro, E.Y.; A Subset of Concurrent PROLOG and its Interpreter; Technical Report TR-003, ICOT; Tokyo; 1983.

[23] Shapiro, Ehud; An Or-Parallel Execution Algorithm for Prolog and its FCP Implementation; Proceeding of the 1987 International Conference on Logic Programming; Melbourne, Australia; 1987.

[24] Tamaki, H. and Sato, T.; Unfold/fold Transformation of Logic Programs; Proceedings of 2nd International Conference on Logic Programming; Uppsala; 1984.

[25] Warren, D.H.D.; An Abstract Prolog Instruction Set; Technical Note 309; SRI International, AI Center, Computer Science and Technology Division; 1983.

[26] Warren, D.H.D.; Or-Parallel Execution Models of Prolog; Proceedings of the International Joint Conference on Theory and Practise of Software Development (TAPSOFT); Pisa, Italy; March 1987. (Also in LNCS 250).

[27] Warren, D.H.D.; The SRI Model for Or-Parallel Execution of Prolog - Abstract Design and Implementation; Proceeding of 1987 Symposium on Logic Programming; San Francisco, California; 1987.

[28] Warren, D.S.; The XWAM: A Machine that Integrates Prolog and Deductive Database Query Evaluation; Tech. Report 89/25; SUNY Stony Brook; 1989.

[29] Yasuhara, H. and Nitadori, K.; ORBIT: A Parallel Computing Model of Prolog; New Generation Computing; 2:277-288; 1984.

[30] Yu, B; Side Effects and Other Implementation Issues in Speculative Optimistic Parallelism in Prolog; in preparation; 1989.

Synthesis of Error-Recoverable Protocol Specifications from Service Specifications

Kassem Saleh   Robert Probert

Protocols/Software Engineering Research Group
Department of Computer Science
University of Ottawa
Ottawa, Ontario, Canada
K1N 6N5

ABSTRACT

Several synthesis methods have been proposed and applied to the design of computer communication protocols. Most of these methods do not use the service specification as a reference (or starting) point in the protocol synthesis process. Consequently, these methods do not guarantee that the synthesized protocol provides the specified services, and therefore must be complemented by a semantic validation technique. In this paper, we propose a new synthesis method which automatically derives protocol specifications from a service specification. Both the service and protocol specifications are modelled by finite state machines (FSM). The resulting synthesized protocol is guaranteed to be free from logical design (syntactic) errors and to conform to the service specification. Finally, the synthesized protocol is augmented by error-recovery patterns to enable recovery from transmission errors caused by an unreliable communication medium. The application of the new method to an example service is also presented.

Keywords: Communication software, error-recovery, protocol design, semantic correctness, syntactic correctness, synthesis

1. Introduction

Protocol design consists essentially of the construction of interacting entities which cooperate to provide a set of specified services to the service users while guaranteeing that no errors will be encountered. We can recognize two types of design errors:

(1)   errors encountered during the progress of interactions between the communicating entities. These errors are often called *logical (syntactic) errors*, and include such errors as deadlock and unspecified reception.

(2)   errors resulting in incorrect service (with respect to the service specification) provided by the designed protocol to the service user. We refer to such errors as *semantic errors*.

Two different approaches to the design of computer communication protocols are *analysis* and *synthesis* [18].

In the *analysis* approach, the protocol designer starts with a preliminary version of the protocol in which the syntactic and semantic validation aspects often have been overlooked. Protocol validation is then performed in a separate post-design activity and is based on analysis techniques intended to detect errors and omissions in the design. The sequence of re-design, analysis, error detection and correction is applied iteratively until the protocol design becomes error-free. Therefore, the analysis approach is very time-consuming. Analysis techniques have been surveyed and classified in [17].

In the *synthesis* approach, many methods have been developed and used to construct or complete a partially specified protocol design such that the interactions between the constructed or completed protocol entities proceed without encountering any logical error and ideally provide the specified services. Furthermore, the syntactic correctness of the synthesized protocol is often a direct by-product of the synthesis method.

Synthetic protocol design methods [2,3,4,5,6,7,8,10,13,18,19] have been surveyed and compared in [9]. Most of these methods, except for [2], [4] and [7], do not use the service specification as a starting point in the synthesis process. Consequently, these methods do not guarantee that the synthesized protocol provides the specified services, and therefore, must be complemented by a semantic validation technique. This has the undesirable effect of eliminating the major advantage of the synthesis approach.

In this paper, we propose a new synthesis method which automatically derives protocol specifications from a service specification. Both the service and protocol specifications are modelled by finite state machines (FSM). The resulting synthesized protocol is guaranteed to be free from logical (syntactic) errors and to conform completely to the service specification.

This paper is organized as follows. In Section 2, we discuss the relations between service and protocol specifications and the rationale for designing protocols starting from the service. In Section 3, we introduce the basic service and protocol specification model. In Section 4, we present our synthesis method and prove the semantic correctness of the resulting protocol specifications. In Section 5, we present the error-recovery patterns we use to obtain error-recoverable protocol specifications when an unreliable underlying communication medium is assumed. This extends and improves upon earlier work by the authors [12]. In Section 6, we present an example showing the application of the method to a simple example service. Finally in Section 7, we conclude the paper.

2. Relations between service and protocol specifications

The distinction between the service and protocol concepts has attracted an increasing level of attention and interest by communication software designers [15]. Presently, each new international standard for a specific protocol is accompanied by another standard for the service specification. We feel that a good understanding of the interrelationships between these concepts is essential for the development of an effective synthetic protocol design methodology.

At a high level of abstraction, a communication system can be viewed as a black box offering some specified communication services to a number of service users accessing the system through many distributed service access points (SAPs). The service specification consists of: (1) the identification of service primitives (SPs) that are available to the service users, and (2) the specification of the possible temporal ordering of SP occurrences at the distributed SAPs. This ordering is referred to as the *global service constraints* [16].

At a more refined level of abstraction, the communication services are provided to the service users by a number of cooperating protocol entities which exchange protocol messages that are not observable at the SAPs. A protocol entity uses the lower (underlying) service functions to relay protocol messages to another protocol entity.

Our communication model is based on the above mentioned architectural principles: the specified service offered to the service users, the protocol entities and the underlying services which are represented by a reliable FIFO (first-in, first-out) communication medium (Figure 1). In this paper, we will refer to upper SAPs as simply SAPs, and we will refer to lower SAPs explicitly when necessary.

Because of their refined nature, protocol specifications are much complex than service specifications. Furthermore, a complete and unambiguous service specification assists in eliminating complex protocol design problems. Therefore, it seems quite natural to start the protocol design process from a complete service specification, as we have done in this paper. Thus, for a comprehensive synthetic protocol design methodology, the task to accomplish is "the design of (N-)protocol specifications from both (N-) and (N-1) Service Specifications".

3. The basic specification model

In this section, we describe the finite state machine model we used to develop our synthesis method. We also define some operations on the model.

3.1. Service specification model

Definition 1. A *service specification* S-SPEC is denoted by a tuple (Ss, Σs, Ts, σ), where:

Ss is a non-empty finite set of service states
Σs is a finite set of service primitives
Ts is a partial transition function between service states (a subset of the product Ss $\times$ Σs $\times$ Ss).
$\sigma \in$ Ss is the initial service state

Definition 2. A *service primitive* $SP \in \Sigma$s identifies the type of service event and the Service Access Point (SAP) at which it may occur. For example, A1 means that the service primitive A may occur at SAP 1. Upper case letters are used to denote service primitives.

Definition 3. For every node representing a service state $s \in$ Ss, OUT(s) denotes the set of SAPs associated with the SPs of its outgoing edges.

Definition 4. The *projection* onto a set X of SAPs (Πx) is a unary function which can be applied to either: (i) a finite state machine (FSM) (S, Σ, T, σ) yielding another FSM (S, Σ', T', σ) in which Σ' is a subset of $\Sigma \cup \{\varepsilon\}$ and T' = T with relabeling to ε of events in Σ not contributing to the SAPs onto which the FSM is projected, or (ii) a set of traces yielding another set of traces in which each trace is missing those events which do not contribute to the SAPs onto which the set of traces is projected, but the order of remaining events is as in the original trace.

Note that transitions labelled with ε indicate changes in state which are not directly attributable to a message reception or transmission at a particular SAP. This is not the same concept as an internal event [16].

Definition 5. A projected S-SPECi (PS-SPECi) is the projection of the (FSM) service specification S-SPEC onto SAPi (PS-SPECi = ΠSAPi S-SPEC) as described in Definition 4. PS-SPECi is represented by (Ss, Σ's, T's, σ), where Σ's is a subset of Σs and T's is a subset of the cartesian product Ss $\times (\Sigma'$s $\cup \{\varepsilon\}) \times$ Ss.

Definition 6. L(S-SPEC) denotes the set of legal *global service traces* observable at all SAPs.

Definition 7. L(PS-SPECi) denotes the set of legal *local service traces* at SAPi. Thus, ΠSAPi L(S-SPEC) = L(PS-SPECi).

3.2. Protocol specification model

The protocol specification consists of a tuple of specifications of a number of cooperating protocol entities. The interactions between the protocol entities through the underlying service must yield the service specification. Protocol entities are modeled by deterministic finite state machines.

Definition 8. A *protocol entity specification* PE-SPEC is denoted by a tuple (Sp, Σp, Tp, σ), where:

Sp is a non-empty finite set of protocol states

Σp is a finite set of protocol events, $\Sigma p = \Sigma's \cup IPE$, where Σ' is a subset of Σs, and IPE is the set of internal protocol events

Tp is a partial transition function between protocol states (a subset of the product $Sp \times \Sigma p \times Sp$)

$\sigma \in Sp$ is the initial protocol state

Definition 9. A *protocol specification* (P-SPEC) consists of several interacting PE-SPECs. In our communication model, we suppose that a one-to-one correspondence exists between PE-SPECs and SAPs.

Definition 10. L(P-SPEC) denotes the set of legal *global protocol traces* observable at the interaction points with the service users (at upper SAPs) and with the communication medium (at lower SAPs).

The interaction between an S-SPEC (modeling service users) and a PE-SPECi is based on the rendez-vous concept, meaning that the synchronization will only occur when S-SPEC and PE-SPECi agree on a given SP. Therefore, no direction is associated with SP occurrences. However, the interactions among protocol entities are not assumed to be based on rendez-vous, rather they are synchronized by the (FIFO) communication medium which reliably transfers an event sent by one entity to be received by another entity. An internal protocol event e can be either received (?e) or sent using the function !(e, X), where X is the set of SAPs to which e is sent.

4. The protocol synthesis method

In this section, we first introduce the transition synthesis rules (TSR) and the synthesis algorithm that are used to transform the projected service specifications into individual protocol entity specifications. Then, we sketch the proof of semantic correctness of the derived protocol specifications. The proof of syntactic correctness is not presented in this paper.

4.1. TSRs and the synthesis algorithm

Definition 11. Transition Synthesis Rules (TSRs). These rules are applied to each of the transitions in PS-SPECi, in which two types of transitions exist:
  a.Transitions labeled by an SP:

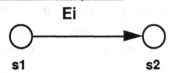

Case 1: s2 is not an initial state and OUT(s2) = {SAPi}.
  Rule a.1: The transition remains unchanged.

Case 2: s2 is the initial state (typically in a reset event).
  Rule a.2: The transition is transformed into the following two transitions:

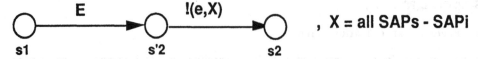

Case 3: Otherwise:
  Rule a.3: The transition is transformed into the following two transitions:

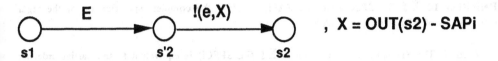

, X = OUT(s2) - SAPi

b. Transitions labeled by ε:

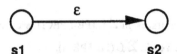

Case 1: s2 is not an initial state and SAPi is in OUT(s2).

    Rule b.1: Suppose E is the label of the transition from s1 to s2 in S-SPEC. The ?e corresponds to this label.

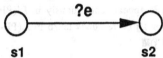

Case 2: s2 is not an initial state and SAPi is not in OUT(s2).

    Rule b.2: The transition remains unchanged.

Case 3: s2 is an initial state.

    Rule b.3: The transformation is identical to Rule b.1.

Synthesis Algorithm. Derivation of protocol specifications from the service specification.
Input: FSM-based service specification (S-SPEC)
Output: FSM-based protocol entities specifications (PE-SPECs).
Steps:
1. Project the service specification S-SPEC onto each SAP to obtain the PS-SPECs.
2. Apply the transition synthesis rules to each transition in the PS-SPECs.
3. Using the algorithms described in [1], remove ε-cycles and ε-transitions to obtain the PE-SPECs as reduced and equivalent finite state machines.

4.2. Proof of semantic correctness

In this section, we prove that the interactions between the derived protocol entities through the communication medium provide the service specificed in S-SPEC.

Definition 12. L(PE-SPECi) denotes the set of legal *local protocol traces* of the protocol entity PE-SPECi.

Lemma 1. ΠSAPi L(PE-SPECi) = L(PS-SPECi) = ΠSAPi L(S-SPEC).

Proof. Both a PS-SPECi and a PE-SPECi preserve the ordering of SPs at SAPi. The projection of each synthesized transition onto SAPi yields the original service transition in PS-SPECi ∎

Definition 13. L'(PE-SPECi) is derived from L(PE-SPECi) by removing all send functions and replacing every receive function with its corresponding SP. For example if A !a ?e D ∈ L(PE-SPECi), then A E D ∈ L'(PE-SPECi).

Lemma 2. L'(PE-SPECi) is the partial specification of the legal interleavings of SPs at SAPi with respect to SPs at other SAPs.

Proof. By the TSRs, the reception of an event corresponds to the occurrence of an SP at another SAP. Therefore, if SP Xi precedes ?y in PE-SPECi, then X precedes Y in L(S-SPEC) ∎

Definition 14. $\Sigma L'$(PE-SPECi) (for all SAPi) denotes the complete specification of the legal interleavings of SPs at all upper SAPs.

Theorem 1. The SP partial order relation in $\Sigma L'$(PE-SPECi) is equivalent to the partial ordering of SPs in L(S-SPEC). In other words, the interactions between the derived protocol entities provide the service specified in S-SPEC.

Proof. We prove this equivalence by showing that all traces in $\Sigma L'$(PE-SPECi) are consistent with L(S-SPEC) and all traces in L(S-SPEC) are preserved in $\Sigma L'$(PE-SPECi).

The first part of the proof is a direct corollary of Lemma 2. To prove the second part, we show that for any pair of contiguous SPs in S-SPEC, the same pair of SPs exists at least once in a L'(PE-SPECi). The contiguous pair of SPs could be of two types: i) AiBi (both SPs appear at the same SAPi): the TSRs guarantee that the same pair of SPs appears contiguously in L'(PE-SPECi), or ii) AiBj (either Ai corresponds to ?a in L(PE-SPECj) or Bj corresponds to ?b in L(PE-SPECi)): the same pair of SPs appears contiguously in L'(PE-SPECj)∎

5. Synthesis of error-recoverable protocols

In this section, we first introduce some basic concepts for error-recovery. Then, we extend our synthesis method to include some error-recovery mechanisms in the derived protocol to obtain error-recoverable specifications. Finally, we summarize the extended synthesis algorithm for deriving error-recoverable protocol specifications and we (informally) prove its semantic correctness.

5.1. Basic concepts for error-recoverable protocols

Ideally, error recovery mechanisms must be transparent to the service user, meaning that only the protocol entities will be involved. Thus, protocol entities alone must detect transmission errors and provide mechanisms to recover from them. Furthermore, the user will not be aware of the occurrence of an error or be involved in its recovery. As a result of these considerations, no modification to the service specification model will be required.

A message can be either an *acknowledgment* or a *protocol* message (control or information). Both types of messages are equally likely to be lost or corrupted due to the non-discriminating nature of the communication medium. Furthermore, an acknowledgment message can be either a positive or a negative acknowlegment. Corrupted and lost messages can be treated similarly by a timeout mechanism that will retransmit the (lost or corrupted) message.

A simple error-recovery mechanism can be used to ensure that eventually each message transmitted by one entity (E1) is properly received by the destination entity (E2). We assume that a timing mechanism, called Positive-Acknowledgment-and-Retransmission (PAR) (Figure 2), exists at the sending entity which starts a timer when a protocol message is sent and stops the same timer when an acknowledgment for the previously sent message is received. Furthermore, when the timer expires after time τ, the protocol entity which started the timer will progress by executing the corresponding timeout transition (labelled by Tm).

The effectiveness of PAR is based on the following reasonable assumptions:

Ignoring corrupted messages: When a corrupted message is received, the protocol entity will just ignore it and will not progress to a new state.

Timeout and message loss: A protocol message will be assumed lost in the channel if, after a time τ equal to the time delay for a message to arrive to its destination and its positive acknowledgment to be sent back, no acknowledgment is received. If the message reaches its destination after its normal transmission time, the effect will be as if the message is ignored.

Fairness: Eventually, after a finite number of retransmissions of a (lost or corrupted) message, the message will be received properly at its intended destination.

Detection of and recovery from duplicate messages can be dealt with by attaching a sequence number for every transmitted message and by attaching the same sequence number to acknowledge receipt of the same message by the destination entity.

A discussion of other error-recovery mechanisms and problems is provided in [4], [11] and [14].

5.2. Extension to the synthesis method

In our synthesis method, we apply the PAR error-recovery mechanism to every pattern of message transmission and reception of protocol messages.

As a result of the application of the transition synthesis rules (TSRs) introduced in Section 4, two possible transmission/reception patterns can occur in the protocol specifications.

Pair of SPs occurring at the same SAP:
When a pair of SPs occurs at the same SAP, we apply the PAR mechanism for every message transmission and its corresponding reception without any modification.

Pair of SPs occurring at different SAPs
However, when a pair of consecutive SPs occurs at different SAPs, we first apply the PAR mechanism for every message transmission and its corresponding reception. Then, we add two other message reception transitions to prevent an unspecified reception error that can be caused by a loss of an acknowledgment message. Figure 3 shows the error-recovery patterns that deal with this case.

The application of the error-recovery patterns for multi-users services requires more attention. At a mixed protocol state (wich corresponds to a service state s for which OUT(s) is not a singleton), an acknowledgment message may be expected from two or more protocol entities. The question that arises is what to do when none or some of the acknowledgment messages are received and what is the meaning of a timeout on an acknowledgment in this case. For multi-users, therefore, SAP identifiers are explicitly encoded in acknowledgments

To avoid a deadlock, we have to make sure that a message sent is received at all SAPs in OUT(n), where n denotes the mixed state. Therefore, the timeout transition must indicate the set of originating entities (X) for which an acknowledgment message has not yet been received. The message will be resent to all SAPs in X.

5.3. Synthesis algorithm for error-recoverable protocols

The synthesis algorithm for deriving error-recoverable protocol specifications is outlined below.

Extended Synthesis Algorithm. Derivation of error-recoverable protocol specifications.
Input: The FSM service specification (S-SPEC) as defined in Section 3.
Output: Error-recoverable protocol (ERP-SPEC).
Steps:
1. Apply the three steps of the synthesis algorithm given in Section 4 to obtain PE-SPECs.
2. Apply the PAR error-recovery mechanism for every message transmission and its corresponding reception in each of the PE-SPECs.
3. For every sequence (!e' ?ack ?e") in any of the PE-SPECs, apply the error-recovery pattern shown in Figure 3, to obtain the ERPE-SPECs.

The synthesized error-recoverable protocol is semantically correct (ΠSAPs L(ERP-SPEC) = L(S-SPEC)). The proof is straightforward since the error-recovery patterns (Section 5.2.) do not introduce any reordering of SPs or protocol messages in the synthesized protocol specifications. The projection of every pattern in each ERPE-SPECi onto SAPi always yields the original SP occurrences as in PE-SPECi (ΠSAPi L(ERPE-SPECi) = ΠSAPi L(PE-SPECi)).The proof of syntactic correctness is also straightforward and is based on the syntactic correctness of P-SPEC derived by the Algorithm, and the correctness of the error-recovery patterns.

6. Example

To demonstrate our synthesis method, we consider the service specification shown in Figure 4. The FSM S-SPEC describes the valid sequences of SPs observable at four SAPs. Our method will derive four protocol entity specifications (PE-SPECs) from the given service specification.

For the given S-SPEC, we have: Ss = {1,2,3,4}, Σs = { A, B, C, D, E}, σ = 1, OUT(1) = {sap1}, OUT(2) = {sap2,sap4}, OUT(3) = {sap3}, and OUT(4) = {sap2}.

Step 1 of the Algorithm: Figure 5 shows the four projected service specifications (PS-SPECs).
Steps 2 and 3 of the Algorithm: Figure 6 show the PE-SPECs after removing ε-cycles and ε-transitions, respectively.
Step 2 and 3 of the Extended Algorithm: Figure 7 shows the error-recoverable protocol specifications.

7. Conclusions and future work

In this paper, we introduced a new method for the synthesis of error-recoverable protocol entity specifications starting from a service specification. Both protocol and service specifications are modeled by deterministic finite state machines. The interactions between the protocol entities and the service users are tightly or strongly synchronized. However the interactions among the protocol entities are based on the sending and the eventual reception of protocol messages exchanged via the underlying communication medium.

The derived error-recoverable protocol specifications have been proved to be both semantically correct (safe), meaning that the interacting protocol entities faithfully provide the specified service, and also syntactically correct, meaning that no deadlocks or unspecified receptions can occur during the interactions. A comparison between our method and another FSM-based synthesis method introduced in [4] has shown that ours is more faithful to the service specifications and moreover, applies to the synthesis of multi-party protocols [12].

Our experience with the method shows that the FSM model requires some extensions to make the service specification complete, unambiguous and more expressive. We have observed that using the strict FSM model, we are unable to express concurrent service behaviours at the SAPs. Also, this approach does not yet take into account some architecturally important information needed for the derivation of complete and unambiguous protocol specifications in general [12]. Currently, we are working on some extensions to the specification model to enhance its expressiveness, clarity and applicability.

Acknowledgements. We gratefully acknowledge support of this work by the Telecommunications Research Institute of Ontario (TRIO) and the Natural Sciences and Engineering Research Council (NSERC), as well as useful discussions with Prof. Hasan Ural and other members of the University of Ottawa Protocols/Software Engineering Research Group.

References

[1]   W.A.Barrett and J.D. Couch, *Compiler Construction: Theory and Practice*, Chapter 3, Science Research Associates, (1979).

[2]   G.V. Bochmann and R. Gotzhein, "Deriving protocol specifications from service specifications", in *SIGCOMM'86*, (1986) 144-156.

[3]   T.Y. Choi, "Sequence method for protocol construction", in *Sixth IFIP Intern. Symp. on Protocol Specification, Testing, and Verification*, (May 1986) 307-321.

[4]   P.M. Chu and M.T. Liu, "Synthesizing protocol specifications from service specification in FSM model", in *Proc. Computer Networking Symp.*, (April 1988) 173-182.

[5]   M.G. Gouda and Y.T. Yu, "Synthesis of communicating finite state machines with guaranteed progress", *IEEE Trans. on Commun.* COM-32 (7) (1984) 779-788.

[6]   Y. Kakuda and Y. Wakahara, "Component-based synthesis of protocols for unlimited number of processes", in *Proc. COMPSAC'87* , (1988) 721-730.

[7]   F. Khendek, G.V. Bochmann and C. Kant, "New results on deriving protocol specifications from service specifications", *ACM SIGCOMM'89 Symp.*, (1989) 136-145.

[8]   P. Merlin and G. Bochmann, "On the construction of submodule specifications and communication protocols", *ACM TOPLAS* Vol. 5 (1) (1983) 1-25.

[9]   R. Probert and K. Saleh, "Survey and critique of synthetic protocol design methods", *Technical Report TR-89-41*, Dept. of Computer Science, Univ. of Ottawa, (Oct. 1989).

[10] C.V. Ramamorthy, S.T. Dong, and Y. Usuda, "An implementation of an automated protocol synthesizer (APS) and its application to the X.21 protocol", *IEEE Trans. on Software Eng.* SE-11 (9) (1985) 886-908.

[11] C.V. Ramamorthy et al., "Synthesis and performance of two-party error-recoverable protocols", in Proc. *COMPSAC'86*, (1986) 214-220.

[12] K. Saleh and R. Probert, "A service-oriented protocol synthesis method", *Technical Report TR-89-45*, Dept. of Computer Science, Univ. of Ottawa, (Nov. 1989).

[13] D.P. Sidhu, "Protocol design rules", in *Second IFIP Intern. Symp. on Protocol Specification, Testing, and Verification*, (1982) 283-300.

[14] A. Tanenbaum, *Computer Networks*, Chapter 4, Prentice Hall Inc., (1988).

[15] C.A. Vissers and L. Logrippo, "The importance of the service concept in the design of data communications protocols", in *Fifth Intern. Symp. on Protocol Specification, Testing, and Verification*, (1986) 3-17.

[16] C.A. Vissers, et al., The Architecture of Interaction Systems. Lecture Notes, Twente University of Technology, The Netherlands, (May 1989).

[17] M.C. Yuang, "Survey of protocol verification techniques based on finite state machine models", in *Proc. of Computer Networking Symp.*, (1988) 164-172.

[18] P. Zafiropulo, et al., "Towards analyzing and synthesizing protocols", *IEEE Trans. on Commun.* COM-28 (4) (1980) 651-661.

[19] Y.X. Zhang et al., "An interactive protocol synthesis algorithm using a global state transition graph", *IEEE Trans. on Software Eng.* SE-14 (3) (1988) 394-404.

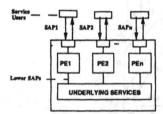

Figure 1. An abstract view of a distributed communication system

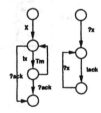

Figure 2. PAR mechanism for error recovery

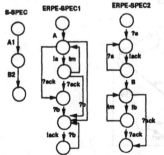

Figure 3. Error-recovery patterns for a sequence of SPs at two SAPs

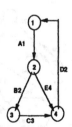

Figure 4. The service specification

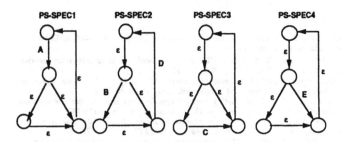

Figure 5. Projected service specifications onto four SAPs

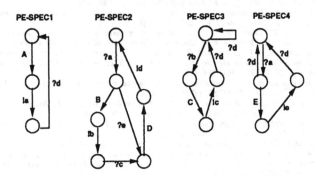

Figure 6. Protocol specifications derived from the service in Figure 4

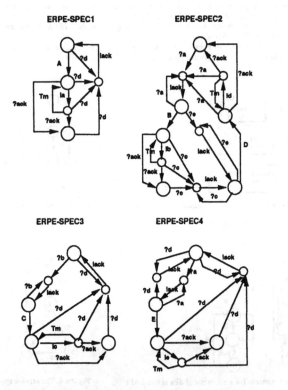

Figure 7. Error-recoverable protoccol specifications

A Parallel Algorithm for Path-Min Queries in Trees

Sung Kwon Kim [1]
Department of Computer Science and Engineering, FR–35
University of Washington
Seattle, WA 98195

Abstract: Given a rooted tree T on n vertices with each vertex v having a label $cost(v)$, preprocess T so that, given a pair of vertices v, w, the minimum-cost vertex on the path between v and w (the path-min of v and w) can be found efficiently. We give a preprocessing algorithm running in $O(\log n)$ time using $O(n)$ processors in the CREW PRAM. After preprocessing, a path-min query can be answered in $O(\log n)$ time using a single processor.

1 Introduction

We consider the following problem, which we call the *path-min query* problem in trees. Given a rooted tree T on n vertices with a label $cost(v)$ associated with each vertex v, preprocess T so that, given a pair of vertices v, w, $MCV(v, w)$ can be found efficiently using a single processor, where $MCV(v, w)$ is the minimum-cost vertex on the path between v and w (the path-min of v and w). This problem was first considered by Chazelle [5], who gave a sequential $O(n \log n)$ preprocessing time, $O(\log n)$ query time solution. For this problem, we give a parallel solution with $O(\log n)$ time, $O(n)$ processor preprocessing complexity and $O(\log n)$ query time. By a query time we mean time needed to answer a query using a *single* processor.

Our parallel computational model is the concurrent-read exclusive-write (CREW) PRAM, which is a class of the parallel random access machine (PRAM) that allows concurrent reads by several processors from the same memory location, but does not allow concurrent writes by several processors into the same memory location.

2 Preliminaries

Observe that we can assume that T is a binary tree. A non-binary tree can be transformed into a binary tree (cf. [1]) by introducing $O(n)$ additional vertices without affecting solutions.

We first introduce two lemmas that will be used in the remainder of this section.

Lemma 2.1 *Given a rooted tree T, one can preprocess T in $O(\log n)$ time using $O(n/\log n)$ processors so that, given a pair of vertices v, w, $LCA(v, w)$, the lowest common ancestor of v and w in T can be found in $O(1)$ time using a single processor.*

Proof. See Schieber and Vishkin [9]. □

---

[1] Research supported in part by NSF Grant CCR-8907960.

Lemma 2.2 *Given a rooted tree T, one can preprocess T in $O(\log n)$ time using $O(n/\log n)$ processors so that, given three vertices $v, w, x \in T$, determining whether or not x is on the path between v and w can be done in $O(1)$ time using a single processor.*

Proof. Let $y = LCA(v, w)$. Then x is on the path between v and w if and only if $y = LCA(x, y)$ and either $x = LCA(v, x)$ or $x = LCA(w, x)$. $\square$

Next, we explain how to "divide" a binary tree when a divide-and-conquer algorithm for problems involving binary trees is to be developed.

Let T be a binary tree with $|T| \geq 3$. Consider a vertex $v \in T$. Deleting v and its incident edges from T leaves a forest consisting of at most three subtrees T_1, T_2, T_3. One (two) of them is (are) empty if v is of degree 2 (1). Define $weight(v)$ $v \in T$ to be $MAX\{|T_1|, |T_2|, |T_3|\}$, where $|T_i|$ is the number of vertices in T_i. A vertex with minimum weight is called a *centroid* of T.

Lemma 2.3 *There are at most two centroids in T; furthermore, if there are two, they are adjacent.*

Proof. See [7] (Prob. 9 on Page 396). $\square$

For each $v \in T$, let $ND(v)$ be the number of its descendants (including itself), and $PRE(v)$, its preorder number. In $O(\log n)$ time using $O(n/\log n)$ processors, $ND(v)$ and $PRE(v)$ for each $v \in T$ can be computed using the Euler tour technique [10]. We characterize the centroids of a tree using $ND(\cdot)$.

Lemma 2.4 *(i) T has two centroids c_1 and c_2 where c_1 is the parent of c_2 if and only if n is even and $ND(c_2) = n/2$.*

(ii) T has only one centroid c whose children are c_1, c_2 if and only if $2 \cdot ND(c_i) \leq n - 1$ for $i = 1, 2$ and $2 \cdot ND(c) \geq n + 1$.

Proof. See [7](Prob. 10 on Page 396, and Page 387). $\square$

Define the *partitioning* vertex of T to be the centroid if T has only one centroid, or the further one from the root of T if T has two centroids. The following facts are immediate from Lemma 2.4.

(i) If $ND(v)$ for each $v \in T$ is known, then the partitioning vertex of T can be found in $O(1)$ time using $O(n)$ processors.

(ii) Let T_1, T_2, T_3 be the subtrees obtained after the partitioning vertex and its edges are deleted from T. Then $|T_i| \leq \lfloor n/2 \rfloor$ for $i = 1, 2, 3$.

Lemma 2.5 *Let c be the partitioning vertex of T. Then a vertex $v \in T$ is on the path between c and the root of T if and only if $ND(v) \geq ND(c)$.*

Proof.

$\Rightarrow$) This direction is easy because c is a descendant of v.

$\Leftarrow$) If c is the root of T, it is obvious. So, assume that c is not the root of T. Then v cannot be a descendant of c (unless $c = v$). Suppose that v is not on the c-to-root path. ce the descendants of c and the descendants of v are disjoint, the number of vertices in

T is at least $2 \cdot ND(c)$ plus one (the root), i.e. $n \geq 2 \cdot ND(c) + 1$, which contradicts to both (i) and (ii) of Lemma 2.4. $\square$

Suppose that $ND(v)$ for each $v \in T$ is known. Let c be the partitioning vertex of T with three neighbors c_1, c_2, c_3. Let T_1, T_2, T_3 be the subtrees containing c_1, c_2, c_3, resp. Wlog, assume that T_1 contains the root of T. Make the root of T the root of T_1 and make c_i the root of T_i for $i = 2, 3$. $ND_i(\cdot)$ will be similarly defined as $ND(\cdot)$ except that only the vertices in T_i are considered with respect to their new root. Then, for $i = 2, 3$ for each $v \in T_i, ND_i(v) = ND(v)$, and $ND_1(v) = ND(v) - ND(c)$ if $v \in T_1$ is on the path from c_1 to the root, and $ND_1(v) = ND(v)$, otherwise. By Lemma 2.5, in $O(1)$ time using $O(n)$ processors, one can determine if each vertex of T_1 is on the c_1-to-root path and, if so, update $ND_1(v)$. So, $ND_i(\cdot)$ can be obtained from $ND(\cdot)$ in $O(1)$ time using $O(n)$ processors. Since $ND_i(v)$ for each $v \in T_i$ is known, one can find the partitioning vertex of T_i in $O(1)$ time using $O(|T_i|)$ processors.

Note that, for $i = 2, 3$, a vertex v is in T_i if and only if $PRE(c_i) \leq PRE(v) \leq PRE(c_i) + ND(c_i) - 1$, because the PRE numbers of the descendant of c_i form a set of contiguous integers $\{PRE(c_i), \cdots, PRE(c_i) + ND(c_i) - 1\}$. So, each vertex can determine in $O(1)$ time which T_i it belongs to. $PRE_i(\cdot)$, defined recursively on T_i, can easily be computed from $PRE(\cdot)$ in $O(1)$ time using $O(n)$ processors.

We now summarize the discussion above. Let T be an n-vertex binary tree.

(i) $ND(v)$ for each $v \in T$ can be computed in $O(\log n)$ time using $O(n/\log n)$ processors.

(ii) If $ND(v)$ for each $v \in T$ is known, then the partitioning vertex of T can be found in $O(1)$ time using $O(n)$ processors.

(iii) Deleting the partitioning vertex and its incident edges from T leaves three sub-trees, T_1, T_2, T_3, each of which has at most $\lfloor n/2 \rfloor$ vertices.

(iv) $ND_i(\cdot)$ for $i = 1, 2, 3$ can be found in $O(1)$ time using $O(n)$ processors.

3 Preprocessing

As shown in Section 2, a binary tree T on three or more vertices has a vertex, called the *partitioning* vertex, denoted by $p(T)$, such that deleting it and its incident edges from T leaves a forest consisting of at most three subtrees T_1, T_2, T_3, each of which has $\leq \lfloor n/2 \rfloor$ vertices.

We build a rooted tree T^* which consists of the root $p(T)$ and its three subtrees T_1^*, T_2^*, T_3^*, defined recursively. In other words, T^* is constructed as follows: Find $p(T)$, make it the root of T^*, delete $p(T)$ and its incident edges from T to get T_1, T_2, T_3, recursively build T_1^*, T_2^*, T_3^*, make their roots the children of $p(T)$, the root of T^*. Clearly, T^* is of height at most $\lceil \log_2 n \rceil$ and can be built in $O(\log n)$ time using $O(n)$ processors, as shown in Section 2. Figure 1(b) shows T^* (solid edges) of T in Figure 1(a).

Let $LCA^*(v, w)$ be the lowest common ancestor of v and w in T^*. Let $PATH(v, w)$ be the path between v and w in T.

Lemma 3.1 $LCA^*(v, w) \in PATH(v, w)$ *for any two vertices* v, w.

Proof. Let $u = LCA^*(v, w)$. If $u = v$ or $u = w$, then we are done. Otherwise, v and w belong to different subtrees of u in T^*, i.e., choosing u as a partitioning vertex and deleting it during the construction of T^* has separated v and w into two different subtrees of

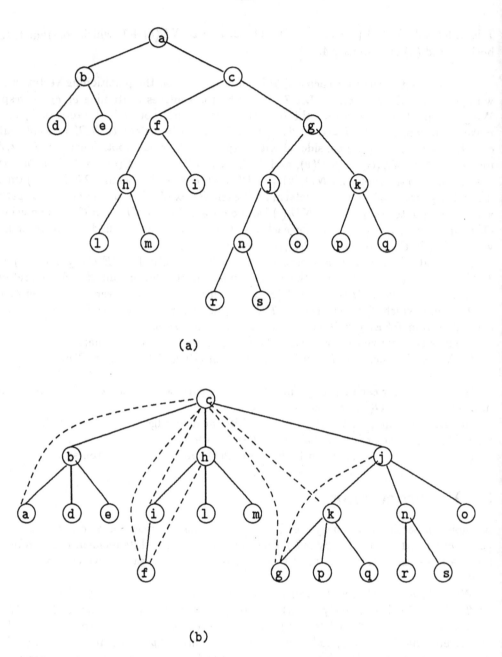

(a)

(b)

Figure 1: (a) T. (b) T^* (solid edges) and T^{**} (solid and dashed edges)

u in T^*. If $u \notin PATH(v, w)$, deleting u could not have been able to separate v and w. $\Box$

Lemma 3.2 *Let* u, w *be two vertices of* T^* *with* u *an ancestor of* w. *If* v *is the neighbor in* T *of* u *on* $PATH(u, w)$, *then* v *is a descendant of* u *in* T^*.

Proof. Suppose that v is not a descendant of u. Then we have two cases to consider.

(i) v is an ancestor of u.

Since $v \in PATH(u, w)$, deleting v during the construction of T^* should have separated u and w into two different subtrees of v; however both u and w belong to the same subtree of v.

(ii) v is not an ancestor of u.

In this case, u and v are unrelated, i.e., they have no ancestor-descendant relationship in T^*. Let $x = LCA^*(u, v)$. By Lemma 3.1, $x \in PATH(u, v)$. Also, $x \neq u$ and $x \neq v$ because u and v are unrelated. Since u and v are adjacent in T, there can be no such vertex x.

From (i) and (ii), v is a descendant of u in T^*. $\Box$

We augment T^* to get a graph T^{**} by adding some new edges to T^*. Let v be a vertex of T^* with k children $v_1, \cdots, v_k$ for $1 \leq k \leq 3$. Then each of the k subtrees of v contains exactly one neighbor in T of v (i.e. exactly one vertex adjacent to v in T). Let a_i be the neighbor in T of v that belongs to the subtree of v rooted at v_i. Consider the paths between a_i and v_i for $1 \leq i \leq k$. Add edges between v and each vertex on the path between a_i and v_i for $1 \leq i \leq k$. We do this augmentation for each $v \in T^*$. Let T^{**} be the resulting graph. Figure 1(b) shows T^{**} (solid and dashed edges) of T in Figure 1(a).

Since the root of T^*, $p(T)$, has at most $3 \log n$ edges in T^{**}, the number of edges in T^{**} is bounded above by $E(n) \leq E(n_1) + E(n_2) + E(n_3) + 3 \log n$ for $n_1 + n_2 + n_3 = n - 1$ and $n_i \leq \lfloor n/2 \rfloor$, which gives $E(n) = O(n)$. We inductively prove that $E(n) \leq 12n - 3 \log n$. The basis case is easy to verify. Assume that $E(k) \leq 12k - 3 \log k$ for all $k < n$. Then

$$
\begin{aligned}
E(n) &\leq E(n_1) + E(n_2) + E(n_3) + 3 \log n \\
&\leq 12(n_1 + n_2 + n_3) - 3(\log n_1 + \log n_2 + \log n_3) + 3 \log n.
\end{aligned}
$$

Suppose that $n_1 \geq n_2 \geq n_3$. Then $n_1 > n/3$ as $n_1 = \max\{n_1, n_2, n_3\}$, and $n_2 > n/4$ as $n - n_1 > n/2$ and $n_2 \geq n_3$. Therefore,

$$
\begin{aligned}
E(n) &\leq 12(n-1) - 3(\log(n/3) + \log(n/4)) + 3 \log n \\
&\leq 12(n-1) - 6 \log(n/4) + 3 \log n \\
&= 12n - 3 \log n.
\end{aligned}
$$

Lemma 3.3 *For each edge* $(v, w) \in T^{**}$ *which is not an edge of* T, *there exists a vertex* $\Delta_{v,w}$ *in* T^{**} *such that (a)* $\Delta_{v,w} \in PATH(v, w)$; *and (b) both* $(v, \Delta_{v,w})$ *and* $(w, \Delta_{v,w})$ *are edges of* T^{**}. *Furthermore,* $\Delta_{v,w}$ *is a descendant of* v *and* w *in* T^*, *and can be found in* $O(1)$ *time using a single processor.*

Proof. Assume that v is an ancestor of w in T^*. Let z be the child of v that is an ancestor of w, and let T_z^* be the subtree of T^* rooted at z. Let $PATH(v, w) = (v_1, \cdots, v_k)$, $k \geq 3$, with $v = v_1$ and $w = v_k$. We shall show that $x = LCA^*(v_2, v_{k-1})$ satisfies (a) and (b).

By Lemma 3.1, (a) is satisfied. To prove that x satisfies (b), we first show that both v_2 and v_{k-1} are descendants of w. Note that if a vertex is a leaf of T^*, then all edges of T^{**} adjacent to it are also edges of T. So, w is not a leaf. By Lemma 3.2, v_2 is a descendant of v. Then $v_2 \in T_z^*$. Otherwise, $v = LCA^*(v_2, w)$ is not on $PATH(v_2, w)$, which contradicts to Lemma 3.1. To show that v_2 is a descendant of w, consider two cases.

(i) $w = z$.

Since $v_2 \in T_z^*$, v_2 is a descendant of w.

(ii) $w \neq z$.

In this case, (v, w) is a newly added edge during the construction of T^{**}. So, one of the neighbors in T of v must be a descendant of w; otherwise, (v, w) could not have been added. Since we know that w and v_2 (but no other neighbors in T of v) belong to T_z^*, v_2 is a descendant of w.

So, we have proved that v_2 is a descendant of w. Proving that v_{k-1} is a descendant of w is another application of Lemma 3.2. Here, w is an ancestor of v_2 in T^* and v_{k-1} is the neighbor of w on $PATH(v_2, w)$.

Hence, both v_2 and v_{k-1} are descendants of w. Since x is the lowest common ancestor of v_2 and v_{k-1} in T^* both (v, x) and (w, x) are edges of T^{**} because there must be edges in T^{**} from v to the vertices on the path between v and v_2, and from w to the vertices on the path between w and v_{k-1}. So, both conditions are satisfied.

Finally, it is easy to see that x is a descendant of v and w in T^* and can be found in $O(1)$ time by Lemmas 2.1 and 2.2. $\square$

We complete preprocessing by associating $COST((v, w))$ with each edge $(v, w) \in T^{**}$, where $COST((v, w))$ is the minimum cost on $PATH(v, w)$. Define the *level* of an edge in T^{**} to be the level of its lower (i.e. further from the root) end vertex. The root is at level 0. Let h be the height of T^*. Then, each edge is at level between 1 and $h - 1$. All edges of T^{**} at level $h - 1$ are also edges in T. $COST((v, w))$ for each $(v, w) \in T^{**}$ can be found in $O(\log n)$ time using $O(n)$ processors in a bottom-up fashion as follows:

for each $(v, w) \in T^{**}$ which is also an edge of T **do in parallel**
$\quad COST((v, w)) = \text{MIN}\{cost(v), cost(w)\}$
for $i = h - 2$ **downto** 1 **do**;
$\quad$ **for each** $(v, w) \in T^{**}$ at level i which is not an edge of T **do in parallel**
$\quad\quad COST((v, w)) = \text{MIN}\{COST((v, \Delta_{v,w})), COST((w, \Delta_{v,w}))\}.$

Since $\Delta_{v,w}$ is a descendant of v and w, $COST((v, \Delta_{v,w}))$ and $COST((w, \Delta_{v,w}))$ are available when $COST((v, w))$ is computed. So, the procedure correctly computes the $COST(\cdot)$'s. Since T^{**} has $O(n)$ edges, the procedure above can be executed in $O(\log n)$ time by assigning a processor to each edge of T^{**}. Our preprocessing is completed. It takes $O(\log n)$ time using $O(n)$ processors.

If we look at the preprocessing carefully, it is not difficult to see that the only step requiring $O(n)$ processors is the one for constructing T^*. The processors do a linear amount of work for constructing T^{**} and associating $COST((v, w))$ with each edge $(v, w) \in T^{**}$. Brent's theorem [3] can be used to reduce the processor complexity to $O(n/\log n)$. An open problem is if T^* can be constructed in $O(\log n)$ time using $O(n/\log n)$ processors. Recently, Schäffer [8] gave a linear time sequential algorithm for the problem.

4 Query Answering

We now explain how to use T^{**} to answer a query $MCV(u, w)$, the minimum-cost vertex on $PATH(u, w)$. Let $v = LCA^*(u, w)$. Then $v \in PATH(u, w)$ by Lemma 3.1. Divide $PATH(u, w)$ into $PATH(v, w)$ and $PATH(u, v)$. We shall explain how to find $MCV(v, w)$ only. $MCV(u, v)$ can be found in the same way.

In the following, $CPATH(v, w)$ will contain a path between v and w in T^{**}. (There may be several paths between v and w in T^{**}.) Briefly, it is a *compressed* path of $PATH(v, w)$ in the sense that $CPATH(v, w)$ contains only a subset of at most $\log n$ of the vertices on $PATH(v, w)$, but it has enough information to compute the minimum cost on $PATH(v, w)$.

Let $x_1, \cdots, x_p$ be the path between $v = x_1$ and $w = x_p$ in T^*. Initially, set $CPATH(v, w) \leftarrow \{x_1\}$ and $i \leftarrow 1$. Find the least index j such that $j > i$ and $x_j \in PATH(x_i, x_p)$. Add x_j to $CPATH(v, w)$. Set $i \leftarrow j$ and repeat the procedure until $j = p$. Clearly, $CPATH(v, w)$ can be found in $O(\log n)$ time using a single processor.

Lemma 4.1 *Let* $CPATH(v, w) = (x_{a_1}, \cdots, x_{a_q})$ *with* $a_1 = 1$ *and* $a_q = p$. *Then* $CPATH(v, w)$ *is a path in* T^{**}.

Proof. We prove the lemma by showing that each $(x_{a_i}, x_{a_{i+1}})$ is an edge in T^{**}. Note that $x_{a_{i+1}} \in PATH(x_{a_i}, x_p)$. Let y be the neighbor in T of x_{a_i} that is on $PATH(x_{a_i}, x_p)$. Then y is a descendant of $x_{a_{i+1}}$ (a vertex is a descendant of itself) in T^*. To show this, first note that y is a descendant of x_{a_i} by Lemma 3.2. Suppose that y is not a descendant of $x_{a_{i+1}}$. Let $z = LCA^*(y, x_{a_{i+1}})$. Then we have the followings:
(a) $z \neq x_{a_{i+1}}$.
(b) z is on the path between x_{a_i} and $x_{a_{i+1}}$ in T^*.
(c) $z \in PATH(y, x_{a_{i+1}}) \subseteq PATH(x_{a_i}, x_p)$.
Thus z should have been added in $CPATH(v, w)$ before $x_{a_{i+1}}$ was added. We proved that y is a descendant of $x_{a_{i+1}}$ in T^*. So, $(x_{a_i}, x_{a_{i+1}})$ is an edge of T^{**} by the way new edges are added during the construction of T^{**}. $\square$

$MIN\{COST((x_{a_i}, x_{a_{i+1}})) \mid 1 \leq i \leq q - 1\}$ is the minimum cost on $PATH(v, w)$, since each $COST((x_{a_i}, x_{a_{i+1}}))$ contains the minimum cost on $PATH(x_{a_i}, x_{a_{i+1}})$. Similarly, $CPATH(u, v)$ and the minimum cost on $PATH(u, v)$ can be found. Then the minimum cost on $PATH(u, w)$ is the smaller of the minimum costs on $PATH(v, w)$ and $PATH(u, v)$. $MCV(u, w)$, the vertex that gives the minimum cost on $PATH(u, w)$, can be found by a straightforward modification of the algorithms discussed so far.

4.1 Path-Min Queries on Paths

If T is a path (i.e. a linked list) of length n, then one can find $MCV(u, v)$ in $O(1)$ time after an $O(\log n)$ time, $O(n / \log n)$ processor preprocessing. Use list ranking algorithms in [2, 6] to rearrange T into an array of size n. Let $C = (c_1, \cdots, c_n)$ be the array of cost's of vertices of T. The problem is to preprocess C so that, given two indices $i \leq j$, $MIN\{c_i, \cdots, c_j\}$ can be found quickly.

Introduce $c_{n+1} = \infty$ and apply the all nearest smaller values problem in [4] to find for each i, $N(i)$, where $N(i)$ is the smallest index such that $N(i) > i$ and $c_{N(i)} < c_i$. Let

T' be the tree defined by $N(\cdot)$'s, i.e. the tree with vertex set $\{1, \cdots, n+1\}$ and j is the parent of i if and only if $j = N(i)$. Preprocess T' by Lemma 2.1.

Our query answering algorithm is very simple. Let i and j be a pair of indices with $i \leq j$.

(i) Find $k = LCA(i, j)$ in T'.

(ii) If $k = j$, then $x \leftarrow k$. Otherwise, $x \leftarrow$ the child of k that is an ancestor of i.

Then it is easy to see that $c_x = \text{MIN}\{c_i, \cdots, c_j\}$. Both Steps (i) and (ii) takes $O(1)$ time using a single processor.

Acknowledgement. The author wishes to thank W.L. Ruzzo for his helpful comments on this work.

References

[1] K. Abrahamson, N. Dadoun, D.G. Kirkpatrick and T. Przytycka, A simple parallel tree contraction algorithm, *J. Algorithms*, **10**, 287–302 (1989).

[2] R.J. Anderson and G.L. Miller, Deterministic parallel list ranking, *Proc. 3rd AWOC.* (Lecture Notes in Computer Sciences, vol. 319) 81–90 (1988).

[3] R.P. Brent, The parallel evaluation of general arithmetic expressions, *J. ACM*, **21**, 201–206 (1974).

[4] O. Berkman, D. Breslauer, Z. Galil, B. Schieber and U. Vishkin, Highly parallelizable problems, *Proc. ACM Symp. on Theory of Computing*, 309–319 (1989)

[5] B. Chazelle, Computing on a free tree via complexity-preserving mappings, *Algorithmica*, **2**, 337–361 (1987).

[6] R. Cole and U. Vishkin, Approximate parallel scheduling. Part I: The basic technique with applications to optimal parallel list ranking in logarithmic time, *SIAM J. Comput.*, **17**, 128–142 (1988).

[7] D. Knuth, *The art of programming: Fundamental algorithms*, Addison-Wesley, Reading, Mass. (1968).

[8] A.A. Schäffer, Optimal node ranking of trees in linear time, *Inform. Process. Lett.*, **33**, 91–96 (1989).

[9] B. Schieber and U Vishkin, On finding lowest common ancestors: simplification and parallelization, *SIAM J. Comput.*, **17**, 1253–1262 (1988).

[10] R. Tarjan and U. Vishkin, An efficient parallel biconnectivity algorithm, *SIAM J. Comput.*, **14**, 862–874 (1985).

Efficient Deterministic Parallel Algorithms for Integer Sorting*

Lin Chen

Department of Computer and Information Science

Ohio State University

Columbus, OH 43210

USA

chen-l@cis.ohio-state.edu

Keywords: Algorithm Design and Analysis, Lexicographic Order, Lower Bound, NC, Parallel Computation, Prefix Sum, PRAM, Resource Tradeoff, Sorting

Abstract

The main result of this paper is several fastest deterministic algorithms including:

- an optimal algorithm which sorts n distinct integers in $O(\log n)$ time using $O(n/\log n)$ processors on EREW PRAM for the case where the integers are in a range linear in n;

- an optimal algorithm which sorts n integers in $O(\log n/\log\log n)$ time using $O(n\log\log n/\log n)$ processors on CRCW PRAM for the case where the integers are in a range linear in n and a constant upper bounded number of integers have a constant lower bounded multiplicity.

Moreover, we present a linear time linear space algorithm for sorting polynomially bounded integers. We also show that our algorithms are the fastest possible on the models of computation used since the run time of our algorithms meets the lower bounds. This also gives a proof that those lower bounds are tight.

1 Introduction

Sorting arises in almost every important computer application. It has attracted the attention of many leading computer scientists. This is partially reflected by the large volume of publications on the sorting problem. Knuth [14] gave an encyclopedic treatise of (mainly) sequential methods. In the past decade, many parallel algorithms have appeared in the literature. Akl [2] even devoted one book to the topic. Parallel algorithms have been implemented on various computational models. Atai, Komlós, and Szemerédi [5] discovered a parallel sorting algorithm which runs in $O(\log n)$ time on a sorting network of $O(n\log n)$

---

*The original title is kept unchanged for this final version although some more general results are mentioned here.

processors. Later, Leighton [17] showed that their algorithm can be improved to run on an n-node fixed-connection network within the same time bound. Reif and Valiant [21] gave a randomized algorithm which runs in $O(\log n)$ time on a fixed-connection network called cube-connected cycles. Their algorithm uses n processors. The computational model used in this paper is the Parallel Random Access Machine (PRAM). Akl and Santoro [3], Bilardi and Nicolau [8], and Cole [11] each gave an NC (polylog time polynomial processors) sorting algorithm on the Exclusive Read Exclusive Write (EREW) PRAM which achieves a processor-time product of $O(n \log n)$. Rajasekaran and Reif [19] (the preliminary form is in Reif [20]) studied the integer sorting. In their algorithm, they assume that all the n integers are in the range $[1, n]$. Their main result is a randomized sorting algorithm which runs in $\tilde{O}(\log n)$ time with $n/\log n$ processors on a Current Read Current Write (CRCW) PRAM. The 'concurrent write' is resolved by priority, which means that each processor has a priority and the processor with the highest priority succeeds in writing in case of 'concurrent write'. They employ the notation $\tilde{O}$ for the complexity bounds of randomized algorithms. A randomized algorithm is said to have resource bound $\tilde{O}(g(n))$ if there is a constant c such that the amount of resource used by the algorithm on the input of size n is no more than $c\alpha g(n)$ with probability $\geq 1 - 1/n^\alpha$ for any $\alpha > 1$. In this paper, we further study the integer sorting. Our parallel algorithms are implemented on the less powerful computational model. All our parallel algorithms work on Arbitrary CRCW PRAM, and sometimes on Common CRCW PRAM or even on EREW PRAM. That is to say, our parallel algorithms always give the correct answer no matter which processor succeed in writing in case of concurrent write, and sometimes we do not allow concurrent write unless several processors attempt to write the same value into a memory cell, or we even do not allow any concurrent read concurrent write at all. We assume that each input integer is in the range $[l, r]$. Let $r - l$ be denoted by d. We give first deterministic optimal parallel integer sorting algorithms for various cases. We also give a deterministic sublogarithmic time parallel stable sorting algorithm for the case where all the integers are bounded by a polynomial in n. The algorithm runs in $O(\log n/\log\log n)$ time using $O(n^2 \log\log n/\log n)$ CRCW PRAM processors. The corresponding sequential algorithm only requires linear time and linear space which obviously beats the $\Omega(n \log n)$ lower bound for sorting by comparison of keys obtained with the assumption that the comparison between two numbers can be done in unit time, which implies that the size of input numbers must be bounded.

2 Known Results

Given a linear order $\leq$ on a set S of n objects $k_1, k_2, \ldots, k_n$, the problem of sorting is to find a permutation σ such that $k_{\sigma(1)} \leq k_{\sigma(2)} \leq \cdots \leq k_{\sigma(n)}$. A sorting is called stable if the resulting permutation has the property that $k_{\sigma(i)} = k_{\sigma(i+1)}$ implies $\sigma(i) < \sigma(i+1)$. The relation $\leq$ when extended to tuples whose components are from S is a lexicographic order if $(s_1, \ldots, s_p) \leq (t_1, \ldots, t_p)$ means that there exists an integer $j \leq p$ such that $s_i = t_i$ for $1 \leq i \leq j$, and $s_{j+1} < t_{j+1}$ if $j < p$. We first briefly review a sorting method called bucket sort, as described in Aho, Hopcroft and Ullman [1]. There are n input integers $a_1, a_2, \ldots, a_n$. The procedure is as follows. Compute the minimum and the maximum of the n integers, denoted by a_{min} and a_{max} respectively. Initialize $a_{max} - a_{min} + 1$ empty buckets. Scan the sequence $a_1, a_2, \ldots, a_n$ from left to ght, placing element a_i in the $(a_i - a_{min})$-th bucket. Finally, concatenate the contents of the buckets to obtain the sorted sequence. The time complexity of the algorithm is $O(d)$ since $a_{max} - a_{min} = O(d)$. When $= O(n)$, the sequential algorithm is optimal. The bucket sort can be extended to sort tuples of integers into lexicographic order. Suppose each tuple has a constant number, say c, of elements in the range 0 to -1. We can sort n c-tuples by applying bucket sort c times. First sort the tuples according to the last element. Then sort the resulting tuples according to the second last element. After the tuples are sorted according to the first element, the result is n tuples in lexicographic order. The space complexity, as well as the time complexity is $O(n)$. Note that the sorting method used to obtain the lexicographic order must be stable. Obviously, we can guarantee that the bucket sort is stable.

In designing parallel algorithm, the following result by Brent [9] is often helpful in improving the processor bound.

Theorem 1 *Any synchronous parallel algorithm taking time t with a total of x elementary operations can be implemented by p processors in time $\lfloor x/p \rfloor + t$.*

The theorem does not address how the processors can be allocated. Below, readers will see that this may not be a trivial task.

Next we take a look at the prefix computation problem. Let Γ be a domain. Let $\odot$ be a binary operator which is required to be associative, but we do not care whether it is commutative or not. Recall a binary operation is called *associative*, if for any three elements a, b, c in the domain, $a \odot (b \odot c) = (a \odot b) \odot c$ always holds. Also assumed is that the computation of one $\odot$ operation can be done in $O(1)$ sequential time over the domain. Now the input is n elements $a_1, a_2, \ldots, a_n$ in the domain. The problem is to compute $_i = \odot_{j=1}^{i} a_j$ for $0 < i \leq n$. Ladner and Fischer [16] showed that the problem can be solved using a circuit of $O(\log n)$ depth complexity and $O(n)$ size complexity. Based upon the idea, Kruskal, Rudolph and Snir [15] gave an algorithm which runs in $O(\log n)$ time with $O(n/\log n)$ processors on EREW PRAM. Later, Cole and Vishkin [12] showed that the prefix computation can be done in $O(\log n/\log \log n)$ time using $\log \log n/\log n$ Common CRCW PRAM processors, in which case no concurrent write is allowed unless several processors attempt to write the same value into a memory cell. Anderson and Miller [4] also gave solution with the same complexity bounds. Recently, Rajasekaran and Reif [19] showed the problem can be solved in $O(\log n/\log \log(P \log n/n))$ time using $P = \Omega(n/\log n)$ CRCW PRAM processors. Based on the parallel prefix computation, Rajasekaran and Reif gave an optimal randomized parallel algorithm for sorting the integers in the range $[1, n]$.

Optimal Algorithms

In this section, we give optimal parallel algorithms for sorting integers. For the n input integers $a_1, a_2, \ldots, a_n$, let $d = \max_{i=1}^{n} a_i - \min_{i=1}^{n} a_i$. We begin with the least complicated case.

3.1 Each integer is distinct

We obtain the algorithm by parallelizing the sequential bucket sort. The minimum of the n integers can be computed by applying the parallel prefix computation. Let the binary operation $\odot$ be min. Obviously it is an associative operation. So we can use the existing algorithm for parallel prefix computation. Computing the maximum is similar. We can also compute the maximum and minimum directly using an algorithm by Shiloach and Vishkin [22]. The time bound T and processor bound P of their algorithm is as follows.

$$
T = \begin{cases} O(n/P + \log \log P) & \text{if } P \le n \\ O(\log \log n - \log \log(P/n + 1)) & \text{if } n \le P \le \binom{n}{2} \end{cases}
$$

Their algorithm is implemented on Common CRCW PRAM.

Theorem 2 *sorting n distinct integers in the range $[l, r]$, where $r - l = O(n)$, can be done by an optimal parallel algorithm in $O(\log n)$ time with $O(n/\log n)$ processors on EREW PRAM, or in $O(\log n/\log \log n)$ time with $n \log \log n/\log n$ processors on Common CRCW PRAM.*

Proof. We first show the result on EREW PRAM. The minimum a_{min} and the maximum a_{max} of the n integers can be computed in $O(\log n)$ time with $O(n/\log n)$ processors. Without loss of generality, assume $\log n$ is an integer and $\log n$ divides n. Denote the input by $\log n$ blocks $A_1, \ldots, A_{\log n}$, where $A_i = a_{(i-1)n/\log n+1}, \ldots, a_{in/\log n}$, for $0 < i \le \log n$. For each block, successively use $n/\log n$ processors and put each a_i in the initially empty buckets. Doing this for one block takes constant time and $n/\log n$ processors. So $\log n$ time and $n/\log n$ processors are needed for all the blocks. Let a bucket have the value 0 if it is empty, and 1 otherwise. Recall the number of buckets is $a_{max} - a_{min} + 1$, which is $d + 1$. Note that $d \ge n - 1$ since each input integer is distinct. Let the binary operation $\odot$ in the prefix computation be '+'. Obviously '+' is an associative operation. Apply parallel prefix computation to the $d + 1$ buckets, each of which has value 0 or 1. This can be done in $O(\log d)$ time with $O(d/\log d)$ processors. According to the result of the parallel prefix computation, we can put n integers in nondecreasing order using $O(\log n)$ time and $O(n/\log n)$ processors. Here we describe the key idea. Let a_i be an arbitrary input integer. If the a_i-th bucket has value k after prefix computation, then we can conclude that a_i is the k-th smallest integer in the input. Thus the sorting can be done in $O(\log d)$ time with $O(d/\log d)$ processors on EREW PRAM. The algorithm is optimal when $d = O(n)$.

Next we consider the computation on CRCW PRAM. The idea is similar to the case of EREW PRAM. We partition the input integers into $\log n/\log \log n$, instead of $\log n$, parts. So each block has $n \log \log n/\log n$ integers. The maximum and the minimum can be computed by Shiloach and Vishkin's algorithm in $O(\log n/\log \log n)$ time if $O(n \log \log n/\log n)$ processors are used. Parallel prefix computation takes $O(\frac{\log n}{\log \log n})$ time and $O(\frac{n \log \log n}{\log n})$ processors using the algorithm by Cole and Vishkin. It follows that the sorting can be done in $O(\log n/\log \log n)$ time with $O(\frac{n \log \log n}{\log n})$ processors on CRCW PRAM. No matter whether we use EREW or CRCW PRAM, the product of time and processor bounds equals $O(n)$, the lower bound of sequential algorithm. So the parallel algorithm is optimal.

.2 Each integer has at most constant multiplicity

uppose each integer appears at most c times. Associate each bucket, say b_i, a list $l_i[1], \ldots, l_i[c]$. Put the ndices of the integers into the buckets as described below. For i from 1 to c do the following:

or each a_k do

    1. if a_k is unmarked, then set $l_{a_k}[i]$ to k

    2. if $l_{a_k}[i] = k$ then mark a_k

Iote that the condition in step 2 may not always be true because of concurrent write and marked a_k's in tep 1. The procedure above can be done in $O(\log n / \log \log n)$ time with $O(n \log \log n / \log n)$ processors. If everal processors attempt to write into a list at the same time, one and only one processor succeeds. The lgorithm works correctly regardless which one succeeds. Since the body is repeated a constant number f times, the complexity orders for the loop are the same. Now the number of integers in each bucket an be counted easily. Let each bucket have the value equal to that number. Apply the parallel prefix omputation. After that, suppose a bucket has value k, and has c_i integers, $0 < c_i \leq c$. We can conclude hat these c_i integers are the k-th smallest to $(k - c_i + 1)$-th smallest integers among the n input integers. "hen we can get the desired result immediately. Thus we have the following theorem.

Theorem 3 *Integer sorting can be done by an optimal parallel algorithm in $O(\frac{\log n}{\log \log n})$ time with $O(\frac{n \log \log n}{\log n})$ rocessors if input integers have at most constant multiplicity.*

.3 Constant number of integers have multiple occurrences

Ve shall exhibit an algorithm for the case in which the number of non-distinct integers is bounded by a onstant. After we place the integers in the bucket, the number of buckets with more than one integer s bounded by a constant. For each of those buckets, we compute the number of integers. It can be arallelized as follows. First mark those buckets which have more than one integer. Let b_i be such a ucket. We need to obtain the number of integers in the input which have value i. Define a new array, ay, $b_1, b_2, \ldots, b_n$.

$$b_k = \begin{cases} 1 & \text{if } a_k = i \\ 0 & \text{otherwise} \end{cases}$$

"hen the number of input integers equal to i is $\sum_{s=1}^{n} b_s$. This can be obtained in $O(\frac{\log n}{\log \log n})$ time with $n \log \log n / \log n$) processors. Sequentially do this for each of those buckets, the number of which is ounded by a constant. Alternatively, we can do this for all those buckets simultaneously using more rocessors. There is a tradeoff between time and processors. But in either case, the time and processor omplexity orders are the same. Once we have those numbers, we can simply use the same idea as nentioned in the previous case. Let the number of occurrences of an integer be the value of a bucket. "hen we can get the location of the integer in the sorted list by applying prefix computation. Hence we ave the following result.

Theorem 4 *Sorting n integers with constant number of non-distinct integers can be done by an optimal arallel algorithm in $O(\frac{\log n}{\log \log n})$ time with $O(n \log \log n / \log n)$ processors on Common CRCW PRAM.*

3.4 Constant number of integers have multiplicity greater than a constant

Suppose in the n input integers, at most c_1 integers have multiplicity greater than c_2. We can get an optimal parallel algorithm by combining the ideas in Section 3.2 and Section 3.3. Note that a key step is to compute the number of integers in each bucket. Once this is completed, sorting can be done by a simple application of prefix computation. First, use the method in Section 3.2 to compute the number of integers in those buckets which have at most c_2 integers. At the same time, identify the buckets which contain more than c_2 integers. The number of such buckets is bounded by c_1, according to the given condition. Now the number of integers in those buckets can be computed using the method in Section 3.3. Since both algorithms in Section 3.2 and Section 3.3 take $O(\log n/\log\log n)$ time and $O(n\log\log n/\log n)$ processors, the sorting in this case can also be done within the same resource bounds. We state the result as the following theorem.

Theorem 5 *Integer sorting can be done by an optimal parallel algorithm in $O(\frac{\log n}{\log\log n})$ time with $O(\frac{n\log\log n}{\log n})$ processors if a constant number of integers have multiplicity greater than a constant.*

4 Sublogarithmic Algorithms

More general cases are considered in this section. We give the corresponding sublogarithmic time parallel algorithms.

4.1 Each integer has bounded multiplicity

Let $f(n)$ be a function of n. Assume the number of occurrences of each integer is bounded by $f(n)$. Obviously, $0 < f(n) \leq n$. The algorithm works almost in the same way as in Section 3.2. The only difference lies in the computation of the number of integers in each bucket. Now the body of the loop is executed $f(n)$ times. Each execution can be done in $O(\log n/\log\log n)$ time with $O(\frac{n\log\log n}{\log n})$ processors or in $O(\frac{\log n}{\log\log n})$ time with $O(\frac{n\log\log n}{\log n})$ processors. Consequently, we have the following theorem.

Theorem 6 *Integer sorting can be done in $O(\frac{f(n)\log n}{\log\log n})$ time with $O(n\log\log n/\log n)$ processors if the number of occurrences of each integer is bounded by $f(n)$.*

We can see from the theorem that, if $f(n) = o(\log\log n)$, the above algorithm runs in sublogarithmic time.

4.2 Bounded number of integers have multiple occurrences

Let $f(n)$ be a function of n. Assume the number of integers with multiple occurrences in the input is bounded by $f(n)$. Obviously, $0 < f(n) \leq \lfloor n/2 \rfloor$.

First we describe an algorithm which takes sublogarithmic time if $f(n) = o(\log\log n)$, i.e., $f(n)$ is of the lower order of $\log\log n$. The idea is the same as in the case that the number of non-distinct integers is bounded by a constant. Place the integers in the buckets. For those buckets with more than one integer,